An Introduction to Nineteenth-Century Russian Slavophilism

Юрий Самарин

An Introduction to Nineteenth-Century Russian Slavophilism

Iu. F. Samarin

Peter K. Christoff

Westview Press

BOULDER • SAN FRANCISCO • OXFORD

In memory of
Professor Theodor Locher

Copyright © 1991 by Westview Press, Inc.

Published in 1991 in the United States of America by Westview Press, Inc., 5500 Central Avenue, Boulder, Colorado 80301, and in the United Kingdom by Westview Press, 36 Lonsdale Road, Summertown, Oxford OX2 7EW

A CIP catalog record for this book is available from the Library of Congress.
ISBN 0-8133-8080-4

Printed and bound in the United States of America

The paper used in this publication meets the requirements of the American National Standard for Permanence of Paper for Printed Library Materials Z39.48-1984.

10   9   8   7   6   5   4   3   2   1

Contents

Acknowledgments

As indicated in the preceding studies, a good many individuals and institutions have favored me with indispensable services. Without these, this project could not have been planned and brought to completion. A number of names have been mentioned in the previous studies; therefore it is not necessary to repeat them. Yet as I conclude this project, I cannot avoid glancing back to its beginning, many years ago, under the expert guidance and warm friendship of the late Professor George Vernadsky. My gratitude to him deepens with every passing year. I am also most grateful to Professor Nicholas V. Riasanovsky, the pioneering and still foremost scholar of Moscow Slavophilism and Official Nationality. His advice after reading sections of this manuscript, and his generous sharing of bibliographical and other information, through many informal personal contacts, and in general his counsel and encouragement have been of major importance in the completion of this work. I also owe sincere thanks to Shirley Taylor for editorial services, which she bravely endured for the fourth time; to Professor George L. Kline for his highly competent and meticulous reading of the manuscript, and for his many invaluable corrections and suggestions; and to Professor Alexander Vucinich for his astute and most helpful evaluation of this study.

But no one deserves my heartfelt gratitude more than my wife, Nancy, who for many years has borne steadfastly and cheerfully the burden of typing first drafts from my longhand. And who, in addition, has constantly responded to innumerable consultations from the most trivial to the most substantive.

It is manifest that while many friends and professional people have contributed to this and the earlier studies, any weaknesses, flaws, or errors are mine alone. Finally a word of gratitude again to the staffs of the Stanford University libraries, particularly to that of the Hoover Library with its rich collection of nineteenth-century Russian periodicals.

Peter K. Christoff
Redwood City

Introduction

The reader familiar with the three earlier studies of this series, on Khomiakov, I. V. Kireevsky, and K.S. Aksakov, will see certain important changes in this fourth and last installment of my work on Moscow Slavophilism. This research project, as indicated in the title, was conceived from its very beginning as a study of "first," "early," "old," or "classical" Moscow Slavophilism, and not as four detached and unrelated literary biographies. Relevant and indispensable as the lives and careers of the individual Moscow Slavophils were, their inclusion here is justified first and foremost on the basis of their respective contributions to "pre-Reform," (pre-1861) Moscow Slavophilism. This period came to an end early in 1861, with the emancipation of the serfs, thus providing us with the generally accepted dividing line between pre- and post-Reform Slavophilism. The division comes after the deaths of Ivan and Peter Kireevsky in 1856 and of Khomiakov and Konstantin Aksakov in 1860.

In the case of Samarin, whose life extended from 1819 until 1876, this pattern does not fit quite as neatly as it does the other early Slavophils. Basically, however, as most students of Moscow Slavophilism have noticed, and as will be brought out in this study, Samarin made his most significant theoretical, as well as practical, reformist contribution to early Slavophilism within its pre-Reform period. I have therefore somewhat abruptly cut off the biographical part on Samarin (Part One) at 1861, though without omitting some pertinent facts belonging to the period 1861–1876.

In terms of the bulk of Samarin's published works, it is clear that he devoted more space to the Western Slavs and the inhabitants of the Baltic littoral than to any other part of the Russian empire. They take more space than even his Slavophilism. But one should not draw erroneous conclusions from this fact. Important as these borderlands (Poland and the Baltic countries) were to the native populations, mostly Catholic and some Protestant, they were peripheral to the Russian empire although the Slavophils were not ready to part with them. Nor were the Slavophils ready to yield to their Catholic and Protestant cultures. For Samarin and the other early Slavophils these areas had a largely negative significance, since the Slavophil attitude toward both the Catholic and Protestant confessions was on the whole though not exclusively critical. The birthplace and geographical and

1

cultural center of Moscow Slavophilism for Samarin and the other Moscow Slavophils was not in Russia's western borderlands but in Orthodox Great Russia and its longtime capital, Moscow. This fact is historically well established despite the considerable amount of time and space that Samarin devoted to Russia's western borderlands and the Baltic littoral.

Even before I had completed my first draft of the Samarin study I was aware of the problem of how to organize and present the views and convictions of the Slavophils and the programmatic content of their writings. It is worth stressing that many of the exchanges with the Westerners during the 1840s and 1850s, out of which Slavophilism grew, were oral and unrecorded. The locale that nurtured Slavophil views and convictions was almost never the academic lecture hall, characteristic of German intellectual life at the time, but was rather the Moscow salon, in which discussion and polemics were spontaneous, therefore unrehearsed, and often unprepared, freewheeling, and largely unrecorded. Also, many of the Slavophil writings were polemical in nature, and polemics, by definition, are not conducive to clear, measured, and reasoned exposition as scoring a point against the opponent often takes precedent over dispassionate factual presentation. Slavophil efforts to secure a journal of their own in which they could give regular expression to well-formulated views failed during the 1840s and the first half of the 1850s. The Slavophils were frustrated by the censorship, which was particularly onerous during the "dark seven years" (1848–1855).

Not the least as a problem of organizing the material was the fact that the early Slavophils were not the most disciplined or the most systematic of writers. Coming from the well-to-do gentry, they were not compelled to write for a living, and since none went into the academic profession, they did not feel the necessity for sustained and systematic research. Some of them left works unfinished, and they often wrote in response to an external stimulus—an exchange at a salon, for instance, or a journal challenge. Kireevsky's attempt early in 1847 to induce his fellow Slavophils to consider a concerted effort at elaborating a coherent Slavophil intellectual-ideological stand came to nought. Although by the end of the 1850s Slavophilism had a body of thought and doctrine, its major contributors remained strongly individualistic, and often idiosyncratic members of the Slavophil camp.

In addition, there was a more fundamental reason why the Slavophils were averse to the creation of a "system" of thought. The very notion of a "system" was uncongenial and alien to them. It was Western, more specifically, German. This point was brought out earlier, particularly in the second and third studies, and is worth stressing again. Once the Slavophils, particularly Konstantin Aksakov and Samarin, got over their youthful infatuation with Hegelianism, they shunned German thought as being cold, one-sided, rationalistic, and heavily academic (*kabinetnoe myshlenie*). They were convinced, as the Westerner Ivan Turgenev was, that the systematic unilinear thinking of the great German academic philosophers, fascinating and imposing as it was, was not the solution to all human problems. And those to whom thought and ideas are synonymous with Western speculative systematic structures are looking in vain at Slavophilism, as they would be at other vital areas of human thought.

The haphazard and often rudimentary and incomplete manner in which the early Slavophils stated their basic views is often baffling and exasperating. As Nicholas Riasanovsky pointed out in 1955, Khomiakov never gave more than a passing reference to the doctrine of *sobornost'* – not even in an essay, much less in a monograph or a treatise although this doctrine is central to his thought and to Orthodoxy. As an adjective, *sobornyi,* it appears in the Orthodox creed, and Henry Gifford has recently called attention to the fact that, in 1915, to L. I. Mandelstam, for one, the notion of "'Russian' and 'National,' 'stands . . . for the Orthodox term *sobornyi,* involving the whole community"[1] Kireevsky gave a similarly brief treatment to his doctrine of the wholeness of the spirit (*tselnost' dukha*), while Konstantin Aksakov, one wonders whether by accident or by design, was no more generous in the elaboration of his basic Slavophil conviction – the choric principle – than the other Slavophils were with theirs. He saw his "moral choir" embodied in the Russian peasant commune.

The four personal contributions that comprise the total of the two dozen published volumes of the early Slavophils were conceived, it seems, without mutual consultations or a deliberate effort to distribute the load. Each Slavophil wrote in the area, and on the subject or subjects, that he chose for himself. And in the case of Samarin, his dissertation subject, which gave him a glimpse into Orthodoxy, Catholicism, and Protestantism, was assigned to him by Moscow University while his study of Riga's history was a bureaucratic assignment. It is not surprising, therefore, that under such conditions the works of the four early Slavophils are poorly coordinated, disparate, occasionally wide-ranging, and certainly not free of contradictions.

Yet, taken as a whole, the published Slavophil heritage bears testimony to a number of fundamental shared convictions. There is, for instance, the pervasive and powerful Russian national consciousness resting upon the foundation of Slavophil Orthodoxy. From the Slavophil writings also emerges the Russian peasant communal organization seen not only as the pillar of Russian historical life but also as a bright promise for the future. The Slavophils' opposition to serfdom was another common view and conviction. On this fundamental ethical, social, and economic question, the contributions of Samarin and Koshelev were particularly noteworthy; indeed, these Slavophils were among the prime movers in bringing about the emancipation of the serfs in 1861.

In general, the Slavophils agreed on most issues, and from the time of the completion of my first draft on this project in 1953 I realized that although it would be easier to write four individual studies, it was the common doctrine that interested me. As individuals they were intriguing, but I was never tempted to concentrate on each one separately for in their own way the Slavophils saw themselves contributing to a common doctrine, particularly Orthodox, particularly Russian. In short, this was not a case of the author with the beautiful word looking for a worthwhile thought and subject. It was, rather, that of one who, having come upon ideas that are worth knowing about, desired to get them across to the reader by the simplest and shortest road consistent with reasonable thoroughness. My decision, therefore, was to take the Slavophils on their terms, and in their spirit. This seemed unavoidable in view of the fact that they were probably among the first anywhere to react, as it were from the outside, to early modern Western industrial civilization. And this reaction should not be lost for either Russia or the West.

It is hoped that from the first three studies and from this fourth and last volume a pattern and a form will emerge indicative of what might be termed the descent of an idea. The "idea" begins on the level of religion and/or philosophy, moves down to that of ideology, and finally reaches the lowest level, that of program, tactics, organization, and action. This order and the metaphor could be reversed, as for instance when it is said that an idea or a principle is based upon such and such religious or philosophical premise. In either case ideology occupies the middle ground. This middle level or area is reasonably well defined, not because it is sharply delimited from those above and below, but because, as in the rainbow, the area of the predominance of the red color, for instance, is quite discernable.

At the stage of ideology ideas acquire potency, accessibility, and relevance; urgency and potency because ideology and ideologues can, and do, exert powerful influences. Ideological views become accessible to large numbers of ordinary people in ways in which philosophy and theology cannot and do not reach them. The relevance of ideology (often cast in the form of exhortations) comes from the fact that in mass urban societies vital concerns and problems, or those presented as such, touch a great number of people. This is particularly true when in rapidly changing societies social, economic, and political problems create a sense of urgency and demand for solutions. In the process, the ideas become adulterated often so greatly that the original idea is almost unrecognizable.

The scheme illustrating the descent of an idea is derived from the writings of the Slavophils as broached in the earlier studies. This should become even clearer further on in this study, but it can be illustrated briefly here. In 1859, a year before Khomiakov died, he published a thirty-page essay in *Russkaia beseda* in the form of a letter to Samarin. The title of the essay-letter is "On

Contemporary Developments in the Field of Philosophy." In it, among other things, Khomiakov says, "It does not enter anyone's mind that the most practical [aspect] of life constitutes only the realization of abstract notions (more or less consciously), and that the most practical question quite often contains in itself an abstract seed, capable of philosophical definition that leads to the correct solution of the question itself."[2] Although Khomiakov seems here to omit the middle stage, of ideology, in other Slavophil works, and Slavophilism as a whole, the middle ground, between religion and/or philosophy and "practical" questions, is present and quite apparent.

Such a view of ideology, entirely independent of Slavophilism, is suggested, among others, by the relationship between certain aspects of the American Declaration of Independence and the Constitution of the United States. The Declaration of Independence in one of its fundamental assertions states that "all men are created equal, that they are endowed by their Creator with certain inalienable rights." Clearly, the notion of human equality goes far beyond eighteenth-century Philadelphia, and could have come from either Christianity or the then predominant view of the state of nature and natural law, or from both. Thus a fundamental principle of religion and/or philosophy is brought to the level of ideology. And it is characteristic of ideology to be concerned with, and point at, the solution of pressing human problems. These can be single, such as liberty. They may concern religious, social, political, and economic questions, or they can arise as some combination of these. But it is a major function of ideology to illuminate and justify the solution of vital and unavoidable problems in terms of ultimate religious and/or philosophical principles. The Constitution with its several amendments contains an exposition of the program, tactics, organization, and type of action for the functioning of a polity on the basis of certain ideological principles, which in turn rest upon religious and/or philosophical premises.

On the level of action, however, we are confronted with historical reality. Here, ideological views and religious or philosophical ideals too often become diluted and degraded. The complexities and imperfections of human life render even the noblest and most worthy aspirations considerably less lofty than the primary conceptions, and sometimes even unrecognizable. Yet it is not difficult to see that, without the constant tug of the idea, the ideal, and the noble, human beings, and humanity in general, would fare worse.

The three stages in the life and movement of an idea correspond to the well-known and long-established agents of the three stages: the philosopher or religious leader, the ideologue or ideologist, and the political leader or man of action. Each one of these seems to require not only the proper aptitude and inclination but also a particular temperament. It is not difficult to single out in history major philosophers, great religious leaders, or outstanding ideologists. It is perhaps even easier to name prominent political leaders and men of action. It is also fairly common to see an outstanding figure who functions on two adjacent levels, such as a combination of ideologist and a man of action. But it is quite difficult to point to an outstanding historical figure engaged on all three levels.

If one were to take Ranke's celebrated injunction, "wie es eigentlich gewesen," too literally, and apply it to Moscow Slavophilism, the result would very likely be one of less than normal or nominal clarity. Reconstructing the poor organization and coordination of the Slavophils, and the consequent disarray, would hardly be a service to history or to the reader. Here arises one of the historian's perennial unsolved questions. How much liberty should he take with his subject in order to provide it with a minimum of order and organization? On the whole, as expressly stated at the end of the study of Aksakov, I have been of the conviction that these studies depart too far from the Slavophil mode of writing and expression, although this has been done in the effort to make Slavophilism accessible to the reader. Neither Ranke, nor quanto history, nor psycho-history, nor cleometrics, nor metahistory, nor as far as I know any of the social "sciences," has given us a precise formula or instrument of measurement that one could apply to historical material of the type presented by the Moscow Slavophils.

What I have tried to do, with the aid of the scheme outlined above, is to present Moscow Slavophilism as predominantly (but not exclusively) an ideological current of thought. Although the Slavophils dwelt for the most part on the middle level, they also stayed in contact with the two adjacent levels. Thus Khomiakov and Kireevsky were primarily concerned with problems of Orthodox theology, and "Russian," Orthodox philosophy, respectively; Aksakov devoted himself to matters of ideology; Samarin touched on the areas of theology and ideology and played a prominent part in the 1861 emancipation of the serfs. Samarin's activity in particular, and also that of Alexander Koshelev and Ivan Aksakov during the 1850s and early 1860s, illustrate the Slavophil descent, however incomplete, to the level of program, tactics, action — in a word, to Slavophil reformism — and incidentally renders empty the claim made in various forms by Chaadaev and repeated by others since then that Slavophilism was merely retrospective utopianism. Throughout these studies I have constantly tried to follow the record and avoid the preconception, which can be, and occasionally has been, quite misleading.

As the only one of the four early Slavophils who lived beyond 1860, Samarin witnessed the growth and evolution of Russian pan-Slavism in the decade from the mid-1860s to the mid-1870s. This study therefore is the proper one in which to make a few cursory remarks on the relationship between the Moscow Slavophilism of the 1840s and 1850s and the ill-defined pan-Slavism of the succeeding two decades. But these two major ideological currents were not all that mid-nineteenth-century Russian ideological thought, literary criticism, and publicistic work produced. In addition to Russian Westernism, the pro-Catholic version of Chaadaev, the liberal variety of Granovsky, Kavelin, and Chicherin, and the radical variety of Herzen, Belinsky, and Chernyshevsky, there were other currents, not so well known outside Russia, that at times touched on Moscow Slavophilism. Two of them were represented by the *pochvenniki* (men of the soil), and by the "men of official nationality."

These currents of thought, each one separate and distinct, yet occasionally, and usually briefly, in contact with Slavophilism, were advocated and defended by a number of outstanding men of letters and ideologists. The literature by and about the various representatives of these ideological orientations is considerable. (M.P. Pogodin, for instance, one of the "men of official nationality," has the unique distinction in Russian letters — possibly in European letters — of having been honored by a twenty-two-volume "biography," *Zhizn' i trudy M.P. Pogodina.*) There are excellent studies of many of the representatives of these schools, and some of pan-Slavism and of the "men of official nationality." To my knowledge, the areas where these currents come close to each other, and where they diverge, remain relatively obscure; yet it is obvious that if we had a reasonably clear notion of how, for instance, Slavophilism was like, and how it differed from, currents of thought with which it is occasionally confused, such as pan-Slavism, we would know more accurately what Slavophilism was, as well as what it was not.

I deal with these four currents of thought in the last two chapters of this study, but not in an effort to summarize the views and writings of a number of highly individualistic and talented authors. Even less are these chapters meant to settle the issue of the complex relationship between the four schools of thought and others. Rather, they are intended to show the need for integrating studies, such as N. V. Riasanovsky's of Official Nationality, and several on pan-Slavism, and to compare and contrast them in greater detail and more precisely than is here feasible.

The concern in this volume remains first and foremost with Moscow Slavophilism, and with Samarin's contribution to it. Since Slavophilism was primarily a school of ideological thought, the emphasis throughout these studies has been on the writings of the Slavophils. In Samarin's case, however, there was a significant departure from writing into the sphere of action and reform. This adds another dimension to Moscow Slavophilism that is frequently overlooked, that is, the practical, "non-utopian." But whether working to bring about emancipation of the serfs or engaged in writing, which he did most of his adult life, Samarin, like the other early Slavophils, was not narrowly or rigidly concerned with a thoroughly logical, systemlike exposition of his Slavophil views and convictions.

Even a cursory glance at the eleven volumes of Samarin's published works reveals a variety of subjects, themes, and approaches.[3] These were called forth not so much by an unwavering preconception of what Moscow Slavophilism should be, but, first, by the growth and development of a precocious youth who as a university student struggled with Hegelianism, and then abandoned it for Slavophil Orthodoxy. Samarin's dissertation, (in volume 5 of his published works) completed when he was twenty-three years old, was as mentioned on an assigned subject, but it gave him an opportunity, among other things, for a historical look at Catholicism, Protestantism, and Orthodoxy. The three confessions were rapidly becoming a fundamental concern for the Slavophils in their constant comparisons and contrasts of Russian and Western cultures. In defining Eastern Orthodoxy, Khomiakov and Kireevsky played the major roles during the 1840s and 1850s. Samarin participated in this controversy during the 1840s and returned to this theme when he published in 1865 five letters, replies to the Jesuit Father Martinov, a more polemical work than his dissertation, prompted by certain Jesuit writings. (This now comprises volume 6 of his works, published in 1887.)

A few months after he defended his dissertation in 1844, Samarin entered government service in St. Petersburg, but he found the work uncongenial. In the summer 1846 he began an assignment in Riga on the staff of governor-general E. A. Golovin. This move, prompted by Samarin's desire to escape the stifling and unrewarding atmosphere of bureaucratic St. Petersburg, inspired his *Riga Letters, History of Riga,* undertaken on assignment as mentioned above, and *Memoranda on the Baltic Question,* contained in volume 7, part one, of his works, and *An Essay on the History of Urban Classes in Riga, 1200–1845* (in volume 7, part two). At the end of the 1860s he returned to this question. This marked a new phase in his polemics with several pro-German authors. That is when he wrote the extensive work, *The Borderlands of Russia,* now volumes 8, 9, and 10 of his published works. In this study of the Baltic littoral, given in historical perspective, the underlying theme is that of Samarin's strongly pro-Russian, pro-Orthodox, nationalistic convictions, which are also a fundamental ingredient of his Moscow Slavophilism.

Volumes 2, 3, and 4 of Samarin's works are especially relevant to his ideological views and convictions, and to Slavophil reformism. They deal with the agrarian problem in Russia, particularly with the *narod,* and the abolition of serfdom. Volume 2 covers the period up to November 20, 1857 (Alexander II's proclamation on emancipation); volume 3 is devoted to a span of less than two years of intense Slavophil concern and work for emancipation, from November 20, 1857, to June 1859, and volume 4 covers the period from June 1859 to April 1864. Samarin's rich and illuminating correspondence (up to 1854), indispensable for biography and for the study of Moscow Slavophilism, takes up volume 12. (His correspondence from 1855 to 1876 has, as far as I know, never been published.) Volume 1 consists of a collection of articles, essays, and reviews on a variety of subjects including the Polish question. It is essential to point out here that a reasonably complete literary biography of Samarin, covering all of his published works, would require a two and possibly three volume treatment.

As was true of the first three studies of this series the purpose here is not to summarize the published works of one of the Moscow Slavophils. Rather, the focus remains on Moscow Slavophilism, specifically, here, on Samarin's contribution to its doctrine, and to its reformism. Samarin's works have therefore been used selectively as was the case in the preceding studies.

Included in this volume is chapter 8 which is about Slavophil views on science and technology, and about Koshelev (1806–1883), who deserves more extensive and thorough treatment than this. Particularly pertinent here is his contribution to Slavophil reformism, to the emancipation and to other reforms, and to modern agricultural technology in Russia. This is strikingly illustrated by his views and reflections on the London exposition of 1851 which he visited.

At least as deserving of a separate study is Ivan Aksakov (1823–1886), who has been accorded in recent years good biographical treatment in both the West and the Soviet Union. He has often been mentioned in these studies but this in no way diminishes the need for a separate full-length work on his Slavophilism. This was seriously considered but had to be abandoned, as he straddles the dividing line of 1861. Any factual and reasonably thorough treatment of his ideological position would take one beyond the realm of pre-Reform Slavophilism into its post-Reform phase, and into the complex pan-Slavism of the 1870s. And these manifestly are beyond the scope of this work. Furthermore, because of his age, (born in 1823), his role in the elaboration of "classical" Slavophilism during the 1840s and 1850s was not quite comparable to that of the four early and older Slavophils.

Finally, one further qualification is necessary, and that is with respect to the importance, more easily sensed and felt than accurately measured and determined, of the debt of the Moscow Slavophils to Western thought and ideas. For example, we could recall Ivan Kireevsky's early impressions of Guizot, and Khomiakov's reading of Western literature, broadly speaking, including Hegel and Schelling. We are reminded of Konstantin Aksakov's youthful enchantment with Homer and Goethe, and of Samarin's early discovery of Lorenz von Stein. And while the Slavophils concentrated on things Russian they continued to read some of the outstanding Western authors in a variety of fields and usually in the original language. Professor N.V. Riazanovsky called attention some years ago to the kinship of Moscow Slavophilism to Western romanticism. In more recent years Professor V. I. Kuleshov, a specialist in literature and history, has given us in his *Slavianofily i russkaia literatura* (1976) the names of a good many Western authors who were well known to the Slavophils. He also calls attention to the Slavophil bond with nineteenth-century "German philosophical Christianity," as well as to Khomiakov's serious reservations about the presumed perfection of Russia's ancient order.

Kuleshov includes both the "allies" of the Slavophils and those whom they renounced. Among the latter were Hegel, Feuerbach, Lamennais, Strauss, Guizot, Thierry, Fichte, Saint-Simon, Fourier, and Comte. More acceptable to the Slavophils were Schelling, "Hegel, taken in a certain way," as for instance Khomiakov's limited use of the dialectic, Baader, Ekstein, Philarete Chasles, Savigny, Henrik Steffens, and Pascal. This incomplete list, chosen here for the purpose of illustration, is sufficiently baffling. How, one wonders, out of the welter of thoughts, ideas, and views, some classical Greek, some Western, and many Russian and Orthodox Byzantine, did Moscow Slavophilism emerge? In these four studies I have tried to record in bare minimum some of the surface manifestations and results of the complex mental process of both the integration and acceptance of certain ideas as well as the rejection of others.

Notes

1. Henry Gifford, *The Times Literary Supplement,* Oct. 24, 1982, p. 1044.
2. Khomiakov, *Sochineniia,* vol. I, p. 287.
3. D.F. Samarin (ed.) *Sochineniia Iu. F. Samarina* (Moscow, 1877–1911). 11 vols. (hereafter cited as Samarin, *Sochineniia*).

PART ONE

THE MAKING OF A SLAVOPHIL

1

The 1820s: Family and Tutors

There is much in Iurii Samarin's life that is reminiscent of the pattern familiar from the study of the other Moscow Slavophils. There are also differences, which will emerge in due course to establish Samarin's individuality, as was the case with Khomiakov, the Kireevsky brothers, and Konstantin Aksakov. Like them, Samarin belonged to the Russian gentry and enjoyed the economic security, social rank, and in general the privileged position that goes with wealth and status. Like them, he possessed a striking intelligence and received his early schooling from private tutors, both Russian and Western. In energy and the capacity for sustained work, however, he surpassed his fellow Slavophils. He left the largest legacy of published works (eleven volumes) as well as other writings that have appeared in scattered publications or are yet not in print and a second volume of correspondence, still unpublished, which would supplement his published correspondence, 1840–1853.

Samarin, born in St. Petersburg in 1819, was the youngest of the early Slavophils (Khomiakov was born in 1804, Ivan Kireevsky in 1806, Konstantin Aksakov in 1817). His father, Fedor Vasil'evich, a wealthy landowner, was equerry to the Empress Maria Fedorovna, the mother of Alexander I. By the beginning of the sixteenth century the Samarins had achieved high rank among the gentry. Their land base at the time was in the Samara gubernia. A Samarin was one of the first to be nominated senator by Peter the Great, a practice followed later by Catherine the Great, Paul I, and Alexander I. His maternal grandfather, Iurii Aleksandrovich Neledinsky-Melitsky, for whom he was named, served as state-secretary under Emperor Paul. A poet, a senator, and a favorite of the widowed Empress Maria Fedorovna, he was doubtless pleased when his daughter, Sofiia Iureevna, Iurii's mother, became the Empress's favorite lady-in-waiting. (Iurii's paternal grandfather, Vasilii Nikolaevich Samarin, married to Princess Meshcherskaia, was, however, a landlord who has not fared well in historical accounts because of his harsh and dictatorial treatment of his serfs.) Thus on both sides of his family Iurii Samarin was in closer touch with the court and the royal family than the other early Slavophils. This is a fact of some significance in his later career.

Iurii's father, born in 1784, was an officer in the Ismailovski regiment; he participated in the military campaigns against Turkey and France between 1805 and 1814 and retired from the army in 1816 as a colonel. Two years later he married and thereafter gave his time and attention to his family and estates. If anyone has compiled a complete list of the landholdings and wealth of the Samarin family it has escaped my attention. Samarin's able biographer, Nol'de, speaks of Iurii's father's "enormous fortune," meaning lands and serfs granted to generations of Samarins by the tsars but gives no specific information beyond a vague reference to estates in the Moscow and Tula gubernias and "along the Volga." Iurii's younger brother, Dmitry, the publisher-editor of Iurii Samarin's works and the source of much biographical information, is more specific, though also incomplete. He says that there were twenty thousand merino sheep, a special project of his father's, on the family Simbirsk estate, and a sugar beet refinery on the Tula estate. Semevsky, the well-known nineteenth-century historian of Russian peasant life, says that on the Samara gubernia estate the Samarins had 2,114 male serfs, and on another in the nearby Syzran district, 322. In addition, the Samarins had on the two estates, respectively, 61 and 400 household serfs, making a total of 2,897 serfs, although male serfs are specified only for the largest number, 2,114.

While the serfs' land allotments of nine to ten *desiatinas,* approximately twenty-seven acres (one desiatina = 2.7 acres), was relatively generous, the serfs on the Samarin estates were on the corvee (*barshchina*) order, not on quit-rent (*obrok*), somewhat freer than corvee and preferred by the serfs. Furthermore, Semevsky states that the 400 household serfs on the Syzran estate were required to do "factory" work of an unspecified nature. Another source lists the Samarin eastern estates, as of about 1861, as the villages of Spasskoe and Vasil'evskoe, on the left bank of the Volga, below Samara.[1] The population of the two villages is given as "up to 2,000," and the extent of the Samarin lands there as 30,000 desiatinas or 81,000 acres.

Recently, on the basis of unpublished archival material, V. A. Aleksandrov has given us sharply outlined portraits of Iurii Samarin's father and paternal grandfather. These do not supply detailed information about the Samarin family estates, but they are extremely valuable in sketching the family heritage in which Iurii grew up. Vasilii Nikolaevich Samarin, the "large" landowner, had estates in the Tula, Tver, Iaroslav, Kostroma, Murom, and Simbirsk gubernias, with about 3,400 serfs in 1788, having increased their number by about 650 in fifteen years. From the records of the Samarin estates, Aleksandrov saw Vasilii Nikolaevich emerge as a "well-read but limited, bilious, thirsty, and cruel serf-owner, a Pharisee and a hypocrite," who deprived the serfs and the village commune of all independence, initiative, and self-government, and created a "police system" on his estates. But for all his rigid control, he could not make his estates prosper, and his son, Iurii Samarin's father, had to rescue them from economic decline.

In contrast to his father, in 1816 F. V. Samarin issued a set of rules and guidelines for his estates with well-defined serf duties and functions, doing away with his father's trivial and annoying meddling in his peasants' affairs. The differences in temperament between father and son were further reflected when Fedor Vasil'evich abandoned his father's agents among the peasants, restored authority to the estate managers, severely limited corporal punishment, and set up record-keeping of peasant offenses. The estate management was urged to encourage commerce among the peasants, and the three-day-a-week corvee, often arbitrarily extended by landlords, was strictly enforced. The village *mir* was not entrusted with administrative duties but was given the right to consider serf needs at general mir assemblies and refer them to the estate management. In addition, the estate manager was obliged to hear serf grievances three times a year against the other estate authorities, and serf meetings were closed to estate authorities. Finally, the village mir or commune could maintain its own treasury supplied with funds from fines, the sale of escheat property, and voluntary contributions. These funds were used to help serfs in case of natural disaster, or to support old serfs without families, or simply loans to serfs. Dmitry Samarin tells us that at one time communal capital on the Simbirsk estate amounted to 50,000 rubles.[2]

Whatever the exact extent of Fedor Samarin's lands, there is no doubt that large acreage, thousands of serfs, and two or more factories provided ample funds for himself and his family.[3] As was customary among the Russian gentry in the late eighteenth and early nineteenth centuries, particularly among the strongly pro-French families, trips to France, especially Paris, were practically mandatory, and Fedor Samarin was no exception. Iurii, the first-born of Fedor's children, spent the winter of 1823–1824, when he was four years old, in Paris with his parents. On this trip, which was only the first of a number of trips for Iurii to Western Europe, Fedor Samarin's main concern in the French capital was to find a tutor for Iurii. After some inquiries he decided on twenty-three-year-old Adolf Pascault. Pascault joined the Samarin household in St. Petersburg soon after the Samarins returned home in 1824, for what was to become a long — and for young Iurii at least — fruitful association. Pascault, called "Stepan Ivanovich," remained Iurii's principal tutor until Iurii entered Moscow University in the fall of 1834 at the age of fifteen.

In the meantime, an important change occurred in the composition of Fedor Samarin's family and its social and intellectual milieu. Late in 1826, when Iurii was seven years old, and the oldest of five children (there were two more boys and two girls), Fedor Samarin left government service and

St. Petersburg and settled his family in Moscow. Two reasons are usually given for this move: the elder Samarin's concern for his children's education, and the management of his estates. Not only was Moscow University, in spite of certain shortcomings, Russia's ranking university at the time, whose professors also often served as private tutors, but also Moscow was more centrally located than St. Petersburg to the Samarin estates.

Pascault, who, in Dmitry Samarin's words, soon became "russified," eventually became a lecturer in French at Moscow University, but he continued to conduct Iurii's education, working out for him a classical curriculum based on Latin and Greek. One of Fedor Samarin's first concerns when the family arrived in Moscow in the fall of 1826 was to supplement Pascault's tutoring of his children by hiring twenty-two-year-old Nikolai Ivanovich Nadezhdin, a graduate of the Moscow Theological Seminary, later Professor at Moscow University and publisher of the well-known *Teleskop*. Nadezhdin remained a tutor of the Samarin children until the middle of 1831.[4]

Pascault taught Iurii French, Latin, geography, and arithmetic while Nadezhdin instructed him in catechism, Russian "by way of Church Slavonic," Greek, history, and, for a while, German; later, a special German tutor was employed. It is not surprising, then, that by the age of ten, Iurii was fluent in French, and what is perhaps more noteworthy, he "spoke freely in Latin." These early years under Pascault's tutoring and guidance left a lasting imprint on Iurii Samarin's character and career. "Classicism in the French pedagogical manner," Nol'de writes, "which lay at the base of Pascault's teaching, is felt in Samarin's whole mental makeup, in his irreproachable logic, in his meticulousness, in the beautiful simplicity of his writing."[5] More recently Gratieux characterized Samarin's letters to Baroness Rahden in French as being "charmantes de pensee et de style."

Valuable as these early achievements were, they did not come without a price. The handicap that beset other gentry children brought up by foreign-speaking nurses, governesses, and tutors did not bypass young Samarin. Speaking French and Latin at ten was admirable, but speaking and writing poor Russian was a heavy sacrifice. Even Pascault was aware of the gap in Iurii's education, and while Nadezhdin's appointment was intended to remedy matters, Iurii recalled many years later that when he entered Moscow University at fifteen he was guilty of ten or twenty of the "crudest errors in [Russian] spelling" in an ordinary dictated passage of several pages. It is also well documented that, although young Samarin could read with ease classical and medieval Latin (he does not seem to have become as proficient in Greek), he was not an easy student for his tutors; he was neither diligent nor well behaved. But he compensated for these shortcomings by sheer ability, so that eventually he wrote in Russian no less proficiently than in French.

A glimpse into the life and education of gentry children, specifically in the Samarin family with the active participation of Iurii's father, is provided by F. O. Buslaev, a fellow student of Iurii Samarin's at Moscow University:

At that time the rich and eminent among the nobility prepared their sons for the university entrance examinations at home. . . . In the gimnazia studied primarily the children of the burghers and local civil servants who . . . acquired very meager knowledge. . . . This explains the urgent need . . . for the establishment in the well-bred, well-to-do families of the most complete and the most proper home schools possible for their children, with an appropriate number of educators and tutors. Such a home school . . . flourished for more than twenty-five years . . . in the home of Fedor Vasil'evich Samarin. . . . During the summer this model school was transferred from the Moscow home of the Samarins to their Izmalkovo estate, twenty versts [12 miles] on the Smolensk road. . . . Every day carriages drawn by a team of four horses punctual to the hour and minutes brought teachers from the city, and took them back.[6]

Clearly, Fedor Samarin made the education of his children a major concern after moving his family to Moscow. Early in the 1830s Nadezhdin's tenure as tutor of the two oldest Samarin boys came to an end, an experience perhaps entering into "his biography more than into Samarin's." In Nol'de's words, the future editor of the ill-fated *Teleskop* used Fedor Samarin's rich library to become acquainted with secular Western culture, particularly with French.[7]

Notes

1. D. F. Samarin, *"Russkii biograficheskii slovar"* (St. Petersburg, 1904), XVIII, 147 (hereafter cited *R. B. S.*); V.I. Semevsky, *Krest'ianskii vopros v Rossii v XVIII i pervoi polovine XIX veka* (St. Petersburg, 1888), II, 415; V. P. Semenov et al., eds., *Rossiia. Polnoe geograficheskoe opisanie nashego otechestva* (St. Petersburg, 1901), VI, 458; B. E. Nol'de, *Iurii Samarin i ego vremia* (Paris, 1926), p. * (hereafter cited as Nol'de, *Samarin*).

2. See V. A. Aleksandrov, *Sel'skaia obshchina v Rossii (XVII – nachalo XIX v.)* (Moscow, 1976), pp. 58, 64; also by Aleksandrov, "Sel'skaia obshchina i votchina v Rossii (XVII – nachalo XIX v)," *Istoricheskie Zapiski,* 1972, no. 89, pp. 248, 294 (hereafter cited *I. Z.*); D. F. Samarin, *R. B. S.,* XVIII, 147.

3. For the purpose of comparison with other gentry families, a few partial figures can be cited. V. G. Orlov, one of the five brothers, favorites of Catherine the Great, possessed, between 1793 and 1824, some 27,000 serfs and 300,000 desiatinas (710,000 acres) of land; the Vorontsovs in sixteen gubernias had 55,000 serfs of both sexes early in the nineteenth century; the Panins, in 1782 had 23,839 serfs of both sexes in many gubernias, and the

Iusupovs had 13,700 serfs of both sexes in the Ukraine and two other gubernias. Aleksandrov, *Sel'skaia obshchina,* pp. 82–85; *I. Z.,* pp. 243–274.

4. There is a discrepancy in dates in the accounts of Nadezhdin's tutorial
duties in the Samarin household. Nol'de states that Nadezhdin spent "two
years" with the Samarins, 1826–1828; Dmitry Samarin, who was tutored by
Nadezhdin, says that Nadezhdin left the Samarins in the middle of 1831. I
have taken Dmitry's statement as more likely to be accurate. Cf. Nol'de,
Samarin, p. 10; D. F. Samarin, *R.B.S.,* p. 134.

5. Nol'de, *Samarin,* p. 9.

6. F. I. Buslaev, "Moi vospominaniia," *Vestnik Evropy,* 1890, no. 12, pp.
519–520, see also Nol'de, *Samarin,* p. 11.

7. Nol'de, *Samarin,* p. 10.

2

The 1830s: Moscow University

Konstantin Aksakov's university years in the middle thirties were a time of important contacts established through his family's social connections, Moscow University, and the Stankevich circle. In the case of youthful Samarin, outside of his family, Moscow University provided him with influential contacts, and its environment assumes a somewhat greater significance in his early life than was perhaps the case with Konstantin Aksakov. Fedor Samarin's large Moscow home on the Tverskaia, though "standing at the summit of Moscow gentry society," did not reach its full prominence until the 1840s, during the second half of which decade Iurii Samarin was no longer living in Moscow.[1]

Neither Dmitry Samarin nor Nol'de tells us much about young Iurii's life during the early 1830s except that he was at home in Moscow, and, it seems, had limited contacts outside his family and his tutors. We also know less about Iurii's father, mother, brothers, and sisters than we do about Konstantin Aksakov and his family. Konstantin's father, Sergei, his younger brother Ivan, and his sister Vera, all with literary gifts and achievements, in a sense competed with Konstantin. In Samarin's case, his light seemed undimmed by family competition. When he entered the faculty of literature of Moscow University at the age of fifteen, in the fall of 1834, Iurii Samarin was, in his own estimate, poorly prepared for university work. Yet scarcely out of the university he would strike his contemporaries, and later students of his works, with his excellent prose. Nol'de declared that he was "one of Russia's best writers" and that pages from his writings were "magnificent models of Russian prose," Struve called Samarin a "first class writer."[2] Although perhaps not in the center of the intellectual ferment of the 1830s — the end of the Pushkin era and the beginning of the Gogol' period — Samarin had the connection of his former tutor, Nadezhdin, who became editor of *Teleskop,* which published Chaadaev's famous essay in 1836. The government's banning of *Teleskop* was an affair, that had repercussions for Russian intellectual-ideological life in the nineteenth century much out of proportion to the relatively few pages of a single essay. Samarin also knew "the poet" of the

Stankevich circle, I. P. Kliushnikov (1811–1895), who was the tutor in Russian literature of a brother and sister of Samarin's.[3]

Samarin was, of course, at Moscow University during one of its most inspiring decades. Although the faculty was only then being enlarged and strengthened, the small but exceptionally lively student body gave the university distinction. As Nol'de, referring to the 1830s and 1840s, points out, every year distinguished names were added to the university student roster: "It is almost possible to say that through the auditorium on Mokhovaia street passed Russia's future cultural and political history."[4] F.I. Buslaev, A. F. Bychkov, P. N. Kudriavtsev, A. N. Popov, Prince V. A. Cherkassky, Count I. D. Delianov (later minister of education), the Armenian historian F. A. Emin, S. M. Solov'ev, P. M. Leont'iev, N. V. Kalachev, the Ukrainian leader N. A. Rigel'man, I. M. Bodiansky, and N. I. Sazonov. And at one time or another during the decade Herzen, Belinsky, Ivan Turgenev, Goncharov, and Lermontov, were in attendance.[5]

This is not to imply that Samarin was actively involved in the intellectual ferment of the mid-1830s. But even as a university student, and despite his father's desire that he concentrate on his studies, he was aware of the stirrings of the decade. As a student, Iurii was impatient with the somewhat artificial routine of academic work, as he had been impatient with his studies under his tutors and with the periodic examinations that his father insisted on, although these helped him to pass his university entrance examinations without difficulty. But there was in him something that attracted attention, for all his impatience and lack of industry. Pogodin, who knew him first as a private tutor and later as a Moscow University professor, ranked him in "first place" in the class of 1838, ahead of Buslaev, Katkov, and Michael Stroev in a three-way second. Buslaev excelled in industriousness, Katkov in curiosity, Stroev was equal to his friends but was less mature; Samarin, Pogodin said, "has much information and possesses the means of acquiring new; he reasons logically and speaks clearly and coherently."[6] Similar evaluations of Samarin at Moscow University were later abstracted from the university records by Nil Popov. In Samarin's freshman year, his essay on Russian style (*slog*) was judged "one of the best." In his sophomore year he took part in the translation from German of August Schlegel's "Theory and History of Dramatic Poetry" and of a work on medieval history, and in his senior year (1838) his collating of Professor Gnedich's translations from the *Iliad* and his study of Derzhavin's work were considered "the best."[7]

But as has long been customary in academic life, the prerogative of grading was not reserved for professors alone. Samarin was one of the many students who have left us impressions of their professors. His reminiscences about his university years were written in 1855, the centennial year of the founding of Moscow University, when he was thirty-five years old. Samarin invited a few graduates to his Moscow home for an informal commemoration; for the occasion, Aksakov wrote his longer and better known *Reminiscence*. Samarin's reminiscences, much shorter and not complete, besides giving us some of his views on various professors, tell us something about his preparation for entrance into the university, about important changes that occurred in the university in the mid-1830s, about the academic atmosphere, relations between students and professors, and, with respect to his future Slavophil career, about the strong legacy of Professor Pogodin's approach to the study and interpretation of Russian history, and its relationship to Western European history.

One senses a certain resentment in Samarin's assertion, early in his reminiscences, that, preparing for the university, he was taught at home in "complete seclusion [*uedinenie*] outside any comradeship."[8] During the last two years of this schooling, between the ages of thirteen and fifteen, Iurii felt "unspeakable fear and trepidation" in spite of the repeated assurances of his tutors that he would do well in the university entrance exams. His discomfort was probably heightened by his isolation and the lack of opportunity to compare his intellectual capacities with those of other students. This rather unusual loneliness for a member of a socially prominent Moscow family seems to have carried over into his university years. Although, in another connection, he mentions Stankevich, Stroev, and Konstantin Aksakov, he did not join any of the Moscow circles, then at the height of their feverish activities, and he does not seem to have formed many warm and lasting friendships in or out of the university during his years as an undergraduate.

From a recently published paragraph of an unpublished letter written by Samarin to a friend on February 1, 1837, we get a glimpse into the inner life and temperament of the seventeen year old university sophomore.[9] In this paragraph, Iurii says that he admires Lermontov's poem *"Death of a Poet"* (Smert Poeta), written immediately after Pushkin's death. The central thought is the confession the dead poet evoked in Iurii. Fedor Samarin had asked Iurii to read to his mother the poet Zhukovsky's letter about Pushkin's last hours. Iurii confesses that he knows little about Pushkin but has "profound sympathy" for the poet and the man who was cursed and insulted, and he says he has been deeply disappointed and hurt that his mother, for some unstated reason, does not appreciate Pushkin. "Would you believe," he asks, "that my mother, the most holy person on earth, unlike anyone else I know, smiled ironically, an irony I never knew in her, and I heard form her lips insults addressed at the bloody specter of the poet at the moment when he left this earth and when human judgment should be silent before the judgement of God."[10]

Iurii goes on to say that he has found a kindred soul not only in Pushkin but also in Lermontov, who has written so admirably about Pushkin's death. He imagines his own fate in Pushkin's: "God did not make me a poet, but he

has granted me fervent passions and a sense of the exalted and the beautiful that silence in me the sense of propriety and the rules of trivial morality.
I, too, . . . could fight a duel, . . . I could easily die a violent death. . . . Who
could be silent when people condemn me, people who do not know the depth
of my heart?"[11] This youthful confession reveals a side of Samarin's nature
that is usually neglected in the stress on his disciplined and logical mind; but
it was this more emotional, and at the same time sterner, side that made him
later accept imprisonment for his convictions on the problem of the Baltic
provinces and helped him endure the wrath of some of his fellow gentry on
the emancipation question.

In the middle 1830s when Samarin began his university studies Moscow
University was in the process of change and improvement. New courses
were introduced, the length of study was extended from three to four years
for all undergraduates, and the quality of the faculty was raised by hiring
young, capable men who had done graduate work in German universities.
Between this new younger faculty especially, and the students, a spontaneous
camaraderie existed — or so at least for Samarin. There is a touch of nostal-
gic idealization on this point in his "Reminiscences." Personal relations between students and professors were the "closest and the simplest." Nothing
stood in the way of their friendly relations, which were characterized by a
"living communion" in which the "professors worked for the students" while
the "students followed the professors." In summary, the "university existed
as something independent, complete, living, direct, and immediately acting
on life."[12]

Yet this well-nigh perfect scholarly community consisted of sharply etched
individuals among faculty as well as students. Samarin says that the professor who cast the strongest spell on him and "many other" students was
Pogodin, a mentor and preceptor whose outstanding asset was the ability to
inspire his students. Pogodin, though born a son of a Stroganov family serf,
had risen to academic rank on his merits. He did not seek popularity, and
his lectures were not distinguished by the "artistic completeness and total
freshness of [V. S.] Pecherin's lectures" on the Greek language: "In the gift
of oral exposition," Samarin says, Pogodin was far behind [D. L. Kriukov,
professor of classical (Roman) literature and history. What marked
Pogodin's lectures was the "independent orientation of his thought."[13]

In 1855 Samarin confessed that he could not recall what Pogodin taught
in the second half of the 1830s. He could not "transmit the content" of
Pogodin's lectures "warmed by deep sympathy for Russian life." But speaking for himself and his fellow students, he says they were "ushered into a new
view of Russian history and Russian life in general." Pogodin was in effect
elaborating on the broad and pervasive theme of the historical-cultural differences between Russia and the West, sharpened by Peter the great and his
successors, and more recently by the Napoleonic invasion of Russia.

Pogodin held that "Western formulas cannot apply to us," and that "in Russian life there are certain principles alien to other nations." He further stressed that the course of Russian history and progress follows "other laws not as yet established by scholarship."

Since all this, Samarin says, was presented without proof or evidence, it is possible that Pogodin's impression on his students in general was neither so profound nor so lasting as Samarin judged it to be. Yet there is no reason to doubt his words that Pogodin "convinced him of the necessity of clarifying the phenomena of Russian history from within itself. This was Pogodin's version in the mid-1830s of that strong and persistent view that Russia had followed a different historical path from that of the West, which one finds in its Slavophil version in the 1840s and 1850s, in Tiutchev's poetry, in Dostoevsky's reflections, and in the ideology of some of the Russian populists in the 1860s and 1870s.

That youthful aristocratic Samarin should have been deeply struck by Pogodin's views is perhaps understandable in view of his family's social and economic position. A young student, accustomed from childhood to Western tutors, French language and literature, and travel in Western Europe, could perhaps assume that his life in Russia was not so different from life in the West. From this perhaps came the inclination to regard Russia's past and present as similar to if not identical with that of the West. But Samarin needed to be reminded, as fellow nobleman Alexander Herzen reminded the readers of his *Kolokol* in his obituary of Konstantin Aksakov in 1861, that "we were in the arms of French governesses, and belatedly learned that our mother is not she but the harassed [Russian] peasant woman."[14]

The delusion lasted for Samarin until the shock caused by Pogodin's claim — for such it seems to have been — that Russia's historical past and Russian life were different from those of the West, as they must inevitably have appeared to a Russian born in a serf family. It is possible to overestimate the importance of this incident; but it would be worse to overlook it when in fact the Russian-Western differences, specifically between the Western confessions and Eastern Orthodoxy, soon became central to Samarin's doctoral dissertation, and to his later Slavophilism; when his views on the Baltic borderlands, the Polish question, and even on the emancipation of the serfs, in a rather special way, were deeply colored by this basic concept of Russia's different, and in the Slavophil view, unique, historical road.

Despite what appears to have been a rather isolated and perhaps somewhat lonely university life, Samarin became acquainted with several men who in time became not merely his friends but also his ideological partners, particularly in connection with his lifelong Slavophil orientation. These new friends were Konstantin Aksakov, Khomiakov, and Ivan Kireevsky, and also

Chaadaev, the poet Lermontov, and — though this was not strictly a new connection, but rather a relationship — his cousin Prince I. S. Gagarin.

It is not always easy to determine with certainty the source of an idea or
conviction accepted by a young, impressionable, but independent and self-
respecting man such as Samarin. In his early life he was prone to significant
and even drastic switches in orientation, and many of those around him were
subject to the same vagaries of time and place. Added to these obstacles of
human complexity, and a general air of instability and unpredictability, there
were also obstacles erected by government censorship, and by the tsar's
harassment and persecution of those he disliked or feared. In such circumstances, tentativeness often seems preferable to rash certainty. With
these cautions, one can attempt to sort out these influences on Samarin.

Before Samarin left Moscow University for the larger world of Moscow
society, one of his new contacts was with Lermontov. Although still in his
early twenties, Lermontov, (b. 1814) was a well-established poet and author.
This relationship, which was recently treated in a brief but illuminating essay
by Efimova, has relevance to Samarin's early intellectual growth. Samarin
met Lermontov in his aunt's home in Moscow in January 1838 (when he was
eighteen); Lermontov was on his way from the Caucasus to St. Petersburg.
During the next two and a half years, until Lermontov's tragic death in a duel,
the sporadic meetings between them seem to have developed into sincere,
if perhaps unequal, friendship; Lermontov had after all, already won for himself a name as gifted poet and prose writer, whereas Samarin five years the
younger, had only a university degree to his credit. (The difference in age,
normally perhaps of little consequence, seems to be a matter of some significance in the case of precocious young men.)

A long entry in Samarin's diary dated July 31, 1841, fifteen days after
Lermontov's death in the Caucasus, indicates that Samarin and Lermontov
met from time to time in various Moscow salons and seem to have seen a
good deal of each other on Lermontov's lasts visit to Moscow in April 1841,
when he was returning to the Caucasus. Lermontov, like Samarin, had been
brought up by Western governesses and tutors, but after two years at Moscow University, 1830–1832, he transferred to a military school in St.
Petersburg. From 1837 until his death he lived in exile in the Caucasus, he
had been sent there because the government found certain lines in "Death
of a Poet" "impermissible" on account of their negative view of the state of
affairs in Russia. The government's censure did not effectively suppress the
poem, of course, and Lermontov was soon being hailed as Pushkin's successor.

In this diary entry Samarin says, "I was in raptures from his [Lermontov's]
verses about Pushkin's death." Samarin's admiration for and attachment to
the young poet grew out of this initial impression. "After two or three meetings," the entry continues, Lermontov "captivated me with his simple at-

titude toward me, and with his childlike frankness."[15] Samarin's pain at the news of Lermontov's death is expressed in the opening words of the diary entry: "Lermontov was killed in a duel with Martynov! The spirit to write has gone! [Lermontov] has suffered the same fate as Pushkin. The heart is involuntarily stifled, and facing this new loss the old [losses] are painfully recalled, Griboedov, Marlinsky, Pushkin, Lermontov. One is horrified for Russia at the thought that not blind chance, but some sort of verdict of faith is smiting her, depriving her of her best sons, her poets."[16]

Samarin's sorrow was compounded by a sense of admiration for the poet, by the great loss for Russia, and by an element of pity. "Pushkin needs no exculpation," he wrote; "But Lermontov was not recognized by all, was understood by few, and almost no one loved him." Yet his death was a "loss for a whole generation," and a "whole nation was dressed in mourning." The entry is in some ways sentimental and self-indulgent, though that's not perhaps surprising in the circumstances. Samarin, on the threshold of breaking away from the narrow confines of home and university into Moscow's intellectual, literary, and artistic world, and soon into four years of exceptionally fruitful postgraduate work, was perhaps a little overwhelmed by the prospects before him, and he had treasured this friendship with Lermontov. He recalled how Lermontov, when they met in salons, "freely turned to me in his conversations and summoned me to him." He knew me, Samarin says, and "I did not hide." On the word of an unnamed third party, Samarin concluded that Lermontov "had a favorable impression of me" — and this opinion of the poet could not fail to please the young, aspiring university graduate.[17] Furthermore, although in the spring of 1840 Samarin was far from a blind admirer of Khomiakov, he noted in his diary that Lermontov "liked Khomiakov." This was after Gogol's garden party given May 9 at Pogodin's Moscow home at which were present, among others, Khomiakov, the Aksakov's, and Lermontov.[18]

Lermontov may well have sensed the exceptional mind and potential in young Samarin. He was doubtless sincere in his association with the promising aristocrat, Lermontov himself moved in aristocratic company — but Samarin probably gained more from their relationship than Lermontov did. Equally important was the fact that Lermontov belonged to the "circle of 16," to which also belonged Samarin's elder cousin Prince I. S. Gagarin (born the same year as Lermontov, thus five years older than Samarin). The existence of this circle at the end of the 1830s was brief and controversial. Its home base was St. Petersburg, and it consisted of sixteen young men, about half university graduates, half young officers of the Guard, all in their early or middle twenties. Like other similar circles it had no formal organization, no membership roster, and no agreed-on program. Some authorities consider it to have been neo-Decembrist, and oppositionist; at least one writer describes it as nonexistent, merely a "crowd of 'golden youth.'"[19] What we do know is that some of the young men whose names are associated with the circle had definite views and concerns even if they did not arrive at a consensus, Samarin became cognizant of these ideas at the turn of the 1830s, and they, even if by mere coincidence, had a significant place in Samarin's later Slavophil thought.

What concerned members of the "circle of 16," not necessarily in the order given here, were the problem of nationality (*natsional'nost'*), central to a sense of national cultural identity at a time when the classical Russian literature was in its promising but early stage; Russia's place in the family of nations; its historical path; its presumed "youth"; emancipation of the serfs; and, more narrowly, Lermontov's nationalistic views of foreigners, specifically Germans, as stated in his "*Sashka,*" (1839) and perhaps less forcefully in "Death of a Poet," which may have played a part in Samarin's later views in *Borderlands of Russia.*[20]

The member of the "circle of 16" with whom Samarin had the most frequent contacts, and the only known published correspondence, was his cousin, Prince Gagarin, the so-called "Paris" Gagarin, who spoke poor Russian, wrote in French, and in 1843 joined the Jesuit order in the West, was one of a small but conspicuous breed of Russian "Westerners" whose French veneer, superimposed on serf-ridden Russia, in the 1840s enraged the Slavophil Aksakov no less than the Westerner Belinsky. Gagarin, who confessed his pro-Catholic leanings in 1836, knew Chaadaev's views on the relationship of Russian culture to Western, and was most probably in ideological debt to Chaadaev. At about that time Gagarin wrote in his diary, "Russia is a young sister in the family of European nations" and the "swaddled infant" in Europe.

Similar views are contained in a didactic, big-brotherly letter in French from Gagarin to Samarin, dated April 2, 1838, and written in answer to a letter from Samarin. Samarin's letter has not been published but Gagarin refers to "la jeune Amerique," and to a statement in Samarin's letter that "la Civilisation de l'Occident est a son declin, . . . le jour de l'Orient est arrive" by which Samarin doubtless meant Russia.[21] These are thoughts that circulated in Russia in the 1830s and 1840s, and to which attention has already been called. Assigning source and authorship to the notion of the "decaying West" (*gniiushchii zapad*) is a difficult and unrewarding task, but it seems to have originated in the West and to have been imported into Russia.[22]

What became Russian about this notion for some in the post-Decembrist generation was that, whereas the West was old and presumably dying, Russia was young and the wave of the future, an idea which the Slavophils found congenial and convenient at times. Kireevsky at the end of the 1820s, and a number of other Russian intellectuals, as already pointed out, were profoundly disturbed about the state of Russian culture, specifically literature, as compared with the achievements of the West. Certainly the Russian state and church going back to the ninth and tenth centuries could not be considered young compared with their Western counterparts, but somehow the bright young men of the post-Decembrist generation found it psychologically satisfying to see Russia's cultural backwardness and its literary barrenness (although the Pushkin era had begun) as sure signs of youth, and of future productivity. Whether Russia was young or old remains a moot question. These young men were, however, prophetic about Russia's future, and about its impending burst of literary creativity to which many of them, and the next generation, contributed.

As members of the "circle of 16," Gagarin and Lermontov, who met in St. Petersburg in 1839, were aware of the general ideas mentioned above; the ideas were talked about in the circle. But they also knew that the circle had arrived at no agreement or consensus, that it had no program, and that there were no views equally common to all its members. Therefore when Samarin met members of the circle in Moscow, in the spring of 1840, he was probably exposed to no more than loosely floating views and ideas. Lermontov, however, after an initial dislike, firmly caught his attention. On July 19, 1840, Samarin wrote to Gagarin that he often saw Lermontov. "Les premiers instants, la présence de cet homme m'était désagreáble; je le sentais doué d'une grande force d'investigation qui lisait dans ma pensee. . . . " Despite the initial uneasiness that Samarin felt at Lermontov's "reading" of his mind, he was sure that the poet could help him "comprehend much."[23]

Precisely what Lermontov helped young Samarin to understand in the spring of 1840 is problematic; it is certain, however, that in the summer, or within about a month of the just mentioned letter to Gagarin, Samarin wrote his well-known letter (dated September 1840) to François Mauguin (1798–1855), a member of the French parliament, then on a short visit to Russia. The letter refers to conversations between Mauguin and Samarin and Konstantin Aksakov, and speaks for both incipient but by no means as yet convinced Slavophils. The letter (ten and a half pages long) begins with a review of Russian history. Despite his later stress on the presumed peaceful nature of the Russian Slavs, Samarin says that Russia's history during the first seven or eight centuries presents "d'un enchaînement de guerres presque perpétuelles." These were civil wars, between appanage princes until the fifteenth century, or external wars with Tatar tribes and Khazars, Pechenegs, Polovtsy, and Mongols or with Poles and Lithuanians.

At the same time, Russia's "spiritual independence" was threatened by the papacy and Catholicism. It had to resist the popes, who, "tantôt par les armes, et tantôt par une propagande sourde et infatigable, s'efforçait d'arracher la Russie à son isolement pour la faire entrer dans le mouvement des peuples occidentaux." Then came the Reformation and Protestantism, and all of northern Europe succumbed, but Samarin and Aksakov contended that Protestantism was a logical outgrowth of Catholicism, and since Russia had never been Catholic, it could not provide fertile ground for Protestantism. Under Peter the Great's pressure, Russia opened its gates to the West and the Russian people were forced to forget their past, and "nous devenons Francais, puis Allemands." The new French and German intrusions in Russia were different from the old Catholic and Protestant. They were secular in nature and threatened Russia's "social order" and its "governmental principle, autocracy." They took hold of the Decembrists, and a whole generation was "seduced" by false Western values and institutions.[24]

During the eighteenth century, young Samarin wrote Mauguin, "nous rivalisions avec les Francais dans la connaissance de leur langue et de leur littérature." Thus a period of exclusive nationalism in Russian history was followed by a "period of imitation," which in turn led us into "un cosmopolitisme pâle et dénué," but this could not last indefinitely. Western influences in Russia had to come to an end, Russia had to discover its own national identity. From now on Russia would borrow from the West only "les résultats matériels de la civilisation, tels que l'industrie; désormais notre développement sera tout excentrique."

In the Moscow salon conversations between Mauguin and Samarin and Aksakov, the young Russian patriots aroused Mauguin's fears that the cultural independence and aloofness from the West, which they espoused might lead Russia to confrontation with the West and to "rêves de conquête embrassant l'univers."[25] Samarin denied any such dreams; the pressing problem for Russia, he wrote, was to accurately and carefully define the components of Russian nationality (*narodnost'*), that is, its religious principle and autocracy. Although he had only begun the long work on his dissertation in which the major topic was the relationship between Orthodoxy, Catholicism, and Protestantism, he saw in D. F. Strauss's *Leben Jesu* (1835–1836) proof that Protestantism is "not a religion but only a negation of Catholicism." In Strauss and Lamennais, "deux hautes intelligences," Samarin found an illustration that the cause of religion in the West was lost.

Returning to early Russian history, and declaring his firm allegiance to the Russian monarchical principle as Russia's great historical achievement, Samarin repeated the later Slavophil fiction, heard, it seems, from Khomiakov in the winter of 1839, and earlier from Pogodin, and firmly fixed in Samarin's and Aksakov's minds, that "there was and there could be no conquest" in Russian history. Samarin held that the relationship between the Normans and the French, and between the Normans and the English, was completely different from that between Normans and Russians, because the Russians, according to the old Normanist theory, invited Rurik and the Normans to Kiev. From this premise Samarin drew a series of far-reaching but dubious conclusions. Not only did old Russia not know conquest, but it also could not know feudalism and military aristocracy as an "independent principle." Furthermore, since Russia had not experienced the "hostile relations of conquered and conquerors," it would be immune to "revolution and constitution." No less idealized than this was Samarin's view of Russia's conversion to Christianity, which, he informed Mauguin, "was introduced among us without war, without force, and with the unanimous consent of the whole people."[26]

In reference to the Kievan period of Russian history, and to the centuries of appanage Russia, Samarin spoke of the "centripetal" phase of Russian history when Russia was seeking its "center," something which it found in Moscow in the fifteenth century under Ivan III. That is when it became embodied in the principle of autocracy. This was achieved after prolonged struggles among Russian princes and against foreigners, and even against Catholicism. This is followed by the paradoxical conclusion, "Thus we have had neither conquest, nor feudalism, nor aristocracy (in the sense of an autonomous principle), and we have had no agreement, no *contrat social* between tsar and people." This "unlimited, united, and peoples' authority," Samarin asserted, "acting in the name of all," was the "sacred heritage of Russian history," and any other form of government "would be tyranny" and would lead to revolutions, religious wars, and other disturbances, as in the West.[27]

What was there in this letter that young Samarin could have learned from, or found confirmation of, in Lermontov (and the "circle of 16") whom he met in Moscow a few months before he met Mauguin? Lermontov's "Sashka" and "Nravstvennaia poema" (1839) are both quite explicit about the search for Russian nationality, the notion of the West's age and Russia's "youth," and a distrust of foreigners, specifically of Germans. What Samarin did not borrow from Lermontov in this letter to Mauguin — not from "Death of a Poet," or from "Sashka," or from the eight-line "Proshchai nemytaia Rossiia" (Farewell, Unwashed Russia) (1840),[28] or from any other poem — is the staunchly pro-autocracy stand. Nor is there any pro-emancipation, anti-serf sentiment, as enunciated in Khomiakov's "About the Old and the New," which Khomiakov read in Kireevsky's home in the winter of 1839. Samarin's unreserved praise of Russian autocracy could not have been inspired by Lermontov, but was probably a deep-seated conviction from Samarin's home and family environment, so deep that even in later life he was unable to shift his views on autocracy to keep up with Khomiakov, and particularly Konstantin Aksakov, when they experienced doubts about government in general, and perhaps entertained occasionally thoughts of Christian anarchism.

Samarin's letter to Mauguin, drafted with Konstantin Aksakov's concurrence, is often cited as a statement of Samarin's early Slavophil convictions. More accurately, it was an incomplete confession of some of his proto-Slavophil views. Even more uncertain, in the charged and highly fluid atmosphere of the time, is Lermontov's ideological position. The friendship

between Lermontov and Samarin, in 1840–1841 was that of a certain congeniality rather than a complete meeting of minds; there were perhaps some
shared convictions, but could one conclude from this that Lermontov was
pro-Slavophil or anti-Slavophil, as has recently been done?[29] Could there
be pro- or anti-Slavophils before Slavophilism? In 1839, 1840, and 1841,
Slavophilism was barely emerging from the ideological ferment of the 1830s;
to speak of Slavophilism as if it had become fully formed then, is to declare
the decades of the 1840s and 1850s (when it and Westernism took form and
content) nonexistent.

Not only Samarin but Khomiakov and Ivan Kireevsky knew Lermontov
and his work and valued it highly. All three, and Konstantin Aksakov also,
had met Lermontov, but he was closest to Samarin. Samarin tells us that
Lermontov made a "very favorable impression" on all his friends, and that
Lermontov "liked Khomiakov more than the rest." Khomiakov in turn saw
in Lermontov (May 20, 1840) "a true talent both as a poet and as a prose
writer." This was said less than a month before the tsar declared *A Hero of
Our Time* "a wretched book," and a witness to the "great depravity of its
author."[30]

The incipient Slavophil circle would have liked to attract Lermontov, just
as the Slavophil families attempted to enlist Gogol' on their side, but it is
doubtful whether Lermontov was ready and willing to join a proto-Slavophil
group. It is also doubtful whether he was ready for the proto-Westerner
camp, for toward the end of his life, as his poem "Spor" Dispute (1841), the
first of his projected cycle *Vostok* (The East), indicates, his gaze was turned
toward the "mystical" East rather than toward the West and toward
rationalism, idealism, and secularism.

For young Samarin, the 1830s were primarily a period of schooling in the
relative seclusion of the family home, and of university work, which seems
to have afforded few contacts outside the lecture halls. Yet these were years
during which the seed was cast that was to bear the harvest in the next two
decades. Circumstances began to change rapidly toward the end of the
1830s as Samarin graduated from the university and enlarged his contacts to
include Lermontov and the "circle of 16." At the same time he moved
toward the Slavophil camp then in the process of formation as it responded
to the challenge of the Westerner camp, also in the process of formation.
Lermontov's premature death in 1841, and the demise of the "circle of 16,"
would soon become memories for Samarin, but Slavophilism, locked in
ideological struggle with Westernism for a generation was to remain a major
factor for the rest of his life.

Notes

1. Nol'de, *Samarin,* p. 14.
2. Ibid., p. 12; P. Struve, "Iurii Samarin. Opyt kharahteristiki i otsenski," *Vozrozhdenie,* Paris, no. 376, June 13, 1926, p. 2. Kavelin, one of Samarin's most determined ideological opponents, said that Samarin possessed a "masterly pen" and a "great writer's talent." K. D. Kavelin, "Nekrolog. Iurii Fedorovich Samarin," *Vestnik Evropy,* 1876, no. 4, pp. 907, 909.
3. See Samarin, *Sochineniia,* XII, 23; S. I. Mashinsky, ed., *Poety kruzhka N. V. Stankevicha* (Moscow-Leningrad, 1964), pp. 487–493.
4. Nol'de, *Samarin,* p. 13.
5. Ibid. Moscow University had 438 students in 1836. With the exception of the period of the Napoleonic wars, this was probably the lowest figure for the nineteenth century. In 1822–1823 the enrollment was 695; in 1823–1824, 768; in 1824–1825, 800; in 1825–1826, 876. In 1837 there were 611 students; in 1838, 637; in 1839, 765; and in 1840, 889 (about the same number as in 1825). The first fifteen years of the reign of Nicholas I were particularly hard on university enrollments. For additional enrollment figures and for ably drawn vignettes of the leading professors at Moscow University, see A. A. Kizevetter et al., *Moskovskii universitet 1755–1930* (Paris, 1930), pp. 83–118. Herzen enthusiastically recalled later: "In disgraced Moscow University, as in a common reservoir, the young Russian forces gathered together from all directions and from all strata of society. In its halls they became purified of prejudices acquired in the domestic environment, reached common ground, fraternized, and once again flowed in all directions, and all strata of society in Russia." Quote from *My Past and Thoughts,* I, 95 in *Russkii biograficheskii slovar'* (St. Petersburg, 1914), vol. Labzina-Liashchenko, p. 270.
6. N. P. Barsukov, *Zhizn' i trudy M. P. Pogodina,* 22 vols. (St. Petersburg, 1888–1910), V, 139 (hereafter cited as Barsukov, *Pogodin*). See also Nol'de, *Samarin,* p. 14.
7. Samarin, *Sochineniia,* XII, 475.
8. Iu. F. Samarin, "Iz vospominanii ob universitete, 1834–1838 g.," *Rus',* 1880, no. 1, p. 18. Nadezhdin's reaction, as recorded in his brief and unfinished autobiography, was similar to Samarin's. He says that while at the Samarin's (1826–1828), he lived, "one might say in complete withdrawal from the world, known to no one, and myself knowing no one except the members of the family in which I found myself." But Nadezhdin (born 1804) does not seem to have been completely at a loss while at the Samarins'. He mentions reading several works form Fedor Samarin's library. These give

us a glimpse into the reading fare that young Iurii had at his disposal. Nadezhdin mentions Edward Gibbon's *The History of the Decline and Fall of the Roman Empire,* in French translation, F. P. Guizot (unnamed works), J. C. L. Sismondi's *Histoire des Republiques Italiennes du moyen age* (presumably all 16 vols.) Henry Hallam's French translation, and unnamed romantic works, "a l'ordre du jour." See P. S. Savel'ev; (ed.) "N. I. Nadezhdin. Aftobiografiia," *Russkii Vestnik,* March 1856, book one, pp. 56–57.

9. See M. T. Efimova, "Iurii Samarin v ego otnoshenii k Lermontovu," *Pushkinskii sbornik* (Pskov, 1968), pp. 42–43 (hereafter cited as Efimova, "Samarin i Lermontov").

10. As quoted in ibid. For the views of Khomiakov and Ivan Kireevsky on Pushkin, see M. T. Efimova, "Tema 'Pushkin i Slavianofily' v Pushkinovedenii," in *Pushkinskii sbornik,* pp. 15–22.

11. Efimova, "Samarin and Lermontov," p. 43.

12. Samarin, "Iz vospominanii ob universitete, p. 19.

13. Ibid., p. 19.

14. Herzen's reprinted obituary is attached to K. S. Aksakov, *Vospominanie studentsva* (St. Petersburg, n.d.), pp. 40–42.

15. V. V. Grigorenko et al., eds. *M. Iu. Lermontov v vospominaiiakh sovremennikov* (Moscow, 1964) pp. 304, 506.

16. See also, A. Vasil'ev, ed. *M. Iu. Lermontov v vospominaniiakh sovremennikov* (Penza, 1960), pp. 210–214.

17. Grigorenko, *M. Iu. Lermontov,* pp. 303–304.

18. Ibid., p. 304. For Sergie Aksakov's account of the party and the many guests, see S. I. Mashinsky, ed. *S. T. Aksakov. Sobranie sochinenii,* 4 vols. (Moscow, 1955–1956), III 186.

19. Ibid., p. 25. Besides Samarin's cousin, Prince Gagarin, the members of the "circle of 16" included the Pole, Count Xevier Branicki, the "semi-Frenchman," Prince A. P. Shuvalov, the Princes P. A. Valuev and A. V. and S. V. Dolgoruki, and Baron D. P. Frederiks. See E. G. Gershtein, "Lermontov i 'kruzhok shestnadtsati,'" in N. L. Brodsky et al., eds., *Zhizn' i tvorchestvo M. Iu. Lermontova. Issledovaniia i materialy.* (Moscow, 1941), p. 89.

20. B. M. Eikhenbaum, ed. *M. Iu. Lermontov. Polnoe sobranie sochinenii,* 4 vols. (Moscow-Leningrad, 1947–1948), I, 17–20; II, 71–121 (hereafter cited as Lermontov, *Sochineniia*).

21. Brodsky et al. eds. *Zhizn' i tvorchestvo M. Iu. Lermontova,* pp. 94–95.

22. In the first volume of this series I made a brief reference to Shevyrev's involvement in a controversy with Belinsky in 1841 over the notion of the "decaying West," which the Slavophils picked up before Slavophilism was fully formed, and which was often but without proof attributed by the Westerners, specifically Belinsky, to Professor S. P. Shevyrev. Ninety-nine

years later P. B. Struve in a detailed and erudite essay traced the source of the "theory" and "aphorism" of the "decaying West" to the French writer Victor-Euphemon-Philarete Chasles (1799–1873), and to the German Baron Ferdinand d'Eckstein specifically, and more broadly to several currents of thought in the West at the end of the eighteenth and early nineteenth centuries. The general, and paradoxically grouped, sources of the notion of the "decaying West," were (1) the 'theocratic' ideology of Saint-Martin, Baader, Joseph de Maistre, de Bonald, and Lamennais, (2) Western romanticism with its idealization of the Middle Ages, and (3) the then incipient "socialist-anticapitalist literature." Each of these, for its own reason, saw the "decaying" of the West, just as early in this century Oswald Spengler saw "Der Untergang des Abendlandes." See P. B. Struve, "S. P. Shevyrev i zapadnyie vnusheniia i istochniki teoriia aforizma o 'gnilom' ili 'gniiushchem' Zapade," *Zapiski Russkogo Nauchnogo Instituta v Belgrade* (Belgrad, 1940), no. 17, pp. 201–263; Peter K. Christoff, *An Introduction to Nineteenth-Century Russian Slavophilism: A Study in Ideas,* vol. I, *A. S. Xomjakov* (The Hague, 1961), pp. 65,67; S.P. Shevyrev, "Vzgliad russkogo na sovremennoe obrazovanie Evropy," *Moskvitianin,* 1841, no. 1, chast' I, pp. 219–296.

23. In Samarin, *Socheneniia,* XII, 54.

24. Samarin, *Sochineniia,* XII, pp. 61–62.

25. Ibid., pp. 63–64.

26. Ibid., pp. 65–67.

27. Ibid., p. 68.

28. See Lermontov, *Sochineniia,* II, pp. 120–121.

29. V. I. Kirpotin, *Politicheskie motivy v tvorchestve Lermontova* (Moscow, 1939), p. 157.

30. V. A. Manuilov, *Letopis' zhizni i tvorchestva M. Iu. Lermontova* (Moscow-Leningrad, 1964), pp. 131–133.

3

The Early 1840s: The Dissertation

No decade of nineteenth century failed to leave its imprint on the life and fortunes of Russia and the West, and the 1840s were no exception. Indeed, certain manifestations of Western and Russian thought of the 1840s extended far into the nineteenth century, and even into the twentieth. From the West under the impetus of French rationalism, utopian socialism, German idealism, and to a lesser extent English empiricism, there came to Russia a strong current of Western anthropocentrism. Man would no longer be merely the measure of all things, he would also be the creator of all things, including the earthly paradises of the future. And to this end perhaps, in 1842, Heine was talking about "Die soziale Weltrevolution," with its implication of global secular messianism. Nothing better symbolized the West's all-consuming faith in man than modern science, perhaps Western man's crowning achievement. It is no accident, therefore, that *Wissenschaft, nauka,* science, came to encompass so much that often the word became a source of obfuscation rather than of precision (*akribeia*) and clarity.

It was no longer sufficient to record the West's great achievements in mathematics, physics, chemistry, and biology, with promise of more to come; now the time had arrived for Saint-Simon's "science de l'homme." In the late 1830s and early 1840s Comte labored mightily to create his "positive philosophy." The first volume of *Cours de philosophie positive,* appeared in 1830, and the last, sixth, volume,in 1842, while John Stuart Mill published his no less weighty *System of Logic* in 1843. For the time being, that is, the first two or three years of the 1840s, there was a meeting of minds between Mill and Comte, and Mill could confess to Comte, with satisfaction, that his "exceptional" lot was, "never to have believed in God, not even as a child."

While Comte was challenging Christianity in the name of the "science of man" and later in the name of the "Great Being" theme, and Mill was doing the same in the name of human logic, D. F. Strauss's *Das Leben Jesu kritisch bearbeitet* (1835–1836) and *Die christliche Glaubenslehre* (1840–1841) were undermining Christianity in the West in a pseudo-theological way. Strauss's denial of the historicity of the supernatural elements of the Gospels and his attack on Christian doctrine succeeded not so much in doing away with belief and religion as in substituting perhaps unintentionally belief in man for belief in God. It is also doubtful that Comte ever succeeded in creating his sixth science (of man), but it is now clear that he made his contribution however unwittingly to the religion of man or more precisely to the worship of man.

Today we are not so certain that those who claimed self-sufficiency for the human being through reason, logic, and science, and its handmaiden technology, thereby denying the need for religion or downgrading it, actually chose atheism. We see them more as cultists, believers in man — anthropotheists rather than atheists, that is total nonbelievers. Placing one's faith and reliance in the human faculty of reason and its concomitants, logic, philosophy, and science, is, in effect, deifying of man, after which the next, inevitable, step, historically attested to time and again, is hero worship, and a variety of cults. Cults in recent times, from one end of the ideological spectrum to the other, have included those of Marx, Hitler, Lenin, Stalin and Mao. The day of *Übermensch,* superman, was at hand in the West, for it seems that Western "scientific" man is no more capable of life without believing than of life without reason and intelligence.

The record from prehistoric times to the present seems to suggest that the human being has no less need to believe, to belong, and to worship than to think and reason. The societies, which in modern times gave rise to the doctrines of papal infallibility and divine right of kings, seemed on the way in certain instances to completing a cycle by returning to the age of the pharaohs when the temporal ruler and the deity were united in one and the same person. For when in the heyday of Western utopian socialisms, of *Le mouvement social,* the 1830s and 1840s, omnipotence (even to the extent of the creation of a new, nobler human being), infallibility (in the name of science or "scientific" doctrine), eternity (the dialectic would presumably come to an end in due course, and the new blessed state of nature would endure) were attributed to man and his society, anthropocentrism and anthropotheism had indeed arrived. Then came Marxism toward the end of the 1840s with its faith in proletarian man with his promise of world revolution, and a new millennium for man without God. There were probably few atheists left in the West, but a conscious and determined effort was being made to put the human being in the center of the universe perhaps even replacing the Christian God, fundamentally conceived as the perfect spirit.

Incipient Slavophilism could hardly have seen this problem with thorough clarity and completeness at the end of the thirties and early forties — we see it now with historical hindsight — but it is evident that the Slavophils grasped the essence of the conflict. Samarin's inner struggle in the first several years of the 1840s was a consequence of his effort, vain in the end, to reconcile speculative (human) philosophy (Hegelianism), and divine Christian revelation, perhaps in some form of Slavophil Orthodoxy.

In his letter to Mauguin in September 1840 Samarin made reference to the work of Strauss and Lamennais. Saint-Simon's views were discussed in the Herzen circle in Moscow in the early 1830s, and also by Kireevsky, Chaadaev, and others.[1] With respect to socialist doctrines and hopes for the future, particularly important for Samarin was Lorenz von Stein's *Der Sozialismus und Kommunismus des heutigen Frankreichs. Ein Beitrag zur Zeitgeschichte,* published in Leipzig in 1842. Within a year Samarin was reading it and was writing a review, "not for publication," as he said to Aksakov. This review from the second half of 1843, in the words of Dmitry Samarin, seems to have survived but has not been published. Nol'de rightly attributes special importance to Stein's book in the formation of Iurii Samarin's political, social, and economic views. He says that its contrasts of "state and society, the political and social questions, its sermon of social justice and organization realizable through a regenerated state," are all in Samarin's later thought — this, while Struve saw at the same time as Nol'de (mid-1920s) Samarin's "Slavophil-populist doctrine, renewed by Lorenz von Stein's ideas on social monarchy."[2]

Yet while the young Samarin was giving attention to practical matters of politics, economics, and social questions at the turn of the 1830s, his major effort was directed at his master's dissertation, its work proceeding in conjunction with new friendships and associations. Among the new friendships that Samarin formed at about the time that he graduated from Moscow University in 1839, none was more propitious than that with Konstantin Aksakov, two years older than Samarin. Our two most reliable sources, Aksakov's brother Ivan and Samarin's brother Dmitry, are in general agreement with respect to the time when Konstantin and Iurii met. Dmitry tells us that in the winter of 1838–1839 Iurii and Konstantin established "close relations"; Ivan Aksakov states that his brother and Samarin, who, up to 1839, were "almost unacquainted," decided to prepare together for their masters' examinations.[3] It was an informal but earnest collaboration, and in February 1840 they both passed their examinations and began work on their dissertations — Aksakov on Lomonosov, Samarin on two prominent Russian clergymen in the reign of Peter the Great, Stefan Iavorsky and Feofan Prokopovich.

With respect to Samarin's future career and lifelong ideological orientation, the year 1840 was fateful in yet another way. It was then that he met the leaders of incipient Slavophilism. The basic facts about the event come from Samarin himself, in a letter he wrote on April 6, 1869, to M. I. Zhikharev, a relative of P. Ia. Chaadaev, (b. 1793 or 1794), thanking him for a photograph of Chaadaev's study on Basmannaia Street in Moscow. Samarin was deeply touched by the gift and recalled fondly his association with Chaadaev, and even more, that "in this same study so faithfully and clearly reproduced I met and became acquainted for the first time with Khomiakov and I. V. Kireevsky."[4] Though Samarin does not give the exact date, it is clear from his other correspondence that it was early in 1840.

Samarin had been introduced to Chaadaev's pro-Catholic views by his cousin Prince I. S. Gagarin. The two had known each other from childhood but seem to have become particularly friendly at about the time Samarin was in his third or fourth year at Moscow University—the time when he was vacillating between Hegelianism and Orthodoxy. Gagarin himself had pro-Catholic leanings as early as 1835, when he first met Chaadaev, and after he entered the Jesuit order he became the first editor of Chaadaev's works.[5] Not all the correspondence between Gagarin and Samarin has been published, but the volume of Samarin's published letters for the years 1840–1853 contains four letters to Gagarin, two from the second half of 1840, concerned with Lermontov, and two (one of which is only ten lines) from the second half of 1842.[6]

Recently Gershtein, relying on long excerpts from a hitherto unpublished letter of April 2, 1838, from Gagarin to Iurii Samarin (a reply to an unpublished letter of Samarin), expresses the conviction that Gagarin, writing in French, cast himself in the role of Iurii's preceptor. Characterized as a man with a "flaming, missionary soul," Gagarin no doubt would have liked to see Iurii follow in his footsteps, but his didactic, insistent letters to Samarin did not achieve their goal. Certainly after Gagarin joined the Jesuit order in the West in 1842, any possibility of a positive influence on Samarin vanished. Yet as already indicated, Samarin read in Gagarin's letter, or heard from him in person while in his third year at Moscow University, about Russia's historical path and its place among the European nations, about the need for emancipation of the serfs in Russia, about the "decaying West," three years before he read this in Shevyrev's well-publicized *Moskvitianin* essay, about young America and old Europe.[7]

The pro-Catholic view came to Iurii Samarin not only from Prince Gagarin but also directly from Chaadaev, whose Moscow salon he visited at the end of the thirties, and where as we have seen, he first met Khomiakov and Kireevsky. For it is worth stressing again that in the 1830s and at least the early 1840s, the informal Moscow salons were open to all, whatever their convictions or leanings toward any future ideological orientations; this practice continued even after the winter of 1844–1845, when the clear break between the Slavophils and Westerners occurred. And so at the age of nineteen (in 1840) Iurii Samarin embarked on a new and broader course than during his student days. The Wednesday evenings at the Kireevsky's and the Monday evenings at Chaadaev's among others, were well known.

In the same letter to Prince Gagarin, dated July 19, 1840, from which I have already quoted, Samarin says that he has started reading for his dissertation. He had finished Iavorsky's *The Rock of Faith* and confesses that Protestantism now appears to him "in an entirely different light." Further he says, "Le peu que j'ai appris depuis trois mois sur certaines questions religieuses m'a deja suffi pour comprendre combien peu en savent Khomiakov et autres."[8] (That same summer, as we saw earlier, Samarin and his equally self-confident friend Aksakov undertook to brief the French deputy Mauguin on Russian history and culture.) This reference to Khomiakov sheds light on the then evolving Moscow Slavophilism, and the roles of each of the four "early" Slavophils. Clearly, Khomiakov played no part in the choice of Samarin's dissertation subject: Iurii says in a draft letter to Khomiakov that the subject was assigned to him "by the university," as was customary at the time.[9] Iurii began reading about it, or at least began reading *The Rock of Faith,* at about the time when he first met Khomiakov and Kireevsky, when, one suspects, the precocious and perhaps brash twenty-year-old Iurii would not have been inclined (though this changed) to defer to the older, more experienced, and more widely read Khomiakov. Samarin was at this point under several "influences": the Orthodox base of his home environment, strengthened later by his friendship with Aksakov, Khomiakov, and perhaps, to a lesser degree, Kireevsky; the pro-Catholic views of Gagarin and Chaadaev; the over-all Russian historical Orthodox environment, a basic component of Russian culture that Samarin would seek to show as superior to its Western counterparts; also Pogodin's inspiration, and possibly Shevyrev's.[10]

Although the Samarins were wealthier than the Aksakovs and closer to court circles, their Moscow home does not seem to have been on a par with the Aksakov and Kireevsky (Elagina) salons as a center of literary, artistic, and intellectual activity in the early 1840s. Konstantin Aksakov's participation in the Stankevich circle in the 1830s and his involvement in Moscow salon activities, his own family's and others, at the turn of the decade placed him a step or two ahead of his new friend and would seem to account for the readiness with which Iurii submitted to Konstantin's leadership, if not domination, in the early stages of their friendship.

The nearly two dozen published letters, some of them only brief notes, that Samarin wrote to Aksakov in 1840 are my principal source on their early relationship. Even assuming that there were no others, the record is at best half-complete, since Aksakov's replies, if they exist, have not been published, so one must beware of easy judgments. The first impression from Samarin's letters is that he continued to use the formal "vy" until early in 1842. This, of course, implies a certain formality in the relationship, or possibly deference on Samarin's part. The first letter, dated by the editor, to the end of 1839 or early 1840, appears to indicate that it was Aksakov who proposed that they prepare together for their master's examinations;[11] yet Samarin's letters reveal a certain anxiety that they were not meeting as often as they should. Samarin mentions Hegel's *Aesthetics,* S. P. Shevyrev's published dissertation on the theory of poetry in ancient and modern times (1837), the

German works on aesthetics by Professors A. G. Baumgarten and K. S. Morgenstern, and a few other books. As Nol'de noticed, Samarin was questioned during his master's examination primarily in the fields of aesthetics and philology, which were "quite unrelated" to his dissertation subject.

Reading the works of Stefan Iavorsky and Feofan Prokopovich and other Orthodox theological writings by way of preparation for his dissertation was Samarin's primary occupation during the year 1840. He was living with his family in Moscow, and during the summer at Izmalkovo, the family estate west of Moscow. Yet one must not conclude from this that Samarin secluded himself in monastic isolation for the duration of his work on the dissertation. Besides meeting Khomiakov and Ivan Kireevsky in Chaadaev's home, and drafting the joint letter to Maugin, Samarin was also reading Gogol', probably his *Arabesques*. At Izmalkovo, where the charms of the summer air were conducive to "indolence and reflection" and "could not better harmonize with my nature," as he confessed to Aksakov,[12] he found time to read some of E. T. A. Hoffmann's works. The works of the German romantics were being read by the prospective Slavophils no less than by the Westerners, and by literary Russia in general, particularly, at the turn of the 1830s, Hoffmann's *Die Serapionsbruder* and *Kater Murr*.[13] Samarin, carried away by Hoffmann's works, wrote Konstantin Aksakov, in a letter dated 1840, "Hoffmann has completely overshadowed for me Goethe and Schiller to say nothing about the Frenchmen," and he wished he could discuss *Die Elixiere des Teufels* with him. Samarin acquired the 1841 edition of Hoffmann's *Samtliche Werke* and continued to read them the following year.[14]

In August 1840 Samarin also came in contact with Ljudevit Gaj, the Croat patriot and leader of the short-lived Illyrian movement. Gaj was soliciting funds with Pogodin's assistance, for his cause (he eventually collected more than 15,000 rubles). Samarin, probably at Pogodin's suggestion, made a contribution. This was his introduction into a phase of the non-Russian Slav problem, about which he would learn more in his later life. At the same time Samarin kept in touch with some of his professors. In the autumn of 1840 he reported to Aksakov "many controversies," and an array of activities. The principal debate was between S. P. Shevyrev (b. 1806) and D. L. Kriukov (b. 1809), professor of Roman literature and ancient history. The subject was, "Is it possible to pray to God through Hegel?" Shevyrev and P. G. Redkin (b. 1808), professor of law, argued about the "primitive state of man." A similar argument arose between Redkin and M. A. Dmitriev, and finally, Samarin says, I had "my controversy with Orlov." M. F. Orlov (1788–1842), a military man of distinction and a signer of the act of France's capitulation in 1814, was apparently attempting to impress Samarin with "some sort of system of his own." Samarin does not explain how he knew Orlov or the circumstances of the controversy, but merely concludes, "It turned out that I, the humble David, should throw down the terrible Goliath."[15]

Although Samarin died a bachelor, he was not averse to feminine company, and some of his valuable correspondence, in his later life, was conducted with Baroness von Rahden. In the winter of 1840 he frequented the well-known salons of Ekaterina A. Sverbeeva and Karolina K. Pavlova (Ianish). Sverbeeva was born in 1808, Pavlova in 1810. That young Iurii enjoyed the company of these older women as well as of the visitors to their salons is made clear in a letter to Aksakov from the same winter. "Yesterday," he says, "I spent a good three hours with Karolina Pavlovna. We examined all the questions that engaged, and still engage, you and me. We talked about Faust, the French, [George] Sand, immortality of the soul, Hegel, love, etc. She read to me several fragments from the recently published Philosophy of Lamennais." He goes on to say, Karolina Pavlovna "told me that you and she argued about whether Hegel acknowledges revelation. . . . Jesus Christ as the Son of God, and it seems, you said that he did." But Iurii had doubts, and told Konstantin, "We need to clarify this question, because I think entirely differently. Hegel understands all history, all development as divine revelation, but does not accept revelation only at a certain . . . " "We talked very long about the immortality of the soul, about the creation of the world, and then we passed over to Shevyrev."[16]

Thus in the first year after Iurii graduated from Moscow University he met Khomiakov and Ivan Kireevsky, took his master's examination, frequented such Moscow salons as those of Chaadaev, Sverbeev, and Pavlov, kept up the reading for his dissertation, proselytized when the French deputy Mauguin was in Moscow, joined in support of Ljudovit Gaj's Illyrian cause, gave considerable attention to Hoffmann, Hegel, and George Sand, and somewhere in the midst of this could write to Konstantin that the "Question of Catholicism and Protestantism, about religion in general, is beginning to become clear to me."[17] This was the life and routine of a member of the Russian gentry, one of a relatively few Russians in a great sea of peasants, poor, illiterate, and discriminated against, for whom physical survival in a state of bondage was the normal and primary concern. And yet neither Samarin nor the other Slavophils could or did remain completely oblivious of the other vast, unredeemed Russia.

In the welter of human complexities and motivations few manifestations of conduct, individual or social, are as frequently displayed as those prompted by the desire to be "the first," "the original," "the greatest" or "the best." Seemingly sustained by pride and vanity, thus far neither the judgments of ordinary people, nor of secular prophets and "experts, " nor of "science" have given us an objective, exact, scientific measurement or determination of what in every instance constitutes the first, the original, the greatest, or the best. This seems to be the case with respect to ideas. For when we pronounce an idea to be first, we may well be referring to "the first" in regard to when it was recorded and acquired significance rather than to the more obscure and difficult when, how, and where it first appeared. The birth of ideas, particularly of those that prove seminal and fecund, is often hidden, elusive, and wrapped in controversy. Since individual and national pride and reputation are involved in such contentions, any possibility of exact factual determination often becomes lost in tendentious claims and counterclaims.

This matter was brought up in the first volume of this study, and again in the preceding chapter but in a general way. With respect to Samarin the basic information is more specific. Early in 1841 he commented in a letter to Aksakov, "By the way, how Shevyrev has talked his head off in his 'A Russian's View of Contemporary European Culture'! [*Vzgliad russkogo na sovremennoe obrazovanie Evropy*]."[18] This long (seventy-seven-page) essay by Shevyrev, which was published in the first issue of *Moskvitianin* in 1841, contains a number of points of contact with the later, relatively well defined Moscow Slavophilism, and specifically with some of Samarin's views, as should soon become clear. Yet neither Shevyrev nor the *Moskvitianin's* publisher, Pogodin, can be considered Slavophils together with Khomiakov, Kireevsky, Aksakov, and Samarin. Throughout the life of *Moskvitianin,* from the first issue in 1841 to the last issue in 1856, there was a close relationship between the journal and the Slavophils, and some of the Slavophils occasionally published in it, since Nicholas I never allowed them their own journal. But the Slavophils never considered it a Slavophil journal, not even during the few months in 1845 when Kireevsky became its editor. During the 1840s Pogodin and Shevyrev mixed socially with the Slavophils, but their relations were at times cool and exacerbated, and the two professors tended to look upon Samarin and Aksakov with the kind of condescension that precocious students, particularly after they have struck out on their own, find irritating. With respect to such important points as Pogodin's that Russia's historical course was different from the West, and Shevyrev's claim that the West was decaying, the Slavophils concurred. But with respect to Slavophilism's positive content, its heart and core, Khomiakov's principle of *sobornost'*, Kireevsky's principle of the wholeness of the spirit, and Aksakov's choric principle, Pogodin and Shevyrev made no contribution.

In summary, what Samarin read in Shevyrev's long essay, early in 1841, was a survey, country by country, of the state of Western culture, its "religion, science, art, and literature." Italy, England, France, and Germany are the subjects of the survey. Shevyrev's pro-Russian bias aroused the ire of the then evolving Westerner camp. The polemics, as usual, generated name-calling, and Shevyrev was soon dubbed "pedant." Yet at the time he was perhaps better informed about the West than were Herzen and Belinsky, neither of whom had then been in the West, and neither of whom had studied any part of the West as thoroughly as Shevyrev had studied Italy.[19]

Shevyrev's essay contains favorable comments on Italian art, poetry, and "vocal music," and, mixed views about England, favorable comments on Byron and Scott (the 1830s were the "high-noon of romanticism in Russia"), also on Shakespeare and Dickens, whose "fresh and national" genius, Shevyrev said, had much in common with Gogol's. Shakespeare's plays at Covent Garden were a reminder that English drama had declined, for there was nothing to match the great bard. Shevyrev's comparison of life in Italy and life in England showed his preference for the former:

> There the ideal world of fantasy and art; here the essential sphere of commerce and industry; there the lazy Tiber on which only rarely one sees a fisherman's boat, here the busy Thames crowded with steamers; there an eternally bright and open sky, here fog and smoke . . . there every day religious processions, here dry religion without ritual . . . there light heartedness, carefree gaiety, here the grave and grim idea of the north.[20]

Of the four Western countries reviewed, France, not surprisingly, received the lowest marks from Shevyrev; in the 1830s and 1840s, at least up to the revolutions of 1848, France and French culture, with few exceptions such as the feminist movement and some of utopian socialism, fared well neither with the Slavophils nor with the Westerners. From a Russian nationalistic point of view, the Napoleonic period was still alive, and French rationalism and secularism held no attraction for Orthodox nationalists and incipient Slavophils. The radical Russian Westerners may not have found fault with French rationalism and secularism, but they had no use for the culture, politics, and economics of bourgeois France under Louis Philippe. Although the French language was still widely used among the Russian gentry, including the Samarins, in correspondence, and sometimes in publicistic work as was the case with Chaadaev, this well-entrenched and durable practice, although rapidly becoming anachronistic, was bitterly assailed by such self-appointed and zealous guardians of the indigenous as Samarin's friend Konstantin Aksakov.

To nonradicals and nonrevolutionaries of all stripes, including Shevyrev, France and French culture were inseparable from revolution. Shevyrev's convictions were evolutionary, pro-organic. For him, all educated Russia fell into two categories, "the French and the German," depending on the influence of the respective cultures. Thus the Russians were confronted with two "critical illnesses": "the Reformation in Germany and the Revolution in France." Both were the inevitable results of the West's departure from the course of "healthy, organic development." After citing some details and specific cases, Shevyrev glumly concluded, "The nation that through abuse of personal freedom has destroyed in itself the sense of religion, has rendered art soulless and science meaningless, had, of course, to push the abuse of freedom to the ultimate extreme in its literature, a misuse restrained neither by laws of the state nor by the opinion of society." He found a few favorable exceptions in the French historical literature, citing the work of Augustin and Amedee Thierry, but on the whole the French literary scene was bleak and foreboding. "One does not truthfully know who corrupts more: literature society or society literature."[21]

If France's glaring shortcoming was "misuse of personal freedom," Germany's "principal malady" was its dwelling in an "abstract world." For the German intellectual, inner life was separate from social, external life. The beginning of Germany's "corruption of thought" its fateful "invisible sickness," went back directly to the Reformation. Prussia as the center of Protestantism became the "hotbed" of German philosophy. Shevyrev declared German poetry in decline and blamed this on the Hegelians, who deem poetry to be "one of the stages of man in his aspiration to all-absorbing philosophy." Schiller and Goethe anticipated Hegel, and German poetry was ready to become the "skeleton of philosophy." Yet he showed due respect for the "great creations of Goethe and Schiller," and for the University of Berlin, with which "Russia was in the happiest relations ... and draws science and scholarship where its source is deeper and more abundant."[22] But Shevyrev could not overcome the curse of deeply entrenched ethnocentrism. This was the same sort of ethnocentrism as in the writings of the Marquis de Custine, running at the same time but in the opposite direction, against Russia.

Germany was the arena where the question of the relationship of science and religion was being debated, and this was for Shevyrev "the greatest" of all questions. Regretting Protestantism's "total, complete freedom, which violates all unity" he declared Protestantism to be "the most savage feudalism in religion" (this is one of a number of thoughts found later in Samarin's dissertation). And lest he be mistaken as being partial to the Vatican, he added that Catholicism was "stagnating in papism's deep-rooted prejudices." Nor did he spare the pope, "That man who first dared call himself the living vicar of Christ, and the visible head of the church. He was the one who gave birth to Luther ..."[23]

But this is not all that Khomiakov, Kireevsky, and the two younger future Slavophils, Konstantin Aksakov and Iurii Samarin, read in Shevyrev's essay early in 1841. Two more topics need to be mentioned here. They also read about the work of the pro-Orthodox Franz von Baader, whom Shevyrev had met in Munich in 1839, and about the "decaying West." Shevyrev had a number of talks with Baader in the course of nearly three months, and later in 1841 in the *Moskvitianin* he published an essay entitled "Christian Philosophy: Conversations with Baader."[24] More will be said later on about Baader's influence on Moscow Slavophilism; Shevyrev seems to have been attracted by his being a "ferocious opponent of papism, and also an opponent of the Protestant party."[25] "The magical fascination of the West still acts powerfully upon us," Shevyrev said, "and we cannot all of a sudden renounce it."[26]

Whether or not the West and Russia liked it, Shevyrev saw the West as the "grumpy old man," advised it "not to be angry with its heir [Russia], inevitably called upon to take possession of its treasures," and was not disturbed that Russia might be demeaned in the process. "Everything foreign but humanly splendid," he consoled his readers, "will be absorbed by the Russian spirit, an all-inclusive, broad and universal Christian spirit, a spirit of tolerance and universal communion."[27]

The centerpiece of Shevyrev's essay, on which this congenial and generous premonition was based, was his three-page quotation from Philarete Chasles. I refer here specifically to the *Schlagwort,* the "winged word," the "decaying West."[28] People living in an age of incessant mass propaganda and advertising need no explanation of "winged words," or catchwords. Nor do we need to be detained for long on the question of the "first," who first proclaimed the West to be "decaying." It is sufficient to be reminded here that Gagarin informed Samarin, at least as early as April 2, 1838, that the West was declining—"l'Occident est a son declin"—that it was old, that America was young, and, so he implied, that Russia also was young. We do not know when and where Samarin first heard these "winged words."[29] They were clearly abroad then, before Shevyrev gave then added impetus, and they continued to float in the air for decades. The Slavophils used the notion for their purposes just as the Westerners used it for theirs, and we hear it reverberating, for instance, in 1867 in Turgenev's *Smoke.* Like folk songs and folk tales, ideas also seem at times to lose their single authors.

But a careful reading of Shevyrev's long quotation from Chasles, and of Shevyrev's own words, bear out Struve's contention that in this instance neither Chasles nor Shevyrev used the verb "decaying," although this was later attributed to the Slavophils by their ideological opponents. In Shevyrev's quotation appear two dozen words characterizing the state of the West, from "decline" "weakness," "powerlessness" to lethargy and "dying," but not "decayed" West. Furthermore, the reference here is to the West's moral, not technological decline. Shevyrev quotes Chasles to the effect that even if the West should "discover 12,000 new acids," invent new "electrical machines," and the "means to kill 60,000 human beings in one second," its "moral world" is "dying if it is not completely dead."[30]

Since civilizations are the product of human activity, it is not surprising to see the biological rhythm of human life also attributed to them. The analogy may be questionable, but its historical accuracy cannot be denied. It was used both before and after the Slavophils. Birth is followed by growth, flowering, decline, and death. Such was the historical course of Oriental, Near Eastern, Mediterranean, and American Indian civilizations; therefore there was no historical precedent upon which to base the possible eternity of Western civilization. Furthermore, in the midst of the ebullient anthropocentric optimism of the Age of Reason there appeared Edward Gibbon's celebrated *History of the Decline and Fall of the Roman Empire* (1776–1788), as if to remind even the most sanguine rationalists of the frailty of man-made structures. This was the effect, although it may not have been the purpose of the author. We do know, however, as mentioned earlier, that a French translation of Gibbon was in the Samarin family library.

During the 1840s and 1850s the Slavophils found it convenient and advantageous to accept the Western prognosis about the West's moral and spiritual decline.[31] Upon this they erected part of their ideological structure. Another, more basic, part rested on the assumed superiority of Russia's Orthodox, communal virtues; the Slavophils were contesting the West on religious, moral, and cultural grounds, unlike perhaps some of the later pan-Slavs who concentrated heavily on the diplomatic-military front.

It is most noteworthy that at the turn of the 1830s with the fortuitous assignment of Samarin's thesis, the youthful Western-bred aristocrat decided to challenge the West on religious grounds. Clearly, no Russian could argue at the time about Russian superiority over the West in the scientific, artistic, and literary or in the social, political, and economic fields. Russia's literary and musical works, with which it was to record perhaps its most noteworthy achievements in the nineteenth century, were too recent and incomplete in the early 1840s to form a solid base for claims of superiority or even equality with the West. By the early forties, Pushkin's brief but illustrious career was over, and Gogol' had scored his greatest literary achievements, but the time perspective which has added much to their luster and reputation, in Russia and abroad, was not yet there. Modern Russian music, which was launched in 1836 with the performance of I. M. Glinka's opera *Ivan Susanin,* like Russian literature, needed two or three decades to become established.

The one national Russian achievement by the end of the thirties, from the Russian point of view, was military, 'martial' not cultural in nature, the defeat of Napoleon, which had occurred a few years before Samarin was born. The memory of it caused a wave of nationalistic euphoria in Moscow at the end of the thirties. For despite the services of generals Winter, Frost, and Mud, it was not they, but the Russian peasant-recruited army that followed the remnants of Napoleon's Grande Armee to France and Paris. Yet the Slavophils, never strangers to much of the best in Western culture, could take no solace in Russian military prowess and imperial sway alone; and since Russia was unable to measure up to the great Western cultural achievements, the Slavophils challenged the West in the field of religion and theology. This was an area in which they thought, the West was sorely deficient — even though, or perhaps because Christianity as a highly ethical religion had by then profoundly affected the spiritual and moral life of the West according to its Catholic and Protestant interpretations.

It would be difficult to place too much stress on the Christian, spiritual, and ethical issues on which the Slavophils concentrated their own positive, constructive thought as well as their most trenchant criticism of the West. As we have already seen, Khomiakov elaborated and strengthened the Slavophil Orthodox challenge to the Western confessions that youthful Samarin had embarked upon on his own when he commenced work on his dissertation. Ivan Kireevsky did the same in the area of philosophy without ever constructing a Slavophil "system," while Aksakov concentrated on the political and social economic sphere, particularly when the Slavophils saw, by the end of the forties and early fifties, the depredations that Western capitalism, industrialism, and individualism were wreaking upon the new masses of industrial workers. Mere landlordism and self-interest cannot account for the fact that the thought of the Slavophils, like much of the great Russian literature of the nineteenth century, particularly the works of Dostoevsky and Tolstoy, is permeated by social, ethical, and spiritual concerns. In all this the Slavophils saw themselves and Russia not as destroyers of the "decaying West" but as successors to, and improvers of, Western culture, first and foremost in religion, ethics, and in general in the realm of human relations. For the Slavophils, as for later generations of Russians, Christianity remained a highly ethical faith, perhaps more so than for some of their Western contemporaries.

It has occurred, particularly in the West, to regret the fact that Dostoevsky, and even more Tolstoy, presumably became lost to art and literature as they stressed the importance of morality and religion. Whether one agrees with their standards on these matters, the top priority of their concerns should be even more apparent today than in their time. There can be no doubt now that Western science and technology, with all their marvelous and beneficial achievements, have also rendered man more destructive than before, thus threatening to destroy all their blessings and even life itself. And this is so because science and technology have failed to provide mankind with the ethics of survival.

True to the religious and moral, concerns that were making their way into the rapidly evolving Slavophil doctrine of the early 1840s, young Samarin made his weighty contribution by way of his dissertation. His subject, the two early 18th century theologians Stefan Iavorsky and Feofan Prokopovich, was sufficiently large to allow him the opportunity to expand on his own ideas. Analysis and evaluation of Samarin's dissertation and its place in Slavophil thought belong to Part Two of this study. In order here is a brief statement about the quality of his research, including his bias, the contents of the dissertation, and his basic conclusions. This was not a modern university dissertation on a small segment of a subject, but a full study on a big theme. Part one, the only part that was published in 1844, deals with Iavorsky and Prokopovich as theologians; parts two and three deal with them as church officials and as preachers. Together with an introduction and the twelve-page "speech" (summary) that Samarin delivered as the opening statement in his public defense of the dissertation, the whole comes to 458 pages in volume 5 of Samarin's Works.[32] Only part one, the part that Samarin defended publicly, was published by Moscow University in 1844 because of fears of censorship, particularly of certain comments about Peter the Great.

Besides the large historical scope, the first and most striking imprint of Samarin's dissertation is its complexity and the highly controversial nature of the subject, no less than an evaluation of Catholicism, Protestantism, and Orthodoxy in a historical setting through the first quarter of the eighteenth century. Archpriest Ivantsov-Platonov, in the introductory essay to volume 5, described the dissertation as the "first remarkable-serious, and for its time in many respects very daring attempt." Following Samarin's own admission in the foreword, Ivantsov-Platonov illustrated the fact that Samarin was not aiming at complete investigation of the three major Christian confessions, or at consultation of all available sources.[33]

On page two of his introduction, Samarin stated that he had a thesis to prove, and he gave his position — "From the Orthodox church preserving in itself all the completeness of undamaged revelation, from the united and one Church of Christ, the Western European world, dropped off, expressing a pretension to be a church, [thus] revealing Catholicism.[34] (This of course is a reference to the eleventh century schism.) Two pages further on, using a phrase closely reminiscent of one in Shevyrev's review of contemporary European culture, referred to above, Samarin characterized Protestantism as "feudalism in the sphere of religion." Throughout the dissertation the problem of Christian ecclesiology remained for him the most sustained single theme. Catholicism, Protestantism, and Orthodoxy are seen not merely as doctrine and dogma but as historical churches touching in a variety of ways the daily lives of the millions of faithful.

But to illustrate that Samarin had a thesis and a bias does not of itself impair the quality of his research. Indeed, the research work of this major in literature, barely out of his teens, shows a rare facility in the use of Catholic theological sources in their medieval and modern Latin, and in historical source materials in Latin, German, and to a lesser extent French, as well as in Russian and Church Slavonic.[35] No less striking, as serious readers and biographers of Samarin have long known, is the penetrating, articulate, and logical mind of the youthful scholar. Although the point of view is strongly pro-Orthodox, the dissertation, even today, has a fresh, vibrant quality.[36]

Samarin scrutinizes such fundamental Christian concerns as what constitutes the Christian church, its organization, its head, the place and role of the faithful in it, its doctrine and dogma, its tradition, ecumenical church councils, and, above all, the central Christian concern for salvation, the main issue in the West, that of justification through faith and works or through faith alone. All these are in a way peripheral to the announced subject, but the study of the careers of Stefan Iavorsky, well known for his pro-Catholic leanings, and Feofan Prokopovich, well known for his pro-Protestant sympathies, gave Samarin the opportunity to explore other related questions. If there is a fault in the analysis, it lies in a tendency to overstate, perhaps out of polemical zeal. This is noticeable, for example, when he speaks of the danger to Russian Orthodoxy from proselytizing Catholicism and Protestantism in the seventeenth century, the first in the South of Russia, spearheaded by the well-organized Jesuit order, the second coming through northwestern Russia. Samarin was, of course, quite aware of the fact that the most serious threat to the Russian church lay within itself rather than on the outside. His highly critical views on Peter the Great's decision to discontinue the Russian patriarchate should become apparent in Part Two of the present work.

Here it should be sufficient to provide a few biographical facts about the two clerics whose works and careers Samarin studied. Stefan Iavorsky (1658–1722), born in a Polish village but in an Orthodox family in what is now the Ukraine, was educated in the Kiev Mogilianski college where the studies were conducted in Latin and in a "strictly scholastic spirit." In 1684 he "outwardly" switched to Catholicism, changed his name to Stanislav Simon, and studied in Catholic schools in L'vov and Liublin, and later in Poznan and Vilna. Three years later he was again in Kiev, went back to Orthodoxy and in 1689 became a monk. Such switching from one confession to another is said to have been fairly common when Orthodox students wished to study in Catholic seminaries. Iavorsky then taught in his alma mater rhetoric, pietistics, philosophy, and theology. In 1697 he became abbot and a close assistant to the metropolitan of Kiev, with whom he traveled to Moscow in January 1700. There Peter the Great heard Iavorsky speak, and when Patriarch Adrian died on October 15, 1700, Peter, seeing in Iavorsky a cleric with Western education, free of the taint of the Moscow clergy, appointed him vicar of the patriarchal throne. But by 1715 the tsar's deepening secularism, his mockery and parodies of the church hierarchy, and his growing leanings toward Protestantism, spelled the end of collaboration between the tsar and Iavorsky.

Feofan Prokopovich (1681–1736), although of a similar background to Iavorsky's, in his adult life developed an inclination toward Protestantism, which in the last decade of Peter's reign coincided with the tsar's views on the relationship between state and church. It should, however, be stressed again that neither of these clerics thought of giving up Orthodoxy. Prokopovich was born in Kiev and was educated at the same Kiev Mogilianski college where Iavorsky had studied a generation earlier. After graduation, Prokopovich entered the Roman Uniate academy, Saint Athanasius, in Rome, where it is said he caught the attention of the Pope. In order to enter the Rome academy, Prokopovich had to convert to Catholicism, which, however, he abandoned for his original Orthodoxy after he returned to Kiev in 1704. Back home, he taught pietistics, rhetoric, philosophy, and theology, writing handbooks in a clear manner, free of scholastic touches.

As an ardent supporter of Peter I's reforms, Prokopovich sang the praises of the reforming tsar and delivered a well-known panegyric on the battlefield after the famous battle at Poltava in 1709: Peter had him translate the speech into Latin. Prokopovich, who was an admirer of Bacon, Descartes, Hobbes, and Puffendorf, welcomed secular learning and stood up against Catholic control of education, as well as against the supremacy of ecclesiastical over temporal authority. In 1716 Peter summoned him to St. Petersburg. Two years later he was appointed bishop of Pskov, and in 1720 archbishop of Novgorod. In the same year he drafted Peter's "Spiritual Regulation" and became a member of the tsar's new Holy Synod, which replaced the patriarchate as the highest office in the Russian church. Perhaps the ultimate in Peter's secularization of the Russian Orthodox church, and its subordination to his will, was his appointment in 1722 of the army officer I. V. Boltin to the newly created office Ober-Prokuror of the Holy Synod.[37]

In his study of the thought and careers of Iavorsky and Prokopovich, Samarin remained firm in his Orthodox position. But in his attitude toward the fate of the Russian patriarchate he seemed relieved that the Russian Orthodox church at the end of the seventeenth century was no longer moving in the fateful direction of Catholicism, that is, of acquiring the functions and image of the state; this he feared could have happened under Iavorsky's leadership. He was no more favorably disposed toward Protestantism, which he felt had, like Catholicism, yielded to rationalism, and had in addition abandoned both church tradition and the church. But he seemed less sensitive then, than later in his life, to the fact that, while the Catholic church was a state as well as a church and Protestantism had splintered into fragments all that was left of the church under Peter I and Prokopovich was transformed into no more than a department of the Russian autocratic state. This, of course, was a travesty on Samarin's and the Slavophils' exalted views of the sublime role of the Christian church in a Christian society.

In the late 1840s and during the 1850s, neither Samarin nor the other Slavophils remained insensitive to the millennial Christian problem of church-state relations, and this perhaps as much as any other factor accounts for the streak of anarchism in Khomiakov's, and particularly in Aksakov's, thought, yet the Slavophils never renounced their loyalty to the Russian autocrat. At the end of 1867, Samarin, in his justly acclaimed introduction to Khomiakov's theological works, spoke out against church statism [*tserkov-*

naia kasenshchina], otherwise [known] as the subordination of faith to purposes external to it, of a narrow official conservatism . . . when official conservatism under the pretext of preservation of the faith . . . tramples upon and suffocates it in its unceremonious embrace, giving the impression to one and all that it values faith for the sake of the service that faith renders to it, then most naturally the opinion arises in society that this is as it should be, that nothing else could be expected of faith, and that actually this is its purpose. This kills all respect for faith.[38]

We shall return in the next chapter to the inner conflict and turmoil in which Samarin wrote his dissertation in the early 1840s. After over three years of diligent work he finished it in the spring of 1843. The year that elapsed between its completion and its defense on June 3, 1844, was particularly trying for him. It was also the year in which the Slavophils and Westerners engaged in the polemical sparring that led to the break between the two ideological camps in the winter of 1844–1845.

Biographers speak of Samarin's defense of his dissertation in superlative terms. Nol'de says that he showed "his sure and profound knowledge, his eloquence, and his skill in argumentation . . . "; there was, he says, "general recognition of his triumph."[39] In Kornilov's view, Samarin defended his dissertation with "great brilliance in spite of the hostile attitude of several university professors, and the defender had a bewitching influence not only on his friends and adherents but also on thinkers of the opposite camp."[40] To this could be added Bochkarev's simple statement that Samarin passed his examination "brilliantly."[41] There is no doubt that during his public defense in the presence of many from Moscow's intelligentsia, Samarin scored a memorable success.[42]

No claim can here be made that the riddle of the two Iurii Samarins who existed side by side in the young graduate student in the early 1840s or, more precisely, were locked in irreconcilable struggle, has been unraveled. As usual in situations of severe inner conflict, we see some of the outward manifestations, perhaps some of the reasons and circumstances, and usually the outcome. But with respect to any precise "scientific" analysis and definition of the factors and forces involved and their often unstable alignments inside the person, we seem to be still in the stage of more or less shrewd guesswork. What is clear to those who have studied Samarin's career is that during the early 1840s, while he was working on his dissertation, preoccupied with questions of religion and theology, he did not labor in monastic seclusion but participated in Moscow's vigorous salon life with its literary, artistic, and ideological concerns. At the same time he wrestled with the problems of Western secularism and rationalism, more specifically with Hegelian idealism, trying in vain to reconcile Hegel and Orthodoxy. This major stream in Samarin's early intellectual life will be examined in the next chapter.

Notes

1. Kireevsky refers to Saint-Simonism in a letter to Koshelev written in the summer of 1833 or 1834; Chaadaev was aware of Saint-Simonism at least as early as 1831. See I. V. Kireevsky, *Polnoe sobranie sochinenii v dvukh tomakh,* ed. M. O. Gershenzon, 2 vols. (Moscow, 1911), II, 227 (hereafter cited as Kireevsky, *Sochineniia*); Peter K. Christoff, *An Introduction to Nineteenth-Century Russian Slavophilism: A Study in Ideas,* vol. II, *I. V. Kireevskij* (The Hague-Paris, 1972), p. 50. Comte attracted some attention in Russia in the 1840s, although not, surprisingly, much among the Westerners. Both Belinsky and Herzen reacted to his "positive philosophy" unfavorably, Belinsky in a letter to Botkin of February 17, 1847, Herzen in his *My Past and Thoughts,* referring to about the same time. See V. G. Belinsky, *Izbrannye pis'ma,* 2 vols. (Moscow, 1955), II, 291; A. I. Gertsen, *Sobranie sochinenii v tridtsati tomakh,* (30 vols). (Moscow, 1954–1966), X, 201, 344, 487 (hereafter cited as Herzen, *Sochineniia*). Awareness of Comte in Russia was considerably stronger in the second half of the nineteenth century. See Samarin, *Sochineniia,* XII, 42; Nol'de, *Samarin,* p. 34. For a highly competent view of positivism in Russia in the second half of the nineteenth century, see Andrzej Walicki, *A History of Russian Thought: From the Enlightenment to Marxism,* trans. Hilda Andrews-Rusiecka (Stanford, Calif., 1979), pp. 349–370.

2. See Samarin, *Sochineniia,* XII, 42, and V, LV; Nol'de, *Samarin,* p. 34; P. B. Struve, *Iurii Samarin, Vozrozhdenie,* no. 376, p. 3.

3. Samarin, *Sochineniia,* V, xxxvi; I. S. Aksakov, *Russkii arkhiv,* 1879, no. 11, p. 301.

4. P. I. Chaadaev, *Sochineniia i pis'ma,* ed. M. Gershenzon, 2 vols. (Moscow, 1913), I, 403.

5. R. T. McNally, *Chaadayev and His Friends: An Intellectual History of Peter Chaadayev and His Russian Contemporaries* (Tallahassee, Fla., 1971), p. 161.

6. Samarin, *Sochineniia,* XII, 53–58.

7. E. G. Gershtein, "Lermontov i kruzhok shestnadtsati," pp. 91–96.

8. In his brief introduction to Samarin's letters for 1840 = 1845, published in 1880, Dmitry Samarin says that he omitted form three letters "expressions that were too harsh." This early reference to Khomiakov was very likely one of them, since only the first half of this letter appears in Samarin's *Works.* The second part, from which this quotation comes, is given by Gershtein Cf. Samarin, *Sochineniia,* XII, 53–54; Gershtein, "Lermontov," pp. 11–112; *Russkii arkhiv,* 1880, book two, p. 242.

9. Samarin, *Sochineniia,* V, lvii.

10. The often elusive matter of "influences" and similarities, intriguing though it is, continues to bedevil the student of Moscow Slavophilism. Thus in a recent Soviet book review the authors say that if one takes as criteria of Slavophilism "bowing before antiquity, criticism of the West, and idealization of national principles," then one could categorize as Slavophils "M. M. Shcherbatov, I. N. Boltin, D. I. Fonvisin, F. M. Dostoevsky, A. A. Grigor'ev, N. Ia. Danilevsky, M. P. Pogodin, and S. P. Shevyrev, and even Emperor Alexander III." See V. I. Kerimov and L. V. Poliakov, "V. A. Koshelev, Estiticheskie i literaturnye vozzreniia russkikh slavianofilov (1840–1850-e gody)," *Voprosy filosofii,* 1986, no. 6, p. 166.

11. Samarin, *Sochineniia,* XII, 7.

12. Ibid. pp. 11–12.

13. On Hoffmann's popularity and influence in Russia and for "Hoffmanniana" in the nineteenth century, see C. E. Passage, *The Russian Hoffmannists* (The Hague, 1963).

14. Samarin, *Sochineniia,* XII, 16–18.

15. Ibid., p. 21.

16. Ibid., p. 24.

17. Ibid., p. 14.

18. Samarin, *Sochineniia,* XII, 24.

19. Struve characterized Shevyrev as "one of the most cultured Russians of his time," and concurred in Pushkin's high opinion of him, and in the respect that Goethe showed for him. Shevyrev spent more than three years in Rome, is said to have spoken Italian "like an Italian," and was Russia's "first Italianist." He visited France and Germany and spent a total of about six years in Western Europe. In the early forties Shevyrev was the "principal intellectual force" behind the *Moskvitianin,* but this journal was no match for Belinsky's *Otechestvenniia zapiski,* published at the same time in St. Petersburg. Shevyrev did not possess the "mighty temperament" of Russia's foremost publicists, such as Belinsky and Herzen, nor the "independent philosophical thought" of Khomiakov, Kireevsky, Chaadaev, or Vladimir Solov'ev, and his "inclination for rhetoric" was no substitute for these qualities. P. B. Struve, "S. P. Shevyrev i zapadnyia vnusheniia. . . ." *Zapiski Russkogo Nauchnogo Instituta v Belgrade,* pp. 213, 215, 217–218, 220–222.

20. Shevyrev, "Vzgliad russkogo," pp. 234, 236–237.

21. Ibid., pp. 246–247, 259–260.

22. Ibid., pp. 269–271, 275–276.

23. Ibid., pp. 280, 287.

24. "Khristianskaia filosofiia, Besedy Baadera," *Moskvitianin,* 1841, no. 3, pp. 378–473.

25. Ibid., p. 286. Much valuable information and interpretation about Shevyrev, and on his relationship with Baader can be found in an unpublished Ph.D. dissertation on Shevyrev by R. M. Arnold Jr. Thus he writes

of "Baader's on-going effort to educate Russia for the role of mediator between Catholicism and Protestantism," p. 131. This work came to my attention too late to be fully utilized here.

26. Shevyrev, "Vzgliad russkago," p. 289.

27. Ibid., pp. 295–296.

28. Struve, "S. P. Shevyrev," p. 203.

29. Gershtein, "Lermontov," pp. 94–95.

30. Cf. Struve, "S. P. Shevyrev," pp. 204, 206, 223, 228–231. For the Shevyrev-Belinsky controversy, which Struve says was begun by Shevyrev, see p. 224. See also Shevyrev, "Vzgliad russkogo," pp. 242–245. This long quotation came from Philarete Chasles' "Revue de la littérature anglaise," *Revue des deux mondes,* November 1, 1840, pp. 363–363.

31. It is not the purpose here to survey the role of the "decline of the West" theme in European history. It is sufficient to stress that it reappeared in a different and much better publicized form in the West early in this century in Oswald Spengler's renowned but non-too-lucid or well-documented *Der Untergang des Abendlandes,* vol. I, *Gestalt und Wirklichkeit* (Munich 1918), vol.II, *Welthistorische Perspektiven* (1922). The Slavophils might have been mildly amused by Spengler's characterization of the Russians as "non-Western," whose ethics, in the words of a student of Spengler's works, were those of an "undiscriminating brotherhood." The period, environment, and context of Spengler's thoughts was no less different from that of the Slavophils' than is our contemporary scene from Spengler's. But concern for the fate of the West has not vanished; on the contrary, it now appears in a more complex and ominous context. A few years ago, in the course of a discussion of U.S. foreign policy, specifically of U.S.-Soviet relations, George Kennan wrote, "Poor old West: succumbing feebly, day by day, to its own decadence, sliding into debility on the slime of its own self-indulgent permissiveness: its drugs, its crime, its pornography, its pampering of the youth, its addiction to its bodily comforts, its rampant materialism and consumerism." Kennan's thesis on this and other points has been challenged by a number of other specialists. See, for instance, Hugh Seton-Watson's reply in M. F. Herz, ed. *Decline of the West? George Kennan and His Critics* (Washington, D.C. 1978), pp. XV, 39–48.

32. In this volume, the dissertation is preceded by a 27 page introductory essay by Archpriest A. Ivantsov-Platonov, and by an equally indispensable 62 page biographical essay by the editor, Dmitry Samarin. See Samarin, *Sochineniia,* V (Moscow, 1880). Parts two and three were not published until 1880, four years after Samarin's death.

33. Ibid., pp. viii–x, 3.

34. Ibid., p. 4.

35. The dissertation does not contain a bibliography, but the footnotes and the text itself reveal wide-ranging and thorough reading. The works of

Iavorsky and Prokopovich, some in Latin, came first. The work also shows careful reading of the Bible, the works of the Eastern church fathers in Russian translation, and a number of multivolume collections of documents such as *Polnoe sobranie zakonov*, (Russia's Complete Collected Laws), as well as of contemporary works such as Hegel's *Aesthetics*. In the words of Gratieux, Samarin used for "du côté catholique, les *Canons et décrets du Concile de Trente*, du côté protestant, la *Confession d'Augsburg et l'Examen du Concile de Trente* parle Dr. Martin Khemnitz." A. Gratieux, trans., *G. Samarine. Préface aux Oeuvres théologiques de A. S. Khomiakov* (Paris, 1939), p. 14. On the papacy Samarin read Leopold von Ranke's just published *Die römischen Päpste, ihre Kirche und ihr Staat im sechszehnten und siebzehnten Jahrhundert*, 3 vols. (Berlin, 1834–1836). These items, and a biography of Innocent III are among the many sources cited in Samarin's footnotes.

36. Writing in 1939 Chizhevsky said; "The scholarly significance of Samarin's dissertation is beyond any doubt. It retains its value up to the present, 95 years later! And not simply on specific points, like [Konstantin] Aksakov's work, but as a whole." D. I. Chizhevsky, *Gegel' v Rossii* (Paris, 1939), p. 178. In the same year Gratieux wrote that Samarin's dissertation could still be read with "interest and profit." See Gratieux, *Samarine*, p. 14.

37. Samarin wrote his dissertation with a time perspective of a century and a quarter. In his consideration of the same period and personalities, Professor Kartashev of the Paris Saint Sergius Orthodox Theological Academy, an authority on the ecumenical councils and Russian church history, had a time perspective of nearly two and a half centuries. He gives more attention to Prokopovich than to Iavorsky and is unsparing in his criticism. He acknowledges Prokopovich's talent, erudition, and ability as a "fighting publicist," and his "intellectual superiority" over his contemporaries. He sees Prokopovich as Peter's "living academy on all questions of church and state." In fact, he says, "Feofan ... became Peter's brain. And further on, "To Peter only the spirit of reform was clear. But he was helpless in giving it precise legal and canonical form." Prokopovich, living in the age of "enlightened absolutism" in the West (Gallicanism in France, and "Josephism" in Austria), and not a stranger to "sophistry," justified the absolute authority of the tsar over state and church. Prokopovich's theorizing, based on Western natural law, resulted, in Kartashev's words, in "overthrowing the whole ancient Russian theocratic structure. Not two supreme parallel authorities, not two sovereignties [*maiesteta*, from *maiestas*], but one. And this single sovereignty the monarch himself verifies with the measure of Divine law immediately, directly, without interference from the church." In contrast to Peter, who was "very careful," Prokopovich gave full rein to his maximalist impulses. As a result, "not a single one of the zealots and ober-prokurors of the synodal period talked of such a radical deduction as . . . Prokopovich. The ideological destruction of the Orthodox canonical order

remained in our history a fortissimo, repeated by no one else [and] only a cloudy oblivion in the course of 250 years." A. V. Kartashev, *Ocherki po istorii russkoi tserkvi,* 2 vols. (Paris, 1959), II, 340–343, 345.

38. Samarin, *Sochineniia,* XI, 333–334.

39. Nol'de, *Samarin,* p.32.

40. A. A. Kornilov, *Ocherki po istorii obshchestvennogo dvizheniia i krest'ianskogo dela v Rossii* (St. Petersburg, 1905), pp. 455–456.

41. V. Bochkarev, *Osvobozhdenie krest'ian. Deiateli reformy* (Moscow, 1911), p. 270.

42. After the defense, which lasted three and a half hours, Sergei Aksakov admiringly wrote "Never have I seen anyone on the podium so free, noble, and moderate." By the last "epithet, " he added, "I wish to say that everything in him was in proportion: inner warmth, and merit, and calmness, and modesty, and deference and audacity. Everyone was enraptured by him, particularly those who raised objection." And to the latter "Samarin answered brilliantly but still not sharply, and not impertinently." Professors S. P. Shevyrev, I. M. Bodiansky, I. I. Davydov, and others raised questions, including defense of the Ukrainian theologians, which Samarin skillfully parried. Chaadaev was also present, divided by his admiration for Samarin's excellence and his own pro-Catholic views. Writing to a friend, he said that on the dais he saw Samarin's "calm, almost triumphal forehead," but that under the umbrella of his dissertation "he destroys all of Western Christianity." Chaadaev claimed that the Catholic church was a "kingdom," not a state, as Samarin said, and he found other points of disagreement, but he still could marvel at Samarin's audacity in dealing with so vast and fundamental a subject. From the Protestant point of view Samarin was taken to task by Professor E. M. Klin (1795–1866), son of a German pastor, who had studied theology in Leipzig and taught Latin at the University of Moscow. He accused Samarin of not having read Protestant sermons. Samarin had, however, been forewarned of Klin's coming attack by Professor D. L. Kriukov, who wrote to Samarin before his defense that Klin considered it his "heilige Pflicht" to accuse Samarin of "premeditated distortion of Protestantism." Herzen, looking at Samarin from a secularistic, materialistic point of view, wrote of his "sorry Orthodox theories." See Barsukov, *Pogodin,* VII, 410–415; "Neizdannye rukopisi P. Ia. Chaadaeva," *Vestnik Evropy,* November 1871, pp. 331–333; *Russkii arkhiv,* 1880, book 2, p. 331; Herzen, *Sochineniia,* II, 356.

4

Early 1840s:
The Struggle with Hegelianism

Reading Samarin's dissertation today one would little suspect that at the time of its writing its author knew anything but a happy, fortuitous immersion in his subject and serenity of mind and spirit. In fact, for the youthful graduate student the early 1840s were a period of Sturm und Drang, as they were, though perhaps with lesser stress, for his friend Konstantin Aksakov. Whatever other problems contributed to the turmoil in the lives of the two young men, there is little doubt that in the eye of the inner storms was Hegelianism, and the Western, particularly continental, penchant for taxonomy and system building.

There was nothing new in the first half of the nineteenth century about the notion of philosophical systems. They were simply in vogue. As with so many "firsts," philosophical systems go back to classical Greece. Recently, for instance, we have been told that Plato's pupil Heraclides of Pontus attempted to describe a Platonic system that included Plato's views on astronomy, the theory of matter, eschatology, ethical doctrines, pleasure, and religion, including the "divinity of stars." For the "men of the thirties and forties" it was not unusual to hear references to Kant's, Schelling's, Hegel's, and even Comte's "system." In fact it seems that the young Russians who were members of the various *kruzhoks* and often visited the Moscow salons in the eighteen thirties and forties talked, if not always very knowledgeably or even earnestly, about various philosophical systems and their respective authors.

But the notion of a philosophical system was not as innocent and as innocuous as it appeared in the sometimes lighthearted atmosphere of a *kruzhok* gathering. Carried to its ultimate end, a philosophical system should encompass all important aspects of human existence, including personal, social, and aesthetic questions, physical environment and the universe, and, of course, philosophical, eschatological, and religious questions. The profoundly anthropocentric character of such an enterprise should be apparent at first glance, for the enigmas and mysteries of so vast an undertaking were presumed to be accessible to the human intellect, if not to the ordinary then to the rare or exceptional. But what appeared to the ancients as an unavoidable necessity—that is, sole reliance on man's own resources in the search for the truth—was not valid for the Christian, for whom revealed truth (as contrasted with man's own acquired knowledge) became supreme. In spirit if not always in results and achievement, philosophical system building as the Slavophils saw it in the 1840s and 1850s was an expression of Western anthropocentric secularism, not far behind which lurked Western anthropotheism—for the intellect that penetrates and explains all is in no need of supernatural assistance.

System building, in the first half of the nineteenth century, was primarily a German enterprise. It is not therefore surprising that in the early 1850s the Slavophils showed considerable concern with the problem. For them, philosophical system building raised two fundamental questions: could human intellect, logic, and science penetrate and unravel the mysteries of human existence and the universe, and could cold intellect and logic serve as the base upon which human relations could be established? From the Slavophil, Orthodox point of view the answer to both questions was in the negative. To the pro-Slavophil Ivan Aksakov, at the time, as to the Westerner Turgenev, the person devoted to systems and abstract systematizing was a *sistematik,* and he was stereotyped as German. The same conviction found expression in Ivan Aksakov's formulation of "the systematism of the German and the absence of systematism in Russia."[1]

Unlike the builders of philosophical systems who relied on human resources in their pursuit of the truth about human existence and the universe, the Slavophils admitted the existence of, and gave priority to, revealed, God-given truth, and together with this they removed themselves from impersonal, often inhuman, frigid logic in human relations. In place of it they would hark back to the Christian ideal of turning the other cheek. That is why Ivan Aksakov spoke of "noble inconsistency" (*blagorodnaia neposledovatel'nost'*). That is why hatred and harm were to be returned not in kind but with forgiveness and love. The difference here is between anthropocentrism and theocentrism, and between anthropotheism and theism.

To say that young Samarin saw these problems clearly, and with all their implications, in the early 1840s while he was writing his dissertation and struggling with Hegelianism would be unwarranted. To say that he became enmeshed in them and had to find a way out is to take into account his serious, several-years-long encounter with Hegelianism, and the problems it raised for him. We have noway of knowing when Samarin became aware of the importance of Hegelian philosophy, but most probably it was while he was a student at the University of Moscow. Hegel was known to young Russia in the 1820s and 1830s, and we saw in the *Kireevskij* study that young Kireevsky attended Hegel's lectures at the University of Berlin in 1830, the year before Hegel died. We also saw in the *Aksakov* study that Hegel and Hegelianism became major topics of discussion in the Stankevich circle in the second half of the 1830s.

When Samarin and Aksakov met in 1839, Hegel became a primary concern – Hegel's *Aesthetics* was, as we have seen, one of the requirements for their oral examinations in February 1840 – and they soon resolved to study together. But perhaps an even stronger inducement than this academic requirement was the pervasive position of Hegelianism in Russian intellectual life at the time. In addition, the young friends were soon to seek, however vainly, solutions to certain basic Slavophil problems in Hegelianism. This early attempt concentrated on Hegel's *Logic,* which they studied during part of 1840 with the help of a Herr Klepfer, a teacher of German. But early the following year Samarin wrote to Aksakov, "Do not expect me . . . at Klepfer's," and tell him that I shall have to stay away "because of my inability to listen to Hegel." Behind this display of undue modesty was Samarin's decision to concentrate on his dissertation.[2]

It is not entirely clear what and how much of Hegel Samarin read during the rest of 1840 while he was concentrating on his dissertation. It is certain, however, that in the winter of 1841–1842 when he was working on the second part of the dissertation he was also engaged in a vigorous epistolary discussion with his friend and classmate at the University of Moscow, A. N. Popov, on the subject of the so-called "developing of the church" (*razvitie tserkvi*) or the evolving, "developing church" (*tserkov' razvivaiushchaiasia*). As Chizhevsky has correctly said, the controversy between the two friends was conducted "in terms of Hegelian philosophy."[3] The record of Samarin's reading of Hegel is somewhat more complete for 1843; in a letter to Aksakov of the summer of that year he says, "I have postponed the *Phenomenology,* for I could not master the chapter on Wahrnehmung [perception] and have taken up the *Encyclopedia* which is easier for me." Although this was a tandem arrangement with the dissertation coming before Hegel, the hold of Hegelianism on the youthful graduate student was strong and steadfast. But lest we oversimplify the state of Samarin's mind at the time it is worth noting that in a post script to this same letter to Aksakov, he added, "I am writing an article about Stein's book, but not for publication."[4]

While Samarin and Aksakov were concerned with Orthodoxy and Hegelianism at the same time, and shared their problems and difficulties, each reacted in his own way, and as noted in the preceding study, Aksakov emerged from the inner conflict perhaps with fewer scars and somewhat more easily than Samarin. Chizhevsky justifiably regretted that "we know very little about how concretely the process of Samarin's departure from Hegelianism occurred." What we do know is that in this process, extending over about four years, Khomiakov and A. N. Popov were major participants in Samarin's inner drama. Aksakov, and possibly indirectly to an extent, Ivan Kireevsky were also involved.

Alexander Nikolaevich Popov (1820–1877) was born in a gentry family in the Riazan gubernia. A year younger than Samarin, he entered the University of Moscow in 1835, during its "glorious Stroganov days," and graduated with an interest in Russian law and history in 1839. Among his friends on the campus were Samarin, Konstantin Aksakov, D. A. Valuev, Buslaev, Katkov, and M. A. Stakhovich, all able undergraduates. In the spring of 1842, he defended his master's dissertation in Russian history, and then left for Berlin where he attended Schelling's lectures for a short time, and then, by way of Munich, went to Montenegro.[5] A year earlier, in 1841, Stakhovich (1819–1858), poet, dramatist, musician, and folklorist, had written to Popov, "I have already read Venelin. Now I will study him, that is, I will memorize him." Iu. I. Venelin (1802–1839), was one of Konstantin Aksakov's tutors. His two-volume work on the old and contemporary Bulgarians (1829–1841) became for many Russians as well as Bulgarians a standard guide to the history, culture, and fate (Bulgaria was then under Ottoman rule) of one of the ancient Orthodox, South Slav peoples. Popov, too, probably took note of Venelin's work before his trip to Montenegro, for the Montenegrins were, like the Bulgarians, under Ottoman rule. In 1847 Popov published the impressions of his trip under the title *A Journey to Montenegro* (*Puteshestvie v Chernogoriiu*), which the historian Bestuzhef-Riumin characterized as "an excellent work, independent [and] written with knowledge of the subject."[6]

The significance of Popov's trip to Montenegro from the point of view of a study of Moscow Slavophilism lies in the fact that he, like V. A. Panov, who visited Dalmatia, Herzegovina, and Montenegro in 1842, and F. V. Chizhov, who spent more time in the Balkans in the early 1840s, supply some of the justification for the broader meaning of the term "Slavophilism." They, acting, so far as I can tell, independently and on individual initiatives, showed a genuine interest in and concern for the oppressed Balkan Slavs, which the four major or "classical" Moscow Slavophils, Khomiakov, Ivan Kireevsky, Konstantin Aksakov, and Samarin, did not show to the same degree during Slavophilism's formative period, the early and middle 1840s. As a young man Khomiakov served in North Eastern Bulgaria as a volunteer in the Russian army during the Russo-Turkish war of 1828–1829, and he always had a fondness for the Balkan Slavs, particularly the Orthodox. Samarin contributed, as we have seen, to Ljudevit Gaj's cause in 1840. In the same year he is said to have collaborated with Pogodin in publishing in Russian Jan Kollar's *Über die litterarische Wechselseitigkeit* (on Literary Reciprocity)[7] but neither he, nor Kireevsky, Khomiakov, or Aksakov thought of visiting the Balkan Slavs or, what is more important, giving much of their time and attention to the non-Russian Slavs. Thus perhaps the most visible justification for the

rubrics "Slavophil" and "Slavophilism" in the 1840s was supplied by some of
the *dei minores* of Moscow Slavophilism.

As both the correspondence between Samarin and Popov for 1841–1842
and Ivan Aksakov's recollections reveal, at that time young Samarin's mind
was not focused on the Balkan Slavs but was intent on his dissertation and
on the "world of the Russian national spirit and life." Samarin and Konstantin Aksakov were, in Ivan Aksakov's words, "ardent admirers of German
philosophical thought and literature," and were in search of the "soil for the
groundless, and up to then errant Russian thought." Furthermore, they
would be satisfied with nothing less than "a complete sort of
'phenomenology' of the Russian national spirit with its history, native
[*bytovye*] phenomena, and even Orthodoxy."[8] The young admirers of Hegel
conceived phenomenology not in the Kantian sense in which a distinction is
made between phenomena and noumena ("things-in-themselves") with only
phenomena being accessible to human cognition; rather, they embraced the
Hegelian notion according to which both phenomena and noumena could
be apprehended by the human mind. This perhaps more than anything else,
accounts for the youthful friends' reading of Hegel in the early 1840s.

The most fundamental aspect of the Russian national spirit as Samarin
conceived it was the embodiment of Eastern Orthodoxy in the historical Russian Orthodox church. Therefore it is clear why in his dissertation, in his
correspondence with Popov, and in his informal discussions with his friends,
in the early 1840s, particularly those with Khomiakov, his concerns with the
problems of ecclesiology were paramount. Whether he compared and contrasted the Catholic and Protestant churches with Orthodox or sought to
define the Russian church as the base of Russian culture, he could not get
away from the profound and irreducible question of whether all matters concerning Christianity, and specifically Orthodoxy, are accessible to the human
intellect, and if so what role is left for revelation in Christian doctrine and
dogma.

Imperfect as the record is, for we shall never recover what was said and
lost in informal conversations, held at salon gatherings, and dinner parties
some of which lasted through the night, we do have the key correspondence
between Samarin and Popov, and between Samarin and some of his other
friends, including Khomiakov.[9] Letter number 84, to Popov, dated by
Dmitry Samarin to the winter of 1841–1842, begins with the words, "The
church is developing [*tserkov' razvivaetsia*], i.e., it constantly brings to its consciousness the eternal inexhaustible truth which it possesses." The appearance on earth of the "God-man" (*Bogo-chelovek*) had to come to an end,
but He left to his disciples "the promise of the Spirit—He created the
Church. The Spirit of God lives constantly in the Church. . . . Consequently the fact of incarnation taking place in the person of the God-man alone is
taking place invisibly in the Church. And so there are two elements in the

Church: the divine and the human." This much, Samarin concluded, was clear; the problem was to determine their mutual relationship.

In his search for this answer Samarin eliminated two possibilities, the Old Testament and the Catholic answers. In the first case the Church had been reduced to a "priestly caste," whereas in the second, a "single person" is designated "in whom the Spirit is constantly concretized, then this person becomes the Church while all the rest are a contingent crowd of people." The relationship here is that of "subjects to the state; they live under the Church but not in the Church. They develop, the Church remains immobile." Samarin could not accept a condition in which, he said, the "Spirit is nailed to one person, to one pulpit." Instead he declared for the "close, indissoluble union of the two elements: the private persons [who] represent the Church, and the Spirit — the developing consciousness of the Church."[10]

That these and other related problems were being discussed orally as well as in writing is clear from Samarin's reference to a conversation between him and Popov in which they considered the nature of church dogma and the role of the ecumenical councils. Samarin drew a distinction between the "unconscious spontaneous conviction of private individuals," which although perhaps correct is merely an "opinion," if in such persons the "Church does not become conscious of itself." When this occurs the Church "becomes a collectivity in the Ecumenical council," and solves its problems "as a consequence of the presence of the Spirit in it." He concluded that in a Church council the members of the Church were as much above an ordinary meeting "as a rational conviction is above opinion."

Samarin was aware of historical development in general, but he placed the development of the church above any other, because "its every dialectical phase is imprinted with the Spirit, every result, every word of the Church is of necessity true. That is why the Church must recognize the very path by which it arrives at truth, and must bless development." The essential question, he wrote to Popov, is not "why the Church is a Church, but can it, should the Church develop." As in his dissertation so in this letter, when he was confronted with a fundamental question he was apt to resort to comparisons and contrasts, probably believing that this clarified matters. "Catholicism realized in itself the immovable church," he said, while "Protestantism, acknowledging the principle of development, was obliged to negate the church and therefore the very content of this development," remaining in "an abstract, fruitless motion." This left the Orthodox church in a category by itself, and the letter ends with his well-known declaration, "Aksakov and I confess the developing Church [*Tserkov' razvivaiushchuiusia*].[11]

This last sentence in Samarin's letter provided the opening words of Popov's reply, in which he said that he would gladly join Samarin and Aksakov in their confession of faith except that he did not understand the "word *development*" as they did. Like his friends, Popov could not condone the "immobile deadness [*mertvennost'*] of Catholicism," but he was equally un-receptive to the "abstract movement of Protestant philosophy," and to the notion that the development of the church was a matter of the "reconcilia-tion of the two opposites." Denial of the dialectic in the development of the church is basic to both Popov's and Khomiakov's point of view. Popov was unequivocal when he said in this letter, "In the Church there is no rational development, apart from immediate life. This dichotomy came to an end in it [the Church]."[12]

It is not necessary to follow every step in the argumentation contained in the Samarin-Popov correspondence. They both argued with unusual maturity, and the letters reveal a remarkable store of information, depth of thought, and facility of expression. Above all they were loyal to Russian Or-thodoxy, and in search of the elusive Russian spirit, which they saw as the essence and the foundation of Russia's future culture. The rest of the salient thoughts in the correspondence on the developing church can readily be summarized. Samarin characterized church sacraments as the "living aspect" of the Church, but his contention that they could be "the subject of the rational development of the Church" called forth Popov's reply that if one admits this, the very "notion of sacrament is destroyed, for being ration-ally comprehended it ceases to be a sacrament."

The questions that Samarin and Popov raised would eventually be reduced to the elusive, millennial problem of the relationship between faith and reason, between man's intellectual powers and divine revelation, between philosophy and religion, and between anthropotheism and theism. Samarin, with Konstantin Aksakov's concurrence, told Mauguin in the summer of 1840 that both Catholicism and Protestantism had departed from the true Christian church, which for him, then as always, was the Eastern Orthodox church. This church in the early 1840s was the "developing church," the union of the "two elements: the Divine and the human." In Samarin's third letter to Popov (no. 86) from the winter of 1841–1842, he ruled out the "ele-ment of personal arbitrariness" but affirmed that the developing church "was and will be constant; [for] there was no reason for it to end."

But then, in the next paragraph he said, referring to a question that he and Popov had evidently discussed in conversation, "With respect to the pos-sibility of a system, it seems to me impossible."[14] The reference here is to theology. In Samarin's words, "The system or the discipline [*nauka*] of theol-ogy is nothing other than the reduction to one logical whole of all dogmas so that ever one of them appears not as an aphorism but as rationally proved, connected both with what precedes and what follows."[15] Here Samarin came upon a crucial stumbling block. As Nol'de noticed in the 1918–1919 Samarin, having denounced Catholic theology in his study of Stefan Iavorsky and Protestant theology in Feofan Prokopovich, "was obliged to come un-willingly to the conclusion that the Orthodox Church denies in general theological discipline, and that 'it does not prove itself.'" This led Nol'de to the unavoidable conclusion, "Such a purely negative thesis did not fit well with his ideas about the inner development of the Orthodox church . . ."[16]

Popov summed up his view of the Church as "a historical, therefore developing moment. . . . [and] the Church as a uniquely unconditional sphere in the life of the spirit exists as a completely finished whole in Divine foreknowledge [*predvidenie*]." Samarin's developing church meant, so far as he could see, that there were two "moments" in the Church: its "immediate life" and it "conscious [life] in dogma." Samarin placed the second characteristic of the Church above the first in the same degree in which "consciousness is above immediacy [*soznanie vysshe neposredstvennosti*]."[17] Popov cited the work of such Eastern church fathers as John Chrysostom and Basil the Great to illustrate how church teaching develops and drew a sharp distinction between teaching [*uchenie*] and dogma, asking, why does "the Church admit development of teaching but not development of dogma?" His answer was that the "Church does not accept dogma as something separate but as part of general revelation."[18]

The crux of the problem, as Samarin well realized, was Divine Revelation, without which there could be neither Christianity nor Orthodoxy. But the Catholic church, he concluded in his third letter to Popov as well as in his dissertation, in "admitting in its sphere the demands of philosophy [*nauka*] of necessity resolves itself in philosophy."[19] Yet in the winter of 1841–1842 Samarin, aware of the result of the submission of matters of Divine Revelation to human reason, was not quite ready to abandon his youthful dream of establishing the phenomenology of the Russian spirit upon the foundation of Russian Orthodoxy by way of Hegelianism.

It is possible that Popov's departure from Moscow for Germany in April 1842 had a more far-reaching effect on Samarin's thought and convictions than one might normally attribute to such an external and chance occurrence. After all, Popov's decision to go abroad had nothing to do with Samarin's dissertation. Owing no doubt to the distance and the slowness of mail, their correspondence became sporadic, and its former focus and intensity were diluted through the introduction on Popov's part of new impressions and new concerns. In addition, the personal encounters in the Moscow salons that played so vital a role in the exchange and stimulation of ideas were now interrupted.

Popov's first undated letter from Berlin, written in 1842, excited Samarin, who in reply reminded him of his promise to send back to Moscow "extracts" from Schelling's lectures. Samarin informed Popov of the opinions of N. A. Mel'gunov (1804–1867), who as we shall see later, attempted to reconcile Slavophils and Westerners, and of I. S. Turgenev, both of whom had recently returned from Berlin. According to Turgenev, "*all decent people* have taken Schelling's side and Hegel is buried," but Samarin asked Popov, "What is Ranke lecturing on?" "I have a special love and respect for this man. . . ."[20] Samarin also asked Popov whether he had read Gogol's *Dead Souls,* which had appeared earlier that year, and told him that he was in "complete agreement" with Aksakov's review of *Dead Souls,* although, he added, "in this case many doubt my sincerity."[21] He had read Johann Adam Möhler's "Symbolism," and although he found nothing new in it, he conceded that its "exposition is beautiful."[22] At Popov's suggestion, he had read Rozaven,[23] and was then reading on his own Friedrich von Hurter's *History of Innocent III,* which he found "much beneath its reputation."[24]

On the central problem that had so engrossed the two young friends during the preceding winter, Samarin said:

I have particularly developed the thought on which we parted ways before you left, on the subject that a church system is impossible and harmful, that is, theology as a science [*nauka*], and that our Church with its silence and seeming indifference to the two attempts to create a system (I mean the works of Stefan Iavorsky and Feofan Prokopovich) has acknowledged the very idea of a system to be false, alien to it, and as being outside its sphere.[25]

Russia was entering a new and great period in its history, Samarin concluded with a touch of youthful exuberance. The time had come for it to "say its word in the sphere of science [philosophy]. On this thought we come together in a friendly manner and to it we shall dedicate all our lives."[26] In this moment of generous self-abnegation for the sake of Russia's future cultural greatness to be based on Hegelianism, he dedicated not only himself and Popov but also Konstantin Aksakov.

Popov's reply, which so far as I know has not been published, came not from Berlin but from Montenegro, home of brave and independent-minded South Slavs, living in one of the most inaccessible parts of the Balkans. Samarin, in a long (three and one-half page) letter dated December 5, 1842, said he was surprised that Popov had left "learned Germany for the living Slav world"; although he welcomed the "interesting and lively news about the Slav world," he could not hide his disappointment at Popov's decision to leave Berlin, and feared that concern for the South Slavs was replacing in Popov's mind German scholarship and philosophy. "Participation in the Slav renaissance," Samarin wrote, "has for some time acquired such a character that it seems to me it renders counteraction necessary." Referring to talk in the Moscow salons, he added, "Many have come to understand the future triumph of the Slav spirit [*slavianizm*] as a triumph of life over philosophy [*nauka*]." To underscore his own priority on philosophy and Hegelianism, a few lines further on he made his well-known and often-quoted declaration, "You know that by science I mean philosophy, and by philosophy — Hegel."[27]

The letter is pregnant with thoughts, sentiments, and convictions that shed light not only on Samarin's state of mind while he was in the middle of his dissertation, but also on certain Slavophil problems while Slavophilism was in the process of formation, as well as on his attitude toward the non-Russian Slavs. His decisive turn toward philosophy and Hegelianism at the end of 1842 is registered in the letter, among other things, in the form of resentment against the "many" in Moscow (by the many, Dmitry Samarin says, his brother probably meant primarily Khomiakov) who "are too inclined to love life as such . . . placing it parallel with philosophy in general, and giving it priority over the latter."[28]

One senses here that Samarin was feeling a certain intellectual and ideological isolation, which, to a mind that was keenly analytical and logical, naturally led toward philosophical speculation. Aksakov's temperament and aptitude were poetic and intuitive. Khomiakov's inner makeup was perhaps even more complex than normally, but he also had a strong streak of the poet in him, and is still considered one of Russia's prominent secondary poets. As for Ivan Kireevsky, whom Samarin seems to have found least congenial among the "Early" Slavophils, his "wholeness of the spirit" doctrine, formulated in the latter part of his life, is Christian Orthodox rather than rationalist philosophical. These differences may account for the fact that Samarin chose to air his views and problems in 1841–1842 with respect to the "developing church," philosophy, and Hegelianism, to Popov rather than to Konstantin Aksakov, although he was in more frequent correspondence with Aksakov in the early 1840s than with Popov, or with the two older Slavophils.

Samarin's attitude toward the non-Russian Slavs, as expressed in the letter of December 5, 1842, to Popov, was rational and cold as compared with Khomiakov's warm sentiments for them, particularly for the Orthodox Slavs of the Balkans. In showing disappointment that Popov might have put the Balkan Slavs in place of German philosophy and Hegelianism, Samarin writes as one who has made a determined turn toward Hegelianism. It was his way to Russian Orthodoxy, and to his grandiose, and as it turned out, empty, dream of grounding the Russian Orthodox church, and through it the Russian national spirit, on Hegelianism. With most of the non-Russian Slavs under foreign (Ottoman, Hapsburg or Hohenzollern) political rule and exploitation, and therefore unable to give free rein to cultural life and creativity, Samarin saw Russia acting in behalf of the other Slavs. Such a role for his native country was fully in tune with his strong sense of Russian patriotism and nationalism. He considered the cultural potential of the Slav world very great, but said that "to seek the Slav spirit in the complexity of all Slav nations seems to me to be a mistaken thought." The ultimate goal of all Slav concerns should be to make Russia the "point of concentration, and of all the completeness of the Slav spirit without any one-sidedness." "Only in

Russia," he said firmly, "has the Slav spirit arrived at self-consciousness conditioned upon self-abnegation." Although, he conceded to Popov, the "study of the history of other kindred nations could explain much in our development," still he did not believe that Russians could receive "anything new" or anything that was not already in Russia.

That Samarin saw at the time the relationship between Russian and the non-Russian Slavs in cultural rather than political terms is clear from one of his concluding statements. The non-Russian Slavs could achieve "liberation from their national one-sidedness and the realization, in themselves, of the all Slav principle is possible only under one condition, to become conscious of themselves in Russia [*soznat' sebia v Rossii*]." Samarin said that he acquired these views from his "three-year study of church history." How the non-Orthodox Slavs were to become "self-conscious" in Orthodox Russia he did not explain, but he stressed that Catholicism and Protestantism were Orthodoxy's "two extreme positions" [*dvukh odnostoronnostei*]. He expressed the hope, however, that Orthodoxy would triumph (presumably over Catholicism and Protestantism), "when philosophy [*nauka*] justifies it." Furthermore, he was certain that the question of the Church depends on the philosophical question, and that the fate of the Church is closely, indissolubly bound up with the fate of Hegel."[29]

Samarin was, of course, not yet a Slavophil, and one cannot say that he was speaking for Moscow Slavophilism as it came to be known later in the 1840s, and in the 1850s; but he probably sensed as well as anyone that what agitated the "men of the forties" was, above all else, the fate of Russian culture. In their cultural and ideological concerns these men split sharply two years later into the Slavophil and Westerner camps. While the Westerners, specifically Belinsky, and the liberal Westerners Kavelin, Granovsky and Sergei Solov'ev, remained indifferent to the non-Russian Slavs, the principal Slavophils, Khomiakov, I. V. Kireevsky, K. S. Aksakov, and Samarin, remained absorbed during the 1840s in the ideological struggle with the Westerners over the future of Russian culture and its relationship to Western culture. They showed a peripheral sort of interest in the non-Russian Slavs at the time, while the *dei minores* among them, F. V. Chizhov, A. N. Popov, and V. A. Panov, were sufficiently concerned about the Balkan Slavs to visit some of them in the early 1840s. These individual visits had little relevance to the Slavophil-Westerner controversy. "Russophil" would have been a more accurate designation than "Slavophil."

In the spring of 1841 when Popov left for Germany, Samarin felt deeply about the departure of a friend who had been most responsive to his concerns about the Orthodox church, Hegelianism, and the "developing church" that he and Konstantin Aksakov were presumably confessing at the time. Popov's absence from Moscow was compensated for by a closer tie between Samarin and Aksakov, although their relationship was rapidly changing.

In spite of Samarin's rising self-assertiveness in his relationship with Aksakov, during the two and a half years that followed Popov's departure from Moscow in April 1841 the two young future Slavophils held together. They presented an informal united front against Khomiakov and Ivan Kireevsky. The two sides were divided by the "generation gap," but more fundamentally by the young men's staunch adherence to the notion of the "developing church," and Hegelianism. Furthermore, as the Slavophil and Westerner camps began to assume a semblance of ideological coherence the contest for adherents sharpened. Thus, as we shall see in the next chapter, the Slavophil camp attempted to attract Granovsky while the Westerners, Herzen in particular, had hopes of enlisting Samarin on their side.

The ideological crisis that Samarin was undergoing at the time was reflected in his critical attitude toward Khomiakov and Kireevsky. Although this important phase in the evolution of Moscow Slavophilism is not as well documented as one would wish, there are signs that point the direction in which matters were moving. Samarin, who in July 1840 (as we have seen) was critical if not scornful of Khomiakov's knowledge of religious matters, in the following year wrote to Aksakov, "Just now I received the *Moskvitianin*. How very bad it is! How low has Khomiakov stooped in his point of view!" In 1840 Khomiakov wrote a poem "On the Transfer of Napoleon's Ashes." Now in the *Moskvitianin* for March 1841 he published a sequel, "More About Him," in which he attributed Napoleon's fall to "Him, Who placed limits on the seas." Samarin's comment was, "As if it is not in general revolt, and not in history but in something else that God's will or the law of necessity is disclosed." Dmitry Samarin's comment on this was that "the sharpness" of his brother's response to Khomiakov's verses showed "how little were Khomiakov's views shared by Samarin and Aksakov at that time."[30]

Samarin's vexation over what he considered to be Ivan Kireevsky's meddling boiled over into indignation in 1842. His annoyance seems to have started earlier, for on October 23, 1841, he wrote in his diary: "My argument with Kireevsky has strongly shaken me. Is it possible that in fact I have been carried away by a phantom?"[31] Perhaps Kireevsky was not tactful. Intimidation must have left sensitive and self-confident young Samarin with a strong sense of resentment. In a letter to Aksakov (in which he used the familiar *ty* in place of the formal *vy*) he referred to a recent conversation between them that seems to have involved the question of the "developing church," and Kireevsky's opinion of it. "A strange man is Kireevsky!":

Today I saw him and he, with a triumphant look on his face, asked about my controversy [with Popov]. This seemed to me more than immodest, and if anything got in the way of my wish to reply to him harshly it was simply a sense of pride. I did not wish to show him that he had touched a vital cord. And what are they [Khomiakov and Kireevsky] joyful about? As if we have enslaved ourselves to each other? ... It is possible that a disagreement might arise between us, and probably not once, but they cannot pull us apart, ... Yes, for all that "wir gehen vereint dem nächsten Tag entgegen."[32]

One of the less well illuminated relationships among the early Slavophils is that between Ivan Kireevsky and Samarin. A principal reason for this is the absence of any published correspondence between them. Of the 2,048 letters of Iurii Samarin that his brother Dmitry collected (probably not all the letters that Iurii wrote), not a single one was to Kireevsky, while 217 were addressed to Aksakov and 11 to Khomiakov, and 81 to Koshelev. Similarly, Kireevsky's published correspondence, also incomplete, and consisting of about 3 dozen in volume 1, and 39 in volume 2, contains none to Samarin, although one of these letters, of the spring of 1847, was addressed to his Moscow friends, and one would assume that Samarin was included.[33]

In addition to his parents, to whom Samarin wrote 53 letters, according to his other editor Peter D. Samarin, the largest number went to Aksakov.[34] This, among other things, reflects the special relationship and friendship that existed between the two younger Slavophils. But it also illustrates the coolness between them and Kireevsky, which Samarin revealed in 1842, and which is hinted at by Ivan Aksakov, who was also cool toward Kireevsky. This seems to have been a matter of personality frictions caused by personal characteristics and idiosyncracies, for when in the winter of 1844–1845 the showdown with the Westerners came, the Slavophils, rallying around Khomiakov, were able to present a united front. Certainly there is no indication that in later years the evolution of Slavophil thought was seriously hampered by temperamental and personality differences.

But in the early 1840s Samarin, with Aksakov's moral support, struggled with the problem of Orthodoxy and Hegelianism while both were out of sympathy with the two older Slavophils. At the same time Samarin worked on his dissertation, finishing part one in the summer of 1841, part two in December 1842, and part three in the spring of 1843. Samarin's inner conflict is well summed up in three letters, one to Khomiakov written in September 1843, in Khomiakov's reply of October 15, and in Samarin's letter to Aksakov from Kazan of December 31, 1843. In his letter to Khomiakov, Samarin says that they shared many convictions but were divided on the crucial question of the relationship between "religion and philosophy." Working on his dissertation, and thus having to concentrate on one phase of the church, the "appearance in it of the Catholic and Protestant principles," Samarin had reached the conclusion that "Catholicism, making a claim to exclusiveness, is at the same time philosophy [*nauka*] and a state." His view of Protestantism was no more charitable, since, he said, "acknowledging complete freedom for philosophy and the state, and denying the exclusiveness of the Church, it denies, together with this, the Church and religion in general."

This left the Orthodox church in a class by itself: "Our Church is not philosophy, and it is not a state: it acknowledges itself only as a Church." In this manner Samarin reduced the triangular relationship between church, state, and philosophy to a dual problem, the relationship of philosophy and the church. Seeing agreement with Khomiakov on the matter of the state, he posed the crucial question: Since "philosophy exists as a separate sphere from the Church, is it subordinated to it, or, conversely, is the Church subordinated to philosophy?" Still securely in the grip of Hegelianism, he concluded, "I think that if philosophy exists as a sphere of the spirit separate from art and religion, then it must be the supreme sphere, the last phase in the development of the idea."[35]

Khomiakov, writing in reply to this letter a few weeks later (October 15, 1843), said that he was pleased to get it "despite the state of mind in which it was written." Khomiakov was not surprised, and recalled a recent conversation with Samarin and Aksakov during which "I promised both of you inner struggle . . . and that it would begin in you earlier than in him." It came sooner than he had expected, he commented. Using the term *nauka* in Samarin's sense of philosophy, Khomiakov wrote: "Philosophy being untrue to itself up to now confuses the *acknowledged* [*priznannoe*] with the *conscious* [*soznannoe*], and (do not laugh) suffers constantly from that defect for which it blames the mystics." Khomiakov found this fallacy in different ways in both Schelling and Hegel. Distinguishing between "philosophy (analysis) and life (synthesis)," he says that reconciliation depends on whether "analysis is strictly true to itself." There was, he acknowledged, a legitimate sphere for philosophy, and he hoped to see Samarin with restored "freedom of life," which would "convict of a lie the excessive claims of philosophy— the anatomy of the spirit."[36]

In the second part of the letter Khomiakov turned to Samarin's dissertation with the words, "I find in it much, and many truths, and I am even ready to defend it against you." He felt that Samarin was unfair to his own dissertation yet he came down hard on it: "In it there is no candid love for Orthodoxy. And yes, philosophy does not demand love," for "You see only the negative side of Orthodoxy, its antagonism toward the other teachings." In the "disclosing of the disharmony of the other teachings" Khomiakov saw the "only right of philosophy on life," and concluded, "The innermost recess of life and its inner sources are not accessible to philosophy, and belong to love alone." He saw in Samarin's dissertation the "sincerity of the scholar although not the sincerity of the believer that Kireevsky asked for." Khomiakov found the dissertation "dear" to him, and thought that it would be "beneficial" if it could become well known, although "perhaps it would be more beneficial outside Russia than among us."[37]

Almost as an afterthought, on his last page of the letter, Khomiakov turned to Hegel, in a comment that he found not only Hegel but Western thought in general wanting on the problem of epistemology "The French, the English, and the Germans have already argued not a little about the tree of knowledge, and constantly left aside the supplement of *good* and *evil*. This is connected with my long-standing argument with you." Khomiakov was always very skeptical of the unqualified supremacy of logical knowledge, and here he says: "Knowledge, as logical knowledge, has nothing in common with the knowledge of good and evil." He concluded that "Hegel's error . . . stems from the one-sided academically arrogant [*shkol'no-gordoe*] notion of knowledge in general."[38]

When Khomiakov, the mathematics major from the University of Moscow, and the inventor of a steam engine later, wrote about the limitations of logical knowledge, he was likely to be heeded by his fellow Slavophils who did not have his mathematics and mechanical background. Ivan Kireevsky (whether under Khomiakov's influence or not is hard to tell) soon spoke skeptically of German academic philosophy (*kabinetnoe myshlenie*), while in the early 1850s the Aksakov brothers, Ivan particularly, and Koshelev showed concern for German "systematism" and declared themselves in favor of "noble inconsistency" (*blagorodnaia neposledovatel'nost'*) in human relations. Dmitry Samarin was perhaps not far from the mark when he stated that Khomiakov's letter to Samarin "contains in itself, as an embryo, all of Khomiakov's views revealed later in his theological works."

The five or six weeks after receiving this letter from Khomiakov must have been a particularly difficult and trying time for Samarin. After three years of arduous work, he had finished his dissertation, and he doubtless had reason to believe that his research was of high quality, but Khomiakov's frank although not inconsiderate letter could not have given him the peace of mind that he probably wished more than anything else at the time. A year earlier he himself had had serious doubts about the work: 'I pronounce a condemnation of my dissertation, and I destroy it.' His doubts extended to Hegel, to whom the 'fact of the church was almost entirely alien . . . his philosophy of religion is in many respects unsatisfactory.'[39] Now these doubts returned even more intensely, and Khomiakov, the man whose opinion by now he probably valued above all others, had added his criticism of the dissertation and of Iurii's infatuation with Hegel and German idealism.

At his father's suggestion, Iurii left Moscow at the end of November 1843 for a six weeks' tour through eastern Russia. From Kazan on the last day of the old year he wrote a frank letter to his friend Aksakov. He began with a complaint about Aksakov's horrible handwriting. He was delighted to get two letters from him, but then came the letdown, for he looked at them, he says, as "at hieroglyphics to which I do not have the key!" He was glad to hear about Granovsky's success and was annoyed by Pogodin's and

Shevyrev's "inadvertence," (a matter to which we shall return.) Then Samarin unburdened on the changing relationship between them. Although he does not say so in the letter, he no longer needed his Virgil to guide him through Moscow society but could stand on his own feet. "Listen Aksakov!" Samarin began, "You have long been angry at me because recently I have begun to disagree and argue with you more frequently. I am glad that you have finally expressed everything that is in your heart."

Samarin was not arguing with Aksakov for fun: "No, I argue with you because for a long time I have carried on a heavy, tormenting argument with myself." For some time, he confessed, I have been "in the most painful state of mind." Questions that had long disturbed him were now demanding "a decisive yes or no" answer. "It seems the split within me has never been so powerful. It is unbearably oppressive and melancholy for me. . . . I spent many nights in the village [Izmalkovo] without sleep, in bitter tears and without prayer." Toward the end of the letter Samarin pleaded that Aksakov should not be "vexed" or "annoyed" and should not "condemn." "More than ever before I need your complete, trusting sympathy."[40]

Samarin returned to Moscow in mid-January 1844, and during the next few months he talked much with Khomiakov, often well into the night. There is a record that on January 31, 1844, Samarin read an essay, it seems on philosophy, to a small group. The affair lasted until five o'clock in the morning. Another similar evening, at Samarin's, ended at four in the morning. Dmitry Samarin has told us that his brother left no account of his inner state of affairs after returning to Moscow in mid-January 1844 but between then and his public defense of his dissertation on June 3 the decision had been made, and it was a decision for a lifetime. The proud, self-reliant, and self-confident young aristocrat had come to the end of a double-track road. Crestfallen but not vanquished, he knew that the time had come to choose one of the two paths that he had tried to straddle for several years. There was no way of straddling them when they led in opposite directions, one toward God, the other toward man, one compelling man to place his trust in Revelation, the other in man's all-powerful reason. Chizhevsky's astute observation that Samarin's and Aksakov's rejection of Hegelianism was "a rejection of all philosophy" may go too far. But there is no doubt that Moscow Slavophilism, to which Samarin made a fundamental and most significant contribution, was a profoundly Christian Orthodox school of thought; and this, of course, meant that the sphere of Revelation was subject to no human proof or verification by any means at the disposal of man.

Notes

1. N. P. Koliupanov, *Biografiia Aleksandra Ivanovicha Kosheleva* (Moscow, 1892), II, appendix p. 61 (hereafter cited as Koliupanov, *Koshselev*). It

is not the purpose here to focus on philosophical systems and "systematism" or on their presumed absence in Russia, but that this problem gave concern to some of Russia's best philosophical minds in the present century, as well as in the 1840s and 1850s, should be apparent from the following statement of the philosopher Frank about V. F. Ern's philosophy: "Ern's theoretical construction in essence erases every distinction between philosophy and religion. When he asserts that Russian philosophical thought is 'always concrete,' when he sees that the sign of Russian philosophy consists of the absence of *system,* when he includes in the body of Russian philosophy not only the poetic works of Tiutchev, Dostoevsky, Tolstoy but even the *personal life* of Gogol' and Pecherin, who . . . in his own words never wrote a single philosophical work, . . . then every possible definite concept of philosophy . . .disappears." See S. L. Frank, "Filosofskie otkliki. O natsionalizme v filosofii," *Russkaia mysl',* 1910, book 9, p. 167.

2. Samarin, *Sochineniia,* XII, 25. For Dmitry Samarin's comments see V, xxxix.

3. Referring to the early 1840s in general terms, Chizhevsky says, "Among Samarin's notebooks, and in his legacy have turned up conspectuses of the *Encyclopedia, Phenomenology,* and the *History of Philosophy.*" These conspectuses (reminiscent of Bakunin's, made independently several years earlier) are testimony to Samarin's careful reading of Hegel. See Chizhevsky, *Gegel' v Rossii,* p. 176.

4. Samarin, *Sochineniia,* XII, 42.

5. As we turn to a brief consideration of some second-echelon Slavophils, such as A. N. Popov, we are confronted with the problem of determining who was, and who was not a "Slavophil," then as well as later. It is therefore useful to consider here the recent succinct and lucid formulation of the problem by the Soviet scholar Dudzinskaia: "In the works of some foreign and Soviet historians the notion 'Slavophilism' is interpreted too freely. Some authors call Slavophils all promoters of the Slav renaissance; others — scholars — Slav specialists; a third category — people who are more or less interested in Slavdom, i.e., lovers of the Slavs ['*slavianoliubov'*]; a fourth see the beginning of Russian Slavophilism even in the seventeenth century, and bring it to the first World War, and several even to contemporary times. In the literature one encounters the mention of Polish, Bulgarian, Czech slavophilism." Dudzinskaia ends her summary by saying that she "considers Slavophilism as one of the orientations of Russian social thought which existed in the middle of the nineteenth century." See E. A. Dudzinskaia, "Russkie slavianofily i zarubezhnoe slavianstvo," in V. A. D'iakov et al., eds. *Metodologicheskie problemy istorii slavistiki* (Moscow, 1978), p. 261. More recently, Soviet scholarship has given further attention to the historical and semantic problem of the terms 'Slavophil' and 'Slavophilism.' See, for instance, N. I. Tsimbaev, *Slavianofil'stvo. Iz istorii russkoi obshchestvenno-*

politicheskoi mysli XIX veka (Moscow, 1986), pp. 5–55; V. A. Koshelev, *Esteticheskie i literaturnye vozzreniia russkikh slavianofilov 1840–1850-e gody* (Leningrad, 1984), pp. 6–15.

6. Popov's *A Journey to Montenegro* as well as Panov's and Chizhov's travel impressions from the Balkans have remained beyond my reach. Popov did not obtain the academic position in Moscow he wished, and in November 1845 was appointed to the staff of the Senate in St. Petersburg. The following year he moved to the Second Section in charge of legal matters where he remained for the rest of his life. He kept up his interest in Russian history and contributed an essay to D. A. Valuev's symposium, *Sbornik istoricheskikh i statisticheskikh svedenii o Rossii* (Moscow, 1845); "Ob opek i nasledstve, vo vremia russkoi pravdy," pp. 96–113. Later Popov published in the Slavophil *Moskovskii sbornik* (1846) his "O sovremennom napravlenii iskusstv plasticheskikh," pp. 9–46, and the following year, "Shletzer, razsuzhdenie o Russkoi Istoriografii" *Moskovskii sbornik* (Moscow, 1847), pp. 397–484. This work also appeared as an undated, 87-page pamphlet, and was highly praised at the time by the older A. I. Turgenev. Later Popov contributed to *Russkaia beseda* and other journals. He ranged up and down the long period of Russian history, publishing in 1857 *Materialy dlia vozmushcheniia Sten'ki Razina* (Moscow, 1857), and toward the end of his life was working on the "year 12," the Napoleonic period. As a young man he lived in Khomiakov's home for a while, frequently visited Elagina's salon, and later kept up a valuable correspondence with her, Khomiakov, Samarin, Koshelev, Stakhovich, and others. His end of the correspondence, if published, has not been available to me, except for two key letters to Samarin from the winter of 1841–1842. See *Russkii arkhiv*, 1886, no. 3, pp. 320–362; 1888, book 2 pp. 480–504; P.M. Miakov, "Popov, Aleksander Nikolaevich," *Russkii biograficheskii slovar'* (St. Petersburg, 1905), XIV 514–517. For Bestuzhev-Riumin's views of Popov's work, see p. 514. See also *Russkaia starina*, May 1882, pp. 459, 461, 463–464.

7. Koliupanov says that Pogodin published Kollár's work in *Otechestvennye zapiski* in 1840 but he does not mention Samarin in this connection. Professor Petrovich, however, who is critical of Pogodin's translation of Josef Dobrovsky's *Institutiones*, says, "In 1840 Pogodin and Samarin published ... another badly mauled translation, that of Jan Kollár's work on Slavic reciprocity." See M. B. Petrovich, *The Emergence of Russian Panslavism, 1856–1870* (New York, 1956), p. 26; See also Barsukov, *Pogodin*, V, 455. How much Samarin contributed in this teacher-student collaboration is not clear.

8. *Russkii arkhiv*, 1879, no. 11, p. 301. Chizhevsky was accurate when he said that "Orthodoxy for Samarin, if not identical with the 'Russian spirit', is at least extremely close to it." Chizhevsky, *Gegel' v Rossii*, p. 177.

9. On June 3, 1844, Vera Aksakova wrote to her brother Ivan, then in Astrakhan, "Several days ago there was a supper at Samarin's. The guests went home at six in the morning, and yesterday there was a farewell for Granovsky, until three in the morning." *Russkii arkhiv,* 1910, no. 2, p. 303. Dmitry Samarin in editing his brother's works singled out three of Iurii's letters to Popov, numbers 84, 85, and 86 in volume 12, as particularly pertinent on the question of the church, and also published two of Popov's replies in the appendix. See Samarin, *Sochineniia,* XII, 82–95, 458–471; also V, XLI–XLIII.

10. Samarin, *Sochineniia,* XII, 82–83.

11. Ibid., pp. 84–85.

12. Ibid., pp. 458–460.

13. Ibid., pp. 84, 461.

14. Denial of the possibility of a final church "system" here is, as Chizhevsky noticed, a criticism of the Catholic church, which to Samarin and Popov seemed to be an institution rationalized into formal, legalistic immobility. See Chizhevsky, *Gegel' v Rossii,* pp. 177–178.

15. Samarin, *Sochineniia,* XII 93–94.

16. Nol'de, *Samarin,* p. 24.

17. Samarin, *Sochineniia,* XII, 462, 464.

18. Ibid., pp. 84, 466.

19. Ibid., p. 94.

20. Ibid., p. 95.

21. This review was refused by Pogodin for the *Moskvitianin* and was published privately as a pamphlet. For the details, see Peter K. Christoff, *K. S. Aksakov: A Study in Ideas* (Princeton, N.J.,) 1982, pp. 88–97.

22. The reference here is to J. A. Möhler's *Symbolik, oder Darstellung der dogmatischen Gegensätze der Katholiken und Protestanten nach ihren öffentlichen Bekentnnisschriften* (Mainz, 1832). Möhler was a well-known Roman Catholic theologian, active first at Tubingen then at Munich.

23. The Jesuit J. L. Rozaven de Liesseques (1772–1851) spent a number of years in Russia after 1814, and in Dmitry Samarin's words converted a number of prominent Russians from St. Petersburg's high society to Catholicism. It is not clear from Iurii Samarin's wording whether he read one or all three of Rozaven's works cited by Dmitry Samarin, they are all on the polemics between Catholics and Orthodox. Iurii found Rozaven's writing "very wise, but it is possible to reply to everything."

24. The reference here is to *Geschichte Papst Innocens III und seiner Zeitgenossen* (Hamburg, 1834–1842). For Samarin's more complete references to his reading in his letter to Popov, including the Bible, see *Sochineniia,* XII, 86, 92–93, 96–97.

25. Ibid., p. 96. This letter is simply dated, probably by Dmitry Samarin, as 1842.

26. Ibid., p. 97.
27. Ibid., p. 98.
28. Ibid., p. 98–99.
29. Ibid., pp. 99–100.
30. See ibid., pp. 25–26; V. A. Frantsev, ed., *A. S. Khomiakov. Stikhotvoreniia* (Prague, 1934), pp. 87–89, 92.
31. Samarin, *Sochineniia,* V, xii.
32. Ibid., XII, 28–29.
33. See ibid., p. vii; Kireevsky, *Sochineniia,* I, 9–111; II, 215–290.
34. Of the more than two thousand letters of Iurii Samarin's that Dmitry collected and edited, only 262 were published in volume 12 of Samarin's works. Recently 73 of Samarin's letters to Baroness Edith Fedorovna Rahden, all written between 1861 and 1876, some in French, some in German, and some in Russian, have been published in English translation (Terence Scully translated from the French, Helen Swediuk-Cheyne from the German, and Loren Calder from the Russian). The volume also has an excellent introduction by Loren Calder. The publication includes 59 of Baroness Rahden's replies also in English translation. It is clear, however, that even with this valuable addition, and an occasional other publication of some letters, only a small part of Samarin's correspondence has thus far appeared in print. See Loren Calder et al., *The Correspondence of Iu. Samarin and Baroness Rahden (1861–1876). Translated from The Second Edition of D. Samarin, Moscow, 1894* (Waterloo, Ontario, Canada, 1974). Professor Tsimbaev has recently stated that the Slavophils left more than 9,000 letters housed in seven Soviet archives, and that about 2,000 letters were written by Samarin. See Tsimbaev, *Slavianofil'stvo,* p. 95.
35. Samarin, *Sochineniia,* XII, 131.
36. A. S. Khomiakov, *Polnoe sobranie sochinenii* (Moscow, 1904), 8 vols., VIII, 228–229 hereafter cited as Khomiakov, *Sochineniia.* For this letter see also *Russkii arkhiv,* 1879, no. 11, pp. 305–307.
37. Khomiakov, *Sochineniia,* VIII, 229–230.
38. Ibid., p. 231.
39. This is part of a long statement of Samarin's quoted by his brother Dmitry. See Samarin, *Sochineniia,* V, LXV.
40. Ibid., XII, 45–46.

5

Middle 1840s: In the Slavophil Camp

Since the emphasis in the preceding chapter is on Samarin's concern with Hegelian philosophy it would be normal to conclude that during the early 1840s he was so engrossed in Hegelianism, and in his own dissertation, that he had no time for anything else. Such an impression, however, is not borne out by the facts about his contacts, activities, and other interests during those trying and crucial years. It was during the late 1830s and early 1840s that he established most of the personal relationships that were to influence, in one way or another, his life and career. Without attempting to give a complete account of them all, we can at least single out those that shed the most light on Samarin's thoughts and convictions.

The two principal categories into which Samarin's friendships, associations, and contacts fall are the Slavophil and the Westerner. Among the Slavophils, already referred to, were Khomiakov, I. V. Kireevsky, and probably Peter V. Kireevsky, who was not in the front line of the Slavophil camp. Konstantin Aksakov, as pointed out, was Samarin's closest friend. Later Samarin became friendly with Konstantin's younger brother, Ivan Aksakov (1823–1886). In the 1850s Samarin and Koshelev (1806–1883) were drawn together primarily by their interest in the emancipation reform. This was also true of Prince V. A. Cherkassky (1824–1878). The minor Slavophils who should be mentioned here were A. N. Popov (1820–1877), D. A. Valuev (1820–1845), V. A. Panov (1819–1849), and F. V. Chizhov (1811–1877). Later on in sympathy with some aspects of Moscow Slavophilism, according to individual inclinations, were several younger men, including V. I. Lamansky (1833–1914), A. F. Gil'ferding (1831–1872), the older historian I. D. Beliaev (1810–1873), and N. P. Giliarov-Platonov (1824–1887).[1] Perhaps in a class by himself was the poet F. I. Tiutchev (1803–1887).

In the last few years (after this portion of the revised manuscript on Samarin had been completed) a number of valuable studies have appeared in the Soviet Union. Those to which I have had access are of the highest scholarly quality, and this is in part because their authors have utilized many archival, unpublished materials. These shed new light on important aspects of Moscow Slavophilism, and on the personal relationships within the Slavophil circle.[2] Dudzinskaia concentrates on the late 1850s, and the Slavophils' participation in the emancipation reform of 1861, whereas Koshelev and Tsimbaev provide a wider treatment of Slavophilism encompassing the 1840s and 1850s. The problem of terminology, which in turn is closely related to accuracy and precision, and which has been endemic to Khomiakov, Ivan Kireevsky, and Konstantin Aksakov studies, and now to that of Samarin, occupies an important place in these recent studies.

Central and particularly elusive and disconcerting is the one exact and generally agreed upon definition of the terms 'Slavophil,' and 'Slavophilism.' The bewildering meanings, connotations, and usages of these terms, before and after the 1840s. and to the present, remain an unsolved and perhaps an insoluble problem. Replacing 'Slavophilism' with a new, invented term after its usage of nearly two centuries is futile even if feasible. Nor is reducing everything to Slavophil and non-Slavophil or to black and white a solution to the problem. Such a pair of categories would in fact evade the issue of what Slavophilism actually was, for its complexities, qualifications, and contradictions cannot be ignored.

Koshelev and particularly Tsimbaev give much attention to this basic problem of the meaning and usage of "Slavophil" and "Slavophilism." Koshelev's monograph states the problem at the outset: "Confusion in the interpretation of Slavophilism begins with the equivocal [*neodnoznachnykh*] interpretations of the term," and he goes on to point out that the Slavophils, who did not like the designation — as I have noted more than once in the earlier studies of this series — had their individual preferences. Konstantin Aksakov preferred the term "Russian orientation" to Slavophilism. Samarin preferred "Moscow orientation," and Khomiakov, "Slav-Christian orientation." A. I. Koshelev likes the untranslatable *samobytniki*.[3] Some of the Westerners, too, such as K. D. Kavelin, P. V. Annenkov, and Chernyshevsky, had qualms about the designations Slavophil and Slavophilism.

Tsimbaev in the introduction to his survey of Moscow Slavophilism observes, quite correctly, "Clarification of the *different* meanings of the word 'Slavophil,' during the *various* periods of its existence, could serve as a necessary and beneficial introduction to the study of Slavophilism." "The fate of the word 'Slavophil' is a captivating page in the development of the lexical content of the Russian literary language of the nineteenth century," he says, and he considers that the etymology of this designation, seldom seen in historical works, is "unconditionally essential," because of the "vagueness of the words, 'Slavianophil,' 'Slavophil' and 'Slavophilism.'"[4]

In a rich fifty-five-page chapter, and later in the conclusion, Tsimbaev examines the problems, citing the opinion and comments of half a dozen Soviet scholars and multi-shaded meaning of "Slavophil" and its derivatives. In the opening years of the nineteenth century A. S. Shishkov's book, *Deliberation*

about the Old and the New Style in the Russian Language (Rassuzhdenie o
starom i novom sloge rossiiskogo iazyka) was being read in Russia and its
author was soon dubbed a "Slavianofil." This "old believer, schismatic, old
word devotee," who admired the Church Slavonic language, provoked
retorts from the poet I. I. Dmitriev, who probably invented the word
slavianofil about 1803. But what began as a linguistic literary argument acquired shades of a social political nature in the second decade of the
nineteenth century while Russia was enduring the Napoleonic invasion and
its consequences. The controversy became known as the Shishkovist-
Karamzinist dispute.[5]

This episode, which should be known for the birth of the term 'Slavophil,'
is stretched by some to signify a pre-Moscow Slavophil or a proto-Slavophil
movement.[6] The Moscow Slavophils were, of course, acquainted with
Shishkov's views and cognizant of his later career as Minister of Education
(1824–1828); Konstantin Aksakov's father, Sergei Aksakov (1791–1858), had
himself experienced the Shishkov-Karamzin controversy as a young man.
Tsimbaev is probably on solid ground when he concludes, speaking of the
Moscow Slavophils: "Among them there were no connections with
Shishkov's ideas, even in the sense of nonacceptance or spurning."
Khomiakov, for one, as Tsimbaev points out, considered Shishkov's views
"obscure," and the "circle of his demands, 'narrow.'"[7]

Following in considerable detail the tortuous path of the designation
Slavophil, Tsimbaev says that in the 1830s it appears "as if it was invented a
second time." As pointed out in the Aksakov study, the Slav linguistic,
literary, and cultural renaissance of the first half of the nineteenth century
flourished especially among the Western Slavs, and it was during the 1830s
that the untranslatable verb form of Slavianophil or *"slavianstvovat"* ("to
Slavophilize?") came into existence, though this had little relationship to the
as yet undeclared Moscow Slavophil group.[8] In the first half of the 1840s,
this formation took on a variety of shades and meanings, some of them
deprecatory, as it began occurring in the evolving polemics between
Slavophils and Westerners.

In this mid-decade period, Herzen played a leading part in denigrating
the Slavophils, using in the process a variety of semantic forms of the term
Slavophil.[9] Belinsky also used the term derogatorily. Occasionally, too, the
Slavophils were, to their chagrin, lumped together with the men of Official
Nationality. But even though Khomiakov and a few of the *dei minores,* including Panov and Chizhov, made trips in the 1840s to the South Slav lands,
Moscow Slavophilism evolved with its basic concern with Russia's future cultural course vis-à-vis the West.[10] Some scholars have indeed suggested that
"Russophilism" or "Russian orientation" would have been a more appropriate designation than "Slavophilism." The Slavophils themselves
preferred the term *Moskovskoe napravlenie,* "Moscow orientation."[11]

During the 1840s and later, the Moscow Slavophils were occasionally identified with Pogodin's and Shevyrev's *Moskvitianin,* which began publication in 1841. As I have pointed out, this connection was never a strong ideological one, and the *Moskvitianin* did not become a Slavophil organ. Differences, to be brought out later in this study, separated the Slavophils from the *Moskvitianin* and counterbalanced the similarities.

It does not seem necessary here to follow the term "Slavophil" on its tortuous and tortured road through the nineteenth century. "On the borderline between the nineteenth and twentieth centuries the words, 'Slavophilism' and 'Slavophil' acquired in Russian publicistics yet another shade of meaning . . . . they became an ennobled synonym . . . for nationalism, great-power chauvinism, aristocratic reaction, [and] Russification."[12] They also, curiously, to some became synonymous with the word "liberal." The equally twisting path of this word from the early nineteenth century into the twentieth has led it from one meaning to its opposite, and the path is strewn with ambiguities, difficulties, and contradictions. In Russian writings, the word is often applied to the Moscow Slavophils as well as to others. That is why it is of concern here. The word "liberal" came to Russia from the West, so its origin and Western evolution are of obvious relevance.

Down through the centuries, liberty has meant different things to different people, and the definition of liberal has also differed.[13] The word "liberals" entered the English political vocabulary early in the nineteenth century when the Tories named their opponents "liberals." In fact they were "first called *liberales,* and the Spanish form was used in England "with the intention of suggesting that the principles of those politicians were un-English." The political-ideological game played in England then is strikingly reminiscent of the manner and circumstances in which the small group around Khomiakov and Ivan Kireevsky were dubbed Slavophils by their ideological opponents.

English liberalism of the mid-nineteenth century, probably the best-known variety at the time, was characterized as "freedom from the constraints of the state" or in Hobbes's words, "The liberties of subjects depend on the silence of the law." Locke, while admitting the necessity of the state to guarantee peace, security, and property, or, in his words, "life liberty, and property," also stood for the "classical economic doctrine of laissez-faire." But by the end of World War I the "British Liberal party broke into two, the right-wing or laissez-faire element joining forces with conservatism and the radical, *etatiste* element merging with socialism." In the United States, liberalism never played the same role as in England; it had no Liberal party, and toward the end of the nineteenth century the radical movement, the Populist, was not "liberal" but "progressive," a connotation that is still quite noticeable in the use of the term liberal.[14] With the depression and the Roosevelt administration in the early 1930s came social welfare legislation,

and since then complete laissez-faire has gone out so that the word "liberal"
has become "a sobriquet for 'socialist.'"[15]

Western liberalism in the middle of the nineteenth century was a secular,
political, economic doctrine and practice. It may not have been antireligious, but neither was it known for its zeal in Christian piety.[16] In
politics it stood for constitutional limitations on the power of the government, often in written form as in the United States, and economics for laissez-faire, probably its best-known doctrine. In contrast, the Moscow
Slavophils were known for their devotion to Slavophil Orthodoxy—never
perfect, of course, but far removed from Western secularism. Their social
and economic ideal was embodied in the historical Russian village commune, in the preservation of which after the Emancipation Reform they
played a prominent part. In the political sphere their naive faith in a nobler
autocracy than the one that existed rendered them unreceptive and skeptical of written constitutional guarantees. On none of these major counts do
the Slavophils qualify as liberals.

The Moscow Slavophils did, it is true, stand for freedom of speech,
religion, and assembly, but it is a moot question whether these were
transposed Western liberal values or were derived from the Slavophil
doctrine of *sobornost'*.[17] Even if one accepts Western liberalism as their
source this cannot outweigh the nonliberal core of Moscow Slavophilism.
"Reformist" might be a more apt designation for Slavophilism, particularly
with respect to the emancipation of the serfs, Russia's overriding problem
of the time. Certainly the Moscow Slavophils would have been more consistent and more convincing had they divested themselves of their possessions
and joined the peasant communes on their estates, but in fact they took the
opposite road, the bourgeois, capitalistic, entrepreneurial road—that led to
factory ownership in addition to their landed estates. In the case of Chizhov it ended in railroad construction and the accumulation of very considerable personal wealth.

If the Slavophils were never thoroughly united, the Westerner camp was
even less homogeneous and harmonious. Thus there was a wide gulf between the pro-Catholic Westernism of the man who in effect initiated the
Westerner-Slavophil controversy in the 1830s, Chaadaev (1794–1856), and
his admirer Prince Gagarin (1814–1882), and Belinsky's and Herzen's radical revolutionary Westernism. There were also fundamental differences between these two types of Westernism and that of the liberal, academic
Westerners, Kavelin (1814–1885), S. M. Solov'ev (1820–1879), T. N.
Granovsky (1813–1855), and later, of Chicherin (1828–1904).

Pogodin (1800–1875) and his friend and colleague at the University of
Moscow, S. P. Shevyrev (1806–1864) are usually classified as among the
"men of official nationality."[18] The numerous references to Pogodin and
Shevyrev, particularly to Pogodin, in the first three studies, and in this one,

are ample evidence of the ties between them and the Slavophils. Yet Pogodin was for a while also close to the so-called *pochvenniki* ("men of the soil").[19] He also seemed at home with representatives of the non-Russian Slavs, as well as among the Russian pan-Slavs of the late 1860s and early 1870s.

Moscow's vigorous salons in the first half of the 1840s placed Samarin in contact not only with the male literary, artistic, and intellectual strata of the old capital, but also with the small but gifted and unique group of salon hostesses.[20] He was perhaps most at home in the company of Ekaterina Aleksandrovna Sverbeeva, (1808–1892), Karolina Karlovna Pavlova, nee Ianish (1807–1893), and Aleksandra Osipovna Smirnova, nee Rosseti (1810–1882).[21] In the early 1860s he began, as indicated earlier, his correspondence with Baroness von Rahden.

Although this is not intended as a complete list of all of Samarin's contacts, friends, and correspondents, two foreign visitors to Moscow should be, named here the French Deputy Mauguin, already mentioned, who, in Khomiakov's words, "thought that our tsars were Mohammedans — so!" and the German scholar, and specialist on agrarian affairs, Baron August von Haxthausen who arrived in Moscow in 1843, three years after Mauguin's visit.

Those of Samarin's friends, relationships, and correspondents that warrant separate studies include the members of the Slavophil circle. Particularly relevant here would be the Samarin-Khomiakov and the Samarin-Konstantin Aksakov relationships; also the Samarin Ivan Aksakov friendship, which is particularly important with respect to Samarin's career in the late 1850s and for the rest of his life. The same is true of the Samarin-Koshelev, and Samarin-Cherkassky relationships.[22] Samarin's contacts with Shevryev and Pogodin have been mentioned often enough to suggest that more detailed and complete studies are needed. Of the various contacts between Samarin and the Westerners, none would produce a more fascinating study than that between him and Herzen, two of the brightest minds of the "marvelous decade," who also encountered each other in the middle 1860s. Although in 1847 in the "thick journals" Samarin engaged in polemics with Belinsky, Belinsky's death the following year cut short their encounter. Samarin's controversies with Chaadaev, and with the liberal academic Westerners S. M. Solov'ev, Kavelin, and Granovsky, and later with Chicherin are all worth more careful and complete examination than that which can be accorded them here.

Also more pertinent to a standard biography of Samarin than to this study, which focuses on his career up to, and including the Emancipation Reform of 1861, would be a thorough study of the Samarin-Baroness von Rahden correspondence, 1861–1876. Edith Fedorovna von Rahden (1825–1885), a native of the Baltic province of Courland, was of German descent. She is characterized by Nol'de as a person with a "completely outstanding mind, depth of mood, and noble firmness of character." As a Fraulein, lady-in-waiting, to the Grand Duchess Elena Pavlovna, she was in close touch with the imperial palace in St. Petersburg. In her modest quarters in a wing of the Mikhailov palace she had her informal circle, most active during the emancipation reform period.[23] There, the woman whose motto is said to have been "Wahrheit gegen Feind und Freund" received Iurii Samarin, Nicholas Miliutin, Prince Cherkassky, Ivan Aksakov, F. M. Dmitriev, Chicheerin, Kavelin, Turgenev, and others whose interest in the emancipation of the serfs brought them together in spite of different ideological orientations.[24]

The unlikely friendship between Samarin and Baroness Rahden did not begin until 1864, although they had met earlier, when they saw each other in Ragatz, Germany, where the Grand Duchess was visiting. From then on the friendship endured until Samarin's death. It was an unlikely relationship because it involved two strong personalities, highly gifted, self-confident, and dedicated, she to her Baltic German heritage and culture, he to his Orthodox Russian Slavophil principles. That there were strains is clear from their correspondence. But it is also a fact that mutual respect and admiration overcame all obstacles in what seems to have been a uniquely platonic relationship.

Different and perhaps less trying was Samarin's presence in the early 1840s in E. A. Sverbeeva's Moscow salon, on Tverskaia, whose hostess was referred to by her contemporary A. I. Turgenev as "Récamier-Sverbeeva."[25] Eleven years older than Samarin, Sverbeeva was born a Princess Shcherbatov, distantly related to Chaadaev, of whom she is said to have been quite fond. Prince N. B. Golitsyn later characterized her as "wise, educated, and beautiful," in whose Moscow salon from the mid-1830s on the "representatives of university science and scholarship, poets and writers, Westerners and Slavophils often met." Although as a good hostess she welcomed all who could contribute to her parlor conversations, and although she was fond of the foremost Westerner of the late thirties and first year or two of the forties, P. Ia. Chaadaev, she, in Golitsyn's words, "inclined her sympathies toward Slavophilism." This is explained by her "conditions of life, kinship ties, and personal inclinations.

Ever conscious of the duty and function of the hostess, Sverbeeva avoided partisanship and "softened the sharpness of opinions of those who were near to her, while the influence of her husband, a sober and skeptical observer . . . prevented her from enthusiastic doctrinairism." A. I. Turgenev, who had known Madame Récamier and her salon well, wrote in 1845, a few months before he died, "Sverbeeva is still amiable as formerly, in heart and soul, and even in thought, although the latter is sometimes concealed by an ambiguous smile. My soul blossoms out in her presence."[26]

Samarin and Konstantin Aksakov, younger and less sophisticated than Turgenev, doubtless enjoyed and profited from the conversations and discussions in Sverbeeva's salon, and seem to have found her company fascinating. This made it easier for them to visit her parlor and to remain there on occasion, as pointed out earlier, until early in the morning. But neither the incipient young Slavophils nor any of the other salon habitues of the early 1840s had to confine themselves to any one parlor or hostess. The usual salon was open once a week, therefore those wishing more frequent encounters made the rounds of several salons. Samarin was in this category.

Samarin's correspondence for this period, particularly his letters to Konstantin Aksakov in 1840, 1841, and 1842, mentions the Pavlova salon perhaps as often as the Sverbeeva, and as noted earlier, it was at Pavlova's that he discussed in 1841 in a three-hour session with her, "Faust, the French, [George] Sand, immortality of the soul, Hegel, love, etc.," and added, "Karolina Karlovna said to me that you and she debated whether Hegel recognizes revelation, [and] Jesus Christ as the Son of God, and you presumably said that he acknowledges this."[27] Samarin disagreed with Konstantin and possibly also with Karolina Karlovna but did not state his views.

In a recent Soviet edition of Karolina Karlovna Pavlova's poetry the best of her poems are said to be "distinguished by the depth of her spiritual ruminations, by an exquisite and rich musicalness, and high poetical mastery."[28] Pavlova was born in Moscow but was of German descent on her father's side (Janisch) and of French and English on her mother's. She was fluent in several languages and wrote in Russian, German, and French. She made Russian translations from Schiller, Heine, Goethe, and other German poets, also from Molière, Chénier, and Hugo, and from English, including Thomas Campbell and Sir Walter Scott and some of the Scottish folk poetry, of which she seemed particularly fond, as well as Lord Byron and Thomas Moore. She also translated from the Polish and from classical Greek. In addition, she rendered some of Zhukovsky's and Pushkin's poetry into German and French. She also left some prose. During her lifetime, which spanned most of the nineteenth century, she was perhaps best known in her role as one of the leading Moscow salon hostesses.

As a girl of nineteen she fell in love with the Polish poet Mickiewicz (1798–1855) while he was in Russia at the end of the 1820s. Her marriage in 1837 to the actor, translator, and minor Russian author Nikolai Filipovich Pavlov (1803–1864), a man who was released from serfdom as a boy of eight, was, according to Panaev, a marriage of convenience—but mainly, it seems, for Pavlov. Panaev says that it had two purposes: to assure Pavlov adequate income (Pavlova is said to have owned 1,000 serfs), and to add status to his serf origin. Later, Pavlov's gambling losses threatened the family income

and added to the strain of the marriage.[29] But in the first half of the 1840s
their Moscow salon was one of the most active.[30]

Gromov raises the question of Pavlova's relationship to Moscow
Slavophilism and asserts that she "was published in the Slavophil press, and
the principal representatives of this orientation of social thought customarily praised and propagandized her work." The extreme right in the person
of Baron E. F. Rosen attacked her, Gromov says, as a "decided partisan of
Moscow scholasticism, that is Slavophilism." Rosen—in much the same
terms as the liberal Westerners—criticized the Slavophils' defense of the
Russian peasant commune and their "fusion of these individualities into one
mass." Rosen presumably based his attacks on Pavlova's novel, *Double Life*
(Dvoinaia zhizn'), but Gromov flatly states that "there is no Slavophilism
whatever in the novel," and cites Shevyrev's review in the *Moskvitianin* in
1848 as being "more negative than positive."[31] Here again we are faced with
the questions, was the *Moskvitianin* a Slavophil organ, and were Pogodin and
Shevyrev Slavophils? This is a question we shall return to later on. If they
were, one must demonstrate what their contribution to Moscow Slavophilism
was, just as it is possible to show with reasonable accuracy what each of the
"early" Slavophils—Khomiakov, Kireevsky, Aksakov, and Samarin—contributed to "classical Slavophilism."

By the spring of 1845, Samarin had arrived at two decisions that were to
influence his career for the rest of his life. He had chosen Slavophilism as
his ideological orientation, and he had recently submitted to his father's
wishes to join the Russian civil service in St. Petersburg. We saw that the
first decision, made under Khomiakov's guidance and inspiration, also
resulted in what appears to have been Samarin's free choice of Khomiakov's
leadership in matters of religion. Joining the civil service may not have been
as difficult and traumatic as his choice of Orthodoxy over Hegelianism, but
that decision was no more spontaneous than the first.

Samarin had had hopes of following an academic career, especially after
defending his dissertation with considerable success. Entering government
service was not his choice but that of his father, who believed in the discipline
of work and service. Iurii served the government conscientiously, and made
the most of some exceptional opportunities during his tenure (1844–1853),
but he was not content to be just another bureaucrat. The other early
Slavophils did not look kindly on the bureaucracy, and the period from about
1842 until Samarin left Moscow for St. Petersburg on August 7, 1844, was
one of rapid decline of Konstantin Aksakov's authority in his relationship
with Samarin, perhaps not unconnected with Iurii's potential new career.

As noted in the preceding volumes of this study, the middle 1840s marked
a watershed in Russian ideological life, just as they were a time of key
decisions for Iurii Samarin. In fact, these two developments, one national,
Russian, the other personal, concerning the life and career of one of the

"men of the forties," were closely related. Yet this period, from the point of view of Moscow Slavophilism and Samarin's career, is more noteworthy for its purport and promise than for its actual achievement. It must not be forgotten that Khomiakov's doctrine of *sobornost',* Ivan Kireevsky's doctrine of the wholeness of the spirit and Konstantin Aksakov's choric principle were not clearly elaborated and stated until the 1850s. Similarly, although Samarin had given indication of his intellectual brilliance in his dissertation and its defense, and was successful in his work in the Baltic provinces in the late 1840s, his single greatest contribution to Moscow Slavophilism, and to Russia, that is, his participation in the Emancipation Reform—belongs to the 1850s and later decades.

In addition to the final split between Slavophils and Westerners, the middle forties were marked by some competition for new adherents, each camp making informal efforts to bolster its ranks. The Slavophils, who, unlike the radical Westerners and the "men of official nationality," could not have a journal of their own during the reign of Nicholas I resorted to the publication of several annual symposiums. But the very loose nature of the ideological camps, characteristic of Russian circle and salon activities of the 1830s and 1840s, make it impossible to speak of organization, rosters, and membership as was the case with political parties in the West, and later in Russia.[32]

This does not mean that adherence to one ideological camp or another was not well established, or well known, and that no efforts were made to entice individuals from one camp to the other. This probably happened even when attempts at proselytizing were not overt and explicit. In the words of Professor Malia, "for Herzen there was no more promising and attractive person in all of Moscow" than young Iurii Samarin, seven years Herzen's junior, while Nol'de says that, "Herzen, with whom in 1843 after his return from exile, Samarin became very friendly, and who by the makeup of his mind was in many respects inwardly close to the latter," found Samarin then as later a challenge that could not be ignored.[33]

Herzen's diary for the last month of 1843 and the early month of 1844 contains a number of entries on Samarin that shed much light on the thinking of both protagonists. The earliest was recorded on October 26, 1843, and refers to both Samarin and Aksakov, who, as we saw in the Aksakov study, presumably wished to erect their "Slav-Byzantine structure" on the basis of "contemporary philosophy," and to arrive "through Hegel at Orthodoxy."[34] Less witty, and more informative, is Herzen's next mention of Samarin, in the entry for November 10. "A lengthy and extremely interesting conversation with Samarin. He agrees that he cannot clearly develop logically his idea of the immanent co-existence of religion and philosophy." Human complexity and inner contradictions account for the fact that often "thought destroys that which has been accepted by fantasy and the heart."

In Samarin's thought, as also in that of the other Slavophils, Herzen found "Slavianism inseparable from the Greek [Orthodox] religion. The church is one and that is our church; they expect that Catholicism and Protestantism will equally acknowledge its truthfulness. This is the most desperate hypothesis of all."[35] After Samarin's return from his trip to the Volga region in January 1844, Herzen wrote (January 18): "[Samarin] is beginning to view with horror the impossibility of sticking to their [the Slavophils'] Orthodox-philosophical position. The noble structure of his mind does not permit him to come to rest in a formal, external co-existence, or better said, on a juxtaposition."[36]

These impressions were recorded at the time of Samarin's severe inner conflict, which was shortly to be resolved in favor of Slavophilism and Khomiakov's leadership. Herzen's next reference to Samarin was made on June 5: "Yesterday Samarin defended his dissertation. An incomprehensible conjunction of lofty dialectical ability in this man with pitiful Orthodox theories, and with exaggerated Slavianism. This contradiction is particularly striking because in him logic is decisively predominant over everything else."[37] At the end of the year, Herzen was still hopeful that Samarin could be "saved"; the entry for December 4, says: "I wrote to Samarin. I could not, and indeed I did not wish to restrain myself, not to state in full my opinion about the Slavs [Slavophils], about that arid chatter, narrow point of view, stagnation, etc."[38] The letter referred to has not been found, nor has Samarin's reply, if there was one, and the references to Samarin in Herzen's diary cease at this point. Herzen's exasperation with Samarin at the end of 1844, at the time of the final break between Slavophils and Westerners, was probably reciprocated by Samarin. Their mutual respect and the desire for further debate were not ended, however; the confrontation was revived twenty years later.

While Herzen would have welcomed in his camp a young man of the intellectual capacity and promise of Iurii Samarin, Kireevsky toyed with the idea (idle, as it developed) of drawing in Herzen and, particularly, the somewhat more compatible Moscow University professor T. N. Granovsky, who had been attracting considerable attention in Moscow intellectual circles in the winter of 1843–1844 with his highly successful public lectures on Western medieval history. Relations between Granovsky and Khomiakov were cool, however; and both Granovsky and Ivan Kireevsky, though they enjoyed a certain compatibility and mutual respect, knew that their ideological differences could not be bridged. On the contrary, they were both at this time trying to get permission from St. Petersburg to publish their own journals.[39]

The vagaries of human nature and autocratic government account for the fact that while the tsar's administration would not allow the moderate Granovsky his own journal, and denied the same to the Slavophils, it favored the "reptile press" of the capital, and allowed the radical Belinsky to publish his works in Russia's most influential journals during the 1840s, the *Otechestvennye Zapiski* (Notes of the Fatherland), 1839–1846, and *Sovremennik* (The Contemporary), from the end of 1846 when Belinsky became the "heart of the journal," until his death in May 1848. Herzen, who was Belinsky's foremost collaborator, had left Russia more than a year earlier never to return.

The abortive Slavophil effort to take over Pogodin's *Moskvitianin* when Ivan Kireevsky became its editor for three issues in the summer of 1844, convinced them that if they were to have a publication of their own it would have to be annual symposiums, if and when the censorship allowed them. In this manner the first of several annual Slavophil publications was born. The first one appeared in 1844 under the editorship of Dmitry A. Valuev (1820–1845), under the title *Simbirskii sbornik*. This publication has remained unavailable to me, although Valuev's contribution, *Razriadnaia kniga 1559–1605 gg.* (Cadastral Book 1559–1605), supplemented, corrected, and edited, was recently published in Moscow.[40] The second symposium, also edited by Valuev, appeared the following year.[41] Among other things, it illustrates the unreliability of classifying people at that time solely according to the journal to which they contributed.

The *sbornik* that Valuev edited shortly before his premature death in 1845 was presumably a Slavophil publication, although its Slavophil contributors were limited to Khomiakov (who incidentally, was a relative of Valuev's), A. N. Popov, and Valuev himself (and not Ivan Kireevsky, Konstantin Aksakov, and Iurii Samarin, who was then in St. Petersburg); there were also articles by such non-Slavophils as K. D. Kavelin, T. N. Granovsky, and S. M. Solov'ev.[42] The unreliability of journals as absolute or automatic guides to the ideological orientation of its contributors during the late 1830s and 1840s is further demonstrated by *Otechestvennye zapiski,* which, though retaining the name, changed owners, editors, or both, during its long existence (1839–1884).[43]

In preparation for *Simbirskii sbornik,* which included his study of *mestnichestvo,* place order in Russian society, Valuev spent time searching for historical materials in his native province of Simbirsk. A year later, in 1843, he went to Paris and London in quest of sources and data on the Abyssinian and Irish churches. On this trip, while in Prague, he met Hanka, Šafařík, and Palacky. This was his introduction to the non-Russian Slav world, which he held in high esteem, and whose culture and future he considered inseparable from Russia's.[44] The two parts of Valuev's symposium were heavily but not exclusively dedicated to subjects of Russian and Slav history. Part one, 310 pages, also included a brief translation from the Hebrew in reference to Khazar history, and Valuev's perhaps somewhat unexpected essay for a symposium on the Slavs, "Khristianstvo v Abissinii" (Christianity in Abyssinia). The second part contained a 194-page monograph on the legal and political order of the towns in medieval Dalmatia, translated from the German of Alexander von Reutz.[45]

Khomiakov's contribution, the seven-page "In Place of an Introduction," written in the same general interpretative way as his "Semiramida" or notes on universal history, provides virtually no dates although it follows a general chronology. It contains little in the way of concrete data, facts, and names to support its biased and dogmatic conclusions. The story begins, with republican and imperial Rome and ends with about the tenth century. The reign of Constantine the Great is given special consideration, for the eastern half of the Roman empire was "more enlightened, and more independent in spiritual matters than the Roman world, and for this reason accepted for itself the Christian principle in a more vital way, and more profoundly," than the West. A few centuries later when the Slavs arrived on the scene and came in contact with the Germanic tribes in northern and central Europe they demonstrated in their social order the "sacred nature of the family and humane sentiments" as well as their "natural communes." This led Khomiakov to another well-known Slavophil contention, that "conquest is in general alien to the Slavs," and that what is characteristic of them is the "holy war for the fatherland," not the "unjust war of the conqueror."[46]

Orthodoxy, which, in Khomiakov's view, appealed to the democratic, egalitarian, agricultural Slavs, made rapid progress among them while "Catholicism entered the rich premises of their owners and tribal princes." Thus the formal aristocratic nature of Western Christianity contrasted sharply with Slav Orthodoxy. "Rome distorted the spiritual principle, Germany distorted the communal principle. Happily, the Western temptation did not penetrate Russia, Serbia, and Bulgaria. Poland, however, succumbed to the "love of power of the Roman clergy." In spite of Poland's defection — clearly, Khomiakov identified Slavdom with Orthodoxy — he concluded: "If not the embryo, then the possibility of renewal for mankind reposes in the Slav world."[47]

The views and convictions expressed by Khomiakov in this brief essay in 1845 are also to be found in Samarin's dissertation, and Valuev's writings. They were shared, too, by Ivan Kireevsky and Konstantin Aksakov. It is difficult to establish the ultimate source of these convictions, although Samarin seems to have entertained them as early as any of the Slavophils. What is more certain and more pertinent from the point of view of the study of Moscow Slavophilism is that by the middle forties they seem to have become common Slavophil property, well embedded in the Slavophil consciousness and attitude.

Of Valuev's contributions to the symposium, a twenty-four-page foreword and the equally long "Christianity in Abyssinia, " the first is more pertinent to this study as it contains a number of his Slavophil views and convictions, also shared by the other Moscow Slavophils. But the second is a more noteworthy performance by a twenty-three-year-old author of uncommon industry, initiative, and intelligence. This essay, which prompted Khomiakov to dub his young relative "Abissinets-Valuev," ("Valuev the Abysinian") is profusely documented, giving evidence of reading in Latin, French, German, and English, most of it done in London and Paris in 1843, while he was also studying the Irish church. These seemingly disparate subjects are indicative of young Valuev's brand of Slavophil church ecumenism. Not surprisingly, he is critical of Catholicism and Protestantism, and sees the hope of Christian unity in a return to Orthodoxy.[48]

In his forward Valuev humbly acknowledges Russia's cultural debt to the West, and is grateful for Peter the Great's work, but all this must lead Russia to "its own independent life and conscious thought," not to imitation of the West. "Russia must utilize its new, untouched, and fresh powers,"[49] for it was in the fortunate position of choosing freely what to accept and what to reject from abroad. Although Valuev admired the achievements of German science and scholarship, he regretted "its rationalistic pride," and was convinced that "for Germany in general, religious questions are closed." As in the case of the other Slavophils, so also with him, there was the occasional recognition that, after all, he had been brought up on Western languages and literatures. And so he tempered his strictures of the West, for as he said, "to renounce the West completely would mean that we renounce ourselves."[50] Still a man of the thirties as well as of the forties, Valuev was conscious that Russia's greatest cultural deficiency was in literature and philosophy. He regretted the absence of a Russian Walter Scott or Goethe, but Russia was stirring, for he knew that Pushkin and Gogol' had already appeared.

Obsessed with German philosophy, like most of the men of the thirties, and often using the term *nauka,* as Samarin did, to mean philosophy, Valuev ruefully marked the great distance that separated the West from Russia. Before Khomiakov had fully elaborated his doctrine of *sobornost',* Kireevsky his doctrine of the wholeness of the spirit, Aksakov his choric and communal principles, and Samarin his principles of Orthodox, social communality, Valuev vaguely but firmly foresaw the Slavophil insistence on the inseparability of religion and philosophy, or perhaps more accurately, a philosophy based on Orthodoxy. In his view, the "Roman-Catholic and the German-Protestant" philosophy, each in its own way, had worked out the problems of the respective major nations and their kindred peoples. Now it was time for Russia to do the same for itself and its kindred Slav nations. But it must do more than that, for, he concluded, "in the history of the West itself there are hundreds of phenomena for which Russian and Orthodox philosophy must find a completely different solution from that which Westerners have thus far found."[51] This touch of early Slavophil messianism together with the several general Slavophil principles were enunciated, per-

haps somewhat naively, by a bright young aristocrat in poor health and destined never to contribute to another Slavophil symposium.

The Slavophils published two more symposiums in the decade of the forties, *Moscow Literary and Learned Symposium,* 1846 (Moskovskii literaturnyi i uchenyi sbornik) and *Moscow Literary and Learned Symposium for 1847*
(Moskovskii literaturnyi i uchenyi sbornik na 1847 god). Samarin, who left
Moscow for St. Petersburg in the summer of 1844, did not contribute to the
Valuev *sbornik,* or to the 1847 issue; for the 1846 issue he wrote a book
review, and we shall return to this in the next chapter. The final Slavophil
symposium was *Moscow Symposium. Volume I* (Moskovskii sbornik),
published in 1852. This, too, has no contribution from Samarin.[52] His absence from Moscow and his preoccupation during the mid-forties with work
in St. Petersburg and the Baltic provinces probably account for the paucity
of collaboration; this is not, however, a sign of lack of interest in Slavophil
affairs.

When Shevyrev queried Samarin in the spring of 1846 about the impression that the Slavophil symposium of that year produced in St. Petersburg,
Samarin was ready with a reply. In a letter dated June 6, about three weeks
after the appearance of the symposium, Samarin wrote: "I can say the impression is most favorable . . . they read it everywhere, and in all circles, and
everywhere it produces talk, controversy etc. One praises it, another
upbraids it, but no one is indifferent to it." *Otechestvennye zapiski,* which
Belinsky had left two months earlier, had not yet changed its orientation and
Samarin still considered it Slavophilism's principal foe, he told Shevyrev that
the journal had "abruptly turned the hill." The articles in *Otchestvennye
zapiski* about the symposium, Samarin says, are proof that "our orientation
has become predominant and that to ignore it would be dangerous for the
success of the journal."[53]

Despite this enthusiasm, Samarin, perhaps showing overconcern for his
own contribution, believed that "in general the symposium was not and could
not be appreciated on its merits." His review of Count V. A. Sollogub's
Tarantas was, he wrote, "too elaborate" and yet "produced a stronger impression than the others." "Did I not talk nonsense?"[54]

According to the archopponent Vissarion Belinsky, Samarin's review did
have unquestioned merit. In a review essay, "A View of Russian Literature
in 1846" (*Vzgliad na russkuiu literaturu 1846 goda*), Belinsky admitted that
the Moscow symposium, "despite its Slavophil orientation, includes several
interesting articles, one of which is the review of *Tarantas,* particularly
remarkable for its wise content, and masterly exposition."[55] In a letter to
Herzen, written from Odessa, July 4, 1846, Belinsky, though outspoken in
his general criticism of the Moscow symposium, nevertheless admitted that
"Samarin's review is intelligent but malicious, and even sensible in spite of
the fact that the author's starting point is the indecent principle of meekness

and humility. And he is a villain, he provokes me in the name of *Otechestven-nye zapiski.*"[56]

Samarin, in the letter to Shevyrev of June 6, 1846, described Khomiakov's contribution to the symposium, "Russians' Opinion of Foreigners — A Letter to a Friend" (*Mnenie Russkikh ob inostrantsakh. Pis'mo k priiateliu*), as "Superlative . . . too rich in content, and too condensed, and it was absolutely unappreciated by anyone except Tiutchev." A. N. Popov's essay, "About the Contemporary Orientation of the Plastic Arts" (*O sovremennom napravlenii iskusstv plasticheskikh*), "also passed unnoticed"; F. V. Chizhov's letter "About the Work of Russian Painters in Rome" (*O rabotakh Russikh khudozhnikov v Rime*), and verses by I. A. Aksakov, N. M. Iazykov, and P. A. Viazemsky "in general depended on one's taste." Samarin's overall conclusion was, "The success of the Symposium proves without a doubt that a new [Slavophil] journal in Moscow will be successful . . . and that Pushkin's prophecy that Moscow journalism will kill St. Petersburg's will be realized."[57]

Most of all, Samarin praised Khomiakov's rambling yet incisive, and provocative thirty-eight-page essay.[58] Like the other Moscow Slavophils, Khomiakov found Russia's "student dependence on the Western world" intolerable, and he characterized Western history as "crude particularism" or occurrences in their "accidental concatenation without any inner bond." This was the "general system of history" in the West up to the mid-1840s. When one allows for the differences in wit, artistic narrative, fidelity to sources and documents, and degrees of shrewd guessing, the "system remains the same in Ranke as in Hallam, and Gfrörer as also in Neander, Thierry, and Schlozer."

To be sure, efforts were made in the West to "elevate history to the level of true science," some were of a religious, some of a philosophical nature, but they all failed. No attempt in the West to elaborate the unifying principle of history was as outstanding as Hegel's, but it merely demonstrated the "unlimited arbitrariness of the learned systematizer."[59] Although he displayed the customary Slavophil respect for Hegel's genius, Khomiakov could not accept his system: "This great mind so profoundly comprehending the insignificance of contemporary historical science" could not solve the problem. Hegel's difficulty, as Khomiakov saw it, was reduced to this, that "in mathematics as in history, one sees Hegel in a basic defect, which lies at the very foundation of his logic — that is, the more or less conscious confusion of what in the logical order of things is an effect with what precedes it or is the cause or initial phase." Having found no satisfaction in the work of Western philosophers and historians, he conceded that "a certain one-sidedness in historical concepts and judgments is unavoidable." But recognizing implicitly some merit in Western scholarship, he concluded: "What has been achieved by one nation is supplemented and perfected by other nations. . . .

This supplementing of the works of our European brothers was our task and our duty."[60]

A number of other early Slavophil notions are scattered about in Khomiakov's essay—for instance, the view that Russia's "spiritual forces are still sprightly and fresh," and that Russia, unlike the Western nations, is "a living organic commune," in contrast even to his favorite Western nation, England. Khomiakov quotes Disraeli's observation, "English manners save England from English laws," and goes on to say that formalism's great defect is its "constant pretending to replace every moral and spiritual force."[61]

After some sharp criticism of French utopian socialism and communism, particularly with respect to their "destruction of marriage," Khomiakov concludes: "Western thinkers are moving in a perpetual closed circle because the idea of the commune [*obshchina*] is inaccessible to them. They cannot proceed further than association (*druzhina*)." He also found fault with the Western concept of family, and speaking of himself and the Russian gentry, regretted that "From childhood we jabber foreign words and feed on foreign thought; from childhood we become accustomed to measure everything around us with a measure that does not suit us," and among other things, confuse our sense of family, "with the Englishman's feudal notion of 'home' or with German kitchen-sentimental domesticity [*Häuslichkeit*]."[62] Samarin, so lately in the grip of Hegelianism, no doubt agreed with Khomiakov's characterization of German philosophy as "one of the greatest phenomena of human thought,"[63] but at the same time he could agree with Khomiakov's criticism of Hegel, which he had heard more than once during the long and trying salon sessions and in private conversations.

Toward the end of his letter to Shevyrev about the 1846 Slavophil symposium, Samarin briefly mentions F. V. Chizhov's contribution, "On the Works of Russian Painters in Rome," (*O rabotakh Russkikh khudozhnikov v Rime*).[64] The author of this article, one of the early, "minor" Slavophils, was a unique personality, who deserves a full-length biography. In his versatility, wide-ranging interests and pursuits, and intellectual endowment, he was closer to Khomiakov than to the other Slavophils. He was born in 1811 in an impoverished gentry home in old Kostroma, on the Volga about two hundred miles northeast of Moscow, and died in 1877, after a career easier to create in fiction than in life, leaving a fortune, according to one source, of about six million rubles.[65]

After graduating from the Kostroma gymnasium (instead of relying on private tutors as gentry families usually did), and having passed, on the testimony of Ivan Aksakov who knew him well for many years, "through the difficult school of toil and poverty" Chizhov graduated from the University of St. Petersburg in 1832 with a major in mathematics and physics.[66] Soon after, he was appointed an assistant in geometry. There in 1834, he met Gogol' who taught briefly at the university. In 1836 he published his dissertation on a subject in physics, and the following year a book on steam engines, using the work of George Stephenson and two other English authors. He remained in his academic post until 1840. But while still a university student he became interested in art, literature, and history. One result of this was his publication in Russian translation of Hallam's *History of European Literature XV and XVI Centuries*. Two years later he translated from English and edited a work under the title *Prizvanie zhenshchin* (The Calling of Women). In the meantime he had left for Western Europe where he remained during most of the period from 1840 to 1847.[67]

When he returned to Russia after travel and various periods of residence in Germany, France, Italy, Austria, and the Slav lands, Bohemia, Slovakia, and in the Balkans in Serbia, Dalmatia, Croatia, Slovenia, and Montenegro, he was arrested by the Third Section on the complaint of the Vienna government. In the opinion of L. V. Dubel't, head of the secret police, he "arouses discontent among the people with the [Vienna] government, organizes conspiracies, and incites to revolt."[68] Given a number of questions, Chizhov submitted written answers. (Ivan Aksakov and Samarin followed the same procedure when they were arrested by the Third Section two years later.)[69] The government banished Chizhov, "a useless dreamer," from both capitals, and he settled in the Kiev gubernia, where he went into the silk business. During six years of "solitude," in Aksakov's words, he was in the company of only "books and worms." Many years later his letters on silk production were published as a book "distinguished not only for its technical but also for its literary merits, and particularly for its artistic recreation of the mores and life of the worms." At the same time he read extensively in the history of philosophy; he left copious notes and "folios of systematic excerpts" from his readings.[70]

Like many another Russian, Chizhov's life was greatly changed by the Crimean War. After the war, he abandoned the silk business and moved to Moscow and became an entrepreneur. In 1858 he published *Vestnik promyshlennosti* (Journal of Industry), and for the next two decades he was a leader in railroad construction and ownership, in industry, commerce, banking, and steamship navigation. But the beginning of his new career coincides almost exactly with the end of "classical" Slavophilism, and the development of pan-Slavism, and is therefore outside our concern here.[71]

During the classical Moscow Slavophil period, the 1840s and 1850s, Chizhov was as we have seen, away from Moscow for many years, first because of his travel and residence in Western Europe, and then because of his banishment to Kiev. Yet he is usually considered one of the *dei minores* of Moscow Slavophilism, and rightly so. Even more than Panov, and A. N. Popov, he lends credence and content to the designation "Slavophil," usually resented by the Slavophils but not entirely misplaced or undeserved. He spent more time than Panov and Popov among the non-Russian Slavs, particularly among the South Slavs, and seems to have been more active in their behalf in spite of the fact that his first contacts with them were a matter more of chance than of conviction. For the South Slavs, these contacts were particularly welcome in view of the fact that all of them, except the Serbs, lived under foreign domination.

In his "Vospominaniia," Chizhov states that he stopped in Prague, where he met Hanka, Šafařík, and others on the way from Russia to the West, and that in 1843 he visited Istria, Dalmatia, and Montenegro. He returned to Istria the following year to "transport church plates, chasubles, books," all sent to him from Russia.[72] But he says that the "biggest trip" to the Slav lands came in 1845 when he visited Croatia, Slovenia, Serbia, the Adriatic coast, and Montenegro. In his words, "Montenegro was the last place that completely attached me to the Slavs and compelled me involuntarily to concentrate all my notions on this question, about which up to then I had had no inkling."[73] In connection with Chizhov's trip to Montenegro, Aksakov adds, without comment or explanation, "He somehow succeeded in helping the Montenegrins to unload arms on the Dalmatian coast." The arms were presumably to be used against the Turks. Modzalevsky repeats this bit of information, but again without giving a source.[74]

Chizhov interrupted his stay in the West for a visit to Moscow in 1845, possibly because while in Dubrovnik he found himself penniless. By then he had spent almost five years in the West. From his published correspondence with the painter Ivanov and also from the diary that he kept for almost forty years, beginning in the middle 1830s, one can get a good picture of his views and convictions.[75] Particularly valuable to this study are the dozen letters written between 1842 and September 1845, from Dusseldorf, Venice, Lyon, Paris, Zagreb, and Vienna.[76] In a letter from Paris dated May 31, 1844, he says that he attended Mickiewicz's lectures and found his "mystical principles" more than he could endure; "after the lecture I had an awful headache," he complains. A. N. Popov was also in Paris at the time and apparently delivered financial help to Mickiewicz from "Khomiakov, Shevyrev, N. V. Putiata, and other Muscovites." Chizhov met Mickiewicz personally, admired his "moral purity," enjoyed his conversation; although "his convictions are different from mine,[he wrote], we became very close."[77] The Slavophils had not lost their respect and concern for the Polish poet despite the Polish revolt of 1830–1831.

In Zagreb in June 1845 Chizhov found himself in "a completely different world." He became keenly aware of the strain between the Croats and their Hapsburg overlords and the Magyars. The more he became convinced that "The Magyars look upon us with hatred, and say that we are Russian propaganda," the more pro-Slav he became. But in Vienna, two months later, his indignation was directed not against the Magyars and Hapsburgs but against the "St. Petersburg journal promoters," whose "loathsome and despicable activity" he thoroughly resented. Their only concern was to reprint everything from the French, German, and English. Is this literature?" he asked. At the same time "they mercilessly berate everything that's their own," and this included Gogol', Iazykov, and Khomiakov, who was "full of the noblest Russian sentiments," and he vowed to publish his own journal in Moscow.[78]

In a second letter from Vienna, dated September 1, 1845, he says, "Tomorrow I'll leave for Russia," convinced that the all-Slav consciousness was growing stronger. "Several nations look upon Russia as upon the sun that must light up a new period of life. The Russian language must become the language of the Slavs, at least the literary and political [language]. The Russian faith – the faith of the Slavs." All this, Chizhov implied, he found among the Balkan and Hapsburg Slavs, some of whom "are not even of our faith." Pressburg (Bratislava), capital of Slovakia, was particularly pro-Slav, and he concluded, somewhat cryptically, "It seems the minister intends to intercede for a permit for me to publish a journal in Moscow." The only condition for this journal would be that "it would not be a translation from the West. It will contain everything that is its own, and Slavic. The Slavs are in raptures at the prospect.[79]

The journal that Chizhov envisioned in 1845, but was never secured for him by the unnamed minister, would have been a voice for Russia and the oppressed Slavs. It would have espoused the cause of all-Slav cultural unity, and, in Chizhov's dreams, it would have been based on Slav linguistic, and Christian Orthodox principles. But his plans and reality were separated not only by the suspicion and mistrust of the tsarist administration, but also by many centuries of history that held one Slav nation apart form another in religion, culture, and politics. Furthermore, among the "early" Moscow Slavophils, particularly Konstantin Aksakov, the conviction was strong during the 1840s that Russia's own pressing cultural, social-economic, and political problems were sufficiently intractable without taking on those of the rest of the Slavs.

Samarin, absent from Moscow during the second half of the 1840s except for an occasional visit home from his job in St. Petersburg and the Baltic provinces, showed little interest in the problems of the non-Russian Slavs that concerned Valuev, Popov, Panov, and Chizhov. His attention was directed to the problems of the Baltic Germans, Latvians, Estonians and Lithuanians, and, of course, Russia's relations with those people and the Poles. Like Ivan Kireevsky, Konstantin Aksakov, and even Khomiakov, during this formative Slavophil period, he found Russia's own problems his primary concern.

Notes

1. The difficulty of classifying a number of persons whose names appear on these pages, without more extensive research than is here possible, is illustrated by the case of Giliarov-Platonov. The son of a Kolomna priest, he graduated from the Moscow Orthodox Academy. He was particularly interested in heresies and the Russian church schism. In 1855 he left his theological pursuits and between 1856–1863 served on the Moscow censorship committee. This service was temporarily interrupted in 1857 when he was sent by the government to Western Europe to gather information on Jewish rabbinical schools, and on Jewish literary activities. He participated in the Emancipation reform, served in the Ministry of Education, and from 1867 on devoted himself to publicistic work. Earlier he had contributed to the Slavophil *Russkaia beseda,* and in the 1860s and 1870s to Ivan Aksakov's several journals, and to other publications. He knew the Slavophils well, and although twenty years younger than Khomiakov, and never one of the early Slavophils, he wrote to Ivan Aksakov in 1886, a year before he died, that "for Khomiakov I was even the *only* person [*edinstvennym chelovekom*] with whom he acknowledged his complete agreement." Without a thorough study of Giliarov-Platonov's career and writings such a claim would be difficult to confirm. In the same letter he also stated that the "late Iu. F. Samarin deferred to me, in my opinion in excess of what was deserved." See "Iz bumag N.P Giliarova-Platonova," *Russkii arkhiv,* 1889, book 3, p. 268.

2. Three studies published in the last few years are the previously cited E. A. Dudzinskaia, *Slavianofily v obshchestvennoi bor'be* (Moscow, 1983); V. A. Koshelev, *Esteticheskie i literaturnye vozzreniia Russkikh slavianofilov 1840–1850-e gody.* (Leningrad, 1984); and, also previously cited, N, I. Tsimbaev, *Slavianofil'stvo. Iz istorii russkoi obshchestvenno-politicheskoi mysli XIX veka* (Moscow, 1986).

3. Koshelev, *Slavianofily,* pp. 6–7.

4. Tsimbaev, *Slavianofil'stvo,* pp. 3, 5.

5. Ibid., pp. 6–8.

6. As was indicated in the Aksakov study (and will be shown later in this one), a form of Slavophilism and pan-Slavism have been traced to the middle of the seventeenth century and Jurii Krizanic; Professor V. I. Lamansky (1833–1914), an outstanding Slavicist, usually considered one of the later Slavophils, saw a strand leading to Slavophilism from the controversy between the Western nominalists and realists. On the other hand, no less a historian than V. O. Kliuchevsky could declare "Slavianophilism [is] a history of two or three parlors in Moscow, and two–[three] files in the Moscow police [office]." See Tsimbaev, pp. 56, 61.

7. Ibid., pp. 13–14.

8. Ibid., pp. 17–18.
9. Ibid., pp. 19–23.
10. See Christoff, *Xomjakov,* pp. 69–70.
11. Tsimbaev, *Slavianofil'stvo,* pp. 29–30.
12. Ibid., p. 46.
13. What follows is based on the factual and authoritative essay by Maurice Cranston, "Liberalism," In *The Encyclopedia of Philosophy* (New York-London, 1967), IV, 458.
14. Ibid., p. 458.
15. Ibid., p. 460.
16. It is correct to say, as has been said of Khomiakov, that he "did not care for the word 'liberal' [and] avoided its application to the Slavophils. Liberalism in his mind was tied to 'religious indifference.' This predetermined the cautious attitude of the deeply believing Khomiakov toward the European liberals and their Russian followers." Tsimbaev, *Slavianofil'stvo,* pp. 126–127.
17. In his emphasis on K. S. Aksakov's theory of the "non-statism" (*negosudarstvennost'*) of the Russian people (*narod*), Tsimbaev says that Aksakov derives from it the "idea of the existence of the inalienable peoples' rights (freedom of speech, opinion, press, the autonomy of the inner life of the people)." See ibid., p. 163. This presumed "non-statism" of the Russian people as seen by Aksakov, was in turn an expression of Slavophil Orthodoxy.
18. This ideological current, to which I shall return in Part Two, has received thorough expert treatment by Professor N. V. Riasanovsky. See his *Nicholas I and Official Nationality in Russia, 1825–1855* (Berkeley, Calif.) 1959; rev. ed., 1967, also two articles by him: "Nationality in the State Ideology During the Reign of Nicholas I," *Russian Review,* January 1960, pp. 38–46; and "Some Comments on the Role of the Intelligentsia in the Reign of Nicholas I of Russia, 1825–1855," *Slavic and East European Review,* 1957, no. 3, pp. 163–176.
19. About the *pochvenniki* see also Chapter 17.
20. Tsimbaev calls attention to the "active and equal participation" in the Slavophil salons of a number of outstanding hostesses such as A. P. Elagina, O. S. Aksakova, E. A. Sverbeeva, A. P. Sontag, N. P. Kireevskaia, M. V. Kireevskaia, E. M. Khomiakova, E. I. Popova, V. S. Aksakova, L. S. Aksakova, E. I. Elagina, E. A. Cherkasskaia, A. F. Aksakova, E. F. Tiutcheva, A. N. Bakhmeteva. He concludes that their roles are yet to be studied in detail. Tsimbaev, *Slavianofil'stvo,* p. 78.
21. In the preceding three studies of this series the circle (*kruzhok*), salon, and "evenings" have often been mentioned on the assumption, perhaps unwarranted, that the distinctions between them were obvious. In the Aksakov study a derogatory opinion of the circles was cited from I. S. Turgenev's

Sportman's Sketches. A much different view of the circles, salons, and "evenings," and I believe a more truthful one, was given many years later by Aronson and Reiser. The period covered by these authors is from the latter part of the eighteenth century through the 1850s, with heavy emphasis on the thirties and forties, decline having set in by the late 1840s. The authors list in addition to Moscow and St. Petersburg, provincial towns in which circles and salons existed. Exclusive of formally organized literary and artistic societies, they name more than two hundred circles and salons, the great majority of which were active in the first sixty years of the nineteenth century. The circles, like the salons, informal and without organization, were often of short duration. Consisting predominantly of young people, in their late teens or early twenties, they sometimes lasted only two or three years, as was the case with the *Liubomudry* (Lovers of Wisdom) in the 1820s. Organized literary societies lasted longer, but the big difference was in the "element of creativity." The circles, say the authors, "create literature whereas the official societies are nourished by it." The salons, which often observed designated "evenings" such as Saturdays at the Aksakovs' were inspired by French prototypes and were more durable than the circles, but the "Circle was more connected with writers while the salon [was more connected] with readers"; "If the circle helps us to shed light on literary productivity then the salon sheds light on the question of literary consumption." The same could be said of ideas as of literature. See M. Aronson and S. Reiser, *Literaturnye kruzhki i salony* (Leningrad, 1929), pp. 36–37, 301–306, 312.

22. For an excellent but limited treatment of this subject, see Richard Wortman "Koshelev, Samarin, and Cherkassky and the Fate of Liberal Slavophilism," *Slavic Review,* June 1962, pp. 261–279.

23. Korsakov, author of a biographical sketch of Baroness Rahden, stresses the compatibility and friendship between her and the Grand Duchess Elena Pavlovna, and quotes K. P. Pobedonostsev, who knew them both well, how they established in the Mikhailov palace a center "for the cultured society of St. Petersburg" where matters of state, science, scholarship, and art were discussed. There during the late 1850s the two women, who favored reform, met with the principal movers of serf emancipation. Baroness Rahden also showed concern for the wounded during the Crimean War, and did Red Cross work during the war of 1877–1878. She maintained her connections with Western European personalities, including the German emperor and Bismarck. Despite her unwavering loyalty to Protestantism she translated into German Samarin's well-known introduction to Khomiakov's theological works, and Khomiakov's *Tserkov' odna* (The Church Is One). See V. Korsakov, "Rahden, baronnessa Edita Fedorvna," *Russkii biograficheskii slovar* (St. Petersburg, 1910), XV, 369–371.

24. See A. F. Koni, Rahden (baronessa Edita Fedorovna)," in F. A. Brokhaus and I. A. Efron, eds. *Entsiklopedicheskii slovar'* (St. Petersburg, 1899),

XXVI, 68. Reminiscing about intellectual activities in St. Petersburg, presumably in the year 1841, Prince Meshchersky says that Soph'ia Nikolaevna Karamzina, daughter of the prominent historian, received guests "daily. . . in the evening," and that he did not "catch among the living Pushkin and Lermontov," but that he met there "Zhukovsky, Prince Viazemsky, Dmitriev, Pletnev, Count Bludov, Tiutchev, Sobolevsky, Khomiakov, Turgenev, Valuev, Count Vladimir Sologub, Iu. Samarin, and also intelligent persons among foreigners and diplomats. Properly speaking, the Karamzin home was the only one in St. Petersburg in whose parlor people gathered not for worldly gossip and rumors but exclusively for conversation and the exchange of thoughts." A. V. Meshchersky, "Iz moei stariny. Vospominaniia," *Russkii arkhiv,* 1901, no. 1, p. 101.

25. Prince P. A. Viazemsky spoke of Sverbeeva as presiding in her parlor over a "bureau d'esprit et de poesie"; Prince Meshchersky compared Soph'ia N. Karamzina with the celebrated Récamier – but Karamzina's salon did not have the love, intrigues, notoriety, and scandal of Récamier's. "P. Ia. Chaadaev i E. A. Sverbeeva (Iz neizdannykh bumag Chaadaeva)," *Vestnik Evropy,* 1918, January–April, pp. 233–234; Meshchersky, "Vospominaniia," p. 102.

26. Golitsyn, "Chaadaev i Sverbeeva," pp. 233–236.

27. Samarin, *Sochineniia,* XII, 24.

28. P. P. Gromov and N. M. Gaidenkov, eds., *Karolina Pavlova. Polnoe sobranie stikhotvorenii* (Moscow-Leningrad, 1964), p. 2.

29. See "Iz pisem k N. F. Pavlovu ego priiatelei," *Russkii arkhiv,* 1894, no. 2, p. 214.

30. P. P. Gromov says in his introduction to Pavlova's poems: "In the course of the forties a very wide circle of people representing different literary-social orientations gathered at the Pavlovs' for their literary evenings. Here came Viazemsky, Baratynksy, A. I. and I. S. Turgenev, Gogol', Herzen, Ogarev, Granovsky, Pogodin, the Aksakovs, the Kireevskys, Khomiakov, Shevyrev, Fet, Ap. Grigor'ev, Polonsky, and others." See Pavlova, *Stikhotvoreniia,* p. 8. After Pavlov introduced Panaev to his wife, the memoirist recorded his impression of her in the following words: "In front of me stood a tall, slender lady with a *stern and majestic* air, like lady Loch-Leven of Sir Walter Scott. In her pose and in her gaze there was something calculated, rhetorical. She stood between two marble columns, and with a sense of her merit slightly nodded her head in response to my bow, then stretched her hand to me with the grandeur of a theater queen. . . . It seemed to me that at that moment I should fall on my knees." See I. I. Panaev, *Literaturnye vospominaniia* (Leningrad, 1950), p. 177; also quoted by Gromov in Pavlova, *Stikhotvoreniia,* p. 9. For reminiscences of her early life, see "Moi vospominaniia," *Russkii arkhiv,* 1875, no. 10, pp. 222–240.

31. Pavlova, *Stikhotvoreniia,* pp. 34–35.

32. For two unsuccessful Slavophil efforts (1848–1855) to arrive at a generally agreed "written program," see S. S. Dmitriev, "Slavianofily i slavianofil'stvo (Iz istorii russkoi obshchestvennoi mysli serediny XIX veka)," *Istorik Marksist,* 1941, book 1, p. 88.

33. See Martin Malia, *Alexander Herzen and the Birth of Russian Socialism, 1812–1855* (Cambridge, Mass., 1961), p. 300; Nol'de, *Samarin,* p. 30. The Herzen-Samarin relationship has not escaped the attention of scholars, but what is usually noticed are their mid-1840s contacts. See, for instance, N. S. Derzhavin, "Gertzen i slavianofily," *Istorik Marksist,* book 1, 1939, pp. 132–133, 135–136, 138. Herzen thought then that Samarin could "still be saved" (p. 135). Professor Riasanovsky also calls attention to their meeting in London in 1864, and their correspondence of that year. This exchange is more significant than the earlier because they were more mature and more experienced, and knew Russia and the West much better than they had twenty years earlier. Furthermore, Herzen's empiricist Westernism and Samarin's Orthodox Slavophilism were by then firmly established. See N. V. Riasanovsky, *Russia and the West in the Teaching of the Slavophils: A Study of Romantic Ideology* (Cambridge, Mass., 1952), pp. 159–162. See also "Perepiska Ir. F. Samarina s A. I. Gertsenom v 1864g," *Rus',* 1883, no. 1, pp. 30–42; no. 2, pp. 23–30. Samarin engaged in some proselytizing of his own. In a letter to Aksakov early in 1844 he says that he would visit Granovsky, and added: "It would be well if you also come to Granovsky's. We will both attack him by surprise. This man is obviously wavering." See Ch. Vetrinsky, "T. N. Granovsky, *Zapadniki i slavianofily v 1844–45 gg.,*" *Russkaia mysl',* July 1896, p. 130; Samarin, *Sochineniia,* XII, 47. Sergei Solov'ev, as usual in the case of the Slavophils, sounded a dissenting and sour note in his evaluation of Samarin, saying that Samarin "became at the beginning a Slavophil because of lack of a scholarly education." Quoted by P. B. Struve, "S. M. Solov'ev," *Russkaia mysl',* 1915, book 10, p. 21.

34. Herzen, *Sochineniia,* II, 311.

35. Ibid., pp. 314–315.

36. Ibid., p. 327.

37. Ibid., p. 356.

38. Ibid., p. 391.

39. For more details on the Kireevsky-Granovsky relationship, see Christoff, *Kireevskij,* pp. 104–108.

40. See V. I. Buganov, ed., *Razriadnaia kniga 1559–1605 gg.* (Moscow, 1974).

41. Its full title is *Sbornik istoricheskikh i statisticheskikh svedenii o Rossii i narodakh ee edinorodnykh i edinoplemennykh,* (Moscow, 1845), vol. I (hereafter cited as Valuev, *Sbornik*).

42. See for instance the table of contents of Valuev's *sbornik*.

43. For a significant change in the list of contributors to the *Otechestven-nye zapiski* before and after 1839, when Belinsky became its guiding spirit, see A. G. Dement'ev et al., eds., *Russkaia periodicheskaia pechat' (1702–1894)* (Moscow, 1959), pp. 273–286.

44. S. S. Dmitriev, an authority on Slavophilism, states that Valuev's pro-Slav views expressed in his *Sbornik* "influenced the Russian Slavist-his-torians—A. F. Gil'ferding, V. I. Lamansky, N. A. Popov, [and] A. A. Maikov." See *Bol'shaia sovetskaia entsiklopediia* (Moscow, 1971), 3d ed., IV, 261.

45. The original monograph (Dorpat, 1841) has the title *Verfassung und Rechtszustand der dalmatinischen Küstenstädte und Inseln im Mittel Alter. Aus ihren municipal-statuten entwickelt. Ein Beitrag zur Kenntniss slavischer Rechte* (The Political Structure and Law of the Offshore Islands and Towns of Dalmatia in the Middle Ages. A Contribution to the Knowledge of Slavic Law).

46. Valuev, *Sbornik,* pp. 1, 4.

47. Ibid., pp. 5–7.

48. For some biographical information on Valuev, [also Voluev] see "Biografiia D. A. Volueva," *Russkii arkhiv,* 1899, no. 9, pp. 130–139. This is believed to have been written in 1846 By V. A. Panov.

49. Valuev, *Sbornik,* pp. 3, 5.

50. Ibid., pp. 9, 13.

51. Ibid., p. 17.

52. Although the name of V. A. Panov, who died at the age of thirty in 1849, does not appear on the title pages of the 1846 and 1847 symposiums, he is known to have been their "publisher" (*izdatel'*). He also collaborated with Dmitry Valuev, a relative, on the 1845 symposium. Like the rest of the Slavophils, Panov came from the gentry. The son of a wealthy Simbirsk land-owner, he was educated at home and graduated in philology from Moscow University. He was a frequent guest at the salons of Elagina, the Aksakovs (to whom he was related), the Samarins, Khomiakovs, and other Moscow salons. In 1840 he met Gogol', ten years older, at the Aksakovs', and was possibly infected by Konstantin's adulation for Gogol's writings. From this developed an uncommon relationship. In the words of one of Gogol's biog-raphers, Panov, "upon learning that Gogol was soon to set out for Italy . . . spontaneously offered to accompany him and share the cost of the trip. . . . Vasily Panov's proposal could not have been better timed. The young man, pale, slender, and sickly looking, with . . . a naive expression behind his spec-tacles, seemed a likely candidate. Gogol' accepted," and on at least one oc-casion later referred to Panov as a 'man near to my heart.' Henri Troyat, *Divided Soul: The Life of Gogol,* trans. from the French by Nancy Amphoux (New York, 1973), pp. 221–222; see also, *Russkaia starina,* 1889, no. 1, p. 153. Acting as Gogol's secretary as well as companion for about two years, Panov

made copies of *The Inspector General, Dead Souls,* and *The Wedding.* In 1842, Panov then twenty-two, spent four months in Dalmatia, Herzegovina, and Montenegro, and wrote a number of short works on the history of Montenegro, Croatia, and Bulgaria. In the words of Professor V. I. Grigorovich, an authority on the Slavs, who was himself in the Balkans in the middle forties, "Panov together with D. A. Valuev, 'is worthy of being considered among the first pioneers of Slavic studies.'" See B. Modzalevsky, "Panov, Vasilii Alekseevich," *Russkii biograficheskii slovar'* (St. Petersburg, 1905), XII, 261–263.

53. This view contrasts sharply with one he held at the time of the emancipation reform, when he complained to Ivan Aksakov, "A whole generation has been nurtured and inspired by Belinsky while Khomiakov is known and appreciated by 5–6 persons." Quoted in N. G. Sladkevich, "K voprosu o polemike N. G. Chernyshevskogo so slavianofil'skoi publitsistikoi," *Voprosy istorii,* 1948, no. 6, p. 78.

54. Samarin, *Sochineniia,* XII, 441–442. The *Moskvitianin* had apparently rejected Samarin's review a year earlier. In what seems a clear reference to this rejection, Khomiakov wrote Samarin, June 23, 1845, "I am sorry that our friends did not decide to publish your essay on *Tarantas,*" *Russkii arkhiv,* 1879, no. 11, p. 319. Sollogub's story (*povest'*) *Tarantas* appeared in 1845. Written in the form of a travelogue, "it included broad pictures of life in Moscow and St. Petersburg, and in provincial and small towns, of gentry estates and peasant settlements." It contained a variety of portraits of members of "high society, gentry merchants and civil servants" and "sharply mocked the views of the Slavophils." N. I. Iakushin, "Sollogub, Vladimir Aleksandrovich," Russkie pisateli," *Biobibliograficheskii slovar'* (Moscow, 1971), p. 600.

55. See V. I. Kuleshov, ed., *V. G. Belinsky. Sobranie sochinenii v trekh tomakh,* 3 vols. (Moscow, 1948), 679 (hereafter cited as Belinsky, *Sochineniia*), III, 679.

56. M. Ia. Poliakov, ed., *V. G. II, Belinsky. Izbrannye pis'ma v dvukh tomakh* (Moscow, 1955), II, 280 (hereafter cited as Belinsky, *Izbrannye pis'ma*). See also V. S. Nechaeva, *V. G. Belinsky. Zhizn' i tvorchestvo 1842-1848* (Leningrad, 1967), p. 281 (hereafter cited as Nechaeva, *Belinsky*).

57. Samarin, *Sochineniia,* XII, 442–443.

58. Listed in the table of contents in Khomiakov's *Works,* 1911 ed., under the title "Mnenie Russkikh ob inostrantsakh" are the following topics: "Eclecticism of imitation.—Analysis and synthesis.—Hegel's system of history.—Karamzin.—Gogol'.—Suvorov's major.—Doctrine of women and marriage.—Scattered landholding [*cherezpolosnost'*].—Godunov and Mikhail Fedorovich.—The struggle of life with education.—Hope of rebirth." See Khomiakov, *Sochineniia,* I, vii.

59. Ibid., pp. 35–36.

60. Ibid., pp. 37, 37n.

61. Ibid., pp. 43, 55, 61.

62. Ibid., pp. 48–50, 64–65.

63. Ibid., p. 62.

64. While in Rome, Chizhov became a friend of Gogol', and also of the Russian painter Aleksander Andreevich Ivanov, who was devoting himself "to a single huge painting, *Christ Appearing to the People.* A philosophical summa, a pictorial synthesis, this enormous labor was devouring him alive. . . . He considered himself invested by a holy mission." In September 1842 Chizhov, together with Gogol' and the pro-Slavophil poet N. M. Iazykov (1803–1846), Khomiakov's brother-in-law, and well known for his anti-Westerner poem "K nenashim" (To Our Adversaries, 1844), took up residence in a house on the strada Felice, 126; Gogol's apartment was on the third floor, Iazykov's on the second, Chizhov's on the fourth. Troyat, *Gogol',* pp. 188, 299; also K. K. Bukhmeier, ed. *N. M. Iazykov. Polnoe sobranie stik-hotvorenii* (Moscow-Leningrad, 1964), pp. 394–395. This led to, among other things, a valuable correspondence between Chizhov and Ivanov, for whom he solicited in the spring of 1846 among the Moscow Slavophils a fund of 6,000 rubles to ensure Ivanov's support in Rome for two years. See "Nikolai Vasil'evich Gogol." Pis'ma k nemu A. O. Smirnovoi, rozhd. Ros-set. 1844–1841gg., *Russkaia starina,* 1890, no. 7, p. 211.

65. See Vadim Modzalevsky, "Chizhov, Fedor Vasil'evich," *Russkii biograficheskii slovar'* (St. Petersburg, 1905), XXII, 380.

66. I. S. Aksakov, "Fedor Vasil'evich Chizhov (iz rechi I. S. Aksakova, proiznesennoi 18 dekabria 1877g.)," *Russkii arkhiv,* 1878, no. 1, p. 131.

67. Modzalevsky, "Chizhov," pp. 876–877; *Literaturnoe nasledstvo* (Moscow, 1952), no. 58, p. 776.

68. *Russkaia starina,* 1881, no. 1, p. 191.

69. The questions submitted to Chizhov and his written answers were published under the title "Vospominaniia F. V. Chizhova," with introductory remarks by Professor V. I. Lamansky, in *Istoricheskii vestnik,* 1883, no. 2, pp. 241–262. (Hereafter cited as Chizhov, "Vospominania").

70. Aksakov, "Chizhov," p. 133.

71. Much information about Chizhov's entrepreneurial activities has recently appeared in print, although as far as I know no full-length biography has yet come out, nor has his extensive diary been published, except for selected items. For his activities and views during this period, see N. I. Tsimbaev, *I. A. Aksakov v obshchestvennoi zhizni poreformennoi Rossii* (Moscow, 1978), in which Chizhov's diary is quoted several times: A. J. Rieber, "The Moscow Entrepreneurial Group: The Emergence of a New Form in Autocratic Politics," *Jahrbücher für Geschichte Osteuropas,* 1977, Band 25, Heft 1, pp. 1–20; Heft 2, pp. 174–199; "The Formation of La Grande Societe des Chemins de Fer Russes," 1973, band 21, heft 1, pp. 375–391; Th. C.

Owen, "The Moscow Merchants and the Public Press, 1858–1868,"
Jahrbücher, für Geschichte Osteuropas, 1975, band 23, heft 1, pp. 26–38.
These works, particularly the first, include much archival, hitherto unpublished material. See also V. Ia. Laverychev, "Russkie kapitalisty i periodicheskaia pechat' vtoroi poloviny XIX v.," *Istoriia SSSR,* 1972, no. 1, pp.
26–47.

72. Chizhov, "Vospominaniia," p. 243. For his harassment by the Austrian
officialdom, see his letter to A. V. Nikitenko, *Russkaia starina,* 1904, no. 9,
p. 683.

73. Ibid., p. 244.

74. Cf. Aksakov, "Chizhov," pp. 132–133; Modzalevsky, "Chizhov," p. 378.

75. Chizhov left his diary to the Rumiantsev Museum in Moscow with the
stipulation that it should not be made public until forty years after his death
(1917). The diary seems to be rich in information about the middle decades
of the nineteenth century. For some published items on Gogol', see
Literaturnoe nasledstvo, no. 58, pp. 776–785.

76. See "Iz pisem F. V. Chizhova k khudozhnikku A. A. Ivanovu." *Russkii
arkhiv,* 1884, no. 2, pp. 391–422.

77. Ibid., pp. 399, 401.

78. Ibid., 402–403.

79. Ibid., p. 404.

6

Middle 1840s: In Government Service

When in the summer of 1844 Samarin entered government service at the age of twenty-four, he in effect deprived himself of the possibility of an academic career. This decision, made under paternal pressure, did not preclude scholarly research, however; nor did it discourage him from high-quality publicistic work, which, as we have noted, Belinsky quickly recognized in Samarin's review of *Tarantas*. On these matters comparison with Konstantin Aksakov is suggested at once. In the literature about the Slavophils Aksakov is customarily considered their historian, yet in terms of linguistic qualifications, thoroughness of research, clarity of logical exposition, and the number of publications, Samarin was superior to Aksakov.

Samarin was not happy about having to give up his preferred career and his disappointment and distaste for government service was shared by the other Slavophils, particularly by Konstantin Aksakov. The Slavophils disliked bureaucracies in general, in their minds products of Western formalism and legalism, and they also wanted to make a point of their opposition to the tsarist government by having nothing to do with the St. Petersburg bureaucracy. Their attitude was not one of revolutionary conviction, but rather one of intellectual and philosophical opposition. Samarin's joining the government was in a way joining an unfriendly camp.

To be sure, they were at times exceedingly angry with the government. The closing of Kireevsky's *Evropeets* in 1832, the government's unwillingness to permit a Slavophil journal during the reign of Nicholas I, and the censorship over the Slavophil symposiums were followed by the incarceration of Ivan Aksakov and Iurii Samarin at the end of the forties, by government harassment of Konstantin Aksakov and his father over "Russian" beards and dress, and the banning of all Slavophil publications after the 1852 symposium and the filing of dossiers in the Third Section.[1] The Slavophils, with good reason, were resentful and uneasy, but they were still patriotic Russians who had faith in the principle of a nobler autocracy. It can be said, too, that they found it easy to look askance at government service since they were all affluent and did not need additional income.[2]

While in the summer of 1844 Samarin could have had only a partial picture of the Slavophil attitude toward government service, as compared with that outlined above, he did not want to be part of the government. On May 8, 1846, Smirnova wrote to Gogol' that Samarin's "situation is most difficult. He serves in the government on his father's wishes, and with the horrible conviction that he will accomplish nothing for Russia." A week later she again informed Gogol' that Samarin "finds himself in a most difficult struggle with his father, who ties up every free movement of his. From this come the attacks of his friends for his falling away" from the presumed true Slavophil course.[3]

The strain within the Samarin family over Iurii's future and career was reflected in the relationship between Konstantin Aksakov and Iurii Samarin. The friendship of the two young men, as already noted, was rapidly evolving in the two years before Samarin departed for St. Petersburg, and not in the direction that could have pleased Konstantin, accustomed to consider himself the senior partner in an unequal relationship. On this matter A. O. Smirnova's correspondence with the Aksakovs, edited by N. M. Pavlov and published in 1896, sheds much light. Although Gogol', a close friend of both Smirnova and the Aksakovs, was the central figure in the correspondence, the Samarin-Konstantin Aksakov relationship is also illuminated. The correspondence contains among other things, part of Konstantin's "farewell" letter to Samarin, undated by Pavlov, but most likely of the second half of 1844.

High-minded, inflexible Konstantin would not budge from the "straight road," and would shun everything "that we consider rotten and contaminated." The sermonizing letter further tells Samarin that "life will take its own" and that life must be "a moral deed and a moral road."[4] Certain about himself but not about Samarin, he says, "I am convinced that if we met we would not get along at all. I would appear to you a ridiculous, and even an inane madcap, while you [will appear to me] cold, and even perhaps an egotist. You will probably insist on your own . . . and I will take my road." Konstantin stated the case curtly in a four-line stanza, which also probably belongs to the same time:

> Neither the tug of the soul,
> Nor the voice of the heart;
> But the bond of conviction
> Kept us from moving apart.[5] (United us.)

Here he professed to be motivated in his relationship with Samarin by that devotion to principle and ideal, well known throughout the ages, that brooks no interference from friendship or consideration for other human beings.

Samarin's published correspondence contains a letter to Konstantin Aksakov (dated 1844 and probably, from the sequence of letters in which it appears, written in the second half of that year) that may be Iurii's reply to the above letter of Konstantin's, and his verse. Certainly the letter indicates that the strains and stresses that had affected the Samarin-Aksakov friendship by the end of 1843 were serious enough to have interrupted the former easy contact, because Iurii begins his letter by telling Konstantin that he has recently seen Pogodin, and that "I learned much about you from him."[6] He then thanks Konstantin for his "candor and rectitude," and says that Konstantin's words have dispelled many "rumors, slanders, and what not else." He was ready to stretch his hand to Konstantin and embrace him as before, but there was no way of going back to their earlier and unequal relationship: "I love you now as before, although I do not agree with you about many things and shall argue [with you] till my last gasp. What revolts me most are not your opinions but your uncommon exclusiveness and exigency." Paraphrasing Konstantin's letter, Iurii says, you seem to say, "I am impetuous, you also can be impetuous"; further on he says "recast yourself in my image and likeness." Although Iurii admitted that his view of Konstantin's position was "exaggerated and in the form of a caricature," he left no doubt that he would not compromise with his decisions and his self-respect.

What divides us now, Iurii says, is nothing "substantial," otherwise "I would bow to necessity and part with you." At the root of the problem, he tells him frankly, is "your intolerance and a certain lack of a sense for that reality in which we live. This almost always compels you to be unfair in your judgments of other people, including me." It is, he says, difficult for him to explain his position to Konstantin, and admonishes him, "do not hurry with the break with me." Whatever has come between them, "we shall inevitably come together when you recognize the possibility that *another person* can have the same orientation, and the same convictions as you." Iurii ended the letter with the words, "as for me, I shall never part with you."[7]

Somehow (any subsequent exchange is apparently lost), their friendship weathered the storm, helped along by the Aksakov family, who were fond of Samarin and appreciated his abilities. Ivan Aksakov, who was himself in government service, was particularly sympathetic. Writing from Astrakhan on February 8, 1844, he asked, "I would like to know if Kostia has calmed down, and if his relationship with Samarin has been thoroughly clarified?"[8] This was, of course, before Samarin's defense of his dissertation, and before his departure for St. Petersburg. Less than a week later Ivan inquired about the date for Samarin's public defense, and on June 24, overjoyed, wrote home, "I am very, very glad about Samarin's success, but then I expected it." Such "brilliant success," he exulted, "remains as eternally bright memories."[9]

After sending hearty congratulations to Samarin, Ivan—with his older brother in mind and for his sake—praised the benefits derived from "visiting worldly society." There, he says, one "acquires dexterity, presence of mind, poise," qualities that when combined with "true worth and talent" assure "brilliant victory." Thus twenty-one-year-old Ivan, the voice of experience, was advising his older brother, and concluded, "I hope that before Samarin departs for St. Petersburg he will return to Moscow, and will part with it, and Kostia, as one should,"[10] When the news reached him from home that Konstantin had not gone to Moscow from the family estate at Abramtsevo to see Samarin off, he wrote on July 22, 1844, "You write that Kostia did not go to Moscow for a farewell for Samarin . . . It's a pity . . . indeed a pity." Still not yielding to his older brother's prejudices, Ivan concluded that Samarin would make an "excellent diplomat" if he decided to join the foreign service: "I would have done the same thing if I were in his place, i.e., I would have chosen the same career."[11]

Samarin was not prepared to find contentment in St. Petersburg, and in his first letter to Konstantin from the capital (dated September 10, 1844) he wrote that although he was in his second month there, he could "not tell him anything" about it; he had seen little of "high society," and had found it the same everywhere, "dead and boring." The "civil servant circles" did not brighten his early days in the capital any more than gentry society. He claimed that he "almost" did not know this well-publicized segment of the tsarist bureaucracy, but that the thinking people in it held the "deeply rooted conviction" that the government can "do nothing," that it is "powerless," and that no tsarist edicts, "institutions," or any measures could change anything"[12] Iurii saw in the capital "a certain calm, an apathetic despair. This is a spiritual death in its most frightful aspect. In this circle everything is extinguished: zeal for the common task, readiness for self-sacrifice, indignation, everything, absolutely everything. . . . This ugly mute force is the most horrible enemy that one can encounter."

There is no reason to suspect Samarin of ulterior aims, but this was a letter to Konstantin, and he knew what to say. In St. Petersburg, he wrote, "you will never see the common people, except workers. Since I came here I have not heard a Russian song, not the voice of a muzhik. Later I learned that it is forbidden to sing here."[13] He mentioned a number of persons whom he was seeing. The list included N. I. Nadezhdin, his former tutor in Moscow and now a confirmed *chinovnik* (civil servant). In the home of the Westerner N. I. Ketcher, a friend of Herzen, and translator of Shakespeare, he saw Belinsky and M. S. Shchepkin, the renowned Moscow actor, then playing in Gogol's *Revizor* (The Inspector General) on the St. Petersburg stage, and Smirnova.

Peter Samarin, Iurii's younger brother, who edited this segment of Iurii's letters, tells us that a month earlier (on August 10, 1844) Smirnova, "known for her beauty and her mind, and for her friendship with Zhukovsky, Pushkin, and Gogol' . . . returned from abroad and settled in St. Petersburg." His brother's acquaintance "beginning at this time," soon developed into a lifelong friendship. Iurii mentions Smirnova in his first letter to Konstantin: "The most remarkable person in Petersburg, in my opinion, is Aleksandra Osipovna Smirnova. I see her often and we discuss Gogol'."[14] Smirnova (nine years older than Iurii) played the dubious and uneasy role of the middle person in the unequal relationship between Samarin and Gogol' who was a year older than she and by 1844 well established as one of Russia's foremost writers.

It seems certain that Samarin was first in Gogol's presence, and probably met him, at the Aksakovs' toward the end of 1839, for on December 25 Vera Aksakova wrote to her brothers Grigorii and Ivan that Gogol' was visiting them. "On Saturday when Gogol' read [from *Dead Souls*], Samarin was here as Konstantin's guest. He also listened and after the reading drew a portrait of Gogol' which is sufficiently lifelike." This portrait does not seem to have survived, but we do have an entry in Samarin's diary made soon after his encounter with Gogol'. His enthusiasm matched that of Konstantin:

Yes, we can consider ourselves happy that we have been born contemporaries of Gogol'. Such people are born not once in many years but once in ages. His is one of those original artistic natures in which there is nothing studied, nothing borrowed, nothing calculated for effect. The world of his inner contemplation is infinitely diverse. . . . Fortunate is the person who succeeds in grasping Gogol', and who can justify his exaltation for himself and for others. . . . I would not waste words with those who would censure Gogol' or would not unconditionally stand in reverence before him. I would turn away from them, and these people would lose all moral authority over me, and all right to have any influence on me.[15]

In the five years that separated Samarin's first meeting with Gogol' and his reintroduction to him through Smirnova, Samarin had read and reread Gogol', reflected on his art and discussed it with others. He had, of course, read Konstantin Aksakov's controversial review of *Dead Souls,* Dmitrii Samarin dates a six-page letter that Iurii wrote to Konstantin about *Dead Souls* to late 1842 or early 1843, after reading Konstantin's review, and reading *Dead Souls* for the second time. In the letter, Iurii admits that he also considered a review and even began writing one, but having seen Aksakov's, he says, "I was completely satisfied and postponed this matter."

Konstantin "had said about *Dead Souls* everything that could and should be said, presenting the nature of Gogol's contemplation, the act of creation, and setting aside the question of content." He dismissed the matter of content as premature, saying that "we have before us only the beginning," obviously referring to the expected sequel to *Dead Souls.*

While Samarin expressed satisfaction with Konstantin's review, and associated himself with it, he was less than sanguine in his remarks about Shevyrev's two reviews of *Dead Souls.* Samarin was probably unaware that

Shevyrev was Gogol's preferred critic. But for young Iurii, Shevyrev, while "refuting several vulgar accusations cleverly and wisely," achieved nothing more. Shevyrev's reviews "not only do not clarify that impression which *Dead Souls* could not produce on any unprejudiced and nonphilosophizing reader, but on the contrary [Shevyrev] muddies Gogol', dims the meaning of his great creation, and spoils the pleasure."[16] Iurii did not merely disagree with Shevyrev; he saw no merit at all in Shevyrev's reviews of *Dead Souls,* and he devoted much of the remainder of the letter to further disparagement of his former professor.

When Iurii finished with Shevyrev, he turned to the views on *Dead Souls* held by an unnamed group which he probably met in the Moscow salons (their views, he says, were "not stated in print," and therefore did not elicit a published reply. These people deprived themselves of the "enjoyment of an artistic work,"[17] because "How is it possible to be joyful and delighted when the artist presents on the stage a whole series of pitiful, ridiculous, and repulsive phenomena, taken from that reality in which we live, which is our reality, our native land! One should weep and be sorrowful and not laugh." He acknowledged that the unnamed group "expressed sincere, respectful love of what is their own, what is native," but he found their love "too narrow, hence easily turning into despair." These were "people of little faith." He accused the group of being too selective about their love of Russia: they "loved [something] in her, not her."

Those whom he considered as "incapable of understanding" Gogol' and *Dead Souls,* he continued rather disingenuously, suffered not from any sort of natural inability but as a "consequence of the false conviction of the understanding [*rassudok*]." Clearly, Russia in the state of serfdom did not present a dismal picture for the vast majority of its population because of their "false convictions of understanding."[18] He was on firmer ground when he maintained that it was not truthful to say about Russia that "there is nothing exalted, ideal, actual, but only filthy contingency, only the dark side." Not even centuries of iniquitous serfdom could push a vast and awakening nation into total and unredeemable depravity: "Shadow alone does not constitute the picture."[19]

The third part of Iurii's letter to Konstantin raises the question whether *Dead Souls* is a satire, as presumably at least some in "the group" claimed, or a "poem," which was Samarin's definition (and also Gogol's, the word *poema* appears in capital letters on the cover of the first edition as described by Gogol' himself). A satire, Samarin argued, is born when "poetry becomes an expose of the present," and this occurs if the poet is "incapable of perceiving with love the objects that surround him and elevating them to the pearl of creation (speaking in the words of Gogol')." In Gogol', as in Horace, Iurii found the "eternal antithesis ruling out harmony," for the simple reason that "in life itself there is no harmony." Thus Horace saw through the darkness of his own time and place the "dawn of renewal beginning in the north, in the forests of Germany."[20]

Seeing in Gogol's *Dead Souls* not a mere negation of the present in Russia, or a satire, but the promise of a life-encompassing poem, Iurii concluded: "There is no poet who is so far from satire as Gogol', for in every other poet, for example in Zhukovsky, there is much more of the satirical principle than in Gogol'." Gogol' had thus far, Iurii admitted, revealed the "dark side" of Russian life, but he took solace from "those beautiful lyrical passages in which the poet himself reveals and pours light on its other side for us.[21]

Efimova infers—I believe correctly—that Samarin's initial contacts with Aleksandra Smirnova in St. Petersburg, soon after he arrived there in the summer of 1844, were prompted by his desire to get to know Gogol'. He suggested as much in his first letter to Konstantin from the capital. Gogol' was still in Rome, but he and Smirnova were in correspondence, so when Samarin, in whom Smirnova took a warm, patronizing interest, expressed a desire to know Gogol', she made it her responsibility to bring them together through correspondence. Gogol', who was always most concerned with his own problems and was often less than warm and considerate in his relations with his Slavophil friends, was not much inclined to interest himself in someone even as bright and promising as this young admirer. Smirnova was thus uncomfortably in the middle; but this did not daunt her.

Captivated and impressed by Iurii's character and mind, Smirnova saw to it that he initiated his correspondence with Gogol'. According to Efimova, Samarin, on Smirnova's advice, sent Gogol' a copy of his just-completed dissertation, along with a "short" note; this was in 1844, presumably in the latter part of the year.[22] Gogol', showing his usual crankiness, complained to Smirnova; December 24, 1844 from Frankfurt, "I cannot get the most essential things done, and now you entangle me with Samarin. Without you he certainly would not have written me a letter." Just when Gogol' acknowledged the receipt of the dissertation, and at what length, is not exactly clear. On September 19, 1845, Smirnova wrote to him: "Samarin is getting ready to write you a long letter. Do not shrink from him. He is superbly wise and loves you for your living soul and for [your] *Dead Souls*." And again she advised him, October 30, "If Samarin writes to you from Petersburg, answer him, and do not avoid him.[23]

The first letter to Gogol' that appears in Samarin's collected works is dated by his brother Dimitry to March 1846. It seems clearly to have been written in reply to a letter from Gogol', for the opening sentence of this long (five and a half page) letter says, "It is good that you wrote to me first, for it seems, I could not decide to begin a correspondence with you." He goes on to say, "I have long wished from my heart to become friends with you, even before I became acquainted with A. Os. [Aleksandra Osipovna]."[24]

This first letter suggests that Samarin may have sought Gogol's friendship and correspondence not so much for literary or aesthetic reasons — although his admiration for Gogol's work was certainly genuine — as for spiritual ones, in hopes of satisfying certain moral and religious longings, which, so far, had probably not found response in Khomiakov or Ivan Kireevsky. Samarin still, in 1846, had certain qualms about Khomiakov as a religious thinker, and it was not long before that he had been torn between Hegelianism and Orthodoxy and greatly resented what he considered to be Kireevsky's maneuvering to separate him from Konstantin Aksakov. By the time Khomiakov's and Kireevsky's contributions to Slavophil Orthodoxy and philosophy became manifest in writing in the next decade, Samarin had acquired a sense of respect for the elder Slavophils (in 1867 he considered Khomiakov worthy of being a "teacher of the Church.")[25] By that time, too, the Slavophils, including Samarin, had been severely shaken in their respect for Gogol', after he published (in 1847) his ill-fated *Selected Passages from Correspondence with Friends* (Vybrannye mesta iz perepiski s druz'iami).

In 1846, however, Gogol' was still preeminently a moral guide in Samarin's eyes, and Samarin's letter to him written from St. Petersburg in March of that year is, in a rather literal sense, a young man's confession of faith, and a young man's search for moral and spiritual strength.[26] It was his "inner voice," Samarin says, that led him to seek out Gogol's friendship, he was convinced that Gogol' could do him "much good." He admitted to a sense of pity for himself: people looked on him with "cool condolence as upon a sick person condemned to death." He had spent several years "under the yoke of general mistrustfulness" and had felt hostility toward several persons, including Gogol'. But this burdensome period was now over. He joyfully welcomed Gogol's "first approving greetings," and finally, he says, "I heard from you too that I am saved, that you do not fear for me." Thus Samarin found it possible to say to Gogol' everything that he would "say to his own brother in the spiritual sense."[27] Samarin diagnosed his malady as one of the "most common of our time," for which no cure existed. It was

> [the] one-sided development of the intellect extinguishing sentiment and undermining the will, the wholeness of moral existence, the harmony of the spiritual powers and abilities; [all] violated in me by the exclusive preponderance of thought developing rapidly and in isolation, and the lulling of my other abilities. I think, say, and defend one thing in words, but in deed I submit to something else. I have convictions, but I have neither faith nor love.[28]

But this did not seem to disturb Samarin, for he says, "I am conscious of this and do not suffer from it." He admitted, however, that "half my soul has withered and grown numb." Furthermore, he knew how all this had come about. In childhood and youth in his home he knew "only the religious-moral measure," the slightest and most involuntary deviation from which, he said, "filled me with contrition." "I emerged from this primitive condition not by myself" but as a result of external influence, when by chance, he says, he picked up some works of unnamed contemporary French authors that "powerfully shook me up." He saw in them "the proud revolt of the personal spirit against the cosmic order." This in the "ideal image of contemporary poetry" presented him with a strong temptation that soon "captured him. The end result of this experience was to push him into "loneliness and spiritual anarchy." His attitude soon changed and his former "candor" disappeared, while he deliberately repressed in himself "all the immediate movements of the spirit," subjecting everything "to rigorous analysis." In all this, he concludes, "I succeeded beyond [all] expectations."

While this internal turmoil was going on, Samarin told Gogol', "I was able to throw off . . . all submission to religious principles and family customs." Imperceptibly but surely, everything became the "object of inner dispute," and the "criminal desire for doubt and inner rupture became . . . the desired end." At this juncture he met "our common friends" — meaning the founders of Slavophilism — which led to "endless disputes." He refrained from involving Gogol' in detailed accounts, concluding, "I will only tell you in general, that they helped me run faster through the whole cycle of philosophical negation. This, in a few words, is the history of my thought."[29]

Halfway through his letter to Gogol' Samarin found himself in the same general area where he had been all his young life, before he chanced upon the French works. "Christianity," he wrote "encompasses in itself not only a teaching, but . . . creativity and the principle of life. We have become accustomed to separate these two aspects, but they are inseparable." Here he seems to include artistic and literary creativity. At this point the letter becomes a combination of a confession and an exposition on the essence of Christianity. He was convinced, now in 1846 (as he had not been a few years earlier), that Christianity and logic did not mix. "He who wishes to understand it logically, as we understand every other doctrine will never understand it." The very notion of logic here was false, for "only one who lives it can understand that which is living." Confessing once more, he says, approaching Christianity "with the demands of logical comprehension," I had no choice but "to end up where the most recent philosophy ended up, that is, at the total negation not only of Christianity but, in general, of all primordial existence, which is independent of knowledge." This was inadmissible to young Samarin since, "destroying life, thought proves itself worthless in creating anything living from itself." Thus the principle of creativity asserts itself in its right as an autonomous [*samobytnoe*] principle independent of thinking."

With simple candor, Samarin admitted the obvious, that he had arrived at the "acknowledgement of the living truth . . . as a result of philosophy [*nauka*]."[30] He had arrived there, and only then had realized the "full cost

of what I had lost." In the process he had also lost sight of the fact "that conviction and faith, that the concept of love and the reality of love, that word
and deed, are not one and the same." While he was still in Moscow, he was;
only occasionally aware of the "one-sidedness" of his "development." But
the move to St. Petersburg in the summer of 1844 altered that. "Here everything was alien if not outright hostile." In the capital, he was confronted with
a "silent intangible enemy" which threatened to "recreate me from head to
foot." He was rescued from this nightmare by Aleksandra Osipovna Smirnova. Cowed and incensed by his well-meaning but unfeeling father,
pestered by the self-righteous rigidity of his insensitive friend Aksakov, and
living in the cold and uncongenial capital, Samarin readily found comfort in
Smirnova's company. "She valued in me precisely what the world did not
value, and about which it laughed," he told Gogol'. He had become indifferent to the "world" of St. Petersburg out of a sense of "moral self-preservation."[31] His pro-Slavophil point of view was accepted with "curiosity,"
though he "never had any influence on anyone." Referring to the millennial
Christian problem of faith and reason, although in somewhat different language, he says, this is the "sickness of my soul." It is "so well known, so
widespread in our time," and much to his sorrow, there seemed to be no cure
for it. Even thought itself was threatening because it was out of control.
"The idea develops of itself, without any external stimulus, and runs its
course according to the laws of logical necessity."

Far from seeing the panacea for all the personal and social ills of his time
in man's mind and reasoning faculties, as many of his Westerner contemporaries claimed to see, he concluded his "unfinished" letter to Gogol' by
casting doubt on the "laws of logical necessity." In accordance with these
laws, one conviction is replaced by another, already conditioned by it, but
never will conviction by itself give birth to faith; the concept of love will not
warm the heart; knowledge will not pass into creativity. "Everything living,
creative is not acquired but falls from Heaven. I believe that it falls on
everyone, but I do not even have the strength either to beg for it or to wish
for it."[32]

In view of Samarin's long "confessional" letter to Gogol', and a shorter
one, dated St. Petersburg, July 6, 1846, which was carried abroad by one of
Iurii's brothers while in search of cure,[33] there seems little doubt that
Samarin's reasons for seeking contact with Gogol' were intensely personal.[34]
Literary, aesthetic considerations are almost unnoticeable. In this letter to
Gogol' of July 6, 1846, scattered hints, and Smirnova's occasional references to Iurii's difficulties with his father, assume the form and intensity of a
painful confession. "My external relations with family and friends," Samarin
complained, "are becoming more difficult from day to day."[35] He admitted
that his father had sacrificed much for his sake, including his "position in the
world and at court," by moving his family to Moscow to "become engaged

exclusively in my upbringing." But his father's "daily" and even "hourly" concerns for his son's education and upbringing soon assumed the inescapable tedium and constraint of a straitjacket. "My father," Iurii says coldly, "looked upon me as upon his creation. This was almost inescapable, but just the same no less harmful. . . . They punished me ceaselessly and compelled me to repent, forcing tears and repentance on me when I was not at all to blame." In this manner, "unconditional submission became a habit."

In sharp contrast to Sergei Aksakov's treatment of Konstantin, Fedor Vasil'evich Samarin showed little tolerance or understanding when his son Iurii expressed a desire for an academic career. A "fighting officer" in almost all of Russia's wars of the early nineteenth century, he vetoed Iurii's choice, decreed government service, and sent him to St. Petersburg. Iurii's request for a trip abroad was also denied, and while still in Moscow, he told Gogol', "my father blamed me for the very manner of my thought. He looks with a suspicious eye on my friends and yours, on Khomiakov, Aksakov, Pogodin, and others." He maligns them, and "clearly demands of me that I break up with them. Of course I shall never do this. . . . He got me accustomed from childhood to stifle indignation to the sense of violated fairness, to cry and beg forgiveness when I was not guilty."

As if putting up with his father's callous treatment was not enough, Iurii had also to endure Konstantin Aksakov's importuning. Toward the end of the letter he says to Gogol': "Aksakov writes letters in which he threatens to break up with me if I do not accept his manner of thought. . . . He sees in him [man] not a living whole . . . but a rigorous syllogism on two legs. . . . For him the whole human race is divided into unconditionally white, and unconditionally black. Thus lately in a letter to me he reviled Aleksandra Osipovna Smirnova because she was acquainted with people whom he calls villains. . . . How sad it is that you are not here. You alone could have a mollifying and pacifying influence on us all."[36]

The role in which Samarin cast Gogol' in the summer of 1846 was clearly not that of the great artist-writer but that of the moral, religious guide and arbiter. He did not suspect that in half a year Gogol' would publish a work that would profoundly shock his Slavophil friends, and many others, and cause them to lose faith in both Gogol' the artist-writer and the moral, religious preceptor that young Samarin imagined him to be. Gogol's biographers and now Efimova have told us much about the appearance, early in January 1847, of Gogol's disturbing and controversial *Selected Passages*. Samarin was stunned, for he, unlike the other Slavophils, saw in Gogol', as already stressed, more than the great writer and creator of *Dead Souls*.

Not everything that Samarin wrote as a reaction to Gogol's *Selected Passages* is available to me. He says, for instance, in his letter to Konstantin Aksakov from Riga (dated by Dmitry February 1847) that he wrote a "long letter" to Gogol' after reading *Selected Passages*, but did not send it.[37] In this letter Iurii concurred "almost word for word" with Konstantin's views of *Selected Passages*. He found the "pride of the hermit the most dangerous of all the kinds of pride, for it clouds the consciousness . . . of his calling. . . . All this public repentance, this testament, etc. — all this does not pour out of the heart, but is carried out in accordance with some sort of duty." Samarin was particularly dumbfounded by Gogol's lack of a need of "sympathy with the public," a reaction that doubtless pleased Konstantin, who made much of the difference between the gentry, the "public," and the *narod,* the people. Samarin now saw in Gogol' "unbearable pride," and deplored, "how alien he has become to everyone!"[38]

Gogol's images of landlord, peasant, and woman, as given in *Selected Passages,* were all askew. Even though Samarin did not join in Aksakov's blind adulation of the *muzhik* and the *narod,* he, like the other early Slavophils, accorded a central place for the *narod* in the general Slavophil scheme. Furthermore, in the end he probably did more for the emancipation of the peasant and the serf than any of the other "early" Slavophils. But at the beginning of 1847 he regretted Gogol's highly patronizing attitude toward the Russian peasant which so outraged Konstantin Aksakov. All in all, Gogol's "open Gospel" [*otverstoe Evangelie*][39] thoroughly shook young Samarin when he thought that he had earlier found in Gogol' a tower of strength and Christian virtue. Still despite Gogol's many faults and weaknesses, despite his nasty treatment of Pogodin, and his "deliberate silence about Moscow," the old capital, so dear to Konstantin's heart, Samarin urged that the Slavophils should not team up against Gogol'. This would only irritate him and estrange him from them. They should write to him individually.

Vocal and unsparing as the Slavophils were in their reactions to *Selected Passages,* this bitter episode did not spell the end of Gogol's relations with them. Samarin remained concerned for Gogol' as a man and a writer, and perhaps also as a possible recruit to the Slavophil cause. For the remainder of Gogol's life (he died on February 22, 1852), Samarin was either in the Baltic provinces (until March 1849) or in exile, mostly in Kiev, up to 1853, when he left government service to return to Moscow. If he corresponded with Gogol' during this period, Dmitry Samarin found no letters, or at least published none in volume 12 of Iurii's works. Possibly while on leave of absence from Kiev, Samarin together with Khomiakov attended Gogol's reading of the first two chapters of volume two of *Dead Souls.* A decade or more later he reminisced about this in an unpublished letter to Smirnova (October 3, 1862) from which Efimova quotes: "'I am deeply convinced that Gogol' died because he was conscious of how inferior his second volume was compared with the first. He was conscious but did not wish to admit to himself that he was beginning to paint reality in rosy colors.'"[40]

Without access to Samarin's unpublished correspondence it is not possible to follow his reasoning step by step. It seems clear from Efimova's quotations, however, that he considered neither the *"optina* [monastery] monk," nor the "St. Petersburg civil servant [*chinovnik*]" to possess the "ideal of the Christian frame of mind." But like the rest of the Slavophils, at least as late as 1859, he gave vent to his faith in the Russian *narod,* and as Efimova noted, also to his Slavophil messianism. Writing to Smirnova (March 13, 1859) he says: "'One cannot fail to recognize that in all Europe there is only one people that carries Christ in its heart, only one for whom the bond connecting earth and Heaven has not been severed, whose aspirations continually and of themselves turn heavenward while their fingers make the sign of the cross on the occasion of every event, whether sad or joyful.'"[41]

The question whether Samarin was "attempting to reconcile the irreconcilable" following "that road of religious quests which destroyed much in the genius artists, [Gogol']"[42] and whether religion, specifically Christianity, destroyed Gogol' the artist (the claim of some of the Westerners), remains unanswered. Down the centuries, Christianity has inspired some of the world's greatest art, architecture, music, and literature. For centuries it preserved and transmitted the art of literacy, without which Europe's written literature might have been impossible. Christianity and religion did not ruin such authors as Dante, Milton, Dostoevsky (in some of his writings). Why and how did it ruin Gogol'? Is it not possible that Gogol', consummate writer that he was, was also a fallible human being, and in his *Selected Passages* misinterpreted and misused Christianity and religion, among other things? is it not true that in doing so he caused deep distress and agonizing for some of his most devoted and loyal friends, including Samarin? We cannot claim here that the riddle of Gogol' has been solved, but the Slavophil answer merits at least as much attention as that of the Westerners.

The move to St. Petersburg in the summer of 1844 ushered in a difficult and trying period for Samarin. Going into government service meant giving up hopes of pursuing an academic career, and the friction caused by the elder Samarin's insistence on the course he had chosen for his son did not soon diminish, even though they were apart. Away from his Slavophil friends, who did not approve of his new career, Iurii sought companionship and understanding among a different circle of friends in St. Petersburg. Gradually, the strains in his relations with his fellow Slavophils eased, but only after he had unburdened himself to Gogol' and then, like the other Slavophils, was rudely let down by the man they so greatly admired.

Notes

1. Section 3 of chapter 4 of Tsimbaev's study of Moscow Slavophilism is devoted to an excellent factual account and interpretation of the

government's attitude toward the Slavophils and its hostile treatment of them during the reign of Nicholas I and later. See Tsimbaev, *Slavianofil'stvo,* pp. 122–136.

2. N. V. Berg, four years younger than Samarin, who after graduation from the University of Moscow discovered that "nearer to me than all others was the Slavophil circle," describes Khomiakov as "very rich," and says that he sold "part" of his property "for one million rubles." A. I. Koshelev, he says, had an "annual income of 100,000 rubles," while the "Samarins were also not poor," and he concludes that the "Elagins, Kireevskys, Panov, Sverbeevs, Pavlov (who stood with one foot in the Slavophil circle and the other in the Westerner) were not in need, and did not serve [in the government]." N. V. Berg, "Postmertnye zapiski," *Russkaia starina,* 1891, no. 2, p. 242.

3. V. I. Shenrok, ed., "Nikolai Vasil'evich Gogol." Pis'ma k nemu A. O. Smirnovoi. 1844–1851, "*Russkaia starina,* 1890, no. 7, pp. 208, 211 (hereafter cited as Shenrok, "Smirnova k Gogoliu").

4. "Iz perepiski A. O. Smirnova s Aksakovymi," *Russkii arkhiv,* 1896, no. 1, p. 142.

5. Ibid., p. 143.

6. Samarin, *Sochineniia,* XII, 48.

7. Ibid., p. 49.

8. *Ivan Sereevich Aksakov v ego pis'makh,* 4 vols. (Moscow, 1888), I, 73.

9. Ibid., p. 155.

10. Ibid., p. 156.

11. Ibid., pp. 173–174.

12. Samarin, *Sochineniia,* XII, 141.

13. Ibid., p. 142.

14. Ibid., p. 143.

15. L. Lansky, ed., "Gogol' v neizdannoi perepiske sovremennikov (1833–1853)," *Literaturnoe nasledstvo* (Moscow, 1952), LVII, 580 (hereafter cited as Gogol', "Neizdannaia perepiska").

16. Samarin, *Sochineniia,* XII, 30. See also Christoff, *Aksakov,* p. 92n. S. P. Shevyrev (1806–1864) published his two part review of Gogol's *Dead Souls* in *Moskvitianin,* 1842, no. 8, pp. 207–228; no. 9, pp. 346–376.

17. Samarin, *Socheneniia,* XII, 32.

18. In a recent essay of exemplary scholarship Professor Kline aptly says that the Moscow Slavophils "took over and polemically sharpened Hegel's distinction between understanding (*Verstand* = *rassudok*) and reason (*Vernunft* = *razum*)." To this topic we shall have to return. See George L. Kline, "Russian Religious Thought," in Ninian Smart, et al., eds., *Nineteenth Century Religious Thought in the West* (Cambridge, Engl. 1985), II, p. 182.

19. Samarin, *Socheneniia,* XII, 33.

20. Ibid., p. 34.

21. Ibid., pp. 34–35. Samarin's views of Gogol's work have been ably and perceptively examined, and in greater detail than they are here, by Efimova. She calls attention to several interesting points – that Samarin stressed that Gogol' brought out life in its completeness, whereas the satirical author deals only with the "dark side" of life, and that Samarin and Belinsky disagreed decisively in their views of Gogol'. "For Belinsky the emotional content of *Dead Souls* is in the merciless negation of reality." Although it was stressed above that Samarin approved of Aksakov's review of *Dead Souls,* Efimova states that the positions of the two young friends with respect to *Dead Souls* are "very close" but not identical. She says that Konstantin in his zeal to elevate Gogol' to the same plane as Homer and Shakespeare "is ready to be touched even by the negative personalities in *Dead Souls,*" whereas "for Samarin, Sobakevich, Nozdrev, Manilov are 'repulsive persons and are phenomena with which our reality treats us.'" See M. T. Efimova, "Iu. Samarin o Gogole," in *Pushkin i ego sovremenniki* (Pskov, 1970), pp. 137, 138 (hereafter cited as Efimova, "Samarin o Gogole').

22. Efimova, "Samarin o Gogole," p. 139.

23. See N. L. Meshcheriakov et al., eds., *N. V. Gogol'. Polnoe sobranie sochinenii,* 14 vols. (Moscow, 1940–1952), XII, 411 (hereafter cited as Gogol', *Sochineniia*); Efimova, "Samarin o Gogole," p. 139; Shenrok, "Smirnova k Gogoliu," *Russkaia starina,* 1890, no. 6, pp. 651, 653.

24. Efimova, "Samarin o Gogole," p. 139; Shenrok, "Smirnova k Gogoliu" *Russkaia starina,* 1888, no. 11, p. 137; Samarin, *Sochineniia,* XII 240. (The same letter published by Shenrok in 1889 is dated simply 1846). Shenrok, who edited the installment publication of some of the correspondence from and to Gogol', gives valuable information about Gogol' and his correspondents. He attributes "Gogol's moral authority" to his "exceptionally high place" in literature, and says that Gogol' took upon himself the "responsible burden of his preceptorial activity." Before the Gogol' – Samarin correspondence, "Samarin already shared with other intelligent youths admiration of Gogol'." The love of Gogol' on the part of the "talented Slavophil" found in Smirnova "a heartfelt, kindred response." She in turn wrote to Gogol', "Samarin loves you frightfully," and Samarin, "your great dilettante," also "worships you." For her, Samarin was a "wonderful pearl among our youth." See *Russkaia starina,* 1888, no. 7, pp. 55, 59, and no. 10, p. 134; 1889, no. 7, pp. 163–165.

25. Samarin, *Sochineniia,* VI, 369.

26. This letter, as mentioned earlier, was first published by Shenrok in *Russkaia starina* (1889, no.7, pp. 167–171), and dated simply 1846. It was republished by Dmitry Samarin in 1911 in Iurii Samarin's collected works. The citations here are from this publication. It is not the purpose here to give a complete account of the Gogol' – Samarin relationship. Gogol' is dis-

cussed only to the extent necessary to shed light on the evolution of Samarin's Slavophilism.

27. Samarin, *Sochineniia*, XII, 240–241. Gogol' was aware of Samarin before Samarin met Smirnova. This awareness was most likely the result of the contacts between Gogol' and the Aksakovs. At any rate when Gogol' wrote to Konstantin from Gastein, May 24, 1843, he inquired about a number friends including Samarin, thinking, it seems, that Samarin was the author of a review of *Dead Souls*. See Gogol', *Sochineniia*, XII 186. The fatherly, patronizing attitude which Gogol' took toward Samarin once he overcame his annoyance at Smirnova for bringing Samarin to his attention, is evident in several of Gogol's letters to his young correspondent. From Frankfurt, December 24, 1844, Gogol' in a letter to Iurii characterized his dissertation in these words: "The book shows a capacious mind, and the great gifts with which God has rewarded the author are obvious. But the substance of the subject itself, as you know, is a priestly matter [*delo popovskoe*]." After Gogol' read Iurii's letter-confession he wrote to him from Rome, January 3, 1846, "you are saved, saved by sister [Smirnova], and the love of Christ." Gogol's advice on what to do and how to behave in the "world" of St. Petersburg was given in several letters. See Gogol', *Sochineniia*, XII, 411; XIII 25–26, 86–87, 99–100.

28. Samarin, *Sochineniia*, XII, 241.

29. Ibid., pp. 242–243.

30. Ibid., p. 243.

31. Ibid., p. 244.

32. Ibid., p. 245.

33. Ibid., pp. 175–176.

34. Dmitry Samarin chose not to include this letter in volume 12 of Iurii's works, which contains his correspondence from 1840 to 1853, despite the fact that this letter and several others of Iurii's had been published by V. I. Shenrok twenty-two years earlier. See *Russkaia starina*, 1889, no. 7, pp. 167–176.

35. Whether Iurii's Moscow friends sensed the elder Samarin's opinion of them or not is not clear. But early in 1846 Iurii complained to Konstantin from St. Petersburg that his Moscow friends had abandoned him. "Khomiakov has entirely forgotten me," he says, and "only Katerina Aleksandrovna [Sverbeeva] writes to me [and] seldom." Samarin, *Sochineniia*, XII, 173.

36. *Russkaia starina*, 1889, no. 7, pp. 172–173.

37. Efimova, who had access in the Lenin Library to "several" draft copies of Samarin's letters about Gogol's *Selected Passages,* and quotes from some of them, says that this book "overshadowed" for Samarin all other issues. It "sharply" changed his attitude toward Gogol', for now Gogol's insincerity struck him, as the "'false sound offends the ear'." Efimova concludes that

Samarin was also offended by the "extremely crude primitivism of Gogol's sermonizing," and felt that the book had done "harm to the general cause of Christianity." Efimova, "Samarin o Gogole," p. 142.

38. Samarin, *Sochineniia,* XII, 189–190.

39. The word *"otverstoe"* modifying *Evangelie,* presents more than the usual difficulty of rendering Russian into English. Dal' gives as equivalents "finished," "completed," and also, in the verb form, "to avenge." The section of the letter in which this word appears is uncomplimentary to Gogol'.

40. Efimova, "Samarin o Gogole," p. 146.

41. Ibid., p. 147.

42. Ibid., p. 147.

7

End of the 1840s:
Reviews, Riga, and Prison

During the approximately two years that Samarin spent in St. Petersburg before he was sent on a special assignment to Riga, he served first in the Ministry of Justice, then in the Senate, and early in February 1846 he was transferred to the Ministry of Interior. Here he became a member of the committee for the study of the peasant order in Livonia. This position, as Dmitrii Samarin remarked, although of short duration, was Iurii's unexpected but portentous exposure to the peasant question. This question in turn, with its focus on the emancipation of the serfs in Russia, later became Samarin's principal contribution to reformist Slavophilism.

Iurii's unhappiness in St. Petersburg over his relationships with his father and with Konstantin Aksakov, and his general dissatisfaction with life and work in the capital, did not result in undue self-pity or idleness. Despite his aversion to the government bureaucracy, he seems to have been conscientious about his duties, and furthermore he found time to write and publish a good deal, including two relatively brief but noteworthy works. Both were in the form of book reviews. The first, already mentioned, evaluated Count V. A. Sollogub's *Tarantas,* the second, written in Riga early in 1847, was called "About the Historical and Literary Opinions of *Sovremennik*" and consisted of three reviews of works by Kavelin, A. V. Nikitenko, and Belinsky.[1]

Although these two early works of Samarin's are in the category of literary criticism, their content is heavily ideological. Particularly in his reply to Count Sollogub, and even more in his attempts to refute the views of Kavelin and Belinsky, Samarin in effect became immersed in the Slavophil-Westerner polemical fray. This happened to come toward the end of Belinsky's life (he died on May 26, 1848), and it was therefore one of his last direct encounters with Samarin and the Slavophils. Herzen had left Russia in January 1847; whether or not this was intended only as a trip to the West, he was never to see Russia again. This, of course, removed him both from the journal polemics at home and from possible personal encounters with the Slavophils such as occurred during the several years before his departure from Russia. Before the end of 1847 he was already disillusioned in the possibility of a socialist triumph in the West, and like the Slavophils, borrowed from the West the thought that the West was dying or decaying. He soon proclaimed his faith in his "Russian socialism," based on the "Slavophil-discovered" Russian peasant commune, but without the religious Orthodox garb that the Slavophils cast upon it.

The Slavophil camp, led by Khomiakov, Ivan Kireevsky, Konstantin Aksakov, and Samarin, had formed by 1846–1847; though it was not yet in command of a finished and detailed ideology, it had taken a stand against Russian Westernism. The camp of the Westerners was perhaps even less coherent and unified than that of the Slavophils. Chaadaev, who with his pro-Catholic stand in the early 1830s called forth by 1839 the first pro-Orthodox Slavophil reaction, was pushed by circumstances into the background by the mid-1840s. His views aroused little sympathy and less following in Russia. His voice for the rest of his life (he died in 1856) remained that of a solitary and isolated pro-Catholic Westerner. It is not therefore surprising that Samarin did not engage him in ideological battle in the press. But since Chaadaev died at the very time that the reform for serf emancipation was entering its crucial stage, he could not have seen that Slavophilism was more than retrospective utopianism, his early view of Moscow Slavophilism, thoughtlessly repeated since then.

The other two currents of Russian Westernism, which for lack of more precise definitions are designated as liberal, represented in this case by K. D. Kavelin, and radical, represented by V. G. Belinsky, called forth Samarin's response. The specific works reviewed by Samarin in the 1847 article were Kavelin's "A View of the Juridical Order of Ancient Russia" (*Vzgliad na iuridicheskii byt drevnei Rossii*), published by Belinsky in *Sovremennik,* and Belinsky's "A View of Russian Literature for 1846" (*Vzgliad na russkuiu literaturu 1846 goda*).[2] Kavelin's lengthy essay, on a seemingly obscure subject, and Samarin's response aroused considerable polemical passion; as in the case of the controversy between Konstantin Aksakov and Sergei Solov'ev, what was at stake was ascertaining not merely the nature of the ancient Russian social, economic, political, and moral state, but also the nature of Russia's future ideological orientation. This perhaps more than any other consideration accounts for the Slavophils' insistence that the ancient Russian order was communal rather than clan.

At the time, Samarin was twenty-six years old. Vasilii Davydov, who was also of the gentry, and who later (1855) became Iurii's commanding officer in the militia, recalled his first meeting with Samarin in one of the St. Petersburg salons. He remembered Iurii as a "young man of medium height with golden-tinted hair, very white face, and slow, somewhat open-legged gait." There was nothing remarkable about him "except the timbre of his voice and particularly the quality of his speech which involuntarily attracted attention to itself. . . . Even then he was known as an extremely capable, learned, and well-informed man, and a pleasant conversationalist. . . . He stood out strikingly in our common society," and after his Riga Letters and his incarceration he acquired an "exclusive halo in society."[3]

There was, however, a lighter side to Samarin's personality which did not escape his close friends, and certainly not Sergei Aksakov. Writing to his son Ivan, November 3, 1849, he provided him with news about their Slavophil friends: Khomiakov was suffering from his eyes; "Samarin is extremely busy . . . he works very much and at the same time keeps up with everything: he hunts, dances, plays chess with Korf, and *amuses everyone.* He wrote to me describing one of his hunts but sadly I have not received the letter." Four years later (March 9, 1853) Sergei Aksakov wrote to Turgenev with whom, among other interests, he shared a passion for hunting: "I hope that Khomiakov will write about venery, and Samarin about shooting wild boar and wild goats."[4]

Count V. A. Sollogub's satirical novel *Tarantas* (Stagecoach), which had appeared in book form in 1845 (the first seven chapters were published in 1840 in Belinsky's *Otechestvennye zapiski*), is superficially a travelogue through part of Russia. It has been characterized as a "talented" work, but a "strange mixture of belles lettres and publicistics."[5] The point of view is moderate or liberal Westerner, not favorable to the Slavophils. Samarin's review of *Tarantas,* published in the Slavophil symposium *Moskovskii sbornik* of 1846, takes a not unexpected pro-Slavophil position, and it tells us a good deal about Samarin's own Slavophil position and his contribution to "early" Slavophilism.

The theme of *Tarantas* is an encounter of two generations. This was a theme that was quite familiar in Russia at the time, and Sollogub provides an interesting framework. A young man, Ivan Vasil'evich, and an older man, Vasilii Ivanovich, meet on Moscow's main street, Tverskaia, and then travel together by stagecoach to the village of Mordassy. Along the way, they discuss many matters. Ivan Vasil'evich has traveled widely in the West and has reflected with concern on what he has seen, heard, and learned. He represents the younger Russian gentry who in the first half of the nineteenth century were no longer satisfied to merely copy the West. Whereas members of the Russian gentry of the eighteenth century were quite content with their French education, dress, language, manners and mores, the post-Napoleonic war generation, though French-educated, wanted to be Russians. This, of course, was truer of the incipient Slavophils of the 1840s than of the young Westerners, although even among them, few if any would have slavishly followed the West.

Ivan Vasil'evich is, in fact, a generalized type of Moscow Slavophil, somewhat superficially and condescendingly conceived. Vasilii Ivanovich is Sollogub's intended sympathetic character. Samarin, of course, takes the side of the younger man, and he points out that whereas the character represented by Vasilii Ivanovich is not new and could be found in the works of Fonvizin, Griboedov, and others, Ivan Vasil'evich is new and is delineated "more profoundly... more clearly and more completely." Among the topics the two characters discuss, Samarin notes particularly that of the "rupture between life and consciousness." He says that Ivan Vasil'evich's early, shallow, imitative Westernism, before he saw the light, was a result of Peter's reform, which "roused only the upper [strata] and alienated them from the lower class. The reform had no direct influence on the common people." Overlooking such negative effects of Peter's reforms on the *narod* or peasantry as serfdom, army recruiting, and the poll tax, he concluded that Peter merely sanctioned the existing arrangement between gentry and peasantry.[6]

Samarin was less strident and perhaps less steadfast in his esteem of the *narod* than Konstantin Aksakov, but he detected the ever present issue of nationality (*narodnost'*) in the stagecoach journey through the Russian countryside. The very purpose of the trip, Samarin concludes, was to "study *narodnost'*." As a good Slavophil, he saw the "common people, uneducated but harboring in the simplicity of an uncorrupted spirit the profound meaning of love for truth and the good." Ivan Vasil'evich, he says, belonged to that generation that was "innocently atoning for the sin of false education," for the falsely educated person was a "Russian returning from abroad, who is some sort of a fool in ugly garb, chattering in French and despising our way of life." Ivan Vasil'evich is redeemed because he has returned from the West "with respect and love for his native land."[7]

Samarin's references to *nauka* in this review are less precise than they were a few years earlier when he defined *nauka* as philosophy, and philosophy as Hegelianism; now he seems to have in mind philosophy when he excuses Ivan Vasil'evich's "mistrustfulness" of *nauka. Nauka*, he says,

> came to us from abroad in forms that were inaccessible to the majority, [and] with a content alien to out nationality [*narodnost'*]. It has not yet succeeded in becoming transformed into our native possession. It has not yet freed itself from its false contempt for life, and condescending to life, it frightens it with the impertinence of its demands, thus becoming repulsive with its proud pretense to all-inclusive knowledge.[8]

Having firmly joined the Slavophil camp a year or two earlier Samarin (this most "Europeanized" of Slavophils in Tsamutali's view) now boldly took his stand against exuberant and unrestrained mid-nineteenth-century Western secularism and anthropocentrism.

Although Samarin had not long since turned away from his Hegelian way of thinking, he now clearly had no doubt that he needed to believe, as well as to use his considerable intellectual powers. Ivan Vasil'evich, he says, was a youth brought up "in a foreign manner," but not truly in the "French manner," not in the "English manner," not in the German, but just in an "abstractly foreign manner," because none of the respective cultures could be transplanted to Russia — but "only in the non Russian." In his educational program, neither the need to think nor the need to believe would be neglected; and education, and, it could be added, indoctrination, its often present fellow traveler, would play a major role in the Slavophil scheme of things. As Samarin sadly said, the Russian gentry, like Ivan Vasil'evich, had to *"learn* to love' Russia.[9]

One more salient subject in Samarin's review of *Tarantas* should be mentioned here, that of art. In conformity with the views of the other early Slavophils, but without any compulsion, Samarin favored art with a social purpose. He found this in a good many writers but particularly in Gogol' and Dickens, and concluded that "it did not harm their artistry."[10]

Whereas Samarin's ideological bias is obvious throughout his review of *Tarantas,* his opinion of *Sovremennik,* often meaning simply Belinsky, becomes apparent in the opening paragraph of his remarks in the three-part article (1847). Contrasting the "Petersburg journals" with the "Moscow orientation," he says: "They invented . . . its name of Old Believers and Slavianophils," which seemed to them to be "very entertaining." But which in fact contributed to the confusion surrounding the term Slavophil. Referring indirectly to Konstantin Aksakov's "Russian" dress, he reproached *Sovremennik* for dwelling too long on this "rich theme" while neglecting the thought of the "Moscow party." Small wonder, Samarin concluded, that the Petersburg party "attributed to the so-called Slavianophils that which they never said and never thought; that a large part of their accusations, for example, a desire to resurrect the dead past, does not at all apply to them, "In general," *Sovremennik* was the victim of a "misunderstanding," whether deliberate or accidental.

But Samarin did not stay on the defensive very long. He took the other "literary party" seriously and jumped into the polemics with the Slavophils' "literary opponents." Declaring his disappointment with the first number of *Sovremennik,* he listed three principal "accusations" against it: the "absence of unity of orientation and agreement with itself," the "one-sidedness and narrowness of its manner of thought," and its "misrepresentation of the manner of thought of its opponents."[11] Samarin's purpose was to "prove" these contentions. With respect to the matter of unity and agreement behind *Sovremennik,* he could make a case, since those who backed it in one way or another were not of one conviction.[12] Samarin's second and third points are standard polemical accusations.

The first of the three works that Samarin reviewed in this long article was Kavelin's essay on Russia's ancient juridical order. He found in it one overriding thought that was "stated if not proved",[13] and he devotes the rest of the thirty-five pages on Kavelin to a Slavophil refutation of Kavelin's thesis, that is, that Russia's ancient order was characterized by blood, clan relationships; Samarin's counterthesis is that this order then, as in his own day, was communal, social, and Orthodox-inspired.

Although Samarin's refutation of Kavelin's thesis is hardly a strictly scholarly, well-documented, factual historical essay, Kavelin's seventy-page "review" of Russian history is no sounder. (In spite of its title, "A View of the Juridical Order of Ancient Russia," it covers the period from pre-Kievan times through the reign of Peter the Great). One wonders why Kavelin resorted to the fairy-tale manner of recounting Russia's past. His central thesis, that the ancient Russian order was based on blood, clan ties, contains a single two-line quotation from an unnamed chronicler (p. 326) and nothing more. He cites no sources, legal or historical, and no documents or the conclusions of historians, in support of his self-confident, assertive, freewheeling treatment of the subject. Kavelin could have done better than that. Both Kavelin and Samarin were obviously carried away by the polemical nature of their exchange and by the serious ideological stakes involved in the subject. Their respective interpretations of Russian history, and their views and convictions about the blood, clan versus the communal social concept, although not without merit would have carried greater weight if they had been more factual, historical and less polemical. Such an exchange could have contributed to the solution of an important Russian historical problem. As it was, Kavelin in the search for an ideological advantage tended to denigrate Russia's past in the hope of demonstrating the necessity of borrowing from the West, and Samarin, for a similar polemical advantage, perhaps overestimated the quality of Russia's past and institutions. Samarin's goal was to establish historically Russia's self-sufficiency in the area of social, economic, and religious values and institutions.

The several points pertinent to the discussion here are all ancillary to Kavelin's primary theme. Without any reference to place, age, political or social conditions, without sources and data, without even mentioning Ewers, Kavelin simply declares, "In most ancient times the Russian Slavs had *exclusively* a clan order, founded only upon blood relationships"[14]; they "did not have any notion" of any other relationships. Kavelin reiterates this theme throughout the essay in various ways and contexts with the sole purpose of buttressing his basic contention.[15] Closely allied to the clan in Kavelin's mind was the family, and occasionally he uses the terms synonymously, as when he says that the Russian Slavs had "a purely family, clan order without any admixtures."[16]

The explanation of the prolonged existence of the clan-family, blood order among the Russian Slavs is implicit in Kavelin's assertion that such incursions into the Russian Slav lands as those of the Avars, Khazars, Normans, and Tatars did not result in "colonization of the conquerors among the natives, and a mixture with them." Those of the Varangians who settled among the Slavs were completely absorbed, and the "purely family" Russian order, which was "created by nature, not by thought," persisted; this was in spite of the fact that two completely disparate influences, at about the same time, the Christian and the pagan Germanic, exposed the Russian Slavs to the principle of individuality or personality. Using the term German or Germanic broadly, to include the Varangians, Kavelin, while not uncritical of the "barbarian-German," admired the "profound sense of the individual *person*" that the German developed early as he came in contact with Roman civilization: "From the very beginning, all relations among the Germans were impressed with this principle of individuality [*lichnost'*] expressed in strict juridical forms."[17] He regrets that this development had no effect on what he considered to be the Russian clan, blood order, which remained alien to the principle of personality.

This principle of individuality and the opposite Slavophil communal principle were at the heart of the Kavelin-Samarin polemic. For Kavelin, personality or individuality found justification not only in early Germanic and, it seems, pre-Christian Roman culture, but also in Christianity itself. His way of reconciling the notion of individuality in non-Christian cultures and in Christianity called for recognizing Christianity as the ennobling and consummating force in the equation.[18] Whereas the Germanic tribes in their "endless wars" and encounters with Rome "early developed ... a deep sense of individuality," among the Russian Slavs "the principle of individualism did not exist." This was the state of affairs until the time of Peter the Great, when "individuality on Russian soil entered into its unconditional rights."[19] This is to say, Russia had to import the concept of the individual person from the West.

Kavelin admits the existence of communes in Kievan Russia, but he does not say why, how, or precisely where they came into existence. "Settlements become communes", he says vaguely, and then goes on to declare, somewhat paradoxically, "The further development of the communal order consisted of its greater and greater disintegration." Within the communes, there were "endless" struggles and agitation. The clan order evolved at the same time with the communal, "from immemorial times," and "when the communal order became completely destroyed," families began to function independently, assuming all authority. In this manner "blood vengeance" appeared. But this "blood order could not develop social spirit and civic virtues," and it became necessary to "vest authority over themselves in a foreigner."[20] Thus the Varangians were called in.

In his rapid and selective review of a thousand years of Russian history, Kavelin saw the growth of the clan principle from the reign of Iaroslav the Wise (1019–1054) to the rise of Moscow in the fourteenth century.[21] Although the communal principle was "hidden" under the "Varangian layer" it asserted itself strongly in the north of Russia, in Novgorod. Kavelin seems to connect Novgorod's commercial preeminence in medieval Russia with the communal principle but does not explain what the interaction was. He merely says, "Novgorod remains for us the model of the original Russian-Slav communal order," stamped by the "absence of . . . a firm, juridical principle of individualism, as created by public spirit that characterizes our ancient domestic life."[22]

More generalizations, conclusive in Kavelin's view, are contained in his remarks about the reigns of Ivan IV and Peter the Great. Asserting that "in ancient Russia there was no juridical order," and associating the existence of the principle of individuality with juridical norms, he maintains that, while the notion of individuality had appeared in Russia earlier, "in Peter the Great the individual person on Russian soil entered into its unconditional rights, renounced immediate, natural, exclusively national definitions, and conquered and subjected them to itself. All of Peter's private life, all of his political activity is [only] the first phase of the realization of the principle of individuality in Russian history."[23]

As I have shown in my preceding three studies, at least some of the Slavophils' heavy criticism of most of Peter's reforms and innovations was a reaction to the extravagant claims made in Peter's behalf by the Westerners. But at the same time it cannot be here maintained that the Slavophils were more judicious than the Westerners in their polemical views and judgments of Peter's reign. The heat of the polemic is clearly not conducive to the establishment of historical veracity.

Summing up Kavelin's views on how Christianity revealed man's inner world and human individuality, Samarin resolutely says, "No, this is not enough!" This "self-determining" notion of the individual person gives "only the negative side of Christianity." Kavelin had forgotten its "positive side," the "new yoke and sweet burden which are imposed upon man by the very act of his liberation." Against Kavelin's view of personal freedom and individuality as an end in itself, Samarin advanced the notion of the Christian church. "Man, renouncing his individualism . . . submits himself unconditionally to the whole. This self-abnegation of everyone in favor of all men is a free principle, but at the same time [it is] an unconditionally obligatory union of men among themselves. This union, this commune consecrated by the eternal presence of the Holy Spirit, is the Church." Kavelin thought that he had found the principle of individuality in Christianity, but in effect he had secularized it through a "certain subjection of religion" in the Hegelian manner, "to a philosophical comprehension [*osmyslenie*] of history;"

Samarin also found it in Christianity, but he kept it in the Christian church, as he and the Slavophils conceived it.[24]

Having seen a close bond between the commune and the Christian church, Samarin elaborated on the principle of individuality and the "personal arbitrariness of all men." He affirmed that the Slav "communal order was not founded on individuality, and could not be founded on it, for it presupposes the highest act of personal freedom and consciousness — self-abnegation." In the commune, "Everyone has renounced his personal sovereignty."[25] This thought appears several times in Samarin's review of Kavelin, and in his summary he again says that the "communal order of the Slavs is founded not on the absence of individuality but on the free and conscious abnegation of its sovereignty."

The concept of personal freedom and individuality as conceived by Samarin fits into the Christian notion of the brotherhood of man under the fatherhood of God, for absolute personal freedom, freedom that is not self-limiting, is incompatible with one's free choice of the Christian brotherhood. It is not therefore surprising that Samarin saw in Kavelin's extolling of the Germanic concept of freedom something that had "neither an end nor a way out."[26] That is what absolute personal freedom was to him. This raises certain basic questions to which regrettably no answers can be given. What is the origin and content of the Western — Kavelin's Germanic — concept of individual freedom, and the individual person? Was it Roman, pagan, Germanic, or Christian? Or was it a fusion of some or all of these? And if so, in what proportion did each element enter into the combination?

Neither Kavelin nor Samarin raised the questions formulated here. However, what Samarin seems to have perceived more clearly than Kavelin was the mid-nineteenth-century Western trend toward secularism. Samarin saw that the principle of individuality in the West was being defined not in accordance with Christian, Biblical concepts but in secular, legalistic, political, and economic terms. How far this trend has gone in the West since then can be illustrated by the fact that today in the name of personal freedom the Biblical injunction "Love thy neighbor as thyself" is increasingly replaced by "Sue thy neighbor as thine adversary."

To young Samarin, the Christian concept of self-limited personal freedom in the name of the common good had a Providential implication. He conceived the Russian nation as being permeated by, and resting upon, the "communal principle," which, in turn, "saved the unity and integrity of Russia, and again both in 862, and in 1612, created the state out of itself . . . ." The communal principle constitutes the foundation, base of all Russian history past, present, and future." He saw all manifestations of Russian life as being implanted in the "fertile depth" of the communal principle: "No deed and no theory that renounces this foundation will achieve its aim or survive."[27] The bond that Samarin saw between the Russian nation, state, and Christian unity and brotherhood was formulated as follows:

A united state commune [*gosudarstvennaia obshchina*] encompassing the whole of Russia, is the ultimate aspect, the expression of land [people's] and church unity. All these forms are different from one another, but they are only forms, only phases in the gradual expansion of the one communal principle: a single need to live together in concord and love, a need realized by every member of the commune as the supreme law . . . carrying its justification in itself and not in the personal arbitrariness of each and every one.[28]

We may never know how Samarin arrived at his views on the relationship between Christianity, the individual person, and the Russian peasant commune. They seem to have become formulated in his mind within a year or so after he left Moscow for St. Petersburg in the summer of 1844. This raises questions about the problems and issues that the Slavophils discussed in the Moscow salons in the mid-forties, when Samarin was abandoning Hegelianism for Slavophil Orthodoxy and the Slavophils and the Westerners were engaged in the ideological polemics that led to the rupture between them in the winter of 1844–1845. Were the views expressed by Samarin on personality, individualism, individual freedom, Christianity, and the commune in the mid-1840s his own, or were they the common property of all the early Slavophils, the result of their salon discussions?[29] We saw that Konstantin Aksakov held similarly strong views in the 1850s, and, as already pointed out, Khomiakov and Ivan Kireevsky were also partisans of the same highly idealized Russian peasant commune. But Samarin was in the vanguard of early Slavophilism when he published a reasoned, coherent defense of it, thereby making a major contribution to one of the cardinal ideological ideals of the Slavophils.

In doing so Samarin sacrificed the long, painstaking preparation that he knew was necessary in order to provide Slavophilism with a solid factual and historical foundation. He stated his conviction on this matter in his letters to Konstantin Aksakov from St. Petersburg. Writing at the end of 1844 about his busy routine, he said, "I continue to study Russian history little by little;" early the next year, somewhat distressed about Slavophilism's premises, he confessed, "We have as yet proved nothing, or very little; everything that we assert about our history, about our people, about the special characteristics of our past development, all this has been guessed at and not deduced."[30] But at the same time he did not hesitate to take on the Westerners Kavelin, Nikitenko, and Belinsky. Clearly, Samarin the scholar and historian yielded to Samarin the Slavophil polemicist.

It is not surprising that as Samarin looked at Russia's past, and read a good deal more into its remote peasant commune than was historically and factually justified, he painted a picture that was a goal and an ideal rather than a historical reality. At the same time he remained unmoved by what the West had to offer in place of the commune. Guizot's triad of individuality, authority, and Christianity in reference to the Western European historical development ignored the "eastern half of Europe, which was little known to him," and therefore he was unaware of the Slav communal principle. The best that the West could offer in place of the Slav commune were "different kinds of artificial associations, the theory of which is stated in Rousseau's *Contrat Social.*" At fault here was the Germanic principle of individualism which gave birth to nothing more than an "artificial, conditional association," a problem that also caught Ivan Kireevsky's attention. Samarin reiterated this thought, which he seems to have first found in Lorenz von Stein's work on socialism. He reproached Kavelin for failure to take note of Adam Mickiewicz's well-publicized lectures on Slavic literature at the College de France (which began in December 1840), in which Mickiewicz called attention to the variety of historical and still functioning Slavic communes. Thanks to "Mickiewicz's eloquent voice," Samarin says, "the eyes of many people, including those of George Sand, turned to the Slav world, which they understood as a communal world . . . not only with curiosity but with a sort of sympathy and expectation."[31]

Comparing the Western world and Russia's past, as sketched by Kavelin, Samarin saw a different picture. To him, the Western principle of individuality was cold, legalistic, harsh in itself, and it flourished in a harsh and forbidding human environment. Samarin had read Lorenz von Stein's *Der Sozialismus und Kommunismus des heutigen Frankreichs* in 1843,[32] and from this, as well as from Slavophil discussions of French utopian socialism, then in its heyday, and possibly from other sources, he gained some understanding of the astonishing new industrialism that was drastically transforming England and parts of Western Europe.

In 1846, the year before Samarin wrote this review of Kavelin's work, the corn laws had been repealed in England, a triumph for liberalism or for unregulated, uncontrolled, and unbridled laissez-faire economic individualism. This may have been a boon to a relatively small group of British entrepreneurs, but it was not at all a boon to the growing millions of British men, women, and children who were employed in mines and factories, ten, fourteen, or more hours a day. Such measures as the Reform Bill of 1832, which acknowledged the power of the bourgeoisie in England, and the Factory Act of 1834 had not done much to ameliorate the misery of the British worker, who during the 1830s and 1840s was without any effective organization, despite Chartism. He had no union protection, or the later and at least partial defense of social legislation.

While in the name of individual freedom and initiative factory and mine owners could carry on without any control or restraint, millions of their workers, including women and children, languished in misery and hopelessness. One need not go beyond the Michael Sadler parliamentary reports on mine and factory conditions in the 1830s or the Anthony Ashley Cooper parliamentary reports, or Charles Dickens to see that there was more truth than rhetoric in the words of the English historian who recently said that "Marxism was born in the slums of Manchester." Nor is there any difficulty in accounting for Thomas Carlyle's concern when he wrote in *Past and Present* (1843), "I venture to believe that in no time since the beginnings of society, was the lot of those same dumb millions of toilers so entirely unbearable as it is even in the days now passing over us."[33] This is the type of individualism that A. F. Gil'ferding characterized as "wolf freedom," and that Samarin and the Slavophils would strenuously try to avoid, relying on the ancient and still functioning Russian peasant *mir,* then more commonly referred to as *obshchina* (village commune).

In an eight-point summary of his criticism of Kavelin's essay, Samarin first objected to Kavelin's method, which he characterized as analytical and inapplicable in this case.

(1) Elevating the notion of the individual person to that of human being could not be done logically, "because the analytical process never develops of itself into a synthetic process."

(2) The "idea of *narod* appeared not as the natural fruit of the development of individuality, but as a direct reaction to it, and entered the consciousness of the leading thinkers of Western Europe from the sphere of religion." (3) The Western world is now calling for the "organic reconciliation of the principle of individuality ... with the demand[s] of the commune." (4) "This demand coincides with our substance."[34]

In the existence of the commune, and the need to counter prevailing Western, laissez-faire liberalism, Samarin found the "point of contact between our history and that of the West." Point 5, his primary justification of the communal principle, repeated for emphasis, was, "That the communal order of the Slavs is based not upon the absence of personality, but upon its free and conscious renunciation of its sovereignty." (6) Christianity brought "consciousness and freedom" into the national order of the Slavs while the "Slav commune, becoming dissolved, so to speak, accepted in itself the principle of spiritual communion, and became, as it were, the temporal historical aspect of the church." (7) From this it followed that Russia's "internal history is defined as the illumination of the national communal principle by the communal church principle." In this manner, Samarin, like the other early Slavophils, saw a Providential bond between Eastern Orthodoxy and communality (*obshchinnost'*) or between *sobornost'* and *obshchinnost'.* In Samarin's view, this bond was the heart and core of Moscow Slavophilism. In the final point of the summary Samarin voiced his pro-Slav sentiments. He saw Russia's "external history" as aiming at the preservation of political freedom for Russia and "all Slav" nations, through the creation of a "strong state form which does not exhaust the communal principle, but also does not contradict it."[35]

This summary of Samarin's Slavophil ideological position, given mostly in his own words, conveys with considerable accuracy his thoughts, convictions, and motivation. But there was yet another component of his pro-Slavophil and anti-Kavelin attitude, more difficult to determine and weigh, that is, the psychological factor. In the middle of his reply to Kavelin, and obviously irked by Kavelin's extolling of the Germanic concept of individuality, Samarin says, "In other words, it remained for the German to make a human being of himself; [now] the Russian must first make a German of himself in order to learn from him how to be a human being."[36] At one and the same time Samarin expressed the integrated sentiment of personal self-respect and national pride, which was, and still is, a basic and powerful component of nationalistic ideologies.

Although in the available information about the Samarins there is no suggestion that they were in the forefront of Gogol's admirers, as was the case with the Aksakovs, Khomiakovs, and Kireevskys (Elagins), one should not draw the same conclusion about Iurii Samarin. As we have seen, his pro-Gogol' sentiments and ardor did not lag far behind Konstantin Aksakov's. And as stressed, before the men of the thirties and forties, including the Slavophils, felt Russia's greatest cultural deficiency, as compared with the West, to be in the field of literature. Yet literature, even when it relies on folk motives, as was often the case with romanticism, is the product of the creative individual. With the best of French and German literature available to Iurii in the original, he did not need to be told that Shakespeare, or Goethe, and Schiller, yes, even George Sand, did not engage in creative literary activity on orders from their respective parliaments or societies.

Samarin, like the other Slavophils, was fully aware of the role of the individual of talent and genius in literature, art, science, and in general in human creativity, and there was no thought on his part to do anything but to encourage and support such individuals, as was the case with Gogol'. This reminder is necessary since during the polemics with the Westerners, the Slavophils were often accused of wishing to stifle the individual person for the sake of the commune. They were aware of the problem. This, rather than facile and direct copying of Western liberal ideas, was behind their advocacy of freedom of religion, speech, and expression.

The commune, as Samarin saw it, did not stand for the indiscriminate and obligatory leveling of Russian society to the plane of mediocrity. Rather, while caring for the physical needs of all its members—its principal but by no means sole function—the commune would furnish the indispensable economic base for everyone's full self-realization. One did not need to have read Thomas Gray's "Elegy written in a Country Church-yard," to be aware of the countless individuals whose talents could never emerge from obscurity. An observant Russian landlord moving among his serfs could easily see the talent that was wasted. However, the self-realization of the individual as conceived by Samarin would ultimately redound not to the greater glory of the self, but through an act of free and ready self-abnegation would contribute to the benefit and brotherhood of all. This, of course, is the point at which harsh reality rudely intrudes upon the sublime.

One gifted person who was rescued from the wasteland of Russian serfdom was A. V. Nikitenko, whose essay "On the Present Trend in Russian Literature" (*O sovremennom napravlenii russkoi literatury*) was the subject of the middle part of Samarin's review.[37] Although Nikitenko is often considered a moderate Westerner, Samarin begins his remarks by saying, "No literary party can call him entirely its own." This was so because Nikitenko's literary views and opinions had not been given "systematic" form and expression. This remark came about half a dozen years before Koshelev and Ivan Aksakov began vigorously debating the subject of German "systematic thought" against Russian "nonsystematic thought."[38] Nikitenko's article, published in the first issue of *Sovremennik* for 1847, was presumed to be his "literary manifesto," for it contained his views on the purpose of Russian literature. Nikitenko declared, in Samarin's words, that art should be "sympathetic to all social questions."[39] Samarin found inconsistencies in Nikitenko's views and not much to provoke a vigorous debate.

This was not, however, the case with Belinsky, to whom Samarin devoted the last thirty pages of his long article. He begins his remarks with an unkind and unsupported cut. Although Belinsky was not "a stranger to aesthetic feeling," he "was always under the influence of alien thought." Here the affluent young Iurii, who enjoyed a variety of educational and cultural opportunities, confronting the impoverished Belinsky, is at his polemical worst. Belinsky lived on "borrowed thought," Samarin says, which is not bad in itself, and is in fact often necessary. Unlike the gentry, who often spoke German in the nursery, Belinsky had learned of German idealism at second hand. His major deficiency, however, was his inability to make what he borrowed his own. Samarin explained the "uncommon ease" with which Belinsky changed his point of view by saying that the "cause of the change was not in him but outside him."[40] Thus in his opening paragraph or two Samarin set the unfriendly and biased tone of his remarks. Since he does not seem to have known Belinsky personally, he probably acquired his antipathy for him from Konstantin Aksakov. It is, however, clear that Belinsky thoroughly reciprocated the negative sentiments of all the Slavophils.

But even the best of personal relations could not have endured when subjected to the strain of divergent and zealously defended ideological positions. By late 1846 and early 1847, Samarin was firmly in the Slavophil camp, even though its ideology had not yet become fully formulated, while Belinsky, nearing the end of his life, had become committed to a radical, socialistic, secularistic point of view.[41] Writing from this ideological position, Belinsky was in several fundamental ways Samarin's antithesis.[42] Their ages in 1847 were thirty-six and twenty-seven, respectively, and because of the censorship both had to be cautious and circumspect in their public statements, disguising their views on social, economic, and political matters as literary criticism.

In his "View of Russian Literature for 1846" (*Vzgliad na russkuiu literaturu 1846 goda*), written a little more than a year before his premature death, Belinsky appears in the role of the foremost defender of the "Natural School" (*natural'naia shkola*) in literature and literary criticism. This informal group, insisting on literary realism, included also Herzen, Turgenev, D. B. Grigorovich, and others, but agreement on this point should not be taken to mean unanimity of all views and convictions. Belinsky defined the common concern when he wrote, "About us, in us, and around us, that is where we must seek both the questions and their answers." Perhaps still reacting to German speculative academic thought, he emphasized, "The importance of theoretical questions depends on their relationship to reality," and he would therefore exclude "romanticism," "dreaminess," and "abstractness."[43]

Although he was highly critical of Slavophilism, Belinsky did not take an absolutely negative attitude toward its advocates. "We repeat," he says, "the Slavophils are right in many respects, but nevertheless their role is purely negative, although it is useful for a while." Referring to what he considered the Slavophils' excessive devotion to Russia's past, specifically to the pre-Petrine period, he asserted, "They have forgotten that the new Petrine Russia is as young as North America, that there is much more in its future than in its past."[44] Belinsky's tendency to overemphasize the importance of Peter the Great's reign both as a symbol and as a historical dividing line in Russia's past, is quite understandable. As mentioned in the Aksakov study, it is doubtful that on closer examination Belinsky would have approved of such Petrine and post-Petrine developments in Russia as the extension of serfdom to the Russian factories, the poll tax, which fell heavily on the impoverished peasantry, and the iniquitous army recruiting system for life time service mainly borne by the poor and underprivileged.

Nor did Belinsky have a way of knowing in 1846, when he wrote this essay, how the still rudimentary Slavophilism would evolve. He would probably not have sanctioned Khomiakov's doctrine of *sobornost'*, Kireevsky's doctrine of wholeness of the spirit, and in general the Slavophils' pro-Orthodox convictions. But he might not have objected to the Slavophil principle of communality, to Konstantin Aksakov's priority of *zemlia* over state and government, possibly even to the anarchistic touches in Khomiakov's and particularly Aksakov's thought.[45] And if Slavophil inconsistencies and contradictions resulting from their support of the principle of autocracy seem strange to us, one has to keep in mind the time and the complexity of human nature exemplified also in the career of their contemporary Friedrich Engels, who "For two decades . . . maintained the dual roles—so apparently incompatible in spirit—of capitalist manager and socialist theoretician."[46] Belinsky would have found nothing wrong with the Slavophils' indignation against tsarist censorship, particularly during the "dark seven years" (1848–1855), and he is most likely to have seen the beneficial side of Samarin's practical contribution to the emancipation of the serfs in Russia. These and other aspects of Moscow Slavophilism which became manifest at the end of the 1840s and particularly during the 1850s were, of course, unknown to Belinsky.

Belinsky's perspicacity and exceptional critical sense convinced him, even during Slavophilism's formative period, of one truth: "So-called Slavophilism, without any doubt, is concerned with the most vital and most important questions of our public life." He tended to exaggerate Slavophilism's numerical strength, however: "There are many Slavophils among us, and their number is still increasing." Slavophilism's "positive side," he said, consists of "some sort of nebulous mystical premonitions of the victory of the East over the West," but the Slavophils were incapable of understanding the West," because they measure it with an Eastern yardstick."[47] This nonargument provoked the reverse nonargument in Samarin, who accused the Westerners of not understanding Russia because they measured it with a Western yardstick.

Whatever the manner of measuring Russia and the West, there was tacit agreement between Belinsky and Samarin that the two parts of Europe had followed different historical paths.[48] This idea, whatever its origin, was, as already pointed out, associated with Pogodin's name by his students during the 1830s and 1840s, and aroused much controversy later in the century. In the opening page of his review of literature for 1846 Belinsky says that the history of Russian literature, "like the history of Russia itself, is not similar to the history of any other literature." A few pages farther on he is more specific: "We finally understood that Russia had its own history, which is not similar to the history of any of the European states. . . . From this he concluded that Russia's past must be studied "on the basis of itself alone," not in terms of a general European pattern with which Russia had nothing in common.[49]

Referring to members of the Russian gentry, to those in Russian society who had been Westernized since the days of Peter the Great, and who could visit the West, Belinsky paused to consider the profound and lasting inner split that this had caused in Russian society as well as within individuals. "Many among the Russians," he says, "depart for there [the West] as resolute Europeans but return . . . with the sincere desire to become Russians." Is it possible, he queried, that the "Slavophils are right, and that the reform of Peter the Great only deprived us of our national character, and made us into

people who are neither here nor there [*mezhdoumki*] . . . ?"[50] Denying the
Slavophil view, Belinsky asserted that Peter's reforms were essential, and
that they had achieved their goal, but that now the "time has come for Russia to develop on its own, from within," Thus he cast himself in the unaccustomed role of the moderate, the middle of the roader, reproaching "in the
name of humanity, both those who have rushed into fantastic nationality
[and] those [who have rushed] into fantastic cosmopolitanism."[51] The
secularization of Russian literature since Peter the Great had brought it by
the mid-1840s a degree of maturity and achievement that made it possible
for it to stand on its own merits. The time has "irretrievably passed,"
Belinsky asserted, when "every foreign mediocrity seemed to be superior to
every Russian talent."[52]

All this passed the censorship. Belinsky's reference to Samarin's review
of *Tarantas* in the Moscow symposium of 1846 was, as we have seen,
laudatory with respect to its "intelligent content and masterly exposition."
Belinsky was not so well disposed toward Samarin in the confidential pages
of his correspondence,[53] but it is perhaps fair to say that Samarin was less
kind to Belinsky in his published remarks than Belinsky was to him.

The so-called "Natural School" (*Natural'naia shkola*) in Russian litera-
ture, whose founder, in the opinion of Belinsky and other westerners, was
Gogol', caught Samarin's attention. He objected to what he considered the
extremism of the Natural School, portraying the seamy side of contemporary
Russian life exclusively, and attributed its vogue in Russia to the influence
of French literature. But even among French authors the common people,
Samarin said, were spared from criticism. This was not so with the Natural
School, which "badly understood its model," and which, he unjustifiably said,
shows "no sympathy toward the *narod*." Then young Samarin formulated a
basic truism that later in the century, and in this century, became the subject of bitter recriminations in the ranks of the Russian intelligentsiia. "But
the *narod* is voiceless," Samarin wrote, "the *narod* does not know what
people write about it, the *narod* does not judge itself; [rather], others judge
it."[54] Then and later, all sorts of self-appointed spokesmen for the *narod*
appeared in Russia, not the least conspicuous among whom were the Moscow Slavophils.

Samarin himself wasted no time in assuming the role of champion of the
narod. "we are separated from the people," he says, and he characterizes
this as the "unavoidable consequence of Peter's reforms." It was perhaps
easy for a son of a prominent gentry family to overlook the centuries-long
social, economic, and cultural differences between his own class and the
enserfed peasants, and to attribute the gulf between the two to the work of
Peter the Great. Peter, of course, made his contribution to the estrangement
of the gentry from the peasantry, but Samarin would have had difficulty in
proving that no class separation existed before Peter's reign. He was

probably closer to the historical truth when he said that gentry "rapprochement with the *narod* is perhaps even more necessary for the educated class than for the *narod* itself," and that the "first step" should be taken by the educated people.[55] Implied here is the Slavophil "going to the people" urge, which Konstantin Aksakov soon stated more forcefully and explicitly.

Belinsky welcomed the vigorous interest in the study of Russian history during the 1840s, stimulated in part by the Slavophil concern for Russia's past and institutions. But he could not understand or condone the Slavophil contention, probably inspired by distant and vague Byzantine notions, that "humility" was the characteristic trait of the early Russian Slavs. Pogodin had given currency to this notion, and both Iurii Samarin, his former student, and Konstantin Aksakov, subscribed to it, although another Slavophil, Peter Kireevsky, publicly rejected it.[56] The view that the old Russians were meek and mild-mannered in contrast to the warlike and quarrelsome Western Europeans did not need heavy criticism. A few facts and examples from Russian history were sufficient to bring out the fallacy of such contentions, and Belinsky brought these forth without difficulty:

In general it is rather strange to see in humility the reason why the insignificant Moscow principality subsequently became first the Moscow kingdom and then the Russian empire, gathering under the wings of the double-headed eagle as its own possession Siberia, Little Russia, White Russia, Novorossiia, the Crimea, Bessarabia, Lifliandiia, Estlandiia, Courland, Finland, the Caucasus.

For him the Appanage period of Russian history "was as little a period of love as of meekness; it was rather a period of carnage which had become habitual." But the same sort of thing in the West was given juridical garb so that the "very coercion and oppression assumed the aspect . . . of law."[57]

On the intricate and ever present cultural and psychological question of Russia's relationship with the West, Samarin repeated D. A. Valuev's formulation of 1845. The gist of Valuev's views in which Samarin concurred was that Russia could benefit from the West's "science, its lessons and its experiences," but that it was time for the Russians to give thought to the problem of how to "work out by ourselves and from within ourselves the inner principles of our moral and intellectual life." It was no longer right for Russia to accept convictions "together with the latest fashion from Paris or a [philosophical] system from Germany." The Russians must not be disturbed that through Peter the Great's work they received the "possession of the Western world," since it in turn had received the "inheritance of the ancient world." To take advantage of the "lessons and experiences" of the West, and to become acquainted with this "more educated world was for Russia unquestionably a necessity," but what it would actually accept was "presented for our choice."[58]

Belinsky and Kavelin stressed in *Sovremennik* the importance for Russia of the universal and the "human" (*chelovecheskoe*). It was nobler and worthier than the narrowly national. Samarin accepted these "benign counsels," but was concerned about the difficulty of "sorting out" the "human" and universal from the national. Must we take the "universally human on faith" he asked; and who is to determine what is "universally human"? The Catholic church, he pointed out, is convinced that its teachings "are unconditionally true for all times and all nations," while Frenchmen during the eighteenth century held that the "French language is the language of mankind," and that "French mores are decidedly universal." Samarin's comment was, "We believe neither the one nor the other."[59] It is not clear what answers Belinsky and Kavelin gave to these questions.

Along with young Samarin's considerable knowledge of Western societies and institutions, along with his not insignificant readings in the Western literatures, and in Russian history, and his adroitness as a polemicist, went a propensity for fostering striking illusions about the common Russian people, the *narod*. His reply to Belinsky displays an early endorsement of Slavophil populism based upon uncritical and often unqualified adulation of the *narod*. This early populism was in turn to remain one of Slavophilism's most enduring and contagious myths. Samarin's convictions about the *narod* were sustained by the constant and often explicit comparisons and contrasts between Russia and the West. The compulsion in the men of the thirties and forties to measure Russia against the West, although by no means new, has remained a primary feature in Russian intellectual-ideological life ever since. This was true of both Slavophils and Westerners as they ranged over a wide cultural spectrum that often brought them not merely to disagreements but also to opposite conclusions.

Viewing the common Russian people, the peasantry, not as a vast mass, much of it in the clutches of serfdom, but as a people in the Rousseavian garb of undefiled, noble rustics, Samarin defends the Russian attitude. The Russians, he says,

do not feel toward it [*narod*] the inherited historical disdain with which the [Western] medieval aristocracy looked upon it. We are not contaminated with the calculating egotism and the predilection for formal legalism of the Western middle class. In response to the groans of the hungry we do not come down upon a dead letter. We are separated from the people, but not because we deliberately severed our interests from their welfare; rather, because there was a moment in our history when the welfare of our whole land demanded this separation as an all-national sacrifice.

This and more, Samarin conveniently attributed to Peter the Great, but that was apparently not sufficient salve for his gentry conscience. And so we see him early in his Slavophil career adopt the view that the impoverished, enserfed, and abused Russian peasantry, the *narod,* was the paragon of

Christian and human virtues, including humility, wisdom, and nobility of character.

Speaking not only for himself but for the gentry in general, Samarin says: "We do not understand the people, and for this reason we have little trust in them. Ignorance — that is the source of our errors." The way in which the gentry could remedy this was to get to know the people, but first "we must learn to love it."[60] Then the gentry could draw close to the people. Why was it necessary for the privileged, educated, affluent gentry, by the mid-1840s in some respects quite Westernized (and this was true of Samarin himself as well as of the other Slavophils), to want closeness and rapprochement with the illiterate *narod*? Fear of peasant revolts, economic self-interest? Perhaps, but while such selfish motives cannot be excluded, if they alone were behind the Slavophil attitude toward the people, Samarin and his friends would have called for government vigilance and greater repression of the *narod*, and it should be kept in mind that Russia at the time was more than 90 percent rural. Instead, Samarin exhorts the gentry to go to the countryside to learn, for

> the people has preserved in itself a kind of healthy consciousness of the equilibrium between subjective demands and the rights of reality, a consciousness that has been muffled in us by the one-sided development of the individual person [*lichnost'*]. To the people's unclouded reason, the edifying lessons of life come directly and unobstructed. The people has access to the meaning of suffering and the gift of self-sacrifice. All this cannot be taught and bought, but is immediately communicated from one who has it to one who does not have it.[61]

There can scarcely be any doubt that Samarin saw the need for rapprochement between the gentry and the Russian peasantry primarily in educational terms — that is, in terms of the wisdom of Christian living and *vospitanie*, not as *obrazovanie* or formal schooling, which, particularly when tinged with Western ideas, leads to the "one-sided development of individuality." As pointed out earlier, Samarin conceived, at least as early as 1846, the Russian Slavophil way of life as being firmly established on the twin principles in his mind closely related, of Christian togetherness or brotherhood, and communality, historically and socially embodied in the *mir* and *obshchina*. And these he saw preserved in the Russian village.

On March 5, 1849, Samarin was detained for twelve days in the SS. Peter and Paul Fortress in St. Petersburg. The arrest was caused by his *Letters from Riga*, which he wrote as a result of his concern with the Baltic question that so occupied his mind during the period 1846–1849. Much biographical information covering this period is given by Iurii's brother Dmitry in his long introduction to the two-part volume 7 of Samarin's *Works*, his *Letters from Riga*, dated May-June 1848, and his *History of Riga*. Nol'de in his biography of Samarin also provides a pertinent discussion of the period, and more

recently Calder has summarized these and other events from Samarin's biography.[62] Here, as in the preceding three studies, the concern is with
Slavophil ideas, Samarin's primarily, and not with a comprehensive literary
biography.

The *Letters from Riga,* which were written during Samarin's two-year
residence in Riga beginning in July 1846, could not have passed the censorship and were therefore circulated in handwritten form. They reached,
among others, Count A. A. Suvorov, the governor-general of the province,
whom Samarin considered strongly pro-German, Count P. D. Kiselev, and
Count L. A. Perovsky, the minister of the interior. Samarin gave Count
Perovsky copies of the letters when he finished his Riga assignment and
returned to St. Petersburg in the summer of 1848. Suvorov was very indignant over the letters, and when he complained about them to Perovsky and
got nowhere, he went directly to the tsar.[63] Samarin was arrested on March
17, 1849, and after his release, Nicholas II summoned him to the palace for
a fatherly scolding. Samarin, remorseful, stood before the tsar, who asked
him, "Do you know what consequence chapter five of your work could have?
A new December 14."[64]

What did chapter five of the *Letters from Riga* contain that prompted the
tsar to arrest the son of a prominent and favored gentry family? The answer
involves many complex issues. It must be remembered that Russia's central
problem at the end of the 1840s was the emancipation of the serfs, not industrialism and its possible consequences; industrialism had not yet made a
deep impression in Russia, although the economic, social, and political
problems that it created in the West were, of course, felt and appreciated by
the Russian intelligentsia. But in addition to these new and often intersecting problems, the Ottoman empire in the Balkans was shaken, with Serbs
and Greeks on the way to independence, and the West was in the grip of
powerful nationalism. This was soon to result in the unification of Italy and
Germany, and to overflow into a new wave of European imperialism. Contrary to some predictions that the social economic question born of modern
industrialism would overshadow and even displace the national question,
this did not happen in the nineteenth century, and not even in the twentieth.
Side by side with the "social" question, nationalism in various guises remains
a potent factor in the lives of people and nations to the present.

In this respect Samarin and his fellow Slavophils were very much in the
current of the times, for Russian nationalism, an important ingredient of
Moscow Slavophilism, was soon forcefully demonstrated when the British
and French invaded the Crimea. Nationalism seems to be unfailingly
capable of arousing a counternationalism in the aggrieved party or nation,
as in the case in Russia during the Napoleonic wars. In Samarin's *Letters
from Riga,* the nationalistic adversary, as he saw the problem, was the Baltic
German gentry. This did not please the tsar, who was mostly German him-

self, nor could it have pleased those of German descent in high administrative positions such as Count K. V. Nesselrode, the minister of foreign affairs; Count A. Kh. Benckendorff, head of the Third Section; General P. A. Kleinmichel, minister of communications; and General L. V. Dubel't, who was in command of the corps of the gendarmerie.[65]

But Samarin made it quite clear in the opening pages of his *Letters from Riga* that the problem in the Baltic provinces was not merely that between German and Russian. It also involved class antagonisms between the landowning gentry, mostly of German descent, and the landless peasantry, and between the Lutheran and Catholic gentry and the Orthodox *narod*. In addition to these intersecting issues there was the problem of the rising national aspirations of the indigenous populations of Latvians, Estonians, and Lithuanians. The tsar, looking at the problems of the Baltic provinces from his fixed position of self-preservation, that is, the safeguarding of his regime and the status quo, was perhaps justified in seeing in Samarin's *Letters from Riga* a possible incitement to rebellion.

In his *Letters from Riga,* Samarin went back to the beginning of the thirteenth century. In chapter five he reached the contemporary scene, and it is this chapter that is of most interest in connection with Samarin's Slavophilism,, and with Moscow Slavophilism in general.[66] Despite Samarin's considerable study and research on the subject, he cast himself as much in the role of the Slavophil publicist as of that of the historian, a calling for which he again displayed considerable gifts. His pro-Russian, pro-Orthodox, pro-peasant, pro-Slavophil bias is apparent in his treatise as well as throughout the six volumes that he devoted to the Baltic littoral during his life.

As with all Slavophil writings, religion and ideology are mixed in Samarin's writings. To be Russian and Slav, the Slavophils thought, was to be Christian and Orthodox. Theology and cultural-historical questions were not separate from each other. For the sake of convenience and organization of material, I have had to make some arbitrary separations; I discuss the peasant problem and the emancipation question alone, and the theological-religious questions also alone (both in Part two). In terms of the extent of the work, Samarin devoted the most space to the problem of the Baltic littoral and Russia's Western borderlands (the second largest topic in terms of space is that of religious and theological issues, and the third is that of the peasant question and the emancipation of the serfs). Volume 7, part one, of Samarin's *Works* consists of the Riga letters and the history of Riga; part two is on Riga's class structure, 1200–1845. Volumes 8, 9, and 10 contain his extensive polemical involvements on the problem of Russia's northwestern and Western borderlands (volume 10 is particularly rich in historical material; these three volumes, consisting of six issues (*vypuski*) and over 1,500 pages, were published abroad from 1867 to 1875, on the well-founded assumption that they would not have passed the censorship at home.

Samarin's attitude toward the Baltic Germans represents a complex of ethnic, cultural, and religious elements. The great majority of the Slavs, including the three major ethnic groups in Russia, Great, Little, and White Russians, and most of the Balkan Slavs, Bulgarians, Macedonians, Serbs, and Montenegrins were Orthodox. The Poles were Catholic, the largest Catholic Slav nation, and their presence, contiguous to Russia, confronted the Slavophils with a most uncomfortable riddle which they never solved. As Catholics, the Poles could not be included in the Slavophil world, and as Slavs they could not be completely excluded. The Slavophils thought the Poles had gone wrong a thousand years earlier when they accepted Christianity from the West instead of from the East.

The Baltic Germans, on the other hand, were not only non-Slav, they were Lutherans, and Lutheranism was, of course, a much more recent development than Polish Catholicism. It was true that Russia's claim on the Baltic littoral was of relatively recent origin, dating from the reign of Peter the Great, to the early eighteenth century, when it was incorporated into the Russian state, and it included the non-Slav and non-Orthodox Lithuanians, Estonians, Latvians, and Finns. But Samarin regarded the claim as permanently settled; the problems, therefore, were Russia's legitimate concern.

Samarin's two-year stay in Riga was his true initiation into the broad, fundamental, and intricate peasant question. Although serfdom in the Baltic provinces had nominally ended in 1819, the lot of the peasantry there remained miserable, and Samarin took their side as against the Baltic Germans. This approach to the Baltic peasant problem coincided with the activities of the Russian Orthodox church, which had already initiated missionary work in Latvia and Estonia.[67]

Summing up the problem confronting the peasants of Lifland, Samarin pointed out the recent (1841–1846) intensive but fruitless activities of the local gentry and bureaucracy to improve their lot, and then pointed out three main categories of problems that had to be solved before improvement could come. Without specifying amount or conditions, he says that the peasants must be given the right of "hereditary use" of lands from the landlords' estates; at the same time the maximum of peasant obligations to the landlord must be accurately determined, and on the "demand of the peasants" their obligations to the landlord must be changed from work requirements to quit rent (*obrok*); finally, "gentry arbitrariness" must be curbed and controlled by laws from the "supreme authority."[68] This provision was essential as long as the local administration, police, and court system were in the hands of those who insisted on their right to the inviolability of the land. Here we see Samarin, the moderate reformer, standing up for the Lifland peasantry, many of whom seem to have been Orthodox (and largely, it seems, Old

Believers), against the gentry class to which he himself belonged, who were, in this case, German and Lutheran. Thus the socio-economic, the national, and the religious issues were fused in such a manner that it is virtually impossible to isolate and measure accurately the weight and importance of each component.

It is not surprising in the circumstances of the time that Samarin's criticism of the Baltic German gentry was construed as criticism of the Germans in general, and that his views and opinions did not go unchallenged, first by the tsar and others and later by such as Julius Eckardt, Woldemar von Bock, and Carl Schirren.[69] But it is one of the paradoxes of Moscow Slavophilism that Samarin, who temperamentally and intellectually was perhaps better prepared than the other Moscow Slavophils to know and appreciate German culture, and who seems to have enjoyed his frequent trips to Germany and the West, should appear to be the most critical of the Germans. Yet his apprehension (especially later, in the 1860s and 1870s) that Germany might be a threat to Russia not merely in the Baltic provinces but in the very heart of Russia, was more farsighted and prophetic than speculative or alarmist.

Samarin's approach to the study of the history of Riga and the Baltic borderlands was careful and systematic, and intense. His painstaking research, uncharacteristic of the Slavophils, occupied all his free time while he was in Riga. He wrote to Konstantin Aksakov from Riga, November 10, 1847: "Although it is ridiculous to repeat one and the same thing, I am literally swamped with work. I work day and night till three or four in the morning."[70] Since after the arrest of F. V. Chizhov in April 1847, the government was particularly suspicious of the Moscow Slavophils, Samarin conveyed most of his impressions about Riga by word of mouth, during two brief visits to Moscow, one in November 1846, the second in December 1847, when he was in the midst of his feverish studies in Riga.[71] Dmitry Samarin summed up the principal topics on which his brother briefed his Moscow friends in person as, first, his impressions of the Ia. V. Khanykov Commission on which he served in Riga, connecting this with the "question of the emancipation of the serfs in Russia." He also informed them about the peasant question in Lifland and about the role of the Landtag convoked in September 1847; about the going over of the Letts to Orthodoxy; about the "condition of the Helots in which the Russians in the Baltic provinces found themselves," and about the struggle the commission would have with the "local German public authority etc."

There is no reason to question this summary of Dmitry Samarin's, nor his conclusion that his brother in his Baltic assignment was dealing with "practical questions, proving the necessity of cooperating with the government in their solution."[72] This brief quotation focuses attention at once on three major Slavophil concerns. Samarin's Moscow friends were doubtless in wholehearted agreement with him in his pro-Russian, pro-Orthodox stand.

Next they were confronted, early in the evolution of Moscow Slavophilism, with the possibility, and in Samarin's view necessity, of descending from the levels of theology and ideology to that of reform and action; and finally they had to reconsider and modify their attitude toward the government of Nicholas I. Although Samarin had entered government service against his wishes, he was nonetheless the most progovernment of the Early Moscow Slavophils, and his pro-Russian, pro-Orthodox stand tended to soften Aksakov's antipathy toward the government, which was, after all, the only instrument capable of implementing pro-Russian policies in the Baltic littoral.

After Samarin returned to Moscow in July 1848 with his final, clear, handwritten copy of his *Letters from Riga,* he circulated the manuscript confidentially among his friends, Khomiakov, the Aksakovs, and the Sverbeevs. He also made it available to Metropolitan Filaret, A. P. Ermolov and Count S. G. Stroganov. Dmitry Samarin is not unduly partial to his brother when he says that since there was no "political press" in Russia at the time, and since there was no knowledge among the Russian public as to the state of affairs in the Baltic provinces, Iurii's Riga letters "aroused great interest." It was, he continues, the "first attempt to present for consideration from a social, public point of view one of the large questions of our internal policy." Iurii's friends, including "K. S. Aksakov, completely shared the view on the Baltic question that runs through the letters."[73] Metropolitan Filaret responded favorably, and expressed the desire to raise funds for a Russian trade school in Riga. Ermolov and Count Stroganov were appreciative but noncommittal. Government circles in St. Petersburg, at least those close to the tsar, were alarmed and indignant. The Third Section thought it best to put Samarin in prison to give him time to think things over. Samarin's brief incarceration does not seem to have changed his views about the Baltic German gentry, however, nor about any of the problems that he became concerned with during his two years in Riga. That assignment focused his attention on the peasant problem in the Baltic area, and, even more significantly from the point of view of Moscow Slavophilism, it turned his attention to the question of the emancipation of the serfs throughout the vast Russian empire.

Notes

1. The complete title of the first review in Samarin's Works is "Tarantas. Putevye vpechatleniia. Sochinenie grafa V. A. Solloguba," first published in *Moskovskii sbornik* (Moscow, 1846), pp. 543–568, see Samarin, *Sochineniia,* I, 1–27. The second, much longer, is under the title "O mneniakh *Sovremennika,* istoricheskhikh i literaturnykh," first published in Pogodin's

Moskvitianin, 1847, no. 2; Samarin, *Sochineniia*, I, 28–108. In my discussion here I have used the two reviews as they appear in Samarin's *Sochineniia*.

2. For Kavelin's essay, see K. Soldatenkov and N. Shchepkin, eds., *Sochineniia K. Kavelina*, 4 vols. (Moscow, 1859), I, 305–379 (hereafter cited as Kavelin, *Sochineniia*), for Belinsky's, see Belinsky, *Sochineniia*, III, 641–683. Belinsky's friend, the well-to-do liberal Westerner V. P. Botkin, writing to Belinsky from Moscow on November 25, 1847, said that Samarin published in *Moskvitianin* "some sort of Slav manifesto" in response to *Sovremennik*. "In reality it is the same mystical-social fog." *Literaturnoe nasledstvo* (Moscow, 1955), LXII, 40.

3. Vasilii Davydov, "Samarin-opolchenets. (Iz vospominanii ego druzhinnogo nachal'nika po opolcheniiu 1855g.)," *Russkii arkhiv*, 1877, no. 5, pp. 42–43.

4. See A. A. Dunin, ed., "Materialy po istorii russkoi literatury i kul'tury. I. S. Aksakov v Iaroslave. Po neizdannym pis'mam k nemu S. T. Aksakova i ego sem'i," *Russkaia mysl'*, 1915, book 8, p. 117.

5. See S. A. Vengerov in Brokhaus Efron, *Entsiklopedicheskii slovar'*, St. Petersburg, 1900, LX, 757b.

6. Tsamutali in his factual and perceptive review of the Samarin-Kavelin controversy cites Samarin's admission that there was much that was sensible in Kavelin's view of Peter the Great's reforms. This, Tsamutali says, was more than the other Slavophils were willing to admit. See A. N. Tsamutali, *Bor'ba techenii v russkoi istoriografii vo vtoroi polovine XIX veka* (Leningrad, 1977), p. 73; Samarin, *Sochineniia*, I, 62–63.

7. Samarin, *Sochineniia*, I, 11–12, 13, 15.

8. Ibid., p. 9.

9. Ibid., pp. 9, 10.

10. Ibid., p. 27.

11. "O mneniakh *Sovremennika*," in ibid., pp. 28–30. 12. *Sovremennik*, published in St. Petersburg from 1836 to 1866, underwent a number of significant changes in personnel, contributors, and orientation. Late in 1846 its publishers were N. A. Nekrasov and I. I. Panaev. Its official editor was the "liberal" Professor A. V. Nikitenko, member of the St. Petersburg censorship committee. These were not radical Westerners, but the guiding spirit and "soul" of *Sovremennik* was the ardent Westerner Belinsky. In addition to Belinsky, those who backed it in 1846–1847, and who can be counted as radical Westerners, were Herzen and N. P. Ogarev. But there were also a good many contributors of liberal or vaguely defined ideological persuasions. This category included Ivan Turgenev, I. A. Goncharov, T. N. Granovsky, Kavelin, V. P. Botkin, P. V. Anenkov, S. M. Solov'ev, V. I. Dal', and others. See A. G. Dement'ev et al, eds., *Russkaia periodicheskaia pechat'* (*1702–1894*) (Moscow, 1959), pp. 240–242.

13. Samarin, *Sochineniia*, II, 30.

14. Kavelin, *Sochineniia,* I, 312.

15. Ibid., see, for instance, pp. 311, 315, 321–324, 326, 330, 331–332, 336, 344, 347.

16. Ibid., p. 312.

17. Ibid., pp. 313, 318, 323. I have in most instances translated the Russian *lichnost'* as "individual," for it seems that the present Russian *individualizm* had not come into use at that time. (Dal's dictionary, 1863–1866, does not give it, Ushakov's of 1935 does). "Individualism" is the opposite of "commune and communalism," but since communalism does not preclude the development of personality (*lichnost'*), I have at times rendered *lichnost'* as "personality." This is a matter of context and of "sensing," not of precise or unmistakable equivalency.

18. Kavelin considered the sense of personality and individuality as being an expression of man's "inner invisible spiritual world" of which in pre-Christian times there was only a vague and imperfect realization. But with the coming of Christianity, man's inner, spiritual world was "placed infinitely higher than the external, material world." Perhaps somewhat unexpectedly from one arguing against the commune, he says, "The first Christian communes represent a variegated mixture of people of different tribes and classes, rendered equal and united by the truth, by a thirst to join in heavenly spiritual life. Thus in early Christianity arose for the first time the idea of the infinite unconditional dignity of the *human being and of the human individual.*" Ibid., pp. 316–317.

19. Ibid., pp. 318, 320, 369, 370.

20. Ibid., pp. 325–327.

21. Ibid., p. 331.

22. Ibid., 337, 339.

23. Ibid., pp. 364, 369.

24. Samarin, *Sochineniia,* I, 34–35. Recently Tsamutali, using the same passage with a couple of excisions, has stressed the basic disagreement between Samarin and Kavelin on the relationship between the individual and society. Thus he states that Samarin, in contrast to Kavelin, "advances Christianity as the principal force in historical development, liberating the individual person for [the sake of] its complete subordination to the religious commune, the church. This idea of Samarin's . . . is the most important and most essential element in the Slavophil concept of the history of Russia. Samarin was the first to state this thesis with great clarity." See Tsamutali, *Bor'ba techenii,* p. 66.

25. Samarin, *Sochineniia,* I, 52.

26. Ibid., pp. 63, 64.

27. Ibid., p. 51.

28. Ibid., p. 52. For Samarin's more detailed criticism of Kavelin's position, see Tsamutali, *Bor'ba techenii,* pp. 65–74.

29. Tsamutali conjectures, and with good reason, that with respect to the "close interlacing of the communal principle with the Christian idea" young Samarin was speaking for all the early Slavophils. Tsamutali, *Bor'ba techenii,* pp. 74–75.

30. Samarin, *Sochineniia,* XII, 147, 156.

31. Ibid., I, 37, 39–41. For further details about Samarin on George Sand and the Slav world, see Tsamutali, *Bor'ba techenii,* pp. 68–69.

32. In a letter to Konstantin Aksakov, Samarin added a postscript in which he said, "I am writing an article about Stein's book." This letter, dated by Dmitry Samarin to 1843, was probably written in the summer of that year. Iurii finished the essay review of Stein's work toward the end of the year as is apparent from another letter to Aksakov dated Kazan, December 31, 1843. This review, however, as mentioned earlier, does not seem to have survived. Samarin, *Sochineniia,* I, 42, 46.

33. Quoted by William L. Langer, "The Social Question," in Allan Mitchell and Istvan Deak, eds., *Everyman in Europe: Essays in Social History* (Englewood Cliffs, N.J., 1974), II, 98.

34. By the middle 1840s the dismal working conditions in the industrial West were becoming well known among the Russian intelligentsia, including the Slavophils. Western utopian socialism, particularly French, attempting to cope with the new problems as pointed out, was also well known. Although Russia was scarcely beginning to feel the new industrialism on its own soil, and had as its foremost problem the emancipation of the serfs, some Russians, including the Slavophils, were beginning to consider solutions to the West's industrial problems in anticipation that they might become their own. Thus was born the well-known Petrashevsky circle in 1845. The literature on this circle is extensive, and even cursory perusal of it is beyond the scope of this study. It should be sufficient to note here that its founder was Mikhail Vasil'evich Butashevich-Petrashevsky (1821–1866), in whose home in St. Petersburg young members of the gentry and the classless intelligentsiia (*raznochintsy*) gathered. Its best-known adherent was the young Dostoevsky. But among its members were M. E. Saltykov, N. S. Kashkin, A. N. Pleshcheev, V. N. Maikov, S. F. Durov, N. Ia. Danilevsky, N. A. Speshnev, V. A. Miliutin, and others, counting at one time up to fifty. Its ideological inspiration came from the works of Proudhon, Fourier, Feuerbach, Comte, the Decembrists, Belinsky, and others. From this circle emerged several smaller circles, one led by Shchedrin, Miliutin, and Maikov. The Petrashevsky circle came to an end in April 1849 when the government arrested its members, including Dostoevsky. Herzen, who was in Western Europe at the time, as already concentrating on his "Russian socialism" based on the Russian peasant commune. For summaries of the activities and the written output of the Petrashevtsy, see J. L. Evans, *The Petrashevskij*

Circle, 1845–1849 (The Hague-Paris, 1974); Leonid Rasky, *Sotsial'nye voz-zreniia Petrashevtsev* (Leningrad, 1927).

35. Samarin, *Sochineniia*, I, 64.

36. Ibid., p. 43.

37. Born a serf in 1805 on an estate of Count N. P. Sheremetev, young Nikitenko was fortunate to have a father who, although a serf, attracted attention with his singing voice, and who studied French, among other subjects, in the estate school. Nikitenko was taught by his father, but his serf status kept him out of the Voronezh gimnaziia. Attracting attention with his keen mind and self-improvement, he was elected in 1824 secretary of the Russian Bible Society. Before the end of the year, on the initiative of Prince A. N. Golitsyn, minister of education, Count Sheremetev granted Nikitenko his freedom. From then until his death in 1877, Nikitenko led a distinguished and eventful life. As a student at the University of St. Petersburg, he first concentrated on political economy and Adam Smith's views on national wealth; early in the 1830s he changed to Russian literature, and received his doctorate in 1837. In the meantime he was appointed to the St. Petersburg censorship committee (1833–1848), served as a professor in his alma mater, and briefly as editor of *Sovremennik* in the middle 1840s, and again in 1861 as editor of another journal. He was elected to the Imperial Academy of Sciences in 1853. Perhaps his greatest achievement was his two-volume memoir-diary, published after his death, which he began to keep at the age of fourteen and continued to the end of his life. See M. Lemke, ed., *A. V. Nikitenko. Moia povest' o samom sebe i o tom chemu svidetel' v zhizni byl. Zapiski i Dnevnik (1804–1877gg.)* (St. Petersburg 1904–1905). From the fairly extensive literature on Nikitenko, see A. P. "Nikitenko, Aleksander Vasil'evich," *Russkii biograficheskii slovar'* (St. Petersburg, 1914), XI, 296–305; B. P. Zotov, "Liberal'nyi tsenzor i professor-pessimist (biograficheskii ocherk), *Istoricheskii vestnik*, 1893, no. 10, pp. 194–210; no. 11, pp. 511–558; no. 12, pp. 800–832.

38. I gave some attention to this subject in my earlier studies and shall return to it briefly later on in this one. Recently, V. A. Koshelev raised the question in his already cited *Esteticheskie i literaturnye vozzreniia russkikh Slavianofilov 1840–1850-e gody.* (Leningrad, 1984); see, for instance, pp. 11, 29.

39. Samarin, *Sochineniia*, I, 60, 65–66.

40. Ibid., pp. 80–81.

41. It is difficult to identify Belinsky's socialism with any one of the many forms of socialisms that existed in his day. He knew of a variety of French utopian socialisms. Thus in the 1830s the Saint-Simonism of the Herzen circle most probably reached him, and in 1837 he was critical of Lamennais's *Les paroles d'un croyant*. Nechaeva states that he could have heard about

Pierre Leroux from Herzen, Ketcher, Annenkov, and Granovsky, and particularly through Panaev's translation of Leroux's articles. From 1842 on, Belinsky encountered Leroux's ideas in the works of George Sand, and could have read them himself in the original, as by then he is said to have read French. George Sand soon evoked his strong admiration. In the middle forties, among other views and ideas circulating in the rich ideological atmosphere in St. Petersburg and Moscow, in spite of the censorship, were those of Auguste Comte. In this case Belinsky's friend V. P. Botkin, "with his propaganda of positivism," no doubt caught Belinsky's ear. And in the last complete year of his life (1847) Belinsky heard a good deal about the Petrashevsky circle, disagreeing, as we shall see, with V. N. Maikov, a young member of the group. See Nechaeva, *Belinsky,* pp. 35–37, 40, 54–58, 301, 307.

42. Belinsky not only had some familiarity with Western socialist thought of his time, but he knew through friends who read the German *Deutsche-Französische Jahrbücher* of 1844, to which Marx contributed. He was probably approving, as V.P. Botkin was, that the Hegelian dialectic was being adjusted to apply to "questions of practical life." He also may have been aware that P. V. Annenkov and N. I. Sazonov corresponded with Marx in the latter half of the 1840s, but as Reuel' suggested, these three moderates "were far from being receptive to the Marxist ideas." See A.L. Reuel' *Russkaia ekonomicheskaia mysl' 60–60-kh godov XIX veka i marksizm* (Moscow, 1956), pp. 180–183.

43. Belinsky, *Sochineniia,* III, 665–666.

44. Ibid., p. 653.

45. While during the middle 1840s the Slavophils in Moscow were searching for a way to embody the principle of communality and the historical and still functioning Russian peasant commune into their ideology, Herzen, after he left for the West in January 1847, incorporated the idea of the same peasant commune into his "Russian socialism." At the same time Westerners in St. Petersburg were considering a variety of Western European socialisms. Particularly rich in content on this subject is the serialized monograph by V. I. Semevsky, "M. V. Butashevich-Petrashevsky v Sibiri . . .," " *Golos minuvshego,* 1915, no. 1, pp. 66–87; no. 3, pp. 18–57; no. 5, pp. 43–84; no. 12, pp. 35–75; and 1916, no. 2, pp. 41–61; no. 3, pp. 48–68; no. 4, pp. 174–192.

46. H. H. Rowen, ed., *From Absolutism to Revolution, 1648–1848* (2d ed., New York, 1968), p. 306.

47. For Belinsky's more realistic appraisal of the weakness of Slavophil influence in Russia, see his letter to Kavelin of December 7, 1847. Belinsky, *Izbrannye pis'ma,* II, 380–381.

48. Aware of the vagueness of the lines separating West from East and of the cultural connotations of these designations, the Slavophils, first Dmitry

Valuev in 1845, and then Samarin made an effort to define the terms. Thus a little later Samarin says, the "East [*Vostok*] . . . means not China, not Islam, not the Tatars, but the Slav Orthodox world of the same ethnic group, the same faith with us, [and] made conscious of its unity and strength by the appearance of the Russian state. . . . The West means the Roman-German or Catholic-Protestant world." Samarin, *Sochineniia,* I, 98.

    49. Belinsky, *Sochineniia,* III, 641, 644, 654.

    50. Ibid., pp. 651, 652.

    51. Ibid., p. 659. As Mordovchenko and the other editors of Belinsky's *Izbrannye pis'ma* noticed, Belinsky disagreed with what he considered to be the "abstract cosmopolitanism" of V. N. Maikov, the bright young Westerner, who died in 1847 at the age of twenty-four. Belinsky's "revolutionary-democratic patriotism" was actually closer to the Slavophil position on this subject than to that of some of the more cosmopolitan Westerners. See Belinsky, *Izbrannye pis'ma,* II, 457.

    52. Belinsky, *Sochineniia,* III, 650.

    53. Belinsky's criticism of the Slavophils in his long letter to K. D. Kavelin, December 7, 1847, is condescending. He would not, he said, "stand on ceremony" either with the Kireevsky brothers, whom he did not know, or with Konstantin Aksakov, whom he knew well. "Where do you see Samarin's ability?" he asked Kavelin. Though Samarin was a young man of "knowledge and a many-sided education, who speaks several foreign languages, and who has read the best in them," he was also "a man of the world," who "has treated us, you and me, *du haut de sa grandeur* . . . and you reply to him on bended knee." Belinsky cautioned Kavelin not to be too quick to promote anyone to the ranks of talent and genius; Samarin, he declared, was "no better than the rest [of the Slavophils]; abomination arises from his articles." See Belinsky, *Sochineniia,* III, 679, and *Izbrannye pis'ma,* II, 378–380.

    54. Samarin, *Sochineniia,* I, 90.

    55. Ibid., pp. 91–92.

    56. Like the other Slavophils and Belinsky, Peter Kireevsky concurred in Pogodin's view that "there is a fundamental, striking difference between Western (Latin-Germanic) European history and our history." Subscribing to the Normanist theory of the origin of the Russian state, he also agreed that in the "West the states were founded on *conquest,* which did not exist in our case." But he objected to, and refuted, Pogodin's "gloomy and unjust" depiction of the ancient Russians. He could not understand how Pogodin could conceive of the ancient Russians as meek, peaceful, and resigned people who '*voluntarily submitted to whoever came along first,*" and "willingly accepted foreign lords" who "*conquered and held [them] in subjugation.*" Pogodin would find little to be proud of in this sort of history. Furthermore, "such a strange notion would be a unique and unprecedented phenomenon in the annals of the world, and we would find it difficult to think

with love of its [Russia's] past life." Kireevsky also reminded Pogodin of the exploits of Russian arms, saying, among other things, that "during the Tatar incursions not a single Russian town was captured without the most desperate resistance." See P. V. Kireevsky, "O drevnei russkoi istorii (Pis'mo k M. P. Pogodinu)," *Moskvitianin,* 1845, no. 1, pp. 11–14.

57. Belinsky, *Sochineniia,* III, 657–658. Nol'de sees Guizot as the principal source of the notion "that conquest played a tremendous role in the history of the West." See Nol'de, *Samarin,* p. 35.

58. Samarin, *Sochineniia,* I, 101–102.

59. Ibid., p. 103.

60. Ibid., p. 91.

61. Ibid., p. 92. In Moscow Khomiakov followed the reaction to Samarin's review-articles. About those critical of Samarin he wrote to Shevyrev in 1847, "[They say that] Samarin's articles are good, but that they are dark and unfounded while Kavelin's [article], although not as well written, is solid and consistent." See *Russkii arkhiv,* 1878, no. 5, p. 60.

62. See Dimitry Samarin, ed., Introduction to Samarin, *Sochineniia,* VII, part 1, i–cxxxv; Nol'de, *Samarin,* pp. 37–49; Calder et al., eds., *The Correspondence of Iu. Samarin and Baroness Rahden, 1861–1876,* pp. 3–29.

63. For Samarin's dissatisfaction with Suvorov's attitude and policies, see Samarin, *Sochineniia,* VII, part 1, 103–105, 111, 142, 158; for Dmitry Samarin's resentment of Suvorov's "Teutonomania" (*Tevtomaniia*), see p. lxxiv.

64. For an account of this episode in Samarin's career from one who was close to government circles at the time, see Nikitenko, *Diary,* I, 390–391. See also Dmitry Samarin's comments in Samarin, *Sochineniia,* VII, part 1, pp. LXXXIII–LXXXVI. A similar version is given by V. P. Zotov, "Liberal'nyi tsenzor i professor-pessimist," *Istoricheskii vestnik,* 1893, no. 11, p. 551.

65. Dmitry Samarin states that in the "high government circles only L. A. Perovsky and Count P. D. Kiselev openly acknowledged the correctness of [Iurii's] view on the Baltic question." The fact that the letters were circulated in longhand created an aura of secrecy and subversion about them which did not help Samarin in his confrontation with government officials. See Samarin *Sochineniia,* VII, part 1, lxiii.

66. The complexities of the problem of the Baltic littoral are obviously beyond the scope of the present work. Recently Professor E. C. Thaden, who has been concerned for some years with Russian and Baltic problems, contributed to and edited, a collective work under the title, *Russification in the Baltic Provinces and Finland, 1855–1914* (Princeton, N.J., 1981). This large volume is a cooperative work of five American academic specialists on the Baltic nations. E. C. Thaden's contribution, in addition to the Introduction, is "Part One: The Russian Government," pp. 15–108. This is followed by M. H. Haltzel's "Part Two: The Baltic Germans," pp. 111–204; A.

Plakans's "Part Three: The Latvians," pp. 206–284; T. U. Raun's "Part Four: The Estonians," pp. 285–354; and C. L. Lundin's "Part Five: Finland," pp. 355–457. Although the studies, as indicated in the title, are concerned with the period after 1855, they also contain information on Samarin's views on the Baltic problem at the end of the 1840s as well as during the 1860s and later. The individual studies are supplied with up-to-date bibliographies. The term "Russification" often connotes intimidation, compulsion, and force. Historically, however, this has not necessarily been so, and while this subject cannot be here explored it might be worthwhile to mention that the process of Russification has at times been voluntary, and perhaps spontaneous, as when, for instance, individual West Europeans went to Russia and chose to stay there. For some examples, see Sir Robert Bruce Lockhart, "The Scots in Russia," *Penguin Russian Review,* 1948, no. 4, pp. 65–78.

67. Haltzel has recently stated: "The liberation of the peasantry in Estland in 1816, in Kurland in 1817, and in Livland in 1819, actually resulted in the worsening of the peasant lot "because they were given personal freedom without land." As he explains, "In 1836 an Orthodox bishopric was founded in Riga to put pressure on its large and influential colony of Russian Old Believers"; in the same year an Orthodox seminary was established in Pskov and its students were taught the Latvian and Estonian languages. But there seem to be no figures on the relative strength of the Orthodox population of these provinces. See Thaden, ed., *Russification,* pp. 5–6, 122; see also two works by E. C. Thaden: *Conservative Nationalism in Nineteenth-Century Russia* (Seattle, Wash., 1964), p. 195, and "Samarin's 'Okrainy Rossii' and Official Policy in the Baltic Provinces," *Russian Review,* 1974, no. 4, pp. 406, 409.

68. Samarin, *Sochineniia,* X, 429–430.

69. Samarin's correspondence with the German-born Baroness von Rahden, which began only in 1864, did not suffer; but all these matters refer to a later period, well beyond the 1861 cutoff date of this book on early Moscow Slavophilism. Haltzel gives a good summary of the German response to Samarin and Samarin's "Social Darwinist position" in Thaden, ed., *Russification,* pp. 126–128.

70. Samarin, *Sochineniia,* XII, 198. From a letter from Samarin to A. N. Popov from Riga, May 4, 1847, we know that he wrote at the time two memoranda on the authority of public prosecutors and lawyers over peasant courts, a work on the Old Believers in Riga (which does not seem to have survived), and a historical review of the Baltic region. He also wrote the eighty-page review of Kavelin's, Nikitenko's, and Belinsky's works, and the history of the city class structure of Riga (*Letters from Riga* and *History of Riga*), about which he had "gathered much material," including "evidence from German chroniclers about the peaceful spread of the Orthodox faith in Lifland up to the coming of the Germans." Ibid., pp. 282–283.

71. For Dmitry Samarin's account of Iurii's activity in Riga see ibid., VII, part 1, xxxv–xxxvi.

72. Ibid., pp. xxxvi–xxxviii.

73. Ibid., p. L.

8

The 1850s: The Slavophils on Science, Technology, and Farming—Koshelev

When the news reached Russia of the overthrow of Louis-Philippe in February 1848, and of the spread of revolutionary fervor eastward, the tsar was ready to react. The decrees on censorship and thought control that were already in force were tightened and supplemented by new measures, thus initiating the "dark seven years" of the reign of Nicholas I. The Slavophils were among the prime targets of suspicion and repression. In accordance with this new policy the government ordered the arrest of F. V. Chizhov in April 1848, then of Samarin on March 5, 1849, and immediately following this, on March 18, of Ivan Aksakov (1823–1886).[1] In spite of these events in 1852 the Slavophils published, under Ivan Aksakov's editorship, the first number of a projected series of four Slavophil symposiums, but again the government struck, and more issues were banned. These were discouraging and perhaps inhibiting developments, but the Slavophils were not intimidated. For the remaining years of the reign of Nicholas I, what could not be published at home was occasionally published abroad, as in the case of Khomiakov's theological essays. Furthermore, because of government repression the Slavophils exchanged thoughts and views in their valuable, uncensored correspondence, much of which has survived.

Were this study to aspire to a thorough and complete coverage of Early Moscow Slavophilism, one of the leading candidates for separate, individual treatment would be Aleksander Ivanovich Koshelev (1806–1883). As the year of his birth indicates, he belonged to the older generation of Slavophils, and in his youth was associated with Ivan Kireevsky in the Society of the Lovers of Wisdom in the 1820s in Moscow. His father, Ivan Rodionovich, coming from an old gentry family, entered Oxford University at seventeen and studied there for three years. Later he married Dar'ia Nikolaevna Desjardins, who was born in Russia of a French immigrant family, one of a small but significant minority of Westerners who willingly became "Russified." As the mother of Aleksander Ivanovich she imparted to him an appreciation of Western culture and literature, which he never seems to have given up.

From Koshelev's *Memoirs,* which he began to write in 1869, we know that he and Ivan Kireevsky became close friends in the early 1820s while they were being tutored by several of the same Moscow professors.[2] About five years later Koshelev met Khomiakov in Moscow; the ideological tie that would hold them together in the 1840s and 1850s had not yet evolved, but they moved in the same social circles and had many friends in common. In 1826 Koshelev, after receiving a diploma from the University of Moscow, joined the staff of the Ministry of Foreign Affairs in St. Petersburg. In June 1831 he left Russia on the first of more than a dozen trips to Western Europe.

In Germany Koshelev met Schleiermacher, and F. K. von Savigny; in Weimar he was invited in 1831 to the home of the eighty-two-year-old Goethe. In Geneva, where he went next, he met, among others, the Italian statesman and economist P. L. E. Rossi (later, minister of the interior to Pius IX), whose lectures in French Koshelev described as superb. He also attended lectures by outstanding professors in botany and chemistry, some in the lecture hall, and some in the homes of the professors, but no one impressed him as much as Rossi. Rossi's lectures on law and political economy (he reviewed the doctrines of Say, Malthus, and Ricardo) confirmed in young Koshelev "genuine liberalism ... which is seldom found among us, for among our so-called liberals one meets people who for the most part are imbued with Western doctrinairism, and who are guided more by feelings and rules of despotism than by true love of freedom and free thought."[3] He gave much credit to Rossi for his later work in the cause of the emancipation of the serfs and reform in Poland.

From Switzerland Koshelev went to Paris, where once again he was received in socially and intellectually prominent circles. A letter from Rossi introduced him to Guizot, Cousin, Michelet, Thierry, and others. At the end of May he arrived in London. Here, thanks to his impressive connections, he was present in the House of Lords for the passage of the Reform Bill of 1832.[4] Thus in a single year the young Russian aristocrat and future Slavophil was exposed to some of the best Western minds in theory, literature, and scholarship. All this doubtless flattered him, and possibly fed his vanity. But neither then nor later in his life, after additional trips to the West and increased admiration for some of its cultural and technological achievements was he ready to turn his back on Russia.

Dissatisfied with his poor English, on his return to Russia, Koshelev applied himself to the task of improving his knowledge; he says in his *Memoirs,* "in several months I learned English so that I was able to read English journals, and make excerpts from them." Such proficiency in the English language was essential to him, as his duty in the Ministry of Foreign Affairs was to keep the tsar informed about the foreign press. Nicholas I, however, objected to his manner and called him a "mauvais homme."[5] Koshelev was of a more practical bent of mind than Ivan Kireevsky and Konstantin Aksakov, and from about 1835 to 1845 he applied himself to the management of his considerable estate, and succeeded in making profitable the formerly neglected and mismanaged lands of the Dolgorukis.[6]

As I have indicated more than once in this and the preceding studies, information about the possessions and financial affairs of the Slavophils, and it seems of the Russian gentry in general, is often fragmentary and incomplete. The early Slavophils are generally described as wealthy, well-to-do, affluent, but they were not all equally rich. Koshelev was probably the wealthiest among them, or at least the most generous in supporting the Slavophil cause during the 1850s. Semevsky in his standard two-volume study of the peasant question in Russia quotes Koshelev, in reference to the year 1847, that he had on his estate, presumably Pesochnoe, "3,500 census souls".[7] But this is probably an incomplete number. Jerome Blum in his authoritative study of agricultural conditions in Russia points out that wealth in Russia through the nineteenth century was measured not by the extent of the land owned, but by the number of male serfs or "census, revision souls," that a landlord had on his lands. However, the "magnates and even the men of moderate wealth made up a very small minority of the nobility."[8] Compared with the Panins' 24,000 serfs in the 1780s, the Orlov brothers' 27,000, early in the nineteenth century, and the Vorontsovs' 55,000 serfs — and there were some even larger — Koshelev's 3,500 serfs was a modest number, though it was larger than that of most landlords.

But neither the extent of the land nor the number of serfs assured the profitability of an estate. The quality of the land, its geography, topography, and climate, and as much as any other factor, its management, determined the income that it produced. It seems that in this respect Koshelev's estate was very much superior to others. Koshelev and his family spent the winters in Moscow but much of the rest of the year in the Riazan gubernia attending to the business of the estate. At the end of the 1830s this routine was interrupted when Koshelev made two trips to Western Europe in search of medical treatment for his wife. In more normal years, he tells in his *Memoirs,* while in "Moscow we moved little in the so-called grand monde — at balls and night affairs, but spent our time primarily with our good friends, the Kireevskys, Elagins, Khomiakovs, Sverbeevs, Shevyrevs, Pogodins, Baratynskis, and others." Regularly three times a week they gathered at the Elagins', at the Sverbeevs', and at the Koshelevs'. Here, he says, appeared the *"first rudiments of the struggle* between the incipient *Russian* orientation, and the then reigning *Westernism.* Almost the sole representative of the first was Khomiakov, for Kireevsky and I and many others still belonged to the latter." As the leading Westerners in Moscow he lists Granovsky, Herzen, N. F. Pavlov, and Chaadaev. From the context it is fairly clear that in 1869 he was reminiscing about the late 1830s, although the events and personalities that he refers to would place these developments in the early

1840s; the middle forties had not arrived, at any rate, for he says that despite strong disagreements "between these two orientations, there was not yet even a word about a rupture."[9]

Koshelev's skillful estate management was not achieved without difficulties and friction with other landowners who particularly disliked his liberal attitude toward his serfs. Koshelev was disturbed by the existence of serfdom on his lands, and in Russia in general, and wished to see it ended. This belief seems to have intensified when in the summer of 1847, under the influence of Khomiakov and Ivan Kireevsky he "became immersed in the reading of theological works," including the writings of "John Chrysostom, Basil the Great, and Gregory the Theologian." These Eastern Orthodox church fathers, and other theological works, without completely displacing "political books and journals," induced him "to strongly entertain the thought of emancipation of the serfs."[10] Although he was primarily a man of practical concerns and action, emancipation of the serfs was for him a Christian, ethical problem as well as one with strong economic, social and political implications. This is forcefully borne out in a letter he wrote to Ivan Kireevsky on October 27, 1852, in which he says that he cannot understand how Kireevsky, a Christian, was "not tormented by the thought of having human beings in the state of serfdom."[11]

Koshelev's Christian Orthodox ethic called for compassion for one's fellow man, and for "the brotherhood of man under the fatherhood of God." The aristocratic side of Koshelev disturbed that he as a Christian was the owner of fellow human beings, had also a practical complement that was concerned with improving the productivity of his land with the modernization of agriculture on his estate, and in Russia in general. Since the health of Koshelev's wife necessitated frequent trips to Western Europe in search of a cure, Koshelev had opportunities to study conditions and improvements abroad. Between 1849 and 1851 he made three trips to the West. The second of these, in the first two months of 1851, was a brief one, to bring his wife back from Baden; but in August of 1851 Koshelev went to London for the express purpose of seeing the Crystal Palace Exposition, and particularly the agricultural machinery.[12]

Koshelev's activities at home and abroad during the late 1840s and early 1850s, as well as his reading, his impressions, reflections, and reactions, are fascinating. Obviously, our primary concern is with his contribution to Moscow Slavophilism, and even that can only be sketched; but all that he did and thought had a bearing on his Slavophil views. His interest in agriculture was always foremost. In 1850 he joined the Lebedian Society (*Lebedianskoe Obshchestvo*), which had been founded in 1847 by landowners in the central agricultural guberniias of Tambov, Orel, Tula, Riazan, and Voronezh for the purpose, in broad terms, of improving and modernizing Russian agriculture. Khomiakov became a member in 1851, and Samarin joined in 1853. Although Koshelev was not entirely happy about the way in which the society functioned, in September 1852 he was awarded its gold medal for services to the society and to Russian agriculture.[13]

In his travels, Koshelev kept careful and detailed diaries recording his observations on both agriculture and social conditions, to which he was alertly receptive. About Holland, a country that particularly fascinated him, he noticed in the summer of 1849 the draining of the Haarlem Sea and the new steam pump near Leiden that poured the water into the Rhine. He visited several farms where he saw "charming cows," and where "cleanliness, tidiness, and conveniences were everywhere amazing." He observed processes of cheese and butter making, and he had facts and figures on milk production and the yield per cow.[14] He visited a poor folks' home in Haarlem, and an orphanage in Amsterdam. His earlier impression that there were no poor in Holland, he says in his diary, proved to be wrong.[15]

The three trips that Koshelev made to Western Europe between 1849–1851 coincided with turbulent revolutionary events there. The complexity of modern Western life and the sometimes parallel, sometimes intersecting, and sometimes conflicting political, social, and economic forces released by the new industrialism were not lost on him or on the Moscow Slavophils. The Aksakovs carefully followed events and developments in the West; Khomiakov spent much of 1847 in England, and in other Western European countries, and for him as well as Koshelev, first hand observations were supplemented with reading in Western history and literature.

Koshelev's careful diaries show that on board ship from St. Petersburg to Germany in 1849, for example, he read Jacob Venedey's three-volume *England*, published in 1845. Among the things that he liked about the old Saxons was their communal organization. "Khomiakov, [K. S.] Aksakov, and others," he noted "say that the commune is a distinctive Slav institution. [But] Venedey states and proves that among the ancient Saxons the commune was both the owner of all lands, responsible for all its members, and the complete distributor. I am convinced that in every young nation the family and the commune are in full force and are not at all the sole possession of the Slav tribes." While he was in Dresden he read two pamphlets by Count László Teleki, the Hungarian ambassador to France, *Die Deutsche Hegemonie* and *Die Russische Intervention*. In The Hague, he read Xavier Marmier's *Lettres sur la Hollande*, and von Ditmar's *Freundliche Erinnerungen an Holland*, which he particularly enjoyed. Also in The Hague he read A. M. I. Lamartine's two-volume *Histroire de la révolution de 1848*, and the first volume of Bomon E. de Vassis's six-volume *Histoire des états européens depuis le Congres de Vienne* (Paris, 1843–1853), which deals with Belgium and Holland. His reading in Ostend consisted of Adolf Hellferich's *Belgien in politischer, kirchlicher, pädagogischer und statistischer Beziehung* (1848), and in Paris he read Louis Blanc's journal *Le Nouveau Monde*, having al-

ready read his *Organisation du travail,* which he considered "completely inapplicable in practice."[16] In Paris he also followed the published controversy between Lamartine and Louis Blanc.

Together with Samarin's reading of Lorenz von Stein on socialism and
communism in France earlier in the decade, and the Slavophils' general
familiarity with French utopian socialism, the Slavophils, as illustrated by
Koshelev, had a good knowledge of the works of some of Western Europe's
most reputable historians and publicists. In addition, between 1847 and
1851, Khomiakov and, even more, Koshelev, in their extensive travels in the
West observed keenly the deep and far-reaching changes that industrial
capitalism was leaving in its wake. Nor did the revolutions that swept from
Paris to Vienna and Budapest escape the attention and concerns of the
Slavophils. The "social question" of which young Samarin was so well aware
in the early 1840s came into focus as never before. It is a small wonder that
Khomiakov dreamed at the time, even though perhaps for a few fleeting moments, of seeing an industrial commune, *phalanstery,* emerge from the Russian peasant commune.[17]

At the base of the economic, social and political turmoil in the middle of
the nineteenth century were the scientific and technological discoveries and
changes that were revolutionizing the productive process. These in turn
were bringing about unprecedented changes in the class structure of
societies and in the lives of millions, and at an ever faster and faster rate. A
superficial view of Moscow Slavophilism might lead one to the conclusion
that most if not all of this bypassed the Slavophils, who were comfortably
ensconced in their Moscow town houses and country dachas. Yet it should
be obvious that that was not the case. And no Slavophil has provided us with
more hard evidence that the Slavophils were among the best informed Russians about the revolutionary changes in the West than Koshelev.

Of his frequent travels to Western Europe none satisfied him more or
rewarded him more richly with impressions and new ideas than the brief visit
to London and its Crystal Palace exposition of 1851. The trip lasted little
more than a month — from August 7, when he left Moscow, to soon after September 6, when he left London for the return trip (the journey from Moscow
to London — by boat from St. Petersburg to Swinemunde, then by train from
Berlin to Cologne, Lille, and Calais, and on — took nine days). Koshelev's
diary from this trip is the substance of his ninety-seven-page illustrated
"Journey of a Russian Landowner to England for the World Exposition"
(*Poezdka russkogo zemledel'tsa v Angliuu na vsemirnuiu vystavku*), which was
published in the Slavophil symposium *Moskovskii sbornik* for 1852.[18]

Koshelev himself, now settled unequivocally in the Slavophil camp,
financed this publication, and approximately a quarter of it is taken up by
his article, but it also includes contributions from all the other early
Slavophils except Samarin, as well as some by the pro-Slavophil historian I.

D. Beliaev and a seventy-page historical essay, "Pskov i Livoniia," by one of the leading moderate Westerners, Sergei Solov'ev.

Koshelev's diary-essay is handsomely illustrated with twenty-five well-reproduced etchings, four of buildings, including a large one of the Crystal Palace, and twenty-one of a variety of agricultural machinery displayed by the various countries, all dominated by the British exhibit. Given the great number of national pavilions and the richness and variety within them, Koshelev's impressions and reactions are remarkably complete and detailed. Nor is it easy to miss, despite his keen eye and impressionable mind, his simple basic concern and purpose for attending the exposition, that is, his practical interest in agricultural machines. "The principal aim of my trip to England for the exposition," he says in his diary entry for August 21–25 and 28–31, "was the study of English agriculture," particularly the "section of English agricultural implements and machinery."[19]

In many phases of economic activity England was represented with "complete brilliance," but in the realm of agriculture "it decisively surpassed all remaining nations." The works of English agricultural mechanics were exhibited "beautifully — without boasting and frankly."[20] By means of annual exhibitions, awards, and patents, agricultural machinery had become an essential part of any well-ordered farm in England and Scotland. All the leading inventors and builders of agricultural machines, including Garrett, Ransome and May and Crosskill, Barrett, Hornsby, had exhibits at the Crystal Palace, showing altogether "no fewer than 135 pieces." For Koshelev, one of the "most stunning things" was that there were "no less than 16 mobile steam engines," the power of which was applied in "threshing, winnowing, cutting straw and root vegetables, pressing of grain, flour grinding, and others." He thought the "moving steam engines" by Garrett, Clayton and Shuttleworth and Tuxford and Son, were most remarkable.[21] The last, according to the accounts of English farmers, was particularly desirable. Koshelev was tempted to buy one, except that no machines were as yet available for sale, and furthermore they were all designed to burn coal, for which he would have to substitute wood; also, he knew that he might have difficulty in maintaining the machine because there were no trained mechanics in Russia.

Koshelev devoted five days to examining agricultural machinery at the exposition. He studied the English steam plows, Lord Willoughby's and Usher's of Edinburgh. He found both unsatisfactory for different reasons, and much preferred the American plows for their construction and light weight.[22] Tile-making machinery for tiles for drainage as well as for construction caught Koshelev's attention. He looked at hollow bricks and other construction materials for building peasant and workers cottages, "for improving the condition of the laboring classes." He also visited several model cottages in the countryside and obtained a plan and construction sketches, expressing concern for the poor housing conditions of the Russian peasant confined to his primitive *izba.*[23]

As Koshelev moved through the national exhibits — English, American, French, Italian and others — he not only observed the machines and objects that were displayed but also reflected on the larger issues and objective conditions that determine the nature and productivity of agriculture. On the whole, he most admired English agricultural machinery and implements, but he ranked the United States second only to England, and concluded that American agriculture was even more "interesting" than the British farms, perhaps because there were greater similarities between farming in Russia and the United States than between Russia and England. He attributed this to "Soil, climate, abundance of land with insufficiency of working hands, and many other circumstances more or less common to us and the North American states." For this reason, he says, "I have long had a strong desire to visit this country and to study on the spot several questions that are before us for solution, which have already been solved there or are approaching final solution." Thus he went to the American exhibit of agricultural machinery with "special curiosity," and found the objects on display "small in number" but "rich in content."[24]

Koshelev was particularly interested in the American reaper or harvesting machine, not only for the practical reason that it was a key instrument in the agricultural process, helping to bring in the harvest, but also because he was well aware that the backstraining chore of harvesting was usually performed by peasant women. In a report to the Lebedian Society the following year (1852) Koshelev, recommending the harvester, said, "This implement should relieve the heaviest labor of women, who are even without it burdened with various physical sufferings. Probably everyone will happily take advantage of the first possibility to pay his debt to humanity." He was convinced that although the new harvesting machines might be imperfect as yet, they would be improved, and would in time "completely abolish the onerous . . . sickle."[25]

The McCormick reaper, made in America and a centerpiece of the exhibition, was very impressive. Koshelev was familiar with the Husey and Garrett machines, but he preferred the McCormick harvester, which was already in extensive use in America but was just being introduced into Europe. In the Moscow symposium article, he cites the *Farmer's Magazine* for February 1851, saying that 500 McCormick reapers were produced in the United States in 1848, 1,500 in 1849, and 1,600 in 1850.[26] When the McCormick and Husey harvesters were tested by experts, "in the presence of many viewers," Koshelev says, "the first was incomparably superior to the latter," and it was awarded the "Council-medal." Even *The Times,* in a long account that Koshelev quotes, praised the McCormick reaper, which was powered by two horses attended by two farmers.[27] On August 23 Koshelev went to "the

Manor farm Great Wymondby," thirty-one miles from London, and followed
a McCormick reaper at work. He considered the English breed of horses
stronger than the Russian and concluded that in Russia they would have to
use four, or perhaps use oxen instead of horses. He summed up the efficient
operation of the McCormick machine under eight points, the last being its
price — $115 or about 150 rubles — and ordered one to be delivered by boat
in St. Petersburg. He also bought two plows and one cultivator, and considered their price very reasonable.[28]

Koshelev also took particular note of several butter churns, one American,
two English, a French, and a Belgian, Duchene, all of which were awarded
medals. The American churn was also made in Moscow by the farm equipment mechanic, Wilson. Koshelev preferred the American and English
churns, and wished to order a Belgian sowing machine, which could not be
done at the exposition.[29]

Besides the agricultural machinery, Koshelev also looked at the exhibits
of agricultural products, and he found time to tour the exhibits of manufac-
tured goods in the pavilions of the various nations represented in the exposition. Although he was half French, he was not at all enthusiastic about most
of the French exhibits. He praised a French grain separator (for which he
could not find a sketch), made in Lyon; but on the whole, he says, "France
made a painful impression on me." He was saddened to see that "This
republic, this nation of liberal and social thoughts sent to the Exposition only
articles of luxury and fashion," and he enumerated pieces of jewelry, vases,
silks, and so on. He also saw French surgical instruments, turbines, and
some chemical preparations, but he observed with a heavy heart that in this
republic's exhibit he found "nothing made, invented, or perfected with the
purpose of rendering the articles cheaper and accessible to the people
[*narod*]." He concluded that the French pavilion "can serve as an irrefutable
commentary on the opinions and actions of this nation."[30]

On the other hand, in the exhibits of Switzerland, Italy, Spain, Portugal,
Turkey, Greece, China, and others, Koshelev found articles that were useful and often artistic as well. Though he deplored luxury articles on which
"human labor is squandered so vainly and uselessly," he was very satisfied
to see so many well-made articles and goods destined for common consumption. He admired the paper made in England and America, and also their
newspapers and book printing, including the publication of the Bible in
England in 150 languages.[31] He also admired German and English cutlery,
and he examined English and French silks, and in this case gave the French
the edge on patterns and designs. He found English and American advances in steamship construction most promising.[32] And from all these observations he derived admiration for English laissez-faire economics, which, it
should be added, if one were to overlook the miserable lot of the English
mine and factory workers at the time, never looked better.

Koshelev summed up his conclusions under four points (1) No nation in the world had achieved more than England in practically all branches of industry, and whoever wished to learn about modern industry had to go to England; (2) laissez-faire is superior to all other ways: the "theory of Louis Blanc and in general . . . of the other French theoreticians demanding that the government intervene in all industrial production, and render them active cooperation, has been victoriously refuted by the example of England," which had reached the highest level of industrial development without government help or interference; (3) England, although "bending its knee" before its king and seemingly an aristocracy, is in fact "if not the most communal then of course the most public spirited" nation, concerned with reducing the cost of goods and thus making them accessible to the people (that this also meant greatly increased profits for the entrepreneurs he did not seem to notice; (4) "In England more than anywhere else science is directly and extensively applied to the various industries."[33]

While Koshelev was in London, he did not miss a Sunday service in the Russian Orthodox church, and in the *Moskovskii sbornik* article he urged his readers to tend to the Russian "tree of enlightenment" onto which "Holy Orthodoxy was long since grafted," and which had young and strong branches. At the same time, he noted: "In the West, science, art, industry, and many other manifestations of human activity have achieved significant development." Therefore his advice to his fellow Russians was, "Let us study Europe and its enlightenment." But in true Slavophil manner he cautioned his readers to be discriminating in their attitude toward the West, and not to accept its "luxury, its immorality, its coolness toward religion, its show of cleverness [*umnichanie*]." The Russians "should not imitate the West but should study it."[34]

In the opening pages of his description of the exposition in the Crystal Palace Koshelev gives the reader a brief travelogue of his trip by train from Swinemünde to Calais. This and two essays, published later, on the railroads, then in their first quarter-century, reveal his position on the subject, and on the whole also the Slavophil attitude toward this portentous Western invention. In Lille, he compared and contrasted the German, Belgian, French, and English railways. He says that he had traveled extensively throughout Europe but that "I have not found better organization of railroads than in Germany." Trains moved faster in England than in Germany and often followed each other by only minutes. In France they were also faster than in Germany and the diner was superior, but the German trains had on-time dependability unmatched by English and French trains. In Germany it was always possible "to quench one's hunger and thirst," whereas in England "refreshment rooms" were not always easy to find. In France this aspect of train travel was "excellently appointed." He liked the Belgian trains, although on some of the runs they shook a good deal because, he was told, of the thinness of the rails, and their constant use. No trains anywhere in Europe reached the speed of the English "Express trains," up to ninety versts (about sixty miles) per hour.[35]

Not the least attraction of train travel was the opportunity for sightseeing, and of observing the rapidly changing vistas as the trains moved through the countryside. And if this marvelous Western invention was good for the West, what about railroads in Russia? Although by the middle of the century railroad construction had already begun there (the St. Petersburg-Moscow line was completed in 1852),[36] the question of their desirability and utility for Russia was still debated, and so was the construction of a railroad network for the vast empire, and its possible center or centers.

But for the banning of Slavophil publications after 1852, Koshelev very likely would have become a participant in the debate about the Russian railroads as soon as he returned from the London exposition. If the muzzling of the Slavophils channeled their epistolary discussions during the early 1850s in the direction of farming and "theological dogmatics" as has been suggested, in Koshelev's case, at least, the question of the Russian railroads was not forgotten but merely postponed.[37] When in the new reign of Alexander II, the Slavophils obtained permission to publish their *Russkaia beseda* (1856), Koshelev wasted no time. In its first issue he entered the debate about the railroads with the radical Westerner *Sovremennik*. The question at issue was not the desirability of the railroads, since both journals favored them, but where the center of the Russian network should be located. Zhuravsky, the author of the *Sovremennik* article, favored Orel, whereas Koshelev, as a good Slavophil, advocated Moscow.

It is not necessary to go into the details of this controversy. My purpose is to summarize Koshelev's views on the Russian railroads, and to point out their common Slavophil justification, and their relationship to the broader Slavophil views on the place and role of science and technology in the Slavophil scheme of things. First it is characteristic of a Slavophil, like Koshelev, to try to give a "national" or "popular" character to the railroads. In place of *zheleznaia doroga,* "iron road" or railroad, he used the word *chugunka* (from *chugun* = cast iron) as being "livelier and shorter" than *zheleznaia doroga,* and furthermore as being in the "popular language."[38]

Moscow, seen by the Slavophils in the dual role as the geographical center of European Russia, and also as its cultural, religious, and historical national heart, was uniquely suited to become the center of a network of railroads radiating in all directions. In addition, Koshelev stressed the military and strategic importance of the new fast means of transport, emphasizing at the same time their indispensability to modern industry and agriculture, particularly in countries like the United States and Russia where raw materials as well as finished goods and passengers had to be transported over great distances. He summed up his views on the railroads by saying that they would meet new needs in "agriculture, industry, commerce, internal government, and general education."[39] Continuing the controversy with Zhuravsky and the *Sovremennik* over the center of the Russian railroad network, he again argued for Moscow, and once again compared Russia and the United States, repeating in the process a well-known Slavophil myth. "In Europe there are old lands and old people, in America old people but new lands, in Russia — new lands and new people.[40]

A number of years ago in the second study of this series, I cited Professor Kizevetter's characterization of Koshelev as the person who introduced the "harvesting machines in Russia."[41] Kizevetter probably had factual justification for this assertion. But whether Koshelev was the first or not, his position as a leading Russian authority on farm machinery, modern agricultural methods, and living conditions on the farms of Western Europe and in its villages can scarcely be questioned. It is doubtful whether in the middle of last century there were Russians of any ideological persuasion who were better informed than Koshelev about the latest Western scientific and technological advances in agriculture, or who were better prepared to utilize them on their lands.

Among the Slavophils, Koshelev was the authority on modern farming, but he was not alone in taking an interest in science and technology and their application to farming and the industrial processes. Kireevsky also had knowledge of these matters. He is considered the philosopher-theologian of the Slavophils, impractical and dreamy, yet as early as 1832 he gave thought to some of the basic scientific and technological changes then under way in the West. He welcomed the steam engine because it would be "beneficial for mankind in general and for the future success of industry." But he also saw some of the personal and social problems that would arise. "Millions of people must seek new means of livelihood," particularly in view of the fact that the steam engine was at the "beginning of its application," and he expected to see labor and occupational displacements on a very large scale.[42] Not without misgivings, he recorded six years later that industrialism was becoming the "mainspring of social life."

When in 1845 Kireevsky became the editor of Pogodin's *Moskvitianin* for a brief period of three or four months, he introduced a new section on farming with an apology to the readers of a "literary-scholarly" journal. He stood for prudence and good judgment on the subject. Rural economy could no longer be a matter of "custom and old tradition," but neither should one accept the new when it is untested and unproved. The new science of agriculture was complex, and dependent on "chemistry, botany, technology, mechanics, and other similar studies." Conscious of the fact that the West was ahead of Russia in agriculture, the Slavophil estate owner concluded that "experience and rational knowledge of foreign systems and discoveries" marked the road that Russia should follow. Professor I. A. Linovsky of the

University of Moscow was to be in charge of the section on rural economy, the purpose of which was the "betterment of agriculture in our fatherland."[43] In the early 1850s Kireevsky, then immersed in Orthodox theology, seemed unconcerned with questions of political economy and farming, but the poor harvest of 1855 brought him back on farm soil, and he sought Koshelev's advice about purchase of a threshing machine.

Of all the Moscow Slavophils, Khomiakov, by virtue of early aptitude and university training, was, in theory at least, the best qualified to deal with matters of science, industry, technology, and modern scientific farming. He majored in mathematics at the University of Moscow, but his restless, inquisitive, and retentive mind would not be confined to any single area. He studied painting for a brief time in Paris, and a few years later fought as a volunteer against the Turks in Bulgaria during the Russo-Turkish war of 1828–1829. He was a gifted poet. He also dabbled in mechanical invention, and at the end of the 1840s obtained a patent in England for his steam engine, the "silent" *Moskovka,* which he exhibited at the Crystal Palace exposition in 1851.[44] Although the *Moskovka* seems to have made but slight impression then and on posterity, it reveals something about the complexity of the man who is generally considered the father of Moscow Slavophilism. Throughout his adult life, Khomiakov was deeply concerned with the broad range of Russia's internal problems — cultural, economic, social, and political — and with the inevitable question of the relationship between Russia and the West. Always a devout Orthodox believer, he elaborated, particularly during the 1850s, his Slavophil theological views.

One aspect of the baffling and beguiling problem of Russia's relationship to the West was the Russian attitude toward modern science and technology, and their often intractable offspring, modern industrialism and modern agriculture. As Koshelev attempted to formulate his and the Slavophils' position toward the exposition in the Crystal Palace, he was actually dealing with an important phase of the relationship between Russia and the West. But the Moscow Slavophils did not need the great London exposition in order to think about, and react to, early nineteenth century science, technology, and industrialism. In spite of the fact that Khomiakov's *Moskovka* proved impractical, he continued to invent and tinker at about the same time that he was writing some of his best theological essays, and in 1855 he was trying to interest the government in a "conic bullet," and a new warhead for shells and grenades.[45]

The exposition in the Crystal Palace, which to Khomiakov's deep regret he could not visit, evoked in him a sense of nostalgia for England and things English, and a general admiration for the "material" culture of the West. But this was not the first time that he reflected on modern industrialism, technology, and science. In 1843 he published a ten-page description of the Moscow exposition, then in progress, under the title, "A Letter to Petersburg about the Exposition." With characteristic Slavophil bias he looked askance at the social and moral consequences of Western industrialism and urbanization while preserving respect for modern science and technology. Like Koshelev in London, Khomiakov regretted the amount of what he considered to be luxury goods at the Moscow exposition. Luxuries were not necessary; the needs of the people should be satisfied first. "In general," he wrote, "I am not a big lover of factory production, for I am gladdened by the old [kind of] crafts and cottage industry, the origin of which is lost in [past] centuries, and which is based on true need, and has been improved by long-standing habit."[46]

Though he admired some of the brocades and other articles at the Moscow exposition, Khomiakov could not resolve the paradox born of the old and the new. "Even more I am gladdened by that industry," he continued, "which does not introduce on a large scale the immorality of the factory order [*byta*] but is reconciled with the sanctity of the family and the harmonious quiet of the communal order in its organic simplicity, for here, and only here, is strength, and the root of strength."[47]

Two years later, in 1845, Khomiakov published a similarly short article in Pogodin's *Moskvitianin* under the title "Letter to Petersburg apropos of railroads." The article begins with the assertion, "All or almost all are agreed on the necessity of railroads," first of all for military and strategic uses (if other nations could move their troops and supplies rapidly, then Russia had to be able to do the same). Not without a touch of gloating he advised his correspondent that "we can and will reap the fruit of others' labor." He himself was very interested in the possibilities of a French invention for propulsion by means of compressed air instead of steam; he also commented on reciprocal action engines (*forces de retour*) and regretted that the "problem of the aerostat has not yet been solved." But he had no doubt that "many forces up to now useless to man, will become his tools, and many impediments will be transformed into his aids."[48]

Confirmed Slavophil though he was, Khomiakov felt no compunction about a certain type of borrowing from the West. Since the reign of Peter the Great, Russia had "imitated" the West, and it would continue for long "to benefit from its inventions." His justification for this was simple and clear: In the realm of abstract and applied sciences, "the whole civilized world constitutes one whole, and every nation utilizes the discoveries and inventions of other nation[s] without humiliation to its own dignity, [and] without the loss of its right to independent development."[49] This succinct statement contains the heart of the Slavophil distinction between material and nonmaterial culture. It reveals their conviction that mathematics and the physical sciences are universal, hence no nation has a special claim on them, and their belief that on moral, ethical, and religious matters Russia could take its own characteristic stand. What this attitude failed to take into account is the fact that through industrialism, and its inevitable urbanization, science and technology cause drastic and often sudden changes in the mode of life, in human relations, and in mores and morals. In turn, these changes do not leave traditional ethical and religious views and values untouched. The two spheres — physical sciences and technology, and human relations — were not then, nor are they now, as separate and autonomous as Khomiakov pictured them.

With the customary Slavophil partiality toward Moscow, Khomiakov saw the old capital as the only possible center for the Russian railway network. In his characteristic manner of not adhering to a single subject even in a short essay, and still concerned with the problem of cultural borrowing, he elaborated on this favorite theme. Having declared his obvious fascination with what is logical, rational, and scientific, he made an effort to establish the proper relationship between it, and man's broader and more complex nature. Borrowed cultural elements, he says, are "reworked and assimilated by the [new] organism in accordance with its inner and elusive laws. They are subjected to unavoidable changes" which are beyond the "practical understanding [*rassudok*] . . . . [for] life always precedes logical consciousness, and always remains broader than it."[50]

In his long and detailed essay-diary on the London exposition Koshelev left a highly personal view of his travels and observations, but it should also be clear from the preceding pages that he did not go to London naively curious and uninformed. Khomiakov and Ivan Kireevsky had already stated in print (and doubtless also in conversation in the Moscow salons) their opinions and convictions about modern industrialism, science, technology, and their application to agriculture. In the company of the Moscow Slavophils the steam engine and the railroads were most likely discussed in the second half of the 1840s, as Kireevsky and Khomiakov had mentioned them earlier in print. In other words, when Koshelev went to the London exposition in 1851 he and the other Moscow Slavophils had already some knowledge and appreciation of Western scientific and technological achievements. The Slavophils had seen enough of the new trends in Western technology and industrialism to have some knowledge of them, and also a sense of uneasiness about the psychological and social effects of modern industrialism on the ever growing millions of newly displaced and urbanized farmers and peasants.

As the owners of large landed estates and many thousands of serfs, and living in a country that was still overwhelmingly agrarian, experiencing then the early intrusions of modern industrialism, the Slavophils gave priority to their own and Russia's agricultural problems. Here, as noted by Kizevetter, Koshelev, and, it could be added, the other Moscow Slavophils, were in the front ranks of those in Russia who advocated, and by their own actions illustrated, the necessity for the modernization of their own and Russia's farming. This was to be achieved through modern science and technology. It is manifest therefore that the Slavophils had no qualms or reservations about borrowing these from the West, just as they did not hesitate to invest in Western agricultural machinery.

Yet it must be said that, however wise and proper the road the Slavophils chose may have been, they fell short of solving Russia's baffling agricultural problem. The vastness of the empire and the enormous complexity of its agriculture defied the best that anyone, including the West, could offer. Science and technology, including the latest farm machinery, would doubtless help, but they were irrelevant in the removal of the first, and most pressing, obstacle to Russian farming at the time, that is, serfdom, and serf labor.

Even today, people still cannot control the vagaries of geographical, topographical, and climatic conditions of this very northern country, in which the growing season is short and unsuitable for the production of most cereals, vegetables, and fruits. But the Slavophils, like other concerned and thoughtful Russians, realized in the middle of the nineteenth century that science and technology, while not a panacea, offered an important avenue for the improvement of agricultural productivity. They were prepared to take advantage of this on their own estates, and in Russia in general, even if this meant importing them from the West. But that did not mean that Russia would put aside its prerogative to its own religious, ethical, and social views and values.

Notes

1. On Ivan Aksakov's brief incarceration, see Stephen Lukashevich, *Ivan Aksakov, 1823–1886: A Study in Russian Thought and Politics* (Cambridge, Mass., 1965), pp. 28–30. Borozdin, who knew both Ivan Aksakov and Samarin, wrote in his reminiscences, years later, that whereas in Ivan Aksakov "his prejudice against the Emperor Nicholas remained during his whole life," from Samarin he heard "a completely different response about the majestic person of the emperor who honored him with a long conversation about the Riga letters." See K. A. Borozdin, "I. S. Aksakov v Iaroslavle (Otryvok iz vospominanii)" *Istoricheskii vestnik*, 1886, no. 3, pp. 629–630.

2. See *Zapiski Aleksandra Ivanovicha Kosheleva (1812–1883 gody)*. (Berlin, 1884), pp. 6–7, 22 (hereafter cited as Koshelev, *Zapiski*).

3. Ibid., pp. 38–39.

4. Ibid., pp. 42–43.

5. Ibid., p. 47. See also V. Stroev, "Koshelev, Aleksandr Ivanovich," *Russkii biograficheskii slovar* (St. Petersburg, 1903), IX, 386.

6. Koshelev describes in some detail his purchase, in 1835, of Count V. V. Dolgoruki's estate at Pesochnoe, about 180 miles southeast of Moscow, and about 60 miles southeast of Riazan. He paid 725,000 rubles for 9,500

desiatinas (25,650 acres) of good agricultural land. He does not give the number of inhabitants on the estate, nor on the old family estate, Smykovo. In another source the population of Pesochnoe (apparently in 1902) is given as "up to 3,000." According to the same source, at the time of the emancipation of the serfs, "Pesochnoe was the principal holding in the extensive and well-managed estate of Al. Iv. Koshelev." In addition to Pesochnoe, Koshelev owned the neighboring villages of "Mikhei, Krivel', Vasil'evka, and others," for a total of about 12,000 *desiatinas* or 32,400 acres, "and one of the best wine distilleries in the guberniia." The distillery did 43,000 rubles of business a year. According to the same sources, some time after the emancipation reform Koshelev acquired the village of Lakashi with "up to 700" inhabitants. These incomplete figures are indicative of Koshelev's affluence, which made it possible for him to finance some of the Slavophil publications in the 1850s. Cf. Koshelev, *Zapiski,* pp. 47, 52–54; V. P. Semenov et al., eds., *Rossiia. Polnoe geograficheskoe opisanie nashego otechestva.* (St. Petersburg, 1902), II, 321, 489–490. The only figure about the Samarins that I have been able to find is that they had 30,000 *desiatinas* or 81,000 acres on their Samara estate along the left bank of the Volga (Semenov, VI, 458). According to a recent Soviet work, in the Samara and Syzran districts Samarin had 23,810 *desiatinas* (64,287 acres) of arable land, forest, and meadows, and 2,897 male serfs, 461 of whom were household serfs; these figures are probably incomplete, however. See E. A. Dudzinskaia, "Obshchestvennaia i khoziaistvennaia deiatel'nost' Iu. F. Samarina v 40–50-kh godakh XIX v." *Istoricheskie zapiski,* 1984, CXI, 317.

7. See V. I. Semevsky, *Krest'ianskii vopros v Rossii v XVIII i pervoi polovine XIX veka,* 2 vols., (St. Petersburg, 1888), II, 186.

8. Blum says that incomplete figures collected in 1777 show that "32 percent of the serf owners for whom data were available had fewer than 10 male serfs, 30.7 percent had 10 to 30, 13.4 percent had 30 to 60, 7.7 percent had 60 to 100, and only 16.2 percent owned over 100." Fuller but still incomplete figures for 1834 show that "84 percent of serf owners owned less than 101 males, and 16 percent owned over 100" or the "same proportions as those for 1777." But a change was in progress. "By 1858 the proportion of serf owners with less than 101 had decreased. Now only 78 percent of the serf owners were in this category, and 22 percent owned more than 100. The division of serfs between the two groups, however, remained unchanged. The men with less than 101 male serfs had 19 percent of all male serfs, and those with 100 or more owned 81 percent." Jerome Blum, *Lord and Peasant in Russia: From the Ninth to the Nineteenth Century* (New York, 1964), pp. 367–368.

9. Koshelev, *Zapiski,* p. 55.

10. Ibid., p. 64.

11. N. P. Koliupanov, *Biografiia Aleksandra Ivanovicha Kosheleva,* 2 vols., (Moscow, 1889–1892), II, 83–84 (hereafter cited as Koliupanov, *Koshelev).* For a more detailed look at this letter, see Christoff, *Kireevskij,* p. 291. Slavophil concerns with the problem of the emancipation of the serfs, as part of the larger "social question" in Russia, not only during the 1850s but also during the 1840s, receive due attention in Tsimbaev's *Slavianofil'stvo.* See, for instance, pp. 167–168, 178–179.

12. In one of his highly competent works on the emancipation period Zaionchkovsky refers to the interest in new agricultural machinery in the West and in Russia. Thus in 1853 the brothers Butenop sold "almost 140 thousand rubles worth of agricultural machinery" in Russia. But the use of such machinery was more widespread in the Baltic area and in parts of Poland, than in Russia proper. See P. A. Zaionchkovsky, *Otmena krepostnogo prava v Rossii* (2d ed., Moscow, 1960), p. 10. See also Dudzinskaia, "Samarin," p. 320.

13. Koliupanov, *Koshelev,* II, 215–217.

14. Koshelev's own estate included 1,300 *desiatinas* or about 3,500 acres of arable land, and about one thousand cattle, of which about three hundred were milk cows. After carefully observing various Western breeds, Koshelev ordered English, Dutch, and Tyrolian calves, and built a "warm cowbarn for them." Ibid., p. 196.

15. Koliupanov reproduces long excerpts from Koshelev's travel diaries both in the text and in the appendix to volume 2 of his biography of Koshelev. See esp. Appendix pp. 115–117.

16. Ibid., pp. 201–203.

17. See Khomiakov, *Sochineniia,* III, 468; P. K. Christoff, "A. S. Khomiakov on the Agricultural and Industrial Problem in Russia," in A. D. Ferguson and Alfred Levin, eds., *Essays in Russian History: A Collection Dedicated to George Vernadsky* (Hamden, Conn., 1964), pp. 143, 149, 157.

18. *Moskovskii sbornik* (Moscow, 1852), pp. 145–243.

19. Ibid., p. 163.

20. Ibid., p. 164.

21. Ibid., pp. 164, 165, 167.

22. Ibid., pp. 167–169, 173–185.

23. Ibid., pp. 187, 191–192, 197–198.

24. Ibid., p. 199.

25. Koliupanov, *Koshelev,* II, 219.

26. *Moskovskii sbornik,* 1852, p. 199.

27. Cyrus Hall McCormick (1809–1884) patented his reaper in 1834 and began its manufacture on a large scale in 1847. His son Cyrus Hall McCormick (1859–1936) became first president (1902–1919), and board chairman (1919–1935) of International Harvester Co.

28. *Moskovskii sbornik,* 1852, pp. 202–203, 208, 211.

29. Ibid., pp. 212–214.

30. Ibid., pp. 215, 224–225.

31. Ibid., pp, 228, 233.

32. Ibid., p. 239.

33. Ibid., pp. 236–237.

34. Ibid., pp. 242–243.

35. Ibid., pp. 151–152.

36. The first short line from St. Petersburg to suburban Tsarskoe Selo (Pushkin) and Pavlovsk was in operation in 1837. The literature on construction of the Russian railroads is quite extensive. For information on this first railroad and on the St. Petersburg-Moscow line, and for an authoritative discussion of Russian railroads up to 1860, see William L. Blackwell, *The Beginnings of Russian Industrialization, 1800–1860* (Princeton, N.J., 1968), pp. 274–275, 279–302. See also W. M. Pintner, *Russian Economic Policy under Nicholas I* (Ithaca, N.Y., 1967), pp. 131–152; J. N. Westwood, *A History of Russian Railways* (London, 1964), pp. 25–34. For the early period of railroad construction, see R. M. Hayward, *The Beginning of Railway Development in Russia in the Reign of Nicholas I, 1835–1842* (Durham, N.C., 1969).

37. In 1918 Professor Kizevetter edited nineteen letters from Koshelev to Ivan Aksakov, written between 1853 and 1860, and stated in his editorial comments that the censorship, "this catastrophe visited upon the Slavophils," was such as to make impossible any "free act," and "rendered every human being a 'separate visitor of life.'" A. A. Kizevetter, ed., "Iz perepiski moskovskikh slavianofilov. A. I. Koshelev i I. S. Aksakov," *Golos minuvshago,* 1918, no. 1–3, p. 232 (hereafter cited, Kizevetter, "Koshelev to Aksakov").

38. *Zheleznaia doroga* is of course a translation of the German *Eisenbahn* and the French *chemin de fer.*

39. A. I. Koshelev, "Soobrazheniia kasatel'no ustroistva zheleznykh dorog v Rossii," *Russkaia beseda,* 1856, no. I, *kritika,* pp. 148–149, 151–152, 154–155, 157.

40. *Russkaia beseda,* 1856, no. III, *kritika,* pp. 91–92.

41. Kizevetter, "Koshelev to Aksakov," no. 7–9, p, 170; Christoff, *Kireevskij,* p. 136.

42. I. V. Kireevsky, *Sochineniia,* I, 106–107.

43. Ibid., II, 115, 117–118; Christoff, *Kireevskij,* pp. 294.

44. The "Description of the 'Moskovka,' a new rotary steam engine, invented and patented by Alexis Khomiakov of Moscow," all in the original English, and several pages of charts and figures of the engine are appended at the end of volume 3 of Khomiakov's *Sochineniia,* 4th ed., (Moscow, 1914). See also Christoff, *Xomjakov,* pp. 99–100.

45. Khomiakov, *Sochineniia,* VIII, 204–205, 212–213; Christoff, *Xomjakov,* p. 105.

46. Khomiakov, *Sochineniia,* III, 86–87.

47. Ibid., pp. 87–88. For a more detailed discussion of Khomiakov's views on this and related topics, see Christoff, "A. S. Khomiakov on the Agricultural and Industrial Problem in Russia," pp. 129–159. Not only Khomiakov and Koshelev found fairs fascinating and important for technological progress in Russia and elsewhere. Ivan Aksakov published in 1858 a volume on Ukrainian fairs. Part I of his study, beginning with Kharkov, contains accounts of eleven Ukrainian town fairs. Part II, in Aksakov's words, is a "monograph on commodities" (*monografiia tovarov*), and includes such items as silks, cloth, woolens, iron, and copper goods, and so on. His descriptions and comments are often accompanied by pages of figures and statistics. See I. S. Aksakov, *Issledovanie o torgovle na ukrainskikh iarmarkakh* (St. Petersburg, 1858).

48. Khomiakov, *Sochineniia,* III, 104–108.

49. Ibid., p. 115.

50. Ibid., p. 117.

9

The 1850s: Samarin's Studies
and Emancipation of the Serfs

If Samarin does not play a prominent part in the elaboration of the Slavophil views on science and technology and their application to agriculture during the late 1840s and early 1850s, the explanation is certainly due at least in part to his absence from Moscow from August 1844, when he entered government service, until February 1853, when he left it. During these eight and a half years he was in Moscow only occasionally, and usually for only short visits. He was, therefore, away from his Slavophil friends, and away from the Moscow salons where questions of science, technology, and agriculture were doubtless discussed among the plethora of topics that circulated in them. Moreover, the nature of his civil service assignments, particularly the one in Riga, directed his attention toward the question of Russia's borderlands and their relationship to the Russian state and society. His interests lay in such questions as the role of the government and Russian culture, and of such numerically small but highly influential minorities as the Baltic Germans; the relationship between the Lutheran upper stratum and the peasant population that served them, whether Orthodox Russian, Estonian, Latvian, or Lithuanian; their rising national consciousness; the problem of serfdom; and the attitude of the government toward the Baltic minorities — the issue that caused his brief incarceration in March 1849.

Samarin was never out of touch with his Moscow friends for long; whether in Riga or in Kiev, while on the staff of the Bibikov inventory commission, he kept up his correspondence with his family and with the Moscow Slavophils, except Ivan Kireevsky, toward whom he seems to have remained quite cool.[1] In a letter Samarin wrote to Konstantin Aksakov from Simbirsk in October 1849, he said that he needed to study a number of subjects, such as certain aspects of agricultural work. "Then I will take up the project of steam-navigation — a very important article, then the schismatics, after that census of cities, and the grain trade at the wharves."[2] Six years later, in a brief article entitled "Two Words about Nationality in Science" (*Dva slova o narodnosti v nauke*), published in *Russkaia beseda* (1856), he defended the standard Slavophil view that the physical sciences were universal and the common heritage of mankind. With respect to the social sciences and humanities, however, although his definition was imprecise, Samarin contended that different views and interpretations could exist, and in fact were a matter of long-standing practice. Defining the purpose of science as "achieving the essence of the phenomenon," he held that "discoveries in the sphere of mechanics and natural sciences and the improvements introduced" by various nations in the "material" realm are "simply and indisputably imitated." But in the humanities and social sciences things were different. Giving history as an example, he stressed that the way the Catholic Bossuet saw the Reformation was quite different from that of Protestant English and German historians.[3]

Samarin's primary concern in the years 1846–1853 was, as Nol'de has shown, peasant reform. Chapter 2 of Nol'de's biography of Samarin has the title, "Preparation of the Peasant Reform, 1849–1858" (*Podgotovka krest'ianskoi reformy 1849–1858*): "The history of Samarin for the years 1848–1863 is the history of the peasant reform," Nol'de says, and adds, "not the whole [of Russian] history."[4] Even in Samarin's *Riga Letters,* concerned with a Baltic historical problem, the issue of serfdom was never far from him. The Baltic littoral and serfdom were also wrapped up in the important issue of Russian nationality. In a letter to Konstantin Aksakov from Riga in April 1848, Samarin commented, "My present preoccupations are closely tied with what takes place in front of my eyes," and this, he complained, left him neither the time nor the inclination for anything else. "The systematic oppression of the Russians by the Germans, the hourly insult to the Russian national consciousness in the persons of its few representatives – this is what now makes my blood boil. . . . "[5]

The same sort of temporary deflection from the central concerns of the Moscow Slavophils that was a consequence of Samarin's Riga assignment was also a consequence of his quasi-exile to Kiev in the early 1850s. When Ivan Aksakov approached Samarin for a contribution to the projected second volume of the *Moskovskii sbornik* (soon suppressed by the government), Samarin wrote to him (June 10, 1852) from Kiev saying he wished that he could prove to his friends that the "experience in [government] service, and in life, has in no way changed my convictions." But he blamed office work for his inability to turn to anything else, and it was not merely lack of time. He confessed, "I am not in a position to free my thought from concerns of the service, and to concentrate on something else."[6]

Such reassurance that he still held Slavophil convictions was doubtless appreciated in Moscow even if he himself may not have needed it. He was, indeed, on the way to becoming the Slavophils' principal spokesman and moving force in regard to the emancipation of the serfs. Perhaps, more than

Khomiakov and Koshelev, he was already convinced that no amount of science and agricultural machinery could make any real difference in Russian agricultural and industrial production so long as serfdom existed. The first and indispensable step toward the modernization of Russian agriculture, and economic life in general, was the emancipation of the serfs.

Prior to the revolution of 1917 no other change in modern Russian history touched the status and lives of so many Russians, so relatively suddenly, and so deeply as the emancipation of the serfs in 1861. This can be said despite the views of those at one extreme, that the change was nothing short of robbing the landlord of his rightful property in land and souls, or of those at the other extreme, that the reform of 1861 was only a superficial measure that brought no true equality, no freedom, — nor, it could be added, utopia or paradise on earth. But by the standards of the often bumbling, often tortuous, never perfect, course of factual historical change, this was a memorable event.

Although the Slavophils were not the first in the nineteenth century to show concern for the Russian serfs and for their emancipation, they took, as is well known, a prominent part in bringing about the reform of 1861.[7] And none of them surpassed Samarin in expertise and awareness of the endless intricacies and complexities of emancipation, nor in the resolve to see the reform through to its realization. Once again it is necessary to stress that, like the other early Slavophils, Samarin proposed no radical solution. As a well-to-do land and serf owner he was not ready to surrender his estates. But he was determined to help bring about emancipation with certain land concessions to the peasants, even though he knew it would arouse the animosity of some of his uncompromising fellow landowners.

But emancipation, fundamental and essential as it was, would not automatically set Russia on the course of a modern, scientifically and technologically strong, free labor economy. The question who would control and direct such an order was as much political as it was economic. Samarin, whose monarchical convictions were stronger than those of the other Moscow Slavophils had no doubts about the future political course of Russia; but he was less certain about the direction of its economy, and at the end of the 1840s he was engrossed in the subject of economics. In a letter to Khomiakov which Dmitry Samarin dates to the middle of August 1849, he wrote that, since mid-May, "I have been constantly preoccupied with political economy, and have devoured up to 15 rather thick volumes."[8] Many of these works were theoretical, and he came to the conclusion that "this science (or more precisely, this type of deduction from the historical development of the national economy in the West) deserves neither that disfavor with which . . . many respectable people look upon it, nor that tremendous importance attributed to it by those who see in society a company of stockholders . . . and in the life of man a process of food digestion [*pishchevareniia*]."

With respect to Russia, granted certain exceptions, economics, he said, should be studied "not with the aim of applying it in matters of advice and instruction, passing it as infallible, but for one's own education." The exceptions that Samarin stated parenthetically were, "for example about the superiority of free over forced labor, about the advantage of free exchange, about the harm of all artificial stimulation of industrial activity, and several others." His sound judgment led him to the realization that economics was not a science in a class with physics and chemistry and that its usefulness was real but limited. Russians could derive certain benefits from it, as he himself was doing, but as a good Slavophil he was on guard lest Western values should intrude in the realm of "advise and instruction."[9]

Samarin was critical of the individualism that lay at the heart of the doctrine of *laissez-faire, laissez-passer*: "French and English economists ridicule to their heart's content the *ateliers nationaux* and other fictions of the socialists," and that was justified on the ground that man is moved to labor "by need," and does so freely; but the Russian conservatives when they condemned French socialism did not realize "that they undermine equally the *ateliers nationaux* and our [Russian] serfdom." Yet he was disturbed by the conclusions that he arrived at as he reasoned about the state of affairs in Russia. Since the landlord had the "duty to feed" the peasant, the peasant did not feel a strong desire for work. Furthermore, the landlord not only used the peasant's labor but "often put his hand on the fruits of that labor." The "idea of freedom [was] inseparable from the idea of abandoning agriculture," since peasants with any capital, "mental" or financial, would leave the village for the town, and therefore agriculture, Russia's most important economic enterprise, would be in dire straits. Although he was concerned about the Russian national economy, it is inconceivable that his own economic interests, and those of the other Russian landowners, were not foremost on his mind.

The ultimate result of Western political economy was the "unachievable goal" of what on the one hand he described as "la participation du plus grand nombre possible aux bienfaits de la propriete territoriale [and on the other] l'emploi des procedes de la culture en grand." The commanding thought in the West was the "idea of personal property," leaving no middle ground "between subdivision of the land to infinity, and proletarianism." Without elaboration or explanation Samarin stated his (and the Slavophils') preference in the form of a rhetorical question: "Is not the desired reconciliation contained in communal ownership?" The problem of capital accumulation was prominent in the works that he read. "Personal credit," he told Khomiakov, was considered in the West as the "highest degree in the development of credit." But he wondered, why in Russia, in view of the "obvious extreme scarcity of money capital, was personal credit so highly developed among the merchants?" Khomiakov would now understand, he said somewhat apologetically, "what sort of reconciliation I expect from political economy"; from his point of view, he added, "it is at least harmless."[10]

The schematic order in the descent of an idea through the three major, but usually not sharply delineated, stages — in the case of the Slavophils, from religion (Orthodoxy), through ideology, to program and action — is perhaps best exemplified in Samarin's career. After abandoning Hegelianism for Orthodoxy in the early 1840s, he chose religion over philosophy as the ultimate source of his basic and guiding principles. This accounts for his adherence to the communal principle, which, as pointed out in Chapter 7, he associated with the Slavophil principle of Orthodox *sobornost'*. Having wrestled strenuously with philosophy and Hegelianism only half a dozen years before, he could not completely forget them, all the more so since Western political economy triggered in his mind issues and ideas that he considered basic.

Toward the end of the same letter to Khomiakov (of August 1849) Samarin says, "I am not sorry that I used half a year for it [political economy]"; his study has, he says, given him the urge to "write an article about the contemporary muddle [*bezalabershchina*] in Western Europe," though he would not do so, he says modestly, because there would be no readers for it. He had a theme clearly in mind: he wished to show that "between the proud pretenses of abstract thinking and the wild debauchery of the triumphant press, between Hegel's philosophy and French communism, there is the closest and most lawful of bonds, but which up to now have not been identified."

Elaborating on what he considered to be at the heart of the Western "muddle," he came down hard on Hegel, his former mentor and idol. Human nature was "re-educated or more precisely mutilated by Hegel. Everything rational is actual or only the rational is actual." This is to say "only that is acknowledged as rational which has been deduced by thought from itself alone, *that which is created by itself.*" The end product of all this is that the "knowledge of thought about itself is the supreme manifestation of truth abolishing everything preceding." Truth cannot act on man because "it is his creation. In this manner the bond is severed, in which from time immemorial humanity believed (*religiia* from religare, to bind), between Supreme Truth . . . the Principle of all existence, and the finite manifestation of existence in the human person."[11]

In this manner individuals are deprived of the Supreme Truth, and are left to "acknowledge its law in man alone — in the personal contingency of his demands." This "leads inevitably to the unconditional and manifold autonomy of the person, to that cankerous principle against which no society can stand up." Furthermore, "Where is the human being who would order his inner life according to the deductions of logic; and is it not always the reverse, that submissive logic justifies that which man has come to love, or has accepted on faith, or that which habit has thrust upon him?"[12] He had resolutely discarded all simpleminded notions of man's nature and inner makeup. Logic, that marvelous manifestation of the human intellect, was not for him the source of "Supreme Truth." For a believing person to have acknowledged this would have been tantamount to substituting anthropotheism for theism, and as in the case of Europe and the United States, in recent years, it would have probably resulted in a variety of anthropomorphic cults.

There is no evidence in this letter to Khomiakov of conscious schematism or of a strict schematic order. Yet Samarin touches in it on Slavophil Orthodoxy in terms of which he descends to the middle level, and deals in general terms with ideological principles. Then he takes the final step, down to the plane of programming. Here, after "swallowing" the fifteen-odd volumes on Western political economy, he suggests that the "desired reconciliation" between Western individualism and Western socialism, or more precisely the varieties of Western utopian socialism, is "communal ownership." He, like the other Moscow Slavophils, saw in the Russian peasant commune a historical form of long standing, as well as a living institution of still considerable vitality. It held the promise for the future, which, unlike the schemes of Western socialists, did not have to be created out of theory and speculation.

There was a certain smugness in the Moscow Slavophils' notion that the socialist order for which many in the West were groping was already in existence in Russia and only needed certain adjustments, the principal one being emancipation of the serfs. What the Slavophils simply bypassed was the future place and status of the gentry, including, of course, themselves. It is worth stressing again that at the turn of the 1840s, Samarin, like his fellow Slavophils, did not include his own estates in the "communal ownership" that they all so ardently defended for the peasantry. An equally important and perhaps an even more fateful omission was the Slavophils' inability, or unwillingness, to face the problem of modern industrialism that was already marching eastward from England. We saw in the earlier studies that at the same time that Samarin was cramming on Western political economy, Khomiakov, it seems independently, was telling Koshelev that he hoped to see an industrial commune or (Fourierist) "phalanstery" evolve in Russia. Thus the vital, unavoidable, and tremendously complex problem of the coming of industrialism to Russia was dismissed with a pious dream.

In the early 1850s, however, neither the mechanization and modernization of agriculture in Russia, nor its general industrialization, was as basic to Russian society as the emancipation of the serfs. This reform, which had already come to Western Europe, with its economic, social, moral, and political implications, was absolutely essential if Russia was to move out of the Middle Ages and take its place in the forefront of modern European nations. Both Westerners and Slavophils were aware of the inevitability of emancipation, particularly after the outbreak of the Crimean War in 1853. The war soon demonstrated to Western European and Russian alike how backward the Russian social, economic, and political order was, because the backwardness was evident in an antiquated military machine that was woefully inadequate in logistics. As even the tsar had to recognize, emancipation of the serfs was only the necessary, long overdue, first step on the long, tortuous, and costly road to modernization. Compelled by this recognition and by fears of a popular revolution, the tsar in 1856 took the initiative for the Emancipation Act.

Soon after Khomiakov died in September 1860, Samarin was asked by the Society of Lovers of Russian Literature, whose chairman Khomiakov had been a few years earlier, to write his obituary. With the emancipation reform then in the last stage of its realization, Samarin, quite naturally, concentrated on Khomiakov's views on serfdom. He wrote a five-page obituary, but apologized for the limited amount of source material that was available to him at the time. The principal points that Samarin made, while covering a period of eighteen years, refer to events and views which, regrettably, are not always precisely dated.

The first reference that Samarin makes is to two articles that Khomiakov published in 1842 prompted by the tsar's ukaz of the same year about the so-called "obligated," *obiazannye,* peasants. As Professor Blum explains, serfs could now negotiate with their landlords for "freedom and the right to till a piece of seigniorial land in return for dues and services they continued to pay to the landowner."[13] Samarin's reaction was that the ukaz of 1842 was "in many respects inadequate, untested, and regrettably remained almost without application." But he saw it as being "superlatively conceived" as a beginning. Khomiakov was one of few to greet it as such, and he wrote another article publication of which the censor blocked. His purpose, in which Samarin fully concurred, was to show that "it was possible to pass over from personal sovereignty and arbitrariness to voluntary agreements."

The peasant commune, Samarin points out, lay at the center of Khomiakov's thought, "setting aside the question about the right of the individual person." Khomiakov "based the future order of things on purely land relations between the landowner and the peasant commune." He was convinced that the "inviolability" of the commune must be preserved "in all future transformations": it was "a native product of national life" and the "most trustworthy means of ensuring the peasant's right to land," and it provided the "moral milieu in which the best traits of the national character were saved from the contagious influence of serfdom." Samarin quotes from a letter he received from Khomiakov, which ends with one of Khomiakov's best-known rhetorical flourishes: "The *mir* supports in [the peasant] the sense of freedom, the consciousness of his moral dignity, and all noble impulses from which we expect his rebirth. . . . A Russian human being will not get into heaven alone, but a whole village cannot be denied entry."[14]

This is essentially a restatement of the fundamental Slavophil principles of *sobornost'* and *obshchinnost'* (communality) or the Orthodox, Slavophil religious foundation in conjunction with its secular counterpart, communality, which, they believed, was embodied in the historical Russian *mir* and village commune. Samarin concurred in these Slavophil principles in 1860, as he had since the second half of the 1840s. He also affirmed Khomiakov's belief that "it is easier for a whole society [commune] to acquire land . . . than for separate proprietors," and that whereas in 1842 Khomiakov admitted the possibility of compulsory labor by the peasant for the landlord, in 1849 he criticized the "inventory rules," designed to establish clearly the relations between landlord and peasant in the West of Russia, for not allowing the peasant to substitute quit rent (*obrok*) for corvée (*barshchina*).

Khomiakov, Samarin admitted, had reproached him in another letter, saying, "You have studied in detail the economic aspect of the question [of emancipation], but you have paid scant attention to its moral aspect," and had reminded him of the thought of an anonymous Frenchman: "L'esclavage déprave le maître plus que l'esclave."[15] In a letter to Samarin tentatively dated by the editor to the middle of 1848, Khomiakov sought a way out of the dilemma of serfdom and thought that Samarin had found the essential formula. Samarin now, in 1860, in turn attributed to Khomiakov, if not authorship, at least early advocacy of a fundamental Slavophil principle on emancipation.

I have already emphasized how important the Moscow salons of the 1840s, particularly those held in Slavophil parlors, were in the evolution of Slavophil views and principles. This can justly be said even in the absence of stenographic or other detailed and accurate reports on the informal but frequent salon gatherings. This large lacuna in the historical record often makes it impossible to determine with accuracy the authorship of ideas and views. But as I have noted before, the often elusive "first" or the parentage of an idea is of no particular concern here. Much more important is the precise content of the idea, what was done with it, and the purpose for which it was used.

When Khomiakov wrote to Samarin in the summer of 1848 he referred to the younger Slavophil's formulation rather than authorship of a basic Slavophil principle on emancipation: "Thank you for having hit upon that juridical form that expresses the meaning with the greatest clarity and distinctiveness, that is, about the existence among us of two rules equally strong and sacred: the hereditary right to property [for the gentry], and also the right to hereditary use," for the peasants.[16] As if returning the compliment, a dozen years later, Samarin says, "Khomiakov was among the first to understand the need for the complete emancipation of the peasants, allowing them ownership of land by means of a redemption payment." In fact these were two complementary Slavophil principles, possibly coming out of the Moscow Slavophil salon, but it was Samarin's lot to try to see them realized through the program of the emancipation reform.

Several other points that Samarin stressed in his obituary of Khomiakov, though of a more personal nature, shed light on Slavophilism in general. Certainly the social status of the gentry, its landed wealth, and serf labor with its problems, concerned Samarin as much as Khomiakov. Also of common concern were the economic interests of the Slavophil gentry, their mode of life, and the nagging moral Christian problem for those who owned serfs. This was a problem that Koshelev would not let his fellow Slavophils forget. No less keenly aware than Alexander II that serfdom had to go from "above" lest it cause an explosion from "below," the Slavophils welcomed Alexander II's initiative on emancipation. In Samarin's words, the tsar's proclamation of November 20, 1857, was greeted by Khomiakov "as an early joyful ringing of bells [blagovest] announcing the coming of day after a long agonizing night."[17]

Toward the end of Khomiakov's obituary Samarin mentions Khomiakov's memorandum on emancipation of the serfs. This was presumably inspired by the tsar's decision to proceed with the emancipation reform. But Russian public opinion of the 1850s, however restricted its freedom was, did not wait for the tsar's rescript of 1857.[18] The Crimean War, which came to an end with the Peace of Paris of March 30, 1856, served as a catalyst for an outburst of public discussion. The glaring weaknesses of Russia's internal order called forth unsolicited memoranda to tsar and government not only on emancipation of the serfs, but, as in Konstantin Aksakov's *zapiska* of 1855, on a wide range of social, economic, political, and moral problems.[19] Khomiakov's indictment of conditions in Russia contained in the lines of his well-known poem "To Russia" (*Rossii*), written in 1854, was another way of protesting against the status quo.

It is not surprising that Samarin did not remain silent in the midst of this limited and temporary but undeniably strong and sincere outburst of public concern for conditions in Russia. In his usual logical fashion, he put first things first: serfdom had to go before any fundamental improvement in Russian life could come. The immediate result of his concern for the elimination of serfdom was his long (119-page) *zapiska*, "About the State of Serfdom, and on the Transition from It to Civil Liberty," (*O krepostnom sostoianii i o perekhode iz nego k grazhdanskoi svobode*). Dmitry says that his brother worked intermittently on this memorandum for two or three years, edited and revised it several times. In April 1854 Iurii wrote to Konstantin Aksakov: "The other day I finished a rather extensive memorandum about serfdom, and about the various measures that in my opinion will facilitate the way out of it. Now I am copying it, supplementing it, and then I shall subject it to strict analysis in our circle, and finally I shall launch it."[20]

The burden of serfdom, both as a personal and as a national Russian problem, had been on Samarin's mind since at least the mid-1840s. This memorandum, Samarin's first statement on the subject, written while the Crimean War still continued, is a comprehensive, logical, and cogent exposition in favor of emancipation. After a four-page introduction, the first third of the memorandum deals with the underlying issues of emancipation. The subsections are titled, "The influence of serfdom on public morality," "The influence of serfdom on the political welfare," and "The influence of serfdom on the national economy" (this is the longest single subdivision in the memorandum).

Samarin then turns to more specific problems under subheadings such as "Negative or precautionary measures against further development of serfdom," followed by "Prohibition of transfer of peasants to households for domestic service," and "Prohibition of transfer of whole settlements from quit rent [*obrok*] to corvee [*barshchina*]."[21] The reasons for the last two provisions were a mixture of gentry self-interest, and concern for the majority of the serfs, the agricultural peasants. Samarin observes that such household serfs as "village administrators," carpenters, coopers, gardeners, and others were essential for the running of an estate; moreover, they could not be found as free hired hands, and even if they could, "many landlords would not have the means" to pay them. Worse still, the transfer of serfs from the fields to the landlord's household "severs the moral and native bond" between the two categories of peasants, and this in turn "permanently alters their mutual relations." The household peasants get the notion that they are superior to the field workers, and that this gives them the right to live at the expense of those who till the soil. This, Samarin maintained, is actually so, since the field hands assume the "taxes and draft for the army," for the household serfs.

On the *barshchina* and *obrok* problem Samarin's motives were also mixed. As the law stood, transfer from *obrok* to *barshchina* was prohibited with certain exceptions, of which he disapproves: the purpose of the law should be "to stop transfer [of peasants] to *barshchina* as a matter of speculation undertaken by the landlords for the purpose of increasing their income at the expense of the welfare of the peasants." But he qualifies this criticism by saying that this prohibition should not prevent the landlord's using "all compulsory means against delinquent *obrok* peasants."[22] This was particularly important for the landlord on estates where collective responsibility, *krugovaia poruka*, did not exist.

The last third of the memorandum is concerned with various aspects and problems of "Voluntary deals between landlords and Peasants," and a number of other issues. (Voluntary deals, of course, became irrelevant as soon as the tsar declared in favor of universal compulsory emancipation.) Samarin mentions the ukaz of 1846 about the so-called obligated or service peasants, *obiazannye poseliane,* and regretted that the measure was a dead letter as it did nothing to "encourage deals," by failing to remove the obstacles in the way of their realization.[23] He gives considerable space and attention to the relationship between landlords and the peasant *mir* or *obshchina.* Peasant assemblies (*skhodki*), peasant representatives (*starosty*), and other peasant functionaries, their election, activities, and duties; the role of *mir* and landlord in police, judicial, social, religious, and administrative matters; problems between landlords and peasants and their solution; financial, economic, and labor relations between landlords and peasants; the role of the government in the triangular relationship (peasants, landlords, and administration) — these and related matters are discussed in some detail.[24] Finally, Samarin stresses the importance of "public discussion of the question" of emancipation, and the "Necessity of the living example from above."[25]

As in the case of economics, so also with respect to the emancipation problem in Russia, Samarin did not hesitate to read in Western history if he could learn from the Western experience. While the Crimean War wore on, and revealed more and more of Russia's internal weaknesses, Samarin drew the conclusion that just as Prussia, defeated and humiliated after Jena and the peace of Tilsit, found the strength and will for "its internal renovation," so Russia could come out of the war experience reformed and stronger than before. It needed its own "Stein, Hardenberg," and should look not to Vienna, Paris, and London for its strength but inside Russia.[26] Its long overdue "renovation," *obnovlenie,* had its indispensable starting point in the emancipation of the serfs. Other reforms were to follow it.

Whether Samarin favored emancipation of the serfs or other badly needed internal reforms as necessary for the revitalization and strengthening of Russia, or as a way of preserving its indigenous, Orthodox, communal cast — or both — his notion about how the changes were to be made followed Slavophil thought — that is, they were to be sponsored and initiated from above. This can be said in spite of certain anarchistic proclivities already noticed in Khomiakov's and particularly in Aksakov's thought. Here we encounter in Samarin a basic political problem with strong social and ethical implications. In the middle of the triangular relationship, mentioned above, stood an ancient and in Samarin's time still living fiction of Russian public life. It concerned the relationship between tsar and *narod,* the common people.[27]

In spite of the considerable evidence that the *narod* was not as gullible or as innocent in its thoughts of the tsar and his authority as it is sometimes presented, the myth that the tsar was the protector of the *narod* against the gentry and the venal civil servants lived on. And during the nineteenth century the early Slavophils, Khomiakov, Kireevsky and particularly Konstantin Aksakov, were among its exponents. Samarin's position, however, was marked by a certain ambiguity; certainly his views on the subject seem to have undergone a change in the second half of the 1850s. Deeply involved in the emancipation reform in a way in which the other early Moscow Slavophils were not (Kireevsky, of course, died in 1856, and both Khomiakov and Konstantin Aksakov died in 1860), Samarin came to look at the peasantry, the narod, more soberly than the other Slavophils ever did.

The fact that most of Samarin's correspondence for the period from 1853 to his death in 1876 has not been published makes it impossible for anyone without access to the Samarin archives to reconstruct fully his views and convictions. But the considerable evidence in his published works, written both before and after 1853, gives us the foundation for at least some tentative conclusions. Thus, for instance, in his memorandum on emancipation (mid-1850s) he makes references to the relationship between tsar, narod, gentry, and the civil service (*chinovnichestvo*), and his preference is for people, *narod,* and tsar. He is against the gentry and the civil servant.

In a passage from the memorandum, often quoted, Samarin refers to the triangular relationship in these words:

> The gentry has separated the common people from the Tsar. Standing . . . between them, it conceals the common people from the Tsar and does not permit the people's complaints and hopes to reach him. It hides from the people the bright image of the Tsar so that the Tsar's word does not get to the simple people, or does so in distorted form. But the common people love the Tsar and yearn for him, and the Tsar for his part looks with love upon the common people. . . . And some day, reaching over the heads of the nobles, Tsar and people will respond to one another, and reach out their hands to one another.[28]

All members of the gentry, Samarin says, including those in government service, as well as all civil servants, "not excluding the clergy," are "suspect in the eyes of the common people." Furthermore, the "common people do not believe in intermediaries, [and] in their notions tsar and government are never merged."

The clear anti-gentry bias contained in a good many pages of Samarin's memorandum on serfdom is particularly telling in reference to the justification of serfdom. Here we see another fiction that was current among the gentry. To his own query as to "why 22 million subjects," who served tsar and state by paying taxes, doing army service, and performing other state duties, were "outside the law . . . [and were considered] as dead property of another class," Samarin gave an unequivocal answer: "In order to justify this injustice, they sometimes resort to the supposition of some sort of a deal by virtue of which the government arms the gentry with serfdom, at the same time placing on them responsibility for the peasants, [that is] the duty to take care of them, feed them in years of poor harvests, provide them with housing, and protect them from all injuries." While this might have soothed the conscience of some of the gentry, Samarin held that such an explanation "could not stand the most superficial criticism."

The justification of gentry authority, in Samarin's words, was "obviously invented in most recent times." Its purpose was to find a rationale for serfdom, when in reality serfdom "has begun to head for decline." Here, as in the Slavophils in general, and specifically in the case of Konstantin Aksakov, Koshelev, and Samarin, we encounter strong moral rather than legal limitations on the authority of the tsar. Political power was indivisible, or in Samarin's words, "State authority with all its duties, and all its moral responsibility before all the people, is subject neither to alienation nor to division." Supreme state authority was above all classes and was "equally close to all." In Samarin's simile, it was "as blood freely circulating in all the veins of the human body."[29]

This highly sublimated notion of authority in an autocracy was particularly characteristic of Konstantin Aksakov. But Koshelev's views on the role of tsar and government, though different, were no more down-to-earth than Samarin's and Aksakov's. In 1862 he published in Leipzig a pamphlet (it could not be published in Russia) in which he discussed among other things the convocation of a Zemskaia Duma, and argued against a written constitution for Russia. The Zemskaia Duma was to be summoned by the tsar, who would proclaim in his manifesto the Russian "Magna Charta," containing half a dozen basic principles. There would be "no authority above and outside the law." All proposed laws would be submitted for a "preliminary consideration to the Zemskaia Duma," and "without its deliberation no law could be proclaimed." The individual would be protected, for "no one could be subjected to any punishment or penalty without a court order." The state budget and accountability on revenue and spending "would be submitted to the Duma annually and in good time." The national representatives could submit to the Duma for deliberation gubernia matters and opinions, and finally, petitions from the Duma could be addressed to the tsar.

Koshelev prefaced his outline of what his Russian "Magna Charta" should contain with some typical Slavophil statements about "freedom of speech and action, guarantee of personal and property" rights, and "participation in public affairs." Like the other Slavophils, he stood for evolutionary changes and improvements consistent with Russia's cultural heritage: "We must accept what history has created for us," and work on changes and improvements from there.[30]

What is strikingly absent from Koshelev's "Magna Charta," and from the political thought of the early Slavophils, is any provision for legal guarantees. Neither personal rights nor the relations between tsar, state, and

Zemskii sobor were entrusted to legal or court protection. Khomiakov and the other early Slavophils abhorred what they called the penetration of classical pagan legalism into Roman Catholicism, and its eventual diffusion into Western culture, and they were on guard against legal guarantees — even in constitutions, particularly written constitutions.[31] On a somewhat more fundamental level, this sometimes almost anarchistic (in Khomiakov and Konstantin Aksakov) phobia was perhaps an expression of the difference between nineteenth-century Western anthropocentrism with its ultimate offspring, anthropotheism, and Slavophil Orthodox theism. Western constitutions particularly since the French Revolution had become secularly inspired and permeated even when lip service was paid to Christianity and the Christian God.

To Western eyes, and those of some Russian Westerners, the highly quixotic Slavophil views on the relationship between people, tsar, and Duma appeared totally incongruous and inapplicable. The tsar was conceived not as the absolute and often capricious ruler that he historically was, but as a benevolent servant of the people, who, in Konstantin Aksakov's view, relieved the noble people from daily, pedestrian, political chores, thus presumably enabling them to concentrate on the life of the spirit. Among the Slavophils this notion found support in a popular fiction that added a special turn to basic class antagonisms. In accordance with it the gentry, to which all early Slavophils belonged, stood in the way of the harmonious relations between tsar and people. Thus the only recourse the people had against mistreatment by the gentry was appeal to the tsar.

When Koshelev declared in the opening paragraph of his pamphlet that he knew of French, German, Belgian, Spanish, and Italian written constitutions but knew of no true freedom under them, he also expressed his appreciation for the unwritten English constitution,[32] though in his outline for a Russian Magna Charta he made no provision for either a written constitution or for any other legal limitations on the tsar's authority. Yet he and his fellow Slavophils would not tolerate lawlessness, and they relied for the protection of their estates on the enforcement of Russian laws. (Today, one wonders whether there is a choice between the strong Slavophil aversion to legalism and constitutional guarantees, and the pervasive and compulsive legalism in the West that allows people to sue anyone for almost anything, at any time.)

Without recourse to Samarin's correspondence after 1853 it is not possible to determine with certainty where he stood after the middle 1850s with respect to the people, the *narod.* It seems, however, that compared with his friend Konstantin Aksakov, he had a soberer, if not an absolutely detached, view of the Russian people. He had more experience in estate management, and saw the peasantry at closer range than did Konstantin. While he was on assignment in Riga, and later, while he was working on Bibikov's inventory commission in Kiev between 1849 and 1853, he saw Russian serfs under non-Russian, and non-Orthodox masters, and reacted with much sympathy for the Orthodox Russian peasantry.[33]   And in the late 1850s, while deeply involved in the emancipation reform, he observed at close range gentry, peasantry, court, and government. All this seems to have cast a different light on Samarin's view of the mythological relationship between tsar, people, gentry, and church.

Writing to his friend I. P. Arapetov, one of the lesser activists in the emancipation reform, on April 22, 1861—that is, at the end of the early, Moscow, or classical Slavophil period—Samarin said:

A manifesto, a uniform, an official, an *ukaz,* a governor, a priest with his cross, an Imperial Order—all this is falsehood, deception, fraud. To all this the *narod* submits, just as it puts up with cold, blizzards, drought, but it does not believe in any of it, does not acknowledge it, does not yield its convictions. To be sure, before the *narod* stands the image of the tsar who has been separated from it, but this is not the tsar who lives in St. Petersburg, appoints governors, issues imperial Orders, and directs the army, but some other tsar, a half-mythic impostor, who tomorrow may pop out of the ground in the form of a drunken clerk or a demobilized soldier.

In Zaionchkovsky's words, to the peasantry "this was not the actually existing Aleksander II but a good and fair tsar defending their 'muzhik rights,' who could [also] appear before them in the image of a new Pugachev."[34] From the above evidence, incomplete as it is, it would appear that in the late 1850s Samarin modified somewhat his earlier and more idealized view of peasants and people. His knowledge of peasant unrest in Russian history, of the peasants on his family's estates, and of the peasantry in general as he became immersed in the emancipation reform, led him to the conclusion that the appearance of another "impostor" was not impossible. And the consequences of such an occurrence for both peasants and tsar would be quite disturbing to him. This view of the *narod* was obviously different from that of Konstantin Aksakov, who was boldly assuring the tsar in the middle 1850s that he had nothing to fear from the people.

Samarin's belief in the necessity of emancipation was based primarily on a recognition of the facts—that the people believed that nothing could reconcile them with serfdom any longer, and that the "Tsar had for long considered granting them their desired freedom." "Three hundred thousand landlords are not without cause alarmed by the expectation of a frightful upheaval, [and] eleven million serfs are firmly convinced of the existence of a mute, long-standing conspiracy of the gentry against Tsar and people."[35] As Samarin recognized, the issue of emancipation, which united the tsar and the people against the gentry, in effect isolated the gentry class from the rest of Russian society and placed it in extreme jeopardy.

It was inevitable that as Samarin became increasingly involved in Russia's twin irreducible and undeferrable problems, the emancipation of the serfs and disposition of the land, his views on these and on Slavophilism in general should change. What up to the mid-1850s had been theoretical and ideological issues, now quite suddenly became pressing programmatic reform concerns. After the proclamation of Alexander II of March 1856, emancipation and the land question were thrust abruptly from the level of ideology to that of a workable program and tactics. While Khomiakov, and particularly Konstantin Aksakov, the Slavophil ideologist par excellence, could not easily adjust to active reformism, for Samarin, Koshelev, and Ivan Aksakov, this adjustment was essential as well as temperamentally more palatable.

Having stated his views on certain moral, historical, and political aspects of serfdom, Samarin sought to buttress his position in favor of emancipation by turning to its economic side or to mid-nineteenth-century notions of free labor as contrasted to compulsory or serf labor. The middle part of his Memorandum is devoted mostly to this subject. Relying heavily, although not exclusively, on his reading in Western political economy, he cited John Stuart Mill's *Principles of Political Economy*.[36] Not surprisingly, Samarin held that free labor is more productive than compulsory, serf labor, and, with respect to Russia, that quit rent (*obruk*) work was more productive than *corvee* or *barshchina* work. He was particularly critical of *barshchina*, and quoting from an article by Vil'kins, written in 1843, agreed that "in general under the *barshchina* [practice] the advantages of the peasants are diametrically opposed to those of the landlord." In other words, the less the peasants worked for the landlords the more they liked it, and the less the landlords got out of their lands. Samarin simply stated that the "worst worker is the slave [*nevol'nik*]." Barshchina not only rendered the worker unproductive but also subjected him to all sorts of abuse by unscrupulous landlords, including "forceful encroachment on the part of the landlord" upon the fruits of the serfs acquired during their free days.

Still another disadvantage of forced labor for all concerned—serf, landlord, and Russian society—was its drag on the mechanization of agriculture. Samarin's question under the then existing conditions in Russia, was, why "invent or acquire machinery, sacrifice considerable sums for the sake of constant saving of time and labor when labor and time do not represent definite value for the Russian landlord?" His conclusion was that in economic life "selfless love for betterment and desire for labor cannot replace the living feeling of need." In economics, need or necessity was the "mighty mover" of people.[37]

The many problems that beset Russian agriculture in the middle of the nineteenth century induced some Russian landlords to turn to the West for solutions. But Samarin, who was willing to learn from Prussia's experience, was skeptical this time. The "brilliant successes of agriculture in England

and Germany" induced some in Russia to turn to the West while "others were carried away by blind imitation of Western examples." This, he said, tended to disregard the peculiarities and special problems of Russian agriculture. In addition to serfdom, which did not exist in England and the German lands, Russian farming was troubled by the subdivision of landholdings. Samarin considered this detrimental to both landlord and peasant. The landlords who had to cope with such complications as soil exhaustion, years of poor harvests, elimination of some crafts, and "capricious luxury," were now confronted with the problem of shrinking estates. In addition, the landlord was carrying the "obligations of an insurance institution." If the landlord did not have a "reserve for the dark day," how would he support the peasants "during years of hunger, or after fires, cattle-plagues, or other misfortunes?"[38] Thus he was conscious of a definite but poorly defined economic obligation of the landlord to the serf.

Like Konstantin Aksakov and others who wrote memoranda in the middle 1850s on the state of affairs in Russia, and how to bring about changes and improvements, Samarin probably hoped that his memorandum would reach the court. At any rate he intended it for the widest possible circulation and influence. This of course imposed certain limitations on the content of the Slavophils' memoranda, and on their public expressions of opinion. The government was particularly suspicious of the democratic, egalitarian, socialistic aspects of the Russian village commune, the historic *mir*, which the Slavophils admired and wished to preserve.[39] It is not therefore surprising that Samarin did not completely bypass the question of socialism, most prominent in the revolution of 1848 in France, and not irrelevant to the peasant question and emancipation of the serfs in Russia. The historical Russian *mir*, increasingly referred to as the *obshchina* since the days of the Slavophils, was in their eyes the cornerstone of Russia's social-economic and administrative village life. In addition, having endowed it with ethical-Christian content and meaning, they saw the commune not only as the historical, and then still functioning institution, but also as the foundation of Russia's future Christian-socialist order (socialist, that is, for the peasants, since the Slavophils did not volunteer to include their own estates in the common pool of land.

Having concluded that the "weakening of the main springs of national productivity" in Russia was the "direct consequence of the present state of the working serf class," Samarin raised the question whether the brief experience of state socialism in France in 1848 was the answer for Russia; "Of course the questions and passions agitating France at that time were completely alien to us," but they aroused much interest in Russia. Referring obliquely to government circles, he says, "They could not find words for the condemnation of the socialists. [But] in vain!" He saw in secular, centralized, government-imposed French socialism in 1848 the same sort of injustice and stifling of productive forces as in Russian serfdom; but it was not for Russians to "cast stones at the socialists." The difference between French socialism in 1848 and Russian serfdom was that the "socialists hoped to bind together it [labor] with the voluntary consent of the masses, while we are satisfied with their forced submission."

The negative and undesirable character of French socialism of 1848 for Samarin comes through clearly and forcefully in his evaluation, but he is circumspect and evasive about socialist images. "We have become accustomed," he says, "to represent every socialist as a sort of scarecrow in whiskers, with a long beard, with a beastly stare, and in tatters. He might appear as such because of external circumstances, but the theory itself does not at all require such a tragic setting."[40] Given Samarin's circumlocution, one can only speculate about what socialists and socialist teachings Samarin had in mind that did not conform to the stereotype that he described.

Like the other early Slavophils, he reacted negatively to revolution, and to secular, if not outright atheistic, formal, legalistic, and politically instituted regimes, whether socialist or others. His Slavophil convictions inevitably led him to the old Russian indigenous, organic peasant commune, which in their most euphoric moments the early Slavophils believed to be inspired by Christianity. The profound Slavophil distaste for quick, deliberate, purposeful social engineering, as contrasted to the slow, organic process, seems to be behind Samarin's thoughts on French socialism in 1848. This also illustrates how difficult it was to prepare the Slavophils for the ever accelerating pace of change in a world increasingly subject to the impact of the relentless march of scientific-technological developments. Such a change in Samarin's time was reflected in the early scientific and mechanical inventions on the industrial and agricultural fronts. Some of these, as we have seen, were already coming to Russia with far-reaching implications in the realm of human relations there as everywhere else.

The middle and latter part of Samarin's *zapiska* contains much information about voluntary deals aimed at emancipation of the serfs, including his discussion of the government measures of 1842, 1845, 1847, and 1848, all dealing with landlord-serf relations. He also discusses the inventory system worked out for Russia's western provinces, and rejects its application to Great Russia. His views and arguments against serfdom and in favor of emancipation are forceful and well sustained. He advocated emancipation with land for the peasants and remuneration for the landlords while the government assumed the responsibilities for the serfs that had hitherto fallen to the conscientious landlord. His stand rests upon extensive knowledge and firm convictions. Today, this emphasis on voluntary deals between landlords and serfs has a hollow ring through no fault of Samarin's. Why devote so much time, and space, and hope to a form of serf emancipation that touched an insignificant number of serfs and landlords? The answer lies in the events surrounding the memorandum as pointed out, and on its timing.

Dmitry Samarin says in his biographical sketch of his brother that "Already in 1853 he [Iurii] undertook the writing of his memorandum 'About the State of Serfdom and About the Transition from it to Civil Liberty,' but it was finished and given circulation only in 1856.[41] (Samarin made it clear in his letter to Konstantin Aksakov of January 12, 1856, that he had already finished the memorandum.)[42] If Alexander II had made his declaration of March 30, 1856, to the Moscow nobility about his desire to see serfdom abolished "from above" a few months earlier, Samarin's extensive discussion of voluntary emancipation deals would have been superfluous. Yet the discussion contains much information that sheds light on Samarin's personal and Slavophil position on emancipation in general.

Some of Samarin's views can here be summarized. Whatever other considerations he may have had for wishing to see an end to serfdom, and we have already paused at the economic issues, his principal reasons were two. Serfdom was incompatible with Christianity, or, as he put it simply toward the end of the memorandum, in Russia there is an old custom of landlords granting freedom to serfs in their wills. This, Samarin says, was a "precious indication of the disturbing consciousness of the incompatibility of the Christian principle of brotherly communion with the right to dispose of one's fellow man as property." This was a nagging problem for all the Slavophils, of course. But for Samarin, no less compelling a reason for emancipation was his own keen awareness, stated earlier in the memorandum, that the patience of the serfs was running out. This was expressed in the form of "indignation, murders, and attempts on the lives of landlords and those in management," and these were increasing, as were attempts at arson and other acts "which are locally hushed up and do not reach high government circles." The choice for Russia was between "a peaceful or a tragic" solution.[43]

Anyone attempting to establish an exact order or gradation of the motives for Samarin's measured, reasoned, and in view of the circumstances, convincing advocacy of emancipation runs into difficult problems. While wishing and hoping for the immediate emancipation of the serfs with land, and eventual full legal independence from the landlords, he outlined certain transitional duties owed by the peasant to the landlord. These included redemption of peasant loans from the government in order to reimburse the landlords for lands to be conceded to the peasants, and preservation of the bulk of the gentry estates. In a word, Samarin was not ready to sacrifice the interests of his class in the name of a completely egalitarian, communal, one-class Russian society.[44] Konstantin Aksakov might have been tempted by such a solution of the problem of serfdom. Samarin, however, feared, as the memorandum clearly shows, that even a moderate emancipation reform such as the one he advocated would meet with strenuous resistance from the more conservative elements among the gentry and government circles.

The inventory system that Samarin considered proper for Russia's western provinces was not applicable to the Great Russia gubnernias. In the first place, emancipation would render it obsolete; in the second, there were the ethnic, religious, and cultural differences. Anyone familiar with Russian history, he said, "should understand that the relations between the landlords — Poles and Latins [i.e. Roman Catholics], toward the Orthodox Little Russians and White Russians . . . carrying in them external and inner signs of centuries-long systematic oppression must be materially different from the everyday [*bytovye*] relations of these classes in the Great Russian regions."[45] Samarin's experience on the Bibikov inventories commission in Kiev, like his service in Riga and the Baltic provinces earlier, tinged (as will be stressed in Part Two) his views of the Catholic and Protestant gentry within the Russian empire, and on Catholicism and Protestantism in general.

The long memorandum ends on a note, heard on occasion earlier in it and sporadically in the writings of the other early Slavophils on this and other matters, that the question of emancipation should be open to "public discussion" (*glasnoe obsuzhdenie voprosa*).[46] While on the surface this might seem like a page borrowed from mid-nineteenth-century Western liberalism and constitutionalism, its spirit and substance had little in common with them. The Western constitutional freedom of speech was intended to lead to binding majority decisions, and perhaps to Montesquieu's checks and balances. There was none of this in the highly idealistic Slavophil view of "public discussion." It would call for no constitutions, no binding parliamentary majority votes, no compulsory power of majority-enacted decisions. In fact it shunned all these. Konstantin Aksakov, in particular, took an extremely rarefied view of vox populi. What Samarin meant by "public discussion" was the freedom of articulate Russia to be heard and thereby contribute its knowledge, experience, and wisdom to the solution of an extremely complex national problem. This was meant to aid and guide the tsar (here appearing as the highly idealized Slavophil enlightened philosopher-king) in his decisions not to limit his presumed benevolent authority.

Two questions must now be raised with respect to Samarin's memorandum on emancipation of the serfs: what was its significance for his participation in the emancipation reform, in the approximately five years that followed its completion, and what impression did it make on those who read it? While precise answers to these questions elude us, some clarification of both should be achieved in Part Two which among other matters will consider Samarin's active, practical work for the emancipation of the serfs. It should be sufficient to record here on good authority, that some of those memoranda were noticed and considered on the highest level of decision making in Russia at the time, the imperial court in St. Petersburg.

Nol'de tells us that Samarin, who normally was not given to boasting, said in the fall of 1856, "My memorandum is in circulation and has met with great success." His first cousin and good friend, Prince D. A. Obolensky, who was in government service and close to court circles, noted in his diary for October 8, 1856, "During the past week the Grand Duke Konstantin Nikolaevich requested me to furnish him with Samarin's memorandum on the state of serfdom." When the Grand Duke asked his brother, Alexander II, whether he had read Samarin's memorandum, the tsar replied that he had not, but that he had heard about it, "it seems from [the Grand Duchess] Elena Pavlovna,"[47] who knew Samarin personally, and had solicited his views on the emancipation question.

There were, of course, persons working on emancipation of the serfs who were closer to the tsar than the Slavophils were, but few, if any, contributed more toward the reform through the printed page. Once the Slavophils were granted freedom to publish their own journal, and could engage in "public consideration" of emancipation, they lost no time. Alexander Koshelev became the publisher and editor of *Russkaia beseda* (1856–1860), aided by several co-editors, including Ivan Aksakov in 1858 and 1859. Then between March 1858 and April 1859 appeared the Koshelev-financed supplement, *Sel'skoe blagoustroistvo* (Peasant Welfare), dedicated exclusively to the problem of emancipation. Koshelev, Samarin, and their friend and collaborator on emancipation, Prince V. A. Cherkassky, contributed to it "more than 20 articles defining its orientation."[48]

In his distinction between the physical and social sciences Samarin held the view that the physical sciences lent themselves to precision, objectivity, and universal acceptance in a way in which the social sciences and humanities did not. Therefore personal and national preference and bias were much more pronounced in these than in the physical sciences. But Samarin gave more attention than this to his work and involvement in the Baltic littoral, where he felt that the Russian element and nationality were insulted and mistreated by the German nobility. This was happening while the Russian government did little or nothing for the Russians. However, in the early 1850s this issue was overshadowed by the problem of the emancipation of the serfs, and of Russia's economy. These in turn raised a number of highly complex religious, ethical, social, economic, and political issues. The extensive readings in the Western literature on political economy that Samarin undertook at the end of the 1840s to increase his understanding of Russia's present and future economic problems did not convert him either to laissez-faire liberalism or to any form of Western socialism. He remained loyal to Russia's peasant communal order, and was now firmly critical of

Western individualism on economic as well as philosophical and religiously based ethical grounds.

Like so many other Russians at the time, Samarin knew that the key to the future well-being and development of Russia was the highly complex problem of serfdom. Emancipation had to come first. His memorandum on emancipation shows that he was not completely free of a certain idealization of the Russian peasant order, but he was noticeably more realistic about the peasants than Konstantin Aksakov was; and form his reading and his observation on his family estates he knew, as Alexander II believed, that if the government did not take the initiative with respect to emancipation, the serfs would take matters into their own hands.

Notes

1. As I pointed out in Chapter 4, Samarin's published correspondence for the years 1840–1853 contains letters to Khomiakov, N. A. Popov, I. S. Aksakov, S. T. Aksakov, many to Konstantin Aksakov, and also to Gogol', Pogodin, Shevyrev, his parents and his brothers, and to A. O. Smirnova and others, but none to Ivan Kireevsky. See Samarin, *Sochinenia,* vol. XII.

2. Ibid., p. 207.

3. Ibid., I, 109, 111–113.

4. Nol'de, *Samarin,* p. 50.

5. Samarin, *Sochineniia,* XII, 199–200.

6. Ibid., p. 225.

7. Semevsky's standard two-volume study of the peasant question during the eighteenth and first half of the nineteenth centuries is rich in factual material and interpretation about various Russians, mostly from among the landowners, who for various reasons considered the emancipation of the serfs. Thus, Prince V. V. Golitsyn (1643–1714) wished to free the serfs with the *"land that they cultivated."* But this plan like all the rest before 1861 remained unfulfilled. A few other examples, chosen more or less at random, should illustrate the continuous and fruitless concerns. I. T. Pososhkov (1652–1726), son of a silversmith and an able self-taught "economist-publicist," is best known for his *Book about Scarcity and Wealth,* finished in 1724, but first published in 1842. A mercantilist, he took a middle position on serfdom, and toward the end of his life himself acquired an estate with seventy two serfs. Semevsky, however, says, "Pososhkov foresaw the possibility of freeing the peasants." In 1766 I. P. Elagin, on the precedent in Prussia, Denmark, Holstein, and Mecklenburg, suggested to Catherine II that the state take the initiative in granting the serfs on the royal estates hereditary use of a certain amount of land. Catherine II herself, in Semevsky's words, "once dreamed of freeing the peasants," and toward the end of the eighteenth century A. N. Radishchev, among others, favored the

elimination of serfdom. See V. I. Semevsky, *Krest'ianskii vopros v Rossii v XVIII i pervoi polovine XIX veka,* 2 vols. (St. Petersburg, 1888), I, 2–3, 5, 29–30, 213–223. For valuable, more up-to-date information, including the Decembrists on emancipation, see Blum, *Lord and Peasant in Russia from the Ninth to the Nineteenth Century,* pp. 536–574.

   8. Samarin, *Sochineniia,* XII, 430. Nol'de, who quotes more than a page from this five-and-a-half-page letter, surmises that among the authors that Samarin read at that time were the economist and political analyst Jean-Baptiste Say (1767–1832), considered by some a "vulgarizer" of *The Wealth of Nations*; Professor Karl Heinrich Rau (1792–1870), author of the three-volume *Lehrbuch der politischen Ökonomie* (Heidelberg, 1826–1837); Pellegrino L. E. Rossi (1787–1848), economist, jurist, diplomat, political figure, admired by Koshelev; and Frédéric Bastiat (1805–1850), economist and social philosopher, defender of free trade. Samarin also read about communism and anarchism, including Proudhon, and Louis Blanc. See Nol'de, *Samarin,* pp. 54–55.

   9. Samarin, *Sochineniia,* XII, 430.

   10. Ibid., p. 431.

   11. Ibid., pp. 431–432.

   12. Ibid., pp. 432–433.

   13. Blum, *Lord and Peasant,* pp. 548–549.

   14. Samarin, *Sochineniia,* I, 246, 247.

   15. The same thought was eloquently stated by Alexander Radishchev in 1790 in his celebrated *Puteshestvie iz Peterburga v Moskvu.* For the pertinent passage in English see J. P. Scanlan, G. L. Kline et al, *Russian Philosophy . . . .* (Chicago, 1965), I, 74–75. For Radishchev's warning of a possible serf uprising, see Ibid., pp. 75–76.

   16. "Pis'ma A. S. Khomiakova," *Russkii arkhiv,* 1879, no. 11, p. 331.

   17. Samarin, *Sochineniia,* I, 248.

   18. Among those who wrote memorandums at the time, Dmitry Samarin listed, in addition to his brother Iurii, K. D. Kavelin, the liberal Westerner, also Prince V. A. Cherkassky, friend of Samarin and Koshelev, along with Koshelev himself, and the right-wing M. P. Posen. See Samarin, *Sochineniia,* II, 17. Kornilov gives us a more detailed account of this short-lived but revealing outburst of public opinion in the mid-1850s. After a brief characterization of K. S. Aksakov's "remarkable *zapiska,* " he describes Koshelev's memorandum to the tsar as being on the subject of the economic condition of Russia; it advocated the "immediate convocation of the representatives of all the Russian people." The fate of the memorandum was "sad and comical." Koshelev, like the other Moscow Slavophils never a favorite of the tsar, wrote to Pogodin on July 9, 1855, with obvious annoyance that Khomiakov, who had castigated corruption in Russia in his poem "To Rus-

sia," should write about the "pseudo-church," Samarin about the "pseudo-government," Kireevsky about the "lie" in Russia in general, while he would write about "pseudo-gentry and serf" in Russia. Among the former or active members of the bureaucracy, M. P. Pozen and P. A. Valuev wrote memoranda, and as already mentioned so did K. D. Kavelin, early in 1856. See A. A. Kornilov, *Obshchestvennoe dvizhenie pri Aleksandre II (1855–1881)*, pp. 21–23. See also Barsukov, *Pogodin*, XIV, 48–49. For a fuller and more up-to-date discussion of this subject see M. V. Nechkina, ed., *Revoliutsionnaia situatsiia v Rossii v seredine XIX veka. Kollektivnaia monografiia* (Moscow, 1978), pp. 84–94.

19. For details of the Aksakov *zapiska*, see N. I. Tsimbaev, "Zapiska K. S. Aksakova, 'O vnutrennem sostoianii Rossii i ee mesto v ideologii slavianofil'stva.'" *Vestnik moskovskogo universiteta*, ser. Istoriia, 1972, no. 2, pp. 48–51; also Christoff, *K. S. Aksakov*, pp. 423–424.

20. Samarin, *Sochineniia*, II, 17n. Dmitry quotes here from an unpublished letter of Samarin's. See ibid., XII, 222.

21. Ibid., II, 21, 30, 37.

22. Ibid., pp. 79–81.

23. Ibid., p. 90.

24. Ibid., pp. 97–121.

25. Ibid., pp. 129–132.

26. Ibid., p. 19.

27. Recently in a useful monograph Daniel Field quotes Lenin's view of the long-standing myth on the *narod*-tsar relationship. "[There are] millions and tens of millions of Russian workers and peasants who until now have been able naively and blindly to believe in the tsar-*batiushka* [-father], to seek relief from their unbearably hard circumstances from the tsar-*batiushka* 'Himself,' and to blame coercion, arbitrariness, plunder, and all other outrages *only* on the officials who deceived the tsar. Long generations of the oppressed, savage life of the *muzhik*, lived out in neglected backwaters, have reinforced this faith. . . . [Peasants] could not rise in rebellion, they were only able to petition and to pray." Daniel Field, *Rebels in the Name of the Tsar* (Boston, 1976), pp. 1–2. In a differently focused study, going back to Russia's Byzantine heritage, Cherniavsky deals with "The Myth of the Tsar and the myth of the People." He supports the view that Russian political theory of the sixteenth century derived from the sixth-century Byzantine author Agapetus. The dual, divine-human nature of the ruler, in Agapetus's words, means that "Though an emperor in body be like all other, yet in the power of his office he is like God, Master of all men. For on earth, he has no peer. . . . For though he be like God in face, yet for all that he is but dust, which thing teaches him to be equal to every man." Cherniavsky saw a wide range of theoretical possibilities in this formula, and noted that "any epithet

or image from God to miserable sinner" could be encompassed. Michael Cherniavsky, *Tsar and People: Studies in Russian Myths* (New Haven, Conn., 1961), pp. 2, 45.

28. Samarin, *Sochineniia*, II, 33. I quote Field's English translation (Field, *Rebels*, p. 1), which Field took from the Russian version quoted by M. N. Pokrovsky, "Krest'ianskaia reforma," A. I. Granat, *Istoriia Rossii v XIX veke* (St. Petersburg, n.d.), III, 78.

29. Samarin, *Sochineniia,* II, 31–32, 34.

30. A. I. Koshelev, *Konstitutsiia, samoderzhavie i Zemskaia Duma* (Leipzig, 1862), pp. 22–23.

31. Long after the end of the Slavophil period, in 1882, Ivan Aksakov was adamant in opposition to any Western-model constitution for Russia: "The tsar cannot grant a constitution; this would betray the people, it would be treachery." Rather, the solution for Russia was something that "would hold Russia to its historical, political, and national basis. This solution is a *Zemsky Sobor with direct elections* from all classes: peasants, landowners, merchants and clergy." The coronation of Alexander III could be the proper occasion for such a manifestation. "The presence of a thousand peasant delegates will suffice, without need for further compulsion, to silence any constitutional agitation [by Western-type liberals], and will serve as a universal confirmation of autocratic power in the real, national, historical sense. Like wax in a flame, all foreign, liberal, aristocratic, nihilistic and similar notions will melt before the people." Quoted from G. M. Hamburg's translation of P. A. Zaionchkovsky, *The Russian Autocracy in Crisis, 1878–1882* (Gulf Breeze, Fla., 1979), pp. 289–290.

32. Koshelev, *Konstitutsiia,* pp. 5–6.

33. The so-called "inventories" or regulations of 1847–1848, though intended to determine the "mutual rights and obligations of owners and serfs," applied only to Russia's western provinces annexed from Poland. The commission that worked on the "inventories" was under the governor-general of the province, D. G. Bibikov. The inventory regulations were never introduced "in Russia proper." If adhered to, the inventory regulations were expected to relieve the serfs somewhat. But the fate of the inventories became quite controversial. Here we shall cite only Samarin's and Koshelev's views as given in Florinsky's highly competent summary. He says: "Yuri Samarin, an exceptionally keen and well-qualified contemporary observer, maintained that while both the methods used by Bibikov and the inventory rules of 1847–1848 for which he [Bibikov] was largely responsible were objectionable and crude, the reform as whole was favorable to the serfs." But Koshelev, whom Florinsky characterizes as "another authoritative contemporary observer," in his report to Alexander II in 1858, says that the inventories "did not justify expectations; the landowners retained practically unimpaired their powers over the serfs, the peasants made little use of the

safeguards offered to them, and only the police are kept busy and collect no mean profits." But Alexander II, in Florinsky's words, considered the inventories "unduly harsh on the landowners." See M. T. Florinsky, *Russia, A History and an Interpretation* (New York, 1955), II, 779–882. For Samarin's own commentary on the inventories, see *Sochineniia*, II, 1–16.

34. This fragment from an unpublished letter of Samarin's was quoted by P. A. Zaionchkovsky, in *Provedenie v zhizn' krest'ianskoi reformy 1861 g.* (Moscow, 1958), pp. 80–81. The English translation above, with minor changes, is from Field, *Rebels*, p. 23.

35. Samarin, *Sochineniia*, II, 35–36.

36. Ibid., pp. 32–33. He also relied on his reading of *Zemledel'cheskii zhurnal* between 1834 and 1853. This journal is not listed in *Russkaia periodicheskaia pechat' (1702–1894)*, although *Zemledel'cheskaia gazeta* (1834–1905) is listed; see pp. 233–234. The authority cited often by Samarin is Ivan Iakovlevich Vil'kins (1852), author of several works on Western European and Russian agriculture and economics.

37. Ibid., pp. 37–38, 40, 43–44.

38. Ibid., pp. 51, 56.

39. The role of the Slavophils' oppositionism during the late 1840s and early 1850s, although they never called for revolutionary action, has recently been well summed up by Kurilov. "During the period of the 'dark seven years' [1848–1855] they were almost the only ones who openly expressed their dissatisfaction with the existing reality. Belinsky was no longer living, the Petrashevtsy were in penal servitude, Herzen was an emigrant . . . and first turned to Russia with his 'free Russian word' only in 1853. And the time for the revolutionary activity of N. G. Chernyshevsky and N. A. Dobroliubov had not yet come. Under these conditions the Slavophils took upon themselves the basic burden of resistance to the tsarist government, and to the autocratic-serf order *inside* Russia itself. They stood the test without altering their orientation without giving up exposing of the 'imperial regime.'" See A. S. Kurilov, et al., *K. S. Aksakov I. A. Aksakov: Literaturnaia kritika* (Moscow, 1981), pp. 9–10.

40. Samarin, *Sochineniia*, II, 41–42n.

41. Cf. ibid., IX, XIX; Nol'de, *Samarin*, p. 68.

42. Samarin, *Sochineniia*, II, 17.

43. Ibid., pp. 66, 124–125.

44. Ibid., p. 129.

45. Ibid., pp. 88–89.

46. Ibid., p. 129.

47. Nol'de, *Samarin*, pp. 74–75.

48. See *Russkaia periodicheskaia pechat (1702–1894)*, pp. 367–368.

10

Spirit and Meaning of Orthodoxy

When in the summer of 1844 Samarin decided to abandon Hegelianism for incipient Slavophil Orthodoxy he in effect substituted religion for philosophy as the ultimate source of his spiritual life, and of his ideological orientation. This, however, should not be construed to mean that he either wished to or could exclude interest in philosophical questions. This conclusion is justified in view of the fact that his intellectual makeup was not altered by the change in his orientation. Furthermore, the two older Slavophils, Ivan Kireevsky and Khomiakov, also sustained lifelong interest in philosophy. These facts are of more than passing significance in Samarin's career since in his later years he considered himself heavily in debt to Khomiakov on questions of Slavophil Orthodoxy. It is, however, more difficult to determine with certainty Ivan Kireevsky's role in Samarin's spiritual and ideological evolution. What seems well established in the Samarin-Kireevsky relationship, even without the benefit of Samarin's complete correspondence after 1853, is that a certain distance and coolness that characterized it in the 1840s and early 1850s seems to have continued to the end of Kireevsky's life. Yet Samarin must have been well informed about Kireevsky's Slavophil views from Kireevsky's few published works, from discussions in the Moscow salons, and through Khomiakov.

Concerning Samarin's attitude toward Khomiakov we know that not only did Samarin publish Khomiakov's three essays on the relationship of Eastern Orthodoxy to Catholicism and Protestantism, he also collaborated in their translation from the French (in which they were originally published) into Russian. Samarin was also familiar with Khomiakov's germinal *The Church Is One* (Tserkov Odna), which was circulated as an unpublished pamphlet in the mid-1840s, and doubtless discussed in the Slavophil salons. While the personal compatibility between Khomiakov and the much younger Samarin is well established, the Samarin-Kireevsky relationship remains, as indicated in Part One, poorly illuminated. In the early 1840s young Samarin found Ivan Kireevsky too assertive and meddlesome, and I have seen no evidence that Samarin's coolness changed later on. The relationship between the two men is further obscured by the fact, mentioned earlier, that they do not seem to have corresponded.

Yet there is reason for the existence of a firm religious-philosophical and ideological bond between Kireevsky and Samarin. This is suggested first by the somewhat fragmented but authoritative testimony of Iurii's brother Dmitry, and in later years by the work of M. O. Gershenzon. Both Khomiakov and Kireevsky left, each in his own way, indelible marks on Samarin's religious-philosophical Slavophil thinking. This can be said without denigrating the originality of Samarin's thinking and his interest in independent inquiry and analysis. The two older Slavophils did not convert young Samarin from Hegelianism to Slavophil Orthodoxy in 1844; rather, they encouraged him to subject to his own firm intellectual scrutiny the irreducible premises of philosophy and Hegelianism on the one hand, and of faith and Orthodoxy on the other — reason and faith, respectively.

When Samarin decided after the prolonged and painful period of inner quest in favor of Slavophil Orthodoxy, he did so not as a result of a mystical conversion at an altar or in a monastic cell, but in the pangs of a private intellectual struggle stimulated in the Moscow salons. His "manly logic" (*muzhestvennaia logichnost'*) led him eventually to the realization, in Nol'de's words, that "religious truth can be affirmed but it cannot be proved."[1] For to prove religious truth is to prove the veracity of revelation, and to prove revelation is to elevate man's intellect to the level at which he is in a position to discern the divine mystery. Such aspirations inevitably lead to the self-aggrandizement of man, and to his self-elevation toward God, a process which in turn reduces to the vanishing point that which distinguishes God from man.

The "unilinear," "single track" approach of Western rationalism, specifically of German idealism, to history and human problems, well known to the two older Slavophils in the 1840s, became eventually apparent to the struggling Samarin. But behind Hegel's "World Plan" there was the bold claim that history was "subordinated" to a "metaphysical system" purporting to be "systematic." It was in fact not derived from historical experience but "deduced from philosophical abstractions." It posed the fundamental question — unsolved, and perhaps unsolvable — of what truth is and how man arrives at it. To the two older Slavophils the profoundly anthropocentric rationalistic Western way to truth was also indicative of the fragmentation and isolation, from each other, of the human faculties, for patently the human being cannot be reduced, without gross and unwarranted distortions, to reason alone. Hegelian rationalism thus contained not only epistemological but psychological implications, for it tended to distort the fundamental makeup of the human being and the complexity of life.

To these millennial riddles the two older Slavophils gave an answer which, however incomplete and biased, was soon accepted by the younger

Slavophils. This answer, in its barest essentials, consisted of Khomiakov's *sobornost'*, and Kireevsky's *tsel'nost' dukha,* the doctrine of the wholeness of the spirit. By identifying these two fundamental Slavophil premises with the founders of "early," "Moscow," "first," or "classical" Slavophilism no claims are here being made about the paternity or originality of Slavophil ideas. All that I wish to suggest is that Khomiakov and Kireevsky chose to become the sponsors and advocates of these two doctrines, so much so that in the literature on Moscow Slavophilism Khomiakov and *sobornost'* are inseparable, just as Kireevsky and the wholeness of the spirit go together, and both thinkers accepted these principles as the religious-philosophical foundation of Moscow Slavophilism. This integral part of Slavophilism was in turn to survive the nineteenth century and live into the twentieth.[2]

The doctrine of *sobornost'* constituted a foundation stone for Samarin's faith and convictions as it did for all early Slavophils. Although he seems to have been less emphatic about the doctrine of wholeness of the spirit or integral knowledge, he accepted it as completely as that of *sobornost'.* But a certain ambiguity arises here caused by the gaps in our knowledge of the Samarin-Kireevsky relationship. No such problem exists with respect to the better-illuminated friendship between Samarin and Khomiakov.

The most complete source accessible to me on Samarin's views of the "inner wholeness of thinking"—Kireevsky's *vnutrenniaia tsel'nost' myshleniia,*—is Dmitry Samarin's biographical essay of his brother. But ultimately, as Dmitry shows, the source is Iurii himself. It is given clear and colorful formulation in an essay on education published in 1856.[3] Having long since discarded his youthful "castles in the air" (*vozdushniia postroeniia*) in his effort to reconcile Orthodoxy with Hegelianism, now as a full-fledged Moscow Slavophil Samarin saw things differently. Referring to the state of affairs in the West Samarin says:

> "The concept of the spiritual wholeness of man is gradually squeezed out by its fragmentation into separate faculties and powers, each one acting according to its own laws, and in complete isolation from the others. This gives rise to the idea of some sort of box [*iashchik*] with impenetrable partitions. Here in this compartment is the place for dogmatics□this is the pigeonhole for grace. There, behind the partition, is located art□this is the department of taste. Further to one side is philosophy [*nauka*] where no other faculties except abstract thought must penetrate; and there we find morality."

In these circumstances, "it is difficult to admit that all human abilities are subject to a supreme spiritual force," the ultimate meaning of which is "creation of the wholeness of the image of the moral human being." On the view of man and his inner life presented by rationalism, Samarin concluded, "we come to understand the human being as an indifferent receptacle, in which are stowed away various abilities . . . thus discarding the concept of inner wholeness [*vnutrennaia tsel'nost'*]."[4]

As in the case of the other Moscow Slavophils, so also in Samarin's, the polemical way of expressing views and convictions was deeply rooted in Russian intellectual-ideological life and in Slavophilism. Whether he discussed Hegelianism and Christianity, the Western confessions and Orthodoxy, the Jesuits, the history of Riga, Russia's borderlands, Poland or the emancipation of the serfs, and other reforms, Samarin was first and foremost a vigorous polemicist. He was equipped with a knowledge of Latin, French, and German, and a retentive, erudite, and logical mind. He was also capable of sustained work, and possessed a clear and incisive style, and he saw to it that these qualities were mobilized in the service of his unswerving Russian patriotism, and the Slavophil cause.

The polemic style was, of course, ubiquitous in Russian writing in the middle of the nineteenth century and later; Samarin's writing, as well as much of his correspondence, bears an unmistakable argumentative tone, even when the ideas he is discussing are not original. It was, indeed, the tone of nearly all the early Slavophil writing. A competent critic and reviewer wrote soon after Samarin's death, "[Slavophil] ideas swarmed in the private meetings of the circle and they were subjected to heated and many-sided discussion. But in print these ideas were developed by some member of the circle much later, and perhaps sometimes not at all by the person to whom in the main the beginning of the idea belonged."[5] Such delays in publication, as archpriest A. Ivantsov-Platonov elaborated in his introduction to Samarin's published dissertation, were often due to the fact that the Slavophils were not permitted their own journal until 1856.

During one of the early encounters between Samarin and Kireevsky, Samarin's early doubts about the elder Slavophil caused him almost to question the direction he was taking: "My squabble [*spor*] with Kireevsky shook me up strongly. Is it possible that in fact I have been carried away by a phantom? It is necessary to study many things more thoroughly."[6] This was followed by Samarin's letter to Konstantin Aksakov early in 1842, quoted in Part One, in which Samarin expressed his resentment of Kireevsky's whole attitude and his purported satisfaction that Samarin and Aksakov were arguing with each other at the time.

Whether Dmitry Samarin had more information about his brother's relationship with Kireevsky than the few facts given here is not certain, but in his biographical sketch Dmitry rather pointedly excludes Kireevsky from the category of major Slavophils. Referring to Iurii's eventual change from Hegelianism to Orthodoxy, Dmitry says: "The split into two parties, Khomiakov and the Kireevskys on the one hand, Aksakov and Samarin on the other, completely vanished. More and more the concord between Khomiakov, Samarin and Aksakov became established, and in the end it made them prominent as the principal representatives of the Slavophil orientation."[7]

Nol'de is hardly more illuminating on the relationship. He points out that Khomiakov and Kireevsky were much older and "incomparably more mature" than Samarin and stresses the "immediate and direct influence of Khomiakov" on Samarin; "which came later" but seems to exhaust the matter of a possible influence of Kireevsky on Samarin when he says, "Kireevsky by the very characteristics of his quiet, solitary, and modest thought, by his mildness and femininity [*zhenstvennosti*], never produced on Samarin an immediate effect." Nol'de does concede, however, that Samarin's introduction to the two older Slavophils could not have failed to "strengthen his interest in purely religious and theological questions."[8]

Quite a different impression of the Kireevsky-Samarin relationship is conveyed by Gershenzon, who in 1911 edited the two volumes of Kireevsky's works, and the year before published in Moscow his *Historical Notes* (Istoricheskiia zapiski). In this collection of essays he devotes one essay each to Ivan Kireevsky and Iurii Samarin.[9] It may not be absolutely certain who among the Slavophils advanced the idea contained in Samarin's "box," (*iashchik*) (the West was certainly not unaware of it), but there is evidence that it was Ivan Kireevsky, and that Samarin accepted it as one of Slavophilism's negative principles, one that should be counteracted and overcome.

Gershenzon is so certain of Ivan Kireevsky's preeminence in the Slavophil circle that he confers upon him the distinction of "father of Slavophilism," ignoring the possibility that Khomiakov might with equal or greater justice be given the same distinction. The question of Slavophilism's paternity, it should be said, does not seem to have disturbed the early Slavophils, although it has been given some prominence by posterity. Gershenzon is equally certain of the ideological bond between Kireevsky and Samarin to the marked deemphasis if not neglect of the Khomiakov-Samarin relationship. Gershenzon's essay on Samarin begins thus:

> The direct heir of Kireevsky is not Khomiakov, who elaborated the theological-dogmatic aspect of Slavophilism, but Iurii Samarin, and he is the only one at that because it was precisely Samarin who placed at the base of his theory, and further developed, the idea that constitutes the authentic kernel of Kireevsky's theory. The whole "discovery" of Samarin represents nothing other than the further elaboration of the observation made by Kireevsky.[10]

Gershenzon used a combination of psychological and physiological elements to buttress his view of Samarin's dependence on Kireevsky. He saw the "starting point of Samarin's philosophy" in a passage from an unpublished letter of Samarin's to a friend, dated April 6, 1869, in which

Samarin stressed the "existence in man in addition [to others] a core, as a sort of focus from which gushes the natural spring." This, Gershenzon concluded, showed that the "only creative principle in man that determines the whole structure and life of the individual person is the sensory-volitional kernel [*chuvstvenno-volevoe iadro*], which thus centralizes the person and conditions its unity." Gershenzon's principal point is that Kireevsky formulated a well-defined notion of the "nature of human knowledge" based upon the "fact of the spiritual wholeness of man, in whom all faculties are subject to the power of the moral center." The ultimate conclusion from all this was that "vital and substantial knowledge is accessible only to the wholeness of the spirit and cannot be the work of any one faculty."[11]

Yet on the question of the wholeness of the spirit Samarin's role in the Slavophil circle was not completely subservient to Kireevsky's. Samarin, Gershenzon says, repeated Kireevsky, but with "greater precision," and took "a step forward." Samarin did not merely *prove* that knowledge *may* be acquired only through the integral spirit, but *showed* that it is actually *never* acquired in any other way."[12] This epistemological principle, like all Slavophil speculation on philosophy and religion, was based on irreducible Orthodox apophaticism. No amount of philosophizing and theological theorizing, particularly when turgidity is mistaken for profundity, could obscure for the Orthodox Slavophils the conviction that God is unknowable by any means at the disposal of man. For Samarin, of course, this was a premise that could only be taken on faith.

Firmly convinced that human beings are endowed with the capacity for faith and belief no less than with reason, Samarin formulated his stand simply and clearly: "Every man has faith, but one person is conscious of his faith, while another professing his faith in every word and deed is not conscious of it, and may even come to the conclusion that he does not take anything on faith."[13] It is therefore not surprising that he could not admit of "consistent unbelief." Then or now, it is inconceivable that most human beings could exist in total absence of some sort of faith or belief and a sense of belonging. Samarin was convinced that if one thought logically, one could not fail to discover one's own faith. Ultimately one believes in God, or in science, or in science and anthropomorphic gods, or in secular prophets and saviors. Most normal human beings seem to believe as well as think, and often belief and faith go deeper than thought. Complete atheists are probably few in number.

In 1851 Khomiakov stated in the opening lines of his essay "Aristotle and the World Exposition," written on the occasion of the exposition in the Crystal Palace in London, that the "primary character" and "distinguishing feature" of classical Greek civilization was its "deifying of man" (*chelovekoobozhaniia*). Elaborating on this, he saw the Hellenes as "deifying" man, who "was like god [*bogopodoben*] . . . The gods themselves were powerful, rational, beautiful, rich in a human way."[14] But the Greeks soon "understood the accidentalness of external man and began to bow before his reason." Worse yet, he would soon "bow before his own understanding [*razumenie*]." With a single sweep of rhetoric Khomiakov covered a period of many centuries in a few sentences. The "first epoch" of Greek thought was Homer's, the last was that of "silent Socrates, whose eloquent mouth was Plato, a marvelous mind full of every beauty, every fruitful power, every deep Hellenic thought." In contrast to Plato's contribution was the "strict analysis" in Hellenic thought, and it was Aristotle who "completed in Greece the concern with analysis." Thus, Khomiakov concluded, "the further development of reason passed of necessity into the one-sided predominance of abstract understanding [*razsudok*], and as understanding into its one-sidedness, so the unavoidable skeptic dried up, undermined, and uprooted everything living."[15]

Contemplating the course of Western philosophy and its permeation during the Middle Ages by the thought of the "Stagirite," Khomiakov saw a parallel between events in the West then, and in Russia during the eighteenth and nineteenth centuries. Aristotle was essential to Western Europe while it was emerging from the Dark Ages. He proved equally beneficial to the "desert savage, the Arab, and to the forest savage, the German." But his analytical mind, the "strictness of his method, and the abstract generality of his questions" outlived their usefulness, and so there was joy and relief when "Bacon and other great minds freed Europe from Aristotle." What had been a blessing for the West at one time had later become a burden. Similarly, he said: "Not a small favor was rendered to us by Peter [the Great], acquainting us with the sciences and the life of thought of the West, which became our Aristotle. But could it be that we shall never be freed from it and cast off the old saying *magister dixit*?"[16]

Samarin, as we have seen, often used the Russian *nauka* to mean philosophy; Khomiakov makes it clear in this essay that his *nauka* stresses the physical sciences. Peter the Great "introduced among us European science, and through this introduced all of European life." This much was good and beneficial for Russia, but the tsar overstepped the bounds of prudence when he also borrowed "all Western forms, even the most senseless," and—agreeing with Konstantin Aksakov—Khomiakov lamented, "mutilated the beautiful Russian language." Elaborating on Lomonosov's contribution to science in Russia, Khomiakov affirmed: "Science, that is, analysis, by its very essence is everywhere the same. Its laws are the same for all lands, for all times, but the synthesis that accompanies it changes with place and time." Just as Aristotle's usefulness in the West came to an end together with scholasticism, so "Scholasticism in our science, which has not made a single stride forward, scholasticism called academism in our art ... scholasticism in all manifestations of life" must go. The "intellectual enslavement" of Russia, which Khomiakov by implication attributed to Peter the Great and the Russian Westerners, had to end. "The Aristotle of Russia is not dead like the Aristotle of the Middle Ages." It was time for the students "to think with their own minds."[17]

The Middle Ages "subjected themselves to Aristotle as a consequence," in Khomiakov's words, "of the preponderance of analysis in him." Contemporary enlightenment (*prosveshchenie*) on the continent of Europe was in turn dominated by the element of "abstract understanding" (*razsudochnosti*). But finally the rest of Europe turned its eyes on England, and upon the "new miracle of the Crystal Palace and the world exposition." He was disappointed that he could not visit the exposition, and was full of admiration for certain aspects of English life. Not the least was the ability of the English people to preserve some of the best of the old, as they were showing to the world many of the miracles of the new age. "Yes, in England they know how to respect the work of time."[18] This could be said without suggesting blind conservatism, for it would be "difficult to accuse it [England] of stagnation."

Khomiakov had no difficulty admiring the scientific-technological achievements of England and the West, for the London exposition exhibited English as well as other European and American industrial products. But as usual with the Slavophils, he could not concede preeminence to the West in the religious, social, moral, and psychological spheres. He raised the question of individualism in the West, attributing it to the Middle Ages and ever since then, but concluded, "In our time the activity of the individual has been deprived of its grandeur because the individual has lost his meaning." He did not explain why or how individualism was presumably a matter of the past in the West. One can only speculate that he came to this conviction under the impression of the variety of Western utopian socialisms of the 1830s and 1840s, which left the impression with some that social consciousness was replacing individualism.

The wave or the "poetry" of the future, in Khomiakov's words, was not in individualism but in the "political social masses." Although this new "poetry" was not yet well understood, it was superior to "medieval poetry." With this brief introduction he arrived at the choric principle, one of Slavophilism's cornerstones, elaborated most clearly by Konstantin Aksakov. "The melody sung by the soloist is of course beautiful and alluring," Khomiakov began. "It bubbles and it sparkles, it breathes passion and inflames passion, but it is incomparably subordinated to the flowing and harmonious choir in which an endless number of voices blend into one majestic whole. And this is not aflame with petty passion but illuminates the whole soul with the rays of rational harmony." Conscious of the fact that the Slavophils were isolated on this question from both Western liberals and Russia's liberal Westerners, he admitted that there were fewer admirers of the "melodious choir" than of the "individual melody," but then, he said, the task of the choir was more difficult.[19]

One cannot properly or justly reduce Samarin's dissertation on Stefan Iavorsky and Feofan Prokopovich to a single topic. It contains his views on certain aspects of Orthodox, Catholic, and Protestant theology, doctrine, and dogma. It also includes some history, particularly of the period of the ecumenical councils from the fourth to the seventh centuries, and of the three Christian confessions in more recent times. But perhaps nothing was as prominent in Samarin's mind, then and later in his religious reflections, as the subject of ecclesiology. His view of the Christian church emphasized its biblical essence, its organization, and its historical and universal missions. In the early 1840s he, like Khomiakov then and a decade later, left no doubt that by the Christian church he meant the Eastern Orthodox Church. He measured the Western confessions against it and found them wanting, and yet retained the hope, however vain it might appear at the moment, that the erring Western churches would return to the true, Christian and universal church.

Between Samarin's dissertation and Khomiakov's *The Church Is One,* both unpublished in the mid-1840s, and the published theological works of Khomiakov in the first half of the 1850s, there appeared in print in the West a challenge to the Western churches, the Catholic in particular. The author was not one of the "early" Slavophils but one who knew them, and perhaps found himself in sympathy with certain aspects of their orientation. This was the diplomat and poet Feodor Ivanovich Tiutchev (1803–1873). Tiutchev belonged to the generation of Khomiakov and Ivan Kireevsky and, like all the early Slavophils, came from a Russian gentry family. He was not a Muscovite, although he did attend the University of Moscow. Rather, this "almost-foreigner [*pochti-inostranets*]" spent most of his life in Germany and St. Petersburg, a city which he did not really like.[20] Tiutchev's life was one of contradictions and inconsistencies, accentuated by temperament and circumstances. The Tiutchev family, in the words of one of Tiutchev's biographers, "so deeply attached to the land, the faith, and the customs of their forefathers, spoke and read among themselves almost exclusively in French." "In a literal sense . . . French, not Russian, was Tiutchev's parent tongue." And the later intense Russian patriot and nationalist conducted "virtually all his social and family intercourse, epistolary as well as conversational, in the former [French] language."[21]

Receiving his early education from private tutors, as was customary for a gentry son, Tiutchev graduated from the University of Moscow in literature in 1821. There he met, among others, M. P. Pogodin, A. I. Koshelev, V. P. Titov, V. T. Odoevsky, and S. P. Shevyrev. Pogodin grew fond of Tiutchev, visited him at his estate at Troitskoe, on the Kaluga road, and discussed with him the "Turkish question and Pushkin's political views" as well as "German, Russian, and French literature, religion, Moses, the divinity of Jesus Christ . . . Wieland, Lessing, Schiller, Addison, Pascal, Rousseau, and our poverty in writers." Having tasted briefly the social life of Moscow and St. Petersburg, Tiutchev at eighteen arrived in Munich as a second secretary to the Russian mission. He was already "an ardent admirer of feminine beauty," and ready to take advantage of the "holiday of a wonderful youth."[22]

In sharp contrast to the decorous and straitlaced early Slavophils, Tiutchev stands out both as a youth and later in his life. But his long Munich assignment (1822–1837), with occasional travels in and outside Germany, was not completely given over to women. Finding himself in the "Athens of Germany," young Tiutchev was able to move in its distinguished literary and intellectual circles. He won this position thanks to his "agile mind and brilliant conversational powers [which] attracted such distinguished men of letters as Baader, Schelling, Fallmerayer, and Heine." Thus while with Schelling the young Russian "eloquently defended the mysteries of Christian dogma against the latter's [Schelling's] rationalizing inroads." This did not prevent Schelling from characterizing him as "a most remarkable and most cultivated man with whom it is always a pleasure to converse."[23] In Munich, Tiutchev was often a host to fellow countrymen who were traveling or studying in Germany—among whom were Prince P. A. Viazemsky, Shevyrev, N. M. Rozhalin, V. P. Titov, and, in 1830, young Ivan and Peter Kireevsky. Ivan Kireevsky, then a moderate Westerner, wrote home from Munich that Tiutchev "with his presence alone can be beneficial to Russia. Such Europeans among us can be counted on one's fingers."[24] Thus contact between Tiutchev and the Kireevsky brothers, and between him and Koshelev, was established before Moscow Slavophilism was born.

It is not the purpose here to dwell on the poet Tiutchev, although it should be noted that Tiutchev's poetry has risen steadily in esteem since about 1850, and has been recognized and appreciated by personalities as different as the philosopher Solev'ev and Lenin.[25] Tiutchev's prose works, however, particularly his several ideological essays, are of interest because of their clear connection with Moscow Slavophilism. This connection has been noted by Tiutchev's biographers, R. A. Gregg in particular, who bring out the ways in which Tiutchev came close to Moscow Slavophilism in the second half of the 1840s, and also—which is equally important with respect to defining the content of Moscow Slavophilism—how he departed or differed from it.

In 1844 Tiutchev published in the Augsburg *Allgemeine Zeitung,* "Lettre a M. le Docteur Gustave Kolb." His purpose was twofold—to refute the liberal German press view that Russia stood in the way of German unification, and to reply to Marquis de Custine's "savage" attacks on Russia in *La Russie en 1839.*[26] Early in 1849 he published in *La Revue des deux mondes* "La Russie et la Révolution." This article, intended as a chapter in a book, "La Russie et l'Ouest," which he never finished, is said to have been written as a memorandum to the tsar to inform him about the February revolution.[27] In the memorandum Tiutchev criticizes the West, particularly its churches and German, Austrian, and Magyar nationalism, and extols Russia and the Slav world, and shows great concern for the subjugated Czechs, Slovaks, Croats, and Serbs.[28]

These two articles, and a third, "La Question romaine," published early in 1850 in *La Revue des deux mondes,* together with some of Tiutchev's poems, give us the gist of his position. From the point of view of the relationship between Tiutchev and the Moscow Slavophils, "La Question romaine" is the most important of the three articles. Khomiakov, who probably read the two earlier articles also, makes specific reference to it in the opening paragraphs of his first theological pamphlet to 1853, which was his answer — "Quelques mots par un Chrétien orthodoxe sur les communions occidentales"—to M. Laurentie, who had in turn replied to Tiutchev's article. Khomiakov summed up Tiutchev's point of view by saying that he attributed the religious difficulties in the West primarily to the "mixing up [*smeshenie*] in the person of the bishop-monarch [*episkop-gosudar*], of spiritual with secular interests." Although he welcomed Tiutchev's point of view, and noticed with satisfaction that even M. Laurentie "did not question the virtues" of Tiutchev's article, he wondered whether Tiutchev "did not somewhat mix up the cause of the malady with its symptoms."[29]

Koshelev, who knew Tiutchev in the early 1820s in Moscow, as well as later in Munich, was less circumspect than Khomiakov. In a letter to A. N. Popov on February 1, 1850, he commented that Khomiakov was satisfied with Tiutchev's article but he himself did not "approve all his opinions in it." In fact Koshelev come down harshly on his old university friend. He did not consider the article particularly distinguished, and saw in it "more false than true thoughts. His definition of the word 'revolution' and notion of a people's war are simply absurdities. In general it contains many phrases but very little consistency," and the living thoughts that Khomiakov saw in it "found their way there by mistake."[30]

Looking upon the West through the Russian prism, as if the West could be encompassed within a single unified culture, Tiutchev in effect saw the inexact and generalized but nonetheless potent perennial dichotomy between Russia and the West. In his "La Questionn romaine" he stressed the religious differences, and chose to dwell heavily on Catholicism; he glibly dismissed "Le Protestantisme avec ses nombreuses ramifications" with the words "se meurt de décrépitude," except in England, where it preserved some vitality.[31] Catholicism, specifically the papacy, was "la colonne unique" that sustained the Western church. But the Catholic church had long ago succumbed to secularization. And as if echoing the early Slavophils, he declared with unconcealed distaste his opinion of "le fétichisme des Occidentaux pour tout ce qui est forme, formule et mécanisme politique,"[32]

Also like the early Slavophils he was convinced that "l'Eglise est Une et Universelle—mais entre les deux mondes." For him, as for the Slavophils, Christ had given the ultimate answer on this question, "Mon Royaume n'est pas de ce monde."[33] Still in effect in agreement with the Slavophils, he censored Rome for separating itself from the church and thereby violating its unity. That is when it decided to establish "un Royaume du Christ comme un royaume du monde."

Catholicism and Protestantism, each in its own way, Tiutchev says, elevated the "personal I," "du moi humain," in place of the universal church. Rome accepted church tradition and was content "de la confisquer à son profit," whereas Protestantism simply abandoned it in favor of the personal "I." Tiutchev saw this same "I" or ego elevated to prominence in Western life in general, and its "apotheosis" in manmade law as the very heart of Western revolutions. At the same time, the church being no longer "au milieu de la grande société humaine une société de fidèles librement réunie en esprit et en vérité sous la loi du Christ . . . était devenue une institution, une puissance politique-un Etat dans l'Etat." In truth, to Tiutchev the Western church from the Middle Ages on "n'était autre chose qu'une colonie romaine établie dans un pays conquis."[34] Finally, outraged Christian thought and sentiment could no longer be contained, but as the church of Rome shielded the West from the universal church, the protest movement "appeler au jugement de la conscience individuelle-c'est-à-dire qu'ils se firent juges dans leur propre cause." The inevitable end on this road was to elevate and sanctify the "human I," which is "anti-Christian in its essence."[35] This unfortunate development in the West, Tiutchev concluded, was not merely a matter of the last three centuries.

It was no surprise for Tiutchev that the French Revolution summed up its attitude toward Christianity in the words,"l'Etat comme tel n'à point de religion," and this, he said, expresses in general the relationship between the modern state and Christianity in the West. The Western state thus became "étranger à toute sanction supérieure à l'homme." But at the same time that the revolution declared its neutrality on matters of faith it ruled out neutrality toward the Revolution, "Qui n'est pas pour moi est contre moi." In Tiutchev's view, the "sophistry of the new teaching" could not last. Taking a stand on the schism of the ninth century, which was also characteristic of the Slavophils, he said, "De toutes les institutions que la Papauté a enfantées depuis sa séparation d'avec l'Eglise Orthodoxe, celle qui a le plus profondément marqué cette séparation . . . c'est sans nul doute la souveraineté temporelle du Pape."[36]

Tiutchev concentrated some of his severest criticisms of the papacy by way of the Jesuit order, as Samarin did a decade and a half later, and, like the Slavophils, concurred in Pascal's criticism of the Jesuits. But in spite of his strongly negative views on the papacy and on Roman Catholicism in general, he did not completely despair of the West's primary church: the hope, like the light, would come from the east. "L'Eglise Orthodoxe n'a jamais désespéré de cette guérison," and he conceded that "le principe chrétien n'a jamais péri dans l'Eglise de Rome."[37] All that Catholicism had to do was to return to the universal Orthodox church. Thus in effect he reversed the call of Pius IX in his Encyclical to the "Easterns" of 1848.

Tiutchev's views on the Western confessions, particularly on Roman Catholicism, like those of the Slavophils, are sufficiently clear and categorical to need no further elaboration. They show unequivocally and from the point of view of Christian unity, tragically, how irreversible and perhaps irreparable the split in the church had become in the more than a millennium since the East and West in Europe went their separate ways. Nor does the West's centuries-old, "blind," and ill-intentioned inveighing against the "Byzantine" East help the cause of historical fact and reconciliation. Obviously, what was involved in the religious controversy in the middle of the nineteenth century was not merely the historical past, but also the then current sense of regional as well as national, cultural, and individual amour propre.

When Samarin learned of Tiutchev's death in July 1873 he characterized Tiutchev in a letter to the Baroness Rahden as a poet rather than as a religious-political thinker. Yet his concise comments are not without relevance to the question of concern here — that is, how is Tiutchev ideologically related to the Moscow Slavophils? It is not surprising that Samarin was struck by Tiutchev's poetic talent; with the death of Tiutchev, he said, was "extinguished the last ray of the *pléiade* of which Pushkin was the center," and furthermore, "what is figuratively said of poets, comparing them to the stretched chords of an instrument which is always ready to resound at the slightest breath, could be applied to him without any exaggerations. . . . The charms and the pains of poetic childbirth were to him equally unknown." But the paradox that was Tiutchev, well known to his contemporaries, was also noticed by Samarin. The inconsistencies and contradictions in normal men and women are sufficiently striking, but they become magnified and glaring in those of talent and genius. "Curiously," Samarin wrote of Tiutchev, perhaps somewhat self-consciously, "his mother tongue was not familiar to him, and he spoke it only with difficulty, but this ignorance itself, together with a sound knowledge of French and German, led him to discover resources and precision of expression in Russian which no one before him possessed."[38]

Perhaps no one of Tiutchev's contemporaries was in a better position to observe him in his later years and pass judgment on his views and convictions than Ivan Aksakov, who was not only Tiutchev's son-in-law but also his first biographer. One must take with due respect Aksakov's comment on Tiutchev's relationship to the Slavophils; he says that before Tiutchev returned to Russia to live, he "did not know them at all" and "afterwards he was never in particularly close relations with them." Tiutchev, he said, was a person who had "so completely made the Western "European enlightenment his own" that the Russian Westerners must have been amazed to see his "natural love for his fatherland," and "not only [his] faith in the great political future of Russia but also his conviction of the supreme universal calling of the Russian people, and in general of the spiritual element in the Russian nationality."[39]

From Ivan Aksakov's testimony about the relationship between Tiutchev and the four early Slavophils (Khomiakov, Kireevsky, Samarin, and his brother Konstantin Aksakov), it is apparent that this was a case not so much of close association and interaction as of the parallel flow of kindred views and ideas that occasionally touched and then departed and went their respective ways. Even though there was no close continuous contact between Tiutchev and the Slavophils, Khomiakov and Samarin probably could not have completely escaped a certain encouragement and bolstering from some of Tiutchev's views, particularly since these were publicized during the 1840s, Moscow Slavophilism's formative period.

The points of contact as well as those of departure between Tiutchev and the Moscow Slavophils should serve to define their respective ideological positions more clearly. With the help of Professor Gregg's valuable summary one can say that "[both] harbored a deep mistrust for the secularized, materialistic, and rationalistic West," and both believed in the special character and calling of the Russian people, thought to have achieved a high degree of spirituality through suffering and humility. Both chose, on most occasions, to look not at the historical Russian church but at an idealized version, and contrasted its detachment from mundane matters with the "temporal ambitions of the Roman Church."[40] In Tiutchev's poetry and prose, as Solov'ev pointed out, there are clear expressions of a Russian Orthodox messianism, perhaps somewhat more abrasive to non-Russian ears than the similar kind presented by the Moscow Slavophils.

But Tiutchev remained unmoved and untouched by the Slavophils' idealization of the historical Russian *obshchina*. He also was more approving than they of the reign of Peter the Great. They differed fundamentally, as Gregg has properly stressed, on the question of political authority.[41] Whether or not Tiutchev had unswerving faith in the divine right of kings, he was a confirmed monarchist and a believer in the Russian tsar; the Slavophils, despite their contradictory and confusing monarchism, in theory placed their faith in the people, the *narod*. With these points of difference, one asks, was Tiutchev a Slavophil? Solov'ev, Gregg, and others speak of his Slavophilism at times for lack of a more precise designation. Manifestly he was not a complete or true Slavophil. If he belonged to a different category, what was it?

Samarin was in Kiev when Tiutchev published his "La Question romaine" at the beginning of 1850. (He had arrived there on December 2, 1849, in a sort of semi-exile as punishment for his *Riga Letters*.) It is most unlikely that he would not have read Tiutchev's essay some time in the early 1850s, particularly since both Khomiakov and Koshelev read it and reacted to it, Khomiakov as pointed out, in print in the spring of 1853. Samarin and Tiutchev were separated in age by almost a generation, but they had met as early as 1844, probably within months after their separate arrivals in St. Petersburg. On October 2, 1844, Samarin wrote to Konstantin Aksakov, "Tiutchev arrived here recently. Tomorrow evening Viazemsky is supposed to introduce me to him."[42] By the spring of 1847 Samarin was sending greetings to Tiutchev from Riga, as he was doing for other friends and acquaintances in St. Petersburg.[43] But Samarin's relationship with Tiutchev, and indeed the relationship between Tiutchev and the Moscow Slavophils, is important not so much for what Tiutchev may or may not have added to Slavophil doctrine and ideology as for Tiutchev's strong Russian national Orthodox point of view, and as of the early 1850s, because of his growing stature as a foremost Russian national poet. Khomiakov and Samarin were, of course, not trained as professional theologians or philosophers, but neither was Tiutchev, and by 1850 (the year of *La lettre romaine*) there was little that Samarin could learn from Tiutchev about the history and status of the Western confessions vis-a-vis the Eastern Orthodox church. What Tiutchev and the Slavophils had in common, then, beyond the similarities already mentioned, was a profound ethical concern, a concern for life here and now rather than with the hereafter.

It is not unusual to see in Western literary criticism Russian authors, Tolstoy foremost among them, reproached for their religious and ethical preoccupations, as if "pure" art and literature — to say nothing about life itself — can survive without taming and bridling the animal in man. Unconcealed and no far behind the wide-ranging controversies between Slavophils and Westerners of the 1840s and 1850s were basic problems of human conduct and relationships. It is well known, for instance, that the Slavophils and Chernyshevsky started from different premises, one Orthodox Christian, the other philisophical materialist, and that they also disagreed on other important matters, yet their paths converged in their distaste for mid-nineteenth-century Western laissez-faire individualism and the predominance of bourgeois attitudes and values. They differed in their interpretations of the essence of the historical Russian peasant commune, the *obshchina*, but Chernyshevsky saw in the Slavophils' appreciation of it the best part of Moscow Slavophilism. This would probably have been true also of Belinsky had Slavophil views on the commune been fully elaborated before Belinsky's death in 1848.

The Slavophil idealization of the historical and contemporary Russian village commune, which reached its most extravagant level in the thought of Konstantin Aksakov, was tempered in Samarin's own thought. But it is not unwarranted to say that all the Slavophils saw in the commune a providential bond with Orthodox *sobornost'*. The union in love and freedom sanctioned by Orthodox Christianity found its imperfect secular realization in the brotherhood of communal living. Communes had been known to other societies but survived nowhere else in Europe in the middle of the nineteenth century except among the Slavs, principally among the South Slavs and the Great Russians. Both the *zadruga* and the Great Russian *mir* and *obshchina* were functioning institutions in the days of the Slavophils. And whatever attributes the principles of *sobornost'* and *obshchinnost'* had, they also stood for profoundly ethical principles. Mid-nineteenth-century laissez-faire with its often accompanying "wolf freedom" (predatory freedom) had no appeal for the Slavophils and probably for a good many Russian non-Slavophils.

In contrast to Western theological concerns with infallibility purgatory, indulgences, original sin, treasury of merit, justification through faith and good works or faith alone, superrogatory works, predestination, salvation, and denial or ignoring of church Tradition, the Slavophils concentrated on Christian living here on earth. Aided perhaps by Orthodox apophaticism they showed no undue concern for matters of salvation, which so tormented Martin Luther while he was still in the Roman church. Live as complete a Christian life here on earth as possible and leave the rest to God, seems to have been the attitude of the Slavophils. Furthermore, as nontheologians they showed no particular desire for scholastic or other theological hairsplitting. They believed that however imperfect human beings might be, the church was the heart and soul of the Orthodox Christian life. They expected the church to give guidance and inspiration, which in conjunction with the congenial Russian peasant commune would provide Russian social, economic, and political life as well as the individual with the desired Christian milieu. Christianity as a highly ethical religion would lead the Christian through the church to ethical Christian conduct.

Samarin's works, and especially his correspondence, indicate his desire to adhere not only to Slavophil thought but to the way of life of the Orthodox faith. In view of his upbringing in a lay Orthodox Russian family, not untouched by secular Western ways, his interest in Hegelianism was not surprising; the resistance he showed in the end is perhaps not wholly explicable, but it proved that his early faith was stronger than logical argument — though that, too, was of great value. In his remarkable letter-confession to Gogol', in the spring of 1846, Samarin said, "Christianity contains in itself not a teaching alone but at the same time the principle of life and creativity." "Christianity can be grasped not through the intellect alone but by the whole being of man. He who wishes to understand it logically, as we understand any other teaching, will never understand it." With such convictions it is not surprising that the following year he advised his brother Vladimir, "Read the fathers of the Orthodox Church, read them not superficially, not hastily but deliberately and reflectively."[44] One can perhaps safely assume that although Iurii was in St. Petersburg at the time, the Orthodox church fathers, to whom Ivan Kireevsky paid special attention, and who also soon caught Koshelev's attention, were discussed by the Slavophils in Moscow in the early 1850s.

At the age of thirty Samarin made two more decisions that would be reflected in his later life and activities. On January 13, 1848, he wrote to his brother Mikhail, then in Italy, about duty and personal satisfaction. One can find "happiness ... only in self-sacrifice, in forgetfulness of self, in the deed, in labor undertaken for the good of one's country in the feeling of the living bond of one's person ... with the nation to which we belong." His complete, monastic self-abnegation and dedication to the cause of Russia's welfare and to Slavophilism was behind his confession to Aleksandra Osipovna Smirnova on May 25, 1849, that "for me family life ends with my parents' home. I will not become the founder of a new family. I only wish to prolong as much as possible the present relations that bind me with memories of my earliest childhood."[45] For a person who had grown up in a family with many brothers and sisters, Iurii's self-imposed limitations and sense of resignation are somewhat baffling, except that he hints about duty to country and society; and it is beyond question that duty to Russia, to the cause of the emancipation of the serfs, and reform remained the guiding lights of his life.

A major reason for the Slavophil idealization of the *narod,* the illiterate serf peasantry, was their uncomfortable conviction that Orthodox Christianity was preserved and personified in the life of the unspoiled *narod,* not in that of the Westernized and secularized Russian gentry, too often alienated from Russia's Orthodox soil. Among the guilt-ridden gentry – the Slavophils included – the *narod* was not only the toiling mass providing them with sustenance and often luxury, it was also their religious conscience, and their guide to Christian behavior, however imperfect it might be. Writing to Khomiakov from St. Petersburg early in 1846, Samarin in reference to the mixed group of peasants in the Baltic littoral says "For the common people, contrary to the educated classes, religion has not yet withdrawn from life as dry dogmatics and abstract morality, as an object of logical comprehension. The people understands any change in religion as a transformation of the whole of its everyday life."[46]

In the late winter of 1849 when Samarin sensed that his *Riga Letters,* then in circulation in manuscript, could cause him trouble with the government, he decided to prepare his parents. On March 3 he wrote to his father from St. Petersburg to tell him that his fears of arousing official displeasure were being realized. He had learned that the tsar had expressed "his anger at me," and he had been formally told to appear before the minister of interior to explain and justify his conduct and his views. Before going to the Minister's office, "as is proper for an Orthodox person . . . I went to church . . . to pray for myself, and in particular for you and Mother in order that this news would not distress you too much." As for me, he says, "I have surrendered myself unconditionally to God's will."[47]

Iurii's concern for his parents' feelings is, of course, uppermost, but his seemingly natural and unassuming statement about needing spiritual comfort shows the sincerity of his Orthodox beliefs. Further on in the letter he says that if he is put in jail he will simply "rely on God's mercy." He was ready to serve his country, as he saw such service, and he asked for his parents' forgiveness, saying, "I will pray to God that he may send down to you the same kind of firm hope that I now feel."[48]

Only a few months before Iurii wrote this letter he had found confirmation of his Orthodox faith in the *Encyclical Epistle,* which had been sent in 1848 by the Eastern Church to the Pope.[49] Samarin's reaction to the reply of the Orthodox churches and their patriarchs to the "papal bull" was nothing short of exultation, and this by a man not usually given to excessive sentimentality. In a letter of December 1848 to Khomiakov he says that the Encyclical of the Orthodox church was a unique document, and that "from the time of the division in the church [eleventh century] there has been no similar confession of faith."

> What a mystery is this East, immobile, napping, foreign to every formal manifestation of life, foreign even to concern about liberation from harsh violence [all Eastern patriarchates were under Ottoman rule], and to regular organization, but from which suddenly, unexpectedly, after centuries of silence, comes a thought incomprehensible to the West, the depth and the word of which sound as an echo of the time of the apostles!

It is clear from Samarin's letter that he had obtained a copy of the Orthodox Encyclical before Khomiakov, for he says, "I am communicating to you extracts first, because they could give you a conception of the whole; second, because I am not certain that the Synod will not exclude or distort them in its official translation."[50] Samarin's attitude toward Catholics and Russia's Holy Synod is summed up in the critical rhetorical question, "Is it not all the same whether there is one pope or several of them, whether they are in the vestments of the archbishop or in an adjutant-general's uniform?"[51]

But for the Slavophils, and specifically for Samarin, the *Encyclical Epistle* contained a good deal more than a general negative reference to the Catholic church. Out of the complexities in the relations between the Eastern and Western churches during the first eleven centuries of the Christian era one

technical and doctrinal issue, that of the *filioque,* was central to their disagreements, and it has not been overcome to the present. The first two
ecumenical councils, of Nicaea in 325, and of Constantinople in 381, have
left us what is commonly known as the Nicene Creed. This creed is still
professed by all Orthodox, and by many Western Christians, including the
Catholics, but with one crucial difference between East and West, that of
the *filioque.* This clause refers to the procession of the Holy Ghost. In the
Nicene Creed the Holy Ghost proceeds from the Father, based on John
15:26.[52] This creed was also accepted in the West, but some of the Western
churches, particularly in Spain, began to tamper with it, and after a while the
filioque was interpolated to read that the Holy Ghost proceeds from the
Father "and the Son."[53]

The Slavophils attributed utmost significance to the *Encyclical Epistle* of
the Eastern churches; Khomiakov and Samarin, in their zeal, tended to ideal-
ize the ecumenical councils on the decisions of which the Eastern churchmen
relied for their reply to Pius IX. The first seven ecumenical councils were
convoked between 325 and 787, all of them in the Eastern Roman or Byzantine Empire where for the first time in the Roman world Christianity became
legally accepted and protected. But the records of the councils are incomplete and so is our knowledge of their composition and deliberations. From
the first Council of Nicaea in 325 the Christian churches were confronted
with serious and often intractable problems. There were the major heresies
of Arianism, Monophysitism, and Nestorianism, and there were also frequent disagreements within the churches both of the East and of the West
as well as between those of East and West. In 863 the recriminations between Rome and Constantinople resulted in the mutual excommunications
of Pope Nicholas and Patriarch Photius. Thus to the cultural, theological,
and personality differences between the representatives of East and West
was now permanently added the *filioque* in the West, which had been
gradually in the making there for several centuries. This is how matters
stood at the time of the final break between Rome and Constantinople in the
eleventh century, how they appeared in the middle of the nineteenth, and
how they stand at present.[54]

Some phases of this tremendously long and complex relationship between
the churches of the East and the West were better known to Samarin than
to any of the other Slavophils. This was one of the principal benefits of his
dissertation at the University of Moscow. It is not therefore surprising that
he saw the *Encyclical Epistle* of the Eastern churches as a sort of revelation.
In addition to the *filioque,* which is prominent throughout much of the *Encyclical Epistle,* Samarin saw there the determined stand of the Eastern churches on a number of other issues. Thus they questioned Rome's claim to
primacy among Christian cities and gave that distinction to Antioch. "The
Throne of Rome is esteemed as that of St. Peter by a single tradition, but not

from Holy Scripture, where the claim is in favor of Antioch."[55] Declaring its allegiance to the "seven holy Oecumenical Synods" the Eastern churchmen accused the papacy of "supporting and receiving heretical novelties,"[56] of transforming "hierarchical privilege into a lordly superiority," and of "adulterating the divine Creed."

The *Encyclical Epistle,* asserting the authority of the ecumenical councils, declared, "An OEcumenical Council is not only above the Pope but above any Council of his."[57] It was firmly opposed to the autocratic power of the pope and to any changes in what the Eastern churchmen considered eternally established Christian truths: "Moreover, neither Patriarchs nor Councils could then have introduced novelties amongst us, because the protector of religion is the very body of the Church, even the people themselves, who desire their religious worship to be ever unchanged and of the same kind as that of their fathers." Neither pope nor patriarch could be the head of the church, "But until there be this desired returning of the apostate Churches to the body of the One, Holy, Catholic, and Apostolic Church, of which *Christ is the Head* (Eph. 4:15)" there can be no unity in the church.[58]

The *Encyclical Epistle* also referred to the sources of Orthodoxy, and to infallibility. The Orthodox receive their "faith and confession" from "the Gospel from the mouth of our Lord, witnessed by the holy Apostles, [and] by the seven sacred Ecumenical Councils." Further on it said (twenty-two years before the formal proclamation of the doctrine of papal infallibility during the pontificate of the same Pius IX): "Our Church holds the infallible and genuine deposit of the Holy Scriptures, of the Old Testament a true and perfect version, of the New the divine original itself. The rites of the sacred Mysteries, and especially those of the divine Liturgy . . . handed down from the Apostles. . . . The august OEcumenical Councils, those seven pillars of the house of Wisdom."[59]

The bitter tone of the *Encyclical Epistle* and its recriminations against what it regarded as the proud, condescending intrusion of Pius IX into the Orthodox world convey as little Christian charity as the pope's attempt to reach the Orthodox faithful, with or without the concurrence of the Orthodox churches. Pius IX in addressing the "Easterns" declared them "aliens from this holy Throne of the Apostle Peter."[60] That the initiative of Pius IX exacerbated relations between the Orthodox and the Catholic churches was illustrated five years later, during the Crimean War, when the Archbishop of Paris, Marie Dominique Auguste Sibour, preached a "crusade against the Eastern heresy."[61]

It is likely that Tiutchev was aware of the *Encyclical Epistle* at the time his critical views of the Western confessions, particularly Catholicism, appeared in print early in 1850. Certainly Samarin and Khomiakov were thoroughly cognizant of it, and they probably discussed it with the rest of the Slavophils, because the Slavophil Orthodoxy of Khomiakov and Samarin, both in its criticism of the Western confessions and in its positive formulations, depended to a great extent on the *Encyclical Epistle* of the Orthodox churches of 1848.

Neither temperament and inclinations nor external circumstances permitted Samarin at the end of the 1840s to concentrate exclusively on matters of religion and Orthodoxy. Yet as Nol'de has correctly noticed, Samarin was capable of functioning on one or several tracks of thought at the same time. In 1857–1858 — after he had left Kiev and government service and before the emancipation reform, of 1861 when the serf question seemed to engulf him — he engaged in controversy in the columns of *Russkaia beseda*. His adversaries were Boris Chicherin and Sergei Solov'ev and the subject was *narodnost'* or national identity. In 1857 he also made a historical and scholarly study of the emancipation of the serfs in Prussia, and in 1858 he published his views on the Russian peasant commune. In 1856 he wrote an essay on education. He continued his many-sided concerns during the 1860s and early 1870s.

But in this multifaceted career Samarin maintained a clear sense of order and priorities. Neither in the intensity of the pre-emancipation years nor in his post-emancipation assignment in Poland did he lose sight of what constituted the essence of Moscow Slavophilism, its Orthodox religious core. When the stress from the emancipation concerns in Russia and Poland came to an end in the middle 1860s, he returned, as it were, to his dissertation subject by participating with N. P. Giliarov-Platonov in the translation of Khomiakov's theological works from French into Russian — that is, to the "work of Khomiakov" (*delo Khomiakova*), the most theologically oriented of the Slavophils.

The later Western observer of Russian affairs who said, "Russia is not a state; it is a world," may or may not have been a student of Moscow Slavophilism.[62] But there can scarcely be any doubt that the Slavophils made their contribution to the notion that Russia is another world. Khomiakov in his comparison of Aristotle's role in the intellectual and spiritual life of Western Europe in the Middle Ages with that of Peter the Great in Russia, concluded that both had served a purpose, both had eventually outlived their time and usefulness, and that the legacies of both were superseded by more relevant and useful ideas and convictions. What to the Slavophils appeared as Peter's indiscriminate borrowing from the West had to be modified to allow the Russian genius and self-consciousness to assert themselves fully and freely.

For the Slavophils, of course, there was no more characteristic Russian manifestation down the centuries than that summed up in the principles of *sobornost'* and *obshchinnost'* (communality) however imperfectly realized. Eastern Orthodoxy, of which *sobornost'* was an integral part, after nine centuries on Russian soil had become in the minds of the Slavophils thoroughly identified with the Russian national consciousness. During the centuries of Mongol rule over Russia, to be Orthodox was to be Russian, just as in the Balkans during the five centuries of Ottoman rule Orthodoxy became the mark of the various national allegiances, Bulgarian, Serbian, Rumanian, Greek, Macedonian. These allegiances were strongly abetted down the centuries by the decentralized autocephalous nature of Eastern Orthodoxy, and its church organization.

The irreversible fusion of Eastern Orthodoxy and the Russian national consciousness, always present in the minds of the Moscow Slavophils, was never more vital and more vibrant than in the case of Samarin's Slavophilism. The basic and indispensable ingredient of Moscow Slavophilism, the Russian national consciousness (indissolubly integrated with Orthodoxy) perhaps was even stronger and more explicit in Samarin's case than in that of the other early Slavophils. Whatever personal and temperamental differences there were between Samarin and his fellow Slavophils, special external circumstances – notably the Polish rebellion of 1863 and the unification of Germany (1864–1870), neither of which was witnessed by Khomiakov, Kireevsky, and Aksakov – contributed to Samarin's sharper and more strident nationalism. Nor does the Slav congress of 1867 in Moscow seem to have swerved Samarin toward pan-Slavism. The firm and uncompromising nature of his Russian consciousness and Orthodox Slavophil convictions is well illustrated in his correspondence of the period with the Baroness Rahden, in which his staunch and unyielding devotion to Orthodoxy and Russia was equally matched by her unwavering adherence to Lutheranism and her German cultural heritage. Only the personal touches of mutual affection and regard softened their harshest exchanges, and preserved their platonic relationship.

It was in these circumstances that Samarin wrote and published in Prague in 1867 his introduction to Khomiakov's theological works.[63] Two overriding concerns in this essay were the matter of Christian faith, and the nature and role of the church. More than twenty years earlier (1844), he had presented Khomiakov with a copy of his dissertation. Though the two men were separated in age by fifteen years, they established a deep and lasting community of views and convictions, and in the introduction to the theological works of his late friend and fellow Slavophil, Samarin showed not only the lasting quality of the friendship but also his abiding commitment to the Orthodox Christian faith.

The relationship between the Moscow Slavophils and Samarin's fellow translator, N. P. Giliarov-Platonov (1824–1887), and the formulation of Slavophil religious views is interesting but not wholly clear. Giliarov-Platonov, the son of an Orthodox priest, had the theological training that neither Khomiakov nor Samarin had. He was a graduate of the Kolomenskoe theological school, the Moscow Seminary, and Moscow

Theological Academy. He was a professor at the academy (1848–1855) and also a government censor (1856–1863). He was a "publicist of the Slavophil persuasion,"[64] and for twenty years (1867–1887) was editor-publisher of *Contemporary News* (*Sovremennyia Izvestiia*). Giliarov was interested in both Slavophilism and Westernism, in the Jewish question in the West and Russia; he wrote on economics, studied socialism and philosophy, with special emphasis on Hegelianism, participated in work on the emancipation reform, and considered publication of an encyclopedia from "an *Eastern* . . . point of view."[65]

During the 1850s and 1860s Giliarov contributed to the Slavophil *Russkaia beseda* and to Ivan Aksakov's *Den'* and *Moskva,* and in the early 1880s *Rus'.* He also collaborated on *Russkii vestnik.* From the fragmentary evidence available to me (the valuable Samarin-Giliarov correspondence does not seem to have been published) Giliarov is difficult to classify ideologically, although he seems to have espoused, for a time at least, an idiosyncratic brand of Slavophilism. Though he was on friendly terms with the Aksakovs, Khomiakov, and Samarin, he was sensitive – or so it appears – about his plebeian origins, as when he commented in a letter to Prince N. V. Shakhovskoi in 1886, that Samarin was easily let out of jail in 1849 because "he was so-and-so's first cousin, so-and-so's nephew." Similarly, Ivan Aksakov had "important connections not only in Russia" but was "well known at the court [and his wife] Anna Fedorovna actually lived there" (as lady-in-waiting to the empress). In the same letter, however, he also recalled that the "late Iu. F. Samarin stooped before me (in my opinion even above that which was deserved) [whereas] for Khomiakov I was even *the only* person with whom he acknowledged his complete agreement." At the same time (1886) he also felt a certain estrangement from what he characterized as the "neo-Slavophils," Lamansky and Miller. Nor did he have warm sentiments for the "late Gil'ferding."[66] During the early 1850s, his sharp critical views of the official Russian church brought him into some disfavor, but in these views, as well as in some of his positive formulations, he seems to have been close to both Khomiakov and Samarin.

As summarized by Pokrovsky, who was familiar with his biography, Giliarov's views on the church as expressed in his six volumes of published works included criticism of the "bureaucratism" and the "church satraps" in the official Russian ecclesiastical establishment. Giliarov believed that the "life of the church is an expression of faith and love, i.e., freedom in both its applications, speculative and actual. Faith is the free acceptance of truth, love – its free application. . . . Freedom and the church are in reality one and the same." In attacking the "harmful myopic – preservative conservatism," of the official church, he declared himself in favor of freedom of conscience, including freedom for the Old Believers in Russia.[67] Both Giliarov and the two early Slavophils Khomiakov and Samarin continually emphasized the differences between the historical Russian church and the Western confessions, and their Christian church was a highly idealized one conceived in terms of faith, love, and freedom. It should be emphasized, however, that without a thorough study of Giliarov's works and biography one cannot draw final conclusions about the interplay of ideas between the two Slavophils and the younger Giliarov.[68]

Samarin's introduction to Khomiakov's theological works is his last word on the subject of faith and the church, and he generously attributes to Khomiakov merit and distinction, some of which at least belonged to him also.[69] In the early 1840s, Samarin probably discussed his dissertation subject in the Moscow salons and became well acquainted with Khomiakov's views, but it is well to remember that Khomiakov, except in *The Church Is One,* did not state his views in writing and thus make them more completely accessible to this fellow Slavophils until the first half of the 1850s.[70]

Samarin's introduction, cast in the usual polemical form of the period, begins with stress on the indispensable condition for all exchanges of views and opinions, polemical or not, that is, freedom of expression. Using *nauka* in a broader sense than his customary equivalent of philosophy, he quotes Khomiakov as saying that "science needs not only freedom of opinion but also freedom of doubt." Then returning to his more customary use of *nauka* as philosophy, he says that in the West "philosophy looked upon faith from on high," and considered it as a "transitional form." This was particularly striking with respect to the "idealism of the self-determining spirit," leading him to the question, "Must faith disappear from the face of the earth," and must the world stand by while witnessing the consummation of its "uncrowned dominion" as many in the West thought, or should it perhaps be relegated "to the side of the royal road in the new world?"[71] Samarin was actually saying that in the West faith in the Christian God was often being replaced by faith in man, that is, faith in reason and science.

The rectilinear thinking associated with such views was characteristic of the West, and was the offspring of Catholicism and Protestantism. In Samarin's view, Protestantism deriving logically from Catholicism "proclaimed the autocracy of individual reason [and] prepared the kingdom of philosophy, in our view [thus] entering the domain of human conscience and the fate of humanity."[72] Much to his satisfaction, "Orthodoxy remained completely outside this *dialectical development of religious thought* ... [and] did not participate in the self-decomposition of Christianity."[73] In the 1840s Samarin, like the other Slavophils, saw in Orthodoxy a reaction, among other things, to the Western confessions and to Western idealism and rationalism. In the middle 1860s, in addition to these, he also reacted to materialism, which had achieved increased prominence in Western thought since the 1840s.

Assailing what he considered to be "church statism" (*tserkovnaia kazenshchina*) in Russia, and "narrow official conservatism," Samarin expressed thoughts that did not endear him and the Slavophils to the official Russian church. (It was partly on this account that this essay and Khomiakov's theological works were published abroad.) Samarin then took the next step and declared that there should always be room for "honest criticism and lawful condemnation." And although this was directed primarily at "state and public institutions," the Russian church, which the Slavophils considered as "overprotected" by the government, could not be excluded. The desire for improvement and the search for the better must never be obstructed, for such an endeavor was the essence of progress. Then, perhaps somewhat unexpectedly, in the customary Slavophil manner, without writing an essay or a monograph on the role and place of faith in his scheme of things, Samarin declared, "Faith as the expression of the unconditional, the eternal, and the unchangeable cannot, and must not, have any direct relations with this [the political and social] sphere."[74]

Elaborating on the matter of faith, in terms both of what faith was and of what it was not, Samarin said: "Faith by its very nature is not accommodating, and one cannot enter into deals with it.... Faith nurtures patience and self-sacrifice, and reins in personal passions.... Faith is not a stick with which one defends himself and scares others.... Faith serves only him who sincerely believes...." Faith, he added, was in a class by itself, and was "unfailing and unchangeable." With certain lapses in Russian historical reality in mind, he warned, "Demanding of faith any type of police service is nothing else than a special kind of preaching of unbelief...."[75]

It has been stated on more than one occasions in these pages that whereas there was much in Moscow Slavophilism, particularly in the writings of Konstantin Aksakov, that was unhistorical, idealistic, and even utopian, there were also elements in Slavophilism that were down-to-earth, urgent, and eminently practical. This was perhaps more evident in Samarin than in the other early Slavophils. There is scarcely any other sphere of human thought and belief in which it is so easy and likely for a person to fall into an ossified immobility than on matters of faith and religion. Samarin was aware of this when he characterized faith as eternal and unchangeable. But he also knew that in different societies, epochs, and circumstances faith "calls forth particular phenomena," causing in turn changes in thought, art, and practical life. Thus, he says, dogma does not change, but its "logical formulation" and the "determination of its relationship to other teachings — the problem of church studies — develops hand in hand with other disciplines." Similarly the "law of love does not change, but its practical application in family, social, and state life gradually becomes more perfect and broader." In the same manner he saw the "external side of the church" as changing, in its "ritual, custom, disciplinary, and administrative rules," adjusting to new conditions and circumstances. Such changes were essential if the church was to preserve "its contemporaneity and its freshness." For him, the "petrified formations of the seventeenth-century" Russian church were in "direct contradiction to the concepts, demands, and needs of the nineteenth century."[76]

Since this essay was written for publication abroad, free from censorship interference, Samarin felt a certain urgency in speaking out in favor of freedom of expression. In this case it was freedom to speak out on church and religious matters: the "absence of honest, and truthful criticism barricades the approach to the church, and masks the view of its majestic harmony and outline for those standing outside." This gives rise to an "eternal vacillation and wavering between the two poles of superstition and doubt." This is also the source of the type of "conscientious unbelief" that derives *"from misunderstandings."*[77]

Part of the middle section of the essay is given over to lavish but doubtless sincere, praise for Khomiakov's religious views and convictions. Samarin, with unconcealed partiality, praises the older Slavophil for, as he says, "living in the church" rather than merely preaching about it. He admires him for the "indelible traces" that he left, and characterizes him as "a particularly original phenomenon, almost unprecedented among us, of *the most complete freedom of religious consciousness.*" Like all believers endowed with a strong logical mind and keenly aware of the doubts that modern science has cast upon certain aspects of Christianity and the Bible, Samarin raised the rhetorical question, "Have we understood everything that has been disclosed to us, and have we understood it correctly?"

Behind Samarin's criticism of the Western confessions — and this is true also of Khomiakov's and to a certain extent of Tiutchev's — stood the firm and irreducible Slavophil belief in *sobornost'*, in which the individual becomes integrated into the brotherhood of man, or all humanity, under the fatherhood of God. Samarin, looking from this lofty standpoint upon the Western confessions and the central issues that tore them apart during the Reformation, saw in them both what he considered to be an inordinate concern for individual salvation, and how it was to be achieved. This to Samarin was "a peculiar kind of egotism, the egotism of *self-salvation [egoizm samospaseniia].*"[78]

For Samarin and the other early Slavophils, the religious starting point and the inspiration of their ideology was Orthodox Christianity conceived in ultimate terms as faith, freedom, and love. But as usual in human affairs, their ideological principles suffered considerable dilution whenever they were applied to the solution of pressing practical problems. Samarin, like Khomiakov and Ivan Kireevsky, sought the embodiment of Christian principles in the historical Christian church, which they conceived as the guide, counselor, and inspirer in the daily lives of the Russian people. Here they immediately ran into historical reality. When they looked outside Russia, they saw two other major churches instead of the single Christian (Orthodox) church. The Catholic church, in their view, had separated itself from the one true Christian Orthodox church over the *filioque* in the middle of the eleventh century, and the Protestant Lutheran church, following the ages-long Western rationalistic path, broke away from the Catholic church as the Catholic church had abandoned the Orthodox Christian church. Samarin and the early Slavophils believed that the principal reason for this phenomenon was the prevalence in the West of the elements of rationalism, formalism, legalism, and individualism, a strong legacy from its classical Roman pre-Christian past.

In their criticism of the Western confessions, Samarin and Khomiakov found support in the *Encyclical Epistle* of 1848, sent by the Eastern Orthodox churches to Pius IX in reply to his appeal for them to submit to his authority. Khomiakov and Samarin looked upon this document not only as a strong rebuttal of the claims of Rome but also as an equally strong encouragement for their criticism of the Western confessions. Twenty years later, in Samarin's introduction to the translation of Khomiakov's theological works, his views concerning Catholicism, Protestantism, and Orthodoxy, first established at the University of Moscow, were given fuller expression as a statement of his mature Slavophil Orthodox commitment.

Notes

1. Nol'de, *Samarin,* p. 31.

2. The late Professor Lossky suggested that the word *sobornost'* was already being accepted in the West, specifically in England, just as at present it could be said that the Russian *sputnik* and the Czech *robot* have been accepted in the West. Without attempting to attribute ultimate authorship, Lossky says: "The idea of *sobornost'* developed by Khomiakov. . . means a combination of unity and freedom of many persons on the basis of common love for God. . . . It will be easily seen that the principle of *sobornost'* is of value not only for the life of the church but also for solving many problems in the spirit of synthesis between individualism and universalism." With respect to the Slavophil principle of the wholeness of the spirit, which Lossky aptly translates as "integral knowledge," he says that it is "an organic all-embracing unity," and further: "The whole truth is only revealed to the whole man, said Kireevsky and Khomiakov. It is only through combining all his spiritual powers—sense experience, rational thought, aesthetic perception, moral experience and religious contemplation—that man begins to apprehend the world's true being and grasp the superrational truths about God." In Lossky's words, "It is precisely such integral experience that underlies the creative work of many Russian thinkers—V. Solov'ev, Prince S. Trubetskoy, Prince E. Trubetskoy, Florensky, Bulgakov, Berdyaev, N.

Lossky, S. Frank, Karsavin, Losev, I. A. Ilyin and others." N. O. Lossky, *History of Russian Philosophy* (New York, 1951), pp. 407, 404.

3. See "O narodnom obrazovanii," *Russkaia beseda,* 1856, no. 2, pp. 85–106; also Samarin, *Sochineniia,* I, 122–147.

4. Samarin, *Sochineniia,* I, 137. See also ibid., V, LXVI–LXVII. Although Chizhevsky did not specifically stress a bond between Samarin and Kireevsky on the question of the wholeness of the spirit, he clearly brought out Kireevsky's criticism of the philosophy of Aristotle and Hegel for having "fragmented the wholeness of the knowing subject," and in general stressed that "Kireevsky's attitude toward German philosophical idealism was defined very early: as early as 1832." D. I. Chizhevsky, *Gegel' v Rossii,* pp. 22, 25.

5. Samarin, *Sochineniia,* V, XVIII.

6. Ibid., p. XLI, n. 2. Diary entry of October 23, 1841.

7. Ibid., pp. LXXVI–LXXVII.

8. Nol'de, *Samarin,* p. 20.

9. The Gershenzon edition that I have used here was reprinted in The Hague in 1965 from the Moscow, 1910, edition. The Berlin, 1923, edition of *Istroicheskiia zapiski* is different in several ways and it contains an essay on Peter Kireevsky that is not included in the 1910 (1965) edition. The Hague edition contains two essays, "The Theory of the Individual Person (I. V. Kireevsky)" (*Uchenie o lichnosti [I. V. Kireevsky]*) and "The Theory of the Nature of Consciousness (Iu. F. Samarin)" (*Uchenie o prirode soznaniia [Iu. F. Samarin]*), a total of 83 pages.

10. M. O. Gershenzon, *Istoricheskie zapiski,* p. 41.

11. Ibid., p. 42.

12. Ibid., pp. 44, 45.

13. Ibid., pp. 60, 61.

14. Khomiakov, *Sochineniia,* I, 177, 178.

15. Ibid., p. 178.

16. Ibid., pp. 179–180.

17. Ibid., pp. 181–183.

18. Ibid., pp. 184–185.

19. Ibid., pp. 186–187.

20. The characterization of Tiutchev as "almost-foreigner" is from Ivan S. Aksakov's "Fedor Ivanovich Tiutchev (1804–1873)," *Russkii arkhiv,* 1874, no. 10, p. 6. Aksakov's biography, published in 1874 in a complete issue (no. 10) of *Russkii askhiv,* one year after the poet died, is the earliest and in some ways the most intimate biography of Tiutchev. It appeared in book form in 1886. Here I have used the original edition. Ivan Aksakov was Tiutchev's son-in-law, having married Tiutchev's daughter Anna in 1866. Her mother was the first of the poet's two German wives.

21. R. A. Gregg, *Fedor Tiutchev: The Evolution of a Poet* (New York, 1956), p. 2.

22. Ibid., pp. 5–7.

23. Ibid., p. 9. Valerii Briusov quotes these words from Peter Kireevsky's diary in his "F. I. Tiutchev. Letopis' ego zhizni," *Russkii arkhiv,* 1903, no. 11, p. 492.

24. I. V. Kireevsky, *Sochineniia,* I, 43.

25. No less an authority on Russian religious cultural matters than George Florovsky has said: "For the power and force of his aesthetic and philosophic conceptions Tyutchev must be hailed as first among Russian poets," and Zeldin adds, this means "ahead even of Pushkin." Cf. George Florovsky, "The Historical Premonitions of Tyutchev," *Slavonic Review,* December 1924, p. 337.

26. For some reactions in Russia to Custine's book, including Zhukovsky's, who referred to the "dog Custine," as well as the tsar's, Tiutchev's, and Herzen's, see Barsukov, *Pogodin,* 284–287. For a recent treatment of this subject see, G. F. Kennan, *The Marquis de Custine and His Russia in 1839* (Princeton, N. J. 1971).

27. Barsukov gives long excerpts from this article, together with reactions by the tsar, Shevyrev, and others. See ibid., pp. 273–280. Although Ivan Aksakov suggests that the tsar may not have read Tiutchev's essay, he was no doubt familiar with its contents and thesis. See Aksakov, *Tiutchev,* p. 43.

28. Tiutchev was familiar with certain Slavophil views as they were elaborated in the Slavophil symposium of 1847. On April 15, 1847, he wrote to Chaadaev in Moscow referring to Gogol's *Perepiska* and to "votre Sbornik-monstre de Moscou." See P. I. Bartenev, ed., "Pis'ma F. I. Tiutcheva k P. Ia. Chaadaevu," *Russkii arkhiv,* 1900, book 3, p. 412. His personal contacts with the Slavophils during the 1840s are uncertain, although he visited Elagina's salon at least once. It seems some time in 1844 Elagina, mother of the Kireevsky brothers, wrote to Pogodin, "Will you not come this evening to spend a couple of hours with Tiutchev?" Barsukov, *Pogodin,* VII 136.

29. Khomiakov, *Sochineniia,* II, 33.

30. See P. I. Bartenev, ed., "Iz bumag Aleksandra Nikolaevicha Popova," *Russkii arkhiv,* 1886, no. 3, p. 353.

31. See P. V. Bykov, ed., *F. I. Tiutchev. Politicheskie stat'i* (Paris, 1976), p. 136.

32. Ibid., pp. 136, 137.

33. Ibid., p. 139.

34. Ibid., pp. 140–141.

35. Ibid., p. 142.

36. Ibid., pp. 144, 146.

37. Ibid., p. 158.

38. See *The Correspondence of Iu. Samarin and Baroness Rahden (1861–1876)*, ed. and trans. by Loren Calder et al., p. 225.

39. Aksakov, *Tiutchev*, p. 80. Solov'ev, who knew Ivan Aksakov well and thought highly of his biography of Tiutchev, wrote an essay on Tiutchev's poetry in 1895. In addition to the poet's view of nature, compared and contrasted with Schiller's, Goethe's, the classical Greek, and the views of natural scientists on nature, he discussed the spiritual Christian content of Tiutchev's poetry. Toward the end of his essay Solov'ev turned to Tiutchev's views on Christianity and the Russian people, stressing that "for Tiutchev Russia was an object not so much of love as of faith — in Russia one can only believe.'" Solov'ev admitted that the notion of Russia as the "soul of mankind," destined to become the "universal Christian monarchy" not "by blood and iron" but through "love," smacked at times of "the most ordinary chauvinism," but he had no doubts about Tiutchev's sincerity and goodwill toward the West. See V. S. Solov'ev, "Poeziia F. I. Tiutcheva," *Vestnik Evropy*, 1895, no. 4, pp. 749–752.

40. Gregg, *Tiutchev*, p. 134.

41. Ibid., pp. 134–135.

42. Samarin, *Sochineniia*, XII, 146.

43. Samarin remembered Tiutchev in the same manner several times later on. Samarin, *Sochineniia*, XII, 146, 283, 287, 294. In 1849 he mentions Tiutchev twice in Moscow, where both were visiting. See pp. 300, 302.

44. Ibid., pp. 243, 346.

45. Ibid., pp. 243, 346.

46. Ibid., p. 417.

47. Ibid., p. 336.

48. Ibid., p. 336.

49. The complete title of the document in English is, *Encyclical Epistle of the One Holy Catholic and Apostolic Church to the Faithful Everywhere, Being a Reply to the Epistle of Pius IX to the Easterns* (dated January 6, 1848). The edition used here was published by the Orthodox Book Center, South Canaan, Pa.,in 1958. In the opening paragraph of the Introduction it is stated: "The Epistle of Pope Pius IX to which the following document is a reply, was written soon after the accession of his Holiness to the Papacy, and published in the East in modern Greek, manifestly for the purpose of proselytizing such as might thereby be won over from the Oriental Churches to the Roman obedience." The Orthodox reply to Pius IX, a total of thirty-eight pages, is signed by eighteen members of the Holy Synod of Constantinople, four of the Holy Synod of Antioch, and seven of the Holy Synod of Jerusalem. The reply is dated May 1848. For Khomiakov's reaction and the importance he gave to the reply of the Eastern Orthodox churches, see Christoff, *Xomjakov*, pp. 95, 129, 138, 142, 157–158, 163.

50. Samarin, *Sochineniia*, XII, 426.

51. Ibid., p. 428. The head of the Holy Synod was a military man.

52. "But when the Counselor comes, whom I shall send to you from the Father, even the Spirit of truth, who proceeds from the Father, he will bear witness to me. Revised Standard Version.

53. In the notes that accompany the English translation of the *Encyclical Epistle* of the Eastern churches it is stated that "The interpolation of the *Filioque* into the Creed, it is generally agreed, was first made by a Provincial Spanish Council," and that most probably this "took place at the third Council of Toledo, A.D. 589." *Encyclical Epistle,* p. 33.

54. An important step of reconciliation between Rome and Constantinople, recently taken, is described in the following passage: "on Tuesday, 7 December 1965, the Bishop of Rome, Pope Paul VI, and the Bishop of New Rome, Ecumenical Patriarch Athenagoras, lifted the mutual excommunication exchanged in 1054 by means of a 'joint act.' . . . The 'joint act' of Pope and Patriarch reaffirmed their ultimate goal of Christian unity." For this statement, an English translation of the "joint act," and the reactions to it of the Greek and Russian orthodox churches, see Methodios Fouyas, *Orthodoxy, Roman Catholicism, and Anglicanism* (London, 1972), pp. 215–217.

55. *Encyclical Epistle,* p. 14.

56. Ibid., pp. 16, 17.

57. Ibid., pp. 19, 21. For a brief, readable discussion of the role of the Church Fathers and the state of the Christian church during the first seven centuries, see N. P. Karsavin, *Sviatye ottsy i uchiteli tserkvi. Raskrytie pravoslaviia v ikh tvoreniiakh* (Paris, n.d.). On the importance of the Church Fathers to Odoevsky, Khomiakov, and Kireevsky, see V. V. Zenkovsky, *A History of Russian Philosophy,* 2 vols. (New York, 1953), trans. from the Russian by G. L. Kline, I, 138, 184, 211; G. V. Florovsky, *Puti russkago bogosloviia* (Paris, 1937), pp. 255–256, 283–284.

58. *Encyclical Epistle,* pp. 24–25.

59. Ibid., p. 29.

60. Ibid., p. 3.

61. E. V. Tarle, *Krymskaia voina* 2d ed. (Moscow-Leningrad, 1950), I, 482–483.

62. Quoted in Joshua Kunitz, *Russia: The Giant That Came Last* (New York, 1947), p. VII.

63. Khomiakov's three essays have recently been published in Russian under the editorship of the Brotherhood of Saint Job of Pochaev. See A. S. Khomiakov, *Sushchnost' zapadnogo khristianstva. Neskol'ko slov pravoslavnogo khristianina o zapadnykh veroispovedaniiakh* (Montreal, 1974).

64. See A. Pokrovsky "Giliarov-Platonov, N. P.," *Russkii biograficheskii slovar,* (Moscow, 1916), VI, 208.

65. N. V. Shakhovskoi, "N. P. Giliarov-Platonov i A. S. Khomiakov," *Russkoe obozrenie,* November 1895, p. 27 (hereafter cited as Shakhovskoi, "Giliarov and Khomiakov").

66. P. I. Bartenev, ed. "Iz bumag N. P. Giliarova-Platonova," *Russkii arkhiv,* 1889, book 3, p. 268.

67. Pokrovsky, "Giliarov," pp. 214–215. On Giliarov's views of the Russian church in historical and contemporary terms, as well as for a brief but well-documented biographical sketch of Giliarov, see Gregory Freeze, "Introduction" to Giliarov's *Iz perezhitago. Avtobiograficheskiia Vospominaniia* (Moscow, 1886), 2 parts; Oriental Research Partners reprint (Newtonville, Mass., 1977), pp. 1–8.

68. Shakhovskoi mentions the similarity between their views and orientations, which struck Konstantin Aksakov when he attended one of Giliarov's lectures in the Theological Academy, some time before 1855. He suggests that Giliarov as a boy might have heard about Khomiakov's views and ideas from his older brother, who visited Khomiakov at Bogucharovo "twenty years before the acquaintance between N. P. and A. S.." He also stresses the possibility of "independent and parallel developments." On the collaboration between Samarin and Giliarov on the translation of Khomiakov's theological works, he says, "It is a pity that it remains unknown what help was given by Giliarov to Samarin, and what expression was given to Iu. F. [Samarin's] expected 'strict criticism and correction' from him." Shakhovskoi, "Giliarov and Khomiakov," pp. 19, 26.

69. This could be said, I believe, in spite of Florovsky's assertion that under Khomiakov's guidance Samarin "reconstructed his dissertation [and] softened the straightforward dialecticism of his original schemes." See G. V. Florovsky, *Puti russkago bogosloviia,* p. 281.

70. Khomiakov's theological works did not have wide circulation at the time in Russia. With respect to Russia Samarin says that Professor V. I. Lamansky of the University of St. Petersburg was the "first, and almost the only one among us to explain and appreciate on its merit this aspect of Khomiakov's activity." Lamansky published his views in the columns of Ivan Aksakov's *Den'* in 1865. Abroad, Samarin says the most favorable and sympathetic reaction came from "Anglican theologians," whereas the "papists," who did not miss many chances to engage in controversy, "this time were prudently silent." Samarin, *Sochineniia,* VI, 330.

71. Ibid., pp. 330–331.

72. The critical and often sharply worded views about Catholicism that Samarin formed while writing his dissertation in the early 1840s were further exacerbated during and after the Polish rebellion of January 1863. The Polish Catholic penetration of the heart of Russia and Poland's brief control of Moscow during the Time of Troubles was identified with the Jesuit order, and it remained for long a strong and disturbing memory for many

Russians, including Samarin and Ivan Aksakov. Their resentment at what they considered to be a Polish and Catholic-Jesuit thrust into the Slav Orthodox world was heightened during the Polish rebellion and both became involved in a bitter church and national polemic. When Ivan Aksakov took on a written controversy with the Jesuit Martynov, Samarin joined him in the columns of Aksakov's *Den'* in 1865. Samarin's five "letters" addressed to Martynov take up 250 pages of volume 6 of his works in addition to about fifty more pages on the Jesuits in general. It is not difficult to agree with Nol'de that this work of Samarin's does not elevate the general level of his writing. This is so not because Jesuitism as an aggressive proselytizing movement was beyond criticism, but because Samarin in the choice of his approach and words did not uplift the controversy. See Nol'de, *Samarin,* pp. 191–192.

73. Samarin, *Sochineniia,* VI, 332.
74. Ibid., p. 333–334.
75. Ibid., p. 335.
76. Ibid., pp. 336, 337.
77. Ibid., p. 337.
78. Ibid., pp. 344–346.

11

Rationalism, Materialism, and Slavophilism

Among the topics that should become subjects of separate studies or monographs, when one considers the Moscow Slavophils, none would rank higher than their views of, and attitude toward Western philosophy. This is so for a number of reasons. In their own time they witnessed the exuberant culmination of German idealism in Hegel's thought, which they considered as the supreme expression of the Western philosophical genius. They saw the power of the Western intellect, as expressed in both philosophy and science, push in certain cases Christianity into the background as the source of ultimate beliefs, convictions, and values. This occurred as secularism was taking over center stage. Finally they observed Western rationalism give way to various forms of materialism and professed atheism. But while they preserved their respect for the Western philosophical and scientific genius, they were not swept off their feet by it. On the contrary, in the field of human relations they proposed an alternative, rudimentary and incomplete, to Western rationalism and materialism, in the form of Slavophil-Orthodox religious, ethical, and philosophical principles.

If all other characteristics of Russian Slavophilism were disregarded it would still be unmistakably non-Western because it did not emulate Western philosophical system building. Systems of thought, which in the Western tradition go back to classical Greece, became particularly prevalent in the West during the eighteenth and nineteenth centuries. Thus Kant (1724–1804) showed concern in his system for metaphysics, reason, dialectic, the role of categories, noumena and phenomena, practical reason, mathematics and geometry, pure physics, the metaphysical foundations of natural science, the existence of God, teleology, ethics, freedom and necessity, moral imperatives, aesthetics. He also gave thought to the philosophies of nature, history, law, politics, and religion. Hegel (1770–1831), who in his early career had studied the systems of Fichte and Schelling, published his first book in 1801 under the title *Differenz des Fichte'schen und Schelling'schen Systems der*

Philosophie. Later he concentrated on his own rich and many-sided system. The early Moscow Slavophils, whose lives overlapped Hegel's, were familiar with his thought, and Ivan Kireevsky knew him personally as a young man while attending his lectures at the University of Berlin in 1830.

After Hegel's death in 1831 his philosophical system became the center of severe controversy and within a decade his adherents split into Old and Young Hegelians. His celebrated dictum, "the rational is the actual and the actual is the rational," became the center of controversy, but the division took place on a broader front. The Old Hegelians — for instance, Karl Goschel (1781–1861) — attributed to Hegel belief in a personal God and personal immortality. However, Ludwig A. Feuerbach (1804–1872) in his anonymous *Gedanken über Tod und Unsterblichkeit* (Thoughts Regarding Death and Immortality), published in 1830, justified on Hegelian grounds his denial of life after death and saw pantheism in Hegel's system.

Whereas the right-wing Hegelians sought to justify the existing order on the ground that it is rational, the left-wing or young Hegelians during the middle 1830s and early 1840s held that the rational and substantial must triumph over the imperfect alienated state of existing society. This meant that the conservative Hegelian order based on philosophical idealism, Christianity, monarchy, and bourgeois culture should be abolished. The Hegelian Left in Germany soon formed around the work and personalities of Arnold Ruge (1803–1880) and Karl Marx (1818–1883). Ruge, publisher of the *Hallischen Jahrbücher für deutsche Wissenschaft und Kunst,* experienced in 1838 a rapid ideological transformation. By 1841 when he renamed his journal *Deutsche Jahrbücher* he had accepted materialism as the foundation of his ideology.

For anyone concerned with the study of Moscow Slavophilism, the philosophical and ideological developments in Western Europe from the 1830s through the 1860s are of singular importance. This is so because psychologically Slavophilism was a reaction to, and a recoil from, the predominant Western philosophical and religious thought of the time. This is clearly manifested in the case of the two younger Slavophils, Konstantin Aksakov and Iurii Samarin, who in the early 1840s were won over from Hegelianism to religion and Slavophil Orthodoxy. This, as we have seen, was accomplished particularly through Khomiakov's efforts. But in effect the Slavophils were then reacting to more than Western religion and German rationalism. As both Ivan Kireevsky and Khomiakov showed later, they were cognizant of materialistic thought in Germany during the 1830s, 1840s, and 1850s, coming in the wake of German idealism. The two elder Slavophils saw this as the inevitable and natural process of evolution of rationalism into materialism. The thought of Feuerbach, Max Stirner (Johann K. Schmidt, 1806–1856), and David F. Strauss (1808–1874), among others, illustrates the transition from idealism to materialism during the 1830s and 1840s. Nor did "medical" or "physiological" materialism of the late 1850s escape the attention of Khomiakov and Samarin.

The form and content of materialism in Western thought, depending on the epoch and the personalities of its proponents, and on the historical and cultural circumstances, vary considerably. But looking for something recurring or perhaps remaining permanent in two and a half millennia of Western materialism Bertrand Russell concluded in 1950 that "The two dogmas that constitute the essence of materialism are: First, the sole reality of matter; secondly, the reign of law."[1] Lange, in the opening sentence to his masterly three-volume historical survey of materialism, says, "Materialism is as old as philosophy but not older."[2] The relationship referred to here is that between the early atomic theory of matter and the beginning of Greek philosophy, springing from the same source, concern for the substance and laws of man's natural world. This concern is first evident in the sixth and fifth centuries B.C. in the Greek Ionian world, on the west coast of Asia Minor and some of the Aegean islands. But it is essential to bear in mind that from the point of view of historical veracity and chronology, Greek religion, represented by the Olympic pantheon, preceded both Greek philosophy and Greek science. It is worth stressing that even in our present world which places such inordinate faith and reliance on science, we still have abundant evidence of the elemental human need to believe in something beyond ourselves. The compulsion to have faith in a deity, a cult symbol, or a hero persists to the present despite the resolute march of science, materialism, and purported atheism. This elemental need reaches further into our murky anthropological past than the need and compulsion to think and reason, and it seems to be accompanied by the need to belong.

In the Greek world in addition to the interconnection between science in the form of deductive atomic physics, a materialistic philosophy, and a religion centered on the Olympian pantheon, there was also concern for morality. These and the need to belong, were all essential to govern the day-to-day relations between human beings so that they could survive to ponder weightier matters. Thales (640?–546 B.C.), and his pupil Anaximander (611–547 B.C.), both of Miletus on the west coast of Asia Minor, were among the earliest in the Greek world to show concern for mathematics and geometry, astronomy, and philosophy. But it was in Abdera on the Thracian coast of the Aegean, about one hundred miles east of Mount Olympus, that the atomic structure of matter was elaborated. Here in the fifth and fourth centuries B.C. lived for a while Leucippus, probably of Miletus, but it seems associated with Elea, about one hundred miles north of Miletus; also Democritus (c. 460–c. 370 B.C.), "the Abderite," and Protagoras (490?–421 B.C.?) also of Abdera, a friend of Pericles, the "first of the Sophists," and author of the "man-measure" doctrine, one of the best known in classical Greek thought.[3] Although Aristotle of Stagira, about fifty miles across the sea from Abdera, attributed the atomic theory of matter to Leucippus there seems to be no way of making a clear distinction between the views of Democritus and Leucippus. More of the work of Democritus than of Leucippus has survived and for this reason Democritus is better known. In its earliest concept Greek atomism admitted the reality of atoms and void alone. The form of the atoms and their arrangement and position, their different combinations, accounted for the different things we experience.

Since the amount of accumulated factual knowledge about nature in general, and the atom in particular, was extremely meager at the time, the bold atomic theory was the product of the speculative inductive genius of early Greek thought. This means that it was unaided by the results of systematic laboratory data and experimentation. For while the ancient world might have had its share of bright tinkerers and experimenters, and while Alexandria, for instance, might have boasted a "laboratory" as well as a library, the laboratory technique, as an indispensable and constant corollary to the mathematical approach to the study of science, was not a part of the ancient world. Furthermore, it is in the nature of human experience that questions of ultimate beginnings and ultimate ends or eschatology should become matters of philosophy and science as well as of religion. But science and philosophy are totally dependent on the human intellect, whereas religion, specifically Christianity, relies on revelation for its most vital truths. As is well known, revelation and traditional Christianity were assailed by Western materialists as well as by certain Western scientists. Similar doubts and considerations that bolstered the classical Greek materialists were also in evidence in the middle of the nineteenth century. Down the centuries in the Western tradition the varieties of materialism increased in number as different epochs, different historical conditions, and personalities added to the multifaceted character of materialism.

After its initial stage of atomism and materialism, and the concurrent sensationalism of Democritus and Leucippus, in the early fifth century B.C., Greek philosophy entered its most illustrious stage, the fifth and fourth-century spiritual movement of Socrates, Plato, and Aristotle. This was followed by the third-century revival of materialistic thought in the form of Epicureanism. In the field of physics and philosophy Epicurus of Samos (342?–270 B.C.) subscribed to the atomistic theory of Democritus, which was even the case with his opponents, the Stoics. But in spite of the central position of matter in early Greek atomism and physics, Lange says that "generally speaking, the most familiar form of Materialism among the Greeks was the *anthropological*."[4]

The Athens of Socrates, Plato, and Aristotle dominates Greek thought, but it should not be forgotten that most of the leading Greek philosophers and scientist-theoreticians came from the Greek colonies in Ionia, the Aegean shores, and some islands, and from Magna Graecia in the southern part of Italy and Sicily. It is therefore not surprising that in Rome lived and worked Lucretius Carus (96?–55 B.C.), a poet of the Epicurean school of thought. In his great "didactic and philosophical poem," *De Rerum Natura* (The Nature of Things), he deals with matters of physics as well as of psychology and ethics, and displaying a profoundly anthropocentric view of life, inveighs powerfully against the "humiliating terror of the gods." He believed religion, including the Roman pantheon, to be the "source of the grossest abominations" and oppression of mankind, and he denounced the "unreasonable terror of eternal punishment which leads mankind to sacrifice their happiness and peace of mind to the horrors of the prophets."[5] Yet by means of this all-absorbing anthropocentrism, he paradoxically seems to arrive either at some sort of common-man worship or, more likely, at total absence of faith. This latter alternative, however, presupposes that the normal human being can exist without the indispensable human need and manifestation of faith and runs contrary to both human nature and the anthropological and historical record. Those who would deny all gods, including the Christian, must account for the void that this leaves in normal human life. Has the human being in recent millennia existed in total absence of belief, and could he, even in this scientific technological age claim that he has totally rid himself of this need? Is not much of the bravado of what today passes for atheism in truth anthropotheism?

In the long and varied history of Western materialism from the ancient Greeks to the present, the so-called Dark Ages and on up to the Renaissance is a period of relative hiatus. This is not a completely unaccountable phenomenon, for as we have seen, materialism and science have gone hand in hand since the days of Hellenic atomism. The astonishing achievements of the resurgence of science during the Renaissance, accompanied in recent times by an effective technology, have also witnessed an upsurge of modern Western philosophy, including materialism. In the seventeenth, eighteenth, and nineteenth centuries England, France, and Germany led the West in both science and philosophy. It is not therefore surprising that one finds there the concentration of modern rationalistic and materialistic thought. Russian philosophical materialism of the eighteenth century, still rudimentary, and of the nineteenth century when it made its telling impact, including Marxism, was inspired by the West. Up until the second half of the eighteenth century Russia remained largely untouched by both classical and modern Western science and Western materialism, as it had, for various historical reasons, remained outside the current of Renaissance science.[6]

Referring to the West, Lange said:

Although modern Materialism appeared as a system first in France, yet England was the classic land of materialistic modes of thought. Here the ground had already been prepared by Roger Bacon [1214?—1294], and

Occam [1300?—1349?]. . . and Hobbes [1588—1679], the most consequent
[i.e., consistent] of modern Materialists, is at least as much indebted to
English tradition as to the example and precedence of Gassendi [1592—1655].

Lange stressed that Newton (1642–1727) and Boyle (1627–1691) supplied
the "material world-machine" with a "spiritual constructor" but that this, far
from threatening the "mechanical and materialistic theory of nature," merely pacified religion "by appealing to the Divine inventor of the great
machine." In this manner the "peculiar combination of faith and
materialism was permanently established in England."[7]
Down the centuries, a bewildering array of materialistic thought reflecting degrees, shades, interpretations, and varieties of classical Greek
materialism has found expression in the writings of men of talent and even
genius. From the speculative, atomic materialism of Leucippus and
Democritus in fifth century B.C. Abdera to the "Medical" materialism of
Büchner, Vogt, Moleshott, and DuBois-Reymond of the 1850s and 1860s,
which moved along "physicochemical lines, philosophical materialism has
evolved in close contact with the physical sciences, that is, physics, chemistry,
biology, and physiology. But this has not prevented materialistic thought
from moving into realms of human activity which, on the surface at least,
have only a tenuous contact with the physical-mathematical sciences. In the
realm of faith, materialism has often led to atheism or, what is more likely,
to anthropolatry when atheism has been proclaimed.
The varieties of materialism from its inception in classical Abdera pose
difficulties in any consideration of materialism in general, and certainly in
our understanding of the Slavophil reaction to materialism in the middle of
the nineteenth century. The scientific materialism of Leucippus and
Democritus, in Lange's words, "anthropological materialism," was the "most
familiar form . . . among the Greeks."[8] In the teachings of Lucretius
materialism became antireligious as he revolted against the "burden of
religious fear" and "religious terror." Denying any spiritual soul and human
immortality, he stamped materialism with these two permanent doctrines.
But Epicurus modified his stand with respect to the Greek gods and even
"sacrificed" to them.[9] During the Middle Ages in Western Europe we encounter what could be termed nominalistic materialism. Nominalism, particularly appealing in England, not only was opposed to Platonism but in its
affinity to materialism cleared the way for it.
During the Renaissance, the birth of modern science which in the Western
tradition wedded mathematics to the experimental laboratory method,
thereby substituting the hypothetico deductive for the inductive method of
scientific investigation, gave a powerful impetus to the materialism associated with modern Western science. As Campbell has said, the appeal
of materialism throughout the centuries "arises from its alliance with those

sciences which have contributed most to our understanding of the world we live in."[10] In the seventeenth-century French Catholic priest Pierre Gassendi (1592–1655) we encounter a man considered "both as the founder of modern materialism and a leading skeptic and libertine . . . trying to find a *via media* between his faith and the new science." Lange characterized Gassendi as "the propagator of modern Materialism," although he stressed that "Materialism and Atheism are not identical even if they are related conceptions."[11]

With the great advances in science during the eighteenth century in physics, particularly in the work of Newton, and in chemistry in the work of Lavoisier and Priestley, materialism experienced an intensification that was sustained in the nineteenth and twentieth centuries with new scientific discoveries and achievements. Thus in the eighteenth century the varieties of materialism increased. In Campbell's words, "Metaphysical" materialism became prominent in the work of Holbach; in Lange's, in the "Materialism" of "political economy"; in Bertrand Russell's in "scientific materialism" and "revolutionary materialism"; and in Acton's in "mechanical materialism."[12] The nineteenth century contributed dialectical and historical materialism, as well as the "medical" materialism, mentioned earlier, and the twentieth century has made its own contribution to the wealth of materialistic thought.

We have seen that from its inception Greek materialism relied upon, and derived much of its strength and appeal from, natural science. But science usually operates in a circumscribed sphere, and it tends to ask "only those questions that can be answered." Until recently, science seldom ventured into the realm of ultimate beginnings and ultimate ends (eschatology), which have traditionally been concerns of religion, in the Western tradition Christianity, and of philosophy. Science and its twin, philosophy, rely upon intellect and logic, but reason does not function in complete isolation from other human faculties. For instance, in 1857 Khomiakov discussing Hegel's logic declared, "Every philosophy has the capacity to become something akin to faith, or better said, some sort of prejudice." Kireevsky stated a year earlier, "The character of the dominant philosophy . . . depends on the character of the dominant faith."[13] More recently G. K. Chesterton, among others, agreed that "reason is itself a matter of faith." Indeed, hypothesis or theory, the scientific hunch, which has become familiar in modern science, in essence contains an element of faith or belief as well as of intuition and occasionally of chance.

The early Slavophils held modern Western science and technology in high esteem, but they did not consider that either Western science or Western philosophy gave the answers to all human problems and concerns, nor did they find the Western Christian confessions adequate. Their pro-Russian, pro-Orthodox bias was, however, less rigid than that of the official Russian church, and certainly less dependent on and subservient to the state, and heavily reliant on the simple Christian virtues of brotherhood in freedom and love. In his third letter to William Palmer, Khomiakov declared, in a stroke of Slavophil messianism, "Orthodoxy is not the salvation of man but the salvation of mankind."[14] With respect to philosophy the Slavophils lived and worked, as noted earlier, in the transitional period of then dominant German thought, from idealism to materialism.[15] If the Slavophils reacted to these intellectual currents the question is, how well informed were they about that to which they were reacting? Here we encounter a problem to which there seems to be no clear or definite answer.

Owing to the manner in which the early Slavophils, particularly Khomiakov and Ivan Kireevsky, wrote it is virtually impossible to know precisely what they read, for even when they mention a certain author, they are not specific about what work or works they have in mind. Even Samarin who in his dissertation was fairly precise about his reading and sources, after his student days acquired the ususal publicist's disregard for documentation. The second major flaw in the writings of the Slavophils, particularly in the two older ones, was the very obvious absence of concentration on specific themes.

Neither Khomiakov nor Ivan Kireevsky gives us as much as an essay, much less a monograph, on such themes of their concern as, for example, English empiricism, eighteenth-century French materialism, and German idealism, about which they were most critical. Nor did they leave more than scattered references and fragments about their positive central topics, including Khomiakov's concept of *sobornost'* and Kireevsky's doctrine "wholeness of the spirit." The often polemical nature of their writings merely added to the difficulties, particularly since a good deal of their writing took the form of private correspondence (as was the case between Samarin and Herzen) in which scoring points was more desirable than a reasoned and measured presentation of ideas.

In the opening pages of his dissertation on Stefan Iavorksy and Theofan Prokopovich young Samarin, living in an age of philosophical system building in Western culture, stated his views on the matter in clear, concise language. "Every system," he said, "has a pretension to universality. It has to have compulsory force for everyone. Therefore at the beginning of an ecclesiastical system it is necessary to prove that there is actually revelation, and divine authority, and a church." In the Catholic church, he held, two principles, are "forcefully united the ecclesiastical and the philosophical," one matter of revelation, the other of human reason and logic. The end result of this process is that "dogmas lose their original character of free revelation and are reduced to the level of correct deductions." Psychologically this was deleterious for the church because it "loses faith in itself, seeks external support, and summons help from the philosophical principle."[16] Since he and the other early Slavophils maintained that Protestantism was a logical consequence of Catholic rationalism and disregard for the ecumenical—in their opinion Orthodox, church—they attributed the woes of Western Christendom to the powerful intrusion in it of secularist rationalism. How thoroughly the early Slavophils, Samarin and Konstantin Aksakov in particular, were in the grip of that same Western secularism is illustrated by the fact that at the time Samarin put these thoughts down in writing he had barely shaken off Hegelian rationalism.

The early Slavophils were deeply concerned about German idealism and materialism, which they viewed as they did Western culture in general, from their unshakable base of Slavophil Orthodoxy. In their works they refer to the relationship between Hegelianism and the presumed end of modern rationalism, and in this they were somewhat in agreement with Feuerbach, who saw Hegelianism as the ultimate stage in the evolution of modern rationalism. But they could hardly have agreed with Feuerbach's attack on Christianity as "egotistical and inhumane" (in the anonymous *Thoughts Regarding Death and Immortality*, 1830). By 1857 when his *Theogonie* appeared, he had already given himself to a study of the natural sciences, producing among other works *Das Wesen des Christentums* (1841) and *Das Wesen der Religion* (1846).[17] Feuerbach thought all religions were "illusionist" and he declared in favor of a philosophy based upon anthropology and physiology.

Strauss's *Das Leben Jesu kritisch bearbeitet* (The Life of Jesus Christ Critically Examined), which appeared in two volumes in 1835–1836, struck at the very heart of Christianity—its belief in revealed truth. Revelation was nothing more than man's propensity for mythmaking. Revealed truth was a manmade myth. In his *Die christliche Glaubenslehre* (2 vols., 1840–1841) he saw Christianity as a phase in the unfolding of pantheism, and man in the world as the embodiment of God. No less unorthodox and disturbing to the Slavophils was Stirner's *Der Einzige und sein Eigentum* (The Ego and His Own, 1845). This was an apotheosis of egoism, an attack upon reason in favor of will and instinct, and a denial of absolutes, of abstract and general notions and of philosophical systems. Considered by some a precursor of Nietzsche and of anarchism and nihilism, Stirner elaborated on these themes in his later works.[18]

In 1855 Büchner's *Kraft und Stoff* (Force and Matter) appeared in Germany. Ludwig Büchner (1824–1899) was a physician and philosopher, and his highly popular book, which went through more than a dozen editions and many translations, he begins with the fundamental premise that force and matter are identical. He sanctioned the position of the ancient Greek materialists, and felt that modern science was providing new evidence and confirmation of their views. Although he denied religion in general and Christianity in particular, reducing the human being to biological functions, his theory of the mind rejected Karl Vogt's and Pierre Cabanis's notion "which compared thinking to the secretions of bodily organs." Thus, thinking—a brain process—was "not comparable to urine, bile, or other such secretions."[19] Three years before the appearance of *Kraft und Stoff*, Jacob Moleschott (1822–1893) published his *Der Kreislauf des Lebens* (The Circuit of Life, 1852). This was the work of a physiologist, medical doctor, and philosopher, considered by some as the founder of nineteenth-century materialism. Like Büchner, he adhered to philosophical monism, summed up in his famous "No thought without phosphorus," and also like him he maintained that force was inseparable from matter.[20]

The views of Feuerbach, Strauss, Stirner, Moleschott, Büchner, Vogt, and others of similar convictions were known to the early Slavophils. What is not possible to ascertain from the customary Slavophil name references is how many of the works of these authors they read, when they read them, and what was discussed among them. It is quite certain that they read in the original German whatever works they chose since they all knew the German language well; we also know about certain specific works, as for instance Stein's *Der Sozialismus und Kommunismus des heutigen Frankreich*, which Samarin read in 1842, the year of its publication. Khomiakov in discussing materialism mentions Stirner, Feuerbach, and Strauss. But his knowledge and reading in philosophy and religion ranged far and wide, from prehistoric times to his own age, and from China, India, the middle East, Egypt, Greece, Rome and Europe in general, to the Indians of the new world.[21]

Toward the middle of his first letter on philosophy to Samarin (1859) Khomiakov summed up his negative view of materialism in the following words:

> Materialism subjected to the test of logic becomes transformed into a meaningless sound. And yet how many centuries have passed since the time when this meaningless sound passed for the first time for philosophizing [*filosofstvuiushchuiu*] thought! Ancient Greece in the case of some of its wittiest [*ostroumneishikh*] thinkers had already succumbed to its deception.[22]

But not only in Greece had materialism made its appearance. "Ancient India was creating whole schools of materialists even earlier, nor was the West in the "Middle Ages alien to this orientation."[23] Resorting, as he often did, to the sweeping generalization, he declared that "most recent times have seen its [materialism's] development on an enormous scale," stressing in particular "German neo-materialism." His concern for ethical problems led him to the conclusion that these "were equally unsolved in either Hegelian rationalism or in Schelling's gnosticism," the last of Schelling's phases of thought as he saw it. Then came the "transition thought, which appears as the development of matter. How is a transition possible from one to the other?"[24]

Khomiakov looked upon ancient and modern Western materialism from an Orthodox viewpoint. In a summary in *Semiramida* that smacks of religious determinism he says, "Take Christianity out of the history of Europe and Buddhism out of Asia and you will understand nothing in either Europe or Asia."[25] A poet himself, and with an abiding interest in art, he could hide neither his appreciation of Greek literature and art nor his disappointment in Greek religion. He found the contrast striking: "Despite so many evidences of enlightenment, and so many remnants of a poetry [that stands] alone in the world, and a philosophy that yields neither to Hindustan [i.e. India] nor to Germany, it is noteworthy that in Greek literature there is an absence of religious books and even of prayers." He summed up the Greek and Roman attitude toward religion thus: "Do not touch our gods because they are corrupt; do not speak of the unseen because it disturbs the quiet harmony of the visible world."[26] After this it is not surprising that Khomiakov relegated classical Greek and Roman religion to the realm of the Kushite principle.

Khomiakov divided the ancient religions according to the Iranian and Kushite principles, the Iranian standing for freedom, the Kushite for necessity. He further identified the Iranian with the "spiritual worship of the freely-creative spirit or with primordial sublime monotheism," whereas the Kushite meant "recognition of eternal organic necessity derived by virtue of inevitable logical laws."[27] Whereas India and Iran left us complete collections of divine laws . . . Greece did not even feel the need to know what it believed in, and what it did not, or even whether it believed in anything." Only awe, wonderment, and superlatives could render Khomiakov's views of Greek philosophy, of Socrates, Plato, and Aristotle. He contrasted Greek religion with the nobility of Greek art, philosophy, and civic consciousness [*grazhdanstvennost'*].[28]

Kireevsky's knowledge of ancient Hindu and Greek materialism as well as of modern Western materialism was less thorough than Khomiakov's. His reading was more narrowly confined to classical and modern Western and contemporary philosophy. While still in his teens he became interested in Locke and Helvetius (1715–1771), though we are not certain exactly what work or works of these philosophers he read. In a letter to his friend Koshelev written in 1830 he indicated that he had changed his views about Helvetius and would probably share Koshelev's low opinion if he were to reread him. "I shall admit to you that then [when he was in his teens] he appeared to me not only precise, clear [but also] popularly convincing despite the preaching of egoism."[29] Now (at twenty-three), Kireevsky found in Helvetius's "Enlightenment" empiricism, deep-rooted environmentalism, and hedonism, and his negative views toward Christianity, atheistic and materialistic.

Two years later, in 1832, in his published essay "The Nineteenth Century," Kireevsky touched on Western literature and thought. Western rationalism and materialism appeared to him incomplete and negative. All Western philosophical thought, whatever its form and content, "pursued alone the development of the laws of mental necessity, and even most recent materialism is based on purely logical convictions." These convictions were in turn based on the "abstract notions of the laws of our reason but not on the living knowledge of the essence of matter and existence." In this manner it achieves "only *negative* knowledge, since reason that is self-developing is [also] self-limiting."[30] The profound and boundless anthropocentrism of Western rationalism and materialism also seemed self-confining. The self-limitation of nineteenth-century Western rationalism and materialism is even more glaring today when, paradoxically, thanks primarily to Western science and technology, the possibility of making contact with intelligent life elsewhere in the universe increases with each passing day. The time had come, Kireevsky concluded in 1832, "for positive *Historical* philosophy," because "negative and logical philosophy has now completed its development." Speculative thought should now draw closer to "life and reality," and should seek rapprochement with "religious opinions." Religion here was not conceived in narrow, sectarian terms. "Papists, and Jesuits, and Saint Simonists, and Protestant Empiricists and even Rationalists . . . they all come together on one point: in the *demand for a greater rapprochement of religion with the life of people and nations.*"[31]

Kireevsky in 1852 sensed the depth and pervasiveness of Western anthropocentrism and the extent to which it was permeating Western life and culture. Its powerful expression, he said, was logical reason, which was the basic cause of the ninth-century church schism when the church in the West, having "subjected faith to the logical deductions of abstract understanding [*razsudok*] . . . established inside itself the inevitable seed of the Reformation." The Universal Church having thus been disregarded, one "could then see Luther behind Pope Nicholas I," as later one could "foresee Strauss behind Luther."[32] Thus over a period of ten centuries Western rationalism produced first the church schism, then Lutheranism, and by the 1840s Strauss's materialism. But this was not the only way in which Western man succumbed to an excessive opinion of human nature.

Going back to classical Greece, Kireevsky referred to the wonted dialectic which in his day held in its grip some of Europe's foremost minds. In 1838 he was reconciled to the "mutual struggle between two hostile principles," the Russian and the Western. But in 1856 he was skeptical of the dialectic and was critical of Hegel for it. In Chizhevsky's opinion, Kireevsky was the first to see the "inner bond between Hegel and Aristotle."[33] Whether that is so or not, one reads in Kireevsky's last essay that Aristotle's basic convictions (not those attributed to him in the Middle Ages in the

West) were "completely identical with Hegel's convictions. And that manner of dialectical thinking which is ordinarily considered the exclusive characteristic and singular discovery of Hegel constituted even before Aristotle the obvious property of the Eleatic school." This was so true in Kireevsky's mind that "reading Plato's *Parmenides* it seems as if in the words of Heraclitus's pupil we hear the Berlin professor himself expounding on the dialectic as the principle purpose of philosophy and its present task, [and] perceiving in it miracle-working power." But Kireevsky's conclusion was that "Reason [now] stands on the same level — not higher, and sees the same ultimate truth — not farther; only the horizon around it is more clearly delineated."[34]

The Slavophils in effect raised the ancient question of the relationship between reason and faith. They left it as unresolved as before, but the use of the dialectic in the West in the middle of the nineteenth century was disturbing for it was undergoing an ominous change. What to the classical Greeks seems to have been a process of dialogue, deliberation and argument was rapidly becoming in the West one of ideological and social and political power struggle and confrontation. And today unless the new dialectic is abandoned the ultimate "synthesis" would most likely be an atomic eruption between West and East. Clearly humanity could not adhere to any philosophy, religion or cult that would lead it to its atomic annihilation.

In 1852 in his comments on Kireevsky's essay on the nature of Western and Russian cultures Khomiakov was equally critical of Western rationalism and materialism. He considered Protestantism to be profoundly rationalistic and commented, "[The] Feuerbachs of our time began their destructive work" in the days of Zwingli. Seven years later he reiterated his censure of "German neo-materialism" and the "perversion" of Hegelianism by Feuerbach and others. Matter, he said, had replaced spirit, which was the universal "substratum"; German poetry had also been degraded: the "relationship of Heine to Goethe is completely identical with the relationship of Feuerbach to Hegel." The error of German thought, including Hegel's and Feuerbach's, was to "accept *razsudok* [*der Verstand*] for the wholeness of the spirit [*tselnost' dukha*]." Khomiakov had cited in 1849 Stirner's *Der Einzelne und sein Eigentum,* and dismissed it as so much "bookish philosophizing" (*knizhnoe umnichan'ie*). Two years earlier he had summarily declared Strauss and Bruno Bauer to be "quite insignificant" (*dovol'no nichtozhnye*).[35]

After these negative pronouncements on German rationalism and materialism it was perhaps to be expected that Khomiakov would give his opinion of the proper place for human reason. One of his most lucid summaries concerns the function of reason and its relationship to Christian faith and is contained in his last theological essay, published in Leipzig in 1858, in which he says,

The freedom of human reason consists not in creating the universe in its own manner [*po svoemu*], but in comprehending it through the free use of its cognitive abilities independent of any external authority. The Holy Scripture is the Divine revelation freely understood by the reason of the Church. The definitions of the councils, the meaning of the rituals, in a word the whole dogmatic tradition, is an expression of the same revelation, equally freely understood, only in different forms.[36]

For Khomiakov as for Kireevsky, reason alone, however great and gifted the thinker or the philosopher, is incapable of moving beyond limited, imperfect human perception. And despite the great progress of Western science and technology, of which the Slavophils were keenly aware, Western philosophical reason had not advanced beyond that of classical Greece.

Mid-nineteenth-century Western rationalism and materialism, as Kireevsky put it a few months before he died, "stood on the same level – and not higher" than that of classical Greek rationalism and materialism. The ancient Greeks had no choice: both in faith (in anthropomorphic gods), and in philosophy based upon human reason they were inescapably anthropocentric. Nineteenth-century Europe, on the contrary, had a choice in philosophy, but failed to make it. It was up to Russia to come up with its "Russian philosophy." This would reflect Russia's own cultural characteristics but would also be an expression of the "wholeness of the spirit." The future "Russian philosophy" that Kireevsky had in mind but never worked out was not going to be a new phase of Western rationalistic anthropocentric thought but would, in some fashion or other, encompass all of man's faculties and Russian Eastern Orthodox faith.

In his Moscow University dissertation on Stefan Iavorsky and Feofan Prokopovich, Samarin proposed an "ecclesiastical system at the beginning of which it is essential to prove that actually there is revelation, divine authority, and a church." (In a footnote to this assertion he explained that revelation was central to his religious and ideological stand: "Scripture and tradition presuppose the fact of the church but not at all the reverse.") Looking upon the Western confessions from his Orthodox Slavophil vantage point, he noted that Catholicism "begins with tradition," Protestantism "with the scripture." Still, "outside the church neither the authority of tradition nor the authority of the scripture can be proved."[37]

The essence of Samarin's position in the mid-1840s, as also in 1867, was that the "autocracy of personal reason" responsible for the separation of the Roman church from the universal church, and of the Protestant from the Roman, was characteristically Western, and alien to both Orthodoxy and Slavophilism. In his words, "Orthodoxy remained completely outside this *dialectical development of religious thought.*"[38] In 1867, having seen the sad state of Western philosophy as represented by "vulgar" or "medical" materialism, and using *nauka* to mean philosophy, he was relieved to say that the "results that philosophy has attained are connected in a straight ascending line not with Orthodoxy but with Latinism and Protestantism." Idealism that does away with faith "in its own way," and is *"seemingly"* the opposite of materialism, is in reality "its lawful progeny."

Despite his preoccupation with the bond between idealism and materialism, Samarin could not escape in the middle 1860s — only seven or eight years after the publication of Darwin's *On the Origin of Species by Means of Natural Selection* — the heavy impact of science on Western thought and on materialism. Yet materialism that had grown "under the wing of idealism" soon turned against its parent, and finding itself without any kin, "attached itself almost by force to the natural sciences."[39] Samarin could have completed the cycle of Western materialism if he had reminded his readers that it had its birth in ancient Abdera where it had as an integral part the atomic theory of matter.

Samarin, in spite of his awareness of the numerous achievements of Western science, could not hide his disappointment when he judged it to be overstepping its bounds. He noticed with regret that "science looked upon faith from on high [svysoka]."[40] Rationalism, empiricism, materialism, and science in the Western tradition are all of pre-Christian origin, and are the product of man's faculties thus are alien to Christian revelation. While they remain profoundly anthropocentric they have been and still are a powerful encouragement to Western anthropolatry and cultism. It is no mere accident that twentieth-century Europe and America produced some of the world's most destructive cults. Samarin was sufficiently perceptive to see that mid-nineteenth-century Western philosophy and science could come up with no ethics of their own that would ensure man's survival on earth. "For consistent materialism," he concluded ruefully, "violence as an instrument of progress is not at all frightening, therefore one cannot expect from it leniency toward faith."[41]

Russia, Samarin realized, was a special problem. Philosophy was inaccessible to the millions of newly freed illiterate peasants who made up the *narod*, and the *narod* was in danger of falling victim, as stated in part one, to "ecclesiastical red tape," to [*kazenshchina*], or the subordination of faith to narrow official conservatism, and to purposes alien to it. In the West, for centuries after the fall of the Roman empire the Catholic church had no strong temporal power to contend with and it soon constituted itself as a state as well as a church, but in eastern Europe conditions were different. The Orthodox church in Byzantium and later in Kiev and Moscow existed alongside a strong temporal authority. These Orthodox churches did not constitute themselves as states but remained for centuries in the shadow of "ecclesiastical red tape," and in constant danger of being used for the purposes of the state. Samarin recognized the threat in his own day to that highly idealized Slavophil view of Orthodoxy which was conceived as love in freedom and equality. "Demanding from faith any sort of police service is nothing but a preaching of unbelief," he warned: "Among us this preaching has done its job."[42]

Samarin was convinced in 1867 that in the West philosophical idealism no longer counted, and that materialism was rapidly displacing it. He did not, of course, expect from materialism any consideration for faith: materialism "did not even look upon it as a necessary phase in the self-education of mankind, but only saw it as a simple obstacle with which it cannot live in harmony and [therefore] has no reason to stand on ceremony." This accounted for the "singular bitterness of its attacks and for its rude mockery, so sharply in contrast to the chivalrous manners of the late [*pokoinago*] idealism." As for the representatives of the two currents of thought in Russia, he said, "Place Granovsky on one side, and on the other Belinsky (in the last years of his activity) or Dobroliubov and his pupils, and around these two types will be gathered almost all that is stirring among us in the realm of philosophy."[43]

We get the Slavophil reaction to "medical" or "vulgar" German materialism primarily from Samarin, since the Kireevsky brothers died in 1855, the year of the publication of Büchner's *Kraft und Stoff*. (Khomiakov and Konstantin Aksakov died in 1860.) In 1861 Samarin wrote in a letter on materialism to his friend N. P. Giliarov-Platonov, "I read Büchner's *Kraft und Stoff* on board ship in one sitting." This occurred while he was on his way from St. Petersburg to Germany.[44] According to Dmitry Samarin, Iurii's response to materialism was touched off by the quick penetration into Russia of Western materialistic thought particularly with the translation of *Kraft und Stoff* into Russian in 1860, but it is clear from works of the late 1850s to the early 1870s that he was attentive to Western philosophical currents, notably rationalism, idealism, and materialism. He also became keenly concerned with the accelerated pace of Western secularism, dramatically manifested in the advance of Darwinism and Comtean positivism.

The profoundly anthropocentric developments in the West, such as materialism, evoked in Samarin a response on two levels, on the philosophical, and on the more down-to-earth level of ideology. In the absence of a precise scientific determination it could be said that Samarin, with his desire to see reform and improvement of conditions in Russia, was more concerned with ideology than with philosophy. Reliance has here been placed on several of his later works. These include two letters on materialism to Giliarov-Platonov, one of which was mentioned above. We have also mentioned more than once his "Introduction to the Theological Works of A. S. Khomiakov" (1867). Another appeared under the title "Concerning the Works of Max Müller on the History of Religion," written in 1876 in Berlin in German shortly before his death. Samarin's longer "Analysis of K. D. Kavelin's Work, 'Problems of Psychology,'" will be considered later.

The publication of Samarin's letter to Giliarov-Platonov in *Den'* annoyed Samarin because he had not intended the letter for public exposure and Aksakov published it "without my knowledge and consent."[45] In a letter to Prince D. A. Obolensky of December 7, 1870, he apologized for this work, saying that at the time (the end of the 1850s) he was too absorbed with the emancipation of the serfs to give much thought to questions of philosophy. He acknowledged that his thoughts on materialism were stimulated by the reading of *Kraft und Stoff* and said that its author "did not grip me for a single minute" because "I simply felt no strength in him."[46] Büchner's extreme, "vulgar" materialism led to only one conclusion—that "The only consistent and harmonious materialist in whole world is the dumb animal," and he added, to the consciousness of this truth . . . "Büchner has come very close."[47] Samarin was convinced that public discussion of the materialism of Büchner, Moleschott, Vogt, and others of similar persuasion would be sufficient to discredit it.

Conscious of the long historical bond between materialism and some natural scientists Samarin recognized two "orientations" among them. In characterizing the first group he also gave us his views on the relationship between science and Christianity, and Slavophil Orthodoxy. These views, dating to the end of the 1850s, are perhaps fairly representative of early Moscow Slavophilism. The first category of scientists, Samarin says, remain within the limits of their chosen special subjects. Having at their disposal exclusively those means of cognition which are conditioned by the very nature of the subject (experiment, observation, etc.) they are not constrained in their deductions by any data obtained by other means, and from other sources (for example, from Revelation, tradition etc.), and, without rejecting these data, they gradually enrich science with results of a *positive* character.[48]

Other scientists, such as the German "medical" materialists, he asserted, start with "natural science" (*estestvovedenie*) and in a "purely mechanical manner transfer from it fragmentary deductions to an entirely different realm," which to them remains completely dark and unknown. For this reason they tend "to mistake diversities for contradictions", and he regretted that this "negative" school of thought was making an impression in Russia. To the Büchners, Vogts, and their ilk, Samarin concluded, the spiritual world of man, and notions "about God, about the soul, about Revelation" are alien and they "celebrate any discerned contradiction" between the spiritual and material worlds as a "triumph of matter over spirit."[49]

There is no doubt that Samarin remained to the last days of his life true to the Orthodox Slavophil point of view, placing the Christian God in the center of his universe. Although while still a graduate student he showed that he was capable of independent thought on religious matters, he chose to place himself in debt to Khomiakov. He never seems to have forgotten the special relationship that developed between them from the mid-1840s on. As late as June 28, 1870, he could write to the Baroness Rahden, "Ever since the death of Khomiakov I had lost all fear of anyone." And early that year he characterized his older Slavophil friend as "the man whom I venerate most of all in the world."[50] But while Samarin admired Khomiakov for his religious views and his friendship, he preserved his own individuality. Here I believe it is possible to see an important difference in temperament, personality, and historical circumstances between Samarin and the other Moscow Slavophils.

It has been said that Samarin was the most practical minded of the early Slavophils. This assessment is based largely on the leading role that he played in the emancipation of the serfs, a subject that will come up later in this study. In general, however, there seems to have been more of the man of action in him that in his Slavophil friends. The 1850s were the culmination of the era of the "superfluous men" in Russia, of the compulsive talker bogged down in inactivity. Samarin, like others among his contemporaries, sensed the passing of this phase and soon plunged into reform and action. His concern for morality was not only evident, but for a person of his spiritual makeup it was imperative. His conviction, personalized in the mid-forties, that philosophy in its then prevalent forms of German idealism and German materialism could not serve him as the basis for morality was clearly stated in a letter he wrote at the age of twenty-three to his father: "That no good comes of a deed not undertaken for God's glory; that there is no success where there is not the blessing of God, where there is no humble prayer — of this I am completely convinced."[51] This personal conviction became generalized to guide him in his public service.

Toward the end of his life Samarin, while in Berlin for the purpose of publishing the sixth installment of his *Borderlands of Russia,* was intrigued by a recent publication by the German linguist and Sanskritologist, Max Müller (1823–1900).[52] Samarin found Müller's "basic thought of the parallelism in the development of language and . . . belief [*verovanie*], and of the influence of religious data [and] presentations on the form of language, new, rich, and fruitful." Having read all Müller's works except his comparative study of language, Samarin concluded that Müller's "understanding of the history of religion includes an implied confession of complete atheism."[53] Ultimately what concerned Samarin most in his reading of and reaction to German speculative thought, to German idealism and materialism, was the question of down-to-earth ethics and morality. He could not get away from the problem of the daily conduct of human beings and from the principles and beliefs that guide them. Here he found all thought that excluded religion woefully wanting. He was convinced, as he stated at the end of his comments on Müller's work, that "morality without religion is like a plant without roots" (dass Moral ohne Religion einer wurzellosen Pflanze gleicht.)[54]

Yet Samarin's reaction to Müller's thought did not make him lose his respect for German philosophy and literature. He showed a preference for German idealism as against materialism, writing to a friend toward the end of his life, "For every Russian who has completed his education, Germany is in a certain sense also a fatherland, the Germany of Schiller, Goethe, Kant, Fichte, et al., and *this* Germany is disappearing.[55] In view of the resolute march of science, materialism, and secularism in the West, Samarin had a deep concern for human behavior in a world growing irresistibly more complex and more destructive. Could Western man, who had grown up in the Christian tradition, find salvation in the cults of secular prophets? Could even the greatest of these, still human, fallible, susceptible to sickness, passions, and insanity, replace the Christian God, conceived as an eternal and perfect spirit? To these questions and to the secularism and anthropocentrism of the West Samarin gave a negative answer. And the twentieth century has provided no evidence to prove him wrong. Humanity survives today not because Western science and humanism have produced a morality superior to the Christian ethic—yet to be tried in international relations—but because of a primordial fear of universal atomic destruction.

Samarin's reaction to materialism in general was negative and quite predictable. This is also true of the other early Slavophils, particularly of Khomiakov and Ivan Kireevsky, who articulated better than Konstantin Aksakov their opposition to Western materialism, secularism, and anthropocentrism. The alternative to the growing Western faith in secular prophets and saviors was their faith in the theism of Slavophil Orthodoxy.

Notes

1. See Bertrand Russell's introduction to F. A. Lange, *The History of Materialism and Criticism of Its Present Importance,* trans. E. C. Thomas, 3 vols. 3rd ed. (New York, 1950), I, XII.

2. Ibid., p. 3.

3. The complete contention is, "Man is the measure of all things, of things that are that [or "how"] they are and of things that are not that [or "how"] they are not." G. B. Kerferd, "Protagoras of Abdera," *Encyclopedia of Philosophy,* 8 vols. (New York, 1967), VI, 507.

4. Lange, *Materialism,* I, 94.

5. These statements by Lange are based on Book One of Lucretius's *De Rerum Natura.* Copley, a recent translator of Lucretius, concurs in Lange's characterization with his own assertion that "Lucretius is violent and bitter in his hatred of religion." He contrasts Lucretius's attitude with that of Epicurus, who "recommended that his followers go to the temples." Cf.

Lange, *Materialism,* I, 132–133; F. O. Copley, trans; *Lucretius, The Nature of Things* (New York, 1977), pp. XVI, 1–28.

6. The question of native Russian materialism is controversial. There is no agreement on a single definition of materialism, and furthermore Soviet scholars tend to see it as being a basic historical factor in Russia's past whereas scholars of Fr. V. V. Zenkovsky's religious persuasion dispute this contention. Galaktionov and Nikandrov in their history of Russian philosophy cover what they consider Russian materialism (including rationalistic tendencies in some Russian heresies) from the ninth through the seventeenth centuries in twenty-nine pages. Dynnik and his collaborators in their multivolume history of philosophy devote much attention to materialism in general but with respect to Russia are silent on the period before the end of the seventeenth and early eighteenth centuries. Lange's three-volume survey of materialism, completed in the early 1870s, contains much on classical and later French, English, and German materialism but nothing on Russian. Cf. A. A. Galaktionov and P. F. Nikandrov, *Russkaia filosofiia XI–XIX vekov* (Leningrad, 1970), pp. 52–71; M. A. Dynnik et al., *Istotiia filosofii,* 6 vols. (Moscow, 1957–1965), I, 467–485; V. V. Zenkovsky, *O mnimom materializme russkoi nauki i filosofii* (Munich, 1956). For some of the fifteenth- and sixteenth-century heresies, see O. V. Trakhtenberg, "Obshchestvenno-politicheskaia mysl' v Rossii v XV–XVII vekakh," in *Iz istorii russkoi filosofii. Sbornik statei* (Leningrad, 1952), pp. 67–95.

7. Lange, *Materialism,* II, 3.

8. Ibid., I, 94.

9. Cf. Copley, *Epicurus,* pp. xv, xvi, Lange, *Materialism,* I, 209, 255; Keith Campbell, "Materialism," *Encyclopedia of Philosophy, V, 181–182.*

10. Campbell, "Materialism," p. 179.

11. Cf. Lange, *Materialism,* I, 225; R. H. Popkin, "Gassendi, Pierre (1592–1655)," *Encyclopedia of Philosophy,* III, 272.

12. Cf. Campbell, "Materialism," p. 182; Lange, *Materialism,* I, viii, 295; H. B. Acton, "Dialectical Materialism," *Encyclopedia of Philosophy,* II, 391.

13. Khomiakov, *Sochineniia,* I, 267; Kireevsky, *Sochineniia,* I, 246.

14. Khomiakov, *Sochineniia,* II, 352.

15. The emphasis on German materialism here should not imply that no other German thinkers existed in the post-Hegelian period. The names of several have come to my attention, Schopenhauer, E. von Hartman, Nietzshe, Dilthey and Lange.

16. Samarin, *Sochineniia,* V 22–23.

17. H.V. White, "Feuerbach, Ludwig Andreas," *Encyclopedia of Philosophy,* III, 190.

18. Cf. H. V. White, "Strauss, David Friedrich"; George Woodcock, "Stirner, Max," *Encyclopedia of Philosophy,* VI, 25–26, 17–18.

19. Rollo Handy, "Büchner, Ludwig," *Encyclopedia of Philosophy,* I, 411–413.

20. Rollo Handy, "Moleschott, Jacob, *"Encyclopedia of Philosophy,* V 360–361.

21. Any reasonably thorough study of Khomiakov's thought would contain an examination not only of his poems, essays letters, and religious treatises but also of his rich and wide-ranging *Semiramida.* This work, (so named with Gogol's help) under the title *Notes on Universal History* which fills volumes 5, 6, and 7 of his collected works, was first published by Khomiakov's young friend, the Slavic scholar A. F. Gil'ferding (1831–1872), in 1872. Since Gil'ferding began his editorial work on *Semiramida* in 1862 Samarin was probably familiar with it before its publication. Khomiakov did not intend *Semiramida* for publication but it was doubtless informally discussed in the Slavophil salons. Khomiakov began work on it about 1838, and kept it up for the rest of his life, although Gil'ferding in his preface to *Semiramida* says that Khomiakov did not give it much time during the last five years of his life. See Khomiakov, *Sochineniia,* V, XI, XV, XX.

22. Ibid., I, 3304.

23. In *Semiramida,* the author provides the reader with a far-flung, roughly chronological, text and reflections loosely held together. From ancient Hindu and Chinese civilizations through ancient Persian, Mesopotamian, Egyptian, Near Eastern, classical Greek and Roman civilizations, it moves through Western Europe's "dark" and middle ages, Byzantium, the Muslim world, the spread of Christianity in Europe, and Abyssinia, and the American Indian lands. This often comparative cultural study, free and easy in the selection of information and interpretation is too facile in generalization. It abounds in material on religion, philosophy, social and individual values, also contains references on literary and aesthetic matters. Using source materials in Latin, Greek, English, German, French and Russian, Khomiakov also left (at the end of volume one) a fifty-page Sanskrit-Russian dictionary.

24. Khomiakov, *Sochineniia,* I, 305.

25. Ibid., V, 131.

26. Ibid., pp. 250–251.

27. Ibid., 217, 530–531.

28. Ibid., 250, I, 178.

29. Kireevsky, *Sochineniia,* I, 6.

30. Ibid., p. 92.

31. Ibid., p. 93.

32. Ibid., p. 190.

33. Chizhevsky, *Gegel' v Rossii,* p. 21.

34. Kireevsky, *Sochineniia,* I, 110, 233. One can see why Chizhevsky characterized Kireevsky's attitude toward Hegel as "dualistic" (*dvoistven-*

no), adding, "On the one had Hegel is for Kireevsky a great philosopher, on the other hand Hegel's philosophy belongs to the past" (*Gegel' v Rossii,* p. 21). The same, I believe, could be said with equal justice for Khomiakov's attitude toward Hegel.

35. Khomiakov, *Sochineniia,* I, 81, 151, 210, 297, 300–302.

36. Ibid., II, 235.

37. Samarin, *Sochineniia,* V, 23.

38. Professor Kline makes the point "the Slavophils were prepared to assert a dialectical relation among the confessions. Roman Catholicism represents unity without freedom, Protestantism—freedom without unity; Russian Orthodoxy—freedom in unity and unity in freedom." G. L. Kline, "Russian Religious Thought," in Ninan Smart et al., *Nineteenth Century Religious Thought in the West* (Cambridge, Eng., 1985) vol. II, p. 182.

39. Samarin, *Sochineniia,* VI, 332.

40. Ibid., p. 331.

41. Ibid., p. 333.

42. Ibid., p. 335.

43. Ibid., p. 333.

44. The letter was published in Ivan Aksakov's *Den'*.

45. Ibid., p. 541.

46. Ibid., p. 542.

47. Ibid., p. 546.

48. Ibid., p. 551.

49. Ibid., pp. 551–552, 553.

50. "Samarin to Rahden," pp. 131, 159.

51. Samarin, *Sochineniia,* XII, 106–107; VI, 486.

52. Müller's work, for which Samarin wrote a two-part review in German early in 1876, was, *Einleitung in die vergleichende Religionswissenschaft* (Strassburg, 1874).

53. Samarin, *Sochineniia,* VI, 484.

54. Ibid., pp. 520.

55. Ibid., p. 490.

12

National Spirit (Culture): Russia and the West

The views and convictions of the early Slavophils on the Western confessions, and on nineteenth-century Western rationalism and materialism, make it amply clear that their ideology could not rest upon either Western religion or Western philosophy. Furthermore they were quite emphatic in their admiration of Western scientific and technological achievements, and in the person of Koshelev took pains to acquaint themselves with the most advanced Western agricultural machinery in existence in the middle of the nineteenth century. This simultaneous acceptance on the one hand, of Western science and technology on the ground that they are universal, and rejection of the Western confessions and Western philosophy on the other is one of Slavophilism's most characteristic and most persistent legacies.

The criticism to which the Slavophils subjected Western religion and philosophy carried with it the clear and inevitable implication that they would also subject to close scrutiny the moral, social, and economic values that derive from them. And indeed this point can clearly be illustrated by recalling that in their censure of Lutheran religious individualism the Slavophils also underscored their negative attitude toward Protestant social and economic values. The doctrine of togetherness, summed up in the Slavophil concept of communality and *sobornost'*, was as distant and different from the Puritan ethic as the Slavophil commune was from the Protestant stress on individual enterprise.

No less striking is the distinction that the Slavophils drew between their highly idealized Orthodox church and the historical Roman Catholic institution. Attributing the eleventh-century schism in the Christian church to the thought and behavior of the Western church, the Slavophils found it easy to censor the papacy for those lapses in its long historical existence during which it was both a state and a church. The force and compulsion characteristic of states, and authority backed by the armed forces of a church-state, were in sharp contrast to the idealized Orthodox church of the Slavophils, a

Christian communion existing in love and freedom. This, of course, was far removed from the historical Orthodox church, often subservient to the temporal authority, and at times rent asunder by heresies. If the Slavophils could not consider Western Christianity as the source and base for their moral values, they could even less accept the hoary, pagan concepts of materialism, the modern Western dialectic, and anthropolatry as the proper foundation for a moral, social, political, and economic order. Over these fundamental issues the Slavophils in general, and Samarin in particular, found themselves in prolonged and sometimes heated controversy with a number of Russian Westerners.

The subject of Russian Westernism raises questions to which no precise answers have yet been given. Since there was no single homogeneous Westerner movement in the 1840s and 1850s the common practice has been to divide it into three different currents: pro-Catholic Westerners, represented by Chaadaev, liberal Westerners, counting among others the academics Kavelin, Granovsky, and Chicherin, and the radical Westerners, represented during the 1840s by Belinsky and Herzen.[1] In Herzen's whimsical but telling generalization the Russian Westerners had one thing in common, they were "foreigners at home, [and] foreigners abroad."[2]

No less striking than the differences between the three major orientations were the personal differences within each ideological current. It is worth recalling that in the middle of the nineteenth century there were no political parties in Russia. The ideological divisions that existed involved small numbers of individuals, mostly of the gentry. The several currents knew no organization, no rosters, no dues, no official programs, and party discipline. Temperament, education, social position, and changes in one's convictions and beliefs determined one's relationship with those of similar convictions. In addition, youthful instability is often noticeable, as in the altered convictions of young Samarin, Konstantin Aksakov, Belinsky, and others.

The examples that illustrate the principal nongovernment ideological currents have been chosen on the basis of the quality and contribution of the individual representatives, and on availability of source materials. The ideological orientations that evolved in Russia from the 1830s through the 1850s were, as mentioned earlier in these studies, a result of oral and written polemics that were often personal and sometimes bitter.

In the formative and early Slavophil period of Samarin's career no encounter was more thought-provoking for him than those with the radical Westerner Belinsky and the liberals Kavelin and Granovsky. Samarin's ideological skirmishes continued for the rest of his life. Thus in the 1850s he encountered such major challenges as that from the liberal Westernism of Chicherin (1828–1904), and the 1860s from Herzen's changing Westernism. In the 1870s, shortly before his death, Samarin responded to an old adversary, Kavelin, and to a new, and perhaps a friendlier one, General R. A. Fadeev (1824–1883).

The Samarin-Chicherin encounter, although of brief duration, is significant in Samarin's career and in the evolution of Moscow Slavophilism, as it sheds light on both. In the announcement of the program of *Russkaia beseda* in 1856 the Slavophils stated that their journal would strive to develop a "Russian view of science [nauka] and art." The controversy with the liberal Westerners, publicized first in *Moskovskiia vedomosti,* which criticized the Slavophil "Russian view" of science and art, soon shifted to *Russkii vestnik* for the Westerners. Young Chicherin used its columns in his polemic with Samarin.[3]

Chicherin is generally considered a "liberal" Westerner. But the problem of defining "liberal" and "liberalism" was unresolved then and remains such to the present. When viewing Moscow Slavophilism in the middle decades of the nineteenth century one has to keep in mind that this was also the period of the triumph of British liberalism. Whiggery had gradually given way to Liberalism, and the landmark repeal of the corn laws in 1846 was also the beginning of free trade. The period of Lord Melbourne, Russell, and Lord Palmerston was followed by the Gladstonian era (1865–1895) when "Liberalism almost became Gladstonianism." English liberalism, perhaps the most characteristic and fully developed form in the West, was in the days of Moscow Slavophilism a secular, middle class, capitalistic, individualistic, laissez-faire, parliamentary and constitutional force, which showed little if any concern for the underprivileged or for the abject state of the rapidly growing class of English mine and factory workers. Therefore to characterize Moscow Slavophilism, which was gentry-led, Orthodox, oriented toward the Russian peasant commune, and protectionist, although in the 1850s moving in the direction of entrepreneurship, as a liberal movement, as is often done, is more confusing than helpful.

The difficulty here lies in the fact that neither in English nor in Russian is there a single, strict, precise, usage of "liberalism" and "liberal." Since this semantic problem seems no nearer solution today than it was in the middle of the last century, we are left with the alternative of deducing the meaning of, liberalism, and liberal, from the context in which the terms are used, and this often leads to imprecise guesswork. The controversy that has been narrowed down here to the views of Samarin and Chicherin on the subject of *narodnost'* in science and historical scholarship was in fact broader and engaged the attention of the Slavophils Khomiakov and Konstantin Aksakov in addition to Samarin's, and also that of I. D. Beliaev (1810–1873), a Slavophil-oriented historian, and a specialist in early Russian history. In the second half of the 1850s Beliaev was particularly concerned with the centuries-old existence of the Russian peasant commune and peasant order. His well-known *Krest'iane na Rusi* (The Peasants in Russia) was serialized in *Russkaia beseda,* in six installments, in 1859 before it appeared in book form.[4] The importance of this "classic" work, is that it contributed to the problem of "nationality in science," and to another cardinal Slavophil conviction which concerned the historical origin, nature and fate of the Russian peasant commune. This in turn was one of the major components of the deliberations and debates leading to the Emancipation reform of 1861.

At the time of the Samarin-Chicherin written encounter historians in general focused their researches on relations between states, governments, and dynasties; on diplomacy, wars and the upper classes, and not on the vast majority of common people, such as the *narod* in Russia. The Slavophils and Beliaev made a noteworthy departure from this practice. Beliaev was the author of more than one hundred works, but it is not necessary for us to do more than single out his *The Peasants in Russia.* In this study concentrating on Russia's early peasant order he considered both the communal and the clan (*rodovoi*) form of social organization—a problem which, as we have seen, concerned Samarin and Kavelin a decade earlier—and threw the weight of his discussion on the side of the commune. From the point of view of Slavophil ideology and reformism, Beliaev's *Krest'iane na Rusi* came at a crucial time, that is, when the Slavophils, Samarin in particular, were deeply involved in the emancipation reform, and one of the basic issues was the question whether the peasant commune should be preserved after emancipation.

The early Slavophils, of course, regarded the Russian peasant commune as the ultimate achievement in social organization and the cornerstone of Russia's future economic, social, and Orthodox-ethical public order. Chicherin in the late 1850s perceived matters quite differently. He had a long and noteworthy career as academic historian and expert on Russian legal history (Moscow University, 1861–1867), and as a versatile author of more than a dozen and a half works, some of them of multivolume scope, but he is perhaps best known as a leading figure in the state or juridical school of Russian historiography.[5] The difference between his ideological orientation and that of the Slavophils is as simple as it is striking and fundamental. For him at the heart of the historical process in Russia were the law (the word of the autocrat) and the state. In contrast to this formal, legalistic concept of the spirit and form of Russian society was the Slavophil view of an informal, intimate, Christian-inspired communal peasant order. The fact that the Slavophils idealized the historical Russian commune, and some of them, notably Khomiakov and Konstantin Aksakov, had reservations about the value and function of the state, did not narrow the gap between them and Chicherin, and the other liberal Westerners.

In his four-volume memoirs, *Vospominaniia Borisa Nikolaevicha Chicherina,* (parts of which seem to have been written in the 1890s) Chicherin has a good deal to say about Iurii Samarin, the gist of which is negative and critical. Chicherin came from the same gentry background as Samarin and was, indeed, a friend of Iurii's brother Vladimir from the mid-1840s on. He and Iurii very likely met on some occasion when Iurii, with the government in Riga, returned on one of his short visits to Moscow. In the mid-1850s he considered himself a friend of the Samarins (*priiatel' doma*). He tells us that the eldest of the Samarin sons was endowed with "brilliant gifts," and that his father saw him as destined to be a "future minister" in the tsar's administration. In Chicherin's words, Iurii possessed "uncommon strength of mind, iron will, indefatigable ability for work combined with a gift for the word and the writer's talent, and finally the purest and loftiest character. All this was combined in him to render him one of the outstanding workers in literature as also in the public arena." Samarin's conversation was "lively and brilliant, always in refined worldly form, not infrequently spiced with cold and biting irony or with a cutting joke." He had an amazing talent for imitation," but above all he was devoted to a "false orientation." But to Chicherin, possibly because of Iurii's "burning patriotism" and his siding with Khomiakov, his "point of departure was radically false" and so was his "mind."[6]

Chicherin also says that after the death of the elder Samarin in 1853 Iurii "proved incapable of managing the family estates because his mind was of an "abstract-logical" cast. He accepted on faith certain basic postulates and was content "to repeat Khomiakov's sophistry." He lacked the "basic scientific training," which would not have allowed "that profound hatred toward the West which was nursed by the Slavophil school." It would also have saved him from "soaring in the clouds on the wings of the Slavophil idea, from there hurling thunder upon Western enlightenment and its worshippers." Chicherin found it "difficult to believe what level this contemptuous attitude toward everything European had reached."[7] It is not certain whether these sentiments, which seem to have been recorded in the 1890s, truly reflected his views in the 1850s or were the result of reflections and ideological accretions between the 1850s and the 1890s; nor is it quite certain on what evidence he based his conclusions about the complete and absolute negation by the Slavophils of everything Western, for their writings do not support such an extreme and uncompromising verdict on the West.[8]

We are on more solid ground with respect to the Samarin-Chicherin controversy of the mid-1850s in which Samarin defended not only a personal conviction but also a general and basic Slavophil proposition. The semantic difficulties that existed then have not been removed to the present. The ambiguity of the subject arises from its wording, *"narodnost' v 'nauke."* The usual English equivalents for *narodnost'*-(nationality), (nationalness), are at best unsatisfactory approximations. *Nauka,* science, is hardly less ambiguous.[9] The Russian *nauka,* in some ways like the English science, is a disconcertingly elastic term which can be stretched to encompass the so-called "social sciences" and "human sciences." Yet none of these yields, as does for instance physics, to the method that is a combination of mathematics and controlled experiment.

The Slavophils did not claim that there were two mathematics or two physics, one Russian and the other for the rest of the world. When they defended a special Russian point of view and interpretation they had in mind history and the area of human relations with its religious, philosophical, and ethical implications.[10] It is worth recalling that Samarin no less than other outstanding minds in Russia and the West was in a sense victim of the term *nauka, Wissenschaft*. Thus at one time, as mentioned earlier, *nauka* meant to him philosophy, and more specifically Hegelianism. Dealing with Slavophilism and Westernism in the middle of the nineteenth century, one has to be careful in reading the term *"nauka"* as "science"; often the only approximation to its meaning comes from the context in which it is used.

When *Russkaia beseda* announced that it would promulgate a Russian point of view, Samarin was ready. The first issue (1856) contained his "Two Words about Nationality in Science" (*Dva slova o narodnosti v nauke*), which begins with the statement that he too wished to contribute to the "development of the Russian view in science and art." The theme of the liberal Westerners had already been announced in *Moskovskie vedomosti,* its editor, V. F. Korsh, having declared that science and art admit of only one view, the *enlightened,* consequently the *universally human view* [*obshchecheloveches-koe*].[11] The arguments advanced by Samarin and the Slavophils on the one hand, and by Chicherin and the liberal Westerners on the other revolved around this basic formulation of the issue.

Accepting certain historical principles primarily from Hegel, current in the West in the early nineteenth century, Samarin referred to the "law of historical succession" according to which a certain nation is "called forth to stand at the head of humanity." Thus a part of the past achievements and heritage of all nations becomes its possession. This was so in the "realm of mechanics, the natural sciences," and in general in the "material" sphere of life. All this is "taken over simply and incontestably." But the matter is not so simple when reference is made to the "better part of the intellectual heritage." In the field of literature and art, Samarin said, nationality counts. Dante would not have created the same *Divine Comedy* if he had not been Italian and Roman Catholic. Similarly, Goethe's work embodies one of the "most complete manifestations of the German spirit," and Gogol' would not be recognizable without the wealth "drawn from our nationality." Samarin hastened to add that "speaking of Russian *narodnost'* we understand it as having an inseparable bond with the Orthodox faith, from which derives the whole system of moral convictions that govern the family life and the public life of the Russian.[12]

History was perhaps the most obvious discipline in which different interpretations were a commonplace, as for instance those between Catholic and
Protestant historians of the Reformation, and between Whigs and Tories.
But Samarin went a step further, and again making a distinction between the
realm of "nature" and that of "man," asserted that in "law, in philosophy, in
political economy such sharp contrasts are encountered at every step, that
different points of view and different conclusions are normal and inevitable.
With respect to history these differences are of the very essence of the discipline, for a "mere writing down of what has taken place would be like a
series of meteorological observations of the weather." Samarin found "so-
called impartiality" in the realm of human relations to be often mere "un-
consciousness." For him, "every opinion presupposes a point of view, [and]
every act of thought – a point of departure."

These basic conclusions were also applicable to political economy, which
counted among its proponents physiocrats, mercantilists, and free traders.
And the field of philosophy was not different. There, too, various
nationalities had made their distinctive contributions, and perhaps stretching the point, Samarin concluded that Hegel "derived all his philosophy from
the German language." Returning to an idea he had cherished in his student days, he expressed the hope that Catholic and Protestant differences
could be resolved in the "fullness of the spiritual life of the Orthodox
Church."[13] He saw *narodnost'* not as an end in itself but as serving the cause
of the "gradually broadening boundaries of common human knowledge."
He also took pains to state what he did not advocate, that is "Unreasonable,
unaccountable, and deliberate negation of what is foreign only because it is
foreign." He ended his remarks with the declaration that "in history, universally human principles are not manifested except in a national [*narodnaia*]
milieu."[14]

Chicherin in his answer to Samarin, the two-installment "On Nationality
in Science" (*O narodnosti v nauke*), makes it clear in the opening pages that
he was concerned not only with Samarin's views about nationality in science
but also with Beliaev's views on the peasant commune and with Slavophilism
in general.[15] Samarin and the Slavophils, he said, did not deal objectively
with Russia's past: "They transfer into the past their personal wishes,
demands, and passions, and attribute to their forefathers actions and views
about which the latter never even thought." Small wonder then that "From
this derive that endless number of fantastic notions introduced among us in
Russian history, as for instance the notion of the present form of the peasant
communes." Touching a sensitive nerve for both Samarin and the other
Slavophils, Chicherin flatly stated that "Samarin confuses the religious view
with the view of the people [*narodny*]," and furthermore, "nationality in
science is to us a synonym for exclusiveness, one-sidedness, and therefore
also falsity.

For a person who seems to have had considerable knowledge and understanding of physics and mathematics, Chicherin is curiously naive in saying, "Fact and law—that is all of science, that is its whole assignment," as if physics and human relations were governed by the same strict laws.[16] Admitting that there was much to be learned and much work to be done in "science" in general, he conceded to Samarin that a point of view was essential to "science" but that it should be "worked out from science itself and should not be prepared beforehand." Science, he says, answered to *"umozrenie i opyt."* *Umozrenie* means "speculation"; *opyt* means either "experience" or "experiment." Chicherin, like Samarin at an earlier time, thought of philosophy as *nauka,* or science in the sense of systematic knowledge. He argued that *umozrenie* had "its own logical facts, its own logical laws." These, he held, should not be borrowed but should be "worked out form the science itself." The efforts of German philosophy to achieve this, he admitted, "proved not quite successful," but this did not diminish his esteem of German philosophers, who "have not national but universal significance."[17]

Given the passion of the polemic, distortions were bound to appear. Whereas Samarin and the Slavophils might have been too sanguine about Russia's impending great cultural age (although they perceived it more clearly than Chicherin) Chicherin saw an all too dismal picture. He was disheartened because "Up to now great scientists or scholars have not appeared among us. His conclusion, however, was quite clear: since Russia's "scientific literature was so insignificant" the Russian people needed to "learn, learn, learn!" In order for this to be done, Russia had to "make Western science its own."[18] If by *nauka* Chicherin meant the physical sciences, Samarin would probably have agreed with him, although he would have claimed that science is universal rather than specifically Western; but if Chicherin included in *nauka* the social studies, the humanities, literary studies and ethics, Samarin, as we have seen might not have conceded primacy to the West.

As is customary in polemics, there were usual disclaimers when one side attributed to the other thoughts and views that it claimed not to hold. Chicherin began the second installment of his reply to Samarin with a denial of certain views attributed to him by *Russkaia beseda.* The details are not particularly pertinent, but he rejected any implication that he would ever condemn the Russian people "to eternal, senseless, and submissive imitation of Western models." And whether aware or not, he came close to the Slavophil position when he asserted that "nationality [*narodnost'*] must serve as an expression of universal principles." The question he raised was: "Does the universally human have to descend to the national or does the national have to adjust to the universal?"[19] The Slavophils did not see these two in any sort of inevitable opposition or contest. They admitted the legitimacy of both, and although Russia had lagged for centuries behind the West in cultural achievements they were hopeful about the future. Actually their optimism and hopes were being justified at the very time of the controversy in the emergence of the great Russian literature if nowhere else.

One of Chicherin's main points of disagreement with the Slavophils was the subject of education, conceived in Russian in the twin principles of *obrazovanie* (formal education) and *vospitanie* (informal upbringing). Chicherin was convinced that Samarin claimed undue importance for the organic principle. From grade school through the gymnasium and the university the education of the student was highly structured, and this was as it should be, for "a man begins with studying and ends with independence."[20] Was it so extraordinary to expect as much of Russia? Looking at man's long history from a secularist point of view, he said: "In the primitive youthful state of the spirit all its powers flow into one. Science as such does not exist. Everything unites into one, the religious point of view.[21] But as science develops it becomes "independent."

At the end of the second installment of his reply to Samarin and the Slavophils the twenty-eight-year-old Chicherin attacked the theoretical core of Slavophilism, including its doctrine of the wholeness of the spirit, denying its feasibility. He objected to Samarin's metaphor of the "box" or "trunk" in characterizing the fragmentation and compartmentalization of modern Western life and thought, and opposed his attempt to "sacrifice all the variety of life to the abstract notion of the wholeness of the spirit." He concluded his remarks with the rhetorical question, "Is it possible to unite at present in one great synthesis all the separate spheres of the human spirit, is it possible to order human life as one harmonious whole?" His answer was simply, "We are still far from achieving this."[22]

On two of the principal points of the argument between Samarin and Chicherin, that is, the Russian peasant commune and "nationality in science," the outcome was rather blurred. Chicherin was not on solid historical and factual ground when he claimed that the Russian peasant commune was of recent origin and that its presumed creation was to be found in a legislative act of Russian autocracy. The Slavophils, on the other hand, attributed to the commune qualities and characteristics that no human society is ever likely to have possessed. Both sides, of course, were fully aware of the nature and the course of development of mathematics and the physical sciences, and neither side questioned their universality; in the area of human relations, values, and ethics, however, Samarin and the Slavophils denied the existence and prevalence of absolute, objective standards, presumed to be characteristic of the West, and the evidence was not against them. The historical disciplines as they existed in the West were noteworthy for their frequently questionable objectivity.

Oddly enough, the Slavophils did not seem to realize that in the area of literature, music, and art, where they strongly adhered to the notion of attaining the universal through the national or native, their ideas were actually being borne out. Hindsight and perspective make it possible for us to see the substance and form of the controversies of the 1840s and 1850s in a way that remained partly obscured to the participants in the drama. By 1856 there were already perceptible signs that Russia was on the move culturally. As had been the case earlier with the Italian, Spanish, French, English, and German cultural contributions to the general European, and to the universal cultural heritage, the Russians were doing their part, stamping it in the normal course of events with their characteristic native genius. Reference here is made not to "nationality in science" but to nationality in literature, music and art, and this point could be illustrated without an exhaustive catalogue of names and works.

In literature the age of Pushkin came to an end at the time of his death in 1837, that of Gogol', in 1852. In the late 1840s Turgenev and Dostoevsky had appeared on the scene although most of their best work was ahead, for Dostoevsky particularly in the 1860s and 1870s. In the year before the Samarin-Chicherin controversy Tolstoy made his appearance in print to strike more than one of his compatriots as a young writer of extraordinary promise. Russian music having made its entry on the scene through Glinka's compositions in the 1830s, was on the threshold, in 1856, of a brilliant outburst. The "Mighty Five who came together in 1859 gave to Russian music a distinction that would soon win for Russia a place among the leading musical nations of the world, and the Russian ballet and theater were not far behind. Samarin and Chicherin could not see all this as clearly as we can now. But to the present observer of Russian cultural scene in the middle decades of the nineteenth century their controversy, Chicherin's side in particular, has a certain hollow ring.

During the many centuries when no universal, meaning non-national, world existed, how else could Dante create except as an Italian, or Shakespeare except as an Englishman, or Moliere except as a Frenchman, or Beethoven except as a German? And how else could Pushkin, Gogol', Dostoevsky, Tolstoy, and Borodin create except as Russians?[23] Yet all these and many other outstanding authors, composers, and artists were able to transcend national bounds because they were also profoundly human and therefore universally human. Chicherin and other Westerners leave the impression that somehow the Russian of the middle of the nineteenth century was expected miraculously to shake off all traces of national origin and belonging, abandon his native birth and environment, and create only as some sort of new universal person. On this seminal issue, obviously Samarin and the Slavophils were closer to reality than Chicherin and some of the Russian Westerners were.

In the Slavophil scheme of things, particularly clear in Samarin's case, the three fundamental spheres of human thought and activity were indisputable. Religion and/or philosophy inspires and guides ideology on the middle level of civilized man's existence; ideology in turn points the way to the third level in the descent of an idea, that of social organization, program, action, tactics, and the solution of daily problems and concerns. The Slavophils were very explicit in claiming Orthodox Christianity (not philosophy) as the ultimate source of their convictions and ideology. This Orthodox-inspired ideology, they assumed, motivated and determined their thoughts and practical daily activities. Thus the descent of Slavophil ideas from Orthodoxy through ideology to action seems quite clear. Such passage or progression of ideas is not so obvious in the case of Chicherin, except for his choice of philosophy (not religion or Orthodoxy) as the ultimate source of his convictions. But since he also seems to have considered at one time or another positivism, Hegelianism, and Kantianism, one is not certain what his preference was although he is most often seen as a Hegelian.

The case of Samarin's second ideological opponent considered in these pages, that of Alexander Herzen, is not much clearer. He is variously said to have become a materialist, an atheist, a skeptic, and most recently he has been characterized as a "precursor of atheistic existentialism."[24] The difficulty here is the same one we encounter in other cases of conversion from one fundamental conviction to another, and what, if any residues might be left. To this must be added ambiguities of definition, and the complexities of personal credos: how thorough, how pure, and how unalterable is a change? In the Herzen-Samarin confrontation, what is reasonably clear and certain is Herzen's staunch opposition to Samarin's Christian, Orthodox stand, and Samarin's condemnation of Herzen's incitements to revolution in Russia in the pages of *Kolokol*.[25] But by 1864, the year of our concern here, there was no doubt as to the irreconcilable fundamental convictions of the two protagonists, the Orthodox Samarin and the radical anti-Orthodox empiricist Herzen.

The personal encounter between them that took place in London on July 21, 22, and 23, 1864, was their first meeting in twenty years. These had been two eventful decades not only in the history of Europe but also in the evolution of Moscow Slavophilism, and in the lives of Herzen and Samarin. Herzen had already spent seventeen years in what began as a self-imposed exile in Western Europe. After the revolutions of 1848–1849 he became disillusioned about "old" Europe as incapable of a radical socialist transformation, and turned his eyes upon peasant communal Russia for both the inspiration and the foundation of his "Russian socialism." From 1855–1867 he published in London, and toward the end of its life in Geneva, his famous *Kolokol* (The Bell), copies of which were smuggled into Russia and read or heard about from the tsar's palace to the provincial towns of the empire.

The prestige and influence of *Kolokol* reached a high point in the period of the emancipation of the serfs and the Polish rebellion of 1863, when its radical revolutionary content and tone made their most telling inroads in Russia.

During the same two decades Samarin, as already pointed out, had abandoned Hegelianism for Orthodoxy, served in the tsarist administration in the Baltic provinces, and produced his *Riga Letters* which caused his brief incarceration in the Peter and Paul fortress in 1849. After a brief period of government service in Kiev, he devoted himself to the Slavophil cause and to the issue of emancipation.

When Samarin and Herzen met in London in the summer of 1864, neither of them had any doubts or illusions about the foundation of the other's ideological position; indeed, in view of the circumstances, it is somewhat surprising that the meeting took place at all. What probably made it possible was a certain sense of nostalgia for their youthful years in Moscow of the mid-1840s, and their respect for each other's integrity, character, and ability. Also, there were points of contact between Herzen and the Slavophils on the ideological and programmatic levels. Herzen was no more an admirer of the Western liberal bourgeois order than the Slavophils were – they both criticized its individualism and laissez-faire economics, and its unconcern for the miserable condition of the growing ranks of factory and mine workers, although fear of the rising proletariat was the Slavophils' primary reaction.[26] Like the Slavophils, and perhaps even with some help from them, Herzen had seen, particularly after 1848–1849, the possible value of the existing Russian peasant commune as the foundation for a future socialist communal order. Moreover, in 1859 Ivan Aksakov and Samarin were "active informants and collaborators" on Herzen's *Kolokol*.[27]

Five years later conditions had changed. Herzen had supported the Polish rebellion against Russian tsarist authority and he was in sympathy with antigovernment demonstrations and actions in Russia in 1862–1863. Samarin opposed Herzen's position. In spite of this Herzen was willing to meet with Samarin when he, in El'sberg's words, "broke off (each and every) personal relation with Kavelin, Chicherin and others."[28] Samarin in turn did not avoid Herzen as did such liberal Westerners as Kavelin and Botkin.

No stenographic record was kept of the three days of encounters between Herzen and Samarin. But we are not without some firsthand remarks about them coming from the host. After the seven-hour first-day session Herzen wrote to his friend Ogarev, "A dozen times it acquired that form after which it would have been right to break off both it and the acquaintance." The atmosphere that pervaded the second and third days was not friendlier.[29] The air of intransigence that characterized the talks between forty-five-year-old Samarin and fifty-two-year-old Herzen is strikingly revealed in their correspondence. The letters they exchanged before and after their three days of talks in London are our principal source concerning the content and spirit of the conversations. These letters entitled by Herzen "Letters to My Adversary," were first published by Ivan Aksakov nearly two decades later.[30] The letters are of uneven length, content, and importance. But when they are read as a whole, as a continuation of the verbal polemic in the Royal Hotel, on New Bridge Street, Blackfriars, London, the unbridgeable gulf between them is clear.

Within less than two weeks of his encounter with Herzen in London Samarin was in Switzerland. In a letter from Ragaz of August 3, 1864, he went on the offensive. In the opening paragraph he says, "I spoke to you about the moral contagion that you let loose in the Russian land, and grafted onto hundreds and thousands of young people," and the root cause of it was Herzen's philosophical orientation. Addressing Herzen with the formal *vy,* he said, "You were among the first among us to preach materialism, and you adhere to it even now. It became handy to you as a battering-ram with which you shattered family, church, and state."[31] The materialism that Samarin attributed to Herzen was the "vulgar," "medical" variety, that of Vogt, Buchner, Moleschott, then enjoying a vogue in the West. Herzen's stand seems to have been that of an empiricist. With characteristic clarity and explicitness in another letter from Ragaz, written five days later (August 8), Samarin went to the heart of the matter. "Our dispute, the dispute between Russia and the West, is a continuation of the old dispute between the doctrine of freedom (Christianity), and the doctrine of logical necessity (idealism) or material [necessity] (materialism)." Samarin's conclusion was that "all social and political convictions ultimately come down to these two centers and from them receive meaning, life, and coloring."[32]

In accusing Herzen of "vulgar" materialism, Samarin specifically attributed certain convictions to him: "Besides matter there is nothing and everything that exists is substance or body. That which we call force, spirit, psychological principle is nothing more than an attribute of matter and a manifestation of its purely material changes."[33] Herzen, who was of course thoroughly aware of the Orthodox foundation of Moscow Slavophilism and of Samarin's convictions, had tried to remove this subject from the agenda for their conversations. Nine days before they met he had written to Samarin about their common ground — concern for the Russian people, the *narod* — and wrote to him, "In my sincere, sacred love for the Russian people, for the Russian cause, I do not concede [anything] either to you or to all the Aksakovs."[34] But after receiving Samarin's first "too choleric" letters from Ragaz, following the London meetings, "It would be difficult to imagine two persons in whom the whole moral existence and makeup, the complete holy of holies, all ideals and endeavors, all hopes and convictions are to such a degree different as yours and mine." Although in Herzen's words they were men of "different worlds and different epochs," they still shared the same *"one concern"* — for the Russian people, the *narod*.[35] This was quite a concession on Herzen's part, since a couple of paragraphs farther on he wrote: "I know that you, like all religious people, refuse to admit the possibility of arriving at truth by different routes. But history and science [*nauka*] are against you..." The great advances in Western science and technology, and historical research and scholarship characteristic of the nineteenth century, together with the no less noteworthy achievements in literature, music, the theater, and art, which Herzen does not mention, created the secular euphoria in the West. This tended to obscure the limitations and weaknesses of the human being, giving birth, among other things, to an ever more destructive science and technology, culminating in the twentieth century wars.

Referring to the Polish rebellion without naming it, Herzen abandoned the realm of religion and philosophy for that of ideology. He reminded Samarin of their Moscow days, twenty years earlier: "Like two fighters, we have not only changed places in the course of the long battle but have also switched our weapons." He accused Samarin and the Slavophils (three of whom were no longer living) of "having become Western terrorists, defenders of the Petrine empire, even of gentry civilization, whereas we, renouncing bloody progress [and] the all-absorbing state, stand for *narod,* for commune, for the right to land. Your friends are for Petersburg; we are for — no, we are not for Moscow, we are for the village."[36] Behind this alleged complete reversal of the Slavophil position was the disagreement between Herzen and Samarin about the Polish rebellion. Herzen supported it, Samarin opposed it. Also in the background was the revolutionary unrest expressed, among other things, in widespread fires in Russia. Samarin then, as before and after, was adamantly opposed to revolution as a means of social, political or economic change.

When Herzen stated in the first letter to his "adversary" that presumably his role and that of the Slavophils had become reversed in the early 1860s, he touched on a basic and substantial issues. In saying "We stand for *narod,* for commune, and the right to land," he, in effect, went back to the 1840s, to the period when the Slavophils presumably "discovered" the commune (*mir, obshchina*). But the commune had existed in Russian society, particularly in Great Russian, society for centuries and was still, in the middle of the nineteenth century, a vital peasant institution; so there could be no "discovery" of something that was present in the daily lives of millions of peasants. What the Slavophils did was to help bring the commune and the *narod,* among which it functioned, into the stream of Russian consciousness and discussion, and this they did for their own and later generations.

In the late eighteen forties Herzen, while in exile in the West, turned his attention to the Russian village commune just as in the fifties the younger Chernyshevsky would do the same, but in their case from a philosophical point of view diametrically opposite that of the Slavophils. Herzen was correct when he wrote to Samarin, "For you the Russian people is by preference an *Orthodox* people."[37] There is no doubt that the early Slavophils, and Samarin specifically, saw providential significance in the kinship of the principles of *sobornost'* and *obshchinnost'* (communality). Herzen, looking at the peasant commune from the opposite point of view after his disappointment in the revolutions of 1848–1849, saw it as a purely secular institution and a harbinger of the coming socialist wave in Russia. Samarin and Herzen viewed the Russian peasant commune from quite different basic orientations, and endowed it with correspondingly different meaning and significance. Samarin placed his faith and reliance in revealed Christianity, Herzen placed his faith and reliance in "history and science," or in the products of human intelligence; but neither was short on faith. Herzen's anthropocentrism was both very new and very old.

When in the summer of 1857 Chernyshevsky (1821–1889) entrusted his youthful friend and collaborator Dobroliubov (1836–1861), with the "critical-bibliographical" section of *Sovremennik* two kindred spirits began a short-lived but close collaboration. Both were sons of Orthodox priests, both were uncommonly gifted, and both abandoned the Orthodox hearths in which they had been born. Although much more needs to be said than can be included in these pages, a brief treatment of the Samarin-Chernyshevsky relationship during 1857 will help reveal how two antagonists, one pro-Orthodox, the other pro-materialist, as in the case of Herzen, could find much common ground on the question of the Russian village commune, and on other basic Russian problems. What the Samarin-Chernyshevsky relationship illustrates is the possibility that two advocates, one starting from Orthodoxy the other from materialism and finding considerable common ground on the ideological level, could again part ways on the level of tactics and action.

The many and varied interests and achievements of Chernyshevsky have been recorded by his biographers, and in his works on philosophy, history, literature, literary criticism, aesthetics, political science, economics, publicistic work, and journalism. In 1857, when Chernyshevsky reacted in writing to the views of the Slavophils, specifically to Samarin's, he was not yet thirty, but he had already published such influential works as his master's thesis on *The Aesthetic Relation of Art to Reality* (1854–1856), *Essays on the Gogol' Period of Russian Literature* (1856), *A. S. Pushkin: His Life and Works* (1856), and *Lessing: His Time, Life, and Activity* (1856–1857). He had established contact with Nekrasov's *Contemporary* and was soon to become its dominant spirit, who would elevate it to the foremost journal in Russia. It has been said that while in his teens he studied Latin, Greek, Persian, Arabic, Tatar, Hebrew, French, German, and English, in addition to his native Russian language. Chernyshevsky, though he could not go along with the basic

Slavophil religious Orthodox point of view, took a surprisingly tolerant stand
on Moscow Slavophilism, and specifically on Samarin's ideological position.
He made his views clear in the two reviews he wrote for *Sovremennik* in
March and April 1857, both dealing with the Slavophil journal *Russkaia beseda.*[38]

According to Chernyshevsky in the first of the two reviews, the attitude of
the Russian public toward *Russkaia beseda* was "cool, in part mocking" and
even "hostile." Almost all Russian journals, he noted, looked upon it with
"irony or with reproach." This was in contrast to *Sovremennik,* which "almost alone demonstrated that between the Slavophils and the vast majority
of educated people, rejecting Slavophil ideas about a Russian point of view,
exist above this discordant point, also points of similarity in opinions, consent, and wishes."[39] Although Chernyshevsky did not specifically denounce
the Orthodox convictions of the Slavophils, and the rather explicit bond that
Samarin saw between the principles of *sobornost'* and *obshchinnost',* he did
not spare them from criticism. Defending the Slavophils and *Russkaia beseda* from hostile views, he at the same time censured them when he said that
they were "people who are wrong about much, and about what is important."
The Slavophil journal contained many things which demonstrated that the
Slavophils had "interests dearer and more vital than dreams which can find
in the majority neither sympathy, because they are abstract and inapplicable
. . . nor approval, because they would lead to nothing good if they were
realizable."

What struck Chernyshevsky most about Moscow Slavophilism and
Russkaia beseda at the time were Samarin's contributions to the journal. He
attributed his favorable impression "preeminently to the two superb articles
by Mr. Samarin," published in the first issue of *Russkaia beseda* for 1857.[40]
Chernyshevsky was so impressed by these articles that he pronounced
Slavophilism, if not worthy of "complete approval, then of exculpation and
even sympathy." Furthermore, he stated, there are individual questions
"about which the Slavophils think . . . more justly than many of the so-called
Westerners." Dismissing the question of the controversy between Samarin
and Chicherin about the Russian view of "science" and the relationship of
the national to the universal, which as we have seen, attracted much attention at the time, he found in Slavophilism and in Samarin's views "something
more important and better."[41]

Disregarding the well-established fiction at the time (persisting to the
present in certain circles) that the Slavophils had nothing but hostility for
the West, Chernyshevsky countered that such a "crudely understood accusation becomes a complete slander of them." Furthermore, "They are no less
in sympathy with everything that is actually great and good in Western
Europe than the most implacable [*samye zakliatye*] Westerners." He felt it
necessary to go on record that he was not confusing the "best representatives

of the Slavophils," those primarily behind *Russkaia beseda,* or the "early Slavophils," with those who suffered from the "sins of ignorance." He frankly stated that he could find no fault with the Slavophils because "they do not regard as very enviable the present condition of the life of the people in Western Europe," which in spite of certain expectations is not an "earthly paradise." On the contrary, he asserted, "The mass of people in Western Europe too are still stuck in the mire of ignorance and poverty," and the "pleasures of the Palais Royal" and Parisian fashions cannot make up for this.[42]

The sympathy that the lot of the growing industrial proletariat in the West evoked in Chernyshevsky was matched by that for the impoverished peasantry in France. Her, too, the villains were the exploiters: if the fields were given to "communal cultivation with the aid of improved machinery, the harvest would more than double," and France would not be short of grain; instead, France was in the grip of "selfish exploiters," under a "system branded *l'exploitation de l'homme par l'homme.*"[43] (Abuse, defects, and misery in the material and intellectual life of Western Europe — this is an inexhaustible subject." And he asked, "What is so astonishing, and what is so criminal, if this self-indictment of Europe by its best sons finds an echo among us as well?" While concluding that "Western Europe is not a all a paradise," therefore agreeing by implication with the Slavophils, he hastened to add that the Slavophils were also "in error about many things."[44]

Toward the end of this first review, Chernyshevsky touched on two issues that shed further light on his views of Samarin and the Moscow Slavophils. One is the source and nature of the Slavophil critique of the West, the other is a more difficult and uncertain proposition, the basic convictions, beliefs, and character of the Russian people (the *narod*). A year earlier, Chernyshevsky in *Essays on the Gogol' Period of Russian Literature* had said, "There is not a single essential thought in it [Slavophilism] (absolutely *not a single one*) that was not borrowed from some second-rate French or German writers." This disparaging judgment, often quoted in the literature, was soon altered and softened, doubtless as a result of Samarin's two review articles. The softened judgment is found in Chernyshevsky's remarks of 1857 in the following form: "We must acknowledge that the criticism of the European order, which the Slavophils borrowed directly or at second hand from the best contemporary thinkers, is far from being useless for the clarification of our notions about Europe."[45] It is difficult to see how in the 1856 statement the young Chernyshevsky could attribute by implication Slavophil Orthodoxy, and the inspiration of the Orthodox Church Fathers, Khomiakov's notion of *sobornost',* Kireevsky's doctrine of the wholeness of the spirit, and Aksakov's choric principle among others, to "second rate" Western European thinkers or to any Western thinkers. Nor is the implication justified that the Slavophils had to learn from the West what is right and what is wrong.

The problem of the Russian people, the *narod,* by its very nature, has aroused endless controversy, generated much passion, and settled little. Herzen understood correctly that to the Slavophils the *narod* was profoundly Orthodox while for Dostoevsky the Russians were the "only God-fearing people on earth," destined to save the world in the name of God, Chernyshevsky disagreed with both the Slavophils and with Dostoevsky on this matter. He saw nothing in the *narod* resembling the "abstract fantasies" of the Slavophils. "The common sense" of the *narod* "easily distinguishes the fantastic admixture from the facts." Much of this "admixture" is "selected from the realm of feelings, which are very antipathetic to the Russian character. Neither daydreams of things beyond the clouds nor boasting is in the character of the Russian."[46] When the contrasting views on the *narod* of Belinsky, Herzen, and Chernyshevsky on the one hand, and of the Slavophils on the other, are presented, the heavily subjective nature of the argument strikes one at once. For what science, what technique, has ever penetrated and unerringly ascertained what is in the mind, in the irrational, unconscious, and subconscious mind of a single human being, much less of a large and complex nation? One guess and one conviction as a counter to another guess and another conviction does not establish a scientific fact or scientific truth.[47]

Chernyshevsky summed up his opinion of Samarin's article with these words: "It should be read by every living person and there is nothing to say about it except to praise it, which we have already done."[48] He gave short shrift to the second of Samarin's essays, the one that appeared in the first issue of *Russkaia beseda* for 1857. Of this review devoted to Chicherin's historical works, Chernyshevsky commented that he could have raised "some very serious objections" but had left those to Chicherin, who was capable of taking care of himself. He added that he found "Mr. Samarin's remarks such that each one deserves serious consideration and some must be recognized as just."[49]

Despite the fundamental differences between Chernyshevsky and the Slavophils, including of course Samarin, the April 1857 issue of *Sovremennik* contained more of Chernyshevsky's approval and even praise of certain Slavophil views and positions, specifically in reference to their criticism of the political, social, and economic order of Western Europe. But the real question that the Slavophils had formulated and for which Chernyshevsky had much sympathy was that of the moral issues raised by the social-economic order of the West. The "Individual human being, becoming independent," Chernyshevsky pointed out, "was [actually] left helpless." In England the village population was converted "into farm laborers [*batraki*] whose condition is very sad," while each individual capitalist has under his authority "hundreds of workers — proletarians whose existence is a disaster." Western individualism thus had led to the "appearance in England and France of thousands of wealthy people on the one hand, and to millions of poor people on the other."[50]

As usual in these studies of Moscow Slavophilism the purely literary aspects of reviews and criticism are left to the literary critic. The concern here is with the idea content, and with the social, economic, and political events in Samarin's review of Count Orlov's study of Prussia in 1806. The parallels between Prussia and Russia on two counts were, of course, striking. Both had emerged from losing wars, Prussia in 1806 from a war with Napoleon, Russia in 1856 from the Crimean War, and although serfdom in Prussia in 1806, and in Russia in 1856 may not have been absolutely identical, both societies were in the throes of breaking out of their shackles. If Samarin,, like the rest of the Slavophils, felt a certain exuberance at the time, it was because, although not completely beyond suspicion, they were finally allowed to publish their own journal in the relative freedom of the early years of Alexander II's reign.

Samarin's review focused on the reasons for Prussia's defeat, and the composition, role, and morale of its army. Samarin noticed the trend toward centralization in government in the West during the eighteenth century at the expense of "classes, associations, communes, and private individuals" or at the expense of local self-government. The central bureaucracy expanded, establishing military discipline at the same time that in Prussia the poor were deprived of the means of making a living. Although "serfdom (*Leibeigenschaft*) was considerably softened by law and custom," landlord-serf relations did not permit the development of free labor, and the productivity of Prussian society was stagnant.[51] Between the people and the privileged class stood the government with its growing economic demands upon an oppressed and unproductive populace. Corruption in government circles increased and personal gain replaced the sense of duty. Here as elsewhere in his review, Samarin's preference is clear.

In this review of a Russian work on Prussia Samarin relied to a considerable extent on sources other than Orlov's book. He quoted French and German authors and arrived at a number of conclusions. First, he pointed out, the principal aim of the "science of finances . . . is to fill the state treasury," at the expense of the people. The government should dispense with the "sympathy and counsel of the subjects," using them for its benefit alone. The "wisdom of governing consisted in the ability to divide class interests and set them against each other." The mainstay of the throne is people who are "not in any way connected with the *narod*." "In the army they saw not the people [*zemlia*] . . . but some sort of soulless and dead weapon."[52] It does not take much imagination to see that in addition to serfdom, these five points summarize Samarin's reasons for Russia's loss of the Crimean War, and in all this Chernyshevsky readily concurred. Further-more, the Slavophil antigovernment bias, although perhaps not as strong in Samarin as in Khomiakov and Konstantin Aksakov, still comes through.

In the several pages that followed the critical exposition of conditions in Prussia Samarin touched on a subject that was also a favorite of Konstantin Aksakov, a form of gallophobia. Samarin decried the prominent role of the "French colony" in Berlin in the eighteenth century and the "ruinous imita-tiveness of the French by the Prussian upper class which deprived the government and the upper level of Prussian society of its national charac-ter." These together with the French language (which Samarin used as late as 1853 in his letters to his father) brought to Berlin "French rationality," and "deceptive clarity," and was welcomed by Frederick II and Berlin society. In spite of such implacable foes of this gallomania as Freiherr von Stein, "contempt for German nationality became fashionable while imitation of France was acknowledged as enlightenment." Samarin's conclusion was that "Prussia was conquered by France long before their encounters at Jena and Auerstedt."[53] Here again, what Samarin is saying about French in-fluence on the Prussian ruling circles was equally applicable to his contem-porary Russia, and from his point of view was just as reprehensible. With the possible exception of his reference to French rationalism, Chernyshevsky readily concurred in Samarin's judgments.

The balance of Samarin's review was devoted to the composition of the Prussian army and its role in Prussian society. He was highly critical of the social and rank separation of officers from soldier, resulting among other things in poor morale. The "military cast" was entirely separate from the rest of society, and most noticeably from the serf population which supplied manpower for the army ranks. Samarin saw hope for Prussia in the period following the 1806 defeat in the attitude and statements of a number of in-fluential Prussian aristocrats. The role of the army in Prussian and in Rus-sian societies was perhaps not in all respects identical, but there was enough similarity to cause both Samarin and Chernyshevsky concern at home, par-ticularly in view of the vivid memories of the Crimean War.

Agreeing with much of Samarin's criticism, Chernyshevsky sought the solution of the social-economic problem at home, as already indicated, in the Russian village commune. Although he was perhaps not cognizant of it, the Slavophils, while of an older generation than he, were ahead of him in their awareness and knowledge of certain of the basic changes and their im-plications caused by the rising tide of Western industrialism — as proved, among other things, by Koshelev's keen interest in technological advances. Koshelev was also perceptive in his appraisal of the growing gulf between workers and employers. The "proletariat threatens to attack the people who have property," he wrote A. N. Popov in August 1849 from Ostende. "Com-munism has not been conquered. It is spreading more and more . . . it is persuasive for people who have nothing and who do not wish to work." And he noted the disturbing consequences of industrial unemployment. "Here in Europe matters are such that in the cities a third of the population are on public assistance [*vit d'assistance publique*]. . . . Yesterday I was in Brugge. There of 48 thousand inhabitants 15 thousand receive daily subsistence." Conditions in the Netherlands were no better. "In Haarlem of 60 thousand inhabitants 23 thousand also live on charity. . . . And the number of the poor . . . is constantly on the rise and grows."[54] Obvious here is not only Koshelev's pro-capitalistic bias and lack of sympathy for the new proletariat, and its unemployed but also some of the implications of modern industrial mass employment.

While Koshelev served in a sense as the eyes and ears of the Slavophils in the West, he was not the only one among them conscious of the rapidly changing economic and social conditions. Samarin, as mentioned earlier, became aware of this after reading Lorenz von Stein early in the 1840s, while Khomiakov, no less in touch with events in the West, was informed about them and about the varieties of utopian socialism that offered solutions to the new and complex problems. Some of these matters were discussed in writing at the end of the 1840s by Koshelev and Khomiakov, and most probably orally by the other Slavophils. A ten-page letter in Khomiakov's works dated by his editor "about 1849,"and appearing under the title "About the Village Commune" was most probably addressed to Koshelev.[55]

The letter to which Khomiakov was replying seems to have been lost, but it is not difficult to deduce its content from his reply. The theme of the epistolary exchange was the new industrial order in the West, its effects on the displacement of the peasantry as industrialization caused rapid urbanization with its inevitable slums, and the equally rapid growth of the "ulcer of the proletariat," a then current expression used by the Slavophils as well as by Chernyshevsky. In the West the solution was sought in various forms of utopian socialism, and after publication of the Communist Manifesto in 1848 increasingly in Marxism, while the Slavophils turned to the Russian village commune and to what later M. O. Gershenzon characterized as Russian spontaneous, "unconscious socialism." Khomiakov took this notion a step further than the rest of the Slavophils and dreamed of the evolution in Russia of a new "industrial commune," a "phalanstery." To the Slavophils' fear of peasant uprisings was now added the fear of possible proletarian unrest caused by Russia's slow but growing industrialism — this while the Slavophils, Khomiakov and Koshelev in particular, were branching out into entrepreneurship in addition to estate ownership and management.

In discussing Slavophil views of and reactions to Western industrialism one must constantly bear in mind not only their personal and class economic and social interests, which they never forgot, but also the state of affairs in the West. England as the leading industrial nation in the middle of the nineteenth century was the focus of Slavophil attention, but as pointed out above, Koshelev kept his eyes open wherever he traveled in the West. The 1840s and 1850s were the era of unrestrained laissez-faire economic enterprise when the industrial worker was left alone, unprotected, exploited, and at the mercy of the entrepreneur. He did not have the right to vote, had no union protection, and no social legislation to soften the blows of modern industrialism. But after 1881 Bismarck pioneered sickness, accident, old-age, and disability insurance, intended, paradoxically perhaps, to arrest and discourage the progress of socialism. Similar legislation came to England in 1911, and to the United States after 1932. In the meantime, toward the end of Samarin's and Koshelev's lives, in the 1870s and 1880s respectively, "social Darwinism," and in the United States the era of the "robber barons" were further to underscore the excesses of unbridled "wolf freedom," or of predatory license.

The commune-consciousness of the Slavophils, and of Herzen, Chernyshevsky and others, if not "born in the slums of Manchester," was at least "aided and abetted" by Western industrialism in the age of Dickens. In fact it could be said that in the Slavophil view, if the village commune had not existed in Russia at the time it would have had to be invented, in a way in which Khomiakov visualized a possible industrial commune. What emerges clearly from this difference between the West and the Russia of the Slavophils, and of Herzen and Chernyshevsky, is the ancient conflict of ideas as it appeared in the middle of the last century: total freedom for the utmost expression of the individual contrasted with freedom tempered and ennobled by consideration for other human beings. This is true despite the obvious inconsistency in the Slavophils' reluctance to dispense with their estates and other property and join the peasant commune that they espoused. This, surely, would have been the ultimate measure of their devotion to the commune.

The Slavophils saw themselves as the guardians of Russia's national spirit and culture. These were conceived in terms of the principles of *sobornost'* and communality, and were embodied in the Orthodox church, and the village commune, respectively, two historical institutions that often appeared to them in a highly idealized form. Chicherin saw the commune as a tsar-created administrative expedient of relatively recent origin. Both Herzen and Chernyshevsky had much high regard for the village commune than Chicherin, who was favorably disposed toward the then strong and prevalent Western liberalism. But the radical Westerners saw the Russian commune as the kernel and mainstay of the future Russian secular socialistic economic order, rooted in their materialistic *Weltanschauung.* Herzen, and more resolutely and clearly Chernyshevsky, were ready to resort to revolution in order to achieve the new commune-based socialist order. Thus the Slavophils in contrast to Herzen and Chernyshevsky started from opposite premises — Orthodox Christianity versus materialism. They met on the level of ideology symbolized by the village commune, and parted ways again when they got to the bottom level of program, action, and tactics. Here the Slavophils believed in peaceful gradual change, whereas Herzen, and again more resolutely Chernyshevsky were ready to resort to force.

Notes

1. The pro-government ideological faction, consisting of the so-called "defenders of official nationality," the only ones that had government support, will be referred to in Chapter 16.

2. Quoted by Richard Hare in *Russian Literature from Pushkin to the Present Day* (London, 1947) p. 3.

3. The series of exchanges began with Samarin's "Dva slova o narodnosti v nauke" ("Two Words about Nationality in Science"), which was published in *Russkaia beseda,* 1856, no. I, pp. 35–47. Chicherin's reply, "O narodnosti v nauke" (On Nationality in Science), appeared in *Russkii vestnik,* 1856, May, book one, pp. 62–71: September, book one, pp. 8–27. Chicherin followed this with another article, "Zametki *Russkago vestnika-Russkaia beseda* i tak nazyvaemoe slavianofil'skoe napravlenie" (Remarks of the *Russian Messenger, Russkaia beseda* and the so-called Slavophil Orientation), in *Russkii vestnik,* no. 11, pp. 219–223. Samarin elaborated in his "O narodnom obrazovanii" (On National Education) in *Russkaia beseda,* 1856, no. 2, pp. 85–106. Chicherin replied with his "Zametki *Russkago vestnika* — vopros o narodnosti v nauke" (Remarks of the *Russian Messenger* — The Question of Nationality in Science), *Russkii vestnik,* 1856, no. 12, pp. 312–319. Samarin's reply was written in the form of an article intended for the Slavophil circle only, and was not published at the time. The original manuscript was later found among Konstantin Aksakov's papers and was published in Samarin's works under the title, "Zamechaniia na zametki *Russkago vestnika* voprosu o narodnosti v nauke" (Remarks on the Remarks of the *Russian Messenger* on the Question of Nationality in Science). See Samarin, *Sochineniia,* I, 148–161.

4. A later, book edition of this work appeared under the more descriptive title, *Krest'iane na Rusi. Izsledovanie o postepennom izmenenii znacheniia krest'ian v russkom obshchestve* (The Peasants in Russia: Investigation of the Gradual Change in the Significance of the Peasants in Russian Society) (Moscow, 1891). For an excellent brief characterization of this work and its role in Slavophil views on the emancipation of the serfs, see E. A. Dudzinskaia, "Ideino-teoriticheskie positsii Slavianofilov. . ." pp. 152–153.

5. Chicherin's versatility, which found expression in the fields of chemistry, physics, and geometry, prompted D. I. Mendeleev to nominate him for honorary membership in the Russian society of chemists and physicists. See

V. D. Zor'kin, *Iz istorii burzhuazno-liberal'noi politicheskoi mysli Rossii vtoroi poloviny XIX — nachala XX v. (B. N. Chicherin)* (Moscow, 1975), p. 13. In recent years Chicherin's personality and career have attracted attention among doctoral candidates in the United States. See W. E. Gould, *The Philosophy of Boris Chicherin: From Practice to Theory* (Ann Arbor, Mich. 1971); Elliot Benowitz, *B. N. Chicherin: Rationalism and Liberalism in Nineteenth-Century Russia* (Ann Arbor, Mich. 1966); D. P. Hammer, *Two Russian Liberals: The Political Thought of B. N. Chicherin and K. D. Kavelin* (Ann Arbor, Mich. 1962).

6. See S. V. Bakhrushin, ed. *Vospominaniia Borisa Nikolaevicha Chicherina. Moskva sorokovykh godov* (Moscow, 1929), p. 244 (hereafter cited as Chicherin *Vospominaniia*). Although the title limits the period to the 1840s there is much in this volume that goes beyond the forties.

7. Ibid., p. 246.

8. As is true of most people, Chicherin's views underwent a certain change. Zor'kin says that in the last decade or so of Chicherin's life, when he seems to have reflected upon Slavophilism, his interest in philosophy as related to the concepts of state and law increased. He "cooled off toward positivism," and turned to neo-Kantianism and neo-Hegelianism, which were then enjoying a certain vogue in Russia. (See Zor'kin, *Chicherin*, p. 15.) It is possible to speculate but difficult to be certain how these colored his views of Slavophilism and Samarin except that they could not have disposed him favorably toward Slavophil Orthodoxy. It is more certain, as pointed out above, that he maintained his negative attitude toward Slavophilism. See also Dudzinskaia, "Ideino — teoriticheskie positsii Slavianofilov. . .," pp. 154–155.

9. The Russian meaning of *narodnost'* is no less baffling than its English translation. A dozen years ago Dudzinskaia, stressing the absence of a generally accepted definition of *narodnost'* in Russian, said, "Some understood it as a call to national exclusiveness, reticence, limitation; others as a negation of the West and of universal culture . . . as feeling for old times, and a call backward, and there were those who understood this word, serfdom." Dudzinskaia, *op. cit.,* p. 153.

10. In the heat of the polemics, this all-important distinction tended to be swept away by the misuse of the ubiquitous *nauka*. Fortunately this has not always been the case. For example, recently Kitaev, referring to the controversy between the Slavophils and the liberals in the mid-fifties, said: "*Russkaia beseda* began with establishing the principle of nationality in science — science (here meaning humanistic or 'the human sciences' which the Slavophils could not conceive outside of the religious, national [*narodnoi*] element." See V. I. Kitaev, *Ot frondy k okhranitel'stvu. Iz istorii russkoi liberal'noi mysli 50–60kh godov XIX veka* (Moscow, 1972), p. 74.

11. See *Russkaia beseda,* 1856, no. 1, p. 35.

12. Ibid., pp. 37, 39. In the emergence of Russian Slavophilism *narodnost'* has implications beyond the confines of Russia and the purely Russian, for "The question of national culture was closely bound with those interests that the Slavophils manifested toward the national-liberation movement of the Southern and Western Slavs." See E. A. Duzinskaia, "Burzhuaznye tendentsii v teorii i praktike slavianofilov" *Voprosy istorii*, 1972, no. 1, p. 56. This, one might add, was particularly true of most of the South Slavs who were Orthodox.

13. *Russkaia beseda*, 2856, no. 1, pp. 38, 40–41, 43–44.

14. Ibid., pp. 45–47.

15. In his memoirs, Chicherin was neither charitable nor complimentary toward Beliaev, who, in Chicherin's words, "rummaged among the ancient decrees and charters but was quite incapable of understanding them. He had neither sense nor education and was ready to fantasize endlessly, introducing his own wild inventions into the old texts." Chicherin, *Vospominaniia*, p. 263.

16. See b. N. Chicherin, "On Nationality in Science" (*O narodnosti v nauke*), *Russkii vestnik*, May 1856, book 1, pp. 63–65.

17. Ibid., pp. 67–68. Chicherin's philosophical and political views are matters of obvious importance for the study of his ideological position vis-à-vis the Moscow Slavophils, but any precise and complete definition of them is as elusive as those of *narodnost'* and *nauka*. Thus for Zor'kin he was not only a neo-Hegelian but had also flirted with positivism. To Leontovich he was one of the "conservative liberals," and to Utechin, one of the "classical liberal Westernists." Timberlake considers him a "Western-type" liberal: "In 1856 K. D. Kavelin, B. N. Chicherin and N. A. Mel'gunov formed the first Russian group to refer to itself as the advocates of Western-type liberalism." In Fischer's opinion, Chicherin was "Akin to the *Rechtsstaat* liberals of Bismarck Germany," whereas in the words of Kitaev, who agrees with P. B. Struve on this point, Chicherin was a "conservative liberal or a liberal conservative." Cf. Zor'kin, *Chicherin*, p. 15; V. V. Leontovich, *Istoriia Liberalisma v Rossii 1762–1914* (Paris, 1980), p. 186; S. V. Utechin, *Russian Political Thought: A Concise History* (New York, 1963) p. 105; C. E. Timberlake, ed. *Essays on Russian Liberalism*, Columbia, Mo. 1972 p. 4. George Fischer, *Russian Liberalism: From Gentry to Intelligentsia* (Cambridge, Mass., 1958), p. 19. Much valuable material on this topic and on the period can be found in M. V. Nechkina, ed. *Revoliutsionnaia situatsiia v Rossii v seredine XIX veka* (Moscow, 1978).

18. Chicherin, *op. cit.*, pp. 67–71.

19. *Russkii vestnik*, September 1856, book 1, pp. 10–11.

20. Ibid., p. 15.

21. Ibid., pp. 23–24.

22. Ibid., p. 26.

23. Like the Slavophil Peter Kireevsky, who during the 1830s, 1840s, and early 1850s collected Russian folklore in order to preserve it for future use and inspiration, so M. A. Balakirev, a prominent member of the Mighty Five, undertook in 1860 a long trip along the Volga to gather folk songs. In 1862 and 1863 he did the same in the Caucasus. See I. N. Kovaleva, "Russkaia muzikal'naia kul'tura v gody revoliutsionnoi situatsii (1857–1864gg.)," in M. N. Nechkina, ed., *Revolutsionnaia situatsiia v Rossii v 1859–1861 gg.* (Moscow, 1970), p. 247.

24. See W. C. Weidemaier, "Herzen and the Existential World View: A New Approach to an Old Debate," *Slavic Review,* 1981, no. 4, p. 558. The case for Herzen's "atheistic existentialism" ably made by Weidemaier would have been more convincing, and certainly more complete, if he had not confined the examination of Herzen's writings to the 1840s and early 1850s. Herzen's *Kolokol* period, and the 1860s are left out of consideration. Furthermore, no effort has been made to reconcile Herzen's "atheistic existentialism" with his "Russian socialism," both of which belong to the same period in Herzen's life.

25. Herzen's life story, completely or in part, has been told by a number of biographers; see, for instance, Raoul Labry, *Alexandre Ivanovic Herzen, 1812–1870. Essai sur la formation et le developpement de ses idees* (Paris, 1928), Ia. E. El'sberg, *A. I. Gertsen. Zhizn' i tvorchestvo,* 2nd ed. (Moscow, 1951); Martin Malia, *Alexander Herzen and the Birth of Russian Socialism, 1812–1855* (Cambridge, Mass., 1961).

26. Neither the Slavophils nor Herzen followed their admiration for the Russian peasant commune to its logical conclusion, that is, joining a commune after abandoning their established way of life. In spite of Herzen's "Russian socialism," like his fellow-gentry Slavophils, he was not willing to give up the income from his estates. When at the end of the 1840s Nicholas I ordered his Russian property sequestered, Herzen, then in exile in Paris, was not loath to seek help from the Rothschilds. He made a "fictitious sale" of his property in Russia to Baron James Rothschild, who "in turn menaced Nicholas with refusal of a loan then pending in order to obtain removal of the sequester and transfer of the value of the property to Paris. It was a brilliant coup which Herzen, as well as Rothschild, enjoyed immensely... " Herzen then invested in Parisian real estate, and other ventures. See Malia, *Herzen,* pp. 389, 472.

27. See El'sberg, *Gertsen,* p. 428.

28. Ibid., p. 429.

29. See Herzen, *Sochineniia,* XVIII, 600.

30. See *Rus',* 1883, no. 1, pp. 30–42; no. 2, pp. 23–30. The two installments contain fourteen letters, seven from Herzen and seven from Samarin, written between July 11 and November 2, 1864. Nol'de later found Ivan Aksakov's publication of the Samarin-Herzen correspondence in *Rus'* "full

of obvious errors so that the chronology in my narrative for this year had to be based on guesswork." See Nol'de, *Samarin,* p. 240. For Nol'de's account of the Samarin-Herzen meetings in London in 1864 see pp. 181–185.

31. *Rus',* 1883, no.1, pp. 35–36.

32. Ibid., no. 2, p. 25.

33. Ibid., no. 1, p. 37.

34. Ibid., p. 31.

35. Ibid., p. 33.

36. Ibid., p. 34.

37. Ibid., p. 34.

38. See B. P. Koz'min, ed. *N. G. Chernyshevsky. Polnoe sobranie sochinenii* (Moscow, 1948), IV, 722–735 (hereafter cited as Chernyshevsky, *Sochinneniia*).

39. Ibid., p. 722.

40. The two articles to which Chernyshevsky referred were published in the section *kritika.* The first was a twenty-five-page book review, and an essay, under the long title, "A Sketch of the Three-Week March of Napoleon Against Prussia in 1806. The Work of the Aide-de-camp Count Nikolai Orlov. St. Petersburg, 1856" [Ocherk trekhnedel'nago pokhoda Napoleona protiv Prussii v 1806 godu. Sochinenie Fligel-adiutanta grafa Orlova. St. Petersburg 1856 goda], *Russkaia beseda,* 1857, no. 1, 1–24. The second was "A few Words in Regard to the Historical Works of Mr. Chicherin" (Neskol'ko slov po povodu istoricheskikh trudov g. Chicherina), Ibid., pp. 103–118.

41. Chernyshevsky, *Sochineniia,* IV, 723–724.

42. Ibid., p. 725.

43. Ibid., p. 726.

44. Ibid., p. 727.

45. Ibid., III, 85; IV, 727.

46. Ibid., III, 85; IV, 727. See also Christoff, *Xomjakov,* p. 179.

47. The controversy over the convictions and character of the Russian people, the *narod,* did not stop with the disagreement between Chernyshevsky and Samarin. It continued during the rest of the nineteenth and into the twentieth century, usually reflecting the personal convictions of the protagonists. The Orthodox Samarin held onto the Slavophil contention that the *narod* was Orthodox; Chernyshevsky, a "Feuerbachian materialist," saw it as materialistic in nature. The editor of Chernyshevsky's Diary says that Chernyshevsky considered himself "a follower" of Feuerbach, a biographer considers him Feuerbach's "student." Cf. N. A. Alekseev, ed. *N. G. Chernyshevsky Dnevnik chast' I, 1848–1849gg.* (Moscow, 1931), p. 404; N. V. Bogoslovsky, *Nikolai Gavrilovich Chernyshevsky 1828–1889* (Moscow, 1955), p. 381. See also W. F. Woehrlin, *Chernyshevskii: The Man and the Journalist* (Cambridge, Mass., 1971), pp. 52, 146–147. For a summary chapter on the

view of the Russian people as the controversy evolved in the nineteenth and twentieth centuries, and Chernyshevsky's role in it, see V. G. Baskakov, *Mirovozzrenie Chernyshevskogo* (Moscow, 1956), pp. 709–746.

48. Chernyshevsky, *Sochineniia,* IV, 730.

49. Ibid., 730–731.

50. Ibid., pp. 737, 739–740.

51. *Russkaia beseda* 1857, no. 1, *kritika,* pp. 3–4.

52. Ibid., p. 10.

53. Ibid., pp. 11–13.

54. Letter dated August 29, 1849., P. I. Bartenev, ed. "Iz bumag Aleksandra Ivanovicha Popova" *Russkii arkhiv,* 1886, no. 3, p. 352. See also P. K. Christoff, "A. S. Khomiakov on the Agricultural and Industrial Problem in Russia," in A. D. Ferguson, ed., *Essays in Russian History,* pp. 154–155.

55. Khomiakov, *Sochineniia,* III, 459–482. When P. I. Bartenev published the letter in 1884, one year after Koshelev's death, he stated that he was publishing it from the original supplied to him by Khomiakov's son, Dmitrii. He noted "Everything that has since been written among us about the commune (i.e., the many volumes) is only a relatively weak exposition of what Khomiakov said and elaborated." What "he wrote more than thirty years ago" has lost none of its value and relevance. See "A. S. Khomiakov o sel'skoi obshchine. (Iz pis'ma k priiateliu.) Pisano okolo 1849 goda," *Russkii arkhiv,* 1884, no. 3, pp. 261–269.

13

Memorandum (*Zapiska*) on the Emancipation of the Serfs

In his brief but informative biography of Samarin, Nol'de devotes between one-third and one-half of the narrative to Samarin's participation in the emancipation of the serfs. Perusing Samarin's collected works and published correspondence (up to 1853) today one can readily see that there was no other national or personal problem that concerned him more or that placed a greater demand on his mind, conscience, and energy than ridding Russia of serfdom. Once young Iurii decided to forgo marriage and normal family life, his dedication to public service, as he saw it, proved unalterable. Faithfulness to fact calls for recognition of his keen sense of duty but not for elevating him to martyrdom, a circumstance that does not diminish his rare sense of self-denial.

In the early 1840s when Samarin became aware of the "social" question, this issue in the West was becoming increasingly complex owing to the intrusion of modern industrialism; in Russia, still overwhelmingly agrarian, the "social" question was locked into the overriding issue of the peasantry and serfdom. It did not require much knowledge or penetration to see that serfdom was a millstone around the neck of Russian society, and that Russia could not move forward without first removing it. But serfdom was not a simple economic or social matter. It was a major moral issue, and to the early Slavophils it was also one of Christian morals.

On the question of serfdom during the 1840s and 1850s the early Slavophils, like other intelligent and concerned Russian gentry, were confronted by a difficult and trying decision. They and their ancestors had been accustomed to cheap and abundant serf labor for generations. Yet many of them realized that serfdom in Western Europe as in Russia was a matter of the past. It had to be eliminated "from above," or as Alexander II, among others, well knew, it would be swept away "from below." Some of the early Slavophils were also convinced that forced serf labor was less productive than that of hired free hands. Furthermore, since the Slavophils were in the vanguard of those landlords in Russia who believed that most of the back-breaking agricultural labor could be eliminated by the introduction of farm machinery, they could see little reason for prolonging serfdom. And there was also the ethical problem, which, however obscured by the long-existing custom and the reality of serfdom, had not completely vanished in the middle of the nineteenth century.

Anything so pervasive and detrimental to progress of any kind as serfdom was in Russia, was bound to arouse both reflection and indignation. The Slavophils were neither the first nor the last in the first half of the nineteenth century to ponder the problem of serfdom. For instance, in 1809 Speransky declared against serfdom in his "An Introduction to the Code of State Laws," and in the early 1820s the Decembrist Society included among its principal aims the elimination of serfdom. But as Slavophilism became better defined in the mid-1840s, the thought of putting an end to serfdom became more and more insistent. In 1842 Khomiakov welcomed the well-intentioned but ineffective government decree providing for voluntary emancipation arrangements. Increasingly the emancipation issue claimed the attention of the Russian intelligentsia, including the Moscow Slavophils.

As in the case of the other topics and problems discussed during the 1840s in the Moscow salons, so also with respect to the emancipation of the serfs we have only fragmentary information. But by early 1847 concern among the Moscow Slavophils for solution to the problem of serfdom had caused considerable discussion. On March 17, 1847, Ivan Kireevsky wrote to his sister Maria that among us now "they constantly talk about emancipation, Koshelev, Khomiakov, and others."[1] Maria was disturbed by the fact that she was a serf owner and wished to set her serfs free. Ivan's reluctance was only overcome by Koshelev's admonition which touched the core of his Orthodox faith — I do not understand, dear friend Kireevsky, how you, a Christian, are not tormented by the thought of having human beings in the state of serfdom."[2]

Our concern here is with Samarin's views on, and contribution to, the emancipation of the serfs in Russia. There is no doubt that Samarin's two years in the Baltic area had much to do with placing the problem of serfdom for him in the broader range of the "peasant" question, which inevitably involved the basic issue of the land. Serfdom, peasantry, and land were inextricably bound together, and they remained so in his mind throughout his years of work on the emancipation reform. There were, of course, differences between the Baltic situation and the Russian. In the Baltic provinces the landowning class was heavily Baltic German, Lutheran, and Polish Catholic in Lithuania whereas in the rest of Russia it was Slav and Orthodox. The peasantry in the Baltic area was predominantly Latvian, Lithuanian, or Estonian with Slav Orthodox elements all working for German landlords. These mixtures and cultural-religious differences rendered the situation in the Baltic provinces even more complex than that in Russia proper, where both peasants and landlords were Slav Orthodox. In the Baltic littoral in 1846–1848, Samarin encountered a complex of peasant, economic, land, and social problems, as well as religious, cultural, and national issues, at a time when nationalism was sweeping through all Europe.

Under such circumstances, it was hardly surprising that Samarin acquired a dislike — even fear — of the power and influence of the German minority that was in control of Baltic economic, political, and cultural life — although he had at the same time deep and abiding appreciation of German thought, literature, and of its cultural and educational achievements. His experiences and study in the Baltic area convinced him not only of the complexity of the peasant question there but also of the nature of social stratification and political control. His awareness of the medieval and later town charters of Riga as a means for the perpetuation of control and privilege in the hands of the German minority influenced to some extent his later distrust of Western charters and constitutions as the strongholds of class privileges — which, indeed, most Western constitutions of the middle of the nineteenth century actually were.[3]

Speaking in precise terms, Samarin did not encounter serfdom in Liflandia in the second half of the 1840s, for it had been abolished there by the statute of March 26, 1819. But as Dmitry Samarin makes clear in his long introduction to the *Riga Letters,* the serfs had been granted only "bird" freedom, which left them without land and without "legal definition of the extent of their obligations" to the landowner. Having no land, no capital, and no training for work other than farming, the peasants were left at the mercy of the landowners or of the "German knights."[4] Samarin in the *Riga Letters* rarely refers directly to the problem of serfdom and emancipation, but in his treatment of the social and religious history of Riga he shows a typical Slavophil concern and sympathy for the *narod* — for the underdog, the poor city people and particularly the peasantry, largely of non-German, Baltic, and some Russian stock. Nol'de was correct in observing that the "second half of the forties represents the moment when the peasant cause became transformed for them [the Slavophils] into the basic content of their intellectual and moral life."[5]

Dostoevsky's later "frantic *muzhik-olatry,*" or *muzhik*-worship, so characteristic of Konstantin Aksakov during the 1840s and 1850s, was muted in the thought and sentiments of Iurii Samarin, who was unprepared intellectually and temperamentally for the Aksakov type of peasant idolatry. In his soberer view of the *narod,* Samarin was able to see not only its virtues but also its weaknesses and defects. In the opening pages of the first Riga letter he referred to the conquest of the Lets (*Latyshi*) by the German knights and of the "enslavement" of the conquered population, seeing little "difference between slavery existing until recently in the Baltic region and serfdom that exists among us." Another regrettable consequence of the German "conquest and enslavement was the destruction of the communal system." In addition to these basic and irreducible Slavophil premises, that is, emancipation of the serfs and preservation of the peasant communal order, a third one also appears early in the first letter from Riga. This was the Slavophil fiction that force and conquest were the source and foundation of the class structure of feudalism in the West, and that these were alien to Russia's past and social order. "Oppression, [and] rupture between the upper classes and the *narod*, contempt and violence on the one hand, hatred and thirst for vengeance on the other-such were the conditions of the internal order in all colonies founded upon conquest."[6]

Yet another component of Moscow Slavophilism in general, and of Samarin's in particular, emerges from the opening pages of the same letter, his patriotism and nationalism. Here, as was common throughout nineteenth-century Europe, we see the interplay of nationalism and counter-nationalism. Samarin's Russian nationalism assumed the garb of anti-Germanism, just as the Napoleonic invasion of Russia, an expression of French nationalism, aroused the counternationalism of the Russians. Thus in 1846 as later Samarin saw German nationalism as a threat to Russia. It asserted itself in the Baltic provinces, which he considered Russian territory despite their predominantly non-Russian population, and he countered it with his Slavophil, Russian brand of nationalism. He claimed that the life of the conquered people "was so repressed that it could not develop from within [*samobytno*] while it borrowed nothing from German life."

Although Samarin, particularly in his later career, was not prone to accept Konstantin Aksakov's idealization of the *narod*, in the late 1840s he was not immune to the exalted Slavophil views of old Russian society. Thus in his Riga Letters he characterized it as "a living union of all classes in free communion."[7] Obviously there was no place in such a concept for class animosities and struggles. Small wonder then that he found no room for a *narod* in the Baltic area. Here the German element, largely as a result of old charters renewed periodically, and by means of new ones, secured its privileged and dominant position over the non-German population. Conflict and struggle were the inevitable consequence, particularly as the nineteenth century wore on and nationalism became an irresistible force throughout Europe. Placing the responsibility for the oppression of the non-German elements in the Baltic area on government-appointed administrators, some of them of the German, some of the Russian aristocracy, he indirectly censored the Russian autocracy, which ultimately controlled all administrative appointments. This was basically the cause of his incarceration at age twenty-nine, in March 1849.

But even when the provincial assignment in the Baltic area claimed Samarin's concerns and preoccupation the problem uppermost in his mind was the emancipation of the serfs in Russia, and specifically the question of the land, which was inextricably bound up with the emancipation. This was perhaps the most crucial and bothersome problem for all the Slavophils, since nothing less than their future livelihood depended on it. Without land they would have had no income, since they, with the exception of Samarin and Ivan Aksakov, were opposed to joining the administration of Nicholas I. This explains Khomiakov's deep satisfaction with Samarin's emancipation formula, communicated to Khomiakov in a letter from Riga written in January 1848. Although the letter has been lost, Khomiakov's reply makes amply clear Samarin's basic solution of the land problem:

> For us Russians [Khomiakov replied], now one question is more important than all others, more insistent than all others. You have understood it, and understood it correctly. . . . Thank you for having hit upon that juridical form which expresses its sense with greatest clarity and precision, that is, on the existence among us of two rights equally strong and sacred: the hereditary right to property, and the same hereditary right to use [*pol'zovanie*].[8]

"Use" refers to the use of land. What Khomiakov so gratefully welcomed was Samarin's formula that confirmed the landowner's right to private ownership of land, and the peasant's right to the use of a much more limited area of land, controlled by the village commune, particularly in Great Russia, and sometimes periodically redistributed among the peasants by the village *mir.* Clearly, on the crucial question of land ownership the Slavophils were not ready for the ultimate sacrifice. As much as they admired and valued the historical peasant commune, often in their representations dressed in the most attractive garb, on the issue of the land they were not prepared to abandon their long-standing privileges. They were not willing to give up the right to land ownership and join the peasant commune in which the more fortunate peasants, in return for long hours of work on gentry land, had the right to a small plot of land. (The household serfs, though equally hardworking, had no such right.) Khomiakov found Samarin's formulation of the double standard on the land question, one for the landowner, another for the agricultural serf, quite acceptable. He rationalized the landowners position by saying that only the state had the absolute right to land ownership. In the Slavophil view,, Samarin's formula would soon become the foundation of the emancipation reform.

What Khomiakov was probably not aware of during his exchange of letters with Samarin on emancipation of the serfs and the land question was a brief memorandum, of five pages, that Samarin had prepared at the time on serfdom and the land in Livonia.[9] At the beginning of the memorandum Samarin refers to the unclear origin of serfdom, making a dubious distinction between Russia proper and Livonia. It was a "fact," in his view, that in

Livonia serfdom was the result of "conquest and enslavement" and a matter of "premeditated coercion," whereas in Russian proper it was the "indirect consequence of administrative measures." Even if this was true, one wonders how much difference it made to the Russian serf down the centuries. Samarin made another perhaps truthful but unsupported assertion when he stated that in Livonia the "landowners regarded the peasants as their spoils of battle, and the peasants regarded the landowners as their natural enemies and oppressors."[10]

But whether in Russia or in Livonia, the serf had two inalienable rights: inseparability from the land, and the right to use of the land. With respect to Livonia, Samarin passed judgment of two measures, the statutes of 1804 and 1819. That he favored the first is quite clear. The second statute "recognized the person as free but destroyed his bond with the land," Samarin held that it was essential to confirm in the future the "right of the peasant to land": peasant freedom without land was a "purely negative" right. He found equally unacceptable the "unlimited right to the ownership of land by the landowner," which would leave the peasant landless. Finally, he ruled out a third alternative, the "free contract," because the landowner and the serf would not be on equal footing.[11] In none of these discussions did Samarin specify how much land he thought should be alloted to the peasant, and the implication was that it should go to the commune, not to the individual peasant. Nor did he raise the question of monetary indemnity for the landowner, or of possible other serf obligations such as the old corvee.

In the western borderlands of Russia, where many of the landlords were of the Polish gentry, serfdom appeared to Samarin doubly oppressive. He saw not only the wretchedness of serfdom but also the "boundless contempt of the *civilized, knightly stock* for the rejected *nation* of serfs."[12] While he was in Kiev, working on Governor General D. G. Bibikov's inventory commission, he was constantly reminded of the "oppression of the Poles and the oppression of serfdom."[13] The centuries-old antagonism between Catholic, westward-looking Poland, and eastern Orthodox Russia welled up in Samarin as he contemplated the lot of the Orthodox Ukrainian serfs in the possession of the Polish Catholic gentry. In Kiev even more firmly than in Riga, the problem of serf emancipation assumed cultural, religious, and nationalistic overtones in addition to its simple and fundamental economic and moral aspect. More clearly and resolutely Samarin and the other Moscow Slavophils felt their difference and distance from the Westward-oriented Poles on the question of serf emancipation.

In his capacity as General Bibikov's chief of office, Samarin became well acquainted with the so-called "inventory" system that Bibikov introduced in 1848. This reform has been seen from different angles and has been given different interpretations, but in its most essential aspect it was an effort to accurately define the obligations of the serf to the landowner. This, of course, was not abolition but acknowledgment of serfdom; indeed, it fell far short of emancipation. Yet by insisting on an exact determination of serf obligation it was intended to deprive the landowner of unlimited and arbitrary demands on the serf, which was all too often his lot. Samarin was strongly in favor of the inventories because he saw them as an effort to improve the lot of the serfs.

Notes that Samarin made while in Kiev give us clear indication of his evolving views on the landowner-serf-land question. At the beginning of the 1850s when these notes were made, this triple relationship had entered a vital stage for all the Slavophils. This was the period of the "seven dark years" of the reign of Nicholas I, when the Slavophils were under government suspicion and censorship, forbidden to publish their own journal and more or less threatened with imprisonment in the event of offending the government by speaking about emancipation or any of a number of other sensitive questions. Under such conditions, notes, memoranda, and personal letters, often carried by friends, were the channels of communication.

In his reflections on the crucial triple relationship while in Kiev, Samarin made it clear that the serf should not be left completely at the mercy of the landlord. The peasant, he wrote, "*should* work for the landowner; the landowner *should* provide his peasants with a plot of land. That is why their mutual relations should be *inviolable* and based on justice." What he saw from Kiev, however, were relations characterized by injustice and arbitrariness weighted in favor of the landlord and consequently heavy and oppressive for the serf. Looking forward to possible changes and improvements from the government, he asserted that any new order must rest on the "*concept of the inseparability of the tiller of the soil from the land,* a concept totally alien to Western Europe. This *inseparability* is manifested in a twofold manner, *as dependence of the tiller of the soil on the land*-serfdom, and *as the dependence of the land on the tiller of the soil,* that is the converse relationship, the realization of which is left to the future." Contrasting this with conditions in France and England, Samarin said, "there the farmer can dismiss his workers in all four directions while the landowner can say no to his farmers and turn all his land into a park." But under the conditions in Russia "landlord and peasants are inseparably linked."[14]

These views, expressed by Samarin in his first two years in Kiev (1849–1852), are contained in some random notes that his brother Dmitry found in Iurii's notebooks. They were written under the impact of two noteworthy events, the tsar's manifesto of March 14, 1848, sanctioning the inventories in the Kiev, Volynsk, and Podolsk gubernias, which Samarin considered a step on the way to eventual emancipation of the serfs, and the revolutions of 1848–1849 in the West. Samarin recorded a number of peasant uprisings against the landlords in the western gubernias, and took note of the "social question," of which he had become keenly aware in the early 1840s. This question was becoming more pressing both in the West and in Russia, despite the differences in social, economic, and political situations.

It was during this period that Samarin did a good deal of reading in political economy. Between 1851 and 1853 the Moscow Slavophils turned their attention not only to the moral, political, and economic aspects of emancipation, as illustrated in the lively correspondence between Khomiakov, Ivan Kireevsky, Ivan and Konstantin Aksakov, and Alexander Koshelev, but also to the religious and ideological implications of Slavophilism.[15] Samarin, in Kiev, did not participate in these exchanges, although he was doubtless well informed about the contents of the many-sided discussions; but he was an enthusiastic participant in some of the more practical concerns that the Slavophils were engaged in, including the Lebedian Society (*Lebedianskoe Obshchestvo*), which was founded in 1848 to advance the modernization of Russian agriculture. Both Koshelev and Khomiakov, as mentioned, were active in the society, and Samarin also joined it in 1853 after he returned from Kiev. What the Slavophils realized at the turn of the 1840s, better than the men of official nationality, and perhaps better than the "men of the soil" (*pochvenniki*) and the pro-Catholic, liberal and radical Westerners, was that elimination of serfdom, essential as it was, would not of itself transform an overwhelmingly backward agrarian economy into a modern diversified progressive economic system. Russian agriculture and the Russian economy, particularly in the northern, colder gubernias where the growing season is short, was in need of a long-range program of modern scientific farming using up-to-date equipment and methods. As Koshelev, Khomiakov and Ivan Kireevsky demonstrated, the early Slavophils saw nothing "Western" or "Russian" about science and technology. They were ready to use the latest scientific and technological achievements in order to modernize their agriculture at the same time that they were working for the emancipation of the serfs. On this second crucial issue, the modernization of farming, the Slavophils were not only in the forefront of Russian society, they were also ahead of their time in Russia.

When Samarin left Kiev in December 1852 to return to Moscow, he also terminated his government service, a fact which was officially confirmed the following February. In October of 1853 fighting between Russia and Turkey broke out and the Crimean War was on. It soon caused new and far-reaching consequences for Russia's internal order as well as in its foreign relations. At the end of the year Samarin's father died, and Iurii, then thirty-four-years old, experienced for the first time, and only briefly, some of the problems of estate management. After the death of the elder Samarin, Iurii went to the family's Volga estate, Vasil'evskoe, and undertook its management. For the first time in his still young career he was confronted with peasant life and its problems on a daily basis, and his experiences dissuaded him from uncritical extolling of the *narod*. Nol'de quotes Samarin as saying in a letter from Vasil'evskoe to Sergei Aksakov: "The general impression is so painful [*tiazhelo*] that if there were no hope for the future, if there were no firm conviction that it is for the moment still in our hands, I could not live a week in the village. But it is fortunate for our generation that its task is completely clear. The goal stands [before us] fixed [and] high. No theorizing [*umstvovanie*] could obscure it."[16]

Cognizant, as the rest of the Moscow Slavophils were, that Russia's economy was sadly in need of modernization, Samarin was convinced of the obvious, that the beginning of this long, complex and difficult task was the emancipation of the serfs. Even before the Crimean War came to an end with the Treaty of Paris of 1856, some of Russia's best minds, irrespective of ideological orientation, interpreted their country's military defeat as a consequence of the inequities of serfdom, and of Russia's backward and almost stagnant economic order. Poor, often impassable roads, and inadequate military supplies and provisions contributed no less to Russia's defeat than the strength of Turkey and its Western allies. It is therefore not a mere coincidence that for most of the period that the war continued in the Crimea, Samarin, like a number of other leading Russians, gave his attention to the problem of serfdom. As mentioned above the proposals for emancipation took the form of individual, privately circulated, memoranda, *zapiski*.

Volume two of Samarin's published works contains a number of memoranda that he drafted between 1853 and 1857. But before we look into his evolving views and convictions on emancipation of the serfs it would be useful and timely to review briefly the ideas and opinions on serfdom in Russia during the 1840s and early 1850s of those who were closest to him intellectually and ideologically, that is, his Slavophil friends. Although it has been known for some time that the Moscow Slavophils played a role in the emancipation of the serfs, second to no other school of thought in Russia, and in retrospect, it seems a leading role, their views and their labors in behalf of emancipation do not appear generally appreciated. This is particularly true of those who for various reasons consider the Slavophils as thoroughly conservative if not reactionary, and often confuse them with the proponents of "official nationality."

This is not at all meant to imply that the Slavophils had an exclusive claim on discussion of emancipation or were the first in the nineteenth century to work for the abolition of serfdom. Abolition was a major point in the program of the Decembrists,[17] and although the Slavophils disapproved of Decembrism in general, the older Slavophils, Khomiakov, Kireevsky, and Koshelev, had contacts with certain Decembrists prior to the uprising of 1825.

Those who have looked into the work of the Moscow Slavophils on serf emancipation usually stress — as Semevsky did — Khomiakov's early censure of the wickedness of serfdom. The essay "About the Old and the New" (*O starom i novom*), which Khomiakov read in Kireevsky's home (Elagina's salon) in 1839, contained among other ideas his often quoted condemnation of serfdom as a "brazen violation of all rights"; also his reference to the "abomination of slavery," and the "abomination of legal slavery." Although doubtless sincere, these sentiments expressed by a serf-owning landlord produced no immediate effect other than to inform the company gathered in Elagina's parlor how Khomiakov felt about serfdom. At the same time he perhaps placed too much blame for its existence on Peter the Great, whom he also characterized as "a frightful but beneficial thunder" that had struck Russia.[18]

A few days before the government's ineffective decree "About Obligated Peasants" (*Ob obiazannykh krest'ian*) of April 2, 1842, which provided for voluntary emancipation agreements between landowner and serf, Nicholas I, made clear his views on emancipation: "There is no doubt that serfdom in its present state in Russia is a perceptible and obvious evil for all; but to touch it now would, of course, be an even more ruinous evil."[19] The government had two main fears: it feared antagonizing the peasantry to the point of another Pugachev uprising or worse, and it feared seriously offending the landowning class, autocracy's principal prop. It was obvious in the two decades that preceded the emancipation reform that many educated Russians, from the tsar to the radical Westerners, realized both the evil of serfdom and its unavoidable end. But this was not true of many of the landowning gentry who were opposed to emancipation then and later. Some of these facts should become more obvious and better attested to as we approach the 1860s.

Inseparable from the emancipation of the serfs in Khomiakov's early considerations were the problems of the commune (*obshchina*), redemption payments for the land to be alloted to the emancipated peasants, and the gnawing consciousness of the "state of the proletariat or the landless English workers," as something to be definitely avoided in Russia. In two brief articles on the peasant problem published in 1842 he vigorously defended the peasant commune and *mir*, and the "rule of half-sharing [*polovnichestvo*] or three days' work on the agricultural estates," which in his view had existed in Russia "from time immemorial." More difficult was the problem of the numerous household serfs, who had no land allotted them except for the small kitchen gardens (*ogorody*), and who were, moreover, in Khomiakov's view, not suited for factory employment.[20]

Khomiakov (like all the early Slavophils) always kept an eye on the West while focusing on Russian problems. One of the major concerns through the 1830s to the 1850s was how Russia could avoid the rise of a Western-type proletariat. Intellectually and psychologically, Khomiakov departed from his theme, the peasant question, to state the fundamental Slavophil position on the relationship between Russia and the West. "Accepting in many respects the lessons from nations which have outstripped us in the realm of enlightenment, we must, and fortunately we can, solve vital questions more correctly than our teachers. Only in this manner can we compare ourselves with them, for the student in order to catch up with his tutor must [also] surpass him."[21] True to this unflinching Slavophil conviction, Samarin would later study and learn from the Prussian emancipation reform but would not imitate it. And in his firm conviction, and that of the other Slavophils, they would improve on the Prussian solution by emancipating the Russian serfs with land.

The dichotomy of Western individualism versus commune-consciousness, always uppermost in the minds of the Slavophils, extended to others in Russia, but with variations that were very unlike the Slavophils' commune-oriented thought based on Orthodox *sobornost'*. The religious Christian base was supplanted in Herzen by a secularistic, rationalistic "Russian socialism," in Bakunin by revolutionary thought, and in the Petrashevtsy by varieties of utopian "Fourierist" socialism.[22] The commune also entered in the 1850s the radical thought of Chernyshevsky, and in later decades it would permeate the populist, *narodnik* movement. Although the "discovery" of the Russian peasant commune is sometimes attributed to Baron von Haxthausen he was not the first to focus attention upon it. The essence of the ancient commune (*obshchina*), *mir,* and *artel'*, characteristic of Great Russia, still vital in the 1840,s was "discovered" during the 1830s and 1840s only in the sense that thanks largely to the early Slavophils these institutions were brought to the attention of educated Russia.

But the same sense of informal institutional togetherness that became one of the pillars of the Slavophil ideological edifice was soon perceived as transcending the boundaries of Great Russia. Thus the communal form of organization with its local characteristics and periods of duration, which was also indigenous to the South and Western Slavs,[23] became a major element of the "cultural pan-Slavism" of the first half of the nineteenth century. Mickiewicz's lectures, "Course de la litterature slave," delivered at the College de France in 1840–1842, had a great deal to do with the continuance of interest in, and the reexamination of, the Russian communal order that had been started in Moscow by the Slavophils. Herzen, after reading the lectures described Mickiewicz as "a Slavophil of the type of Khomiakov."[24]

A year before Herzen spoke in the Moscow salons about Mickiewicz's views on Slav literature and the Slav world, Baron August von Haxthausen had also become interested in the Russian communal order. Haxthausen was exceptionally well informed about peasant conditions in Russia, and during his stay in Moscow in the spring and fall of 1843 he heard much from Konstantin Aksakov about Russian peasant life and the village commune. Soon his own views on this and other Russian matters were brought to the West through his publications. Thus in the 1840s while the early Slavophils

extolled the virtues of the peasant commune at home, Mickiewicz was bringing the Slav commune to the attention of his listeners and readers in France
and the West, and Haxthausen did the same in Germany and the West in
print.[25]

Paradoxically perhaps, the radical Westerners, Belinsky and Herzen, were
much freer to express their views publicly on the Russian peasant commune
and on other matters than the Slavophils were, and the Petrashevtsy circle
too, for the four years that it existed in St. Petersburg (1845 to April 1849)
discussed the commune. The Petrashevtsy were of various backgrounds and
diverse social economic views, and their goals were a melange of French
utopian socialism or more specifically of the "anthropological materialism
of Fourier and Feurbach," in combination with the idea of making the Russian peasant commune "the basis of the future socialist commune or
phalanstery."[26] The Petrashevsky circle was in fact a cluster of ten or more
interconnected groups with more than two hundred members. The circle
that met in Petrashevsky's home on Fridays was attended by "men of letters,
officers, civil servants, teachers, students, artists, and even merchants and
commoners."[27] Although they were heavily under the influence of French
socialist thought of Fourier, Saint-Simon, Bazard, Enfantin, Cabet, Proudhon, of Owen and others, many among them looked "with the greatest sympathy" upon Russia's own "commune, *mir* and *artel*'."[28]

But though there was doubtless a point of contact between the Moscow
Slavophils and many of the Petrashevtsy on the question of these old Russian peasant institutions as well as on the desire for the end of serfdom, on
the higher level of the ideologies there could be no common ground between
the Slavophils and most of the Petrashevtsy. For whereas to the Moscow
Slavophils, Samarin specifically, the Russian peasant commune was illuminated by Orthodox *sobornost'*, to Petrashevsky, who referred to "the
famous demagogue Christ who ended his career rather unsuccessfully,"[29] it
was a purely secular institution. Herzen, too, saw the *mir,* commune, and
artel' as social secular developments not confined to the Slavs or Russians.
Nonetheless, in spite of their basic irreconcilable convictions the Slavophils,
Petrashevsky, and Herzen were all distrustful of the course of Western
economic, social and political evolution that was producing the generally
dreaded industrial proletariat.

From the perspective of the end of the twentieth century it is temptingly
easy to pontificate about the fear and dislike of the phenomenon of the
proletariat experienced in the 1840s by the wealthy landowning Slavophils
as well as by the radical Petrashevtsy, and by a variety of utopian socialists
in the West and in Russia. Though the new industrialism, especially in
England where it was most advanced, was spurred on by a laissez-faire ideology that played into the hands of the relatively few self-seeking
entrepreneurs and simultaneously "harassed and brutalized" thousands of

factory workers, young and old, it was the proletariat, not the entrepreneurs, who were looked upon as the blight of society. The proletariat that Marx soon proclaimed the savior of its own class, and of humanity, had acquired an ambiguous status. The Slavophils feared it and thought that it was not inevitable for Russia. Herzen, and Chernyshevsky in the 1850s, although denouncing Slavophil Orthodoxy, wrote, like the Slavophils, of the "ulcer of the proletariat" or of "proletarianism" (*iazva proletariatstva*).[30] During the 1850s they all hoped to avoid the "ulcer" in Russia. They all agreed that this was to come about through the *obshchina,* the village commune, but just how was never very clear. What would lead Russia to socialism through the existing commune at the time of the relentless march of industrial capitalism?

In the case of the Slavophils, the path wa especially obscure. Khomiakov and later Ivan Aksakov dreamed of an "industrial phalanstery" but for the peasants only. The village commune, despite all the Slavophils' glorification of it, was to remain a peasant institution while they themselves not only clung to their private estates but, in the case of Khomiakov and Koshelev, branched out into capitalistic entrepreneurship, as for instance in sugar refining. The commune was good for peasants and for Russia, but the gentry would in effect stay out of it, and above it. If this work had been conceived as a study in human consistency rather than of ideas it would have ended some time ago.

Marx, of course, saw the industrial proletariat in quite a different way. Instead of fearing it and despairing of it, he conceived it as an inevitable and irresistible force destined to play a universal emancipatory role. He and Engels proclaimed this and a good deal more in the famous *Communist Manifesto* published in London in February 1848. It is doubtful, however, that the *Manifesto,* appearing at the outbreak of the revolutions of 1848–1849 in the West, could have produced much of an immediate impression in Russia, though not because it was not allowed in Russia.[31] In fact for a few years before the *Manifesto* was drafted a small group of Russian emigres and visitors to Paris and Brussels were in touch with Marx and other radical thinkers in the West. Among those in the middle 1840s in Paris were M. A. Bakunin, N. I. Sazonov, a member of the Herzen circle in Moscow of the 1830s, Herzen's closest friend, N. P. Ogarev (who was in Western Europe between 1841 and 1846 and then left Russia permanently for the West in 1856), V. P. Botkin, P. V. Annenkov, and G. M. Tolstoy, a Kazan aristocrat who "promised Marx that he would sell his possessions and give him the proceeds," but did not carry out his promise.[32]

The relationship between Karl Marx and a few Russian liberally and radically inclined young men must be confined here to the subject of the Western proletariat: what did the young Russians, specifically the Slavophils, know about it in the 1840s and 1850s, the period of primary concern in these studies? What awareness, if any, had they of Marx's conception of the proletariat, and its role as he saw it in England? What was its universal significance as conceived by Marx and Engels? Any answers to these questions, however tentative, would have to take into account certain basic and unavoidable facts.

When the *Communist Manifesto* appeared, English and Russian societies differed markedly. In England the two feudal classes, the aristocracy and the peasants, had by 1848 been joined by the bourgeoisie and in numerical strength were being overshadowed by it, and even more by the rapidly swelling ranks of the proletariat. In contrast, Russian society was still basically feudal in it structure and stratification, with the vast majority of the impoverished peasantry, many of them serfs, at the bottom, and the numerically small but dominant class of landowners on top. The bourgeoisie and the industrial proletariat were in their incipient stage.

The few young Russians who made contact with Marx and Engels in the 1840s and 1850s belonged to the loosely designated Westerners-Annenkov, for example, was a liberal, nonrevolutionary Westerner; Bakunin as early as the 1840s became established as a radical revolutionary Westerner. Although the early Slavophils were interested in the West and its rapidly changing economic, social, and political life and were keenly conscious of the revolutions of 1848 and 1849, they did not make contact with Marx-not in their travels nor, it seems, in print. They all had traveled in the West, some of them extensively; some had attended a university there.[33] Certainly they were aware of the profound changes that were occurring in the Western economic, social, and political order. But to the Slavophils, and indeed to educated Russia in general, the news from Western Europe, on the surface at any rate, had a certain irrelevance, simply because modern industrialism had scarcely made a dent in the Russian economy, and even more important and more pressing than this was the problem of serfdom, which as the Crimean War was soon to illustrate, was the millstone around Russia's neck.[34]

Any concerted and coordinated Slavophil effort in behalf of emancipation of the serfs in the early 1850s was out of the question even if they could have attained complete concurrence of views. Furthermore, within the Slavophil camp a certain regrouping occurred, although as usual in Slavophil affairs, it was informal and rather spontaneous. From the early 1850s through the reform of 1861 the Slavophil leaders in the struggle for emancipation were young Samarin, Koshelev, thirteen years his senior, and Prince V. A. Cherkassky (1824–1878), properly characterized, as "close" to the Slavophils.[35] Both Kireevsky brothers died in 1856, while emancipation was becoming an urgent issue, and neither Konstantin Aksakov nor Khomiakov both of whom died in 1860, was prominently involved in the emancipation. Whether or not Cherkassky was "heart and soul" a Slavophil has been debated.

Koshelev, who raised the question in his memoirs (*Zapiski*), denied him Slavophil status, regardless of his work on the emancipation reform. Looking back on this period in the 1860s and 1870s, Koshelev said, "Although later he [Cherkassky] was often considered a so-called Slavophil, and has even been placed at the head of this party, he has never been such, and differed from us on the most essential convictions." Specifically, Cherkassky denied the cardinal tenets of early or Moscow Slavophilism: "He did not at all consider the Orthodox teaching of Christ as the basis or our world view, he ceaselessly declared himself against the village commune, and he liked to sneer at the people-as idol [*narod-kumir*], before whom in his opinion Khomiakov and K. Aksakov bowed down." Why, and how then could Cherkassky ever be mistaken for a Slavophil? Koshelev's answer was: "Cherkassky as an admirably wise man acknowledged that in our orientation there was more strength and future than in the opposite, Western orientation."[36] It could be added that Cherkassky, a titled landowner, seems to have found the Slavophil gentry more congenial company than the Moscow Westerners.

Samarin's brief experience in 1853 in managing the family lands merely accentuated his awareness of the emancipation question. Clearly, the growing peasant and serf unrest was to the land-owning and serf-holding Slavophils a most ominous development that threatened not only their possessions but also their lives. Also, the heavy dependency of Russian agriculture on serf labor, and the state of the Russian economy in general, as the Crimean War was daily illustrating, showed how dangerously outdated the country was as compared with the West in science, technology, and modernization. When Samarin began to draft his first memorandum on emancipation of the serfs, in the fall of 1853, as Nol'de surmised, he and the other Slavophils were convinced that serfdom had to end. In great part their concern was based on self-interest, and they were determined that serfdom should be abolished from "above," by peaceful, legal means. They disliked and feared revolutions, and that of course had something to do not only with their economic interests but, even more basically, with an instinct for physical self-preservation and survival.

Yet to say that this, and this alone, motivated the Slavophils to take so prominent a part in the emancipation of the serfs is to neglect other considerations. They were discussing the problem during the 1840s when the issue did not appear nearly so pressing for solution as it became in the middle 1850s. More revealing than this is the fact that in 1852–1853 Khomiakov, Ivan Kireevsky, Koshelev, and Konstantin and Ivan Aksakov conducted a vigorous epistolary discussion of religious, ethical, cultural, and social issues that included ideas on the way Christian ethics impinge upon the question of the emancipation of the serfs. All this and more entered the debates conducted in the "parliament of the Moscow parlors."

The evidence incomplete as it is (for reasons not only of archival difficulties but also of the unrecorded salon discussions) points to a condition in the Slavophil circle during the first half of the 1850s where the emancipation issue could be seen not as simply one of crass economic interest of the landowner. It was also one of a Christian, ethical nature, of concern for Russia's economy, and its national future in general, and as a way to soften the class conflict between landowners and peasants.[37] In addition, the question of timing entered into the Slavophil motivation. The Crimean War was seen as the ultimate proof of the bankruptcy of the serf-permeated order in Russia, and of the inevitability of its abolition. In their views of and desire for emancipation during the 1840s, and well into the 1850s, the Slavophils were ahead of many Russians including the government of Nicholas I, in advocating emancipation. But the Slavophils were sufficiently in tune with the secularist temper of the time in the West and in Russia, to have no illusions that the emancipation reform could be conceived in terms other that social-economic, and political. They left their religious Orthodox considerations out of the public's view.

One point to remember is that until the tsar's edict on the necessity of emancipation of August 20, 1857, which at last made it possible to talk openly of emancipation, the Slavophils had to sidestep the censorship on Slavophil publications by making tactical common cause from time to time with the radical Chernyshevsky, who aired his views in *Sovremennik,* and also with the radical Herzen, who was publishing his famous *Kolokol* in London. The emancipation edict added vigor to their cause and allowed them the opportunity to state their views on how the emancipation of the serfs should best be carried out.

Samarin's participation in the emancipation reform of 1862 is perhaps the best-known aspect of his biography. Certainly it has been emphasized in works published in this century, by Nol'de, by Riasanovsky in his discussion of the Slavophils, and by Dudzinskaia in her recent (1983) treatise on the Slavophils, which concentrates on the second half of the 1850s and the emancipation reform. From this distance it would be difficult to add anything new on Samarin's role in the reform movement in Russia in the decade from the mid-1850s to the mid-1860s. Yet in regard to early, "classical" or Moscow Slavophilism, Samarin's contribution to the emancipation movement is an indispensable last link in the chain of Slavophil thought and action: from the highest level, in their case religion, Orthodoxy (rather than philosophy characteristic of Western secularism) through ideology, to the third and final level of action or reformism. Partly as a matter of external circumstances, the fact that the Kireevsky brothers died in 1856, and Khomiakov and Konstantin Aksakov in 1860 and partly because of personal and temperamental characteristics Samarin, is best known for his practical reformism. But as pointed out earlier, he was not unmindful of the two upper levels of Moscow Slavophilism: its ultimate justification — Orthodoxy, and its ideology.

Samarin finished his lengthy memorandum on the serf question in the spring of 1854; the writing had begun the previous fall, but since as usual the Moscow gentry left the city for their country estates and dachas for the summer, it was not until early in 1855 that, as Vera Aksakova has told us, Samarin went to the Aksakov Abramtsevo estate to share his thoughts on emancipation with his fellow Slavophils. "After the reading" of the memorandum Vera says, "there was much conversation and interpretation."[38] Thus while the memorandum was Samarin's work, he saw to it that it was submitted to the judgment of the other Slavophils. It is, however, more difficult to know whether he eventually received their complete concurrence. Although the government had not yet declared its position in favor of emancipation, the fiasco of the Crimean War was accompanied by new peasant unrest, and also much soul searching together with spontaneous expressions in favor of emancipation.[39] It is not therefore surprising that Koshelev and Cherkassky also drafted emancipation projects, as well as such liberal Westerners as Kavelin, the conservative and Poltava landowner M. P. Posen, and others.

All these emancipation projects or memoranda had an extralegal if not illegal character, since the government had not yet declared in favor of emancipation, and for the same reason, their authors had to rely on voluntary agreements between landowner and serfs. Like these, Samarin's first, and lengthy memorandum (120 pages), as well as the four shorter ones (53 pages), written in August 1857, advocate that emancipation, if at all feasible, had to rely on private, sporadic, and usually uncoordinated agreements between a landowner and his serfs.[40]

The first memorandum, (and its revision on which Samarin worked intermittently for several years) bears the title, "About the Condition of Serfdom and the Transition from that Condition to Civil Liberty." It is divided into nearly two dozen sections of varying length and importance. Samarin starts by confirming the conviction, prevalent in educated Russia, that the Crimean War was being lost on the home front rather than on the battlefield. "We must turn to ourselves and investigate the root causes of our weakness," Samarin begins: "Not in Vienna, not in Paris, and not in London but only inside Russia are we going to win anew the place that belongs to us in the assembly of European nations." And the major obstacle to Russia's internal renewal and strength, he adds, is serfdom. Russia could not hope for any "internal rejuvenation" without first ridding itself of serfdom.[41] Convinced that the issue of emancipation had reached "complete maturity," Samarin called for "firm will" on the part of the government and for the cooperation of the classes most intimately concerned with the problem. Since the muted serfs remained outside the solution of this or any other public issue (except for sporadic peasant uprisings), Samarin was in effect appealing to his own landowning class to take an active part in abolishing serfdom.

These, general introductory remarks are followed by the first section, subtitled "The influence of serfdom on public morality." Declaring serfdom an "undoubted evil" he condemned a bureaucratic pronouncement in 1852 in which "Texts from the Scripture were cited in favor of serfdom." The government came in for more criticism when he denounced its attitude toward emancipation, discussion of which he said, is persecuted by the censor with merciless severity."[42]

If Samarin had ever entertained Konstantin Aksakov's idyllic notions of a communal peasant order in Russia, he showed no traces of them in his memorandum. His recent taste of estate management may have stripped away any lingering illusions about the exalted character of the peasantry in general, and of the landowner as a kindly father of a family of serfs. He tried to dispel any notions of a benevolent patriarchal relationship between landlords and serfs. Declaring his purpose to be "neither to accuse nor to exonerate" but only to clarify existing relationships, he had no doubts that the "landowner enjoys almost unlimited and unaccountable authority of the father in the family, [but that] the peasants see in him not a father, but a natural enemy and would tear themselves away from him" at the first opportunity.[43] In the middle of this relationship, and maintaining it, was the much maligned civil servant or *chinovnik*. The government could not disregard the civil service or the gentry, (also in command of the army) the twin props of its autocratic power.

The status, position, and authority of the "sovereign" landowner enabled him to intrude into every phase of the life of the serfs, including their family relations. The serfs in turn saw the landlord's authority "as a heavy necessity, as violence, the way once Russia submitted to the dominion of the Mongols." Such a relationship could lead to nothing other than to "dissimulation, deceit, and flattery." In this poisoned and degraded atmosphere, "The clever peasant plays the fool in the presence of his master, the truthful peasant unconscionably lies straight to his face, while the honest peasant steals from him, and all three call him their father."[44]

Russia had suffered grave and debilitating effects from serfdom, and their repercussions were felt in every important phase of private and public life, one of the most crucial of which was in its "good political order." Although he knew that serfdom had existed in the West — "in certain lands until not so long ago" — Samarin was convinced that "it was nowhere so historically unlawful as among us."[45]

Politically this was "both harmful and dangerous." But he moved onto less certain historical ground when he theorized about the origin of the state. In the West, he says, the state emerged from the animosity "between tribes, classes, and political parties" with the consequent struggles and the "enslavement of one class of the population by another.... Not so in Russia." This fundamental Slavophil conviction, based more on preconceived notions than on painstaking investigation of the early period in the formation of the modern state, led the Slavophils to a number of idiosyncratic conclusions. The most portentous of these was their conviction that Russia had always followed, and should continue to follow, a path different from that of the Western nation states. Clearly implied here is the Slavophil denial of a universal law of political or state evolution valid for all states.

Samarin argued that Russia was an undivided nation in which in the past, and up to the present, all "classes" supported the tsar, and that every Russian, however far from the throne, "sees himself in the Russian Tsar." In contrast, the French peasant could not but be estranged from the throne, because "Francis [I] was the first courtier of France" and "Louis Phillipe was the Citizen-King."[46] Such specious argumentation on a basic political problem with wide-ranging social and religious implications of course tends to confuse and conceal the complexities and fluctuations, down the centuries, in the relationship between tsar and people. For if every peasant saw himself in the Russian tsar, why were the government of Nicholas I, the gentry, and Samarin himself fearful of another *Pugachevshchina*?

Samarin did not see eye to eye on these matters with Khomiakov, Ivan Kireevsky, and Konstantin Aksakov. "State authority," he declared, "with all its obligations, and with all its moral responsibilities to the whole nation, can neither be alienated nor divided."[47] The more idealistically inclined Slavophils— and this certainly included Konstantin Aksakov—stumbled over attempts to reconcile the authority of the tsar-autocrat with the notion of the tsar as the benevolent servant of the all-wise people (*narod*). Furthermore the Slavophils had to face mid-nineteenth-century Russian reality, and their own gentry interest in law and order.

The centuries-old and unresolved problem of the relationship between church and state or religious and temporal authority appeared in a particularly sharp form in Russia during the reign of tsar Alexsei (1645–1676). There was the Latin or Catholic notion that the "clergy is above the temporal power," or in the free exegetic English translation of Professor Alexander V. Solov'ev's "Sviataia Rus'" (Holy Russia), "the priesthood like the sun was higher than the temporal power—the moon."[48] In a succinct, factual, and lucid manner Solov'ev deals with the notions first of Holy Russia, and then with the emergence after the fall of Constantinople to the Turks in the middle of the fifteenth century, of the related view of Moscow, the Third Rome. Both of these basically religious convictions acquired over the centuries deeply Orthodox messianic content and power, the implications of which affected not only Russian religious life but also its socio-political internal order, and by the nineteenth century Russian diplomatic relations and foreign policy.[49] This was most striking in the case of the liberation of some of the Orthodox South Slavs from the Turks, and in demands in Russia for the liberation of Constantinople from Ottoman rule.

Internally, as Professor Solov'ev has shown, the rejuvenation of the notions of Holy Russia and Moscow the Third Rome occurred early in the nineteenth century. This took place under the influence of the Romantic Movement and the Napoleonic wars, both of which provided a powerful impulse in Russia for Russian nationalism and incipient Moscow Slavophilism.[50] "The traditions of Holy Russia that faded and became forgotten" during the reign of Peter the Great and the remainder of the eighteenth century were revived in the nineteenth century, which in Solov'ev's words

> saw the rebirth in the official ideology, as well as in the political religious literature, of the dream of Russia's greatest perfection as a truly Christian state, and also to a rebirth of the dream of its special providential purpose. Russian thought became deeply involved in the historical task of the fatherland, concerning its bright ideal of Holy Russia, and as in the earlier epoch so also now . . . the ideal and the actual are very far [apart].

Western romanticism, particularly in its English and German forms, left a deep mark both on Russian literature and on early Slavophilism. Its stimulation of interest in the Middle Ages, among other things, was reflected in Slavophil speculation on communal social organization of Russian society. "According to Khomiakov's teaching," A. V. Solov'ev says, "Orthodoxy of itself conditions the special universal mission for Russia." This "thought and mood" he also finds "in the three representatives of the Slavophil teaching— in Khomiakov, Dostoevsky, and Vladimir S. Solov'ev. Their example could show us how closely bound up Russian religious-social thought of the nineteenth century was with the basic channel of the people's ancient consciousness."[51]

Chapter 4 in Cherniavsky's *Tsar and People,* under the title "Holy Russia" based, in his words, on his earlier article on the same theme, begins with a quotation from Dostoevsky: "The Russian *narod* is the God-bearer." This was a somewhat later entry of Dostoevsky into the controversy about the true character and quality of the Russian people, usually conceived in this context as the common people, the *narod.* The question as to whether the Russian people were the "God-bearers" or the most godless came to a head in the late 1840s, toward the end of Belinsky's life, when, while sick in Salzbrunn in the summer of 1847 he wrote his famous letter to Gogol'. There are perhaps few subjects that lend themselves so easily to endless and unresolvable controversy as the religiousness (or its absence) of a vast, historical nation.

Despite sample tests, statistics, questionnaires, and computers, even today science has yet to give us a reliable method of ascertaining and measuring the religiosity of a single person at a given time much less of a large and complex nation. In the summer of 1847 when Gogol' and Belinsky pondered the question of the religiousness of the Russian people, personal preference, opinion, and conviction determined the "truth" of one's position. "In your opinion," Belinsky wrote to Gogol', "the Russian people [*narod*] is the most religious people in the world: that's a lie!" If you look carefully, he said "you will see that by its very nature this is a deeply atheistic *narod*. There is still much superstition in them but there is not even a trace of religiousness." In France, there were "many sincere, fanatical Catholics among enlightened and educated people, and many who have become detached from Christianity, but still stand steadfastly for some sort of God"; but "[The] Russian *narod* is not such. Mystical exaltation is not in its nature. It has too much common sense for this."[52]

At the end of the 1840s we see on the one hand the Slavophils and those for whom the ideas of Holy Russia and Moscow the Third Rome supported their conviction as to the profound Orthodoxy and true Christianity of the Russian nation, together with its Christian mission. In addition to Gogol' and the Slavophils, among those who in later decades expressed this conviction were Dostoevsky and Vladimir Solov'ev, and perhaps also Tolstoy, each in his own way. On the opposite side in the divided Russian intelligentsia stood Belinsky, Herzen, Chernyshevsky, and Dobroliubov in the 1840s and 1850s. Neither side had more than its own convictions and preferences to back up its position; each selected the facts and arguments that could strengthen its ideological stand and avoided those that did not. The most visible evidence, although incomplete, imperfect, and perhaps insufficient, of Russia's Orthodoxy through the centuries, are the thousands of monastic, parish, and other Orthodox churches and shrines constructed throughout the vast land, and the faith that inspired certain extraordinary works of art, architecture, and iconography.[53] And however one may judge the Old Believers, millions of them were willing to endure denunciation, persecution, and even immolation for the sake of their Christian faith. Clearly, myths, whether secular or religious, such as those of Holy Russia and Moscow the Third Rome, are based on faith and commitment not on scientific proof.

While Samarin was away from Moscow during the late 1840s and early 1850s Khomiakov and Ivan Kireevsky brought to a head their differences concerning ancient Russian society. Khomiakov stressed his well-known conviction that "Western life was founded on one-sided reason and on the division of basic principles (antithesis of freedom and unity)," a corollary to the division within Western society as Kireevsky said, of "conquerors and conquered."[54] But in the Holy Russia of the Slavophils such a division was inadmissible. In Khomiakov's paraphrase "The peculiarity of ancient Russia lay in the very fullness and purity . . . of its Christian teaching, . . . *in the complete sweep of its public and private life.*"[55]

This is as far as the agreement between Khomiakov and Kireevsky went. For whereas Kireevsky defended an idealized view of ancient Rus', Khomiakov objected to Kireevsky's conviction that "The Christian teaching was expressed in its purity and fullness in the whole realm of the ancient Russian order, both public and private." Two different types of "formalism" soon appeared in Russia and the West to vitiate the Christian order. In Russia it was "a formality of ritual whereas in the West it was a juridical or rationalistic formality." In Russia, Khomiakov added, by the sixteenth and seventeenth centuries this "one-sidedness" was exemplified in the career of Ivan IV and in the church schism.

In contrast, in 1852 Kireevsky, perhaps carried away by the concept of Holy Russia, was unrestrained in his glorification of ancient Rus'. "In it," he insisted, "there were neither conquerors nor conquered. It knew neither the ironclad divisions of immobile classes, nor advantages for one that were a detriment to another; neither class contempt, nor class hatred, nor class envy. Therefore it did not know the unavoidable birth of this struggle."[56] Yet as Cherniavsky aptly observed, Khomiakov was not completely immune to the idealization of Holy Russia. Further on in the same article Khomiakov, comparing rural, simple, and unspoiled early Russia with the highly organized, legalistic, and often turbulent Byzantium (from which Russian Orthodoxy had come), reached the conclusion that, thanks to its lofty Christian spirituality, Russia "has risen not only higher than Byzantium but higher than all the countries of Europe."[57] When Khomiakov and Konstantin Aksakov donned what they thought was old Russian peasant dress they were trying to show the outward signs of their identification with the *narod,* the embodiment and guardian of Holy Russia.

While the two older Slavophils, Khomiakov and Ivan Kireevsky, were engaged in a largely theoretical controversy about the character and virtues of Russia's ancient public order, Samarin had his feet planted firmly in the peasant soil of Russia. He was trying to formulate a solution to the problem of serfdom that threatened to tear apart the fabric of Russian society. In a rational systematic manner in his *Zapiska* he outlined the basic relationships between tsar, *narod,* or people, the gentry, and the government civil service. Yet even Samarin's relatively factual and hardheaded approach was not completely free of Slavophil fictions that tended to obscure certain basic facts and relationships in Russia's past. Thus he saw the nobility (*dvorianstvo*) as intruding upon the relationship between tsar and people. "The nobility," he said, "severed the common people from the Tsar. Standing athwart them it screens off the *narod* from the Tsar and does not admit to him the people's grievances and hopes." In spite of this the "Tsar from his height looks upon the people with love, and has for long been thinking of its salvation." In turn "the people do not believe in intermediaries. In its notions Tsar and government never merge."[58]

Among the early Slavophils, Khomiakov and Konstantin Aksakov exemplify the dominant role in Moscow Slavophilism of the myth of the people as against another, and perhaps older, myth of the ruler conceived as "saint-ruler," "saint-prince," or God-Prince."[59] But the schism of the seventeenth century and the reign of Peter the Great changed the image of the new emperor in the eyes of the Old Believers to that of Anti-Christ. The early Slavophils cannot be mistaken for Old Believers, yet their cool and critical though not completely negative view of Peter the Great may have strengthened in them the myth of the *narod*. At any rate, this myth reinforced a basic and powerful current in Slavophil thought, particularly when it is seen in conjunction with the myth of Holy Russia. In one brief statement quoted by Alexander Solov'ev, Khomiakov asserted, "We received [our] faith from the purest source, and founded a state on the favorable development of the *mir* communes, and not on the savage brute force of military bands."[60]

Thus Khomiakov claimed for Russian Orthodoxy (not a new Slavophil claim) a more genuine source of Christianity than for the Western confessions. He associated the origin of the Russian state with the early Russian form of communal organization. The Moscow Slavophils saw once again a firm bond between the principles of communality (*obshchinnost'*) and *sobornost'* – unity in love, freedom, and harmony. And from this comes their denial, Khomiakov's in this instance, of force and compulsion in the formation of the Russian state. These myths, together with that of the "Russian soul," are in turn associated with the myths of Holy Russia and the *narod*. Khomiakov accepted them, and also held the kindred belief in the presumed meakness and humility of the people (*narod*), who were also peace loving and God fearing. Yet he was not blind to their normal human weaknesses and their sinfulness.

Khomiakov, like Tiutchev, and later Dostoevsky, while entertaining the myth of Holy Russia, had no difficulty seeing the darker side of the Russian, and of man in general. In prose, and more eloquently in verse, specifically in his well-known *To Russia*, which caused considerable furor during the Crimean War, he lashed out at Russian reality, at its law courts for tolerating "dark injustice," for the "yoke of slavery," for "Godless flattery, pernicious lies," for "deadly indolence," and for all sort of other "abominations." Yet Russia was still the chosen one. Sergei Aksakov exclaimed, "What wonderful verses Khomiakov has written.!" And his younger son Ivan, three years later, could write home from the provinces about the "'stinking swamp' of Russian provincial life" where "continuous abomination, oppression, slavery, vileness" could completely absorb and destroy human beings.[61] As we have already seen, Samarin's reaction to Russian country life at about the same time was similar to Ivan Aksakov's. One can therefore understand A.

V. Solov'ev's quandary that the "chosenness of Russia compellingly fills the hearts of the Slavophils with inexplicable pride despite their preaching of humility,"[62] and, it should be added, despite their awareness and admission of the darker side of Russian life, and of life in general.

But the early Slavophils were not alone in this inconsistency. So were also those whom A. V. Solov'ev designates as the "second-generation Slavophils," of whom the most prominent were Vladimir Solov'ev and Dostoevsky. Pushing into the background the notion of Holy Russia "as a distant task," the Slavophils became enticed by "Russia's greatness and its national peculiarities. This process we can [also] trace to Dostoevsky's sermons, particularly in the *Diary of a Writer,*" dating mostly from the mid 1870s.[63] In A. V. Solov'ev's summary, Dostoevsky, taking as his starting point Khomiakov's convictions, came to two principal conclusions: the "aim of Russia was complete service to mankind, [*veseluzhenie chelovechestvu*]," and that Russia should act as the "guardian of Christ's truth." This role is somewhat easier to concede to Dostoevsky in the 1870s than to Khomiakov, who died while serfdom was still in existence in Russia. But as has happened in history more than once, both before and after the Slavophils and Dostoevsky, any one contemplating this sort of an assignment and mission stands at the top of a steeply inclined plane. The descent into a possible morass is uncontrollable, and often unpredictable as to its course.

In the words of A. V. Solov'ev, "The first step on the road to service" for Russia, "in its foreign policy—was the liberation and unification of the Slavs." As we shall see when we look briefly into the Slav world in the second half of the nineteenth century, this was a more complex and intractable problem than even Dostoevsky's genius could conceive. Dreams and unwarranted assumptions prompted him to entertain the thought that all "Russians wish the resurrection of the Slavs," all of whom, except the Russians, Serbians, and Montenegrins, were then under foreign rule. He assumed that, like himself, all Russians wished for all Slavs "complete personal freedom and the resurrection of their spirit," and that "Russia is the natural magnet that irresistibly draws to itself the Slavs thereby sustaining their wholeness and unity." This of course ignores the wishes of the Western Slavs, particularly the Poles. The first step in Dostoevsky's dream of all-Slav unification, which historically the Slavs had never before known, was the conquest of Constantinople from the Turks. "For this purpose Constantinople, sooner or later must be ours."[64] This was said when Turkey the "sick man of Europe," was not quite so sick as was often believed in the West, when English and French imperialist circles, particularly after the victory over Russia in the Crimean War, had not given up hope of conquering Constantinople, and not many years before German imperialism would dream of a Berlin-to-Baghdad railway.

Like Khomiakov, Dostoevsky was not altogether insensitive to reality. Konstantin Aksakov could say that "Russian history reads like the lives of the Saints," and Dostoevsky could proclaim the Russian people "God-bearers," but on calmer reflection he could also declare that "our people [*narod*] is sinful and coarse: beastly is its image." And in A. V. Solov'ev's words, Dostoevsky "in his novels more penetratingly than all others measured the depth of the Sodomite abyss in the soul of the Russian." But here once more the cult of the *narod* intrudes in Dostoevsky's Russian dichotomy, for "whatever moments of revolt against God the individual Russian might experience, the Russian *narod* as a whole, just the same, goes its own way—the way of the sufferer, and the God-bearer."[65] One is tempted to read here a Slavophil-Dostoevskian version of Rousseau's call for a return to nature.

On the crucial question of the relationship between tsar and people, an integral part of the ideal of Holy Russia, Samarin in the mid-fifties, and Dostoevsky two decades later, seemed to come quite close. Samarin asserted in his *Zapiska,* as mentioned, that every Russian "sees himself in the Russian Tsar"; Dostoevsky stated, "for the people [*narod*] the Tsar is the personification of itself, all its ideas, hopes, and beliefs." This same stream of thought is also discernable in Gogol's controversial *Selected Passages from Correspondence with Friends* (1847), in which the conception of the tsar is embodied in a "mystical and supra-juridical principle." Without mentioning the Slavophils, A. V. Solov'ev concluded in his remarks on Dostoevsky that the "truly Christian, patriarchal relationship of Tsar to people" seen on the "meta-juridical level" makes possible the "raising of the edifice of Holy Russia wherein the eternal norms of the Gospel would be established in the foundation of all political and human relations."[66]

In the section of the *Zapiska* dealing with the effects of serfdom Samarin has a good deal to say about the political administrative structure of Russia. The nobility, including those in service, like the civil servants, from the lowest rank to the "full general," and not excluding the state-supported clergy, all these "government persons" occupying the middle ground between the "simple peasant and the Tsar are suspect in the eyes of the *narod.*" "The Tsar, who for long has thought of giving [the *narod*] the desired freedom," in the opinion of the same *narod,* was being frustrated by other classes and interests. But Samarin concluded, "three hundred thousand landowners are, not without grounds, alarmed by the expectation of a frightful revolution. Eleven million serfs are firmly convinced of the existence of an obscure and long-standing conspiracy of the nobility against Tsar and *narod.*"[67]

If Samarin could find no comfort or hope for Russia in the political and administrative effects of serfdom on Russian society, the next, longer, section of the *Zapiska,* devoted to the "Influence of serfdom on the national economy" gave him even less cause for satisfaction. Relying in part on the

French translation of J. S. Mill's *Principles of Political Economy,* and on other Western sources, he affirmed the greater productivity of free (or freer) labor, as contrasted to forced labor. Thus he cited an article in *Zemledel'cheskii zhurnal* of 1834 in which *barshchina,* compulsory serf labor (usually three days a week), was compared with the freer *obrok* or quit rent obligation paid in cash. His conclusion was that the *obrok* peasant had a considerable economic advantage over the *barshchina* peasant. For the forced laborer, "there were no incentives other than fear," and he cited an article of 1843 in which the author concluded, "The peasant rule [of thumb] on *barshchina* labor was: the less and the worse, the better."[68]

The condition of the *barshchina* serfs was actually worse than it appeared, because the days of the week that were left free for their own work "are not only not protected by formal law from the forcible encroachment by the landlord, but also not by custom, which in many cases among us is stricter and more moral than the law. The concepts of peasant property are so vacillating, so vague, and so arbitrary" that the serf is at the complete mercy of the landowner.[69] Reflecting on the recent revolutions in France, in 1848 and 1849, Samarin took a rather tolerant view of the brief socialist experiment. It was not up to Russians "to throw stones at the socialists." No more in favor of revolutions than before, he concluded that with respect to labor, "The whole difference lies in this, that the socialists hoped to bind it with the voluntary agreement of the masses whereas we are satisfied with their forced submission."

Samarin was not optimistic about the future of agriculture in Russia — although his older Slavophil friends, Khomiakov and Koshelev, were carefully following Western mechanical inventions and agricultural machinery and looking for a brighter future. Samarin wondered why the Russian landowner should expend large sums on modern agricultural equipment when serf "labor and time do not represent for the Russian landlord definite value."[70] The landlord would have to maintain his serfs even if machinery did most of the field work.[71] The simple unavoidable conviction with which of course Khomiakov and Koshelev agreed was that serfdom stood in the way of the modernization of Russian agriculture. To improve that agriculture and increase its productivity would require large capital investments, and considerable scientific and technological expertise, both of which are slow and costly to acquire. And as long as serfdom prevailed there was little that anyone could do to raise the productivity and the standard of living of the Russian peasantry, at the time more than 90 percent of Russia's population.

But even in countries like England, which was in the vanguard of scientific-technological improvements in agriculture and had a considerable accumulation of capital fueling its industrial revolution, the problem was not simple. As large numbers of English farmers were replaced by machinery in the fields and landholdings were consolidated, unemployed and impoverished agricultural workers flocked to the new industrial centers where they swelled the growing city slums. This new mass of people, the emerging proletariat, was a challenge to the industrial age and is still obviously a force that is very much with us. The task of modernizing Russia's farming and economy after emancipation proved to be considerably more complex and difficult than it probably appeared to Samarin and the other Slavophils at the time, yet there could be no question in their minds that the end of serfdom in Russia could no longer be postponed, and that it was the indispensable starting point for any basic improvement in Russian life and agriculture.

The Slavophil conviction that there was more than one way of solving a problem — a "Western" way and a "Russian," Slavophil way — entered into Samarin's consideration of agriculture. Many Russian landowners he said, dazzled by the "brilliant successes" of English and German farming, became enticed into "blind imitation of Western models." They began to talk about introducing in Russia "a breed of tall cattle, improved tools," and so on.[72] After the talks came experiments. Most of these were unsuccessful and tended to discourage confidence in science and technology in general. Of course the situation in Russia was full of peculiarities and complexities that made indiscriminate Western transplants onto Russian soil futile and disappointing, and Samarin concluded that the failures in the use of Western-type farming in Russia ought to be followed by the "study of the distinguishing peculiarities of our village husbandry" in all its aspects in order to find our what stood in the way of the "application of foreign theories" to Russian agriculture. Only when "basic differences" in agriculture between Russia and the West were fully taken into account could the "science of village husbandry be firmly established on our soil, and enter a period of independent development."

Samarin seemed quite aware of the capriciousness of the geographic and climatic factors in Russian agriculture, but the economic, social, and ethical characteristics and problems are what stand out in his *Zapiska*. High on the list of problems was the scarcity of "working capital" and he concluded that the modernization of Russian agriculture would have to await emancipation of the serfs.[73] This touches on a cardinal Slavophil tenet, on the principle of communality, and on the historical Russian peasant commune. "Every industry including agriculture," Samarin declared, must meet three related conditions: "material given by nature, capital, and labor." He defined capital as the "saved up fruit of former human efforts." Moreover, since the "productiveness of labor is in direct proportion to the freedom of the laborer," the productiveness of the landlord's estates could be improved only through free labor, which would make possible accumulation of capital by the landlord, who then could invest in the improvement of his agriculture and manufacturing.[74]

Such mid-nineteenth-century capitalistic enterprise as conceived by the Slavophils was only the explicitly stated part of their scheme. Since they insisted on the preservation of the village commune, the question of its productiveness after emancipation loomed in the background. Whether considering it in its traditional economic functions as an agricultural unit or as a possible industrial commune, a phalianstery, as in Khomiakov's dreams, rationalization of its productivity would require considerable capital. Where would it come from, who would control it, and who would use it? The *mir* possibly? Samarin did not dwell on these questions.

Speaking for himself and by implication for "enlightened landowners" in general, Samarin stated that "together with the consciousness of the immorality of serfdom, its danger, and its harmful economic consequences," certain unfortunate and undesirable thoughts were in circulation — that the conditions of the serfs were "improving daily," that there was no need for legislative action, and that the matter would be resolved in a "natural and peaceful manner." In all this he saw "much truth but even more untruth."[75] For him the time for deliberate and immediate emancipation of the serfs had arrived.

In the next major section of his *Zapiska* Samarin turned to the status of the serfs conceived in terms of three principal relationships — landowner to serf, serf to landlord, and government to serfs. In the brief treatment of the first two in which he commented on the *obrok* and *barshchina* practices, pointing to *barshchina* as the more undesirable he came to two basic conclusions. He saw that serfdom *"as a right of one person over another"* was being "undermined by the softening of the mores," and even more by the "grumbling" of the serfs. On the other hand, he stressed that *"applications of serfdom to economic goals are being systematically exhausted. Personal, aimless arbitrariness kills; constant, clear pressure on the people is increasing."*[76] Only the government could alter this condition, and he expressed the hope that it would soon arrive at a peaceful solution of the problem.

The discussion of serf unrest was one of Samarin's major concerns in the *Zapiska,* and he begins it with a general query: "What is the attitude of the government to the actual question?" "What does it wish?" Should the government choose to become "locked up" with the landowners in serfdom, as in a "besieged city," with all the consequences of such a course, or should it decide on a solution of the problem?[77] Not surprisingly, Samarin chose the second course. After discussing in some detail several government measures on emancipation since 1842 that had proved ineffective, he came to the conclusion that the government had occasionally considered the matter, "it seems, in order to clear its conscience": "Instead of a gradual advance toward the realization of a deeply thought out plan, we see in its actions a certain *vacillation in various directions,"* arousing in society *"alarms* that spring up periodically."[78]

In the next section of the *Zapiska* Samarin briefly characterized several types of serfdom. On the highest rung of his scale he placed the *obrok,* quit rent, serfs; on the lowest, the household serfs, who "did not have their own husbandry" [*khoziaistvo*] and who usually had less independence than the serfs working in the fields.[79] From his early involvement in the emancipation question in the Slavophil salons of the 1840s, from his readings in political economy, and from a negative reaction to the "bird freedom" (freeing the serf without giving them any land) of the emancipation in Prussia, Samarin had acquired a deep and lasting conviction that the Russian serfs must not be left landless.

Since at the time of the writing of the *Zapiska* Samarin could not be certain of immediate action by the government, he could only suggest a number of measures that he thought would prevent deterioration of the lot of the serfs, and some that might even ameliorate their condition. Abroad, he said, serfs were freed either as individuals or as whole societies. In Russia it was necessary to use both forms, although he stressed "whole villages." In a passage that contains much essential Slavophilism Samarin stressed the central position of the *mir* and village commune in the past, and in the "ageless phenomena of the present." He referred to unnamed Russian authors who "prize our village commune as the solid material from which the Russian state was established, and who foresee in it a ready solution, prepared by life itself, for social questions that are insoluble for Western Europe."[80] At the same time he denounced those Russian Westerners who saw in the commune and *mir* obstacles to the solution of Russia's agricultural problem. For him the commune was as much the product of Russian *narodnost'* as the Russian language was.[81]

Another allusion to a sensitive Slavophil nerve came in a section of the *Zapiska* that dealt with the "inventory rules," or inventories that were worked out at the end of the 1840s in Russia's western provinces, where many of the landowners were Poles while their peasants were Ukrainian or Belorussian (that is Catholic landowners controlling Orthodox or Uniate peasants). This was, of course, a matter on which Samarin had firsthand knowledge from his work on the Bibikov Inventory Commission in Kiev. He describes an "inventory" as a "statistical description of every estate . . . containing definition of mutual rights and duties of landlord and peasants," which led to an arrangement that he characterizes as a "contract in the full sense of the word." But because the contract was concluded not by the two sides involved but by the government, it lacked the "*voluntary consent*" of the contracting parties, and it failed to satisfy either the landowner, who felt that he lost too much, or the peasant, who complained that he did not gain enough.[82]

Samarin, who was not entirely without a personal stake in the inventory system, saw it as beneficial for the peasants in the western borderlands but he made it clear that he "did not wish to see it spread" to the Great Russian *gubernias*. There he favored not a formula established by a government bureaucracy and imposed on the two parties, but a "voluntary deal" (*dobrovol'naia sdelka*), worked out by the two sides and "confirmed" by the government. The motivation behind this proposal was no less idealistic than the solution. The procedure he suggested, would, have the effect of *"binding the conscience, of stimulating consciousness of civic liberty, and of moral obligation."* The nationalistic, Orthodox sentiments aroused in Samarin during his service in the Baltic provinces a few years earlier came to the surface again. He resented the "relationship of the landlords, Poles and Latins, with the Ukrainians and Belorussians," both largely Orthodox.[83]

Toward the end of his *Zapiska* Samarin turned at considerable length (more than thirty pages) to the question of "Voluntary deals between landlords and peasants." This was the very limited but at that time almost only way to freedom for a serf, and Samarin's approach to the problem became obsolete as soon as the government declared its policy of prompt, compulsory, nationwide emancipation. There are, however, certain ideas and convictions in this section of the *Zapiska* that shed light on Samarin's later position on emancipation. Among the pertinent points are his conviction that the emancipation of the serfs could be achieved as in Prussia, peacefully, "without violent disturbances and revolutions."[84] He favored the notion (under the circumstances somewhat unrealistical) that landowners and serfs should be equally represented on any administrative body considering the problems of emancipation. On the always touchy question of taxes, fees, and other payments to the government, whether by the landowners or the "peasant society," he favored promptness and conscientiousness. In case of arrears by the peasants he would avoid "unnecessary indulgence" in order to discourage the "carelessness of the negligent payer." Considering briefly the matter of recruiting for military service, a burden borne by the serfs, and a practice often abused by the landlords, he declared himself on the side of the serfs without removing the burden from them. He would take the landowner completely out of it, and leave recruiting to the "village society."[85]

Although Samarin probably spent a good deal less time in the countryside than most of his fellow Slavophils, he seems to have had his hand on the pulse of the village. Thus he was convinced that the *"peasants patiently bear their present condition only because they are sustained by the constant expectation of a better future."* He counseled honesty and fairness for both peasants and landowners, but above all "sensible flexibility by the latter."[86] Yet neither then nor later was he willing to sacrifice what he considered the legitimate interests of the landowner, and indeed his relatively tolerant and benevolent attitude became modified under the harsh conditions of the emancipation reform. In the *Zapiska* he approved of the practice according to which sometimes wills provided for the freeing of serfs after the death of the land-

owner. But for the more usual although still not widespread practice of freeing serfs on private estates, he included a scale of payments to the landowner
varying according to age and work-life expectancy: workers from age 16–
18, 100 rubles; from 18–50, 350 rubles; from 50 to 60, 100 rubles. Wives,
mothers, unmarried daughters, brothers and sisters, children under sixteen,
and those over sixty were to be freed without redemption.[87] This provision
was not as generous as it sounded since all these categories would become
the responsibility of the freed serf, not of the landowner. The redemption
fees Samarin suggested required cash on the part of the serfs, and since most
serfs did not have cash he suggested that there could be a system of loans,
"domestic or foreign," the interest and down payments of which would be
borne by the peasants. "A similar operation," he noted, "was crowned with
complete success in Prussia. . . ."[88]

Fears of peasant violence that show up on the surface of the *Zapiska* in
several passages determine its spirit and overriding motivation. Samarin was
not completely unaware of Slavophilism's Christian roots, but the awareness
comes to him as an apparent afterthought in the conclusion of the *Zapiska*,
in relation to the practice of freeing the serfs by the provision of a landowner's will. Here he alludes to the "obscure consciousness of the incompatibility of the Christian principle of brotherly communion with the right
to treat one's neighbor as property."[89] Serfdom could finally end in Russia
but the tsar had to take the initiative. "The necessity of the living example
from above" had to come. Next to this, public opinion had to be enlisted in
favor of emancipation, and for this the government had to assure the free
and "public [*glasnago*] discussion of the question."[90] Whether Samarin's
Zapiska, which eventually reached the court in St. Petersburg, had decisive
influence or not, on the last two points he soon found himself in agreement
with the government.

Notes

1. Kireevsky, *Sochineniia*, II, 242. This quotation and a brief discussion
of Kireevsky on serfdom appear in Christoff, *Kireevskij*, pp. 119, 286–287.

2. Koliupanov, *Koshelev*, II, 83–84.

3. It is quite common today in the West to identify constitutional parliamentary governments with functioning democracies. But for most of the
nineteenth century, including the middle Slavophil decades, such identification is erroneous and misleading. Parliamentarism and constitutionalism as
they existed then in England, for instance, were not synonymous with
democracy, because on the crucial question of suffrage they fell short of
democratic universalism. As a result, political control was vested in the
hands of powerful minorities (as in Riga). Property qualifications, among
other restrictions, deprived even most males of the right to vote, and

women's suffrage made little progress in the nineteenth century. Thus "in Britain nearly a quarter of even the adult male population remained voteless until 1918." On the continent "Switzerland had universal male suffrage after 1874. In Belgium until 1893 property qualifications restricted the electorate to less than 5 per cent of the population. . . . In the Netherlands, reforms of 1887 and 1896 extended the electorate from 2 per cent to 14 per cent of the population. . . . Spain introduced male suffrage in 1890, Norway in 1898. Finland and Norway pioneered female suffrage in 1907." France, ahead of most of Europe, had "effective universal male suffrage from 1871 onward." In Italy even after the reform of 1882 "only 7 per cent of the population" could vote, and in Germany, while Bismarck "permitted the Reichstag to be elected by universal male suffrage," he left untouched the "decisive power" of the *Bundesrat,* the emperor, and the chancellor. See David Thomson, *Europe Since Napoleon,* 2nd ed. (New York, 1964), pp. 323–324. One can readily agree with Nol'de that particularly after Samarin's Riga experience, for "him constitutionalism forever preserved the taste of class consciousness and the 'trickery' [*plutovstva*] of the upper classes at the expense of the lower." Nol'de, *Samarin,* p. 42.

4. Samarin, *Sochineniia,* VII, viii.

5. Nol'de, *Samarin,* p. 50.

6. Samarin, *Sochineniia,* VII, part 1, 5–6.

7. Ibid., p. 7.

8. See *Russkii arkhiv,* 1879, no. 11, p. 331; also Samarin, *Sochineniia,* VII, part 1, xxxix.

9. Dmitry Samarin found this note among Samarin's papers and published it under the title "Conclusion to the Historical Survey on the Destruction of Serfdom in Livonia" (*Zakliuchenie k istoricheskomu obozreniiu unichtozheniia krepostnago sostoianiia v Liflandii*); see Samarin, *Sochineniia,* II, 433–438.

10. Ibid., pp. 433–434.

11. Ibid., pp. 437–438.

12. Nol'de, *Samarin,* p. 58.

13. Ibid., p. 57.

14. Samarin, *Sochineniia,* II, 15.

15. Reference to the twenty-four letters exchanged between the early Slavophils has been made before in these studies. They were published by N. P. Koliupanov in *Biografiia Aleksandra Ivanovicha Kosheleva* (Moscow, 1892), II, Addendum, no. 8, 41–110.

16. Nol'de, *Samarin,* pp. 60–61.

17. This is perhaps a fair statement in spite of the fact that, as Semevsky pointed out a century ago in his study of the peasant question in Russia, there were differences in the personal views of I. D. Iakushkin, M. S. Lunin, N. I. Turgenev, K. F. Rylev, Nikita Murav'ev, S. Trubetskoi, P. I. Pestel' and

others. Cf. V. I. Semevsky, *Krest'ianskii vopros v Rossii v XVIII i pervoi polovine XIX veka,* 2 vols. (St. Petersburg, 1888), I, 501–517; A. G. Mazour, *The First Russian Revolution, 1825. The Decembrist Movement...* (Berkeley, Calif., 1937), pp. 4–11ff; Jerome Blum, *Lord and Peasant in Russia from the Ninth to the Nineteenth Century,* p. 565.

18. Khomiakov, *Sochineniia,* III, 13, 14, 18, 27.

19. Cf. Semevsky, *Krest'ianskii vopros,* II, 60–61, 65; G. T. Robinson, *Rural Russia under the Old Regime: A History of the Landlord-Peasant World and a Prologue to the Peasant Revolution of 1917* (New York, 1949), p. 62.

20. Khomiakov, *Sochineniia,* III, 78–79, 84.

21. Ibid., p. 83.

22. Seddon has recently (1984) published an exceptionally fine article on the Petrashevtsy, based on research in the archives in Moscow and Leningrad. With respect to the social-economic background of the Petrashevtsy he states that "only a few came from wealthy families ... (for example Speshnev, Kashkin, and Petrashevskii). The majority (over a hundred and fifty of those interrogated) came from the impoverished gentry." He sees the Petrashevtsy as "a transitional stage between the wealthy, leisured intelligentsia of the 1820s and 1830s, and the properly *raznochintsy* intelligentsia of the 1860s, but bearing a much closer resemblance to the latter ..." There was no single philosophical-religious and ideological conviction among the Petrashevtsy; they were "humanists and materialists, anticapitalists, democrats," many of whom saw, as early as 1845, the *obshchina* and *mir* as the kernel of Russia's socialism. Petrashevsky was a bitter critic of Christ while "Nikolai Danilevskii and Aleksandr Beklemishev ... were liberals and liked Fourier because he offered social reform without political upheaval. Some, including many members of Kashkin's circle, were leisure-time socialists ... others, among them Dostoevskii, Maikov, and Miliukov, were Christian socialists," while "Speshnev lost patience with Petrashevskii and ... formed a real revolutionary conspiracy." Seddon is convinced that Chernyshevsky "In *Chto delat'?* ... directly identifies the *obshchina* with the Fourierist phalanstery," something that Khomiakov, apparently independently, also did earlier, in 1849, but Seddon makes no mention of him or of the Moscow Slavophils. See J. H. Seddon, "The Petrashevtsy: A Reappraisal," *Slavic Review,* 1984, no. 3, pp. 435–448.

23. For a recent treatment of the commune among the South Slavs, see the excellent collective work under the editorship of R. F. Byrnes, *Communal Families in the Balkans: The Zadruga* (Notre Dame, Ind., 1976).

24. Another Polish emigre, the historian Joachim Lelewel, who fled to the West after the Polish uprising of 1830–1831, and met Bakunin and other Russians in Brussels in the mid-1840s, was an admirer and advocate of the old Slav peasant commune. For a certain bond between Lelewel and the Mos-

cow Slavophils on the peasant commune, see Jan Kucharzewski, *The Origins of Modern Russia* (New York, 1948), pp. 186–187, 226, 237, 250.

25. Jules Michelet, who attended Mickiewicz's lectures at the College de France, wrote enthusiastically that thanks to Mickiewicz the chair of Slavonic Literatures had "become sacred": "The Russians who attended were as if thunder-struck and stared at the ground while we Frenchmen, [were] moved to the very depth of our souls." Quoted in Kucharzewski, p. 235.

26. Seddon, "The Petrashevtsy," p. 448. The circle was suppressed in 1849 and twenty-one of its members, including Fedor Dostoevsky, were sentenced to terms of exile.

27. Semevsky, *Krest'ianskii vopros,* II, 378.

28. Ibid., p. 386.

29. Quoted in Seddon, "The Petrashevtsy," p. 438.

30. As late as 1857 Chernyshevsky could say in his essay on Haxthausen's studies of Russia's peasant order, that Haxthausen "as a practical man very truthfully foresaw in 1847 the proximity of the horrible explosion of the proletariat of Western Europe. And one cannot but agree with him that the salutary principle of communal ownership is what guards us against the frightful ulcer of proletarianism [*strashnaia iazva proletariatstva*] among the peasant population. See Chernyshevsky, *Sochineniia,* IV, 330–331, also p. 326. See also Dudzinskaia's recent study, *Slavianofily v obshchestvennoi bor'be,* pp. 108, 164–165. Here again, the absence of clear, precise, universally accepted terminology and definitions, and the necessity to generalize lead occasionally to error and unintentional misrepresentation. For example, in the mid-1840s Belinsky justly complained that the term "bourgeoisie" was too vague because of its "multi-inclusiveness and elastic extensibility" (*mnogovmestitel'nost' i elastcheskaia rastiazhimost'*). But instead of designating the proletariat as *iazva* (ulcer), as others were doing, he put the blame on the "large capitalists" whom he saw as the "plague and cholera [*chuma i kholera*] of contemporary France." Quoted by V. I. Kuleshov in his introduction to *P. V. Annenkov Literaturnye vospominaniia* (Moscow, 1983), p. 21 (hereafter cited as Annenkov, *Vospominaniia*).

31. Chagin pointed to a paradox in 1948 when he declared in a public lecture in Leningrad that government "permission for the import of Marx's books in Russia was granted on the basis that the subject of [his] works cannot be applicable to Russia, and [moreover] it represents a sufficiently abstract speculation." This refers to the 1840s and 1850s, for as Chagin made clear, the government's attitude toward the works of Marx and Engels change in the later decades. Chagin stressed the early interest of a number of young Russians in Marx and his works, but concluded: "The influence of the ideas of Marx and Engels in the forties and fifties on social thought in Russia was just the same limited and narrow. Those familiar with them were

first, the circle of such people as Annenkov, Botkin; second, a few progressive circles, and third, revolutionaries and thinkers ... such as Belinsky, Herzen, and Ogarev." He does not, however, shed light on the relationship between Marx and Herzen, who lived in Paris for a brief period and for much longer in London; according to Malia, they did not know each other personally. See B. A. Chagin, *Proniknovenie idei marksizma v Rossiiu 1845–1883* (Leningrad, 1948), p. 10. Referring in a footnote to "Herzen's numerous clashes with Marx," Malia says, "the two never met." Malia, *Alexander Herzen and the Birth of Russian Socialism, 1812–1855,* p. 472 n. 13. The *Communist Manifesto* was first translated into Russian in 1869 by Bakunin.

32. See Franco Venturi, *Roots of Revolution* (New York, 1960), p. 46. A vivid firsthand account of several young Russian admirers of Marx in the middle 1840s was left by the literary critic, memoirist, and friend of Belinsky, P. V. Annenkov (1813–1887). "I arrived in Paris at the end of the spring of 1846 and found a whole Russian colony already established there whose principal and outstanding members were Bakunin and Sazonov." Carrying a letter of introduction to Marx, Annenkov was "received by Marx in Brussels in a very friendly manner," and found him to be "a type of man made up of energy, will power, and invincible convictions." Marx impressed Annenkov, then thirty-two years old, with his insistence on a "positive doctrine" if the workers' movement was to succeed. Annenkov saw Marx again, and also Engels, in Paris in 1848. But for this moderate Russian Westerner this was his last contact with Marx. See Annenkov, *Vospominaniia,* pp. 290–292.

33. Dudzinskaia summed up the Slavophils' travels and studies in the West as follows: "In 1824–1825 Khomiakov was in [Western] Europe. In 1829–1830 the Kireevsky brothers studied in Germany: Peter in Munich, while Ivan in March 1830 attended Hegel's lectures in Berlin, and more than once was in his home, on the invitation of the host. ... The elder Kireevsky was acquainted with Schelling and Oken. Koshelev in 1831–1832 attended in the University of Berlin the lectures of Schleiermacher, [Eduard] Gans, and Savigny [and] in Weimar talked with Goethe, while in Geneva he was captivated by Rossi's lectures. In Paris he became acquainted with the historians Guizot and Thiers and with the philosopher Cousin. In England he met the statesmen Palmerston and Grey, and was a witness to the passage of the historic Reform Bill [of 1832]. ... K. S. Aksakov attended German universities in 1837–1839." See Dudzinskaia, *Slavianofily,* pp. 25–26. One could add that Samarin's travels in the West came in the 1860s and early 1870s, and that Ivan Aksakov was abroad at the end of the 1850s and later.

34. Long before the Crimean War the government was well aware of the burden and danger of serfdom. Thus in 1839 the chief of the gendarmerie, Count Benkendorf, counseled emancipation. "It is better," he advised the tsar, "to begin gradually, cautiously, rather than wait while it [emancipation]

begins from below, from the people." Advocating gradual, quiet measures
he concluded, "But that it is essential, and that the peasant class is a pow-
der keg, on this all agree." Quoted in P. A. Zaionchkovsky, *Otmena
krepostnogo prava v Rossii,* 2nd ed. (Moscow, 1960), p. 58.

35. It has been correctly said that Cherkassky "became close to the
Slavophils" (*sblizivshiisia so slavianofilami*) in the 1850s rather than joined
them. See Dudzinskaia, *Slavianofily,* p. 22.

36. See Koshelev, *Zapiski,* p. 84. Princess Trubetskaia, who with V. O.
Kliuchevsky's help edited the rich and valuable correspondence between
Cherkassky, Koshelev, Samarin, and Ivan Aksakov, stresses Cherkassky's
youthful associations with some of the Slavophils but in general concurs in
Koshelev's judgment, citing the above passage from Koshelev's *Zapiski.*
Thus she says that Cherkassky "was never a Slavophil in the generally ac-
cepted sense of this word." The principal difference was in the fact "at the
basis of all philosophical, historical, social, and political views of the
Slavophils ... lay religious conviction" formed under Khomiakov's influence.
What brought Cherkassky close to the Slavophils was his "conviction, transformed into a belief, in Russia's great mission," and in the early 1850s the
"peasant question." See O. N. Trubetskaia, ed., *Materialy dlia biografii kn.
V. A. Cherkasskago ...* (Moscow, 1901), book 1, pp. 37–38. For a biographical essay of Cherkassky see also O. N. Trubetskaia, "Kn. Vladimir Aleksandrovich Cherkassky," in A. K. Dzhivilegov et al., eds., *Velikaia reforma*
(Moscow, 1911), V, 108–118. On Cherkassky's status as a Slavophil, see p.
110. See also Richard Wortman, "Koshelev, Samarin, and Cherkassky and
the Fate of Liberal Slavophilism," *Slavic Review,* 1962, no. 2, pp. 261–279.

37. Koshelev made the following entry in his diary for March 12, 1850:
"These days in the evenings I have talks with my friends. The principal topic
of our conversation is emancipation. Our notions become clarified. . . . On
Thursday, the fifteenth, and Friday the sixteenth we spent the evening, the
first at Khomiakov's, the second at Cherkassky's, and the only topic of conversation was the destruction of serfdom. " Quoted by V. Ia. Ulanov,
"Slavianofily i zapadniki o krepostnom prave," in A. K. Dzhivelegov et al.,
eds., *Velikaia reforma* (Moscow, 1911), v. 3, p. 177.

38. Quoted in Nol'de, *Samarin,* pp. 61–62.

39. At the beginning of this century Kornilov gave an example of peasant
discontent stirred up by the Crimean War: "The ukaz about the naval militia
of April 3, 1854, and after it the manifesto about the peoples militia of
January 29, 1855, instantly called forth general discontent among the
peasants. . . . The rumor spread that entering the ranks of the militia would
free them and their families from serfdom, and they rushed in crowds to sign
up as soldiers in the militia." In one instance, to subdue unrest in the
Cherkassky and Chigirinsky districts, the government dispatched several
army units. See A. A. Kornilov, "Krestian'skaia reforma 19 Fevralia 1861

goda," in A. A. Kornilov et al., *Krest'ianskii stroi. Sbornik statei* (St. Petersburg, 1905), p. 297. Much factual information on peasant unrest and uprisings with emphasis on the period 1826–1861 is contained in I. I. Ignatovich, "Krest'ianskiia volneniia," *Velikaia reforma,* III, 41–65. The "specter of Pugachev" continued to haunt landowners and the government, as Terence Emmons underscored in the "The Peasant and Emancipation," in W. S. Vucinich, ed., *The Peasant in Nineteenth-Century Russia* (Stanford, Calif., 1968), pp. 47, 52.

40. For Samarin's *zapiski,* and his brother Dmitry's editorial comments, see Samarin, *Sochineniia,* II, 17–190.

41. Ibid., pp. 17–19.

42. Ibid., pp. 20–21.

43. Ibid., p. 25.

44. Ibid., p. 28.

45. Ibid., pp. 30–31.

46. Ibid., p. 31.

47. Ibid., p. 32.

48. The complete title of A. V. Solov'ev's thirty-five-page historical summary essay of the kindred notions of Holy Russia and Moscow, the Third Rome, appeared under the title "Sviataia Rus' (Ocherk razvitiia religiozno-obshestvennoi idei)," in *Sbornik Russkago Arkheologicheskago Obshchestva v Korolevstve S. Kh. S.* (Belgrade, 1927), pp. 77–112. An English translation under the general editorship of Professor Dmitrij Cizevskij was published as a pamphlet thirty-two years later. See *Holy Russia: The History of a Religious-Social Idea* (The Hague, 1959). I have compared the two versions and used both, but have relied on Professor A. V. Solov'ev's Russian original, partly because the unnamed translator has on occasion departed too far from the original (for example, see "Sviataia Rus'," p. 97, and *Holy Russia,* p. 36). Another example of the free English translation deals with the Byzantine notion of the "symphony" or the "complete accord between emperor and patriarch outlined by Patriarch Photius in his Epanagogue" of the ninth century (see *Holy Russia,* pp. 30–31). In the original there is a reference to the "theocratic idea" in the reign of tsar Alexei, but there is no mention of "symphony" (see "Sviataia Rus'," p. 94). The "slight emendations" mentioned in the Foreword to the English edition are actually quite significant, including pp. 39–43, which do not appear in the original. To avoid confusion I have used the spelling "Solov'ev" transliterated from the original instead of "Soloviev," which is given in the English translation.

49. A. V. Solov'ev did not consider the case of Russian messianism absolutely unique. He saw in "La belle France," "Merry England" and "Olde England," and "die deutsche Treue" connotations similar to "Holy Russia," Solov'ev, "Sviataia Rus'," p. 107.

50. For examples of "historical romanticism" and of the use of Holy Rus' or Holy Russia as these appear in the poetry of Fedor Glinka (1812), Ryleev (1821), Pushkin (1824), Kuchelbecker (1827), A. I. Odoevsky (1830), Denis Davydov, and A. S. Khomiakov (1832), see Solov'ev, *Holy Russia,* pp. 39–43. This occurred from approximately 1810 to 1840, "when Russian literature was born in Romanticism." In a recent book covering the same period — the late eighteenth and early nineteenth centuries — secular rather than Orthodox religious romanticism and proto-Slavophil ideas are stressed. See Mark Al'tshuller, *Predtechi slavianofil'stva v russkoi literature* (Obshchestvo "Beseda liubitelei russkogo slova" (Ann Arbor, Mich., 1984).

51. A. V. Solov'ev, "Sviataia Rus'," pp. 99–100. Much pertinent material on the concepts of Holy Russia and Moscow the Third Rome is contained in Michael Cherniavsky's "'Holy Russia': A Study in the History of an Idea," *American Historical Review,* 1958, no. 4, pp. 617–637. See also his *Tsar and People: Studies in Russian Myths* (New Haven, Conn., 1961).

52. Belinsky, *Sochineniia,* III, 710. For a summary of the Gogol-Belinsky controversy, see Cherniavsky, *Tsar and People,* pp. 184–186.

53. Since we have no way of measuring or quantifying either religious or atheistic convictions, perhaps even a crude approximation on the religiousness of the Russian people is better than nothing. In this connection, according to Professor Kartashev, in 1915 Russia had "more than 50,000 churches, 100,000 clergy, up to 1,000 monasteries and nunneries with 50,000 monks and nuns. It possessed four ecclesiastical academies, 55 seminaries with 100 church schools, 100 diocesan schools with 75,000 daily students." A. V. Kartashev, *Ocherki po istorii russkoi tserkvi* (Paris, 1959), II, 317.

54. Kireevsky, *Sochineniia,* I, 206.

55. Khomiakov, *Sochineniia,* I, 212–213.

56. Kireevsky, *Sochineniia,* I, 206.

57. Khomiakov, *Sochineniia,* I, 219; Cherniavsky, *Tsar and People,* p. 163.

58. Samarin, *Sochineniia,* II, 33–34.

59. Cherniavsky, *Tsar and People,* pp. 74–75, 117.

60. A. V. Solov'ev, "Sviataia Rus'," p. 100. Khomiakov's "purest source" was of course, Byzantine Orthodoxy. Yet as Solov'ev stressed, Khomiakov held that the Byzantine empire fell because there Christianity "became estranged from man's soul endeavoring to better his private life and setting aside his public life." This and the "stench of social injustice, depravity, and blood," in Khomiakov's view, caused its downfall. Ibid., p. 101.

61. See V. A. Frantsev, ed., *A. S. Khomiakov, Stikhotvoreniia. Vstupitel'naia stat'ia i primechaniia* (Prague, 1934), pp. xxviii, xxx, 118.

62. Solov'ev, "Sviataia Rus'," p. 102.

63. In the most recent edition of Dostoevsky's works *Diary of a Writer* (Dnevnik pisatelia) begins in 1873 in volume 21. The diary entries for 1876 take up three volumes, 22–24, while volumes 25–26 contain the entries for

1877, with some for August 1880 in volume 26. Volume 27 contains the diary for 1881. See the Soviet Academy of Sciences edition, *F. M. Dostoevsky Polnoe sobranie sochinenii v tridtsati tomakh* (Leningrad, 1980–1984), vols. 21–26 (hereafter cited as Dostoevsky, *Sochinenii*). Dostoevsky, like many other members of the Russian intelligentsia, was then under the impression of an eventful three years that included the Bosnian crisis of 1875, the Russo-Turkish war of 1877–78 for the liberation of Bulgaria, and the treaties of San-Stefano and Berlin, both concluded in 1878.

64. Quoted in A. V. Solov'ev, "Sviataia Rus'," p. 103. See also Dostoevsky *Sochineniia,* v. 23, 48.

65. Ibid., p. 104.

66. Ibid., p. 105.

67. Samarin, *Sochineniia,* II, 35–36.

68. Ibid., pp. 37–38.

69. Ibid., p. 40.

70. Ibid., pp. 42–43.

71. In the fall of 1856 Samarin observed on another landowner's estate Clayton's imported English steam threshing machine do the work in one day that *barshchina* serfs took a whole winter to do by hand. See E. A. Dudzinskaia, "Obschestvennaia i khoziaistvennaia deiatel'nost' slavianofila Iu. F. Samarina v 40–50-kh godakh XIX v.," in *Istoricheskie zapiski,* 1984, no. 110, pp. 319–321.

72. Samarin, *Sochineniia,* II, 51.

73. Ibid., pp. 51–52.

74. Ibid., p. 37.

75. Ibid., p. 58.

76. Ibid., p. 66.

77. Ibid., pp. 66–67.

78. Ibid., p. 75.

79. Ibid., p. 77.

80. Ibid., pp. 83–84.

81. V. A. Koshelev in his already mentioned work, *Esteticheskie i literaturnye vozzreniia russkikh Slavianofilov 1840–1850-e gody* (1984) pp. 80–81, refers to Khomiakov's concept of *narodnost'* as consisting of three main ingredients, or in his paraphrase, "The personality of the people [*narod*] appears within the complex entwining of the elements of 'nation' [*zemlia*], 'state,' and 'faith' (the religion of the people); each of these is compulsory but the *measure* of the influence of each on the personality of the peopl is different. In this sense the essence of the Slavophil concept of *narodnost'* could be reduced to the quest for the most harmonious combination within the interweaving of these elements."

82. Ibid., pp. 86–87. A side effect of the inventories in the Ukraine resulted from the limiting of the amount of labor a serf owed the landlord

to three days a week. During the three days left to the serf he could, for instance, take employment in another landowner's sugar refinery. Thus the refinery owner could hire the "free labor of someone else's serfs for whom, just the same, the pay was received by their landowner." This "new phenomenon coincided with the introduction of the inventories." See Dudzinskaia, "Samarin," pp. 315–316.

83. Samarin, *Sochineniia,* II, 88–89. Volume 2 of Samarin's *Works* begins with a sixteen-page summary of his views on the inventory reform. These notes were not intended for publication. Ibid., pp. 1–16. He returned to this subject in 1863.

84. Ibid., p. 98. Samarin's preparation for participation in the emancipation of the serfs consisted not only of a thorough study of the problem in Russia and its Baltic and Western Borderlands but also of a conscientious 206-page investigation of the emancipation of the serfs in Prussia. This was serialized in the supplement to the Slavophil *Russkaia beseda, Sel'skoe blagoustroistvo,* in 1858. See Samarin, *Sochineniia* II, 195–400. Recently (1982) Dudzinskaia has published a highly competent summary commentary on Samarin's study of the Prussian example. See E. A. Dudzinskaia, "Der 'preussische Weg' in den Schriften des Slavophilen Ju. F. Samarin," in Wolfgang Kessler, at al, *Kulturbeziehungen in Mittel-und Osteuropa im 18. und 19. Jarhundert* (East Berlin, 1982), pp. 245–250.

85. Samarin, *Sochineniia,* II, 110, 111.

86. Ibid., pp. 118, 120.

87. Ibid., p. 127.

88. Ibid., p. 135.

89. Ibid., pp. 124, 125.

90. Ibid., p. 129.

14

The Drive for Emancipation

When Alexander II issued the proclamation on November 18, 1857, that he favored emancipation of the serfs, this "theme became transformed from an illegal one, not only into a legal theme but even into a compulsory one."[1] The nature of the change was easily understandable in a society in which the word of the tsar was the law of the land. Thus the announcement from St. Petersburg at once shifted the focus of the discussion of emancipation, among other things, from concern for private voluntary deals between individual landowners and their serfs to nationwide, compulsory elimination of serfdom under the authority and sponsorship of the government. For Samarin, Koshelev, Cherkassky, and other authors of memoranda on emancipation of the serfs word from the palace also meant that they would no longer dwell in a cloudy realm of uncertainty and apprehension. Prior to November 1857 they did not know whether by expressing views and advocating policies in the form of written and privately circulated memoranda they might not provoke the wrath of the authorities and the censorship. Now, although the censorship did not come to an end, the tsar had declared in favor of emancipation, and this made it easier and safer, for the time being at least, for individuals to state their positions on the serf question.

Numerous works, some of them careful and detailed, have been written on the emancipation reform of 1861, some before and some after 1917, and some in the West. The concern here is not with emancipation of the serfs as such, nor with the valuable work on it of many public-spirited men and women. Our interest is confined to Samarin's participation in the emancipation reform, and to his ideological and programmatic contribution to it. Yet too narrow concentration on Samarin's views and activities would tend to isolate him from the broader intellectual-ideological environment in which he and the Slavophils functioned in the mid and late 1850s.

Viewed against this background it is manifest that Samarin's *Zapiska,* although one of the earliest in its inception, was not an isolated event. Konstantin Aksakov, among the early Slavophils, also drafted a *zapiska* in the spring of 1855, to which reference was made in the preceding study of this series, and which has been ably analyzed by N. I. Tsimbaev.[2] From the point of view of determining the Slavophil attitude toward emancipation of the serfs Koshelev's *zapiska* was no less pertinent and relevant than Aksakov's and Samarin's. In fact, as one of the best-informed and most progressive landowner-farmers in Russia at the time, Koshelev was in a class by himself.

For Koshelev, self-interest and fear of a peasant uprising provided a powerful incentive for immediate emancipation. Knowledge of basic economic forces at work and familiarity with the serf-free societies of Western Europe had convinced him that free labor was more productive than serf labor. And there were the occasional, possibly frequent, pricks of conscience, as when he scolded his old friend Ivan Kireevsky for being insensitive toward the serfs. In the already mentioned letter to him of October 27, 1852, Koshelev said, "They say that some people base the legality of slavery on the words of the apostle Peter: 'slaves, obey your masters!'" He was disturbed that the "Savior more than once speaks about slaves but nowhere does he dishonor the right of domination," but he finally brushed aside his doubts by summing up all that needed to be said on the subject in Christ's well-known admonition, "Love thy neighbor as thyself." This might have satisfied him if he had not been at the time the master and owner of several thousand serfs. How could he love them as himself and still keep them in the state of serfdom? Samarin attempted to account for what he considered to be Kireevsky's complacency on the serf issue by asserting, "I know that you say: I do not oppress my people. I take care to see that they are warm and fed, being convinced that if they were free their condition would be worse, and for this reason I consider it my duty to preserve this situation for the time being."[3] In Koshelev's opinion, such a rationalization was unacceptable and could not be reconciled with Christian ethics.

Koliupanov, who did not solve the riddle of human motivation any more than anyone else has done before or since, not without reason said that in the case of Khomiakov the "starting point in the cause of emancipation was religion," that is, Christianity. In Khomiakov's words, "Speaking in relative terms, the slave owner is always more corrupted than the slave: a Christian may be a slave but he should not be a slave owner." While the circumstances in which these pronouncements were made are such as to remove doubts about their sincerity, they do not seem to reveal the complete motivation that prompted Khomiakov and Koshelev to declare in favor of emancipation of the serfs. Had they actually been following in the footsteps of Christ and the apostles they would have freed their serfs, divided their wealth among them, and joined the peasant commune.

Toward the end of the Crimean War, when its dismal outcome for Russia had become apparent, some of Russia's best minds were moved to action. Despite censorship, the Third Section, and the fact that Nicholas I was still on the throne (though as it turned out not for long), publicistic work became revived. This took the form of the usually unsolicited *zapiski,* of a lively and rich personal correspondence, and the founding of several new journals which reached wide audiences. While there were still unbridgeable ideological, programmatic, and tactical differences between the Slavophils and the two Western orientations, represented by Herzen in *Kolokol* and Chernyshevsky in *Sovremennik,* all were in agreement that serfdom had to go. This tended to establish temporarily, during the last five years of the 1850s, a certain tactical rapprochement even between Orthodox Slavophilism and secular Russian Westernism.

Three of the Slavophils, Iu. F. Samarin, I. S. Aksakov, A. I. Koshelev, and their friend Prince V. A. Cherkassky decided on an informal division of labor, corresponding to their interests and competence. In their *zapiski* Samarin would concentrate on possible reforms of government service and the system of serfdom, Aksakov would concentrate on the court system and justice, Cherkassky on the condition of the state peasants, and Koshelev on "finances and the redemption system."[4] But whether in the *zapiski,* in private correspondence, or on the pages of their own Slavophil journal, *Russkaia beseda,* (*Russian Conversation*) which the government finally permitted in February 1856, the Slavophils were never out of sight of the government censorship. As Tsimbaev put it, "The Slavophil periodical publications were always the object of the special attention of the censor."[5] While this remark is in the context of Ivan Aksakov's several journals, it applies to all the early Slavophils, and to their writings and pronouncements.

Notably absent from the above group of four is Konstantin Aksakov. Samarin, apparently in an effort to make it clear that the four were concerned with practical problems, wrote Konstantin in March 1855: "Would I not be right if I said that you have not seen [government] service, and that you are not acquainted with such service? You have studied neither our rights to property, nor the organization of [social] classes, nor the financial administration, nor the public or private economy."[6] This of course did not deter Konstantin. The *zapiska* that he drafted on the subject was, it is true, read mainly by his father, mother and sisters, and by M. P. Pogodin and other family friends who were always ready to admire him, and yet it is said that Alexander II, too, read it "with pleasure."[7]

According to some of Konstantin's more hardheaded friends as well as later critics, the *zapiska* was on the whole rather esoteric. At the time of its drafting, neither the Kireevsky brothers, both of whom died in 1856, nor Koshelev seems to have been informed of its contents. When it was published for the first time in 1881 (by Ivan Aksakov) Koshelev wrote to Ivan that he had read it "with great pleasure," but he said, "I disagree . . . with your brother about many things. I do not consider that the Russians or the Slavs as a whole are nonpolitical people. And I do not recognize any contrast between the people and the state, etc." The main point of agreement, at least between Konstantin Aksakov and Samarin, was the fear of revolution and "hostility to the Western European constitutional order."[8] It is well to be reminded again that, in the middle of the nineteenth century, Western European constitutionalism was not synonymous with political or social-economic democracy.

Before we return to Samarin's role in the events that led to the emancipation reform of 1861 it is essential to consider briefly the *zapiski* on emancipation that were drafted by Koshelev and Cherkassky. Only thus would we be able to evaluate Samarin's stand on emancipation not only as an individual but also as a member of the Slavophil circle. In this respect Koshelev's part is of singular importance, for among other things it was he, in the words of Princess Trubetskaia, who "early in June 1858 . . . proposed to Prince Cherkassky and to Iu. F. Samarin . . . to establish among them a trilateral correspondence to keep one another informed about the course of the peasant cause."[9] The ultimate result of this suggestion was the invaluable collection of more than 350 letters exchanged at the height of the reform initiative, between these three men and some of their friends. This correspondence was later published, with much biographical information about the three principal correspondents and particularly about Cherkassky, by Princess Trubetskaia with V. O. Kliuchevsky's help.[10]

Koshelev, although a relatively late comer to the Slavophil camp, was prevented from full commitment mainly by his reluctance to accept Orthodoxy at the time, yet he shared the Slavophil concern with the problem of the serfs. He drafted his first *zapiska* on emancipation in 1855, and he also took an active part in sponsoring and financing the first Slavophil journal, *Russkaia beseda* (Russian Conversation), early in 1856.[11] Koshelev took two shares of the total financial burden, and one share each was borne by Khomiakov, Samarin, and Cherkassky. The circulation was never very large, but the journal was published from 1856 to 1860, first as a quarterly and then as a bimonthly. Koshelev was both editor and publisher.

At various times during the four years of publication Koshelev had as coeditors T. I. Filippov, P. I. Bartenev, M. A. Maksimovich, and, toward the end, I. S. Aksakov. From March 1858 until April 1859 Koshelev also published the influential supplement, *Sel'skoe blagoustroistvo* (Rural Welfare). All fourteen issues of the supplement were dedicated to the emancipation problem. During the same period (April–December 1857) Konstantin Aksakov also published the weekly *Molva* (Report), and in January 1859 Ivan Aksakov began the weekly *Parus* (Sail). Both Aksakov publications were banned by the government, however, Konstantin's after thirty-eight issues, Ivan's after two. These activities are symptomatic not only of temperamental differences within the Slavophil camp but also of ideological and tactical differences.

The death of the Kireevsky brothers in 1856 had deprived the Slavophils of two of their oldest friends, while the "generation gap," specifically that between Koshelev, "mentor and inspirer of the younger" Slavophils, on the one hand, and Samarin, Konstantin and Ivan Aksakov, and Cherkassky on the other, soon produced further disagreements.[12] Added to this were the differences in temperament and personalities among the younger Slavophils, such as those between Konstantin and Ivan Aksakov, between Samarin and Konstantin Aksakov, and between Samarin and Cherkassky. But as individual convictions, preferences, and choices are briefly considered here in order to establish as accurately as possible Samarin's ideological and programmatic position we have to guard against allowing internal differences to be magnified to such a degree as to render Slavophilism of the pre-emancipation period nonexistent.

As ideas and convictions were brought out of the sphere of Slavophil Orthodoxy and ideology, where by the very nature of these two stages they presented no problems of application, the Slavophils, like many before and after them, encountered grave difficulties. It was one thing, for example, to subscribe wholeheartedly to Slavophil *sobornost'*, and quite another to apply it in actual personal and social life. And it was one thing to engage in publicistic work and sincerely sing the praises of the historical peasant commune, and quite another to preserve it for the future after emancipation in the face of evolving industrialization and urbanization. Like all those people before and after the Slavophils, who tried to realize basic religious or philosophical ideas and ideals in life, the Slavophils were finding out in the late 1850s that there was no such thing as an easy and guaranteed way in which their notions of *sobornost'* and wholeness of the spirit could enter daily life perfectly and painlessly. Was it after all, possible for the third prop of the Slavophil edifice, *obshchinnost'*, in spite of its long historical existence, to survive in a world of ever accelerating change.[13] That the Slavophils succeeded in extending the life of the village commune beyond emancipation was probably for them a most satisfying achievement. It was also a most noteworthy one, whether one favors the commune or not.

Toward the end of the 1850s the early Slavophils were in general agreement on a number of fundamental convictions and principles: on *sobornost'*, *obshchinnost'*, *tsel'nost' dukha*, and on the presumed uniqueness of Russia's historical path. On the level of program and action they were in general accord about the emancipation of the serfs and other reforms, and in opposition to government censorship and the bureaucracy. They extolled the *narod*, although none as ardently as Konstantin Aksakov, who also spoke eloquently for himself and his fellow Slavophils in favor of freedom of speech, and conscience.[14] They all had an appreciation — in varying degrees — of the classical cultural heritage, and of the great literary, artistic and scientific achievements of the West.

The Slavophils valued and enjoyed the best of Western literature and education, and they praised and appreciated the beneficial results of what at the time was predominantly Western science and technology, but they had serious reservations about both doctrinal and historical Catholicism and Protestantism and they directed some of their most trenchant criticism at Western ethics and mores. Without pretending to lead a crusade against the West, they nonetheless saw themselves as offering to Russia, and also to the West, certain religious and ethical alternatives. Finally, they had a special regard, again differing in degrees, for their fellow Orthodox Slavs of the Balkans, more specifically for the Bulgarians and Macedonians, who, unlike the Serbians, were still under complete Ottoman domination.[15] Slavophilism should be seen as it was — a complex of ideas, personal views, and convictions nurturing several streams which contributed to a single broad current. In accord with its time and place, it was never cast in the form of a centralized, disciplined, and homogeneous political party that could speak with a single voice.

The list of scholarly works in which Slavophil disagreements have received at times cursory, at other times more detailed, treatment is quite long, and no complete catalogue will here be attempted. The selected sources given above illustrate the nature and extent of the problem to which further reference will be made. Here the emphasis is on Samarin's role in the emancipation reform, and on the agreements and disagreements in which he was involved. Some of these were theoretical, matters of conviction and principle, before he became active in the Samara gubernia committee and on the government's Editorial Commission. Others were of a theoretical as well as tactical and political nature once the emancipation of the serfs was on the way to its enactment.

The interplay between the views and activities of Samarin, Koshelev, and Cherkassky sheds light not only on Slavophilism in general but also on Samarin's role in one of the principal changes in Russia's long social history. The policy of the government, that is of Alexander II, toward emancipation was manifestly of central importance, since Samarin, like many other moderates, wished and expected the reform to come "from above."

In spite of the uncertainties of censorship, the early years in the reign of Alexander II were promising for those expecting reform. Early in 1857 the tsar authorized the so-called Secret Committee (changed on January 8, 1858, to the *Glavnyi Komitet* (Main Committee), and in July on his return from Western Europe he appointed to this committee the Grand Duke Konstantin Nikolaevich. Samarin was summoned to St. Petersburg and met the Grand Duke. On August 18, 1857, the committee outlined a feeble preliminary plan of action on emancipation that provided in general terms for three stages: ameliorating the lot of the serfs, encouraging the freeing of serfs by their landowners, and collecting data and information that would lead to the eventual freeing of all serfs. The secret committee also formulated fourteen questions to which it sought answers. It was in response to this activity that Samarin late in August 1857 drafted four *zapiski,* supplements to his long *zapiska* of 1856. This was three months before the tsar made his historic proclamation of November 20, 1857, calling for the end of serfdom.

These relatively short *zapiski* are titled, "On the Right of the Peasants to Land," "What Is More Advantageous, Communal or Private Ownership of Land?," "Should Term Agreements be Accepted?," and a "Project of an Ukaz for Amicable Arrangements" (between landlords and serfs). In a total of fifty-six pages, in addition to the long *zapiska* discussed in the preceding chapter, Samarin provides much pertinent detail in his usual cogent, persuasive manner. The *zapiski* reveal the functioning of logic within a circumscribed sphere, but they also contain some fundamental contradictions, as, for instance, when he defended freedom, consent, and concern for others as in the village commune, and at the same time stood for the autocratic power of the tsarist government. He found it possible to live with the local, self-governing village commune side by side with the absolute authority of imperial St. Petersburg.

The fundamental character of the land question in a nation such as Russia, which in the middle of the nineteenth century was heavily peasant, needs no further elaboration. Earlier, Samarin had agreed with Khomiakov that the landowner had the right to land whereas the serf had the right to the use of land; now, in 1857, he was more specific: "By land we mean only that part of it that the peasants use for themselves, including farmhouse, kitchen garden, pasture, meadow, and plough land," and this right was based not on law but on custom or "history."[16] In ancient Russia, Samarin claimed, the question of whom the land belonged to "did not exist," and the peasants, being free, could move from place to place. But with the rapidly rising state organization the distribution of land to servants of the state replaced "monetary remuneration."

Possibly wishing to avoid offending the reigning family, since these *zapiski* were intended first and foremost for the court in St. Petersburg, Samarin mentioned neither names of rulers nor time or place. He simply referred to *"chaotic fermentation and the time of crisis"* that confronted Russia with two choices, either "establish land for the peasants by laws, or . . . attach the peasants to the land." His justification of the official enserfment of the Russian peasants, nearly three centuries after the event, now sounds glib and self-justifying. There was no "free choice," he said, and when the interests of the "common people," and those of the "service class, the strong and unique organ of governmental authority, [were considered], the latter was inevitably bound to prevail." But he consoled himself by saying that the serfs were not completely victimized, since *"with this sacrifice their right to land was saved for better times."*[17] Thus, Samarin explained, "the historical right of the peasant to the possession [*vladenie*] of land was strengthened under the name peasant land or *mir* land, which constituted the essential condition for their material existence as an independent class." The peasants were "firmly convinced of their right to land," and Samarin soberly advised his readers at court that any attempt to "forcefully expropriate" the peasants would require "grapeshot and bayonets."

In his effort to find an answer to the problem of control of the land in Russia, Samarin arrived at a formula that was intended to satisfy both landowner and peasant. The key words were *vladenie* ('possession'), and *sobstvennost'* ('ownership' or 'property'). In his words, there existed in Russia "two mutually limiting rights to land: the right of possession belonging to the peasants, and the right of property of land, belonging to the great landowners."[18] He admitted the absence of clarity and precision in this formula and asked, "Are these rights compatible, and are they not mutually exclusive?" Could the landowner be considered an owner if "against his will [his land] is left in the perpetual use of another person?" He resorted to French legal terminology to explain the status of the lands that a landowner conceded to his peasants: "Any capital placed, with renunciation of the right of its return, in the form of a permanent loan [*capital inexigible, place a fond perdu*] comprises the incontestable property of the lender or investor, although it is not at his disposal." But he had this reservation: "There is no question about the legality of the right to compensation for the conceded right of disposal."

Samarin suggested three ways in which the landowner could be compensated for the land: payment for the total worth of the land (which, of course, few if any serfs were in a position to consider), "constant uninterrupted payment of a certain percentage in the form of corvée [*barshchina*]" or cash, or "term payments of a certain percentage with amortization of the capital."[19] In these considerations, which seem to be simply economic ones, he was in effect pursuing a double or perhaps even a triple goal, involving a corollary administrative-political and social aspect.

Samarin wished to preserve the "settledness" (*osedlost'*) of the peasant, and clearly did not wish to see the landowner deprived of his farmhands or the country flooded with roaming bands of impoverished and dissatisfied peasants. He condoned the "administrative centralization [that] strengthened and consolidated the political unity of the Russian nation" together with serfdom, and admitted that "now its excess and its harmful consequences have become obvious to everyone." His conclusion, bearing directly on the administrative as well as social-economic functions of the village *mir* and commune was that the "time has come to give scope to regional life." Once again we see the Slavophil dichotomy: defense of local communal autonomy together with national political centralization or the "state unity of the Russian land."[20] The vastness of Russia's territory and diversity of its population required nothing less.

After this brief digression Samarin returned to the emancipation issue. He gives a review of Swedish policies when Sweden was in control of much of the south coast and hinterland of the Baltic, and a review of the Prussian land reform and serf emancipation earlier in the nineteenth century, and then mentions the statute of 1804. This measure of Alexander I "recognized the person as free but destroyed his bond with the land," and it constituted a most serious "violation" of the old and established peasant right to the use of land. Not surprisingly, Samarin called for restoration of the "law of the inviolability of peasant land," and after some discussion of the three alternatives of putting an end to serfdom in Russia—emancipation without land, emancipation with the portion of land consisting of farmhouse and pasture, or emancipation with the land then in the serf's use—he declared, as might be expected, in favor of the third choice.[21]

It is perhaps not superfluous to stress here the fact that Samarin, although convinced of the need for immediate emancipation of the serfs, was not ready to sacrifice the economic interests of the gentry. He showed at times the romantic Slavophil predisposition toward the peasants as against the gentry, but idealization of the peasantry, so unrestrained in his friend Konstantin Aksakov, was not characteristic of him in his *zapiski*. To free the serfs without land and let them shift for themselves would not do, for "given the insufficiency of education, the fact of being unaccustomed to independence, and given the general poverty of the serfs, that would mean sacrificing them to the landowners." Nonetheless, he added although the "landlord would yield forever the right to disposition or possession of the *mir* land, he would preserve his right to its ownership, hence the right to receive income from it." Such income would take the "form of quit rent (*obrok*) or corvée."[22] Samarin, the landowner, would not deprive himself of his livelihood derived from the combination of his lands and the labor of those working on them.

The first and longest of the four supplementary *zapiski* ends with the enumeration of four successive periods that Samarin suggested should be followed. He obviously envisioned a long period leading to the actual declaration, or at least implementation, of emancipation. What comes as a surprise at the end of this *zapiska* is his suggestion that the government should have as "its goal legislation [leading to] the highest condition attainable by a chiefly agricultural people: the status of free *peasant proprietors* [*paysans propriétaires*]."[23]

The second *zapiska*, "What Is More Advantageous: Communal or Personal Ownership of Land?," is nine pages long and therefore by Samarin's standards quite brief. At the outset he is at pains to dispel the idea that Slavophil views are "radical or revolutionary."[24] "In what history," Samarin asks, "does one read that revolutionary principles are implanted in peasant communities more easily than in separate individuals?" In defense of the nonrevolutionary history of the Russian commune, he cited an example — also a favorite of Konstantin Aksakov's — from the early seventeenth century. "From our history it is apparent that the village and town communes cleared Russia in 1612 of homeless vagrants, saved its integrity, and elevated Michael Romanoff to the Moscow throne." He then dismissed the matter by saying that it was idle to be suspicious of the "communal principle from the point of view of the interests of autocratic authority."

Another obstacle in the way of the future acceptance of the village commune was primarily economic in nature. There were some people, Samarin said — meaning the relatively few but vocal and influential Russian liberals — who looked upon the commune established on the land as "unfavorable and harmful." Voices were heard saying, "Sacrifice the economic commune and preserve the administrative commune." The source of this notion was twofold: the first part of the demand was suggested by Western "theories of political economy," the latter by Russia's own historical record.[25] Although the Slavophils are often described in the pre-Soviet, Soviet, and Western historical literature as "liberal," and "liberals," this highly elastic, chameleon-like word is often more confusing than helpful.

Of the three principal components of English liberalism that were known to Samarin and the other early Slavophils, (lukewarm attitude or indifference to religion, parliamentarism and constitutionalism in politics, and laissez-faire in economics) in theory they subscribed to none. Clearly there was nothing in common between Slavophil Orthodoxy and the Puritan ethic, for instance. For reasons already touched upon, Samarin did not favor constitutionalism and parliamentarianism for Russia. He, as also his friend Konstantin Aksakov and the other early Slavophils, stood for the "rights of man," but for different reasons than in the West (deriving from Slavophil *sobornost'*) they were outright contradictory on laissez-faire economics, a problem born of the difference between conviction and practice. With respect to the vast majority of Russian people, the peasantry and the serfs, they stood for communal or communalistic economic enterprise, an integral part of their defense and apotheosis of the village *mir* and commune. As individual landowners and entrepreneurs they were engaged in private, capitalistic enterprises with a strong nationalist-protectionist tinge. Thus their Slavophil convictions and their personal economic practices remained irreconcilable.

Having declared the commune indivisible, and its economic and administrative functions inseparable, Samarin looked into the relationship between the commune and the individual. His conclusion was, "The communal principle, like the individual principle has its advantages and disadvantages." He considered the two indivisible, but his elaboration on the concept of the individual person shows him favoring the communal principle. "A person left to himself has no right to expect anything from others. He could die of hunger while in a rich village or town." In contrast, a member of a "native commune," who has made his contribution to the *mir,* has submitted to its limitations, and even made sacrifices in its behalf, has earned the right to expect from the commune not only help but a share of its benefits.

The administrative commune in Samarin's view was advantageous for the government treasury because it imposed on its members not only a personal but also a collective responsibility (*krugovaia otvetstvennost'*). But even he, although perhaps given less to flights of the imagination about the village commune than some of his fellow Slavophils, conceived it as an expression of the best in Russian peasant life, and of the freedom that presumably prevailed in it. He summed up his thought in the words, "Where there is no free, sincere participation in the common cause there is no commune." Compared, for instance, with "shopkeeper societies," he concluded that these were "caricatures of the communal order."[26] This is a reminder of the Slavophil, most particularly of Ivan Kireevsky's seminal contrast between community and society.[27]

With the rise in the West of economic individualism and competition, liberal laissez-faire, and the "Puritan ethic," the question of whether the commune was detrimental to Russia's economic welfare became particularly sharp from the middle of the nineteenth century and into the twentieth. More specifically and in current terminology, the issue on the minds of many concerned with Russia's future was whether the village commune was detrimental to the modernization and mechanization of Russian agriculture. Among those who were most vocal against the commune were the Russian liberals who favored private ownership of land. They saw the commune as an archaic institution, deeply accustomed to primitive farming, and anachronistic in the middle of the nineteenth century. The Slavophils, as we have seen, were in the forefront of those who worked for the modernization of their farming and of Russian agriculture in general. But they did not consider the village commune an obstacle.

It was a well known fact among the Slavophils in the 1850s that English and German farming were far ahead of Russian farming but Samarin held that the discrepancy could not be attributed to the village commune. It was the result of far more complex causes, and he maintained that "everyone would agree that in our country it is the factories, mills, schools, means of communications, sea transport, judicial and government institutions which lag behind their foreign counterparts as much as our husbandry does." This state of affairs, he concluded, was not the result of any single cause, and it could not be placed at the doorstep of the village commune. He saw the *mir* and the commune as "one of the living native principles of the Russian nation, but it was only an embryo,"[28] and as such capable of growth and development. He argued that comparing the highly productive, individual-ly owned farms of the West with Russia's stagnant communal farming was not a reason for denying the potential of the commune.

Relying on his reading in Western political economy, specifically John Stuart Mill (in French translation), Samarin saw the scarcity of capital as a principal reason for Russia's backward agriculture. From this he concluded that when capital becomes more plentiful, "it will not only not encounter obstacles in communal possession, but on the contrary, will find in it the soil long since prepared for it." Answering perhaps the most commonly repeated accusation against communal landholding, the "disadvantage of the frequent redistribution of land," he concluded that, although there might be some justification for this, the argument was exaggerated. His reasons for this conclusion were that periodic land redistribution did not paralyze agricultural labor, and furthermore the bulk of the land that was in landlords' estates was not subject to redistribution. Communal land reallotment, like all folk customs, was "extremely elastic." Depending on location and climatic conditions, land redistribution could occur annually, once in nine, twelve, or more years, or not at all.[29]

For Samarin and his fellow Slavophils, the village commune conveyed a suprahistorical meaning and significance. It was the embodiment of the spirit of communality, altruism, and Christian togetherness; it was the very essence of Russian *narodnost'*. It had become sublimated and incorporated into Russia's spiritual and physical existence, so much so that he could say that the "village commune is a primary, natural, and indigenous [*pervostepen-nyi, samorodnyi i bytovoi*] fact of everyday life. To object to it would be as useless as it would be to argue against climate, language, or the physiognomy of the people. This must simply be acknowledged." The one quality that he would not attribute to the commune was eternity. If the "natural course of economic development" should demand a change, communal ownership could "easily pass into private." But he cautioned his readers in the royal palace in St. Petersburg that the "corrosive element of individual ownership" should not be lightly allowed to enter the commune, since once the latter is destroyed it can never be restored. He concluded the *zapiska* by urging "ra-tional conservatism" with respect to the village commune.[30] It is a measure of Samarin's awareness of the rapid and irresistible changes in mid-nineteenth-century Europe that he should admit of the possibility that the village commune, the Slavophil holy of holies, might at some time in the fu-ture disappear.

The third and shortest *zapiska,* five pages long, under the title "Should Term Agreements be Accepted?" deals with a technical, legalistic matter, but also sheds light on property relations between serfs and landowners. Samarin referred to Volume IX of the Code of Laws providing for the in-violability of contracts between landlord and peasant. The peasants did not need a contract to establish their right to the "possession" (*vladenia*) of land. This was their "historical" right, "finally confirmed by their attachment to the soil," that is, by the confirmation of serfdom. The contract was needed "for the establishment of its firm relationship to the newer but equally unquestionable right to patrimonial property."[31] From a theoretical Slavophil point of view Samarin made it appear that the peasants and serfs had a more legitimate right to their share of land that the landowners to theirs. The peasants' right was of longer standing than the landowners', and it was "historical," created by time and the genius of the Russian nation, spontaneously, from within and without explicit legalistic formalities.

However, this did not deter Samarin from claiming what the enserfment of the peasantry had established nonhistorically, that is, over a relatively short period of time, and on the initiative of the autocratic government, as the right of the landowner not only to land but also to serf labor. Article 965, Volume IX of the Code of Laws, Samarin says, "obliges the peasants to work three days a week for their landowner." This was the well-known corvée. He approved of it and its "character of an *inviolable* stipulation *without time-limit*."[32] He favored supplementing and clarifying the contracts to confirm the right of the landlord. Keeping in mind that the government had not yet openly declared in favor of universal compulsory emancipation, he hinted that such a policy would be by far the best for Russia.

It seems that in anticipation of the impending government initiative Samarin saw to it that the financial interests of the landowners would be duly safeguarded. He expected the landlord to be compensated for the possible loss of land and such other sources of income as quit rent, corvée, "and various sorts of revenues." If the government had no cash to fully reimburse the landlord, he would consider government bonds paying regular dividends that would ensure the landowner of "constant uninterrupted, unchangeable monetary income." He advised the government that it should not tolerate the annulment of contracts by one side or the other as this would lead to disorders. This could also place in jeopardy the "advantages of the landowners [and] the well-being of the peasants."[33] For the more distant future, he foresaw a growth of population while the land remained constant and there were to be rises in land rents, "powerful growth of industry," and other changes. The *zapiska* ends with Samarin's reminder that the *mir* land "comprises less than half of all the land, for the seigniorial land includes in addition to plough land, tilled by means of corvée, also fallow lands, steppes, reserve land, waste lands, forests, and all sorts of resources."[34]

Dmitry Samarin properly stressed in his editorial comments in Samarin's *Works* the crucial character of the period during which the four *zapiski* were written. According to Dmitry, early in August 1857 Iurii was invited to St. Petersburg by Grand Duke Konstantin Nikolaevich, who was a member of the then Secret Committee. On August 16, 1857, this committee decided as a first step toward emancipation to encourage landowners and peasants to engage in mutual agreements leading to emancipation. Samarin's fourth *zapiska* was under the title, "Project of an *Ukaz* about Amicable Arrangements Between Landlords and Serfs Incorporated in Their Estates."

In this *zapiska* Samarin stressed a number of points that he had made earlier. Among others he again justified the establishment of serfdom on the grounds of state necessity. Its highest "development" occurred at the beginning of the eighteenth century, while such palliative measures as the laws of 1803 and 1819 accomplished very little. This took place because it was becoming ever clearer that it was essential to "bring Russia's productive forces into action by means of uncoerced labor."[35] The rest of the *zapiska* consists of eight topics, mainly concerned with the mechanics of contracts between landlords and peasants. It is striking that in all Samarin's *zapiski,* even though he is unalterably convinced of the necessity for immediate emancipation of the serfs with land, he never downplays the interests of the gentry but takes note of the necessity of compensation for the land to be conceded to the peasants, and of provisions to ensure that the landowner, after emancipation, will still have farm labor for his lands.

Samarin like the other early Slavophils tended to glorify the village commune and the *mir,* but at the same time he seemed to have little concern for their members beyond emancipation. Were these peasants to remain in circumstances which for centuries were inimical to their cultural development? Were the presumed communal virtues of concern for one's fellow beings, of Christian piety, and deep social consciousness all that the Russian peasant needed to adjust to a highly scientific technological age that was upon him, a change that was already shaking up the West? Samarin and his fellow Slavophils were often unequivocal in their admiration for the village commune and the *narod,* and they were equally resolute in their denigration of the gentry and bureaucracy; yet there is no provision in Samarin's *zapiski* to emancipate the peasantry from illiteracy and ignorance as well as from serfdom and give it a voice in determining its own destiny. The implication is clear that after emancipation the gentry would continue as before to hold the position of leadership in Russian society.

Samarin's *zapiski* on emancipation, including the first, longest, and principal one, were not merely an exercise in written eloquence and revealed personal conviction. They had a considerable effect on the course of events in Russia between 1856 and 1861. But as often in such cases, it is difficult to gauge their impact precisely. Nol'de in his highly perceptive and superbly documented biography provides us with much factual information. What we do know with certainty is that Samarin was one of a good many in the Russian intelligentsia openly urging emancipation of the serfs, that he was highly competent, articulate, and unsparing in his efforts for emancipation, and that the final decision was made by Alexander II. Nol'de, who sheds much light on the relationship between Samarin and the court in St. Petersburg, finds Samarin's views as stated in the *zapiski* "unusually moderate and . . . almost pusillanimous," but excuses him by saying that his principal goal was to present emancipation as "unavoidable and necessary."[36]

The "perfection of his form" that Nol'de found so striking in Samarin's *zapiski* perhaps led him to his judgment that it was superior to the *zapiski* of Kavelin, Cherkassky, and Koshelev; but Nol'de was of course aware that the test of any *zapiska* was its reception at the court in St. Petersburg. Obviously, if a *zapiska* were not to become a dead letter it had to be taken into account by the tsar. The Grand Duke Konstantin Nikolaevich's invitation to Samarin would not have come had there not been an already established connection between Samarin and the royal palace. Nol'de states that in the fall of 1856 Samarin's first *zapiska* "fell into the [hands of the] highest circles of the government in St. Petersburg." The intermediaries in this case were Samarin's cousin and friend, Prince D. A. Obolensky, then an official in the ministry of the navy in St. Petersburg, the Grand Duke Konstantin Nikolaevich, and the Grand Duchess Elena Pavlovna.[37]

The Grand Duchess was in Moscow for a few weeks in the summer of 1855 where some of Moscow's leading men were presented to her, including Samarin and Konstantin Aksakov. She talked with Samarin again while attending the coronation of Alexander II the following year.[38] Samarin's principal concern at the time was to see the emancipation issue discussed freely and openly, a matter that he stressed in his conversations with the Grand Duchess. Soon he would insist that "the reform must begin." In this manner Samarin, who, in Nol'de's words, was "much less inclined to pure speculation than his friends Khomiakov and Kireevsky," with his "unerring political interest, almost instinctively pulled down the old abstract dispute closer to earth."[39] Nol'de provides additional information and discussion of Samarin's prestige at the court and with Alexander II without claiming for Samarin exclusive influence on the tsar. He does, however, say about the tsar that "during the winter months of 1856–1857 when Samarin's *zapiska* lay on his desk, there was maturing within him the firm resolve to carry out the emancipation of the peasants in his lifetime."[40] But a similar claim has been made for Kavelin.[41]

Alexander II's equivocal attitude toward the Slavophils remains a moot point. He allowed them for the first time in their existence their own journal, *Russkaia beseda,* as mentioned, and its supplement *Sel'skoe blagoustroistvo,* also for a brief while Konstantin Aksakov's *Molva,* yet the censorship and the Third Section never let the Slavophils get out of sight. Earlier Samarin had been incarcerated by the tsar's father, while the Third Section and Ministry of the Interior suspected the Slavophils of radical, communistic views and convictions. The government does not seem to have had a clear view of the Slavophils and their ideological orientation. Prince

Obolensky, who was in contact with the court in St. Petersburg as well as with Samarin and the Slavophils, says in his memoirs, "When the Sovereign wished to learn what sort of people the Moscow Slavophils were, and when the Third Section could not give him any sort of clear explanation . . . an order was issued to arrest Ivan Aksakov . . . to put the question, what is Moscow Slavophilism?" And indeed Ivan Aksakov was arrested for several days in March 1849 and interrogated by the tsar.[42] Alexander II, most probably following the intercession of the Grand Duke and Grand Duchess, softened his attitude sufficiently to permit Samarin, Koshelev to a degree, and their friend Prince Cherkassky to play leading roles in the emancipation reform.[43]

Samarin's interest in emancipation was clearly not an isolated case. It was shared by the other Slavophils whose concern for the abolition of serfdom goes back to the beginning of Moscow Slavophilism. Emancipation of the serfs, although not in an identical manner, was very much on the minds of a number of leading liberals, in the views of Herzen and Chernyshevksy, and even for some officials in the government. Samarin's more direct involvement in emancipation than that of the other early Slavophils was due in part to his court connections, and to his experience in government. This made him better informed in some matters than Konstantin Aksakov, for one, and also better informed in the eyes of the tsar. Alexander II also seems to have appreciated Samarin's directness and his concern for the interests of the gentry.

Notes

1. See N. P. Popov, "Liberal'no-burzhuaznyi lager' (1853–1858)," in M. V. Nechkina, ed., *Revoliutsionnaia situatsiia v seredine XIX veka* (Moscow, 1978), p. 90.

2. See N. I. Tsimbaev, "Zapiska K. A. Aksakova 'O vnutrennem sostoianii Rossii' i ee mesto v ideologii slavianofil'stva," in *Vestnik moskovskogo universiteta. Istoriia,* 1972, no. 2, pp. 47–60. This brief work, based on extensive, wide-ranging research, including a study of important archival materials, sheds much light on Aksakov's political convictions, and on Slavophil ideology in general.

3. Koliupanov, *Koshelev,* II, 83–84.

4. In addition to his memorandum "Concerning the Monetary Resources of Russia in the Present Circumstances" Koshelev sent to the tsar early in 1858 four more *zapiski:* (1) "About the necessity of the immediate destruction of serfdom," (2) "About the various means of emancipating the peasants," (3) "Hypothetical measures for emancipation of the peasants," and (4) "Hypothetical measures for emancipation of the household serfs." Koshelev, *Zapiski,* Appendix, pp. 33–166.

5. N. I. Tsimbaev, *I. S. Aksakov v obshchestvennoi zhizni poreformennoi Rossii* (Moscow, 1978), pp. 8, 53.
6. Tsimbaev, *"Zapiska* K. S. Aksakova," p. 52.
7. Ibid., p. 53.
8. Ibid., pp. 48, 55.
9. See O. N. Trubetskaia, "Kn. Vladimir Aleksandrovich Cherkassky," in *Velikaia reforma,* V, 111.
10. See O. N. Trubetskaia, ed., *Materialy dlia biografii kn. V. A. Cherkasskago. . . . Perepiska s Iu. F. Samarinym, A. I. Koshelevym, I. S. Aksakovym i proch. Iz arkhiva kn. Cherkasskago.* (Moscow, 1901, 1904), 1 vol., 2 books.
11. The resume of E. A. Dudzinskaia's dissertation on *Russkaia beseda* gives indications of a valuable work on a major phase of Slavophil thought and activity.
12. Richard Wortman, who has dealt ably with internal Slavophil matters during this period, concentrated on three Slavophils, as stated in the title of his essay, "Koshelev, Samarin, and Cherkassky and the Fate of Liberal Slavophilism," *Slavic Review,* June 1962, pp. 261–79. In more recent years the same subject has been included in the works of a number of Soviet scholars, foremost among whom are E. A. Dudzinskaia, whose *Slavianofily v obshchestvennoi bor'be* and a number of articles have already been cited in this text, and also N. I. Tsimbaev, whose essay on K. S. Aksakov and monograph on I. S. Aksakov are cited above.
13. While the paternity of *sobornost'* is usually attributed to Khomiakov, that of the "wholeness of the spirit" to Ivan Kireevsky, and that of *obshchinnost'* to both, there is also a point of view, expressed by Professor Vengerov, that the "Initiative belongs to all of them together and to everyone separately. One person made a hint, another took him up, a third picked up proofs, and in general a thesis was arrived at, the parental rights to which must be equally attributed to all members of the circle inseparably." Quoted in V. M. Shtein, *Ocherki razvitiia russkoi obshchestvenno-ekonomicheskoi mysli XIX–XX vekov* (Leningrad, 1948), p. 121.
14. Recently some Slavophil views and opinions of the *narod* as well as criticism on the same subject by some of their ideological opponents have been summarized in a monograph by Pirozhkova. While for Konstantin Aksakov the Russian peasant was the "highest ideal of man," and Khomiakov was convinced that the *narod* was the repository of virtues not only for Russia but "for all peoples," their friend, Gogol' considered the Russian upper class the "flower of the people." At the same time V. F. Odoevsky expressed skepticism about the virtues of the *narod* and Chaadaev objected to the Slavophils' "arrogant apotheosis of the Russian people." Herzen and Belinsky disagreed with the Slavophils' associating the *narod* with Chris-

tianity and Orthodoxy. See T. F. Pirozhkova, *Revoliutsionery-demokraty o slavianofil'stve i slavianofil'skoi zhurnalistike* (Moscow, 1984), pp. 32–39.

15. In 1860, shortly before the deaths of Khomiakov and Konstantin Aksakov, the Slavophils and some of their friends who were sympathetic to the Slavs signed Khomiakov's well-known *To the Serbians. A Message from Moscow.* The eleven who signed it were Aleksei Khomiakov, Mikhail Pogodin, Alexander Koshelev, Ivan Beliaev, Nikolai Elagin, Iurii Samarin, Peter Bezsonov, Konstantin Aksakov, ,Peter Bartenev, Fedor Chizhov, and Ivan Aksakov. See Khomiakov, *Sochineniia,* I, 404. See also M. Ia. Goldberg, "K istorii polemiki vokrug slavianofil'skogo poslanie k serbam," V. I. Freidzon et al., eds., *Voprosy pervonachal'nogo nakopleniia kapitala i natsional'nye dvizheniia v slavianskikh stranakh* (Moscow, 1972), pp. 197–209.

16. Samarin, *Sochineniia,* II, 146.

17. Ibid., pp. 148–151.

18. Ibid., pp. 152–153.

19. Ibid., p. 154.

20. Ibid., pp. 155, 436.

21. Ibid., pp. 155, 436.

22. Ibid., pp. 159, 160.

23. Ibid., p. 161.

24. In a Soviet publication that has rather recently come to my attention, the author of the introduction to the volume says, "During the 'seven dark years [1848–1855]'" the Slavophils "proved themselves to be almost the only ones to openly express dissatisfaction with the existing reality." He points out that Belinsky was dead, and that Herzen was abroad and his "free Russian word" did not reach Russia until 1853. The Petrashevtsy were in prison, and the time of the revolutionary activity of Chernyshevsky and Dobroliubov had not arrived. "Under these conditions the fundamental burden of resistance to the tsarist government and to the autocratic-serf order . . . was accepted by the Slavophils . . . and without changing their orientation, they did not refuse to expose the 'imperial regime.'" See A. S. Kurilov, ed., *K. S. Aksakov, I. S. Aksakov. Literaturnaia kritika* (Moscow, 1981), pp. 9–10.

25. Samarin, *Sochineniia,* II, 163–165.

26. Ibid., pp. 165, 166.

27. Walicki has written some highly informative pages on Ivan Kireevsky's distinction between *narod,* people, and society (also expressed in one of Konstantin Aksakov's ringing editorials), and on Kireevsky's (and Khomiakov's) sharp criticism of the West's strong adherence to classical or pagan Roman legalism, formalism, and institutionalism. What is not stated with unmistakable clarity is that if there was influence between the Slavophils and the West, represented in this case by Ferdinand Tönnies (1855–1936) and Max Weber (1864–1920), it would have had to flow from Russia to the West. Kireevsky and Khomiakov, who died in 1856 and 1860, respectively,

could not have borrowed from either Tonnies or Weber. See Andrzej Walicki, *The Slavophil Controversy* (Oxford, 1975), pp. 168–177.

28. Samarin, *Sochineniia* II, p. 166.

29. Ibid., pp. 169–170.

30. Ibid., p. 171.

31. Ibid., p. 172.

32. Ibid., p. 173.

33. Ibid., pp. 173–174.

34. Ibid., pp. 175–176.

35. Ibid., pp. 176, 178.

36. Nol'de, *Samarin* p. 67. Recent, highly informative, and more up-to-date summaries of Samarin's *zapiski* than Nol'de's are given in Dudzinskaia, *Slavianofily v obshchestvennoi bor'be*, pp. 90–96. See also, Dudzinskaia, *Samarin*, pp. 321–329.

37. The activities of the Grand Duchess Elena Pavlovna (1806–1874), born Frederike Charlotte Marie of Wurttemberg, of her salon and circle established in 1848, her purchase of the Karlovka estate in the Poltava gubernia in 1849, and its role in her circle, the Wildbad conference of 1857, and the emancipation reform, have recently been brought to light by W. Bruce Lincoln in two works. See his "The Circle of the Grand Duchess Yelena Pavlovna, 1847–1861," *Slavonic and East European Review,* April 1970, pp. 373–385, and *In the Vanguard of Reform: Russia's Enlightened Bureaucrats, 1825–1861.* (De Kalb, Ill. 1982), pp. 154–160.

38. Much information, a significant portion of which apparently comes from archival sources, has recently been provided by Lincoln on the role of the Grand Duke and Grand Duchess in the emancipation reform. For the Grand Duke's "Konstantinovtsy," and the Grand Duchess's salon, see Lincoln, *In the Vanguard of Reform,* pp. 141–162.

39. Nol'de, *Samarin,* pp. 73–74, 79.

40. Ibid., p. 76.

41. The author of a biographical essay focusing on K. D. Kavelin's views and influence on the emancipation reform states that Alexander II was angered when Kavelin's *zapiska* of 1855 appeared in print. Yet earlier the tsar had approved of it. The author concludes that Kavelin's "historical *Zapiska* of 1855 was almost wholly assimilated by those who were destined to bring the liberating reform to life." See B. I. Syromiatnikov, "Konstantin Dmitrievich Kavelin," *Velikaia reforma* (Moscow, 1911) V, p. 138.

42. See D. A. Obolensky, "Moi vospominaniia," *Russkaia starina,* March 1909, p. 507.

43. Concentration on a single subject, in this case Samarin's *zapiska,* tends to distort the broader subject of the emancipation of the serfs in which participated a good many in addition to the Slavophils. For a summary of the *zapiski* of M. A. Korf, Ia. I. Rostovtsev, P. P. Gagarin, M. P. Posen, A. F.

Haxthausen, K. D. Kavelin, A. I. Koshelev (four *zapiski*), Prince V. A. Cherkassky, and Samarin, see P. A. Zaionchkovsky, *Otmena krepostnogo prava v Rossii,* 2nd ed. (Moscow, 1960) pp. 72–92. In addition to the Slavophils and liberal Westerners (Kavelin, Chicherin, and I.I. Pànàev submitted *zapiski*), one must also consider the strong pro-emancipation voices of the radical Westerners, particularly those heard in Herzen's *Kolokol* and Chernyshevsky's *Sovremennik.*

15

Slavophil Collaborators
and the Edict of 1861

Samarin's part in the evolution of the government's policy and the emancipation edict serves as the ultimate measure of the degree to which his views and ideas were realized in the reform. The complicated task that faces the student of his thought and activities in the late 1850s becomes apparent when we are reminded that he was one of many who worked for emancipation, that the final decision was not his but the tsar's, that the emancipation issue was bafflingly complex, and that Samarin was torn between his personal and class interests and the larger concerns for the Russian peasantry and nation – and furthermore, that all this took place in a rapidly changing social and economic environment.

Considering the inefficiency of the tsarist administration and the intricacies of the serf and land questions, the emancipation reform moved quickly in the roughly three years between November 1857 and February 1861. The principal agents that prepared the way for one of the most far-reaching and peaceful changes in Russian history were the gubernia committees organized on Baron M. A. Korf's initiative (staffed by gentry from each gubernia), and the "Editing Commissions," that is the larger central bodies that were assigned to draft the legislation.[1] The committees came into existence in 1857, the commissions on March 4, 1859. In February 1861, as a result of the tsar's edict, nearly 23,000,000 serfs belonging to 104,000 landowners were freed from centuries of bondage that was often not far from slavery. But in the process of emancipation the serfs were relegated to the position of mute, impatient, and sometimes rebellious spectators. It seemed, as if among 23 million serfs, although left illiterate and uninformed, not even a handful could be found to represent those whose fate was being decided! In the summer of 1858 Samarin left Moscow for Samara, having accepted an appointment as member-from-the-government on the Samara gubernia committee. He soon learned that, of the fourteen members of the committee, he could count on only two for support for his stand on emancipation.[2]

Since the focus of this study narrows to exclude a general discussion of the emancipation reform, it is essential to remind the reader of the distortion that, try as one may to avoid it, accompanies concentration on a single person, in this case Samarin. A good example of a comprehensive approach is Semevsky's enduring *Krest'ianskii vopros v Rossii* (The Peasant Question in Russia). Volume two of this work published in 1888, covers the reign of Nicholas I (1825–1855); although a summary, it extends over more than six hundred pages. Here are skillfully and factually presented the views, measures, and policies on the peasant question and emancipation of the government, of the tsar and his officials. The work also touches on Russian literature, specifically on the works of Pushkin, Viazemsky, Griboedov, Lermontov, Gogol', Dal', Sollogub, Grigorovich, and Turgenev. Semevsky then examines the attitudes and convictions of Belinsky, Herzen, Ogarev, Stankevich, Nekrasov, and the early Slavophils. This and a good deal more is included in this masterly work that covers the most relevant spokesmen on emancipation from the extreme left to the extreme right. In the face of such a work, anyone concentrating on an individual cannot avoid a keen awareness of the limitations of the choice, and of the consequent incompleteness and involuntary distortions.

Beyond the immediate concern with Samarin lies the central topic of this and the preceding three studies, and that is Moscow or early Slavophilism. But Samarin's and the Slavophils contribution to the emancipation reform can best be understood if he is not entirely cut off from the rest of the Slavophils. This seems to be so despite his independence of mind and spirit, and his expert knowledge of the emancipation problem in Prussia and Russia. Although Khomiakov and Konstantin Aksakov died in 1860, when work on the emancipation of the serfs had largely been completed, the men with whom Samarin kept in closest touch on this problem were Koshelev and Cherkassky, and to an extent Ivan Aksakov. To be convinced of the role that the three-sided relationship between Samarin, Koshelev, and Cherkassky played in the emancipation reform one need not go much beyond their invaluable correspondence, already mentioned, and published in two volumes ("books") in 1901 and 1904 by Princess Trubetskaia.

Much biographical information is available about A. I. Koshelev, reference to which has already been made. A few more biographical facts will be added in due course as we touch on his relationship with Samarin and Cherkassky during the few feverish years preceding February 1861. In the process certain facts should emerge which shed light on Moscow Slavophilism as it evolved at the end of the 1850s when, in connection with the emancipation of the serfs, serious differences emerged in the Slavophil camp, not the least of which were between Samarin and Koshelev.

As mentioned earlier (Chapter 13) Prince Vladimir Aleksandrovich Cherkassky (1824–1878) occupies a somewhat ambiguous position among the early Slavophils. The Cherkasskys were a princely family that had been prominent in Russia since the days of Ivan the Terrible, though they had lost much of their fortune by the early nineteenth century. Prince Vladimir entered Moscow University in 1840, prepared for university work by Professor O. M. Bodiansky, the well-known Slavicist. During the eight years 1840–1848 he lived in Moscow and on his Tula estate. As a student in the faculty of law at Moscow University he showed interest in Russia's peasant order and in the historical establishment of serfdom, and while in his middle twenties became a member of a nine-man circle in the Tula gubernia and wrote for it a project for possible serf emancipation. But orders came from St. Petersburg at the end of 1847 to abandon the project.[3] Then the revolutions in the West in 1848–1849 put an end to any immediate emancipation plans in Russia.

Both as an undergraduate and graduate student at Moscow University Cherkassky established contact with the Slavophils. Nikolai Alekseevich Elagin, half-brother of Ivan and Peter Kireevsky and two years older than Cherkassky, also a university student, introduced the prince into his mother's salon, then in its prime. There he met both Slavophils and Westerners. A generation separated Cherkassky from Khomiakov and Ivan Kireevsky, while Konstantin Aksakov was seven years, and Samarin five years his senior. In the words of Bezsonov, who knew Cherkassky personally, Nikolai Elagin was warmly attached to the prince. He also says that Cherkassky became "gradually involved" in the Slavophil circle. Bezsonov captured the spirit of the circle and the characteristics of its members in the following lines:

> But whereas K. S. Aksakov, in all similar situations entered directly into a fight to the death, Iu. F. Samarin deliberately lured his adversaries under the blade of his artful analysis, while Khomiakov liked to set one against another, enjoying it from the side, and wholeheartedly laughed at the fruit of his labor. The Prince, in contrast, almost always removed himself from the controversies, and readily withdrew with a jest [*otshuchivat'sia*].

Elaborating on his characterization of Cherkassky, Bezsonov added, "One could sooner find him in heated debates with Khomiakov and K. S. Aksakov, and with the other 'fellow members' than with his true adversaries."[4]

Cherkassky felt deep respect for Khomiakov, but he "became closest to I. V. Kireevsky," with whom he shared a certain sense of "Europeanism"[5] With the younger Slavophils, Konstantin Aksakov and Samarin, Cherkassky's relationship was different. Bezsonov, born in 1828, was closer in age to them than to Khomiakov and Kireevsky, and he knew their university and social milieu and their personal characteristics. Comparing Konstantin Aksakov and Cherkassky, he noted, "Aksakov was too serious about questions that were on his mind, and being a youngster at heart he could not take either a play or a joke on any subject, whereas the jocular side of the subject as well as the jocular side of a conversation, and plays on words were constant inclinations of the prince." Of Samarin he says, "[His] relations with the prince were at first very reserved and almost cool," but later "Samarin became intimately close to the prince and their names together with the third, Miliutin's, became inseparable."[6]

Cherkassky himself, in the brief reminiscences of his student days that he wrote in 1855 on the occasion of the university's centennial, observed that history was the dominant interest on the campus,[7] especially Russian history as taught by M. P. Pogodin, who was noted for his pro-Russian, pro-Slav orientation and his view that the course of Russian history was different from that of the West. That the university studies had an important and lasting, if not exclusive effect on Cherkassky's career is illustrated by the five "periods" into which Bezsonov divides his public life; his Moscow student days and his association with the Slavophil circle, a period of concentration on the "peasant question," another period dominated by the "Polish question," a fourth period concerned with "Moscow city organization," and a fifth, concerned with the "general Slav question and Bulgaria."[8] Here we are concerned with the first two periods, since the last three, beginning in 1863, continue to 1878, well beyond the emancipation reform that coincidentally and conveniently marks the end of "early" or "classical" Slavophilism.

Leaving out of consideration political and tactical differences that emerged in the course of the emancipation reform between Samarin, Koshelev, and Cherkassky, it has been competently attested that Cherkassky differed with the Slavophils on several fundamental Slavophil tenets: on the place of Orthodoxy, and on that of the peasant commune in Slavophil ideology, as well as the Slavophil notion of the *narod*. As noted earlier, Princess Trubetskaia stated in the preface to her collection of letters between Cherkassky, Samarin, and Koshelev that Cherkassky "was never a Slavophil in the commonly accepted meaning of this word." She based this assertion on differences in the "philosophical, historical, social, and political views of the Slavophils." She also stressed that under Khomiakov's influence Slavophilism's foundation was religious, specifically Orthodox, whereas for Cherkassky the "religious side" of life "remained for long as if untouched." It "slipped by" him.[9] From the Slavophil point of view, Cherkassky was also deficient enough in his views on the village commune to provoke K. S. Aksakov to write to him in 1859: "You are an enemy of the commune and therefore in my view you are an enemy of the people . . . Between us a war has been declared."[10]

The credibility of Trubetskaia's characterization of Cherkassky is enhanced when we are reminded that she based her opinion on the written testimony of Koshelev, who, it is well established, knew Cherkassky intimately during the 1850s and was the senior member of the *troika* (Koshelev,

Samarin, and Cherkassky) involved in the emancipation reform. Koshelev and Cherkassky had serious disagreements, however, not only about reform but of a long-standing nature, dating from the time when they both served in Warsaw following the Polish rebellion. In his *Zapiski,* written some years after the emancipation reform, Koshelev states:

With respect to Prince Cherkassky's collaboration I consider it necessary to say a few words. Although subsequently he has often been considered a so-called Slavophil, and sometimes has even been put at the head of this party, in reality he was never such, and parted [ways] with us on the most essential convictions. He did not at all consider the Orthodox Christian teaching the foundation of our point of view; he spoke out repeatedly against the peasant commune, and liked to ridicule the *narod*-idol, before whom, in his opinion, presumably Khomiakov and K. Aksakov bowed down.

What, then, did the Slavophils and Cherkassky have in common? Koshelev's reply to this question was brief and simple: "As a highly intelligent man he recognized that there was more strength and [prospects for the] future in our orientation than in the opposing, i.e., the then Western, orientation."[11]

At the beginning of the 1850s Cherkassky drew closer to the Slavophil circle and in 1851 he contributed an article to the Slavophil symposium. Its theme, in which Cherkassky had an early interest, was "Iur'ev den'," (November 26) — the only day of the year on which serfs could legally move from one master to another. But the censorship banned the symposium. For the remainder of the decade, particularly in its latter half, Cherkassky experienced his most active publicistic period. Two works should be stressed here. His *Zapiska* on emancipation, and his seventy-five-page review essay of two Western works, *"De l'avenir politique de l'Angleterre* par le comte de Montalembert," and *"L'ancien régime el la révolution.* Par Alexis de Tocqueville" (both volumes were published in Paris in 1856). The reviews, dated February 20, 1857, appeared in the 1857 issue of *Russkaia beseda.*[12] The *Zapiska* on emancipation was handed to a government official early in January 1857.

The occasion of reviewing someone else's work, particularly books of uncensored Western authors, was a way in which a Russian reviewer could take advantage of a degree of freedom that the censorship would probably not normally have allowed. Any criticism of government authorities and their policies and practices was that of the Western writer, and presumably not of the reviewer. Cherkassky, agreeably amazed that Montalembert's "truths were obviously and exclusively directed against the system of Louis Napoleon" and frankly admiring of the freedom of expression in France and England, declared that "neither Montalembert nor Tocqueville was indifferent to the notion of an independent national development of each society. They have no sympathy for [state] centralization equally alien to old Europe as to old Russia"[13] He regretted that pre-Petrine Russia was "not in great respect" in certain quarters in Russia, (this struck a chord that was certain to find a favorable response among the Slavophils), for he was convinced that the "new Russia could only rise upon the strong, firm foundation of the old Russia; that the latter protected and rallied our state at the cost of much heavy sacrifice," and that in the process it expended "not a little honest labor and noble daring."[14] As if answering some of the Westerners' charges against the Slavophils, he referred to England as "this classical land of freedom," and quoted Montalembert to the effect that England "dares to believe at one and the same time in historical tradition and in progress; that it has the skill to preserve its monarchy and live in freedom, to turn aside revolution and to escape despotism." For all his admiration of Montalembert's devotion to and love of "freedom" and "human dignity," however, he took little note of the seriousness of England's social, economic, and personal problems, consequences of industrialism that the Slavophils had been critical of.[15]

In the remaining body of Cherkassky's rather remarkable review of a work on England he provided in some detail a summary of English social and political institutions and a discussion of the nature and role of the English aristocracy, as well as of the Whig and Tory parties. He stressed the role of "self-government" in English history exhibiting the characteristic Slavophil antipathy toward excessive centralization and of bureaucracy in general. In a comparison of the laws of inheritance in England and the United States, he favored the practice in the new world where upon the death of the parents property was divided by all children instead of going to the eldest son as in England. Property and inheritance laws in Russia were, he noted, more like those in the United States than those in England.

Cherkassky took note of Montalembert's chapter 11, which discusses English education, particularly the famous "public" schools like Eton and Harrow and the two ancient universities, Oxford and Cambridge. Cherkassky seemed to be interested in the uniqueness and the characteristically English aspects of the educational system, but he pointed out that Montalembert "pays little attention to the means of educating the children from the lower classes, from the urban and agricultural workers' classes."[16] Cherkassky was struck by the "medieval character" of English universities, and by the fact that, in Montalembert's words, "Nowhere in the world do the Middle Ages appear to be so alive . . . as at Oxford and Cambridge."[17] Yet Cherkassky was quite aware of the modern scientific and scholarly achievements of these universities. He also had something to say about the English parliament and the Church of England. The role of the aristocracy in these two institutions was, he commented being replaced by "triumphant democracy," but he did not believe that that would result in the "perversion of the free English order." He had no doubt that the two basic traits of

English public life, "respect for another's opinion" and the "dominance of open discussion [*glasnost'*] in England in all matters," would not come to an end.[18]

Very clearly, Cherkassky was familiar with both volumes of Tocqueville's earlier work, *La Democratie en Amérique*, which had appeared in 1835 and 1840. The problem of administrative centralization in France and America that had concerned Tocqueville also concerned Cherkassky and the early Slavophils in its Russian context. Cherkassky announced his distaste for centralization early in his review by stating with approval that it did not exist in old Russia. He returned to this subject and declared Tocqueville's chapter entitled "Des effets politiques de la décentralisation administrative en Amérique" a "most substantial word of political wisdom." He pointed out the difference between political and administrative centralization, everywhere urging support for the first and weakening of the latter."[19] Like Tocqueville, the Slavophils saw administrative centralization as undesirable and harmful, and it is not farfetched that Tocqueville might have had some influence on them on this point since he publicized his views on this matter before the Slavophils.

Cherkassky agreed with Tocqueville that centralization and its "abuse" lead to despotism and that "Democracy . . . without independent regional institutions is powerless." For the Slavophils, of course, the many-sided peasant commune and *mir,* and the old *veche* were the local and regional institutions that would assure basic autonomy and self-government without impairing the existence and function of the monarchy, and indeed of the whole empire. But Cherkassky regarded the village commune and *mir* simply as useful local administrative organs, without the social, economic, ethical, and even Orthodox religious values that the early Slavophils tended to read into them. On the whole, Cherkassky agreed with Tocqueville's antirevolutionary views, and he says that Tocqueville is in favor of the "maintenance of the inner public equilibrium ensuring it beforehand against violent upheavals."[20] This, Cherkassky said, was Tocqueville's "firm conviction" running throughout his book. There is no doubt that it was also Cherkassky's. Here too, as in Montalembert, Cherkassky was particularly interested in the discussion of property and inheritance. He cited figures given by Tocqueville to illustrate the degree to which landholdings in France had been fragmented, noting that farms in France between 1790 and 1855 had increased in the ratio of two to three, he drew the conclusion that making available "to the lower classes wide access to land property is the best and essential foundation for the conservative principles of the new society." Here, indeed, Cherkassky clearly departed from the Slavophil position on the economic functions of the Russian peasant commune, and several paragraphs later he underscored his conviction by agreeing with Tocqueville that "land property well organized and expanded among the lower classes is the last anchor of salvation for the contemporary state in Europe."[21]

The lessons from French history, before and after the Revolution, were clear for Cherkassky as they were for Tocqueville. Lesson one was the "harmful consequences of centralization"; lesson two, the "most substantial ulcer of old France, closely tied to the first, was the separateness [*razroznennost'*] of classes, and their political estrangement from each other."[22] He devotes a few paragraphs to elaborating the reasons why the French aristocracy was alienated from the peasantry and the peasantry from the middle class, and he agrees with Tocqueville that the increasing migration of the French gentry to the cities, particularly to Paris, was a bad thing. He seemed to imply that France's experiences should be a lesson to Russia.

Since Cherkassky's reviews were published in *Russkaia beseda* it is a safe assumption that the early Slavophils read them. Samarin, we know, had read Tocqueville's *L'ancien régime et la révolution* soon after it was published. His collected works, published in 1877, contain a three-paragraph commentary on the book that Dimitry Samarin found written in pencil on the cover of Iurii's personal copy. These remarks — obviously for Iurii's own use and not meant for publication — begin with the declaration, "Tocqueville, Montalembert, Riehl, Stein, are Western Slavophils. All of them in their basic convictions, and in their ultimate demands are closer to us than to our Westerners." Unlike Cherkassky, who in his reviews was concerned with ideological and political problems, Samarin jumped into the sphere of philosophy before he got to the question of the *narod*. The central contemporary question in the West, as in Russia, was, "Is the autocratic sovereignty of abstract rationality [*razsudok*] in the structure of the human soul, civic society, and the state lawful?" In the West, the "tyranny of abstract rationality in the realm of philosophy, faith, and conscience" was matched in life by the "tyranny of the central authority."

The commentary goes on to say that *razsudok* is ubiquitous in the West: "La manie de tout administrer, de tout réglementer, de substituer partout une regle déduit d'un principe abstrait a la tradition et a la libre inspiration." He probably went as far as he would ever go in denouncing governments when he asserted that the "lawful sense of anguish and surfeit evoked by the absolute power of abstract rationality and governments lies in the fundamental endeavors of Montalembert, Tocqueville, and *Russkaia beseda.*" But he also saw a major difference between the Russian and "Western Slavophils." In the West the latter turned to the aristocracy, because "there it better than the other parties realizes 'living Toryism'." This strong cultural and political force had no counterpart in Russia. We in Russia, Samarin states, "turn to the common people for the same reason for which they sympathize with the aristocracy."[23]

"With us," Samarin goes on, giving full reign to his Slavophil sentiments, the *"narod* sustains in itself the gift of self-sacrifice, the freedom of moral inspiration, and respect for tradition. In Russia the only refuge of Toryism is the dark hut of the peasant." In contrast to this, he added, "in our palaces [and] university halls blows all-parching Whiggism." But there was still another difference between Russia and the West. Both Toryism and Whiggism grew out of the same soil whereas in Russia "Whiggism was grafted from without." Clearly Samarin identified "Russian Whiggism" with Russian Westernism, and liberalism and showed little enthusiasm for either. In Russia, he says, the "struggle between Whiggism and Toryism in the realm of faith, philosophy, and administration is much more complex than in the West." It was in fact a "struggle of the *people's* everyday life [*byt*] with non-national [*beznarodnoiu*] abstract *civilization.*"[24]

The obvious differences of opinion and convictions between Samarin and Cherkassky reflected in their partial reactions to the works of Montalembert and Tocqueville could not stand in the way of cooperation once they both became involved in the emancipation reform. Cherkassky's *Zapiska* (on emancipation) shows clearly that there was no such thing as a monolithic Slavophil program on emancipation, or on any other matter, on which unwavering conformity was expected. We are still in that phase of Russian public life when the loose discussion circle, not the tightly organized and disciplined political party prevailed.

The principal *Zapiska* on emancipation that Cherkassky drafted late in 1856 and early in 1857 was about fifty-five pages long (it was later supplemented by more than a dozen shorter additions). It begins with a brief introduction, and is divided into fifteen topics, each of which is discussed and elaborated upon. It concludes with a four-page summary.[25] As in the case of Samarin's *Zapiska,* and indeed of all other *zapiski,* whether by Slavophils or Westerners, the time of their drafting and submission is of obvious relevance to their contents and form. Before November 20, 1857, opinions had to be phrased with care; ideas were guarded. Cherkassky's *Zapiska,* written almost a year before he knew where the government stood on emancipation, is typically conditional and tentative.

For instance, in the conclusion to the *Zapiska* Cherkassky states that the government need not look for "immediate and radical transformation of serfdom." He would have been content with the removal of some of serfdom's "main abuses, and with the healing of some of its most painful ulcers." He urged the government to pass legislation in order to prepare public opinion to work for and accept emancipation, which was indeed a civic duty and should be given "free and even [public] written consideration." At the same time, the government should encourage "industriousness" and self-reliance among the peasantry. He believed that the most desirable form of emancipation was that which freed the serfs "with land," but at the same time he considered it advisable that "two or three million" serfs be freed without land. These peasants, (presumably from among the household serfs) would respond to Russia's growing need for labor in factories and agriculture, and they could be a mobile work force, which could go wherever it was needed. Cherkassky envisioned a transitional period of some fifteen to twenty years, after which would come emancipation of the serfs *"with preservation for them of property in land and communal government."*[26] At the same time the landowners would be fairly compensated for the loss of their lands to the freed serfs.

Realizing that he belonged to a minority of the Russian gentry, Cherkassky spoke out against the landowners who would indefinitely postpone emancipation on the ground that Russia's first need was administrative reform, glaringly obvious after the Crimean War. Although he did not deny this need, he cautioned that emancipation could not wait for other internal improvements since in every society there is always need for administrative reform. His *Zapiska* ends with an admonition that Russia should follow the example of Prussia after Jena and Tilsit, and of the "great Stein." Elsewhere in this first *zapiska* and its supplements Cherkassky refers to the emancipation of the serfs in Prussia and Austria in such a way as to make it clear that he, like Samarin, has had a good deal of history, both Russian and Western.

In this connection one encounters in Cherkassky a suggestion — rare in the nonrevolutionary pro-Slavophil literature on emancipation — that the government and representatives of classes other than the gentry should participate in the reform. In a *zapiska* addressed to the Grand Duchess Elena Pavlovna after the tsar's rescript on emancipation, Cherkassky suggested that the gubernia committees "for the sake of the most many-sided study of the task should summon in their midst for consultation not only landowners and nobility but also peasants of excellent minds and morality, as well as persons of all other classes who are intimately informed about the peasant order and needs, in particular the best members of the village clergy." The data, opinions, and suggestions obtained in this manner, he thought, "will receive special completeness and importance, and will approach . . . the beautiful example represented by the famous English parliamentary investigations (Parliamentary Inquiries)."[27] Clearly, when Cherkassky made this suggestion to the Grand Duchess he was imagining a different political and social order from the one the tsar was willing to tolerate.

Cherkassky was no more able than other Russian intellectuals to ponder emancipation, or as the government preferred to say the "betterment" (*uluchshenie*) of the peasant order, without also dwelling on other aspects of Russian public life that were in need of "betterment."[28] One of the several issues that Cherkassky spoke out on has to do with the possible rush to the towns and cities of freed serfs. While he wished to see some of the serfs become free laborers to fill the need for factory workers, he also wished to control the possible rapid influx of villagers into the cities where they might fall victims to unemployment. His purpose was to maintain a balance between towns and villages by the creation of additional *"mir* communes" *(mirskie obshchiny).*[29] Presumably these were to be administrative in character and would have none of the other attributes of the historical Russian commune, conceived by the Slavophils as a spontaneous expression of the Russian spirit over a long period of time, and which could not be the result of a quick stroke of "social engineering."

Although for over a century Koshelev's Memoirs *(Zapiski),* correspondence, and other works, including the two-volume (3 books) unfinished biography by N. P. Koliupanov, have been major sources of information and opinions on the emancipation reform, and on other possible reforms; on Slavophilism, Westernism, and other tendencies no complete full-length biography of Koshelev has yet been published. From the references made in this and the preceding three studies it is apparent that he had an important part in the evolution of Moscow Slavophilism in spite of the fact that he is not usually included among the "early" Slavophils. The principal reason for this is that by the time he joined the Slavophil circle at the turn of the 1840s, — thereby moving from the status of friend to that of colleague — the Slavophil religious-philosophical and ideological positions had largely been established by Khomiakov, Ivan Kireevsky, Konstantin Aksakov, and Samarin. Koshelev moved resolutely into the Slavophil circle as the Slavophils were entering the third and last sphere of their concerns, that of reform and politics. By temperament, inclination, and choice he arrived in the right place (for him) at the right time.

Because of his wealth and his reputation as publisher and chief editor of the 1856 *Russkaia beseda* and also *Sel'skoe blagoustroistvo,* in the eyes of the government Koshelev probably stood out as the Slavophil par excellence. At any rate, he served on the Riazan gubernia committee on emancipation, although a little later he was refused appointment on the government Editorial Commission. This happened while Samarin and Cherkassky, a generation younger and not so experienced in estate management nor so well informed about the latest developments in modern agriculture, were appointed on the Editorial Commission in St. Petersburg. As might be expected, Koshelev resented this slighting by the tsar's principal representative in the emancipation reform, General Ia. I. Rostovtsev. This in turn, not altogether surprisingly, had an effect on his relations with Samarin and Cherkassky.

In recent years, research in the Soviet Union has provided us with much additional information about the pent-up energies during the thirty-year reign of Nicholas I, and their release, partial though it may have been, after his death. Between 1855 and 1860 150 new journals and newspapers appeared — among them, as already mentioned, *Russkaia beseda, Sel'skoe blagoustroistvo,* and Konstantin Aksakov's *Molva.* The sudden outburst of journalistic and publicistic activity, much of it of distinction, whether it came from the radical, liberal, or Slavophil press, helped maintain the usually high level of nineteenth-century Russian periodical literature.

In addition to the three Slavophil journals during this period there were also the "liberal" *Russkii vestnik,* which later changed orientations, published by M. N. Katkov, whose contributors included, at one time or another, Kavelin, Chicherin, S. M. Solov'ev, Turgenev, Dostoevsky, and many others. *Atenei,* published by the moderate liberal E. F. Korsh, appeared as a weekly and later as a bimonthly for less than two years (1858–1859).[30]   Among the leftist Westerner journals were the well-known *Otechestvennye zapiski* and *Sovremennik,* mainstays of Russian literary criticism and publicistic work. During the period under consideration Chernyshevsky was the driving force behind *Otechestvennye zapiski. Sovremennik,* already with a long and distinguished record entered a new phase in late 1856 when N. A. Dobroliubov became associated with it. In time, he, along with Chernyshevsky, who had become a permanent contributor in 1854, came to dominate the journal, displacing the liberal Westerners V. P. Botkin, P. V. Annenkov, and I. I. Panaev. Herzen's famous *Kolokol* was, as previously mentioned, being regularly smuggled into Russia, and it even proved possible for some of the Slavophils to air their views in its columns.[31]

Such crossovers occurred often enough to illustrate two important points: one, that whether an orientation was liberal, radical, or Slavophil, ideologies and political programs were not so firmly and unequivocally cast, nor ideological loyalties so unbending, as to preclude all line crossing; second, that the need to achieve the emancipation of the serfs was so pressing that some of the Slavophils were willing, however temporarily, to make common cause with radical Westerners such as Herzen and N. P. Ogarev in order to bring about an end to serfdom. Nor were these tactical rapprochements observable only from the Slavophil camp. Chernyshevsky, for instance, found it possible to approve much in the Slavophil stand on the village commune, in their views of the West, and in their general ideological position, remaining all the while firmly attached to his materialistic revolutionary convictions. This and a good deal more has been brought out in some of the latest Soviet researches on the Slavophils.[32]

In addition to his estate management and his concerns for the publication of *Russkaia beseda* and *Sel'skoe blagoustroistvo,* Koshelev remained deeply involved in the emancipation problem. He also found it possible to continue his frequent trips to the West. Early in the summer of 1858 while the gubernia committees on emancipation were being organized, Koshelev tells us, the governor of his Riazan gubernia asked him to join its committee as a member "from the government." He replied that he would accept provided that he would not be bound to "support all the opinions and demands of the ministry of internal affairs."[33] He accepted the appointment after he was assured that he would not need to forfeit his freedom of judgment and choice, but it soon became clear that he would never take the next step in the working out of the emancipation reform, that is, he would not be appointed to the Editing Commission.

It remains now to turn to Koshelev's *zapiski* on emancipation, which along with the *zapiski* of Samarin, Cherkassky, and certain non-Slavophils who had convictions and suggestions on emancipation of the serfs are a primary source on the subject. The appendix to Koshelev's *Zapiski* includes a letter of 1847 from Koshelev to the Minister of Internal Affairs L. A. Perovsky, on the "betterment" of the status of landowner's serfs. This two-page letter, written a decade before the post-Crimean War flow of *zapiski* to St. Petersburg and the official government declaration in favor of emancipation, deals with the problem of the so-called obligated (*obiazannye*) peasants. By the decree of April 2, 1842, a serf could enter into agreement with his landowner to receive freedom and the right to till a piece of the master's land in return for dues and services that he would continue to pay to his landowner. Only about 25,000 male serfs achieved the new status, however Koshelev, knowing well that the majority of landowners did not wish to change the conditions of the serfs, asked permission of the Minister of Interior to organize a committee to look into the matter. Perovsky, after consulting with the tsar, advised him to confine himself to his serfs and estates, and set a good example for the other landowners.[34]

In this as in his later pronouncements on the peasant question Koshelev had several considerations. He stood for emancipation, and while he did not play up the Christian motive, neither did he hide it, giving it what he considered appropriate consideration.[35] This was true, though less noticeably, of Samarin. The Slavophils, who were not only conscious of the predominantly secular age in which they lived were also quite aware of their own economic interests, and refrained from insisting that the struggle for emancipation should rest upon an Orthodox Christian base alone. They knew that in France during the Revolution and in Prussia after the Napoleonic wars serfdom came to an end in the course of political and economic changes, and not as a result of religious crusades. In a similar manner in the United States slavery would soon be abolished after a bloody civil war. The Slavophils did not see the Russian Orthodox church under the Holy Synod (with which they did not always see eye to eye) as moving into a position of leadership in the struggle for emancipation—any more than the Catholic church in France or the Protestant churches in the United States, with some minor exceptions, led in the struggle for the emancipation of the slaves.

Another strong consideration against serfdom in Koshelev's view was the complexity of the economic aspects of the institution—involving questions of labor and land (their extent, quality and value). Although he was no more willing than the other Slavophils to sacrifice the economic interests of the landowners, he hoped at the same time to provide the emancipated serf with sufficient land to sustain himself and his family. The serf was expected to pay a redemption fee for the land he was to receive from the landowner, but the quantity, and particularly the quality and value of the land, differed widely not only from one region to another, and within the gubernias, but even on the estates of a single landowner.

Finally in Koshelev's thinking on emancipation there was the nationalistic, Slavophil motivation. This was not weaker in his case than for the other Slavophils. As the most widely traveled among them, he repeatedly saw the fruits of science, technology, and economic development in England, the Netherlands, and Germany. He saw it in housing in England, in roads, bridges, in transportation and communications in the West in general, in provisions for the indigent in Holland, and he was keenly conscious of Russia's lag. And of course he, like all other thinking Russians, did not have to be reminded why Russia had just lost the Crimean War. The Slavophils, who had done much to encourage Russian cultural creativity, particularly in literature, preservation of Russian folklore, and perhaps less directly in Russian music, saw as many others did, that removing serfdom would, in addition to its primary objectives, clear the way for greater cultural activity.

This was Koshelev's conviction, although as his *Zapiska* to Alexander II "On the Necessity of the Destruction of Serfdom in Russia" (early 1858) shows, he had no illusions about the possibility of miracles. He saw in the serfs many human failings such as coarseness, drunkenness, and sloth bred by centuries of oppression, and he did not expect the serf to be transformed overnight, nor to see Russia changed into a modern nation as soon as the serfs were freed. Yet as he observed the peasants on his estates and in the countryside over many years, he was not pessimistic. "Our *narod* is not lazy and not careless," he wrote in the *zapiska*; "With respect to drunkenness, this vice is not worse in the Russian people than in other peoples; and it is not less evident on the gentry estates than in the villages.[36] Serfdom had had debilitating and demoralizing effects on both serf and landowner, and particularly so with respect to the household serfs, the *dvorovye*. Citing official figures for Russia of 1,035,924 household "souls" of both sexes, he stated that actually there were more, and he painted their lot in dismal colors. They are "not attached to the soil, and existed in complete slavery. They have no property and depended completely on their masters' dictates." This condition "acts in a most injurious manner on the morals of both the household serfs and the landowners." The serfs are tempted to give themselves to "carelessness, indolence, and drunkenness," and the landowners tend to regard them "as domestic animals, as things."[37]

At the end of his second *zapiska* to the tsar, also dated early in 1858, Koshelev summed up the conclusions of his recommendations on the emancipation of the serfs under seven main points: (1) The peasants should be freed with land sufficient for them to "exist without privation [*bez-nuzhdno*]." – generally interpreted by the relatively few landowners who favored emancipation to mean the allotments that the serfs had at the time;[38] (2) the serfs should be freed "completely and unconditionally"; (3) this meant "without any transitional period from lesser to greater freedom"; (4) emancipation should come "everywhere at the same time"; (5) serfs should be freed as "*mir* communities and not as individuals or as families"; (6) the landowner was to receive compensation for the land which would become "property of the *mir,* or for quit rent" if the peasants could not pay; (7) emancipation should be achieved "by means of voluntary agreements between landowners and peasants at the instigation of the government, under its supervision and under the threat of having the government carry out the emancipation."[39] In view of the tight government supervision, one wonders why Koshelev thought the agreements could still be "voluntary."

It should be stressed here that while the Slavophils were among the first of the Russian intellectuals to come forth with *zapiski* during the Crimean War and immediately after, there was no such thing as a Slavophil *zapiska*. These were individual efforts stating the views and convictions of single Slavophils. And although the *zapiski* were usually read in a Slavophil salon and met with interested approval, they cannot be considered as party programs or platforms strictly binding on all members. Koshelev's *zapiska* was his own. Indeed, many of his contemporaries regarded his proposals for emancipation, including his desire for the "destruction of serfdom," as quite "radical."

Samarin, in particular, was shocked by Koshelev's arguing for complete emancipation with land, and for allotments to be redeemed with government help over a twelve-year period. Samarin, in Koshelev's words, said, "No! do not send these *zapiski*; they will frighten St. Petersburg and force it to go backward." Cherkassky's views on emancipation were more moderate than Koshelev's, but he nonetheless urged Koshelev to go ahead: "No! Send them by all means. Although your *zapiski* are actually radical that is not a misfortune. . . . St. Petersburg must be bombarded." Many years later Nol'de referred to Koshelev's reputation as that of an "extremist" (*krainii*). This, he said, cost him his appointment on the Editorial Commission.[40]

Koshelev did become a member of the Riazan gubernia committee, however; Samarin was appointed to the Samara gubernia committee, and Cherkassky joined the Tula committee. But all three men were in the minority of their respective committees in their staunch support of emancipation. The story of these committees has been told many times and well, and there is no need to go over this ground again. Much of the best factual information on the subject comes from the three-way correspondence of Koshelev, Samarin, and Cherkassky (edited by Princess Trubetskaia). Our chief concern here, however, is not with the details of the committees' activities but with the question of the motivation that lay behind Samarin's drive for the emancipation of the serfs and, in a broader sense, the place of Samarin's views in the overall Slavophil stand on the serf question. The span of time in this instance is quite short, from the first meeting of the Samara gubernia committee on September 25, 1858, to the dissolving of the Editorial Commission on October 10, 1860.

This period of little more than two years was a time of intense activity for all who were concerned in the portentous changes that were under way. Samarin found it particularly trying to "argue at the same time against the landlords and against the government," and he complained in a letter to N. A. Miliutin that in the Samara committee he was in the minority, one of four "against eleven or twelve." Such were the conditions, he wrote, while the "bitterness of the conservatives grows from day to day: intrigues, slander, impertinences, rudeness, lying, hypocrisy, dishonesty to such an extent that every session costs a person a year of his life, and adds a lock of gray hair."[41] Samarin fell ill probably as a result of the overwork and stress and on the advice of his physician, went to Western Europe for several months in the fall of 1859. Between September and December 1859 he visited Germany and Italy (at the height of the Risorgimento); he returned to St. Petersburg on December 2, having missed some of the early sessions of the Editorial Commission.

While Iurii worked for the Samara committee, two of his brothers, Dmitry and Peter, served on the Riazan and Tula gubernia committees, respectively. The majority of the Riazan and Tula committees, too, were opposed to emancipation. Most landowners feared losing their possessions, privileges, and status, and were openly hostile to the Samarins, and to Koshelev, Cherkassky, and other landowners who were actively working for the emancipation. According to Kornilov, Iurii Samarin "was forced to leave his home armed and accompanied by bodyguards." Cherkassky was threatened with a duel, and Koshelev's relations with his fellow landowners became extremely unfriendly and strained.[42] Echoes of the difficulties and obstructions that the three friends encountered in their gubernia committees are often heard in their correspondence.

In 1857 and 1858, along with work on Russia's emancipation question, Samarin was engaged in reading and research on the Prussian peasant reform. He wrote to Princess Cherkasskaia, November 18, 1857, that he had been reading H. F. K. Stein's biography: "It has been long since I have chanced upon a book so *aufregend* [exciting] and so *aufrichtend* [uplifting]. It has precisely been written for us, namely for our situation."[43] In addition to the epistolary discussions with Koshelev, Cherkassky, and on occasion with N. A. Miliutin and others, he also made his views public in *Russkaia beseda* and the new *Sel'skoe blagoustroistvo*.

In a number of issues of this monthly journal that appeared between March 1858 and April 1859 dedicated to the emancipation problem, Samarin planned to publish eight articles on different themes, all of them related to emancipation. Dmitry Samarin says that they were intended as a guide to the gubernia committees in their deliberations, but probably because of the censorship his brother could publish only three. In Samarin's collected works they appear under the general title, "About the Present and Future Organization of the Landowner's Peasants in it Juridical and Economic Aspects." The first was "About the Peasant Land," the second, "About the Unavoidability of a Transitional Period," the third, "About the Peasant Farmstead" [*usad'ba*]."

Serfdom, he asserted in the first article, rests on two "dependencies, that of one person on another (the peasant on the landlord), and that of the cultivator on the land to which he is attached." The "historical substance of serfdom" rested on the second relationship, which was capable of "development," since a village could exist without a landowner but not without land. Samarin, knowing full well that most landowners were not anxious for emancipation and had no desire to part with any of their lands, nonetheless recommended very clearly that the serfs should be freed with land: "Under land, we understand that part which the peasant uses *for himself* and which includes farmsteads, vegetable garden, pasture, plough land, meadowland, and all accessory lands" such as forests.[44] There was, he admitted, small legal basis, though the Code of Laws (*Svod Zakonov*) contained "hints" of the peasants' right to land. The basis lay in what he called the custom or "historical" right of the peasants.

As he had done before, Samarin justified the appearance of serfdom in Russia on the ground of state necessity. In ancient times, when there was a shortage of cash and capital in Russia, the practice arose of paying for services to the state with land. As Muscovy expanded east to the Volga and beyond, and to the south, to the Black Sea, it was easy for the Russian rulers to reward their service nobility with land, for this class was the "unique and powerful organ of the supreme authority." But when the peasants lost their freedom through enserfment in the interest of the state, they retained "their right to land," for the "peasant owned this land since ancient times [*izstary*] according to the right of unquestionable occupation, long before this land became the patrimonial property of the landowner."[45] From this, it ought to have followed that the serf should pay no indemnity for any land conceded to him with emancipation, and that the land would be his according to the ancient practice of occupation, and would therefore not be "given" or conceded to him by the landlord. But Samarin did not see the matter in quite these terms.

Casting himself in the dubious role of spokesman for the peasantry, Samarin declared, "Deeply conscious of its right to land, our people [*narod*] does not, however, *consider that right unconditional and recognizes,* at the same time, the *right of the patrimonial landowner to the same land.*" From this he derived a formula that he had first announced a decade earlier, and that Khomiakov found most satisfactory. It is summed up in Samarin's *"two mutually limiting rights to land*: the right *of use* [*pol'zovanie*] belonging to the peasants, and the right to *property* [*sobstvennosti*] belonging to the landlords."[46] Complaining about the weakness of "our juridical culture," he regretted that these land relationships had not been cast in clear and precise legal form.

From this sort of reasoning Samarin arrived at the "compatibility of the two . . . rights," and defined their respective positions. The landowner had the "obligation to renounce forever in favor of the peasants any immediate disposition of the land that he has ceded." The peasants in turn were to hold this land "on definite conditions and to reward the landowner for the use [of the land] left at their disposal."[47] Although Samarin had acknowledged the peasants' right to land as predating the landlords' right, he still expected the landowners to be compensated for the land they would cede to the peasants. Payment could be made either in the form of corvee or as quit rent. There was also the more unlikely choice (since the serfs seldom if ever had savings or capital) of a "buy-out or payment of the total capital value of the land." In this manner, he concluded, the "right to use becomes a right to property while the right to property of the former landowner is terminated."[48]

In the second article Samarin took considerable pains to justify a transitional period in the emancipation process, ignoring in this manner the immediate, complete, and unconditional freeing of the serfs. It was time, he said, that emancipation achieved with a single stroke of the tsar's pen would cause the landowners considerable economic losses, but the government had no such intentions and Samarin found this reassuring. On the contrary, he asserted, the "principal features of the *transitional* status" in the tsar's rescripts and gubernia committees could go even further than the government. To his rhetorical question, Is "gradualism" possible? he gave the answer, "Gradualness is essential and a transitional stage is possible.[49]

A major consideration in Samarin's view for the transitional, gradual stage in the emancipation process was the necessity to "reeducate" the landowners. This idea was not only new for the gentry but, he said, "even somewhat offensive to our self-esteem."[50] However genuine this sentiment may have been, his primary concerns in this article were economic, social, and even political rather than moral. The question was what would happen to the gentry lands, and income, if suddenly they were deprived of the peasant working hands? If the peasants were set free overnight the landowners would lose the usual three-day-a-week corvée, which, however grudgingly given, was indispensable to the landowners, specifically to those whose serfs were not paying quit rent (*obrok*). And if the freed peasant chose to move to a city or town — likely in some locations — the landlords' estates would be left unproductive.

Although industrialization and its inevitable side effect, urbanization, were beginning to develop in Russia by the late 1850s, if as yet in embryonic form, the country was still overwhelmingly rural, and it was understood by the Slavophils — and many other thinking Russians — that most of the freed serfs could not be realistically expected to pay redemption fees for the land conceded to them, either individually or through the *mir*. From Samarin's point of view, the only alternative was to collect quit rent or utilize their farm labor in the form of corvee for a transitional period of about a dozen years. Unless that was done, gentry estates would be left untilled and unproductive, thereby causing landlords to suffer and the country to go into economic decline. He justified his attitude on the ground that similar arrangements had been made in the emancipation process in Livonia, in 1819, and in Prussia in 1811 and 1816.[51]

The third article in the series, "Ob usad'bakh," is Samarin's analysis of how the peasant lives and why he should be kept on the *usad'ba,* that is, on the farm, though Samarin uses this word in the broadest sense. The word can mean "farm" or "farmhouse," "country house with outbuildings and garden," "with its orchard, kitchen garden," also "homestead, farmhouse." The *usad'ba* was the serf's home, with all that that implied, and Samarin thought it was of great value in "strengthening the settledness of the villagers, and in the prevention of vagrancy."[52] In England, for instance, the landless peasants flocked to cities like Manchester and Liverpool for industrial employment. In Russia, where there was little capital available for rapid industrialization, the peasant once detached from the land would indeed become a vagrant. And not only was there the compelling need to forestall vagrancy and peasant unrest; keeping the peasant on the land was necessary in order to ensure the landowners the labor they needed. The introduction of farm machinery by some of the Russian gentry was intended, among other things, to decrease the landowners' dependence on peasant hands.

Samarin also defines *usad'ba* to mean "living quarters and farm buildings, with the land under them, with kitchen garden, and pasture,"[53] but he also endows it with a special meaning; he says that he could "firmly say that in Great Russia the *usad'ba* taken separately *as an economic unit does not exist,*" for it "could not be sold, could not be bought, and could not be rented." It followed therefore that there was no way of establishing the market value of the *usad'ba,* and that in case of its redemption one would have to "*create an artificial value*" for it. In addition to these difficulties there was the question of who would carry out the redemption in case the decision was made that the serf should buy out his *usad'ba,* "the *mir* or each peasant owner separately?" Yet another complication was that *usad'ba* was not subject to periodic redistribution, as farmlands often were, but was "passed on through heredity from father to son as a personal possession."[54] In other words, every new owner would have to redeem his own *usad'ba* by paying the landowner yearly installments.

Samarin proposed a different arrangement for the part of the landowner's estate that consisted of "fields and arable land, forests, pastures, etc.," of *polia i ugod'ia*. Here the *mir* should become active—first, because in Great Russia it conducted the periodic land redistribution wherever and whenever it occurred; second, because it was probably easier, and on the whole safer, for the landowner to deal with the *mir* than with individual serfs; and third, because the *mir* could through the exercise of mutual responsibility (*krugovaia poruka*) take care of all peasant obligations. Whether the serf's payment was in the form of quit rent or corvee, he would remain in the village, thereby providing the landowner with essential farm labor and also with working hands for the growing number of gentry commercial and industrial enterprises such as wineries, sugar refineries, and woolen mills.[55]

The attention that Samarin gave to the *usad'ba* in this separate article was justified on a number of counts. No less important in view of the fact that the great majority of landowners were opposed to emancipation was his attempt to show that there were certain advantages for the landowners in emancipation. Certainly it would be to the landowner's advantage to have the working hands they needed remain in the villages for at least a dozen years after emancipation and for them to be compensated for the land they conceded to the peasants—land that in many cases would amount to a considerable portion of the total estate. The serfs would obtain legal freedom, retain their homes, and be allotted the land that they already tilled for themselves and their families. The government—which in the circumstances was the decisive factor—would see an explosive internal situation defused, and could attempt to lead the country out of the stagnant condition that had just caused, among other Russian miseries, defeat in the Crimean War.

Indeed, Samarin made clear, the *usad'ba* was very important in the general scheme of things. For the peasant, it was not an item of income but the essential condition of existence, and it would help "forestall vagabondage."[56] Yet paradoxically—and ironically, in spite of the Slavophil and in particular, Konstantin Aksakov's, apotheosis of the *muzhik* and the *narod*—Samarin did not raise a voice in favor of including representatives of the peasants themselves in the deliberations on the emancipation of the serfs. For him, as for his fellow Slavophils, despite their genuine concerns for Russian cultural creativity, national strength, and a certain sensitivity to the needs of the Russian peasant, they remained, above all else, fearful of a possible Russian Jacquerie should serfdom continue.

The individual and class interests that Samarin was trying to safeguard in the face of widespread gentry opposition to serf emancipation were of concern not only to Cherkassky and Koshelev, as we have seen, but also to the generally acknowledged leader and inspirer of Moscow Slavophilism, Khomiakov. At the same time that Samarin was publishing his articles on the emancipation question Khomiakov drafted a letter-memorandum on the same subject, addressed to the head of the Editorial Commission, Ia. I. Rostovtsev. Koshelev's moderation in invoking God in the work on emancipation, and Samarin's reticence in this regard were not shared by Khomiakov. His opening sentence reads: "The task assigned to Russia by God in our time . . . " was to bring an end to serfdom, and he expected this to happen in a few years. His further reference to Russia as a Christian nation was not without a touch of Slavophil messianism.[57]

Then as earlier the relationship between Khomiakov and Samarin (fifteen years younger) was probably closer and warmer than that between any other two Moscow Slavophils. In 1859 when Khomiakov wrote to Rostovtsev he also addressed two letters to Samarin (1859–1860) on contemporary developments in philosophy, published in *Russkaia beseda*. When Khomiakov died in the fall of 1860 Samarin lost a close friend and mentor. Seven years later he paid tribute to him in his well-known introduction to Khomiakov's theological works. How close were Khomiakov and Samarin in the years crucial to the emancipation reform (1857–1860)? Samarin was either in the Samara gubernia, serving on the gubernia committee or after that, in St. Petersburg, on the Editorial Commission, or abroad. We know how thoroughly preoccupied he was with his work during this brief period, and his contacts with Khomiakov in Moscow, personal or by letter, seem to have been limited.

Perhaps these circumstances account for certain discrepancies in Samarin's and Khomiakov's views on emancipation. The motivation in both was multifaceted. There was the Christian consideration, more clearly and loudly proclaimed by Khomiakov than by Samarin; also the galling fresh memory of defeat in the Crimean War, attributable in part to Russia's lag behind the West in economic, technological development, which was in turn closely tied to the existence of serfdom. Perhaps the most potent factors in their motivation were economic self-interest and fear of widespread peasant revolt. Pushed back in the complexities of human motivation, and in the minds and hearts of the Slavophils, were the peasant, the *muzhik,* and the village commune, subjects, as we have seen, of much Slavophil adulation prior to the emancipation reform.

Now, in 1859, Khomiakov declared that emancipation with "simultaneous, uniform, and compulsory redemption is the only rational solution to the . . . problem." This issue, he said, should be settled in one to four years, without the transitional period of a dozen years that Samarin advocated. The peasant should receive land in the amount of two desiatinas per person except in the Novgorod and Trans-Volga regions where it should be three desiatinas (these were somewhat smaller allotments than those advocated by Samarin). The landowner should deal with the village *mir* rather than with individual peasants.[58] This was both more convenient and safer for the landlord. To raise the money to pay the landowner for the land conceded to the peasant, Khomiakov proposed a combination of a government loan, repayment of gentry debts to the government, and sale of government lands, with the government active as agent for both the landowner and the *mir*.[59] Ultimately the peasant would be obliged to repay the government, and the *mir* should deal severely with delinquent peasants; in extreme cases, he suggested, "whole settlements should be sent to Siberia and their land allotments sold." Though "seemingly cruel," the severity would be "true mercy."[60] In the last year of his life Khomiakov's dream of a decade earlier, of adjusting the village commune to serve also as an industrial commune, seems to have been overtaken by the complexities of an industrial scientific age bent, it seems, on creating a new problem for each one that it solves.

The brief statute-proclamation of Alexander II that initiated the emancipation reform on February 19, 1861, was drafted by the conservative Moscow Metropolitan Filaret Drozdov. It provides a background against which can be characterized some of Samarin's Slavophil views on serf emancipation, and their relationship to the position of the government.[61] This seems proper in spite of Samarin's opinion that Drozdov's version "breathes sorrow for serfdom."[62] The tsar's proclamation opens with homage to "Divine Providence and the sacred law," a typical government piety that none of the Slavophils would have indulged in. But the tsar was as aware as the Slavophils were that serfdom in Russia was a matter of custom as well as law, and he also recognized, as Samarin did, that there was a great deal of gentry arbitrariness and excess in the treatment of serfs, and that the partial measures of former tsars to ameliorate the position of the serfs had been completely inadequate. The tsar expressed confidence that the gentry were ready for "sacrifices in favor of the Fatherland" just as Samarin knew that economic and other concessions to the serfs by the gentry were inescapable. The edict states that the gentry were "to retain the right to property of all lands belonging to them," while the peasants "in return for established obligatory services would have constant tenure of the peasant homestead." In addition the peasants were to have a definite but unspecified use of arable land and access to other lands such as meadows, pastures, lakes and rivers, fisheries, forests and hunting grounds, all these referred to as *ugod'ia*.[63]

The edict makes specific reference to the household serfs, of whom at the time there were 1,467,378 according to the tenth census (1858–1859) out of 23,000,000 serfs on about 104,000 gentry estates. Household serfs had rapidly increased between 1829 and 1859 as the expectation of emancipation grew, and the gentry wished to have as few serfs as possible to whom to concede land.[64] The emancipated serfs were subject to a transitional period of two years (Samarin favored twelve) when "they will receive complete freedom and temporary exemptions."

In order to achieve the emancipation of the serfs efficiently and without delays, Alexander II proposed a number of administrative measures, such as creation in each gubernia of permanent bureaus in charge of peasant affairs, and appointment of county arbitrators. But from the point of view of the Slavophil position on emancipation, and Samarin's in particular, no provision in the tsar's edict surpassed in importance the preservation of the village commune and *mir*. We have seen that in the early 1850s the Third Section and the government of Nicholas I looked with disfavor on the Slavophils, suspecting them of radical communistic leanings. In the official edict the village commune and *mir* were to be preserved but the emphasis here was not on the Slavophil's favorite theme, their historical social-economic and quasi-Orthodox nature, but on the administrative functions of these two local peasant institutions. In the tsar's edict they are referred to as "*mir* administrations" and "village societies." These village or peasant societies would be in charge of lands "at the disposal of the peasants for their permanent use" as well as of the "number of obligations in favor of the landowner for the land and other advantages coming from him."

During the two-year transitional period the landowners would maintain order on their estates, hold law courts, and render justice. This temporary extension of the old order was accompanied by the pious hope that landowners and serfs could come to "voluntary agreements" on the many problems arising from the "diverse circumstances on the individual estates."[65] Admonishing the serfs to obey authority on the basis of Romans 13:1, Alexander II referred to the "important sacrifice made by the Noble Gentry for the betterment" of the lot of the serfs.[66]

In Samarin's case one can get a notion of the state of his wealth and possible loss as a result of emancipation from some recently published facts and figures. Samarin had 2,897 male serfs, including 461 in his household (see note 38 above). On his Samara estate there were 2,114, and on the Syzran, 322. The average allotment per serf was 9.5 desiatins (9 desiatins per serf in Samara, 10 in Syzran). This was higher than the average in the two gubernias. The extent of his lands was "about 24,000 desiatins."[67] This would have meant that if his 2,436 agricultural serfs had been allotted 9.5 desiatins each, Samarin would have conceded to them 23,142 desiatins – or virtually his whole estate – for doubtful redemption payments since the serfs had no cash and the state treasury was in trouble. According to information gathered for the Editing Commissions, the average serf holding in the late 1850,s in 43 gubernias was "3.2 desiatins per soul."[68] At this rate as a result of emancipation Samarin would have given up 7,795 desiatins or approximately one-third of his whole estate. His land was not in the most fertile part of Russia, and for this reason, in part at least, he had branched out into sheep raising and the manufacturing of cloth.

In the welter that is often the true state of human motivation, and in Samarin's case specifically, no single concern can be said to have determined his move from ideology to action and reform. There was the matter of economic self-interest, social standing, and fear of a possible peasant uprising. There was the patriotic realization that serfdom was the principal cause of Russia's economic and therefore military weakness during the Crimean War. There was also the Slavophil yearning for Russian creativity, which, though impressive in the field of literature, was drastically handicapped by the near-total lack of participation by those who constituted the majority of the Russian nation. And finally there was the conviction among the Slavophils, as well as among others, that serfdom was morally wrong and un-Christian.

In his steady and strenuous work in the cause of serf emancipation Samarin was neither saint nor villain. Like his fellow Slavophils, he would not sacrifice his economic, social, and class prerogatives and status, nor was he willing to become thoroughly immersed in, and absorbed by, the village commune, which, of course, the Slavophyils constantly idealized. He looked upon serfdom as a moral, social, and economic evil that was keeping the whole Russian nation, not just the peasantry, in abject bondage. In their confrontations with the Russian Westerners, and the West, the Slavophils — and this certainly included Samarin — had no more cherished hope and goal than to see Russia become culturally creative in its own Russian way.

Notes

1. Nol'de, for instance, speaks of commissions in both the singular and the plural explaining that two commissions were originally proposed but that in fact "they functioned in a fused manner although according to tradition the plural has remained in general use." In the literature some authors use the singular, others the plural. Emmons explains that the government created two "Editing Commissions" under Rostovtsev's chairmanship. One was to deal with the general legislation on emancipation, the other with local provisions. Later, a third, Finance Commission, was created also under Rostovtsev. The first two commissions were merged into one, and then divided into Judicial, Administrative, and Economic Departments. The Finance Commission became a fourth department, all under Rostovtsev. Referring to Samarin, Koshelev, and Cherkassky, Emmons gives the correct designations of their appointments on the Samara, Riazan, and Tula gubernias, respectively, as "members-from-the-government." Cf. Nol'de, *Samarin,* pp. 112–113; Terence Emmons, *The Russian Landed Gentry and the Peasant Emancipation of 1861* (Cambridge, 1968), pp. 171, 214–218.

2. The activities of, and problems encountered by Samarin, Koshelev, and Cherkassky in their gubernia committees have been well summarized by Emmons, pp. 171–189. Excellent summaries also appear in the pre-Soviet, Soviet, and Western literature, for example, by V. I. Semevsky, A. A. Kornilov, P. A. Zaionchkovsky, E. A. Dudzinskaia, L. G. Zakharova, N. V. Riasanovsky, and Richard Wortman.

3. Trubetskaia, "Kn. Vladimir Aleksandrovich Cherkassky," in *Velikaia reforma,* V. 109.

4. P. A. Bezsonov, "Kniaz' Vladimir Aleksandrovich Cherkassky," *Russkii archiv,* 1878, book 2, pp. 206–207.

5. Ibid., pp. 205, 206.

6. Ibid., pp. 208–209.

7. See *Kniaz' Vladimir Aleksandrovich Cherkassky. Ego stat'i, ego rechi i vospominaniia o nem* (Moscow, 1879), p. vii.

8. Bezsonov, "Cherkassky," p. 13.

9. O. N. Trubetskaia, ed., *Materialy. . . .Perepiska.* I, book 1, 37–38. See also Trubetskaia, "Cherkassky," p. 110.

10. Quoted in Tsimbaev, *I. S. Aksakov v obshchestvennoi zhizni poreformennoi Rossii,* p. 68.

11. Koshelev, *Zapiski,* p. 84.

12. See V. A. Cherkassky, "O sochineniiakh Montalamberta i Tokvilia." *Russkaia beseda,* 1857, II, kritika, pp. 23–88.

13. Cherkassky, *Ego stat'i,* p. 137.

14. Ibid., pp. 140–141.

15. Ibid., p. 142.

16. Ibid., p. 162.

17. Ibid., p. 166.

18. Ibid., pp. 171, 175.

19. Ibid., p. 177.

20. Ibid., pp. 178, 179.

21. Ibid., pp. 187, 188.

22. Ibid., p. 200.

23. Samarin, *Sochineniia,* I, 402.

24. Ibid., p. 403.

25. For the Cherkassky *Zapiska,* see Trubetskaia, ed., *Materialy . . . . Perepiska,* book 1, 11–67. A number of supplements follow the *Zapiska.*

26. Ibid., pp. 63–64.

27. Ibid., p. 77.

28. Koshelev clearly defined the areas of Russian public life in which "betterment" was badly needed in his *zapiska* of 1858 to the tsar. "We know," he stated, "that the police, courts, and various administrations are poorly organized, and that their functioning is even worse; that extortion and the plundering of the treasury is increasing and is becoming more frequent; that

the government is not in a position to put an end to this evil; that public morality is faltering and weak; that public opinion is completely powerless, and that in the present state of affairs there is no way out of our disastrous situation." The end of serfdom would not immediately change everything but it would "constitute the most essential measure toward its [the situation's] improvement." Koshelev, *Zapiski,* Appendix, p. 79.

29. Cherkassky, *Zapiska,* p. 78.

30. Among other works *Russkii vestnik* published in serialized form Turgenev's *On the Eve* (1860), *Fathers and Sons* (1862), *Smoke* (1867); Dostoevksy's *Crime and Punishment* (1866), *Idiot* (1868), *The Possessed* (1871), *The Brothers Karamazov* (1879–1880); and Saltykov-Shchedrin's *Gubernskie Ocherki* (1856–1857). See A. G. Dement'ev et al, eds., *Russkaia periodicheskaia pechat' (1702–1894)* (Moscow, 1959). pp. 341, 355.

31. Much valuable factual information on contacts between some of the Slavophils and Herzen in the second half of the 1850s has recently been furnished by Dudzinskaia. The Slavophils, she states, traveled to the West after the Crimean War "in order to become acquainted with the state of mind of the European, and particularly of the Slav countries. . . . In addition to the states indicated in their passports [they] also visited England in order to meet with Herzen." During the period 1856–1860 "I. Aksakov, V. Cherkassky, A. Koshelev, and those close to them, P. Bartenev, D. Samarin, A. Popov, A. Gil'ferding, V. Kokorev, and others," visited England. The contacts with Herzen were in the form of "personal visits, letters containing accusatory facts, and also advice as to who should be branded [*zakleimit*], and who should be encouraged," back home. Herzen received from them "plays, materials on government actions, impeding emancipation, news reports dealing with the most vital questions of public life, which because of their unmasking character could not be published in Russia." From 1856 on, and particularly during the deliberations of the Editing Commission, the "Slavophils constantly had, so to speak, 'their own correspondent' in Europe." Dudzinskaia, *Slavianofily v obshchestvennoi bor'be,* pp. 130–131, 137–141.

32. It is not within the scope of this work to give a complete account of Dudzinskaia's research on the Slavophils. Among her publications the most pertinent from the point of view of this study is her well-focused work (1983) on the Slavophils' involvement in Russia's social, economic, and political struggles. This work, based on thorough knowledge of Slavophilism and the period in which it appeared, is a noteworthy achievement. It reveals uncommon penetration of the activities and motivation of the principal actors of the period, both Slavophils and Westerners, and brings to light much archival material. Concentrating on the second half of the 1850s the work tells us much, among other things, about the relationship between Herzen and Cher-

nyshevsky and the Slavophils. See Dudzinskaia, *Slavianofily,* chapter 4; also her "Slavianofily i revoliutsionnye demokraty," pp. 127–166.

33. Koshelev, *Zapiski,* p. 96.

34. Koshelev, *Zapiski,* Appendix, pp. 3–5.

35. In his speech to the nobility of Riazan gubernia at the end of the 1840s Koshelev appealed for an end to serfdom by saying, "Both our Orthodox faith and education [*prosveshchenie*], increasingly expanding, unconditionally demand changes in serfdom." In 1852 in his reflections on a visit to the West, England in particular, he listed among the many things he admired there, also some of the weaknesses of Western culture, including its love of "luxury, its immorality, its coolness toward religion, its show of cleverness [*umnichanie*]." And in his *zapiska* to Nicholas I of 1854 on Russia's difficult financial position he made a reference to "Orthodoxy, which constitutes the essence of all our existence." Again in 1858 he found it necessary to state in his major *zapiska* to the tsar "On the Destruction of Serfdom in Russia": "The real education of every person derives from the basic notion of his relationship to God and men. This fundamental notion is borrowed by our people from the saving teaching of Christ." After this it is not surprising to see in the same *zapiska* his reference to the "sin of owning people." But these random references pale before the spirited and sometimes poignant epistolary discussion among Khomiakov, Ivan Kireevsky, Konstantin and Ivan Aksakov, and Koshelev that took place between 1847 and 1854. Reference to these two dozen letters has been made before, it is sufficient to say here that religion in general, and Orthodoxy in particular, have a prominent place in them. Cf. Koshelev *Zapiski,* Appendix, pp. 6, 27, 49, 60, 74; Koliupanov, *Koshelev,* II, 47–110.

36. Koshelev, *Zapiski,* Appendix, V, p. 64.

37. Ibid., p. 163.

38. According to recently published figures, Koshelev himself owned 5,500 serfs and 9,000 desiatinas (24,300 acres) of land. On his Riazan estate the serfs had 2.74 desiatinas (7.39 acres) per "soul," where the average allotment was about the same. His property included one thousand head of cattle and a winery which in its first year brought him an income of 100,000 rubles. His smaller landholdings, located in three gubernias, amounted to 1,136 desiatinas (3,067 acres) of arable land, and 1,475 "souls." On his Tula and Riazan estates the peasant allotments of 4.17 desiatinas (12.69 acres) were larger than the national average of about 2.74 desiatinas (7.39 acres). But on his estate in the Smolensk gubernia where the average serf allotment was 5.29 desiatinas (14.28 acres) his was 4.23 desiatinas (11.42 acres). In the 1850s he branched out into sugar production, imported agricultural machinery, and worked on improvements. By way of comparison when Samarin's father died in 1853 the children inherited in the Samara and Simbirst gubernias 23,810 desiatinas (64,287 acres) and 2,897 male serfs, most

of whom were on the Samara estate. The land east of the Volga was more plentiful, also cheaper and more sparsely populated, than that west of the river, and the allotments of 9 desiatinas (23.4 acres) on the Samarin estate were relatively large. In 1861 Cherkassky had more than 1,500 desiatinas (4,050 acres) and 416 serfs in the Tula gubernia with a peasant allotment of 2.9 desiatinas (7.83 acres). Most of the information in this footnote, and a good deal more is contained in the three recent works by E. A. Dudzinskaia: "Burzhuaznye tendentsii v teorii i praktike Slavianofilov," *Voprosy istorii,* 1972, no. 1, pp. 52–53; *Slavianofily v obshchestvennoi bor'be,* pp. 60–80, and "Obshchestvennaia i khoziaistvennaia deiatel'nost' slavianofila Iu. F. Samarina v 40–50-kh godakh XIX v.," *Istoricheskie zapiski,* 1984, vol. 110, pp. 317–318.

39. Koshelev, *Zapiski,* Appendix, p. 128.

40. Cf. Koshelev, *Zapiski,* p. 93; A. A. Kornilov, "Iurii Fedorovich Samarin," in *Ocherki po istorii obshchestvennago dvizheniia i krest'ianskago dela v Rossii* (St. Petersburg, 1905), p. 463; Nol'de, *Samarin,* p. 129.

41. Quoted in "Iz zapisok Marii Aggeevny Miliutinoi," *Russkaia starina,* 1899, no. 2, p. 283.

42. Cf. Kornilov, "Iu. F. Samarin," p. 467; Koshelev, *Zapiski,* p. 103.

43. Trubetskaia, ed., *Materialy . . . . Perepiska.* Book 1, p. 84.

44. Samarin, *Sochineniia,* III, 19, 21.

45. Ibid., pp. 25, 26.

46. Ibid., p. 28.

47. Ibid., p. 29.

48. Ibid., p. 30.

49. Ibid., pp. 33, 34.

50. Ibid., p. 35.

51. Ibid., pp. 42, 43.

52. Ibid., p. 46.

53. Ibid., pp. 46–47.

54. Ibid., pp. 48, 51. This same point of the serf's monetary obligation to the landlord or of redemption payments comes up in the correspondence that Samarin exchanged with Koshelev and Cherkassky at that time. In a letter from Samarin to Koshelev dated July 18, 1858 (the time of the article on the *usad'ba*), Samarin says that the serf would "redeem *not his person,* and not the land (according to its market value) but the *obligation* which would be assessed from the peasants for the use of the land. The obligation," he believed, "represents something intermediate between person and land." Trubetskaia, ed., *Materialy,* book 1, part 1, pp. 118–119.

55. Samarin himself employed 400 household serfs in the manufacture of cloth, made from wool produced on his grazing lands. Cherkassky, employed free serf labor in his sugar refinery; Koshelev concentrated on butter, cheese, and leather production, and also on a highly profitable winery

and distillery. Khomiakov ran his sugar refinery with free labor, "with the newest technology and steam power, which for those days was extremely progressive." See Dudzinskaia, *Slavianofily,* pp. 66, 71, 77, 80.

56. Samarin, *Sochineniia,* III, 54.

57. Khomiakov, *Sochineniia,* III, 291.

58. Ibid., pp. 296, 300–305.

59. Ibid., pp. 308–311.

60. Ibid., p. 314.

61. I have used here a 1954 edition of the tsar's five-page edict edited by K. A. Sofronenko, *Krest'ianskaia reforma v Rossii 1861 goda. Sbornik zakonodatel'nykh aktov* (Moscow, 1954).

62. See P. A. Zaionchkovsky, *Otmena krepostnogo prava v Rossii,* 2d ed., (Moscow, 1960), p. 159.

63. *Krest'ianskaia reforma,* pp. 31–33.

64. Although it had become clear during the reign of Nicholas I that the government would not consider emancipation of the serfs without land for the serfs, the landowners wanted to keep to a minimum the land allotted to their serfs for doubtful redemption fees. For this reason they transferred agricultural workers to their households. Thus the ranks of the *dvorovye* grew until the end of the 1850s, when transfer was prohibited, to the relief of the agricultural serfs who in fact supported the large numbers of household serfs. Cf. Terence Emmons, "The Peasant and Emancipation," in W. S. Vucinich, ed., *The Peasant in Nineteenth-Century Russia* (Stanford, Calif. 1968), p. 41; Blum, *Lord and Peasant in Russia,* pp. 455–460.

65. *Krest'ianskaia reforma,* pp. 33–34.

66. Ibid., pp. 35.

67. See Dudzinskaia, "Samarin," pp. 317–318. While the figures in this paragraph are drawn from Dudzinskaia's study, the conclusions are mine.

68. Blum, *Lord and Peasant,* p. 529.

16

Official Nationality

At the end of this fourth and last study of Moscow Slavophilism it would be appropriate to draw certain general conclusions that are supported by the foregoing evidence and interpretations. Before this is done a cursory glance (for no more is here possible) should be directed at another matter which if not cleared will tend to obscure our conclusions about Moscow Slavophilism. At this juncture it is pertinent to determine as accurately as possible what Moscow Slavophilism was not, as well as what it was. Hardly anyone would doubt that it was not the same as Russian Westernism. Here the differences were usually sharp, clear, irreconcilable, and easily demonstrable. A problem, however, has existed since the early years of Moscow Slavophilism when such ideological currents as "official nationality," *pochvennichestvo,* the "native soil" school of thought, and pan-Slavism are mentioned.[1]

In order to deal factually yet with a minimum of detail with the relationship between the Slavophils, the "proponents of official nationality," the "men of the soil" (*pochvenniki*), and the pan-Slavs one would need more than four studies. Fortunately much valuable work, and some of it of the highest scholarly order, as indicated above has been done exploring and defining these three currents of thought, which although at times making contact with Slavophilism have never become identical ideologies. They have preserved their respective identities, as in the nineteenth century, in spite of the fact that precise, unequivocal, "scientific" definitions still elude them, and our terminology today, as in the past, still deals in approximations. The reasons for this are many, and they are mostly, although not exclusively, historical. Moscow Slavophilism began and matured while Russia was still saddled with centuries-old serfdom. The same is true of Official Nationality. *Pochvennichestvo* is primarily a development of the 1850s and 1860s, whereas active pan-Slavism followed the cultural pan-Slavism of the first half of the nineteenth century. It might be said to have culminated in the mid-1870s when Russia fought the Ottoman empire for the liberation of Slav, Orthodox Bulgaria. By the late 1870s Russia was on the way to modern industrial capitalism and the balance of power in Europe had become greatly altered as compared with the period of "pre-reform," early, or "classical" Slavophilism.

Before we consider the differing characteristics of these currents, and distinguish them from Moscow Slavophilism, it is essential to stress certain similarities. All these currents came into existence during a phase of Russian history characterized by the absence of modern legal, organized, political parties. This accounts in part for the absence of the sort of ideological and organizational coherence that could have given these broad ideological currents generally agreed upon party programs and platforms, tactics and voting records, party congresses, and written agendas with membership rosters. Together with these would go all the written records which would have helped us define each ideological current more factually and accurately. This in turn would have lent a degree of precision in determining their similarities and their differences. The censorship, although somewhat relaxed in the second half of the 1850s, was never absent from publications that treated social, economic, political, and religious matters. This limitation was often overcome by publishing abroad as was the case with some of Khomiakov's, Samarin's, and other Slavophil works.

The prevalence during this period of salons, circle, and other loosely held groups, often reinforced by personal ties and the support of a journal, provided whatever unity and cohesion the several currents of thought possessed. As a general rule their members were men of considerable talent, extremely well educated, highly articulate, individualistic, and well informed about both Russia and the West. This circumstance and the absence of party organization and discipline lent to all these movements considerable amorphousness, which leads one at times to question whether the individual within a certain current of thought did not outweigh the current itself. Yet all four schools of thought shared a strong but not necessarily uniform sense of nationalism, a strong feeling for their Russian consciousness (*narodnost'*), and most for Orthodoxy, although no identical concepts of nationalism and Orthodoxy existed. In addition, in all four schools of thought (the occasional use of the term "party" as is sometimes applied to the Slavophils, is unfortunate and misleading) there were degrees and varieties of awareness of social, economic, and political matters. These and other characteristics of the four currents of thought, which should soon become manifest, render the task of dealing with them uncertain and tentative.

Chronologically the earliest current of thought is that of "Official Nationality." It could conveniently be dated to S. S. Uvarov's triple formula of 1833; *pravoslavie, samoderzhavie i narodnost'* (Orthodoxy, Autocracy, and Nationality).[2] Taking individually the components of the government's formula, the Slavophils, who have at times been confused with the men of "Official Nationality," read the formula quite differently from those who were close to the government of Nicholas I. To the Slavophils, Orthodoxy meant Christian faith based upon their exalted doctrine of *sobornost'*, not the Russian church under Nicholas I, whose Ober-Procurator of the Holy Synod was not even a cleric but the "despotic cavalry officer" Count Nicholas Protasov.[3] Autocracy in the idealized Slavophil view stood not for a crude royal dictatorship but for a "'people's' monarchy" (*narodnaia monarkhiia*) in which the tsar is the servant, not the master, of the *narod*.[4] And finally, nationality—*narodnost'*—which often meant nationalism and patriotism to Nicholas I and his administrators. For the Moscow Slavophils, still in an unrealistic manner, it stood for the "'all-human' when the all-human is refracted through the prism of nationality [*narodnost'*]."[5] Thus the government's practice and the Slavophil ideal were separated by a big gap. True to the thought expressed in the title of these studies, concern for ideas is worthwhile in itself, and no attempt will here be made to reconcile Slavophil ideas and ideals, with Slavophil practices, for there is no evidence that the Slavophils were more consistent or less fallible than anyone else.

Voices about the relationship between Slavophilism and "Official Nationality" were heard in the 1840s, and they have arisen ever since, but the controversy assumed a somewhat better defined and perhaps more acute form in the early 1870s. The designation *"teoriia ofitsial'noi narodnosti"* ("theory of Official Nationality") was widely used then to characterize a group of men who were in close accord with the government of Nicholas I, and in the opinion of many critics were subservient to it. Since then this term has become well established in the literature, and its substance and role have been expertly explored in Professor Riasanovsky's well-known work, *Nicholas I and Official Nationality in Russia, 1825-1855.*

Coinage of the term "Official Nationality" is attributed to the liberal nineteenth-century Russian historian A. N. Pypin (1833-1904), who published in 1871 and 1872 a series of articles under the general heading *Kharakteristiki literaturnykh mnenii ot dvadtsatykh do piatidesiatykh godov. Istoricheskie ocherki* (Characteristics of Literary Opinions from the Twenties to the Fifties: Historical Essays). The second section has the title, "Narodnost' ofitsial'naia," the fifth and sixth appear under "Slavianofil'stvo."[6] Pypin compared and contrasted the "system of official nationality" with Slavophilism, among other things, and arrived at several conclusions, stressing two unmistakable characteristics of official nationality: conservatism, and its "close ties with romanticism." The reference to romanticism is primarily to the English and German streams, particularly strong in Russia during the 1820s and 1830s. His low opinion of Official Nationality was summed up in his assertion that it produced a "strange literature" which "pretended to be journalism, and poetry, and science [*nauka*]. There was even a certain animation, or at least noise, which just the same strikes one with its barrenness and stiffness."[7]

During the 1830s and 1840s in St. Petersburg the theory of Official Nationality was heard, in Pypin's words, in "those circles whose members included Grech and Bulgarin, Senkovsky, Kukol'nik, and where it strangely came in contact with literature and the police, with romantic fervor and enthusiastic good intentions [*blagonamerennost'*]." To this roster Pypin also added F. N. Glinka, and he referred to the "dark fanatical obscurantism of the journal *Maiak',* published by S. A. Burachek.[8] Toward the end of the installment on *"narodnost' ofitsial'naia,"* Pypin turned from St. Petersburg to Moscow, and to Pogodin and Shevyrev, in a none too complimentary manner, declaring that they belonged to a "special school which must not be confused with Slavophilism although between them there was still much in common."[9]

As Riasanovsky's monograph and recent Soviet biographical sketches of some of the proponents of Official Nationality clearly show, anyone wishing to concentrate on this subject would have to study a sizable collection of published works written by six of its major representatives. O. I. Senkovsky (1800–1858) left nine volumes; N. V. Kukol'nik (1809–1868), ten volumes; F. N. Glinka (1786–1880), three volumes; F. V. Bulgarin (1789–1859), seven volumes. But these works, and those of N. I. Grech (1787–1861) and S. A. Burachek (1800–1876), could not legitimately be considered part of the heritage of early, "classical," or Moscow Slavophilism, and they have therefore not been included in this and the preceding three studies. Fortunately, as already indicated, much valuable work, mostly by Professor Riasanovsky, and some by Professor V. I. Kushelov of Moscow University, Dudzinskaia, and others, has been done to define Official Nationality. What follows in the next several pages are biographical sketches of the leading proponents of Official Nationality based on the work of these three scholars, and a number of others.

While the six representatives of Official Nationality of concern here were men of different backgrounds, education, social position, and aptitudes, and did not form a tightly knit party or even circle, as a group they differed from the Slavophils in age, and therefore in historical experience and perspective. The oldest among them, Glinka, was born in 1786, the youngest, Kukol'nik, in 1809. They all, except perhaps Kukol'nik, had vivid memories of the Napoleonic invasion. Burachek and Senkovsky were in their early teens in 1812; Grech, Bulgarin, and Glinka were in their middle twenties. There were strong nationalistic, patriotic, anti-French convictions among the men of Official Nationality which the younger Slavophils (born after 1816) could not share in quite the same way.

The second oldest of the six, N. I. Grech, was a third generation descendant of the Prussian Johann-Ernst Gretsch, who had settled in Russia. The Grech family was of Protestant stock. N. I. Grech has been characterized as a "journalist, publisher, educator, and grammarian." He was educated in a military school in St. Petersburg, and in Riasanovsky's words "lived intensely through the nationalist upsurge of 1812." He lost a brother at Borodino. There can be little doubt that Grech's pro-Russian sentiments, like those of all Russians, were aroused and stimulated by the French nationalism and imperialism that were manifested on Russian soil. The tsar, then and later, was not only the commander-in-chief of the Russian army but also the symbol of Russian unity and resistance to foreign invasion, and Grech had "little difficulty in adjusting to the ideology of Official Nationality."[10] Nor did he have any qualms about taking up arms in behalf of the government against Custine's *La Russie en 1839.*[11]

A basic and troublesome issue on which Grech, a member of the "triumvirate" of Official Nationality (Grech, Bulgarin, and Senkovsky) would have disagreed with Samarin, was the role and status of the Baltic Germans in Russian society and administration. Grech, not surprisingly, "had a high regard for the Baltic Germans, noting in particular that their success in the Russian service was a result of their superior education."[12] Samarin, as we have seen, went to jail for criticizing the Baltic Germans' record in the Baltic provinces and in the Russian administration. On the crucial question of serfdom and emancipation, too, the Slavophils and Grech were at opposite poles. At the very time that Slavophilism was in the forefront of the emancipation struggle, most notably through the activities of Samarin, Koshelev, and Ivan Aksakov, Grech condoned serfdom.

In the words of Riasanovsky, "As late as 1859 Grech argued that, although serfdom was unjust, 'the liberation of wild slaves, under conditions of complete moral disorder, of a lack of true, spiritual religion, and of the corruption of our minor officials, will bring upon Russia complete ruin and countless misfortunes.'"[13] One wonders whether in Grech's mind fragmented Protestantism was the only "spiritual religion." Grech's journal, *Syn otechestva* (Son of the Fatherland), published intermittently from 1812 on, was dedicated to "literature, politics, and contemporary history." It was at times a joint venture with Bulgarin, Senkovsky, and others, although their collaboration was not always smooth.[14] "Grech's own relations with Bulgarin ended in a violent quarrel and lasting hostility."[15]

Bulgarin was born in a Polish gentry (*szlachta*) family in 1789. He, too, studied in a military academy in St. Petersburg, and eventually became a "journalist and writer." He was a man of chameleonlike propensities — he managed to fight first for Russia against Napoleon, and then for Napoleon against Russia — but in spite of these switches in loyalty he ended with a lucrative publishing career in St. Petersburg. One of his biographers says that in his younger years Bulgarin was so "Russified" (*obrusel*) that although born a Catholic he attended the "Orthodox church and even studied the Orthodox catechism." (He is also said to have "completely forgotten his native tongue.") In his edition of *Selected Poems of Horace* (1816) he excluded whatever was not "in agreement with Christian morality,"[16] From 1825–1859 he published the *Severnaia pchela* (Northern Bee) in St. Petersburg, thrice weekly at first. Also in 1825, in Professor Kuleshov's words, he became a "paid agent of the Third Section." After 1831 his "political and literary newspaper" appeared daily, soon with Grech's collaboration, and it achieved the high circulation of ten thousand copies, unique for its time.[17]

Severnaia pchela was not only the "only private newspaper that had the right to publish political news"; it was also, it is said, a "semi-official journal of the Third Section," which "baited" Pushkin, Gogol', and Belinsky. Bulgarin, among other things, was engaged in "moralizing edification in the spirit of 'official nationality.'"[18] It is not therefore surprising that Bulgarin's principal purpose with respect to the *Northern Bee* was confirming its obedience and loyalty to the tsar.[19] Obviously in his unprincipled changes of loyalty during the Napoleonic wars, in his attitude toward the Baltic Germans and serfdom, and in his crass servility before the throne, he could share no common ground with the Moscow Slavophils.

Senkovsky, like Bulgarin, was of Polish origin. He was born in 1800, which meant that he was too young to participate in the Napoleonic wars but old enough to have vivid memories of them. He was by far the most gifted of the men of Official Nationality. From 1819 to 1821 he traveled in Turkey, Syria, and Egypt, and in addition to Polish and Russian spoke Arabic, Turkish, French, German, English, Italian, Icelandic, Basque, Persian, and Modern Greek. He also studied Mongolian and Chinese. Between 1822 and 1847 he held the chair of Arabic and Turkish literatures at the University of St. Petersburg; he resigned his academic post to devote himself to journalistic and publishing work, and in the meantime he also served as a censor (1828–1833).

From 1834 to 1856 Senkovsky was the publisher of the monthly *Biblioteka dlia chteniia* (Library for Reading), dedicated to "literature, science, art, industry, news, and fashion."[20] (At various times this journal was published by other men, including Grech.) This publication had a wide circulation. In his writing Senkovsky used a number of pseudonyms, the best known of which was Baron Brambeus. He was known as a "despotic editor," who "did not like Russian literature," and who "looked down upon it." He was also critical of contemporary French literature, which he considered immoral, and since he did not care for the historical novel, he remained unimpressed by Sir Walter Scott. His simple declaration was, "I love morality."[21] He preferred English literature to all others in the West, although he regularly pruned English as well as other Western works before publishing them in *Biblioteka dlia chteniia*. In the 1840s the Triumvirate, which he joined in the 1820s, took up arms against Belinsky's *Otechestvennye zapiski* (Notes of the Fatherland), and in the 1850s it attacked Chernyshevsky, Dobroliubov, and others.

F. N. Glinka, one of the "lesser adherents of the state ideology," was born in Tver in 1789. He followed the familiar route of early training in a military academy, service in the Russian army against Napoleon in 1805–1806, then at Borodino, and in 1813–1814 in the West. He was decorated for bravery in action, and ended his military career as a colonel. Characterized as a "poet, dramatist, and prose writer," he began his publishing career in 1808. From 1816 to 1821 he was associated with the Decembrist movement, favored a constitutional monarchy, and was known for his "incorruptibility and self-denial." He was arrested in 1826 and exiled to the Olonetskaia gubernia. He lived in Moscow from 1835 to 1854, then in St. Petersburg, and finally, from 1862 on, in Tver. His poetry was marked by a strong "religious-meditative current."[22] In Riasanvosky's words, "F. Glinka taught a succinct moral lesson in a poem in which a young widow told her children about their departed warrior father:

"He went thither, to the bright abode of the Heavenly tsar
Because here he had been faithful to the earthly Tsar."[23]

It hardly needs repeating that this sort of obsequiousness before the throne of the tsar, however spontaneous and well intentioned, was quite alien to the Slavophils. They were sincere in their support of the Russian autocracy, partly because of its role in the unification of Russia and in the defeat of Napoleon, partly because it was a symbol of Russian unity and territorial integrity in a vast multilingual, multireligious, multicultural, multi-ethnic empire, and partly because it was the mainstay against revolution. At the same time, the Slavophils had a definite distaste for the Western brand of check-and-balance constitutionalism, which appeared to them, as it did to the radical Bakunin, for instance, more a matter of legalisms and for-malities than of a higher quality of human character and aspiration. The nearest the Slavophils came to the divine-right-of-kings sort of exaltation, apparent in Glinka and the other adherents of Official Nationality, was their apotheosis of the *narod* (not of the tsar).

The youngest of these six adherents of the doctrine of Official Nationality was N. V. Kukol'nik, who was born in 1809 in Vilna, the son of a professor. He is described as a "dramatist and poet," and he was one of the most prolific writers among the men of Official Nationality; his collected works run to ten volumes. As a student (Gogol' was one of his classmates) he dabbled in "free thinking" and "forbidden books," but after 1836, when he began work as an editor, he became associated with the state school of thought, giving vent in his plays and novels to the ideas and attitudes of Official Nationality. For him, a biographer has said, the *narod* was a "passive, faceless crowd." On the subject of the *narod* Kukol'nik did not stand alone, for as Riasanovsky has pointed out, Official Nationality was known for its "skeptical view of the

Russian people."[24] This of course is in stark contrast to the Slavophil view of the narod.

Between the center of Official Nationality in St. Petersburg, and Pogodin and Shevyrev, usually considered the Moscow arm of the same orientation, no complete agreement or unanimity existed. We shall have to return to these two men behind the *Moskvitianin,* but for the present it is necessary to underscore the disagreement between Pogodin and Kukol'nik over the meaning of early Russian history, obviously a large and complex subject which will have to be dismissed here in a few lines. Pogodin took umbrage in the early 1850s at Kukol'nik's play *The Orderly,* in which, he said, the playwright was guilty of "insolent ignorance of pre-Petrine Russia."[25] At the same time, Pogodin as well as Kukol'nik and the other proponents of Official Nationality, and Nicholas I himself, were united in their adulation of Peter the Great, whose reign Kukol'nik celebrated with the words, "Great, divine work! Over our dark country Peter is lighting an artificial sun!"[26] Such adulation was strikingly absent from the ideas and writings of the Moscow Slavophils.

The last of the men associated with the St. Petersburg group of "Official Nationality" to be considered here was S. A. Burachek, born in 1800 in the Chernigov gubernia of "Galician Russians." He studied engineering, and in 1831 became a teacher of shipbuilding in St. Petersburg. Later he published his lectures on "Algebraic analysis." In 1840 he began publication in St. Petersburg of the "literary-political" monthly *Maiak* (Lighthouse or Beacon).[27] Riasanovsky says, "Stephen Burachek, a former naval officer . . . introduced naval terminology into his obscurantist periodical *The Lighthouse.*"[28] Burachek believed Russian literature from Karamzin to Lermontov to be in a state of decay, and Pushkin, he said, having turned to the classics, became an "imitator of pagan and romantic models" whose works were marked by "sophistry and absence of creativity," and whose heroes were "criminal felons" (*ugolovnye prestupniki*). Burachek stamped his *Maiak* with his "extreme sanctimoniousness," and could not make it last more than five years, nor could he make this organ of "militant obscurantism" a profitable financial venture. Yet this "most consistent representative of pure stagnation," as Apollon Grigor'ev characterized him, could be a "hospitable and courteous host."[29]

Mikhail Petrovich Pogodin (1800–1875), has been described by a biographer as a "philologist, historian, archeologist, collector, journalist, publicist, fiction writer, dramatist, translator from various languages into Russian, and publisher." In addition to achievements in many endeavors this son of a household serf eventually became the subject of an unfinished twenty-two-volume "biography."[30] N. P. Barsukov's *Zhizn' i trudy Pogodina* (Life and Works of Pogodin) is in fact a rich storehouse of facts, events, and personalities. It touched on a variety of literary, cultural, political, and other matters during one of the most productive and portentous periods of Russia's history. Pogodin has been characterized as a man of "expansive nature," capable of "generosity" as well as "miserliness," and as being both "good natured and cunning." In his scholarly work he could be guilty of "slovenliness" and "petty pedantry," but also displayed uncommon industry and productivity.[31]

Pogodin was of Great Russian stock like the early Slavophils, and also Orthodox, but his religiousness was heavy on the side of ritual and conformity to established church practices and lacked the theological and philosophical probing of his Slavophil friends. Nor should he be unduly reproached for this, as he chose, early in life, the study of Russian history as his life work. Up to the age of ten he studied at home, and between 1810 and 1814 was tutored by his father's friend A. G. Reshetnikov, a printer by profession. In 1812 the Pogodin home was destroyed in the Moscow fire, forcing the family to move to Suzdal'. Between 1814 and 1818 young Pogodin studied in a Moscow Gymnasium and from 1818 until 1821 in Moscow University in the literature faculty.[32] Then and later he was captivated by Karamzin's *History of the Russian State* (Istoriia Gosudarstva Rossiiskago), the first eleven volumes of which appeared between 1816 and 1824.

An important landmark in Pogodin's career was the year 1835, when he was appointed to the chair of Russian history at Moscow University and gave up the teaching of universal history. This change occurred, as Buslaev has explained, in connection with the trend at Moscow University to stress academic specialization in contrast to the prevailing policy that produces "encyclopedic professors." But the change did not discourage Pogodin from concentrating in consecutive years, first on Nestor and the Primary Chronicle, then on the origin of Rus, followed by emphasis on the Norman period, Boris Godunov, Peter the Great, and others. His emphasis was not on form, exposition, or delivery but on content.[33] This and a good deal more Buslaev got from Pogodin's lectures and autobiography, but he also knew that Pogodin relied heavily as a teacher of Russian history on "chronicles, memoirs, charters, treaties, and other monuments of the past." This approach had obvious merits, except when he demonstrated his latest research results in his lectures, a practice that saw him "rush into specialties, sometimes abruptly and outside of any system."[34]

Although Pogodin did not have the estates and income of the Slavophils, he was able to travel frequently to Western and Central Europe, and even to the Balkans. Between 1835 and 1847, according to one source, Pogodin made five trips to the West (1835, 1838, 1842, 1846, 1847), presumably for his health, and he also traveled abroad "several times in the reign of Alexander II."[35] Of particular importance here are his contacts with the Western and South Slavs, with Šafarík, Hanka, Jungmann, Palacký, Čelakovský, Kollár, Karadžić, Kopitar, Venelin, Bouček, Linde,

Maciejowski, Miklošić, Štúr, and others.[36] Pogodin was among the first in Russia to become involved in the flowering of the Slav cultural renaissance, and he did so to an extent unmatched by the early Slavophils, who during the 1830s and 1840s were on the whole more concerned with the course of Russian life and culture than with the fate of the non-Russian Slavs.

There seems to be general agreement that the predominant influences in Pogodin's early career were N. M. Karamzin (1766–1826) and his history, and the German historian August Ludwig von Schlözer (1735–1809). Schlözer's theory of the Norman origin of the Russian state is still controversial, but it was not so for Pogodin. He was struck by it as a young man, and as a professor he incorporated it in his lectures to leave a lasting impression on the Slavophils, primarily through his students Konstantin Aksakov and Iurii Samarin. While still a university student Pogodin became acquainted with Schlözer's work on the suggestion of his friend, the future prominent paleologist A. M. Kubarev (1798–1881). Kubarev lent Pogodin the first volume of Schlözer's two-volume *Nestor,* which had been translated from German into Russian by D. I. Iazykov.[37]

Reading *Nestor,* Pogodin was particularly fascinated by the work of Saints Cyril and Methodius in the Slav lands of Moravia and Pannonia and by the account of the formation of the Slav language with its many dialects, including the Russian.[38] From that time on, Barsukov says, "Schlözer held him in his grip, and Pogodin became immersed in his researches."[39] Pogodin's youthful imagination, inflamed by the patriotic fervor of the time, as well as by Schlözer's work, prompted the following entry in his diary (February 6, 1821): "I talked with Kubarev about the union of all the Slav nations in . . . one state." All that was needed was "another Peter [the Great]" and "another Suvorov." The big task was to liberate the Slavs from Austrian rule. Winning over Serbia, Pogodin said, would be easy. He would offer the Baltic gubernias to Prussia in exchange for the rest of Poland so that "not a single foreigner could dare say that he is a Russian citizen. What a holiday it would be." Many years later, probably in the early 1870s in connection with his written controversy with A. N. Pypin over the meaning of Slavophilism, Pogodin, speaking of Schlözer's *Nestor,* dated his "attachment to the Slavs" to "the minute when I first read the above-mentioned lines of Schlözer."[40]

From this youthful introduction on, for the rest of his life, whatever his main preoccupation, Pogodin would not forget the non-Russian Slavs. "He became the first chairman of the Slavonic Welfare Society (1858–1875), and was regarded as the 'father of Panslavism.'"[41] His career touched at various times on Official Nationality, Slavophilism, the Native Soil movement, and pan-Slavism, ideologies which, although exhibiting at times a certain closeness, were nonetheless distinct currents of thought to the right of center.

The summary of Moscow Slavophilism's cardinal tenets in Riasanvosky's works, and specifically in his latest, on the images of Peter the Great, makes it abundantly clear that although the Slavophils shared a certain common ground with Pogodin, they also had significant differences—not only on the role of Peter the Great, and his "Westernization" of Russia, but also on the kindred and no less pertinent subject of the role and nature of the Russian autocrat. There was no inclination among the Slavophils to extol the tsar to near-deification, nor would they ever have countenanced the renaming of Holy Russia as "Petrovia" or "Nikolaevia." They believed that autocracy was the best form of government for Russia, but they, particularly Khomiakov and Konstantin Aksakov, urged a type of service state in which the autocrat would be attuned to the wisdom and will of the people, the *narod*. Nor do we find outside of Moscow Slavophilism any emphasis on *sobornost'*, wholeness of the spirit, and communality.

Pogodin's real influence on the Slavophils, notably on Konstantin Aksakov and Samarin, was in the matter of the Norman theory, that Russia, unlike the Western states that were founded through force and conquest, was established peacefully as a result of an invitation. The implication was clear that ancient Russia was morally superior to the barbarian Western nations. When Samarin, as pointed out earlier, got into a public polemic with Belinsky in 1846, and insisted on certain presumed and dubious historical claims such as the peaceful character of the early Russians, their meekness, humility, and Pogodin's notion of the "voluntary invitation to rule" in reference to the Varangians, Belinsky quickly, and in one stroke, showed both Samarin and Pogodin how ridiculous it was to see any connection between humility, love of peace, or as Plekhanov said, "patience, meekness, and submissiveness," and empire building.[42]

Pogodin may not have been as favored by the government as were the St. Petersburg men of Official Nationality and Burachek, but as Plekhanov pointed out, the first issue of *Moskvitianin* (1841) left a most favorable impression of Pogodin and Shevyrev in St. Petersburg, and from then until the end of Nicholas I's reign Pogodin was permitted to publish the journal. The few annual symposiums that the Slavophils were allowed to publish were unceremoniously brought to an end by the censorship in 1852, while the attempt in 1845 by the Slavophils to reorient the *Moskvitianin* under Ivan Kireevsky's direction resulted in failure after three issues.[43] Part of the explanation for this failure is to be found in personality conflicts, part in the absence of concurrence between Pogodin and his Slavophil friends on the significance of Peter the Great and his reforms, the nature and importance of the Russian autocracy, the *narod,* the Orthodox church, and the village commune.[44] Their differences precluded identity between Pogodin's views and those of the Moscow Slavophils.

Various attempts have been made to define Pogodin's somewhat baffling ideological orientation. Korsakov was convinced that "Pogodin was not a Slavophil," and he justified this conclusion on the ground that Pogodin's mind was practical whereas the Slavophils were theoretically inclined. Bestuzhev-Riumin declared, "Pogodin was never a Slavophil."[45] But Irene Zohrab, after careful consideration of the matter, and relying heavily on Pogodin's essay on the Slavophils, published less than two years before his death, concludes, "In his essay of 1873 'The Slavophiles' Pogodin firmly aligns himself with these and considers the journals he edited — *Moscow Herald* and the *Muscovite* — to have been platforms for the expression of Slavophile views." Zohrab is convinced that "there remains no doubt that he [Pogodin] identified himself with the Slavophiles and shared their basic beliefs and aspirations."[46] Pogodin's "profession of faith," coming quite late in his life, was doubtless sincere, and seems to be in line with the fact that in 1860, shortly before Khomiakov's death, Pogodin signed, together with the Moscow Slavophils, the "Message to the Serbians," which had been drafted by Khomiakov. But final judgment on this matter must, I think, await a thorough study of Pogodin's works, correspondence, and biography, for only such a scrutiny can reveal whether his convictions at the end of his life were identical with those of his earlier years.

Still, while there may still be unanswered questions about Pogodin's exact ideological orientation and its relationship to Moscow Slavophilism, there is no doubt about his personal relations with the "early" Slavophils, and some of their adherents. He knew the Slavophils and their families closely for many decades and in several capacities, including that of a private teacher-professor. Therefore what he has to say in his essay "The Slavophiles," about them is of primary importance. Pogodin began his reply to Pypin's articles in *Vestnik Evropy* (The Messenger of Europe) by arguing against the invidious comparison of the Slavophils with the Old Believers, employed by Belinsky in the polemics of the 1840s and occasionally by others since then. He likened the Westerners' campaign against the Slavophils to a "Corsican vendetta," and declared that in the Slavophil-Westerner controversy he was on the side of the Slavophils.[47]

"Initially," Pogodin states, "the Slavophiles were a circle of young people (now long aged or gone to their graves) who knew each other from childhood onwards — or from the school bench." He dates their beginnings to the 1820s, listing four generations. In his words,

The Slavophiles declared themselves from the 1820s and 1830s (Khomyakov, Yazykov, the Kireyevsky brothers, Shevyryov, Koshelyov and others). By the 1840s a new generation was ready (Konstantin Aksakov, Samarin, Popov, Yelagin, Stakhovich, Panov, Valyuyev, Prince Cherkassky). The third generation belonged to the 1850s (Gil'ferding, Ivan Aksakov, Lamansky).

From the 1860s onwards began the fourth generation (the collaborators on
The Dawn (Zaria) Conversation (Beseda) and others).[48]

The monthly *Zaria*, which appeared in St. Petersburg for three years
(1869–1872), had contributions from A. D. Gradovsky, Danilevsky, O. F.
Miller, and others. Its orientation has been characterized as conservative
and pan-Slav. *Beseda*, published in St. Petersburg, was a monthly that appeared only in 1871–1872, with contributions by A. I. Koshelev, Ivan Aksakov, S. Iur'ev, and others. It has been classified as "an organ of the
Slavophil orientation."[49]

Plekhanov in his essay "Pogodin and the Class Struggle" makes two points
that are of particular significance here. He rightly maintains that Official
Nationality preceded Slavophilism, dating it to 1832; more dubiously, he says
that Pogodin's Official Nationality and Moscow Slavophilism were practically identical, being separated only by the difference in Pogodin's and the
Slavophils' social-economic status. "Slavophilism and the theory of official
nationality," Plekhanov says, "represent in substance one and the same
doctrine equally dear to several ideologues of the two social strata but differently understood by them. This was in conformity with the different situation of the strata in society which they represented – the Slavophils, gentry,
and Pogodin, a member of the intelligentsia [from various social classes], a
[*raznochinets*]."[50] The fact that Slavophil ideology rested upon Khomiakov's
doctrine of *sobornost'*, Kireevsky's idea of the wholeness of the spirit,
Konstantin Aksakov's choric principle, and Samarin's association of
sobornost' and communality seem to have escaped Plekhanov. To disap-
prove of these on ideological grounds is understandable; to overlook them
in a factual historical study is less so.

Dudzinskaia in her recent (1983) work on the Slavophils devotes several
paragraphs to Plekhanov's views on Slavophilism and Official Nationality.
She points out that "Plekhanov's concept has exerted a great influence on
the subsequent historiography of Slavophilism, and it has not outlived [its
influence] to the present."[51] In a brief review of Soviet scholarship on
Slavophilism she points to "two tendencies in the evaluation of the
Slavophils" that evolved during the 1940s and 1950s – one represented by V.
M. Shtein, who saw the Slavophils as a "progressive phenomenon," the other
represented by A. G. Dement'ev, who in effect "returned to Plekhanov's
evaluation."[52] During the 1960s, interest and research on the Slavophils
among Soviet scholars increased considerably, culmination in the written
discussion in 1969 in the pages of *Voprosy literatury* (Problems of Literature).[53] In this discussion, of more than a dozen essays by as many participants, two general orientations were noticeable: that of the older
generation, who perceived little or no difference between Slavophilism and
Official Nationality (the Plekhanov position), and that of younger scholars,

who saw in Slavophilism certain more enlightened elements than in Official Nationality.[54]

A few examples should here be given from Dudzinskaia's study of the Slavophils, rich in facts and content, illustrating the differences between Slavophilism and Official Nationality. Although she retains her Marxist-Leninist position, she has a clear vision of the Slavophils. She sees their shortcomings, self-interest, and error, but she also recognizes certain views and convictions that set them apart from Official Nationality and from the "reptil'naia pressa." The Slavophils, specifically the Aksakov brothers, viewed the Russian autocracy quite differently from the proponents of Official Nationality, including Pogodin—or at least the Pogodin of the 1830s and 1840s. Thus in Ivan Aksakov's opinion, Russia's "historical mission" was "to contain autocracy in the state realm, and to achieve this by bypassing constitutional forms." There was also a marked difference in the "historical views" of the Slavophils and Official Nationality, specifically of such historians as Pogodin and N. G. Ustrialov. These two "lowered the role of the people, reducing it almost to zero [even] in the moments of its greatest activity." Furthermore "It is impossible to imagine that Pogodin and Ustrialov could call the reign of Nicholas a 'tyranny' or a 'soul-harming [*dushevrednyi*] despotism,' and Nicholas I himself a 'murderer' [*dushegubets*] as the Aksakov brothers did."[55] As I noted in the preceding study of this series, Konstantin Aksakov, did a good deal in his historical writings to call attention to the part played by the people in the historical process in contrast to the prevailing tendency among historians in general, including the West, at the time to concentrate on the role of the state.[56]

Although the Slavophils as land and serf owners never forgot their personal interests, they were among the most forceful defenders of the peasants' right to some land. In this respect Samarin and Konstantin Aksakov were particularly prominent.[57] But perhaps the Slavophils were in no other respect further away from the backward or indifferent sections of Russian society than they were on the question of progressive modern scientific agriculture. As Chapter 8 above showed, their readiness to appreciate the latest Western agricultural machinery, and to purchase whatever could be utilized in their farming is established beyond doubt. It may seem surprising, even startling, that in the crucial second half of the 1850s, the years leading to the emancipation reform, the Slavophils were closer to the radical left, particularly Chernyshevsky and Herzen, than to the conservative Official Nationality. To be sure, the rapprochement with the radical left was tactical on both sides, as the Samarin-Herzen correspondence of 1864 illustrates, but it did actually take place.[58]

Despite the different socio-economic standing and interests that separated Pogodin and the Slavophils, toward the end of Pogodin's life he identified his views and convictions in general terms with Moscow

Slavophilism, and he may have been justified in doing so; but there is evidence that on a number of issues his reminiscences in 1873 were not completely free of wishful thinking. His idealization not only of Holy Russia and the inception of the Russian state but also of Peter the Great and later tsars has already been mentioned. His identification of the *Moskvitianin* with Slavophilism is also doubtful, particularly his saying that this was true not only during the 1840s but presumably also after 1850 when it passed into the hands of the "young editorial board" (*molodaia redaktsiia*). One need not quarrel with his assertions that the Slavophils were not favored by the government (as the defenders of Official Nationality were), that they looked favorably on Western science, education, on the West's great literature, art and on other aspects of Western life, but that they would not uncritically accept everything Western. Certainly he was well aware of the fact that for the Slavophils, as for him, the sense of *narodnost'* included the unshakable desire to see Russian literature, art, and culture spring up and flourish on Russia's native soil.

In the literature of the middle decades of the nineteenth century, Pogodin's name is nearly always mentioned in connection with that of S. P. Shevyrev (1806–1864), who was, of course, Pogodin's friend, collaborator on the *Moskvitianin* during the 1840s, and colleague on the staff of Moscow University. Shevyrev was born in Saratov of a gentry family and died in Paris. This last fact is symbolic of the life and career of this "poet, critic, and historian of literature," who knew the West and its literature as few other Russians knew them. Pogodin offers a glowing tribute to Shevyrev in his essay on the Slavophils:

> What can one say of Shevyryov, who has been so abused in every way by ignoramuses? I don't think there was a professor anywhere in Europe who was equally familiar with all the literatures, both ancient and modern, with all the European languages, as Shevyryov was. He used to translate Plato and Lucian in his youth. As for German, French, and English literature □it goes without saying! Goethe did justice to his critical perspicacity; Pushkin also congratulated him. He left a whole book about Shakespeare, one about Dante. He knew Italian and Spanish literature as well as he knew Russian literature.[59]

Shevyrev has attracted relatively little attention, except opprobrium, in both pre-Soviet and Soviet studies as well as in the West. He was a specialist in literature and literary criticism, but it is the portion of his work that is closer to the sphere of ideology that is of particular attention here. Specifically, I refer to the late 1830s and 1840s when, he encountered, among other Westerners, his able critic and detractor, Belinsky.

In 1823 Shevyrev joined the well-known "Young Men of the Archives" in Moscow, where he met, among others, Kireevsky. Two years later he helped two youthful friends in translating German theoretical works on literature. His publishing collaboration with Pogodin began in 1827 on the *Moskovskii vestnik*. In 1829 he left for Rome as tutor to Princess Zinaida Volkonskaia's son. He remained there nearly four years, studying classical literature and philosophy, the Middle Ages, and also Italian, Spanish, and English. On his return to Russia in 1832 he was appointed, with Uvarov's support, as an adjunct to the chair of Russian literature at Moscow University. His master's thesis the following year was on the subject, "Dante and His Age" (*Dant i ego vek*). Shevyrev's versatility and wide-ranging interests found expression in a series of research publications between 1835 and 1860.[60] Toward the end of his life he gave a course on Russian literature, "*Storia della literatura russa,*" in Florence (1862), and he lectured on the same subject in Paris.

Of all his works, his essay "A View of a Russian on European Education" (*Vzgliad russkago na obrazovanie Evropy*) seems to have provoked the most controversy. It was published in the first issue of *Moskvitianin* for 1841 and immediately aroused considerable debate. It also helped to sharpen animosity between Shevyrev and Belinsky, and to identify certain elements in his *Weltanschauung* with Moscow Slavophilism. This became particularly noticeable in the middle 1840s as the Slavophil-Westerner polemic became sharper and more exacerbated. The crux of the matter was the state and future of the West and Russia's attitude toward it, summed up in the words "decaying West" (*gniiushchii zapad*).

Shevyrev's works of the mid-1830s reveal a considerable knowledge of classical literature as well as of the literature of Italy, Spain, Germany, England, and France,[61] but it was in a way ironic that he should have died in one of the centers of the "decaying West" whose dismal fate he had proclaimed, with some relish, in 1841. Perhaps no section of Shevyrev's essay of 1841 is so revealing of its basic content and spirit as this assertion: "In our friendly and close relations with the West we are dealing with a person carrying in himself a wicked, contagious malady, one who is engulfed in an atmosphere of dangerous breath. We kiss him, share his mental fare, drink any of [his] cup of sentiments."[62] The lesson was clear. Russia should follow its own road or suffer the consequences of the Western contagion.

Yet Shevyrev should not be burdened with complete responsibility for so sweeping a condemnation of the West. The notion of the decaying West was not his own. As Pogodin made clear, it was born in the West. Pogodin, writing in 1873, noted that Shevyrev had said, "The West is decaying," but, he declared, "In the works of the spokesmen of the West, Mill, Quinet, and others, one can point out numerous instances where this thought is corroborated." Pogodin singled out Herzen as having agreed that "One's soul diminishes in the West"; and was this not the same as "the West is decaying"?[63] Many years later, in 1940, in a lengthy essay, P. B. Struve also traced the origin of the "decaying West" to Western Europe.[64] Still in connection with Shevyrev's pronouncement, he concluded that it dated from the late eighteenth century and that it was prompted by the dismal aspects of the life of the workers during the industrial revolution in England. It then found its way "in the writings of William Goodwin, and subsequently influenced French and German writers such as Philarete Chasles and Franz von Baader, in the wake of the French Revolution."[65] Shevyrev, whose "exposure to Western life" was equalled only by those of the Westerners Herzen, Botkin, Annenkov, and Turgenev, concluded (albeit prematurely) that the West had lost its "faith in itself," and that the time had arrived for the light from the East to shine. As in the case of the Slavophils, this sort of reasoning was a boost to Russian Orthodox messianism.

When Shevyrev publicized the notion of the "decaying West," he brought to the fore in the Russian mind the persistent problem of the relationship of Russia to the West in its broadest scope: political, diplomatic, socio-economic, religious, literary-cultural, and psychological. This problem, particularly vital for Russia after the reign of Peter the Great, looms today as the dominant issue not just for Russia and the West but for human survival. During the 1840s when the thought of the "decaying West" became a matter of concern in the Moscow salons and in the Russian periodical literature opinion was split. On the whole the Slavophils sided with Shevyrev, the Westerners against him. But there was at least one participant in the polemic who agreed neither with the Slavophils nor with the Westerners. That person was N. A. Mel'gunov (1804–1867), a "music critic and publicist," a friend of the composer M. I. Glinka. The Slavophils did not consider him "one of theirs"; Belinsky called him a "reconciler" whose articles were characterized by "colorlessness." Mel'gunov's position is aptly summed up in the title of a lengthy biographical essay by Kirpichnikov, published in 1898 under the title "Between the Slavophils and the Westerners. N. A. Mel'gunov."

Mel'gunov came from a gentry family of the Orlov gubernia, and was in the usual fashion brought up by private tutors, Russian and Swiss. As an adult he traveled and lived for long periods in the West. During the 1830s he wrote enthusiastically about the work of Glinka based on Russian folk songs. He also became embroiled in a polemic with Grech and Bulgarin, who did not spare him in their attacks, and in the mid-1840s he became involved in the controversy over the "decaying West." He is said to have "argued against Asiatic, pre-Petrine Russia," and at the same time to have disapproved of Granovsky's presumed scornful attitude "toward the whole East and the Semites." Although Khomiakov and Shevyrev considered him a "one-sided Westerner," he called himself "an exile." The Slavophils, he said, were "alchemists searching for gold in Russian history." "You will come upon many things," he told them, "that are good and sensible, but the main thing is that you will awaken in the Russians the thirst for self-knowledge."

In his concern with the nagging issue of Russia and the West, whether he was at home or abroad, Mel'gunov held firmly to his unheroic middle-ground position. Thus on July 12, 1846, he wrote to Moscow from Lac-sur-Mer in Normandy: "It is not the West that is decaying—it is rather the East that is blossoming. However, in the East as in the West, one segment of the population, and the most significant one at that, carries in itself the possibility of a rebirth and of a great future. This while the other part is actually decaying and is headed for its doom." The future, in his view, lay not with the bourgeoisie and the ruling classes but with the peasants: "The more I become acquainted with the peasantry, with the *narod* of the various nations, the more I see the common bond between them. . . . How much simplicity, purity of mores, and cordiality is here!" But as Kirpichnikov noticed, a year later (July 30, 1847) Mel'gunov wrote to Pogodin from his village Petrovskoe that he was trying to avoid both the "whip and foreign innovations," and that he preferred to remain a "European Russian."[66]

Whatever fault one might find with Mel'gunov's ideological position, in the mid-1840s he was closer to the truth on the crucial question of Russia and the West than most of his compatriots, whether Slavophils or Westerners.[67] The West was neither dead nor dying nor was Russia moribund, but they both had a host of problems. For the West, the most serious problem was that of the new industrialism which was creating vast wealth for the few and for the state while causing unrelieved misery and suffering for multitudes of industrial workers. In Russia, the noose around the neck of the many millions of peasants was the institution of serfdom. Russia's economic, social, political, and military backwardness (soon to be painfully displayed in the Crimean War), the stifling regime of Nicholas I with its censorship, Third Section, and its "seven dark years" (1848–1855) seemed to hang over Russia in a hopeless pall. Yet, perhaps paradoxically, during the thirty-year reign of Nicholas I (1825–1855) Russian culture had begun to "bloom" as never before.

This flowering was most noticeable in the realms of the theater, music, and literature, where in the decades of the twenties, thirties, and on through the fifties there appeared first Griboedov, then Lermontov, Gogol', Turgenev, Dostoevsky, Ostrovsky, and Tolstoy. The gradual maturing of Russia's great periodical literature, and the masters of Russian literary criticism and publicistic work also belong here—Belinsky primarily to the 1840s, Chernyshevsky, Dobroliubov, and Apollon Grigor'ev to the 1850s. In this brief period the principal ideological currents, Slavophilism and Westernism are also registered. Indeed, Mel'gunov saw through the general gloom of the Russian scene in the mid-1840s the blossoming of Russia in several important spheres. But he also had learned that the West, despite its grave problems, was not ready to give up: "It is not the West that is decaying; it is rather the East that is blossoming." West and East had to co-exist despite their respective shortcomings and unsolved problems.

Notes

1. The exploratory and tentative nature of the effort to compare and contrast Slavophilism with the other three currents is based almost entirely on the work of others and is intended as an invitation to further exploration of their similarities and differences, and not as a final or concluding statement on this matter. Although some high-quality published work exists, examples of which are given below, more remains to be done before any definitive conclusions about the interrelationships among these four movements can be drawn. Even then one is likely to be confronted with the manifestly intractable task of drawing boundary lines where often no sharp separation exists. Examples of works published in the West in recent decades are: (1) on official nationality, N. V. Riasanovsky, *Nicholas I and Official Nationality in Russia, 1825–1855* (Berkeley, Calif. 1959), and several articles; (2) on *pochvennichestvo,* Wayne Dowler, *Dostoevsky, Grigor'ev, and Native Soil Conservatism* (Toronto, 1982), Robert Whittaker, "'My Literary and Moral Wanderings': Apollon Grigor'ev and the Changing Cultural Topography of Moscow," *Slavic Review,* 1983, no. 3, pp. 390–407; (3) on pan-Slavism, Hans Kohn, *Pan-Slavism: Its History and Ideology* (Notre Dame, Ind., 1953); M. B. Petrovich, *The Emergence of Russian Panslavism, 1856–1870* (New York, 1956); Frank Fadner, *Seventy Years of Pan-Slavism in Russia: Karazin to Danilevskii, 1800–1870* (Georgetown, D.C., 1962); Ulrich Picht, *M. P. Pogodin und die Slavische Frage. Ein Beitrag zur Geschichte des Panslavismus* (Stuttgart, 1969).

2. The usual English translation of this triad is given above, but occasionally, as in the case of Professor Petrovich, it is rendered as "Nationalism, Autocracy, and Orthodoxy." The significance here is not in the transposition of the components but in Petrovich's translation of *narodnost'* as "nationalism." Cf. M. B. Petrovich, "Russian Pan-Slavists and the Polish Uprising of 1863," in H. G. Lunt, et al., eds., *Harvard Slavic Studies* (Cambridge, Mass., 2953), I, 219, and Petrovich, *The Emergence of Russian Panslavism,* p. 50. In 1956 while in Moscow I raised the question of the meaning of *narodnost'* in this context with a member of the Soviet Academy of Sciences. His opinion was that the Russian term *natsionalizm* may not have come into general use in the 1830s, and that *narodnost'* could have stood for *natsionalizm* in the eyes of the government. The second (1882) edition of Dal' does not contain *natsionalizm* whereas Ushakov's dictionary of 1938 does. The exact meaning of *narodnost'* in the watchwords proclaimed by the government in 1833 remains a moot question. As pointed out in the first

study of this series, there was no question in 1846–1847, after the discovery of the Ukrainian saints Cyril and Methodius Society, that *narodnost'* in the mind of Nicholas I stood for Russian nationalism. This also explains his strong anti-Slav sentiments at the time. See Christoff, *Xomjakov*, pp. 90–93; also "Ob Ukraino-Slavianskom Obshchestve," *Russkii arkhiv*, 1892, no. 7, pp. 347–354.

3. Riasanovsky, *Official Nationality*, p. 224.

4. Tsimbaev, *Slavianofil'stvo*, p. 212.

5. V. A. Koshelev, *Esteticheskie i literaturnye vozzreniia russkikh slavianofilov, 1840–1850-e gody*, (Leningrad, 1984), p. 89.

6. See *Vestnik Evropy*, 1871, no. 9, pp. 301–347; 1872, 11–12, pp. 47–97, 618–678.

7. Pypin in *Vestnik Evropy*, 1871, no. 9, pp. 337–339.

8. Ibid., p. 342.

9. Ibid., p. 347.

10. Riasanovsky, *Official Nationality*, pp. 59–60.

11. For a summary of Grech's role in rebutting Custine's uncomplimentary account of the Russian government, and for Grech's denunciation of Custine's book as "a tissue of lies, inaccuracies, blunders, contradictions and slanders," see George F. Kennan, *The Marquis de Custine and His "Russia in 1839"* (Princeton, N. J., 1971), p. 100. See also Riasanovsky, *Official Nationality*, pp. 114–115, 198.

12. Riasanovsky, *Official Nationality*, p. 145.

13. Ibid., p. 141.

14. For its long and fluctuating history, see Dement'ev et al., eds., *Russkaia periodicheskaia pechat' 1702–1894*, I, 140–144.

15. Riasanovsky, *Official Nationality*, p. 63 n. 64.

16. See Vladimir Botsianovsky, "Bulgarin, Faddei Venediktovich," *Russkii biograficheskii slovar'* (Moscow, 1908), vol. Betankur-Biakster, p. 476.

17. V. I. Kuleshov, "Bulgarin, Faddei Venediktovich," in D. S. Likhachev et al., eds., *Russkie pisateli. Biobibliograficheskii slovar'* (Moscow, 1971), pp. 203–204.

18. *Periodicheskaia pechat'*, p. 188.

19. Botsianovsky, "Bulgarin," p. 476.

20. *Periodicheskaia pechat'*, p. 230.

21. V. I. Kuleshov, "Senkovsky, Osip Ivanovich," *Russkie pisateli*, p. 586.

22. V. E. Vatsuro, "Glinka, Fedor Nikolaevich," *Russkie pisateli*, pp. 244–246.

23. Riasanovsky, *Official Nationality*, p. 122.

24. Cf. V. I. Zaitsev, "Kukol'nik, Nestor Vasil'evich," *Russkie pisateli*, p. 387; Riasanovsky, *Official Nationality*, p. 99.

25. Riasanovsky, *Official Nationality*, p. 113.

26. Riasanovsky has recently stressed this point in a nine-line stanza which he first quoted in 1967. It is from a Kukol'nik play in which he says of Peter the Great,

> I saw how the Great Anatomist
> Split open the decrepit body of Russia
> Changed her rotten insides,
> Put together her cleansed members . . .

This comparison of "Muscovite Russia to a cadaver," it could be added, was unlike the Slavophil view. It was Russian Westerners of the 1840s and 1850s, not the Moscow Slavophils, who in effect seemed to approach Kukol'nik on this issue. See N. V. Riasanovsky, *The Image of Peter the Great in Russian History and Thought* (Oxford, 1985), pp. 114, 120.

27. V. F., "Burachek, Stefan Anisimovich," *Russkii biograficheskii slovar'* (Moscow, 1908), vol. Betankur-Biakster, p. 493.

28. Riasanovsky, *Official Nationality,* p. 121.

29. V. F., "Burachek," p. 494. See also P. M., "Burachek, Stepan Anisimiovich," F. A. Brokgaus and I. A. Efron, eds., *Entsiklopedicheskii slovar'* (St. Petersburg, 1891), IX, 7.

30. In his biographical sketch of Pogodin, K. N. Bestuzhev-Riumin refers to Pogodin's family as "literate, petty-bourgeois [*meshchanskaia*]." See his *Biografii i kharakteristiki* (St. Petersburg, 1882), p. 234. Pogodin's father was a serf who was freed by his master, Count I. P. Saltykov, in 1806.

31. D. A. Korsakov, "Pogodin, Mikhail Petrovich," *Russkii biograficheskii slovar* (St. Petersburg, 1905), vol. Plavil'shchikov-Primo, p. 154.

32. For a summary statement of Moscow University's vigorous growth, which coincided with Pogodin's years as a student and professor there, see F. I. Buslaev, *M. P. Pogodin kak professor* (Moscow, 1876), pp. 3–19. F. I. Buslaev (1818–1897) was a student of Pogodin's, graduating from Moscow University in 1838. Later he became a prominent Russian philologist, an authority on the Russian language, and on ancient Russian literature and art. He began in 1847 as a lecturer in Russian language and literature at Moscow University and later advanced to full professor and member of the Academy of Sciences. He looked fondly on the 1830s when a good many of Russia's brightest students were doing graduate work in the West, primarily in Germany. The group included T. N. Granovsky, P. N. Redkin, and N. I. Krylov, all soon to become professors in Russia. Buslaev also stressed the formation of "two parties, which under the names of Westerners and Slavophils loudly proclaimed themselves in the press during the 1840s." He saw a great difference between those who had studied in the West before embarking on their academic careers as Westerners and who presumably believed that it was "necessary to erase from the face of the earth all dif-

ferences between individual nationalities," and those, like Pogodin and Shevyrev, who "declared nationality [*narodnost'*] to be their [guiding] principle." Buslaev, *Pogodin,* p. 7.

33. Ibid., pp. 9–10.

34. Ibid., pp. 11–12.

35. In 1835 Pogodin visited Germany, Switzerland, and Bohemia; in 1838, Italy, France, England, Holland, and Belgium. While in France he met Guizot and other prominent Frenchmen. In 1842 he "became particularly close to Šafařík" while he was in Prague. Korsakov, *Pogodin,* p. 158. Another author mentions six trips of Pogodin's to the West before the Crimean War. See Petrovich, *The Emergence of Russian Panslavism,* p. 26.

36. Petrovich, *Panslavism,* p. 27.

37. Barsukov, *Pogodin,* I, 54. Much valuable information on Schlözer's personality, scholarship, and relations with other historians, including G. F. Müller, can be found in A. G. Mazour, *Modern Russian Historiography,* 2d ed. (New York, 1958), especially pp. 23–30. Mazour observes (p. 28) that Schlözer was "inclined to accept the Norman theory" of the origin of the Russian state "with some provisions," and he points out that "within two centuries after the arrival of the Normans there was hardly a trace left of Scandinavian linguistic influence upon the Russian tongue. . . . This interpretation [of Schlözer's] even pleased the nationalist and Slavophile elements."

38. For Nestor's Church-Slavonic reference to the work of Cyril and Methodius in Moravia and Panomia, see A. Teodorov-Balan, *Kiril i Metodi* (Sofia, 1934), pp. 150–151.

39. Barsukov, *Pogodin,* I, 55. The rise of Russian national consciousness, stimulated by the Napoleonic invasion, has been a major factor in modern Russian history. Recently it has been ably utilized in connection with the Pogodin-Slavophil relationship by Irene Zohrab in her excellent essay on the Slavophils. This is followed by her translation into English of Pogodin's essay "The Slavophiles," published in the Dostoevsky-edited *Grazhdanin,* nos. 11 and 13, 1873. See Irene Zohrab, "'The Slavophiles' by M. P. Pogodin. An Introduction and Translation," *New Zealand Slavonic Journal,* 1982, pp. 29–87.

40. *Pogodin,* II, 56. Three decades ago in an noteworthy essay, Professor Riasanovsky pointed out a number of similarities between Pogodin and Shevyrev on the one hand and the Slavophils on the other. But he also called attention to differences between them, the principal one being their dramatic divergence on the role and character of Peter the Great. To the Moscow professors he was no less than a "human God." See. N. V. Riasanovsky, "Pogodin and Shevyrev in Russian Intellectual History," in Hugh McLean et al., eds., *Russian Thought and Politics* (Cambridge, Mass., 1957), pp. 149–167.

41. Zohrab, "Pogodin," p. 33.

42. Volume 23 of G. V. Plekhanov's twenty-four volume *Sochineniia* (Moscow, 1920–1927) bears the subtitle, "Westerners and Slavophiles." It contains sixteen essays, book reviews, and a speech, all published between 1908 and 1912, and although most of them are devoted to the Westerners, the author also includes "Pogodin i bor'ba klassov" (Pogodin and the Class Struggle, a 56-page essay), a much shorter one on Ivan Kireevsky, and a brief review of Berdiaev's biography of Khomiakov. Plekhanov showed uncommon competence and comprehension of the principal mid-nineteenth-century Russian ideological currents, but he considered Official Nationality and Slavophilism virtually identical, an opinion that has had considerable influence on many later scholars.

43. Based on information provided by Barsukov, Plekhanov points to personality frictions between Pogodin and the Slavophils in the middle and late 1840s, reflected in such matters as Pogodin's criticism of the Slavophil symposium of 1846, and quotes Khomiakov as saying Pogodin "is not one of ours [*ne nash*]." Cf. Barsukov, *Pogodin,* VIII, 321; Plekhanov, *Sochineniia,* XXIII, 45.

44. No one has done more than Nicholas Riasanovsky to clarify the relationship between the Moscow Slavophils and the men of the Official Nationality. Beginning with his pioneering *Russia and the West in the Teaching of the Slavophiles: A Study of Romantic Ideology* (Cambridge, Mass., 1952), he showed awareness, among other things, of the relationship between Official Nationality and Slavophilism. (See for instance, pp. 9–11). In his 1957 essay "Pogodin and Shevyrev in Russian Intellectual History," he says, *inter alia,* "In general, Pogodin and Shevyrev placed a greater emphasis on the autocratic government and a lesser emphasis on the people than did Khomiakov and his friends" (p. 165). Pogodin, Shevyrev, and Official Nationality are prominent in another Riasanvosky essay of 1957, "Some Comments on the Role of the Intelligentsia in the Reign of Nicholas I of Russia, 1825–1855," *Slavic and East European Review,* 1957, no. 3, pp. 163–176. In "'Nationality' in the State Ideology during the Reign of Nicholas I," *Russian Review* 1960, no. 1, pp. 38–46, he called attention to a number of problems in connection with Official Nationality, including the "narrowly circumscribed role" that it allotted to the Russian people, its defense of serfdom, its limits on education for the people to keep them "in their place," and the agreement between Samarin and Pogodin on the Baltic Germans. Riasanovsky's major works on this and related subjects, *Nicholas I and Official Nationality in Russia, 1825–1855* (1959, 1967) and *The Image of Peter the Great in Russian History and Thought* (1985), have already been cited.

45. Cf. Korsakov, "Pogodin," p. 155; Bestuzhev-Riumin, "Pogodin," p. 233.

46. Zohrab, "Pogodin," p. 43.

47. Ibid., pp. 58–59, 84. The references here (pp. 58–84) are to Zohrab's translation of Pogodin's essay (the Russian original is not available to me); pp. 84–87 are her footnotes to the translation, and pp. 29–58 contain her meticulous introductory essay.

48. Ibid., p. 61.

49. Barsukov called attention to Pogodin's four generations of Slavophils in 1892 (see Christoff, *Kireevskij*, p. 76). Here I have used information supplied by Zohrab, "Pogodin," p. 51, supplemented with that from *Periodicheskaia pechat'*, pp. 519, 535.

50. Plekhanov, *Sochineniia*, XXIII, 96–97.

51. Dudzinskaia, *Slavianofily*, p. 14.

52. Ibid., pp. 16–17.

53. Ibid., p. 18. This increase in Soviet scholarship is is providing Western students with some excellent research, often including new archival material.

54. See V. N. Pavlov, "Spory o slavianofil'stve i russkom patriotizme v sovetskoi nauchnoi literature 1967–1970gg.," *Grani*, 1971, no. 82, p. 196ff. For an incomplete summary see also Christoff, *Aksakov*, p. 331.

55. Dudzinskaia, *Slavianofily*, p. 49. On the same page, states that in an unpublished article under the title "Autocracy Is Not a Religious Truth" (*Samoderzhavie ne est' religioznaia istina*), Ivan Aksakov confined the action of autocracy to state matters, excluding it from religious and private affairs, and from questions of conscience and personal concerns. As Konstantin Aksakov saw it, the autocrat's authority was "not a right but a duty and an obligation." In the presence of such convictions it is not surprising that the "Slavophils considered that the free union of tsar and people was violated by Peter I."

56. Ibid., pp. 51–54. The Slavophils compared Kievan culture favorably with that of the West, noting that women in the court of Iaroslav the Wise (1019–1054) were treated in a humane, civilized manner whereas in Khomiakov's view the old Germans were crude and cruel as illustrated in *The Ring of the Nibelung* in which "Siegfried beats his wife Krimhilde" (p. 51).

57. Ibid., pp. 55–56.

58. Here again Dudzinskaia gives us much factual information. Without minimizing the fundamental starting points — for the Slavophils, Eastern Orthodoxy, and in her opinion, for Herzen and Chernyshevsky, materialism — she notes instances in which Chernyshevsky looked favorably on the Slavophils for their views: on the West (pp. 44–45); on the preservation of the Russian village commune "the principal Slavophil bastion" (pp. 97, 105–111, 126), on Slavophil criticism and condemnation of serfdom (p. 164) — this and more, while his young friend and collaborator Dobroliubov (1836–1863) characterized the Slavophil *Sel'skoe blagoustroistvo* as the "'most humane and most effective journal on the peasant question,'" (p.

100). Herzen appreciated Slavophil efforts to "clear the road for the independent development of Russian national culture" (p. 45), and he warmly approved of the Russian village commune (p. 134). See Dudzinskaia, *Slavianofily v obshchestvensoi bor'be.*

59. Pogodin, "The Slavophiles," p. 64. In a cogent analytical chapter of *Russkaia filosofskaia estetika (1820–1830-e gody,* (Moscow, 1969), Iurii Mann says that Shevyrev was "a critic, historian, and theoretician of literature to the end of his life" (p. 150), correctly implying that he was not exclusively a dedicated ideologist. "Shevyrev was irritating, trivial, and obstinate and particularly toward the end of his life, envious and tricky. He possessed the special gift of provoking antipathy and of placing himself in ridiculous situations" (p. 150). Although Mann's monograph is limited to two decades, his highly informative chapter "Young Shevyrev" also sheds light on the rest of Shevyrev's career. Thus we learn of an early conflict of ideas between Shevyrev and Bulgarin when Shevyrev, then twenty years old, stood for the "Europeanization of Russia" (pp. 151–153); this stand was unlike his later position on the "decaying West, and of [his] dwelling on the infallible holiness of Russia" (p. 153). We also learn of Shevyrev's romantic antisystematic stance at a time when systematic thought was associated with German philosophy and scholarship (pp. 155, 176, 183). (This topic was of course, debated by the Slavophils in the early 1850s.) But as Shevyrev "drew close to the notorious official nationality," Mann says, he fought "against Hegel" in favor of the German "theosophist" Franz Baader, who valued "Russian Orthodoxy highly." He also provoked the displeasure of the "later Ivan Kireevsky" with his attacks "against the Hegelians" (p. 186).

60. Two of his best-known early works are *Istoriia poezii* (History of Poetry, 1835) and *Teoriia poezii v istoricheskom ee razvitii u drevnikh i novykh narodov* (Theory of Poetry in Its Historical Development Among the Ancient and Modern Peoples, 1836). Later on and at intervals he published his major work associated with his teaching at Moscow University, *Obshchee obozrenie russkoi slovesnosti* (General Review of Russian Literature, 1837) and *Chteniia po istorii russkoi slovesnosti* (Readings in the History of Russian Literature, in 4 vols., 1845, 1846, 1858, 1860). A. I. Balandin, "Shevyrev, Stepan Petrovich," *Russkie pisateli,* p. 701.

61. Much pertinent information and interpretation on this topic is contained in the unpublished doctoral dissertation of Richard M. Arnold, Jr., on Shevyrev, pp. 2–36.

62. F. A. Brokgaus and I. A. Efron, *Entsiklopedicheskii slovar'* (St. Petersburg, 1963), vol. 77, p. 363.

63. Pogodin, "The Slavophiles," p. 65.

64. P. B. Struve, "S. P. Sevyrev i zapadnye vnushenija i istocniki teorii-aforizma o 'gnilom' ili 'gnijuscem' zapade" (Shevyrev and Western Suggestions and Sources of the Theory-Aphorism about the Decayed or Decaying

West), *Zapiski russkago nauchnogo instituta v Belgrade* (Belgrad, 1940), pp. 200–263. See also Christoff, *Kireevskij*, pp. 398–399.

65. Arnold, *Shevyrev*, pp. 124, 130.

66. For the above quotations see A. I. Kirpichnikov, "Mezhdu Slavianofilami i Zapadnikami. N. A. Melgunov. Istoriko-literaturnyi ocherk, po neizdannym dokumentam," *Russkaia starina*, 1898, no. 12, p. 570.

67. For a recent study of some Russian Westerners, see Derek Offord, *Portraits of Early Russian Liberals: A Study of the Thought of T. N. Granovsky, V. P. Botkin, P. V. Annenkov, A. V. Druzhinin, and K. D. Kavelin* (Cambridge, 1985).

17

The "Native Soil" Movement and Pan-Slavism

The difficulties encountered in trying to draw a sharp line between the Slavophils and the proponents of Official Nationality are no less real than those that arise from an attempt to separate the Slavophils from the "men of the soil," the *Pochvenniki.* The central position that Pogodin occupies in Russian intellectual and ideological life in the middle of the nineteenth century is once again illustrated by the fact that Native Soil Movement or *Pochvennichestvo* had its tangible start in 1850 when the so-called Young Editorial Office, *Molodaia Redaktsiia* of Pogodin's *Moskvitianin,* passed into the hands of A. A. Grigor'ev (1822–1864), A. N. Ostrovsky (1823–1886), E. P. Edel'son, and several others, [two of whom, P. M. Sadovsky and I. F. Gorbunov, were actors.] "Close" to the editorial board were A. F. Pisemsky (1821–1881) and P. I. Mel'nikov-Pechersky (1818–1883).[1] The management of the *Moskvitianin's* affairs remained in Pogodin's hands, and the uneasy collaboration between the bright young men and Pogodin was short-lived. It lasted until 1853, although according to information in Egorov's edition of Grigor'ev's *Memoirs,* Grigor'ev continued to serve the *Moskvitianin* until 1855 in the "capacity of critic, poet, and translator."[2]

Grigor'ev's unstable and often agitated career provides, among other things, an illustration of the difficulty of resorting to journals for the purpose of identifying ideological currents. Even *Sovremennik* (The Contemporary) and *Otechestvennye zapiski* (Notes of the Fatherland), which are usually considered radical journals, were by no means radical over the whole span of their existence. Grigor'ev in his relatively short life of forty-one years was associated with more than a dozen and a half periodicals in the capacity of editor, publisher, or contributor, and it is virtually impossible to identify him with any single one, but his collaboration on Pogodin's *Moskvitianin* was longer than that on any other journal.[3] In addition to this difficulty it is essential to bear in mind that Grigor'ev was first and foremost a literary critic, and a writer of prose and poetry (matters which cannot be of concern here).

398

His ideology therefore cannot be sought, as is also true of Belinsky, another literary critic, in ideological monographs or treatises since such were prohibited by the government. It has to be reconstructed, however incompletely, from references often scattered in time and place. Furthermore, given the ever present censorship, it was often necessary for anyone touching on political-ideological matters to resort to Aesopian language.

Before turning briefly to Grigor'ev's *Pochvennichestvo,* we must call attention to two external but not irrelevant differences between the Moscow Slavophils and Grigor'ev. Grigor'ev was of the generation of the younger Slavophils, of the Aksakov brothers and Samarin, and he was of humbler birth than the Slavophils. For most of his life he and his family lived not in the northwest, gentry section of the city but in the plebeian *Zamoskvorech'e,* the area south of the Kremlin and beyond the Moscow River. This and the Taganka region, to the southeast of the Kremlin and south of the Iauza River, a tributary of the Moscow River, were the Moscow that Grigor'ev considered home.[4] The section of the city "contained by the river's horseshoe bend" was the "residential district of Moscow's merchants and minor civil servants," and it "gained renown as the setting of A. N. Ostrovsky's early plays of the 1850s."[5] The combination of birth in the family of a civil servant, childhood and youth in the *Zamoskvorech'e,* and a life of low pay and poor financial management (he was imprisoned for debt) gave Grigor'ev an outlook on life markedly different from that of the well-to-do Slavophils.

When Grigor'ev entered the law faculty of Moscow University in 1838 he had already shown a fondness for literature, the theater, and foreign languages. In 1843, having graduated the preceding year, he left suddenly for St. Petersburg in order to escape from "family dogmatism." He returned to Moscow early in 1847 after deciding that the life of the *chinovnik* was not for him, and soon entered into an unhappy marriage. For ten years he survived as a "writer of prose, poetry, [and] as a dramatist, translator, and theater critic," contributing to a variety of journals. He traveled in Italy, France, and Germany for about two years (1857–1859) as tutor to Prince Trubetskoi's son. As in the case of the Moscow Slavophils, commitment to elusive *narodnost',* native soil, and organic growth and evolution did not dampen his appreciation for some of the best in Western literature. He translated from Beranger, Byron, Heine, Goethe, Schiller, and Shakespeare, and was familiar with German idealism, and partial to Schelling, but his volatile temperament pushed him at one time into "sharp transitions from religious mysticism to atheism."[6]

Given the unsettled nature of Grigor'ev's character and career, even this tentative determination of his relationship to Moscow Slavophilism becomes hazardous. Yet based on a number of his publications and on the works of B. F. Egorov, R. T. Whittaker, V. Ia. Lakshin, P. Lobov, and W. Dowler, a notion of his ideological position becomes possible. It is striking that

Grigor'ev's available correspondence, from December 1842 to September 1863, consisting of more than two hundred letters (most of them addressed to Pogodin), contains only one letter to an "early" Slavophil, to Koshelev. It is dated March 25, 1856, and although the reason for it was the possibility that the *Moskvitianin,* then actually at the end of its existence, might pass into the hands of the Slavophils, Grigor'ev makes several points that reveal his attitude toward Moscow Slavophilism. He was convinced that he and the Slavophils served the same cause "but looked upon it from different points of view." He considered his views as representative of "one of the shades of our common orientation." "Principally," he said, "we differ in our views on art." In his opinion, for Koshelev and the Slavophils, art and literature "have only a secondary [*sluzhebnoe*] meaning" whereas "for us it is completely independent, and if you will, it is even above science." Grigor'ev's reference here is to the Slavophil defense of the notion of art with a social purpose.

But there were also other differences. Still professing pro-Slavophil sentiments, Grigor'ev said, "We are convinced only of the special superiority of the Great Russian principle over all others, therefore here we are more exclusive than you are."[7] He then turned to the difference most often cited whenever Slavophilism and "Native Soil" movement are compared and contrasted—that is, what role did the peasant and merchant classes play in Russian society? Among other things in his comments on this subject he revealed the somewhat intangible but nonetheless strong bond between his *Pochvennichestvo* and the Moscow district he came from, *Zamoskvorech'e.* Like the Slavophils, he was convinced that the future of Russia "reposes only in the class of people, guarding the faith, mores, and language of our forefathers, in the class not touched by the falsity of civilization." "However," he went on, "we do not respect the peasantry as such alone." It is "in the middle, manufacturing, and primarily merchant class that we see the old, primordial Rus with its bad and good, with its originality [*samobytnost'*]."[8]

From these ideological differences Grigor'ev drew certain conclusions relative to Russian literature. The *Pochvenniki,* for example, were more inclined "to admire Pushkin" and the Slavophils "to admire Gogol'."[9] But they agreed "on the theory of the independent development" for Russia, and also on "the immutability of Orthodoxy"—by which he meant, presumably, something other than the current status and role of the Orthodox church in Russia, of which neither he nor the Slavophils fully approved. Furthermore, he said of the Slavophils, "We (at least I personally) freely accept you as elders, and ourselves as pupils."

In 1859, after his travels in the West, Grigor'ev, apparently reconsidering his favorable estimate of the Slavophil "elders," turned on the man who deserved this designation more than any other—Khomiakov. In a long letter to Pogodin of August 26, 1859, Grigor'ev inquired, "Have you . . . read the brochure by our great sophist: 'Derniers mots d'un chretien orthodoxe'?" Having read it himself he *"understood* how our dearest and cleverest sophist deceives himself and others!"[10] Egorov explained this stricture by pointing to Grigor'ev's annoyance with Khomiakov's "religious treatises."[11] Khomiakov's religious works were too outspoken to be printed in Russia and had to be published in Paris and Leipzig, but Grigor'ev, toward the end of his life, thought there should be a more pronounced break between Slavophilism and the official Orthodox church.

Grigor'ev's experiences in Catholic Italy and France as well as in largely Protestant Germany had given him insight into the questions Khomiakov was dealing with; his main complaint, in his own censorious language, seemed to be that Khomiakov's statement of the questions was too indirect:

The idea of Christ and the comprehension of the Bible, expanding [and] broadening with the broadening of the consciousness of the *commune,* [and] of *sobornost',* is in contrast to the benumbing idea of Christ and the cessation of comprehension of the Bible in Catholicism. [This is] also in contrast to the fragmenting [*rasdroblenie*] of Christ into individuals, and the arbitrary personal interpretation of the Bible in Protestantism. Such is the broad meaning of the brochure – small in size but great in content, if its meaning could be liberated from the yoke of its Byzantine entanglements.[12]

Partly in consequence of differences in personal attitudes and choices, partly because of a higher degree of secularization of thought in Grigor'ev's *Pochvennichestvo* than in Moscow Slavophilism, Orthodoxy did not have as important a role in Grigor'ev's scheme of things as in Slavophilism. From his youth when German idealism caught his attention, to his later career, when he was absorbed in literature and literary criticism, he seems to have given little attention to the study and contemplation of religion. His primary concern was with the organic in life and literature, which in turn was inspired by early nineteenth century Western, secular romanticism. The *pochvenniki,* like the early Slavophils to a point, were caught up in the spell of German romanticism.

Wayne Dowler has recently pointed out in a monograph on *pochvennichestvo,* particularly in its second phase, that Dostoevsky, freed from Siberian exile and military service in 1859, became associated with it. This extension of *pochvennichestvo,* reaching well into the 1860s, and also Dostoevsky's relationship with Moscow Slavophilism are themes of considerable importance and complexity, deserving thorough treatment. Our concern in this study is, of course, with the earlier period, and for this Dowler's work also contains valuable material, that is on the *pochvennichestvo* of the 1850s. With respect to Apollon Grigor'ev, the principal spokesman of the *pochvenniki during the 1850s, Dowler cites from a letter of Grigor'ev's to N. N. Strakhov, dated September 23, 1861, in which he declares:*

"I was and remain a Slavophile. The narod, the *zemskii sobor,* ... that is what I believe in."

Grigor'ev's views on several matters were at odds with those of the Slavophils—not only on the roles of the peasantry and the merchant class and on the nature and purpose of art, but also on the presumed superiority of the Great Russian ethnic group, on the degree of influence of romanticism, and on what Dowler terms Grigor'ev's "localism," that is, his "love for color and diversity" as against the Slavophil wish "to turn all Russia into Moscow."[13] The common ground they shared, if not always in absolute unanimity, embraced such matters as the organic notion of art and culture, the necessity for Russia's indigenous cultural growth, the immutability of Orthodoxy, and the extension of the life of the *zemskii sobor,* commune, and *artel'.* That is to say, Grigor'ev was closer to the truth when he saw *pochvennichestvo* not as identical with Moscow Slavophilism but as a variant of it or as deriving from it.

In the historical literature of the last two centuries it is not unusual to see pan-Slavism (usually loosely defined) and its origin being attributed to the Catholic Croatian priest, Juraj Krizanic (1618–1683). Thus Fischel considered him "the first apostle of Panslavism." To Hans Kohn he was "One of the few forerunners of modern Pan-Slavism," and Michael Petrovich has pointed out that "Russian Panslavists of the nineteenth century hailed Križanić as a progenitor of Russian Panslavism."[14] It cannot be the purpose here to focus on the varieties of nineteenth-century pan-Slavisms, such as Croatian, Czech, or Polish in addition to Russian. Much less is it possible to examine the views and convictions of all leading pan-Slavs. The purpose in this case is severely limited. It is to look into a few aspects of Russian pan-Slavism of the second half of the nineteenth century with a view to pointing out some similarities as well as differences between Moscow Slavophilism and Russian pan-Slavism.

Among the intractable issues here in the closing pages of this study is the perennial problem of terminology and precise definition of Slavophilism and pan-Slavism, to which could be added those of pan-Russism, pan-Orthodoxy, and pan-Byzantinism—the problem, that is, of establishing clear dividing lines between them and, of determining the points at which these isms pass into their respective messianisms.

In the preceding volume, I emphasized the fact that during the first half of the nineteenth century only the Russians and Serbians, of all Slav nations, were politically self-governing while the rest of the Western and South Slavs lived under German, Austrian, or Ottoman rule. The literary, linguistic, and cultural renaissance that raised the national consciousness of these Slav nations, ruled by non-Slavs, was considerably strengthened during the second half of the nineteenth century (in part at least as counterreaction), when

Italian and German nationalism found expression in the unification of Italy and Germany.

The various nationalisms with their usual tendency to spill over into jingoism and messianism furnished the setting that accompanied the rise of pan-Slavism. By the end of the nineteenth century, Russian nationalism and messianism had to contend with pan-Germanism and the *Drang nach Osten,* and it is not clear which was more provocative, pan-Germanism or pan-Slavism. It is manifest, however, that the age of innocence that gave birth to Moscow Slavophilism was gone, and although Samarin's premonition in the mid-1860s that the Baltic area might become another Schleswig-Holstein did not come to pass until 1914, his reading of the changes in Europe was not faulty. For the rest of the nineteenth century and well into the twentieth, pan-Germanism proved to be more of a driving force in European affairs than pan-Slavism.

In a real sense, both these ideologies were synthetic and esoteric; therefore they lacked the inspiration and driving force of genuine mass movements. A pan-German empire as conceived by Heinrich Treitschke, Friedrich Naumann, or Hitler, for instance, had never existed, nor was a single all-Slav realm stretching from the Adriatic Sea to the Pacific Ocean ever entered in the historical record. Neither had been a historical reality, and both were born of the dreams and fantasies of a handful of theoreticians. Yet from the 1870s on, these two pan-movements were major factors in the political-diplomatic, and military calculations in both Berlin and St. Petersburg, and certainly no less for the Kaiser's government than for the Tsar's. The pan-Germanism of Bismarck and his immediate successors was accompanied by an outburst of German imperialism. During the two decades from 1875 to 1895, Africa was divided among the Western European imperialist powers. (It was nine-tenths independent before 1875, and only one-tenth independent after 1895.) In this scramble for African territory Germany acquired one million square miles in Togo, Cameroun, German Southwest and German East Africa. In addition the *Drang nach Osten* and the Berlin-to-Baghdad railroad became major factors in German foreign policy.[15] At about the same time Russia was extending its empire in Central Asia, a move devoid of any cultural or ethnic connection with pan-Slavism.

But in the pages that follow all political, diplomatic, and military developments as well as pan-Germanism, the foil for pan-Slavism and vice versa, must be left out, as only several pan-Slavist personalities can here be mentioned and their views summarized. In this review, it is well to remind ourselves again that since three of the four "early" Moscow Slavophils died before the emancipation reform (the Kireevsky brothers in 1856, Khomiakov and Konstantin Aksakov in 1860), it is impossible to know what their reactions might have been to the Russian pan-Slavism of the late 1860s and 1870s.

We have seen that even the early Slavophils, who socially, culturally, and educationally belonged to the same milieu and were in friendly personal relations, did not ever come to a complete agreement on all points of Slavophil ideology. Lack of agreement is even more apparent in the more heterogeneous pan-Slav group, which, despite two attempts at all-Slav congresses—in Prague in 1848 and Moscow in 1867—achieved no unity of purpose, program or action.[16] The Slav Benevolent Committees in Russia from the late 1850s through the 1860s and 1870s, although assisting Slav causes such as Bulgaria's struggle for liberation from Ottoman rule in 1877–1878, were not the sort of organization whose central purpose was an ideologically articulated unitary pan-Slav movement. When Russian pan-Slavism of the 1860s and 1870s is mentioned, we refer primarily to a number of individual exponents of pan-Slav views having no single program or organization to bind them together. There was considerable disparity, for instance, between the pan-Slavism of the scientist and social theoretist Danilevsky and that of the poet Tiutchev. Yet it is undeniable that there were points of contact between them and between a number of other theoreticians. Not the least of the binding threads between several prominent Russian pan-Slavs was a sort of Orthodox messianism.[17]

In his standard and indispensable work on the Slav benevolent societies in Russia after the Crimean War, Nikitin has given us a highly readable factual account based on both published sources and archival material.[18] Of great value to the student of Slavophilism and pan-Slavism is his long chapter (102 pages) entitled "The Slav Congresses of the Sixties." The Crimean War was the watershed that saw not only the initiative for the creation of the Moscow Slav Benevolent Committee, but also a reversal in the attitude of St. Petersburg toward the Slav question, or, more precisely, toward the South Slavs. The government of Alexander II, unlike that of Nicholas I, did not object to Russia's involvement in the struggle of the South Slavs for independence from Ottoman Rule.[19] Nikitin attributes primary roles in the post-Crimean period of agitation in favor of the Orthodox Slavs of the Balkans to Konstantin and Ivan Aksakov.

An unpublished *zapiska* on the Eastern Question drafted by Konstantin Aksakov contains the following passage: "Turkish authority in Europe is a shame for Christendom willingly endured up to the present by the powerful nations. This must disappear. What is to follow? The Slav nations must be liberated, and constitute, according to their nationalities, separate principalities. They must be under Russia's protection, as is the case with Serbia now.[20]" In the creation of the first Slav Committee, that of Moscow, the leading roles belonged to Ivan Aksakov, the "heart" of the circle that organized the Committee in the winter of 1857–1858, to the Moscow Slavophils, and to the Bulgarian Naiden Gerov.[21] The process followed was in accordance with the Slavophil way of doing things, proceeding from a *kruz-*

hok. Konstantin Aksakov, however, did not belong to the circle that backed the Moscow Slav Committee; in 1860 Ivan Aksakov said somewhat enigmatically of his brother, "Formerly in Moscow he regarded the Slav cause quite indifferently." Although there is some uncertainty about the complete list of backers of the Moscow Slav Committee, Ivan Aksakov emerges as its most ardent supporter. Khomiakov was another strong supporter, also Pogodin, A. V. Rachinsky, and Khomiakov's Bulgarian friend Savva Filaretov, who was one of a number of Bulgarians in Russia, some of whom were studying at the universities of Moscow and St. Petersburg and received financial help from the Slavophils and others. Koshelev, Samarin, and Khomiakov also subsidized Gerov's Russian-Bulgarian dictionary.

Besides the Slavophils, who were the prime movers behind the Moscow Slav Committee, the supporters also included such "liberals" as S. M. Solov'ev, M. N. Katkov, F. I. Buslaev, and such nonparticipants in the Slavophil-Westerner controversy as the "therapeutist" F. I. Inozemtsev and the "economist technologist" M. Ia. Kittary.[22] Nikitin makes it quite clear that a Russian did not have to be a Slavophil or a pan-Slav to have a fondness for the other Slavs, in this case the South Slavs. The preference in Russian intellectual publicistic circles for the South Slavs as distinct from the Western Slavs was not accidental, and it helps to expose some of the fallacy of Western anti-pan-Slav propaganda before World War II.

As Khomiakov and others in Russia knew at the end of the 1850s, and this was scarcely a new realization, there was little hope of bringing the Western Slavs into any sort of all-Slav cultural or political union. In his well-known "Message to the Serbians," Khomiakov turned, shortly before his death, to the Orthodox Serbians, who together with the Russians were the only Slavs not living under foreign political rule. In his view, the Western Slavs, specifically the most numerous of them, the Poles, were beyond redemption; they had gone with the Catholic West for much too long to be won over to the true Slav fold which, for Khomiakov, rested upon Slavophil Orthodoxy.

Khomiakov said to the Serbians, "Do not contract diseases from which God has delivered you! Do not forget the example of Poland, your kindred in blood."[23] He castigated "unfortunate Poland, for its Western-like feudal nobility, for its imitation of Western ways and manners, and for the historical road it had traveled. Similar temptations had confronted Russia since Peter I, and he admonished the Serbians to eschew them and not fall into the "errors and sins of Poland," but to remain true to the communal Orthodox ways of its people.[24] He was fully cognizant of the key role of Czech and Slovak scholarship in the linguistic, historical, and cultural aspects of the Slav "awakening" in the late eighteenth and early nineteenth centuries and he regretted the loss of the Czechs and Slovaks to the Western confessions, ways, and culture no less than that of the Poles, yet the brunt of his criticism was aimed at Poland. One does not have to read between the lines of the "Message to the Serbians" to see that much of its sermonizing, censuring, and admonishing was directed at various aspects of Russian public life, and not only at the Western Slavs.

The purposes and goals of the Moscow Slav Committee, and of those in St. Petersburg, Kiev, and Odessa, remained basically charitable and educational, but they were also combined with cultural-ideological functions. The committees were privately supported and had difficulties raising the necessary funds. This can rightly be said despite the willingness of the government of Alexander II to use them on occasion to advance its diplomatic and military goals. The committees were interested in promoting closer relations between the Slav nations but were thwarted in this goal in part at least because the Western and most of the South Slavs were not constituted as independent states. In spite of this, the Moscow Slav Committee, although not officially in charge, was instrumental in organizing the Moscow Slav Congress of 1867, and this occurred despite the hostile attitude of the Austrian government.

In all, Moscow welcomed 81 delegates, of whom 27 were Czechs, 16 Austrian Serbs (plus 12 from Serbia), 10 Croats, 3 Slovenes, and 4 Ukrainians. There were also one Bulgarian, and a few other unattached delegates. Poland, which had revolted a few years earlier, was not represented.[25] This congress, and the concurrently held Slav ethnographic exposition, were not able to coordinate the disparate interests and concerns of the several Slav nations, foremost among which, for all except the Russians and the Serbians, was freedom from foreign domination and oppression. According to Nikitin, "The Russian pan-Slavs encountered the determined and firm resistance of the Slav delegates who went to Moscow for their own purposes.[26]" National independence, or at least autonomy for those who were not free, had to precede any talk of possible all-Slav ties. For it should be remembered that after the partitions at the end of the eighteenth century Poland ceased to exist as an independent state. In 1867 the Czechs and Slovaks were under Hapsburg rule, as were also the Slovenes, the Croats, and some Serbs, while in the southeast the Bulgarians and Macedonians were enduring their fifth century of Ottoman domination. For all these, political independence had to come first.[27]

A biographer of Danilevsky (1822–1886) characterized him as a "naturalist and a philosopher, a publicist of the Slavophil tint." While this is not incorrect it also leaves unsaid a good deal about Danilevsky that is pertinent. A glance at the end of the introduction to the 1966 edition of *Rossiia i Evropa,* which lists his publications, reveals that he was the author of works on statistics and demography, climatology, ichthyology, viticulture, geography, economics, international relations, politics, the Eastern question and Constantinople, Darwinism, and Russia and Europe.[28] The uncommon versatility and productivity of this man of science must be left out of consideration here, giving only a brief view of his *Rossiia i Evropa* as the most characteristic work expressing his "pan-Slavism" and his Russian messianism.

Danilevsky was born in a gentry family in the Orlov gubernia November 28, 1822. He was educated first in private schools and then studied natural sciences at the University of St. Petersburg (1843–1847). After graduating, he became attached to the Petrashevsky circle while also investigating the flora of the Riazan and Orlov gubernias, and met Dostoevsky (one year older than himself). Although Danilevsky is said to have looked upon Petrashevsky's Fourierism as a purely economic doctrine, seeing in it nothing revolutionary or antireligious, he was arrested in 1849 along with many other members of the circle, spent one hundred days in the Saints Peter and Paul fortress and was then exiled to eastern Russia. He was soon transferred, however, to the office of the governor of the Samara gubernia.

During most of the 1850s and 1860s Danilevsky traveled extensively, from the Black and Caspian seas and from the sea of Azov to the White Sea and the Arctic Ocean, engaged in the study of Russia's fisheries. But neither this work, nor his probing into the fields of psychology and geology during the early 1860s, got in the way of what is his best-known publication, *Rossiia i Evropa.* He began this work in 1865, and four years later it made its appearance in installments in the periodical *Zaria.* Serialization was unavoidable, for as Strakhov, collaborator in the publication of this journal, said, the demand in Russia for books like Danilevsky's was not sufficient to pay the cost of publication; it was issued in book form in 1871, and it took fifteen years to sell the two thousand copies that were printed; the strongest demand for it came during the Russo-Turkish war of 1877–1878.

The fact that Danilevsky began work on *Rossiia i Evropa* in 1865 was not a matter of chance and deserves more attention than it usually gets in the Western literature on pan-Slavism. He himself left no doubt as to the events that prompted him to begin work at that time: Bismarck's wars against Denmark (1864) and Austria (1866). In the opening sentence of *Rossiia i Evropa,* Danilevsky says: "In the summer of 1866 there occurred an event of enormous historical importance. Germany, broken into pieces in the course of centuries, began to unite under the leadership of a Prussian minister of genius into one powerful whole. The European status quo has obviously been violated."[29] He also remembered that during the Crimean War, France, England, and Sardinia took the side of Turkey and invaded Russia. He summed up his views on these developments by asking, "What is the source of this indifference to humanitarian, liberal Denmark, and this sympathy for barbarian, despotic Turkey?"[30] Danilevsky stressed early in *Rossiia i Evropa* that he was reacting strongly, although not exclusively, to the military, diplomatic, and political behavior of the West, whereas the Slavophils, not unaware of these, had responded primarily and more characteristically to the Western confessions, culture, and values. Thus Danilevsky's pan-Slavism cannot be severed from the powerful wave of pan-Germanism.

The events of the mid-1850s and mid-1860s served to fortify Danilevsky's conviction that, although Russia and the Western nations had deep roots in Europe, in reality they were two different worlds. To this conviction he attempted to lend, in the era of Western positivism, materialism, and scientific socialism, a secular foundation in the form of his well-known theory of "separate *culture-historical types.*" Strakhov (1828–1896), the "philosopher and literary critic" who was instrumental in the serial publication of Danilevsky's *Rossiia i Evropa,* summed up in his biographical sketch of Danilevsky the basic idea of the work. In his words, the author "rejects the *single thread* in the development of mankind, the idea that history is the progress of some common reason, of some common civilization. There is no such civilization, Danilevsky says; there exist only individual civilizations, there is the development of separate *culture-historical types.*"

Strakhov elaborated by saying that the common view of history was *"artificial"* because it was forced into preconceived notions. Danilevsky's new view was *"natural"* based on "experience, observation, and the careful examination" of the nature of history. He saw *Rossiia i Evropa* as an attempt to "introduce in the science [*nauka*] of history" a revolution similar to that *"introduced by the natural system* in the physical sciences, where up to then an artificial system prevailed." Whether a certain historical period or civilization corresponded to preconceived notions and theories had nothing to do with its actual existence or value. Although at the time relatively little was known in the West about China, this was no reason to exclude it from the flow of history. In Danilevsky's system "China," Strakhov declared, "is as much a lawful and instructive phenomenon as the Greco-Roman world, or proud Europe.[31]" Clearly, Danilevsky, the natural scientist, had a different mentality and different bias from that of the early Slavophils, none of whom had been trained in the natural or physical sciences. It is hardly surprising, therefore, that although Danilevsky was a believing Orthodox Russian, his views in general lack the heavy Eastern Orthodox slant that is at the heart of Slavophil thought and ideology.[32] Ivask explained this difference thus: "Danilevsky was an Orthodox believer but just the same, in his philosophical system, God does not act, does not manifest Himself in history."[33]

In chapter 5 of *Rossiia i Evropa* Danilevsky pointed at the core of his concept of "cultural-historical types." Russia and the other Slav nations were grouped together into a single "cultural-historical type." This in turn accounted for the dichotomy between "Russia and Europe." Danilevsky is clearly using these terms in the cultural and ethnic sense, for he includes the United States in "Europe," and "Russia," of course, stands for all Slavdom.

Danilevsky then enumerated five "laws," which he said determined the various "cultural-historical types." The first referred to language. One language or a group of kindred languages helped hold together a certain cultural-historical type. The second law referred to the necessity of political freedom for the individual cultural-historical type; the third stated that each type is self-generated although not totally removed from the influences of other cultures. The fourth "law," reflecting Danilevsky's advocacy of a Slav federation under Russia's leadership, provided for the "various ethnographic elements" which enjoy independence "to form a federation." The fifth law, derived from Danilevsky's botanical training, referred to "long-living monocarpous plants" which take a long time to reach flowering and fruit bearing but spend their "vital forces" in a relatively short period.[34]

Chapter 5 of *Rossiia i Evropa* begins with a quotation from one of Khomiakov's poems, and chapter 7, 8, 9, and 11 also have as starting points texts from Khomiakov's writings. Clearly Danilevsky thought highly of Khomiakov. He shared Khomiakov's faith in Russia and the other Slavs, particularly those for whom Orthodoxy constituted a long historical and religious tradition. This Slav world was capable not only of its own indigenous culture but also of communicating to the West its Orthodox ethic, which the Slavophils considered superior to the Catholic and Protestant ethics of the West. Like the Slavophils of the 1840s – and certain philosophers before that in the West – Danilevsky believed that the West was "dying" or "decaying," and he used this notion as a convenient starting point for one of the chapters in *Rossiia i Evropa.*

"Is the West Decaying?" (*Gniet-li Zapad?*) is the title of the brief but pithy chapter 7. The chapter begins with a stanza from a poem by Khomiakov in which he sees the "shroud of death" over the West, and the "Awakening of the slumbering East." Danilevsky was aware that the Slavophil view on this matter had changed, and early in this chapter, he asked, "Really, is it possible to assert without joking as Khomiakov and Kireevsky once did, that the West is decaying? The Slavophils themselves, it appears, renounced this extravagance.[35]" He found comfort and encouragement in this Slavophil renunciation by drawing a parallel between Greece and Rome on the one hand, and the West and the Russian-Slav world on the other. "Rome began its triumphant march when Greece became illuminated by the complete splendor of [its] civilization." Could the Slav Orthodox world be denied a similar resurgence to that of Rome while Western civilization, faulty in much as the Slavophils saw it, was still flourishing?

While there were significant differences as well as points of contact between Danilevsky and the earlier Slavophils, there is no denying the fact that he found them more congenial than the Russian Westerners.[36] The heading of the chapter he devoted to them in *Rossiia i Evropa* tells much about his views and sentiments on this matter. Chapter 11 is entitled

"*Evropeinichan'e — bolezn' russkoi zhizni.*[37]" The untranslatable "*evropeinichan'e*" is meant to stand for imitating or aping the West, and that in Danilevsky's view was the "sickness of Russian life." As in the case of the Slavophils, only perhaps more clearly, Danilevsky saw two sides to the reign and reforms of Peter the Great. He welcomed as essential Peter's reforms in the "state" sphere, the dissemination of "military, naval, administrative, and industrial matters." These changes were necessary for Russia's survival, and were desirable even when they were purchased at a high price for the Russian people. But, he queried, what was the sense of forcing people to "shave their beards, wear German dress . . . require the smoking of tobacco, organize drinking bouts [*popoiki*] . . . distort the language, introduce . . . foreign etiquette, change the chronology, [and] limit the freedom of the clergy?"[38]

There is much in *Rossiia i Evropa* that ranges from ancient times to the late nineteenth century, and from China and the Far East to Europe and America. But the sections of the book most relevant to Danilevsky's own time and to the subject of these several studies are devoted to the "Eastern Question," to "Austria and the Eastern Question," to an "All-Slav Union," and to *Tsar'grad* or Constantinople — the standard Russian medieval designation. Danilevsky's dreams and hopes were for a Slav federation headed by Russia and for an All-Slav Union under Russian leadership centered on Constantinople. He affirmed that "Tsar'grad must be the capital not of Russia — but of an All-Slav Union.[39]" In turn this All-Slav Union was essential not only for the Slavs but "for humanity." It would have a total population of 120 million people including the "hostile Polish and Magyar elements," which he estimated at 12–13 million.[40]

The historical and cultural-religious significance of Constantinople as the seat of the Orthodox patriarchate, its geographical position between Europe and Asia, and its growing naval strategic importance in the middle of the Straits (between the Bosphorus and the Dardanelles), all were highlighted in the 1860s and 1870s. The Crimean War had demonstrated what the free passage of hostile forces through the Straits could mean for Russia. In these circumstances, and aware of the imperialistic aspirations of Germany, Austria, England, and France, Russian publicists from Ivan Aksakov and Danilevsky to Dostoevsky, Konstantin Leont'ev, and Vladimir Solov'ev, to mention the most prominent, reacted to the "question of the Straits" and Constantinople. Pan-Slavism entered a crucial phase in the mid-1870s when in Bosnia and Herzegovina, in Montenegro and Bulgaria, unrest against the Turks induced Russia to enter the South Slav struggle for freedom from Ottoman rule, which in 1878 resulted in Bulgaria's liberation. In all these developments Constantinople and the Straits were of primary concern for all the great European powers, including Russia.[41]

For Danilevsky, Prussia's wars with Denmark in 1864 and with Austria in 1866 were sufficient to trigger his fear of the German "Der Drang nach Osten."[42] But Dostoevsky reacted to the "Eastern Question" a decade later under the stimulus of events in the Balkans. In a lengthy, well-documented, and highly readable two-part essay, Kozlovsky dealt, seventy years ago, with the views and convictions of Dostoevsky and Leont'ev on the Slav question and Constantinople.[43] Kozlovsky's opening sentence is Dostoevsky's refrain: "Constantinople must be ours! . . . . Sooner or later, Tsar'grad will be ours."[44] And it is indeed a refrain heard in the *Diary of a Writer*. In June 1876 Dostoevsky wrote, "Yes, the Golden Horn and Constantinople, all this will be ours, and not through seizure, and not through force." He regretted the decision of Peter the Great to move toward the cold, swampy, and barren north to establish a new capital instead of marching toward the warm south and the ancient and venerable pearl on the Bosphorus. How would Russia justify such a move now? His answer was brief and direct. Russia would claim Constantinople, the first legal seat of the Christian Church, "as leader of Orthodoxy, as its protector and guardian, a role foreordained by Ivan III," who took over from Byzantium the double-headed eagle as Muscovy's coat of arms after Constantinople succumbed to the Ottoman Turks.[45]

Ten months later, in March 1877, sensing the rising international tension over the fate of the Orthodox Slavs of the Balkans (Russia did not declare war on Turkey until April 24, 1877), Dostoevsky again turned his attention to the Balkans and Constantinople with his "utopian understanding of history," as he said. He repeated his ideas as to how Peter the Great could have made Constantinople the capital, and briefly he considered the possibility of seeing Constantinople go to the Greeks, but his conclusion was still the same: Constantinople should become the free center of Eastern Orthodoxy under Russia's guardianship.[46] Kozlovsky was correct in stressing that the question of the Straits did not concern Dostoevsky, which could not be said of other intellectuals in Russia. He, the master of portraying ambivalence in his characters, was not himself immune to it. Whereas in November 1877 he could confess that in his "inner conviction" he knew that "there never were such haters, enviers, slanderers, and even open enemies as these Slav tribes," the following year in *The Brothers Karamazov* he pictured Ivan Karamazov's "celebrated revolt" against the injustices in the world partly under the direct impressions of the Turkish atrocities in Bulgaria.[47]

Yet Dostoevsky, like Nicholas I during the Crimean War, saw Russia not as a defender of Slavdom but as a defender of Orthodoxy.[48] (Leont'ev, as we shall soon see, was even further removed than Dostoevsky from pure Pan-slavism. Kozlovsky stresses that Dostoevsky, in contrast to the Slavophils "does not believe in a Slav federation, and on principle does not admit equality between the Russians and the other Slav nationalities." He is "astonished how Danilevsky could speak of equal rights to Constantinople for Russia and the other Slav nations." Thus Khomiakov's "proclamation of the principle of equality of the Slav nations" was "completely alien to Dostoevsky."[49] For Dostoevsky (as for Pogodin earlier, who spoke of the liberation of the Slavs), the "main goal" of the war of 1877–1878 "was religious: restoration to the Eastern Church of its universal meaning." Kozlovsky concludes that "in the purely-Slavophil agitation" of the mid-1870s, "liberation of the Slavs was the principal task," although he does not deny the Orthodox bond that was always basic to Moscow Slavophilism.[50] Confronted with the unsolved problem of terminology, so intimately tied to precision of definition, Kozlovsky concluded that Dostoevsky is often labeled a Slavophil (by Berdiaev, for instance). Dostoevsky himself sometimes considered himself a Slavophil, but Kozlovsky with good reason concludes that Dostoevsky, like Pogodin, Gogol', and Tiutchev, was not a Slavophil, nor was Leont'ev a Slavophil; Dostoevsky, Tiutchev, and Pogodin harked back to the Crimean War and to Official Nationality, rather than to Slavophilism. Dostoevsky's Orthodox Russian messianism thus transcended Moscow Slavophilism and pan-Slavism and became pan-Orthodoxy.

Konstantin Leont'ev (1831–1891), characterized by Evgenii Trubetskoi, not very aptly, as a "disillusioned Slavophil," was of the Kaluga gentry.[51] He studied medicine at Moscow University on his mother's suggestion, served in the Crimean War as a medical doctor before he could complete his medical training, and then practiced medicine for about ten years. In 1861 he married a Crimean girl of Greek descent, and soon left the medical profession to enter the Asian section of the Ministry of Foreign Affairs and served in Turkey (1863–1873) in several consular capacities. Various assignments took him to Crete, Adrianople, Tulcha, Ianina, and Salonica. While in Salonica he visited the nearby Mount Athos Orthodox monastic community and later he spent about a year there. Before returning to Russia he also had a year in Constantinople, a city he knew and greatly valued, for among other things it was the center and the symbol of that Byzantinism without which his life and thought would have been but a hollow shell.[52] At that time he wrote what his editor, Archpriest Fudel', and others considered to be his "basic work, *Vizantinizm i Slavianstvo*" (Byzantinism and Slavdom).[53] In 1880 Leont'ev became an assistant editor of a journal and then a censor in Moscow. He resigned in 1887, went to the well-known Optina monastery where he was secretly tonsured, and became the monk Clement.

In this highly condensed account of Leont'ev's career one can gain much from the meaningful and revealing titles of some of his shorter works.[54] Among them are: "Pan-Slavism and the Greeks" (1873), "Pan-Slavism on Mount Athos" (1873), "Byzantium and Slavdom" (1875), "Russians, Greeks, and Yugoslavs" (1878), "My Reminiscences of Thrace" (1879).[55] What emerges from these and other Leont'ev works and correspondence is neither nineteenth-century Russian Slavophilism, nor pan-Slavism, but a strong, un-compromising Byzantinism and perhaps a somewhat milder Turkism. But the Slavophilism with which Leont'ev has occasionally been associated is simply not there.[56] He was, of course, of a later generation and came on the scene after early Slavophilism had been formulated and therefore func-tioned in a different historical environment; yet he was aware of the Slavophils, and he concurred in some of their views if he did not actually bor-row from them. It has been well said that "From the Slavophils Leont'ev took over the idea of the cultural uniqueness of Russia."[57] But it is even more accurate to concur, as Kline has done, in Rozanov's judgment, that Leont'ev was his own man who "had neither predecessors nor followers."[58]

If Leont'ev could not see much in the past of the Slavs this was to a con-siderable measure a consequence of his deep and overwhelming infatuation with Greek civilization, both classical and Byzantine, and to a lesser degree with Turkish culture. This is apparent from the opening lines of his *Vizan-tizm i slavianstvo*, written in 1875, when the Balkan crisis was rapidly escalat-ing toward the Russo-Turkish war. In his words, "Byzantinism is above all else a special type of education or culture, having its distinguishing marks, its general, clear, sharp, comprehensible, principles, and its definite conse-quences in history." This while "Slavianism taken as a whole is still a sphinx, a riddle," he said. Byzantinism in its "religious, political, moral, philosophi-cal, and artistic" aspects represented a complete and well-defined entity, and he concluded, "We see nothing like this in pan-Slavdom [*vses-lavianstvo*]."[59]

In contrast to the current fashionable, unedifying denigration of Byzan-tine civilization in the Western media, Leont'ev dispassionately acknow-ledged that the West was well on the way to cultural and artistic greatness in the fifteenth century when Constantinople fell to the Turks. But with equal justice he said that the West's "new rapprochement with Byzantium, and through it . . . with the ancient world brought Europe immediately into that brilliant epoch which it is customary to call the Renaissance." Byzan-tinism also came to Russia in the fifteenth century, when the Tatars were conquered, but its influence was limited because it did not find there the same rich cultural-artistic soil as in the West. Yet Byzantinism in Russia (reduced by Leont'ev to the Orthodox "church and tsar" — *tserkov' i tsar*) also "gave us all our strength in the struggle with Poland, with the Swedes, with France and Turkey."[60] As he had said earlier, "The ecclesiastical feeling and submission to authority (the Byzantine stance) saved us in the year 1812."[61]

Considerably more could be said about Leont'ev's Byzantinism. He thought of it as favorable not only to Russia in the past but also, to the West. In chapter 3 of his *Vizantizm i slavianstvo* he raised the question "What is Slavianism?" His answer was that it was simply a "tribal ethnographic abstraction . . . an idea of common blood (although not entirely pure) and similar languages." Absent from the concept of Slavianism were such "distinguishing religious, juridical, everyday life [*bytovye*], artistic signs as comprise in their totality the complete and living historical picture of a certain culture." "Where is the similar clear general idea of Slavianism?" he asked.[62] Not in the old Bulgarian, nor in the Serbian states; there was no equivalent to the notion in the terms "China-ism" or even "Europeanism."

In support of his conviction that there was little of cultural or artistic value in the history of Slavdom, he focused on the past and present of the various Slav nationalities, beginning with the Czechs. He gave some attention to the Slovaks, Poles, Serbians, Croatians, Montenegrins, and Dalmatians, but his severest judgments were reserved for the Bulgarians. Ever present in his pronouncements are his Great Russianism and his gentry consciousness. He displayed considerable knowledge of the past and present of the Slav nations, and a profound veneration for an immovable, retrospective Byzantinism based on quasi-religious Christian and quasi-pagan aesthetic views and convictions.[63] In all this his uncommon memory and intelligence range over more than two millennia, and from the Far East through the Near East to the West. With a mind that saw things in absolute categories, in black and white with no shades in between, Leont'ev has impressed his biographers with his uncompromising, implacable judgments. He also registered some brilliant and penetrating observations on the thought and conduct of men.

There is much truth in Kozlovsky's summary that "Leont'ev . . . frankly hated the Bulgarians, he passionately wished to give away the Czechs to the Germans, 'to be devoured [*na s'edenie*]'; to Russify the Poles; as for the rest of the Slavs, his attitude was one of mistrust and disregard.[64]" The man for whom the salvation of the world was to be found in "regenerated Byzantinism," and in the 'immortality of beauty' could only deplore anything and anybody that stood in the way. And nothing was quite as much an obstacle as Leont'ev's hated Western liberalism, bourgeois culture, and all those among the Slavs, who had turned a receptive ear to the enticements of the liberal-bourgeois way of life. All this contributed to Leont'ev's hated "leveling equality" and to the "erosion of beauty."[65] In the age of national unification in the West, and of national liberation movements in the Balkans where they were aimed at the termination of five centuries of Ottoman oppression and exploitation, Leont'ev remained remarkably blind and deaf to the flow and demands of contemporary life.[66]

After unconvincing efforts to show sympathy and understanding for the Czech Slavic scholarship; the Czechs still had their originality (*samobytnost'*), he admitted, but he added that, surrounded by the more numerous Germans for centuries, "even in the moral personal traits the Czech very much reminds one of the German."[67] The Czechs had entered "earlier than other Slavs, and for longer, into the general stream of Roman-

German civilization," and as a result had not preserved much of the truly Slav in them. Therefore, he concluded, "Chekhia is a tool of German workmanship now turned by the Slavs against Germanism."

Of the Bulgarians Leont'ev says, "The Bulgarians were brought up by the Greeks in the same sense in which the Czechs were brought up by the Germans."[68] His many and keen observations of Bulgarian and Greek lore while in the Russian consular service, particularly with respect to peasant life and mores, served him well when he decided to put his impressions and judgments in writing. In a single sentence he profiled the Bulgarian, the German, the Greek, and the Great Russian: "And so the Bulgarian is psychologically similar to the most solid, patient, calculating German, and is hardly like the cheerful, lively, more magnanimous Great Russian brought up by the Greeks in the Greek manner."[69] The Bulgarians were, he declared, the "most backward" of the Slav nations and the "most dangerous for us."[70] This was so because only in Bulgaria's recent history, "not in Czech, not in Polish, and not in Serbian [history] has there been a struggle between those two forces with which we Russians live and move — tribal Slavianism and Byzantinism. Thanks to the Bulgarians, we stand upon a sort of Rubicon."[71] There is a good deal more of this same sort of criticism.

What disturbed Leont'ev profoundly about Bulgaria, beyond his overwhelming aversion to all things Bulgarian, were the Bulgarian struggle for church independence from Greece, and the drive for political independence from five centuries of Ottoman rule. On March 11, 1870, after a long struggle with the Greek-dominated Patriarchate of Constantinople, the Bulgarians established their autocephalous Orthodox church under a Bulgarian Exarch. This was a major step on the way to Bulgarian political independence, and when that came eight years later, conflicting territorial claims and other differences between Bulgaria and Greece caused further strains in their relations. Leont'ev, who served in the Russian embassy in Constantinople in the early 1870s, was well informed about these matters and left no doubt that his sympathies were on the side of the Greeks and Turks.

Leont'ev's intense dislike of the Bulgarians in general and specifically — for their adherence to their millennial Orthodox church and its liturgy in the Church Slavonic and Bulgarian languages — took scant notice of Bulgaria's role in accepting Christianity from Constantinople in the ninth century, before Western Europe had come out of its Dark Ages, nor of the fact that in the tenth century the Cyrillic alphabet reached Kiev from Bulgaria. Apparently Leont'ev cared little for Bulgaria's contribution to the rich Church Slavonic, which is a major component of the modern Russian language. Given his contempt for the bourgeois order of his day, and for nineteenth-century democratic constitutional tendencies, Bulgaria's egalitarian but changing society seemed to him to offer nothing as compared with the long stratified societies of England and Great Russia. Bulgaria's medieval aristocracy had long since disappeared under the Ottoman sword, and its people had become the lowly *rayah,* herd. In the second half of the nineteenth century, a minority of professional men and merchants, Leont'ev's despised Bulgarian bourgeoisie, was slowly emerging from a sea of illiterate peasantry. One wonders how much more aesthetically satisfying Bulgaria would have been for Leont'ev had it remained after the 1870s under Ottoman political rule and Greek church domination!

The contrast here between Leont'ev and Khomiakov is striking. As a young man and a volunteer in the Russian army, Khomiakov had fought with distinction in 1829 against the Turks at Shumen, the old Bulgarian capital; in 1857–1858 he was one of the founders of the Moscow Slav Benevolent Society. Of the four early Slavophils, he was probably the most pro-Slav and pro-Bulgarian.[72]

In considering the religious and ideological relationship between the Moscow Slavophils and Leont'ev (separated in time by about four decades) one could benefit from Trubetskoi's summary-review essay referred to above. From this and from the works of Leont'ev and the Slavophils the conclusion is inescapable that there was no common ground between the Slavophil doctrines of *sobornost',* wholeness of the spirit, communality (*obshchinnost'*), and their dedicated work (Samarin's in particular) in the cause of the emancipation of the serfs, and Leont'ev's brand of Byzantinism and Turkism.[73] Leont'ev, looking at Dostoevsky's 'rosy' Orthodoxy, with its "dreamy all-human Christianity" (not unlike Khomiakov's notion of *sobornost'*), denounced the thought of a 'universal all-human brotherhood' and declared himself "against an all-Slav union."[74] He would not even consider Constantinople as the possible capital of such a union, a view congenial to some pan-Slavs. Instead he wished to see the old Byzantine capital 'belong *personally* to the Lord Emperor . . . remaining in so-called *union personnelle* with the Russian crown.'[75]

Leont'ev's narrow and idiosyncratic Byzantinism stands in stark contrast not only to Khomiakov's ultimate Christian universalism and cultural concepts, contemptuously dismissed by Leont'ev as the "'pompous feathers' [*pyshnyia per'ia*] of Khomiakov's original [Russian] *culture,*" but also to the views of such of Leont'ev contemporaries as Tolstoy, Dostoevsky and V. S. Solov'ev.[76] Trubetskoi states that for Leont'ev Tolstoy's Christianity was reduced to "simple morality," and to the "moral obligation of love," and as stressed above he had no respect for Tolstoy's and Dostoevsky's 'rose-colored' Christianity.[77] Nor was he more favorably disposed toward V. S. Solov'ev who dreamt "of universal catholicism of the future uniting the Christian church, [and] of a future Russian-Roman theocracy." (Here some influence of Johann Adam Mohler, 1796–1838, should be given more than a passing reference).[78] Trubetskoi was probably close to the truth when he accounted for Leont'ev's isolated religious and intellectual position by concluding that his Christianity was based on fear, not on Christian love.[79]

Both the Moscow Slavophils, and later Leont'ev, accepted the early nineteenth century Western notion that the West was declining or decaying, but they interpreted it somewhat differently. Although all of them reacted negatively to Western bourgeois culture, Leont'ev was more extreme than the Slavophils. For instance, science and technology, which were integral parts of the mid-nineteenth century Western bourgeois order, were received by the Slavophils, as we have seen, with genuine appreciation. On the other hand, it was not difficult for Leont'ev to perceive, as has been stressed by Trubetskoi and brought out in this and the preceding studies, that Moscow Slavophilism produced its share of inconsistencies and contradictions. But whether the Slavophils were more or less guilty of this weakness than others who have covered so wide a range of thought and activity is a moot question.

Although the Moscow Slavophils focussed their attention on Russia's position vis-a-vis the West, and on its internal order, long overdue for improvements, they also gave some attention to the other Slavs. This is illustrated by Khomiakov's *Message to the Serbians* (1860) and by Ivan Aksakov's crucial role in the liberation of Bulgaria in the 1870s from five centuries of Ottoman rule. During the unfolding of the "Eastern Question" Leont'ev remained adamant in his anti-Slav and anti-national and anti-Bulgarian stance. And it must not be forgotten that, among other things, the war of 1877–1878 was an expression of Bulgarian nationalism just as the desire for the independence of Serbia and Greece, earlier in the century, were manifestations of Serb and Greek nationalism. But Leont'ev saw the expression of nationalism anywhere as "a tool of universal revolution."[80]

Nineteenth century European nationalism, with its virtues and faults, was a powerful driving force not only in the Balkans but also in the unification of Italy and Germany and it thoroughly outraged Leont'ev. He was clear and forceful in its denunciation. As an idea it was 'cosmopolitan, anti-state, anti-religious, containing many destructive forces and nothing constructive.' In another connection he referred to 'animal cosmopolitanism,' expressing his contempt not only for nationalism and cosmopolitanism, but also for "democratism." He called on 'all non-radicals' to serve the 'objective ideas of state and church.'[81] But these key institutions in the idealized views of the Slavophils were quite different from Leont'ev's frozen medieval concepts. No less adamant was Leont'ev in his opposition to constitutionalism, a subject on which there was a certain rapprochement with the early Slavophils. For him constitutionalism in Russia could only lead to the "absolute supremacy of *capitalists, bankers,* and *lawyers,*" and this he found to be completely unacceptable.[82]

As so often happens in human affairs, it was easy for Leont'ev to overlook his own contradictions while gloating over those of the Slavophils, nor was

Trubetskoi more charitable toward the Slavophils on this count. In fact nationalism and Christian universalism were no more reconciled by the Slavophils in Russia than they were in the West. Slavophil humanism, a component of the Slavophils' drive for the emancipation of the serfs was not consistent with the strong elements of Slavophil conservatism. And their loyalty to Nicholas I, at times violated by them, went contrary to some of Khomiakov's and Konstantin Aksakov's views of a nobler autocracy than that which existed in Russia. On this as on other issues the Slavophils and Leont'ev were far apart. Finally a word about the Slavophil *slavianoliubie,* "love of the Slavs," and the dead end into which it led the Moscow Slavophils. The Western Slavs, Poles, Czechs and Slovaks as well as the South Slav Croats and Slovenes, all heavily Roman Catholic, were outside the Orthodox Russian and Orthodox South Slav pale. Thus the possibility of an all-Slav cultural and political union remained a chimera pursued by relatively few thinkers.

To anyone familiar with nineteenth-century Moscow Slavophilism and the Russian pan-Slavism of the late 1860s and 1870s, omission of the role played by Ivan Aksakov (1823–1886) must appear glaring, and perhaps inexcusable. There are three principal reasons for this omission: (1) his not insignificant but ancillary role in the birth of Slavophil thought and ideology of the 1840s and 1850s, (2) the length of the study that would have been required to deal adequately with the considerable legacy of his works, correspondence and activities, and (3) the fact that any treatment of his work would have pushed this project considerably beyond the end of pre-Reform or "classical" Moscow Slavophilism.[83] This last consideration is equally valid in Samarin's case in spite of the fact that he was one of the four founders of Moscow Slavophilism in the pre-Reform period. Ivan Aksakov's prominent role in the events that led to the Russo-Turkish war of 1877–1878 and the liberation of Bulgaria could not be more different from Leont'ev's Bulgarophobia. Aksakov concentrated on the Balkan Orthodox Slavs in the 1870s, for he knew, as had Khomiakov and the other signatories of the "Message to the Serbians" of 1860, that from their point of view the Western Slavs were beyond redemption. As events developed, it also became clear that even among the Balkan Slavs, feelings of nationalism were stronger than feelings of pan-Slavism.

Drawing a contrast between the passionate Ivan Aksakov and the "sober politician" Samarin, Nol'de concluded that Samarin "was always quite cool toward the program of the Slavophils in foreign relations although he never renounced it." He was aware that the "Slavs were drawn in various directions, that they had no sincere feelings for Russia, that they are all eyes for the Western countries and are always ready to submit to their 'civilization.'"[84] Samarin's knowledge of the South Slavs was limited and indirect, whereas his contacts with the Western Slavs, particularly the Poles and the Czechs, were direct, personal, and for him disappointing. He was keenly aware that the national consciousness of the Poles and Czechs was much stronger than any pan-Slav desires. In addition, as Kurilov recently observed, the "Slavophils who lived beyond the reform of 1861 — Ivan Aksakov, Samarin, Koshelev, and others — had ceased to represent any sort of ideological or organizational whole.[85]" Although Samarin concentrated on the Polish problem and the Baltic states, in the post-Reform period, he also went back to the Moscow Slavophil period of the 1840s and 1850s once more and published in 1867 his memorable tribute to Khomiakov in his introduction to Khomiakov's theological works.

Casting a glance at early Moscow Slavophilism from the vantage point of the late twentieth century, one is conscious of a certain relevance. The Slavophils formulated a number of goals and ideals (not unlike those in the American Declaration of Independence, that all men are created equal) toward which the Russians, and, by implication, all nations, could aspire. Among these were Khomiakov's doctrine of *sobornost'*, unity in love, freedom and peace, Ivan Kireevsky's wholeness of the spirit, and Konstantin Aksakov's choreic communal principles. They also demonstrated that Slavophilism could descend from the level of ideology to that of a practical reform and change, and in the person of Samarin and others, they played a major role in the Russian reform movement of the 1860s, most notably in the emancipation of the serfs.[86]

In his striking eleven-page essay "The Social Problem in the Eastern Orthodox Church," Florovsky says, "It was the Slavophile school that brought the social aspect of Christianity to the fore in the nineteenth century." He singles out Khomiakov's pamphlet *The Church Is One* (1840s) as containing the essence of Slavophil "Social Christianity." Later, Dostoevsky, among others, thought of the Orthodox Church as "our Russian socialism," implying the social-economic content of the Slavophil concept. The key words in it, according to Florovsky, were "freedom and brotherhood," which also contained "Solov'ev's leading vision." But later Solov'ev "moved in another direction and was seduced by a Romanizing conception of 'Christian politics'"[87] to become what some commentators have termed, perhaps with a certain exaggeration, the "Russian Newman."

While the Slavophils were formulating their basic principles and policies, the West, particularly Germany, in the middle decades of the nineteenth century stepped forward with the vigorous resurrection of two ancient Greek ideas, which although perhaps never completely lost in Europe had receded into the background for centuries. These were the notions of the "dialectic," going back to Elea on the west coast of Asia Minor and to Zeno, in the fifth century B.C., and materialism, the origin of which in the Western tradition has been traced to Thracian Abdera of the fifth century B.C., and to Leucippus and Democritus. The dialectic which to the classical Greeks stood for the art of conversation became in its modern Western version synonymous with confrontation and struggle.

Together with the new rendition of the dialectic in the West, and with a revived militant materialism, scientism, positivism, and scientific socialism, went a powerful drive toward atheism. But the goal of atheism was elusive. Instead of godlessness, those striving for atheism in the nineteenth and twentieth centuries arrived usually if not always at anthropolatry. They might have "killed" the Christian God in some cases but they did not uproot man's primordial need to believe and to belong. These two needs historically predate by much, at least as far as our early murky record goes, man's need to think and reason. In this century, the most scientific of all centuries, Western man still feels so strongly the need to believe and belong that those who have discarded traditional Christianity and other historical religions find refuge not so much in atheism (it is difficult to conceive of a normal human being living in a total vacuum of belief) as in the submission to secular prophets, gods, gurus, cult leaders, and others as in the case of the not so distant Guiana tragedy. For when a secular leader is endowed with omnipotence, infallibility, all-wisdom, and even eternity as has so fatefully occurred in the twentieth century, he is no longer an ordinary human being but assumes the attributes of divinity. That is why much of what has recently passed for atheism is more candidly and accurately described as anthropolatry or anthropotheism. The Slavophils, for all their criticism of the West, particularly of its philosophy, religion, and mores, did not preach a holy crusade against it, and they saw in the West much that was worthwhile. In this age of the possibly uncontrolled atom, humanity can either adopt the peaceful—view of problems, which was also the Slavophil way, and even more accept ages-old tolerance, forgiveness, and respect for others, or stay in the grip of the nineteenth-century Western revision of the dialectic and end it all.

Notes

1. A. G. Dement'ev, ed., *Periodicheskaia pechat'*, pp. 297–298. Soon after the publication of Ostrovsky's play *Bankrot*, in 1850, the young author D. V. Grigorovich (1822–1899), a classmate of Dostoevsky's, called on Ostrovsky one day about eleven o'clock in the morning. In Ostrovsky's sitting room he also met Edel'son, Almazov, Apollon Grigor'ev, and I. F. Gorbunov. Ostrovsky's *kruzhok*, meeting on the second floor of a modest wooden house, made a none too favorable impression on the morning guest, who was struck by the "high opinion" the members of the circle had of themselves. "They considered themselves the center of some sort of new movement, the proclaimers of a new word. They all unconditionally bowed before Ostrovsky, who, regrettably, readily accepted the praises of the circle."

Grigorovich also took note of the "sharpness of their judgments and condemnations." And he concluded, "In this respect Apoll. Aleks. Grigor'ev was particularly distinguished." D. V. Grigorovich, "Literaturnyia vospominaniia," *Russkaia mysl'*, 1893, Book II, pp. 56–57.

2. B. F. Egorov, ed., *Apollon Grigor'ev. Vospominaniia* (Leningrad, 1980), p. 375.

3. A succinct factual picture of Grigor'ev's somewhat flighty relationship with journal owners and publishers can be gleaned from an appendix in Egorov, *Grigor'ev*, pp. 374–376.

4. A map of mid-nineteenth-century Moscow accompanies an excellent essay by Robert Whittaker, "'My Literary and Moral Wanderings': Apollon Grigor'ev and the Changing Cultural Topography of Moscow," *Slavic Review*, 1983, no. 3, pp. 390–407.

5. Ibid., p. 392.

6. A. P. Marchik, "Grigor'ev, Apollon Aleksandrovich" *Russkie pisateli* (Moscow, 1971), p. 280. At the turn of the century Lobov made a brief but thoughtful analysis of Grigor'ev's character, ideological orientation, and relationship with the Slavophils. He sees Grigor'ev as inclined toward a lonely position when compared with Almasov, Edel'son, or the Slavophils. Grigor'ev was torn between two "contradictory principles, the spontaneous, so to say artistic attitude toward life, which was accompanied by or was replaced by the analytical." The first of these Grigor'ev carried with him from childhood; the second was acquired from his acquaintance "with Western European education." Grigor'ev is said to have been particularly sensitive to the spirit of Russian "democratism" and to Moscow Slavophilism when he was subjected to the opposite types of impressions, as was the case with his witnessing "the carnival in Florence." He had high regard for Khomiakov, Kireevsky, K. Aksakov, Pogodin, and Shevyrev; he wrote to Strakhov that politically he "was and remains a Slavophil," and said "I have lost faith in constitutions and the West. Yet he could not condone Konstantin Aksakov's apotheosis of the *narod* as the only hero in Russian history allowing, he thought, no room for the individual. He conceived Russian *narodnost'* as a more balanced phenomenon than being merely an expression of the *narod* or of the purely Russian, and saw this balance in Pushkin's work. Lobov was convinced that Grigor'ev's organic principle had much in common with Khomiakov's and that both were indebted to Schelling. Grigor'ev is said to have summed up his views on Peter the Great by saying that he believed "not in the national substance of pre-Petrine [Russia], and not in the substance of post-Petrine [Russia] but in the organic whole." See L. Lobov, *Pamiati Apollona Grigor'eva* (St. Petersburg, 1905), pp. 3, 6, 11–12. (This is the same as the 1978 Letchworth, Herts, edition.)

7. Grigor'ev's use of the plural "we" in this letter does not seem to be a matter of form but stands for the collective of Native Soil adherents. Much

information on the formation of the Ostrovsky circle is provided by Lakshin in his biography of Ostrovsky. The Ostrovsky *kruzhok,* which had its beginning in the 1840s while Evgenii Edel'son and Tertii Filippov were university students, attracted over a relatively few years a wide range of young men, but in Lakshin's words, it had no definite, "stated roster" (*"opredelennyi spisochnyi sostav"*). In the absence of the gentry salons, those who were drawn to the Ostrovsky *kruzhok* met in various homes and even more often in "coffee-houses, taverns, and wine-shops." In his youthful years Ostrovsky found himself in "Close friendly communication with people of various levels of life, callings, and conditions, which broadened the narrow confines of 'trade' talks." According to a "literary legend," after hearing a moving song at a *kruzhok* gathering, a young man "fell on his knees and begged the *kruzhok* to consider him its own." This is said to have been Apollon Grigor'ev, also characterized as *"neistovyi* [furious] Apollon." Lakshin also says that Grigor'ev was an "enraptured, distracted, unbridled man, beautiful in his purity and passion." V. Ia. Lakshin, *Aleksandr Nikolaevich Ostrovsky,* 2d ed., (Moscow, 1982) pp. 144–145, 150, 152, 154–155.

8. Vladimir Kniazhnin, ed., *Apollon Aleksandrovich Grigor'ev: Materialy dlia biografii* (Petrograd, 1917), pp. 150–151.

9. Ibid., p. 168. There is considerable elaboration and explanation of these and other points in R. T. Whittaker's doctoral dissertation, particularly pp. 172–179.

10. Egorov aptly explained that the complete title of Khomiakov's work is *"Encore quelques mots d'un chretien orthodoxe sur les confessions occidentales, a l'occasion de plusieures publications religieuses, latines et protestantes"* (Leipzig, 1858); Egorov, *Grigor'ev,* p. 301. In the fifth edition of Khomiakov's works this essay appears under the title *Neskol'ko slov pravoslavnago khristianina o zapadnykh veroispovedaniiakh . . . ,* II, 163–248.

11. Egorov, *Grigor'ev,* p. 414.

12. Ibid., p. 301.

13. Dowler, *Dostoevsky, Grigor'ev, and Native Soil Conservatism,* pp. 103–104.

14. Cf. Alfred Fischel, *Der Panslawismus bis zum Weltkrieg. Ein geschichtlicher Uberblick* (Stuttgart and Berlin, 1919), p. 20; Hans Kohn, *Pan-Slavism: Its History and Ideology* (1953), p. 4; Michael B. Petrovich, *The Emergence of Russian Panslavism, 1856–1870* (1956), p. 6; A. N. Pypin, "Literaturnyi panslavism," *Vestnik Evropy,* 1879, III, 600, 602, 605. Volume III of the present series contains a summary of some of the more significant developments in the cultural pan-Slav movement of the first half of the nineteenth century; here the concern is primarily with the 1870s and 1880s. For two lengthy biographical, analytical essays about Krizhanich, his work and mission to Russia, see the recently published *Russian Statecraft: The Politika of Iurii Krizhanich,* translated by A. D. Goldberg and edited with a

long introductory essay by J. M. Letiche and Basil Dmytryshyn (Glasgow, 1985).

15. On pan-Germanism since the beginning of the nineteenth century in Europe, and in North and South America, together with bibliographical references, see the competent essay by Professor F. W. Foerster, "Pangermanism," in Feliks Gross, ed. *European Ideologies: A Survey of 20th Century Political Ideas* (New York, 1948), pp. 742–762.

16. The Prague congress of 1848, often misrepresented as a pan-Slav affair, was considerably less than that. Russia, the most populous and most powerful Slav nation, was not represented because Nicholas I refused Russia's participation, declaring bluntly that the congress "was not our affair." As Riasanovsky, and more recently Professor Orton, have shown, among the reasons for the tsar's coolness was his fear of seeing the status quo in Europe disturbed. In the absence of an official delegation, Russia's unofficial, self-appointed, but quite vocal representative was Michael Bakunin, who happened to be in the West at the time. The congress, far from advancing the cause of pan-Slavism, demonstrated the serious tensions that existed within the Slav world, as for instance between Poles and Ukrainians, Poles and Russians, Czechs and the notion of Austro-Slavism, and the more radical elements who wanted independence from the Hapsburgs. For a concise but thorough review of the Prague congress, and for an excellent "Bibliographical Essay: The Congress as History," see L. D. Orton, *The Prague Slav Congress of 1848* (New York, 1978). For the attitude of Nicholas I toward the congress, see Riasanovsky, *Official Nationality*, p. 164, and Orton, pp. 54–55. In a special work focusing on Russia and the Balkan Slavs in the 1860s and 1870s, Nikitin states that Russia did not have a "single line" approach to the Balkans and simply dismissed the Polish question: "Preservation of the status quo, considering the Polish question within the bounds of the Russian state as an internal matter — these were the fundamental positions of the tsar's government." See S. A. Nikitin, *Ocherki po istorii iuzhnykh slavian i russko-balkanskikh sviazei v 50 – 70-e gody XIX v.* (Moscow, 1970), p. 155.

17. Pan-Slavism can, of course, be considered from various points of view, such as Russian, Polish, Czech, Croat. In a 104-page monograph on this subject, Lednicki touched on a number of aspects and phases in the evolution of pan-Slavism, from Jury Krizanic to Marx and Engels, and to the Moscow Slavophils, to Danilevsky, Tiutchev, Dostoevsky, Bakunin, and Herzen. This is a valuable summary of a highly complex subject written from a pro-Polish, pro-Catholic, pro-Western point of view. See Waclaw Lednicki "Panslavism," in Gross, ed., *European Ideologies*, pp. 808–912.

18. See S. A. Nikitin, *Slavianskie komitety v Rossii v 1858–1876 godakh* (Moscow,, 1960). The Moscow committee is also referred to as the Slav Benevolent or Philanthropic *Society.*

19. In fact, Nikitin, aware of the change in official attitude, says the "government itself looked benevolently upon the preparation occurring in the Balkans for a fight *with Turkey," and was ready to render diplomatic and military assistance. Ibid., p. 344. See also Nikitin's "Vozniknovenie moskovskogo slavianskogo komiteta (Iz istorii russko-bolgarskikh sviazei posle krymskoi voiny)," Voprosy istorii,* 1947, no. 8, pp. 50–65.

20. Quoted in Nikitin, *Komitety,* p. 29. In his conclusion (p. 343), Nikitin brings together Slavophilism and pan-Slavism in the person of Konstantin Aksakov: "the well-known ideologue of Slavophilism, K. S. Aksakov, formulated the fundamental propositions of the pan-Slav program that were at the base of the further development of Slavophilism."

21. Ibid., pp. 31–33. Other committees were later organized in St. Petersburg, Kiev, and Odessa.

22. Ibid., p. 34. In addition to academics and publicists the Russian Slav committees attracted prominent Russian businessmen and entrepreneurs, who had perhaps little interest in ideological matters outside Russia but could help the Slav committees financially. Toward the end of the 1860s the supporters represented a cross section which included "about 30 merchants," as for instance the merchant I. A. Liamin, the bankers G. D. Bezsonov, T. S. Morozov, the entrepreneur F. V. Chizhov, A. B. Tretiakov, K. T. Soldatenkov, and I. K. Babst. Ibid., pp. 64–65, 69. See also Tsimbaev, *Aksakov,* pp. 64, 85–86, 134.

23. Khomiakov, *Sochineniia,* I, 384.

24. Ibid., p. 392. Referring to Ivan Aksakov's attitude toward Poland during the rebellion of 1863, Tsimbaev gives the following apt characterization of the Slavophil view of the Polish question: "In the struggle of Russia with Poland the Slavophils saw the result of the contrast of two worlds, of the Russian and European; of two religions, Orthodoxy and Catholicism; and of two social principles, popular rule [*narodnost'*] and aristocracy." And although the Slavophils considered the Russian-Polish conflict as having universal significance, they saw it "at the same time as an exclusively inter-Slav matter." Tsimbaev, *Aksakov,* p. 108.

25. Nikitin, *Komitety,* pp. 170, 174–175. Lukashevich, citing the N. M. Druzhinin-edited symposium on the Slav question, comments, "It is curious that . . . of the seventy guests from the Slavic lands only eleven were Orthodox, the rest Catholic." Stephen Lukashevich, *Ivan Aksakov, 1823–1886: A Study in Russian Thought and Politics* (Cambridge, Mass. 1965), p. 133.

26. *Komitety,* p. 346.

27. The emphasis here on Slav independence and solidarity, and on the differences between East and West in Europe makes it advisable to be reminded that the early Slavophils never lost their appreciation for the best in Western culture. A century ago Veselovsky, stressing this point, said: "Here are several examples . . . from the works of Khomiakov, I. Kireevsky,

K. Aksakov. Kireevsky considers Leibnitz *great*; Spinoza and Descartes *celebrated,* Hume — impartial . . . . Khomiakov considers Voltaire and Rousseau 'genius activists of the eighteenth century.' He is astonished by Shelly although regrets his errors." In his dissertation Aksakov had good words for the 'enlightenment of the West, although the result of this enlightenment, in its present understanding makes necessary the conscious return to itself.' See Aleksei Veselovsky, *Zapadnoe vliianie v novoi russkoi literature. Istoriko-sravnitel'nye ocherki* (Moscow, 1896), 2nd ed., p. 238.

28. N. I. Danilevsky, *Rossiia i Evropa. Vzgliad na kul'turnyia i politicheskiia otnosheniia Slavianskago mira k Germano-Romanskomu* [1869]. Edited, with an introduction by Iu. Ivask, (New York, 1966), pp. v–xxx. For a full-length biography of Danilevsky, see R. E. MacMaster, *Danilevsky: A Russian Totalitarian Philosopher* (Cambridge, Mass., 1967). MacMaster's harsh verdict on Danilevsky is summarized in his article, "Danilevsky and Spengler: A New Interpretation," *Journal of Modern History,* 1954, no. 2, p. 161.

29. Danilevsky, *Rossiia i Evropa,* p. 1.

30. Ibid., p. 3.

31. Ibid., p. xxvii.

32. The 1966 edition of Danilevsky's *Rossiia i Evropa,* used here, contains four valuable essays supplementing the text. In the order of their appearance they are Iurii Ivask's "Vvedenie" pp. v–xxx (1966), N. N. Strakhov's "Predislovie k chetvertomu izdaniiu," pp. V–VIII (1889), "Zhizn' i trudy N. Ia. Danilevskago," pp. IX–XXXI (1888), and K. N. Bestuzhev-Riumin's "Teoriia kul'turno-istoricheskikh tipov" (1888), pp. 559–610. The brief comments that follow are based on the text and the commentaries in these four essays.

33. Ibid., p. viii.

34. Ibid., pp. 95–96. Since Danilevsky's *Rossiia i Evropa* appeared at the time when the West was exuberant over the progress of the physical sciences, and over Darwinism, materialism, scientific socialism, and positivism, Danilevsky's formulation of "laws" as explaining his theory of "cultural-historical types" is not surprising. But these "laws" raised a serious question. Reviewing *Rossiia i Evropa* in 1877, the populist Mikhailovsky said, "The Slav Danilevsky terminates history with the Slavic "cultural-historical type," but Hegel beginning with ancient Oriental, Greek, and Roman civilizations ends with Germanic civilization, "as the last word of the self-developing spirit. Place these two ideas side by side and everyone would get the feeling . . . that there is something wrong." N. K. Mikhailovsky, *Sochineniia* (St. Petersburg, 1897), III, 873.

35. Danilevsky, *Rossiia i Evropa,* pp. 172–174.

36. Referring to the views of T. G. Masaryk and P. N. Miliukov, Ivask speaks of Danilevsky's "biological nationalism," but denies that Danilevsky

was a "chauvinist-racist": his "hatred of the West" was politically motivated whereas in the cultural sphere "he valued highly Roman-Germanic civilization." Ivask also refers to French and German sources of some of Danilevsky's ideas. Looking at Danilevsky not from a secular but from a religious Christian point of view, Vladimir Solov'ev, and after him Berdiaev, saw in his "teaching betrayal of the universal Christianity of the old Slavophils." For Vladimir Solov'ev, Danilevsky's theory was "incompatible not only with the Christian idea but also with the very historical *fact* of Christianity as a universal religion . . . which cannot be adapted to any sort of special cultural type" (pp. xiii, xx). In addition to the brief but meaningful sections on Danilevsky and Leont'ev, Danilevsky and Dostoevsky, Danilevsky and Vladimir Solov'ev in which differences as well as similarities are brought out, Ivask also supplied a few pages on "Danilevsky and Spengler" (1880–1936). See, Iurii Ivask, ed., *Rossiia i Evropa*, pp. xiii–xxiii.

37. Ibid., p. 283.

38. Ibid., p. 286. See George L. Kline, "Russian Religious Thought" in Ninian Smart et al eds., *Nineteenth Century Religious Thought in the West.* (Cambridge, 1985) vol. 2, p. 191.

39. Ibid., p. 419.

40. Ibid., p. 447.

41. A different view of Constantinople and the Straits was given by A. A. Kizevetter, in 1914. For him they had economic value for Russia, and touched on the "question of existence" for the Balkan Slavs threatened by Turkey. See his review-essay "Rossiia i Konstantinopol'," *Russkaia mysl'*, 1914, book VIII–IX, p. 75.

42. Danilevsky, *Rossiia i Evropa*, p. 285.

43. See L. S. Kozlovsky, "Mechty o Tsar'grade (Dostoevsky i K. Leont'ev)" [Dreams about Constantinople (Dostoevsky and K. Leont'ev)], *Golos minuvshago*, 1915, no. 2, pp. 88–116; no. 11, pp. 44–74.

44. Ibid., no. 2, p. 88.

45. See F. M. Dostoevsky, "Dnevnik pisatelia za 1876 god," Dostoevsky, *Sochineniia*, XXIII, 48–49.

46. Ibid., xxv, 66.

47. Kozlovsky, "Mechty," pp. 89–90.

48. The government Manifesto of June 14, 1853, on the war with Turkey contains no reference to the Slavs under Ottoman rule or to any other Slavs. It ends with the exhortation, "Let us go forward for the Orthodox faith." Ibid., p. 96. For confirmation of Dostoevsky's pro-Orthodox views, see also P. B. Struve, "Velikaia Rossiia i Sviataia Rus'," *Russkaia mysl'*, 1914, no. 12, p. 179.

49. Kozlovsky, "Mechty" pp. 94–95.

50. Ibid., pp. 96–97.

51. This characterization is from the title of a valuable review essay by S. N. Trubetskoi, "Razocharovannyi slavianofil. Vostok, Rossiia i slavianstvo. Sbornik statei K. Leont'eva . . . ." (Hereafter cited Trubetskoi, "Razocharovannyi slavianofil.") The literature on Leont'ev in English, German, and Italian, in addition to Russian, is quite extensive. Valuable bibliographical references, in addition to a summary and an interpretation, can be found in A. L. Ianov's "Slavianofily i Konstantin Leont'ev (Russkaia konservativnaia mysl' XIX v. i ee interpretatory)," *Voprosy filosofii,* 1969, no. 8, pp. 97–106.

52. Kozlovsky says that for Leont'ev, "The future not only of Russia but of all mankind is bound with the future of Tsar'grad." *Golos minuvshago,* 1915, no. 11, p. 44.

53. See I. Fudel', ed., *Sobranie sochinenii K. Leont'eva* 8 vols. (Moscow, 1912–1913), I, iii (Hereafter cited as Leont'ev, *Sochineniia*). In the second installment of his "Mechty o Tsar'grade," Kozlovsky concurs in Archpriest Fudel's opinion of the importance of "Vizantinizm i slavianstvo" as containing Leont'ev's "philosophical ideas and his political ideals." See *Golos minuvshago,* 1915, no. 11, pp. 44–45. Actually volumes 5, 6, and 7 of Leont'ev's works appear under the same general title, *Vostok, Rossiia i Slavianstvo* (The East, Russia, and Slavdom). This versatile medical doctor, diplomat, censor, and monk wrote novels, stories, tales, articles and essays, reminiscences, and other miscellaneous works.

54. The story of Leont'ev's life and work, wholly or in part has been told by, among others, Nikolai Berdiaev, *Konstantin Leont'ev. Ocherk iz istorii russkoi religioznoi mysli* (Paris, 1926); Iwan von Kologriwof, *Von Hellas zum Monchtum. Leben und Denken Konstantin Leontjews (1831–1891)* (Regensburg, 1948); Stephen Lukashevich, *Konstantin Leontev (1831–1891): A Study in Russian "Heroic Vitalism"* (New York, 1967); *Konstantin Leontiev: Analysis, Style, and Atmosphere in the Novels of Count L. N. Tolstoy. With an Essay on Leontiev by Vasily Rozanov and an Introductory Piece by Donald Fanger* (Providence, R. I., 1965); B. A. Filippov, ed., *Konstantin Leont'ev pis'ma k Vasiliiu Rozanovu. Vstuplenie, kommentarii i posleslovie V. V. Rozanova. Vstupitel'naia stat'ia B. A. Filippova* (London, 1981).

55. Leont'ev, *Sochineniia,* V, 7–335. Kozlovsky, *Golos minuvshago,* 1915, no. 11, pp. 44–45.

56. In a summary of the relationship between Leont'ev and the Slavophils, Lukashevich says, "Leont'ev has been called a 'disenchanted Slavophile' by Prince S. Trubetskoi, or a Slavophile of the period of decay of Slavophilism by Paul Miliukov, or finally, 'a latter-day Slavophil' by V. Rozanov. Although later on Rozanov withdrew his statement." Lukashevich's views on the differences between the Slavophils and Leont'ev are clear and valid. See Lukashevich, *Leont'ev,* pp. 163–170. Alexander Ianov lists V1. Solov'ev, B. Griftsov, V. Rozanov, and A. Walicki as among those who did not consider

Leont'ev a Slavophil, and P. Miliukov, L. Tikhomirov, and E. Thaden as those who would not separate Leont'ev from the Moscow Slavophils. See Ianov, "Slavianofily i K. Leont'ev," p. 99.

57. See Kologriwof, *Leontjew,* pp. 59–60.

58. See George L. Kline, *Religious and Anti-Religious Thought in Russia. The Weil Lectures* (University of Chicago Press) Chicago, 1968, p. 39. (Hereafter cited, Kline, *Weil Lectures.*)

59. K. Leont'ev *Sochineniia,* V, 113.

60. Ibid., pp. 116, 137.

61. Ibid., pp. 137, 138.

62. Ibid., pp. 148, 149.

63. Those who write about Leont'ev invariably stress such elements in his character and work as naturalism, aestheticism, and romanticism. This "good, mild man," who could not resist the charms of the Greek, Bulgarian, and Turkish girls," was also capable, in Berdiaev's words, of formulating a "merciless naturalistic sociology." Leont'ev's naturalism was indispensible to his aesthetic,, for "In the laws of nature, active in history he [Leont'ev] sees God and beauty." Kologriwof took note of Leont'ev's "aesthetic criterion of life," and of his "romanticism." Lukashevich devotes chapter 6 of his biography to Leont'ev's "Esthetics of Reaction." In the brief discussion of his relationship with Leont'ev, which came toward the end of Leont'ev's life, V. V. Rozanov (1856–1919) says that Leont'ev felt the "aesthetic fear that liberalism with its equalizing and liberating movement would undercut diversity and therefore the beauty of things, of the social order, and of nature." Rozanov found not even a trace of pretense, hypocrisy, or affectation in Leont'ev, who was for him "like Adam without clothes." When Rozanov went through Leont'ev's library after his death and found the French monograph *Alcibiade,* "Such resurrection of Atheneanism (using an uncommon term), he wrote, of Athenians at the noisy Agora, the passionate struggle of the parties, and the marvelous Hellenic 'na ty' toward the gods and people – this I never saw in anyone as in Leont'ev." But this same Leont'ev "was first among the Russians and perhaps Europeans who . . . discovered the 'excitement' (the living soul, the real meaning of poetry) of Turkism [*turetchiny*] with its militancy and love of women, religious naivete and fanaticism, devotion to God and peculiar respect for man." Like others before and after him, Rozanov recognized the "astonishing" coalescence of Leont'ev and Nietzsche" (1844–1900), and was at a loss to account for "this roaring encounter of Hellenic aestheticism with the monastic words about the strict otherworldly ideal." Cf. Berdiaev, *Leont'ev,* pp. 82–83; Kologriwof, *Leontjew,* pp. 27–30, 175–180; Lukashevich, *Leontev,* pp. 105–133; Rozanov in Filippov, *Leont'ev, Pis'ma,* pp. 26–27, 31, 34–35.

64. Kozlovsky, "Mechty," *Golos Minuvshago,* 1915, no. 11, pp. 61–62, 65.

65. G. L. Kline, *Weil Lectures,* p. 42.

66. In view of Leont'ev's convictions – all too briefly stated in these pages – it is difficult to see how he could be characterized as a "historical successor" of the Moscow Slavophils. More credible but still conditional is Tsimbaev's statement that in the period 1870s to 1890s their "historical successors" were A. A. Kireev, S. A. Iur'ev, S. N. Trubetskoi, L. N. Tolstoy, Dostoevsky, some populists, and several others. See Tsimbaev, *Slavianofil'stvo*, p. 75.

67. Leont'ev, *Sochineniia*, V, 151.

68. Ibid., pp. 153, 154.

69. Ibid., p. 156.

70. Leont'ev's dislike and strictures of things Bulgarian preceded his *Vizantizm i slavianstvo*. See, for instance, his earlier (1873) essay, "Panslavizm i Greki," in *Sochineniia*, V, 9–43.

71. Ibid., p. 157.

72. Leont'ev's baffling life and convictions impressed the late George Florovsky, who devotes to him a number of penetrating and revealing passages. He calls into question Leont'ev's Christianity by quoting Vladimir Solov'ev, among others. Thus "Leont'ev's hopes and dreams do not derive from Christianity, which he, just the same, confessed as universal truth." Florovsky found extremely unpleasant the "aftertaste" of Leont'ev's "constant double-meaning [*dvusmyslennosti*]" and his twofold "measures, the aesthetic and the Christian." In him, Florovsky exclaims, there is "Such a venomous mixture . . . of Nietzsche and Calvin!" Leont'ev did *not* "seek in Christianity truth and faith but only salvation . . . from hell." In "history," he says, Leont'ev saw no religious meaning, in history he remained an aesthete and a biologist, and these completely satisfied him." Florovsky, describing him as "a disenchanted romantic more than a believer," concludes that "Leont'ev should be compared not with the senior Slavophils but rather with such unrepentant romantics as Herzen and Apollon Grigor'ev." Florovsky compared Grigor'ev with Leont'ev and found charity for neither. "Grigor'ev was a man perplexed, disordered, failed, and unhappy"; "he did not possess authentic faith," for in his confession he said, "by Orthodoxy I meant a certain elemental-historical principle which was destined still to live and provide new forms of life and art." Small wonder that Grigor'ev valued the older Slavophils, Khomiakov and Kireevsky, not for their religious and philosophical thought but as "bearers of the 'organic principle.'" Florovsky, the Orthodox archpriest and theologian could find congeniality in neither Leont'ev nor Grigor'ev, these two deeply if not exclusively secular authors. See Florovsky, *Puti russkago bogosloviia*, pp. 303–306.

73. Leont'ev referred to the 'emancipation delusion,' regretted that the old Russian order was 'destroyed by the emancipation process' and considered 1861 the year in which "Russia became sick from the emancipation.' See Trubetskoi, "Razocharovannyi slavianofil," pp. 781, 800, 801.

74. Ibid., p. 788.

75. Ibid., pp. 800–801.

76. Ibid., pp. 796–797.

77. Ibid., p. 804.

78. Ibid., p. 780.

79. Leont'ev and Nietzsche have points of contact as well as of differences, even though Leont'ev's views were "formulated almost a decade before Nietzsche's first works appeared." For a penetrating summary of these see G. L. Kline, *Weil Lectures,* pp. 40, 41, 47–49.

80. Trubetskoi, "Razocharovannyi slavianofil," pp. 788, 789. In 1889 Leont'ev published a pamphlet under the title "National policy as a tool of universal revolution."

81. Ibid., p. 793.

82. Leont'ev, *Sochineniia,* v. 7, p. 170.

83. For Ivan Aksakov's biography see these previously cited works: Lukashevich, *Ivan Aksakov, 1823–1886: A Study in Russian Thought and Politics,* Tsimbaev's *I. S. Aksakov v obshchestvennoi zhizhi poreformennoi Rossii,* though limited in scope, is indispensable, and the brief but informative introductory essay by A. S. Kurilov, ed., in *K. S. Aksakov i I. S. Aksakov. Literaturnaia kritika,* pp. 5–29.

84. Nol'de, *Samarin,* p. 210.

85. Kurilov, ed., *K. S. Aksakov i I. S. Aksakov,* p. 11.

86. Vladimir Solov'ev (1853–1900) during his relatively brief but highly productive career, went as far as to say, when he became disenchanted with Slavophil Orthodoxy, that on the question of the emancipation of the serfs the Slavophils acted "in the name of the Western principle of human rights. On this issue the contributions of several Slavophils (in particular Samarin's) were beyond doubt, but these were not the contributions of Slavophilism." Thus in his polemic with Samarin's brother Dmitry, in 1889 Solov'ev went so far as to imply that the Slavophils were incapable of ethical judgments, that the evils of serfdom were not obvious to them, and that therefore they had to import the "Western" principle of human rights. And this import was from the same West, which engaged in slavery for centuries, and a good portion of which (the United States) maintained slavery in the South longer than serfdom existed in Russia! The quotation above comes from Solov'ev's "Slavophilism and Its Degeneration" (*Slavianofil'stvo i ego vyrozhdenie*) (1889), in V. S. Solov'ev, *Sobranie sochinenii,* 2d ed. (St. Petersburg, 1912–1914), V, 192–193.

87. See Fr. Georges Florovsky, *Christianity and Culture: Volume Two of Collected Works* (Belmont, Mass., 1974), pp. 136–138.

Conclusion

"It is an astonishing time of external slavery and inner liberation." With this ultimate characterization by Alexander Herzen, editor M. D. Gershenzon began in 1910 the volume on the *Epoch of Nicholas I*. In this simple and brief statement Herzen brought out the truth and the paradox that marked the thirty-year reign of Nicholas I (1825–1855). And this reign, contained most of "early," pre-Reform Moscow Slavophilism. But the simple truth conveyed in Herzen's words covering among others the "marvelous decade" of the 1840s to which the Slavophils were major contributors, also exposes the fallacy of adhering unreservedly to logic and "scientific laws" in the realm of human relations. The Third Section and the censorship of Nicholas I that hounded the Slavophils and other talented Russians, far from stifling their ideas and works, witnessed an outburst of ideological and literary artistic creativity unprecedented in Russian history. It was a case of portentous developments occurring in spite of, not because of, external conditions.

The Slavophils, although harassed and censored, and even imprisoned by the tsar's authorities, did not have to endure severe physical punishment. Samarin's and Ivan Aksakov's brief incarcerations, while still young, were more in the nature of temporary eye-opening experiences than periods of great privation and soul-trying suffering. None of the Slavophils was ever in need or deprivation. On the contrary, they were well off. Their families could afford the luxury of Western nurses, governesses, and tutors, and also travel and study in the West, as well as amenities at home that were accessible to only a tiny fraction of the Russian population. Yet from this exceptional position in Russian society they looked up not to their own class, and not to the tsar's government, which made all this possible, but to the common Russian people, the *narod,* the illiterate, underprivileged Russian peasantry, many of whom were in the state of age-long serfdom.

Several major streams formed and nurtured pre-Reform Moscow Slavophilism: Slavophil Orthodoxy, and its striving for an integrated view of the individual and society; a strong national consciousness, fortified by the memory of the not-too-distant Napoleonic wars, a native Russian pride that would not brook slavish copying of the West; and a strong, and as it developed, justified, premonition that Russia would finally have its day in the undeclared literary and artistic competition in Europe. Along with these understandable components of Moscow Slavophilism there was also the rather baffling romantic-utopian adulation of the *narod,* strong at times in all the early Slavophils but most unrestrained in the case of Konstantin Aksakov.

It would not be an error to say that the early Slavophils, like most educated and articulate Russians of the time, experienced a sense of inferiority when they viewed the West's literary, artistic, and scientific achievements and compared them with Russia's own. But the same cannot be said, and certainly not of the Slavophils, when they looked at the West's religious, and moral imperatives, as revealed before their eyes by the early stages of the industrial revolution. The middle decades of the nineteenth century witnessed perhaps the most dismal phase of Western liberalism, individualism, and laissez-faire industrialism. But what in the West was considered freedom of the individual, often appeared in the eyes of the Slavophils as "wolf freedom," or a predatory freedom that was purchased with the misery and suffering of millions in the "slums of Manchester" and other British industrial towns. These deplorable conditions responded neither to the West's Christian ethics nor to its secular humanism. Nor have the ethics of the West, more than a century and a half later, in this highly scientific technological age, been able to solve the twin problems of unemployment and poverty that still plague millions in most free and affluent Western societies.

On the level of religion and philosophy, the early Slavophils left no doubt that neither of the West's two major religious forces, Catholicism and Protestantism, nor its philosophical currents, more specifically the then dominant Western rationalism, held any attraction or promise for them. They saw historical Catholicism as too deeply in debt to classical pagan Roman statism, legalism, rationalism, and authoritarianism and as guilty of separating from the true Christian church, which for them was the Eastern Orthodox Church of Constantinople. This was the church that through the ecumenical councils of the fourth, fifth, and sixth centuries, held in the Byzantine empire, established the doctrine and dogma of the Christian church after it emerged from the first three centuries of official Roman persecution. Thus was born the Nicean creed, among others.

Lutheranism and subsequent Protestantism were for the early Slavophils a logical development of what they considered to be schismatic Catholicism. Luther went a step further than the Catholic church when he first renounced the Eastern Orthodox church and the work of the ecumenical councils and of Tradition and then went on to break away from the established Catholic church itself — and in so doing prepared the way, perhaps unwittingly, for the further splintering of Christianity. To the early Slavophils, Lutheranism, while breaking away from the Catholic and Orthodox churches, also yielded to the strong secular currents of thought in the Renaissance and post-Renaissance periods. In fact, the Slavophils regarded the German rationalism of the eighteenth and early nineteenth centuries as a logical and inevitable extension of Protestantism. To them, Catholicism stood for unity without freedom; Protestantism for freedom without unity; Orthodoxy for unity in freedom. In the political life of the West they saw an excess of individualism, legalism, and constitutionalism, written or unwritten, and not enough Christian togetherness and concern for others.

Yet when the Slavophils looked away from the West and turned their gaze inward, they chose not Russia's official state Orthodox church (although they never renounced their membership in it), but a nonexistent and highly idealized Orthodoxy—something that, for lack of more precise terminology, I have referred to as Slavophil Orthodoxy. The Slavophils sought inspiration and guidance not in the historical Russian church but in the Patristic Orthodoxy of Byzantium of the early Christian centuries. Among the principal reasons for this was the Slavophil coolness toward the contemporary Russian church then under the authority of a Holy Synod, presided over by an army officer. They were unhappy with the seventeenth-century schism that threw millions of faithful Russian Orthodox believers into the ranks of the schismatics, and they—Ivan Aksakov in particular—felt that the Russian church was too heavily under the authority of the tsarist government, and too ritualistic and removed from the daily problems and concerns of the faithful.

When the tsar-dominated church refused to permit the publication of Khomiakov's theological works at home during his lifetime, and officially at least, indicated its coolness toward the Slavophils, the Slavophils turned for their religious philosophical "substratum" to Khomiakov's doctrine of *sobornost'* and to Ivan Kireevsky's doctrine of the "wholeness of the spirit, both of which were inspired by Eastern patristic Orthodoxy, although in Kireevsky's case scholars have also seen Western romantic overtones. One can only surmise that if Kireevsky had ever written his "Russian philosophy" it would have been heavily tinged by ideas about the "wholeness of the spirit," and as in the case of Khomiakov, by the early Christian sense of *koinonia*, fellowship. For the Slavophils, although familiar with the great and fascinating achievements of the classical Greek mind, remained deeply devoted to their Orthodox Christian views and convictions.

There is no doubt that as the Slavophils observed the crucial developments in English industrialization during the 1840s and 1850s, and the spread of industrialism on the continent of Europe, they turned their eyes to the old Great Russian commune, still active in the nineteenth century. This institution lost some but not all of its romantic hues when it was perceived by the Slavophils as the embodiment of the ancient Russian Christian communal spirit that was still important for all members of the communal societies. They firmly believed that this institution, if properly maintained, could satisfy the basic needs of all Russians below the level of the gentry and the growing urban population, without establishing absolute equality among manifestly unequal human beings. This belief presumed that the commune would save Russian society from the all too evident miseries of the West — chronic poverty, homelessness and the ugliness of life for millions of city slum dwellers — this and the excesses of the "robber barons," all of it justified in the name of individual freedom. The initial Slavophil reaction to Western industrialism was so fundamental and so perceptive that it has not yet spent itself. Nor are Slavophil views on other aspects of Russian and Western life irrelevant today.

The village commune, the citadel of the Slavophils' moral, social, and economic order, was abolished by Stalin in the early 1930s, and with this ended Khomiakov's hope that it would branch out to become an industrial commune, a phalanstery. Nonetheless, despite the march of modern entrepreneurial industrialism in the second half of the nineteenth century, with its stress on private property, the village commune survived the Stolypin reforms and the early Bolshevik era. As usual in human affairs the ideal was not realized in the historical reality, and the Slavophil communal dreams fell short of their expectations. But the early Slavophils staunchly upheld their faith in the commune, and could even speak, in the case of Konstantin Aksakov, of Russia as the "Great Commune." He more than the other Slavophils contrasted the common people (zemlia) with the state, perhaps dreaming of some sort of Christian anarchism. It is true that the Slavophils never ceased being loyal subjects of the tsar, nor did any of them volunteer to give their lands to the communes and join the communal life. Indeed, most of them branched out into various private industrial and financial enterprises. Clearly they never shook off their gentry consciousness and many old gentry privileges, despite Ivan Aksakov's pious hopes early in the 1860s that the gentry should abolish its own class. But since this study was never conceived as a test of human or Slavophil consistency it is not necessary to dwell further on this matter.

Before leaving the commune and the communal principle, I should clarify one other issue, and that is the Slavophils' attitude toward the individual and individual freedom. Since the stress placed here on the communal in the Slavophil scheme of things could distort some of their basic positions, it is necessary to emphasize in this summary that, in their view, the individual was neither neglected nor excluded from their considerations. Rather, the individual was conceived as a zoon politikon in the sense of being a member of a Christian community. The Slavophils were thoroughly cognizant and appreciative of the work of such great men as Homer, Shakespeare, and Gogol'. Their own self-respect, Christian consciousness, and the obvious harm to Russian society that resulted from the tsar's suppression of individual freedom and possible creativity prompted them to declare in favor of freedom of conscience, of expression, of assembly, and of what is sometimes referred to as Samarin's "enlightened conservatism," and to work for long-overdue internal reforms. To the Slavophils, as probably to most thinkers in the West, the noblest individual was not the one who would take advantage of "wolf freedom," but the socially conscious person for whom the welfare of his fellow human beings meant more than his own personal aggrandizement.

This concern, in the usual human fallible and not completely disinterested, altruistic manner, was behind the determined Slavophil effort during the 1840s, and even more during the 1850s and early 1860s, to rid Russia of some long-standing evils and weaknesses. The Slavophils knew, as did other Russians of various ideological and political persuasions, that Russia's national security and its place and status in a rapidly changing world were being jeopardized by the age-long institution of serfdom. This inequity with its stranglehold on millions of Russians, and on Russia as a whole, eventually reached the palace and Alexander II. The Slavophils played a role in the emancipation reform of 1861 second to none. They also had a part in yet another form of emancipation—on the literary artistic front. For early or Moscow Slavophilism coincides in time with the birth of the great Russian literature of the nineteenth century and of modern Russian music. The insistence of the Slavophils that Russia look inwardly, not to the West, for the solution of its national problems tended to focus on the native roots of both Russian music and its literature, thus saving their country and the rest of the cultural world from possible feeble imitations of western models. The old institutions of *zemski sobor* and *zemskaia duma* would have been recast to meet mid-nineteenth-century needs and conditions. These and other beginning with the emancipation of the serfs, were on the Slavophil agenda of reforms. Finally, toward the end of the 1850s some of the Moscow Slavophils became earnestly concerned about the fate of their fellow Orthodox Slavs in the Balkans, who were impatient to become free after five centuries of Ottoman rule. Khomiakov's "Message to the Serbians" of 1860, and the eventual liberation of Bulgaria from the Turks, in which Ivan Aksakov was a major force, provide further evidence that complex and sometimes contradictory Moscow Slavophilism was never merely utopian or merely retrospective.

It is now time for one final glance at Slavophilism's true beginning, that is, Slavophil Orthodoxy with its ultimate concern for all humanity, and a world at peace; for the Slavophils made a good deal of the fiction that the early Russians were peaceful in contrast to the ever warring Western lords and knights. Their contemporary Western European current of the dialectic, which did not meet with approval by the Slavophils, was a Western refurbishing and possibly debasing, however brilliantly done, of the ancient Greek model. Ivan Kireevsky, for one, remained cool and skeptical toward the then current Western dialectic as he demonstrated in 1838 and in 1856, the year of his death. In Chizhevsky's view Kireevsky considered the dialectic a philosophy of the past. For it is unquestionable that if the Western version of the classical Greek original were to be pushed today to its logical end it would inevitably lead to the final atomic clash between East and West with an infinitely reduced possibility for a new and higher synthesis. In the place of the modern dialectic they advanced, as we have seen, Khomiakov's doctrine of *sobornost'*, union in peace and love, and with this they hoped for the appearance of the "light from the East."

Bibliography

The practice established in the preceding three studies of Moscow Slavophilism, to take as the basic source the published works of the individual Slavophil, has also been followed in this case. The eleven volumes of *Sochineniia Iuriia Fedorovicha Samarina* published in Moscow by Iurii Samarin's brothers Dmitry and Peter between 1877 and 1910 are the indispensable source for this work. In addition, Iurii Samarin was co-author with Fedor Dmitriev (one monograph each) of *Revoliutsionnyi konservatizm. Kniga R. Fadeeva "Russkoe obshchestvo v nastoiashchem i budshchem" i predlozheniia Peterburgskikh dvorian ob organizatsii vsesoslovnoi volosti* (Berlin, 1875). Valuable research, both before and since the publication of *A. S. Xomjakov* in 1961, has been incorporated into this volume, as in the preceding ones. I have found particularly helpful recent Soviet publications on the Slavophils, which often include information from unpublished archival sources.

Here as in the preceding three studies it has been my purpose to avoid bibliographical repetitiousness and to treat these studies as part of a single work on Moscow Slavophilism, rather than four separate, unrelated monographs.

Books

Aksakov, I. S. *Izsledovanie o torgovle na ukrainskikh iarmarkakh*. St. Petersburg, 1858.

Al'tshuller, Mark. *Predtechi slavianofil'stva v russkoi literature* (*Obshchestvo "Beseda liubitelei russkago slova"*). Ann Arbor, Mich., 1984.

Annenkov, P. V. *The Extraordinary Decade: Literary Memoirs*. Translated by I. R. Titunik; Introduction by A. P. Mendel. Ann Arbor, Mich., 1968.

___ . *Literaturnye vospominaniia*. Introduction by V. I. Kuleshov. Moscow, 1983.

Berdiaev, Nikolai. *Konstantin Leont'ev. Ocherk iz istorii russkoi religioznoi mysli*. Paris, 1926.

Berlin, Isaiah. *Russian Thinkers*. Edited by Henry Hardy and Aileen Kelly; Introduction by Aileen Kelly. New York, 1978.

Blackwell, William L. *The Beginnings of Russian Industrialization, 1800–1860*. Princeton, N.J., 1968.

Blum, Jerome. *Lord and Peasant in Russia from the Ninth to the Ninteenth Century.* New York, 1964.

Bochkarev, V. N. *Osvobozhdenie krest'ian. Deiateli reformy.* Moscow, 1911.

Borovoi, A. A. *Lichnost' i obshchestvo v anarkhistskom mirovozzrenii.* Petersburg-Moscow, 1920.

Borovoi, A. A. and Lebedev, N., eds. *Sbornik statei posviashchennykh pamiati P. A. Kropotkina.* Petersburg-Moscow, 1922.

Calder, Loren, et al., eds. *The Correspondence of Iu. Samarin and Baroness Rahden 1861–1876.* Translated by Terence Scully from the French, Helen Swediuk-Cheyne from the German, Loren Calder from the Russian. Waterloo, Ont., Canada, 1974.

Chagin, B. A. *Proniknovenie idei marksizma v Rossiiu 1845–1883.* Leningrad, 1948.

Cherkassky, V. A. *Ego stat'i, ego rechi i vospominaniia o nem.* Moscow, 1879.

___. *Materialy dlia biografii . . . vol. 1, Kn. V. A. Cherkassky i ego uchastie v razreshenii krest'ianskago voprosa. Perepiska s Iu. F. Samarinym, A. I. Koshelevym, I. S. Aksakovym i proch. Iz arkhiva kn. Cherkasskago.* Vol. 1, Books 1, 2. Moscow, 1904.

Danilevsky, N. Ia. *Rossiia i Evropa. Vzliad na kul'turnyia i politicheskiia otnosheniia Slavianskago mira k Germano-Romanskomu.* Introduction by Iurii Ivask. Foreword to 5th ed. by N. N. Strakhov, and post-mortem essay by K. N. Bestuzhev-Riumin. 5th ed., St. Petersburg, 1888. Reprinted New York, 1966.

Dostoevsky, F. M. *Polnoe sobranie sochinenii v tridtsati tomakh.* Leningrad, 1972–1985.

Dowler, Wayne. *Dostoevsky, Grigor'ev, and Native Soil Conservatism.* Toronto, 1982.

Druzhinin, N. M., ed. *Slavianskii Sbornik: Slavianskii vopros i russkoe obshchestvo v 1867–1878 godakh.* Moscow, 1948.

Durkin, A. R. *Sergei Aksakov and Russian Pastoral.* New Brunswick, N.J., 1983.

Dynnik, M. A., et al., eds. *Istoriia filosofii.* 6 vols. Moscow, 1957–1965.

Dzhanshiev, A. M. *Iz epokhi velikikh reform.* Moscow, 1894.

Eckhardt, Julius, ed. *Iuri Samarins Anklage gegen die Ostseeprovinzen Russlands. Uebersetzung aus dem Russischen.* Leipzig, 1869.

Egorov, B. F., et al., eds. *Letopis' zhizni i tvorchestva A. I. Gertsena 1812–1870 v 4-kh tomakh.* Moscow, 1974, 1976 (Vols. 1 and 2).

Eichenbaum, B. M. *M. Iu. Lermontov.* Moscow, 1936.

Eimontova, R. G. *Russkie universitety na grani dvukh epokh. Ot Rossii krepostnoi k Rossii kapitalisticheskoi.* Moscow, 1985.

El'iashevich, V. B., et al. *Moskovskii universitet 1755–1930. Iubileinyi sbornik.* Paris, 1930.

Emmons, Terence, ed. *Emancipation of the Russian Serfs.* New York, 1970.
Emmons, Terence, and Vucinich, W. S., eds. *The Zemstvo in Russia: An Experiment in Self Government.* Stanford, Calif., 1968.
Evans, J. L. *The Petraševkij Circle, 1845-1849.* The Hague-Paris, 1974.
Fadeev, R. A. *Mnenie o vostochnom voprose. Po povodu poslednikh retsenzii na 'Vooruzhennyia sily Rossii.'* St. Petersburg, 1870.
___. Pis'ma o sovremennom sostoianii Rossii 11go Aprelia 1879–6go *Aprelia 1880.* 4th ed. St. Petersburg, 1882.
___. *Prilozhenie k broshiure Mnenie o vostochnom voprose.* St. Petersburg, 1870.
___. *Russkoe obshchestvo v nastoiashchem i budushchem (Chem nam byt'?).* St. Petersburg, 1874.
Falk, Heinrich. *Das Weltbild Peter J. Tschaadajews nach seinem acht 'Philsophischen Briefen'; ein Beitrag zur russischen Geistesgeschichte des 19. Jahrhunderts.* Munich, 1954.
Fedosov, I. A. *Revoliutsionnoe dvizhenie v Rossii vo vtoroi chetverti XIX v. (Revoliutsionnye organizatsii i kruzhki).* Moscow, 1958.
Fedotov, Georgi. *Rossiia i svoboda (Sbornik statei).* Edited by M. A. Meerson. New York, 1981.
Fischel, Alfred. *Der Panslawismus bis zum Weltkrieg. Ein geschichtlicher Uberblick.* Stuttgart and Berlin, 1919.
Fischer, George. *Russian Liberalism from Gentry to Intelligentsia.* Cambridge, Mass., 1958.
Florovsky, Georges. *Christianity and Culture.* Belmont, Mass., 1974.
Fouyas, Methodios. *Orthodoxy, Roman Catholicism, and Anglicanism.* London, 1972.
Freidzon, V. I. ed. *Voprosy pervonachal'nogo nakopleniia kapitala i natsional'nye dvizheniia v slavianskikh stranakh.* Moscow, 1972.
Frolich, Klaus. *The Emergence of Russian Constitutionalism, 1900–1904: The Relationship Between Social Mobilization and Political Group Formation in Pre-Revolutionary Russia.* The Hague, Boston, London, 1981.
Galaktionov, A. A., and Nikandrov, P. F. *Ideologi russkogo narodnichestva.* Leningrad, 1966.
Garmiza, V. V. *Podgotovka zemskoi reformy 1864 goda.* Moscow, 1957.
Gavin, W. J., and Blakeley, T. J. *Russia and America: A Philosophical Comparison. Development and Change of Outlook from the 19th to the 20th Century.* Dordrecht – Boston, 1976.
Gershtein, E. G. *Lermontov i'kruzhok shestnadtsati.' Zhizn' i tvorchestvo M. Iu. Lermontova.* Moscow, 1941.
Gerstein, Linda. *Nikolai Strakhov.* Cambridge, Mass., 1971.
Giliarov-Platonov, N. P. *Evreiskii vopros v Rossii. Sostavleno na osnovanii statei i pisem Giliarova-Platonova.* St. Petersburg, 1906.

___. *Iz perezhitago. Avtobiograficheskiia vospominaniia.* Moscow, 1886. Republished Newtonville, Mass., 1977. Introduction by Gregory Freeze.

Gleason, Abbott. *Young Russia: The Genesis of Russian Radicalism in the 1860s.* Chicago, 1983.

Glinsky, B. B. *Revoliutsionnyi period russkoi istorii (1861–1881gg.). Istoricheskii ocherk. Chast' pervaia.* St. Petersburg, 1913.

Goldberg, A. D. tr., J. M. Letiche and Basil Dmytryshyn, eds. *Russian Statecraft: The Polilika of Iurii Krizhanich.* Glasgow, 1985.

Goriushkin, L. M., et al., eds. *Krest'ianskaia obshchina v Sibiri XVII-nachala XXv.* Novosibirsk, 1977.

Gradovsky, A. D. *Sobranie sochinenii.* 9 vols. St. Petersburg, 1899–1904.

Gratieux, Albert, ed. and trans. "G. Samarin. Préface aux oevres théologiques de A. S. Khomiakov." pp. 11–29. Paris, 1939.

Gregg, Richard A. *Fedor Tiutchev: The Evolution of a Poet.* New York and London, 1965.

Grigorenko, V. V., et. al., eds. *A. N. Ostrovsky v vospominaniiakh sovremennikov.* Minsk, 1966.

___. *M. Iu. Lermontov v vospominaniiakh sovremennikov.* Moscow, 1964.

Gross, Feliks. *European Ideologies: A Survey of 20th Century Political Ideas.* New York, 1948.

Hucke, Gerda. *Jurij Fedorovič Samarin. Seine geistesgeschichtliche Position und politische Bedeutung.* Munich, 1970.

Iakovlev, V. Ia. [pseud. Bogucharsky, V.]. *Aktivnoe narodnichestvo semidesiatykh godov.* Moscow, 1912.

___. *Iz proshlago russkago obshchestva.* St. Petersburg, 1904. Iankovsky, Iu. Z. *Patriarkhal'no-dvorianskaia utopiia.* Moscow, 1981.

Isakov, S. G. *Ostzeiskii vopros v russkoi pechati 1860-kh godov.* Tartu, 1961.

Ivaniukov, I. I. *Padenie krepostnogo prava v Rossii.* St. Petersburg, 1903.

Ivantyšynová, Tatiana. *Česia Slováci v ideológii ruských slavianofilov. 40.– 60. roky XIX. storočia.* Bratislava, 1987.

Joll, James. *The Anarchists.* 2nd ed. Cambridge, Mass., 1980.

Karsavin, L. P. *Sviatye ottsy i uchiteli tserkvi (raskrytie pravoslaviia v ikh tvoreniiakh).* Paris, n.d.

Kartashev, A. V. *Ocherki po istorii russkoi tserkvi.* 2 vols. Paris, 1959.

Kavelin, K. D. *Chem nam byt'? Otvet redaktoru gazety 'Russkii mir.' V dvukh pis'makh.* Berlin, 1875.

Kennan, G. F. *The Marquis de Custine and His "Russia in 1839".* Princeton, N. J., 1971.

Khomiakov, A. S. *Stikhotvoreniia i dramy.* Edited by B. F. Egorov. Lenningrad, 1969.

___. *Sushchnost' zapadnago khristianstva. Neskol'ko slov pravoslavnago khristianina o zapadnykh veroispovedaniiakh. Po povodu broshiury g. Loransi.* Edited by Brotherhood of St. Job of Pochaev. Montreal, 1974.

___. *Khomiakov i slavianskoe delo.* St. Petersburg, 1877.

Kireev, A. A. *Kratkoe izlozhenie slavianofil'skago ucheniia.* St. Petersburg, 1896.

___. *Slavianofil'stvo i natsionalizm; otviet g. Solov'evu.* Petrograd, 1890.

Kirpotin, V. Ia. *Politicheskie motivy v tvorchestve Lermontova.* Moscow, 1939.

Kitaev, V. A. *Ot frondy k okhranitel'stvu. Iz istorii russkoi liberal'noi mysli 50–60-kh godov XIX veka.* Moscow, 1972.

___. *Slavianofily nakanune otmeny krepostnogo prava.* Gorkii, 1981.

Kline, G. L. *Religious and Anti-Religious Thought in Russia, The Weil Lectures.* Chicago and London, 1968.

Kizevetter, A. A. *Kuznets-grazhdanin (iz epokhi 60-kh godov). Ocherk deiatel'nosti N. A. Miliutina.* 2nd ed. Rostov-on-the Don, 1905.

___. *Posadskaia obshchina v Rossii XVIII stoletiya.* Moscow, 1903.

Kizevetter, A. A., et al. *Moskovskii universitet 1755–1930.* Paris, 1930.

Kniaz'kov, S. A. *19-e [i.e. Deviatnadtsatoe] fevralia 1861 goda.* 2nd. ed. Moscow, 1915.

___. *Kak slozhilos' i kak palo krepostnoe pravo v Rossii. Istoricheskii ocherk.* Edited by A. A. Kizevetter. 2nd. ed. Moscow, 1904.

Kohn, Hans. *Prophets and Peoples: Studies in Nineteenth Century Nationalism.* New York, 1946.

Koleika, Iosef. *Slavianskie programmy i ideia slavianskoi solidarnosti v XIX i XX vekakh.* Prague, 1964.

Kologriwof, Iwan von. *Von Hellas zum Mönchtum. Leben und Denken Konstantin Leontjews (1831–1891).* Regensburg, 1948.

Kornilov, A. A. *Krest'ianskaia reforma.* St. Petersburg, 1905.

___. *Ocherki po istorii obshchestvennago dvizheniia i krest'ianskago dela v Rossii.* St. Petersburg, 1905.

Kornilov, A. A., et al. *Krest'ianskii stroi.* Vol. 1. St. Petersburg, 1905.

Koshelev, A. I. *Chto zhe teper? August 1882.* Berlin, 1882.

___. *Deputaty i redaktsionnyia kommissii po krest'ianskomu delu.* Leipzig, 1862.

___. *Kakoi iskhod dlia Rossii iz nyniashniago eia polozheniia?* Leipzig, 1862.

___. *Konstitutsiia, samoderzhavie i zemskaia duma.* Leipzig, 1862.

___. *Nashe polozhenie.* Berlin, 1875.

___. *Zametki o sudebnoi i administrativnoi reforme v Rossii.* Berlin, 1863.

Koshelev, V. A. *Esteticheskie i literaturnye vozzreniia russkikh slavianofilov (1840–1850-e gody.)* Leningrad, 1984.

Kucharzewski, Jan. *The Origins of Modern Russia.* New York, 1948.

Kuleshov, V. I. *Literaturnye sviazi Rossii i zapadnoi Evropy v XIX veke.* Moscow, 1977.

Kunitz, Joshua. *Russia: The Giant That Came Last.* New York, 1947.

Kurilov, A. S. *K. S. Aksakov I. S. Aksakov. Literaturnaia kritika.* Moscow, 1981.

Labry, Raoul. *Alexandre Ivanovič Herzen 1812–1870 Essai sur la formation et le développement de ses idées.* Paris, 1928.

Lakshin, V. I. *Aleksandr Nikolaevich Ostrovsky.* 2nd ed., Moscow, 1982.

Lednicki, Wactaw. *Russia, Poland, and the West: Essays in Literary and Cultural History.* New York, 1953.

Leighton, L. G. *Russian Romanticism: Two Essays.* The Hague-Paris, 1975.

Leont'ev, K. N. *Sobranie sochinenii.* Edited by I. Fudel'. 8 vols, Moscow, 1912.

Leontovich, V. V. *Istoriia liberalizma v Rossii 1762–1914.* Translated from the German by Irina Ilovaiskaia. General editor, A. I. Solzhenitsyn. Paris, 1980.

Lermontov, M. Iu. *Polnoe sobranie sochinenii.* Edited by B. M. Eikhenbaum. 4 vols. Moscow-Leningrad, 1947–1948.

Leroy-Beaulieu, Anatole. *Un homme d'état russe (Nicholas Milutine)...* Paris, 1884.

Levin, Sh. M., et al., eds. *Kratkii ocherk istorii russkoi kul'tury s drevneishikh vremen do 1917 goda.* Leningrad, 1967.

Lincoln, W. B. *In the Vanguard of Reform: Russia's Enlightened Bureaucrats, 1825–1861.* De Kalb, Ill., 1982.

____. *Nikolai Miliutin, an Enlightened Russian Bureaucrat.* Newtonville, Mass., 1977.

Literaturnoe Nasledstvo. Gertsen i Ogarev. Vol. 62. Moscow, 1955. Also vol. 87. Moscow, 1977.

Lobov, I. *Pamiati Apollona Grigor'eva.* St. Petersburg, 1905.

Lukashevich, Stephen. *Konstantin Leontev (1831–1891): A Study in Russian "Heroic Vitalism."* New York, 1967.

McLean, Hugh, et al., eds. *Russian Thought and Politics.* The Hague, 1957.

MacNaster, R. E. *Danilevsky: A Russian Totalitarian Philosopher.* Cambridge, Mass., 1967.

McNally, R. T., trans. *The Major Works of Peter Chaadaev.* Notre Dame, Ind., 1969.

Maikov, V. N. *Sochineniia v dvukh tomakh.* Edited by G. V. Aleksandrovsky, 2nd ed. Kiev, 1901.

Mann, Iu. V. *Poetika russkogo romantizma.* Moscow, 1976.

Mann, Iu. V., et al., eds. *K. Istorii russkogo romantizma.* Moscow, 1973.

Manuilov, V. A. *Letopis' zhizni i tvorchestva M. Iu. Lermontova.* Moscow-Leningrad, 1964.

Mikhailovsky, N. K. *Sochineniia.* 6 vols. St. Petersburg, 1897. [vol. 4, pp. 434–463 re: Samarin.]

Miliukov, P. N. *Razlozhenie slavianofil'stva. Danilevsky, Leont'ev, Vl. Solov'ev.* Moscow, 1893.

Miller, F. A. *Dmitrii Miliutin and the Reform Era in Russia.* Nashville, Tenn., 1968.

Mitchel, Allan, and Deak, Istvan, eds. *Everyman in Europe: Essays in Social History.* Englewood Cliffs, N. J., 1974.

Mlikotin, A. M., ed. *Western Philosophical Systems in Russian Literature: A Collection of Critical Studies.* Los Angeles, 1979.

Muller, O. N. *Intelligencija. Untersuchungen zur Geschichte eines politischen Schlagwortes.* Frankfurt, 1971.

Nabokov, Vladimir. *Lectures on Russian Literature.* Edited by Fredson Bowers, New York, 1981.

Nahirny, V. C. *The Russian Intelligentsia: From Torment to Silence.* New Brunswick, N.J., 1983.

Nasonkina, I. I. *Moskovskii universitet posle vosstaniia dekabristov.* Moscow, 1972.

Nechkina, M. V., ed. *Revoliutsionnaia situatsiia v Rossii v seredine XIX veka.* Moscow, 1978.

Nikitin, S. A. *Ocherki po istorii iuzhnykh slavian i russko-balkanskikh sviazei v 50–70-e gody XIX v.* Moscow, 1970.

___. *Slavianskie komitety v Rossii v 1858–1876 godakh.* Moscow, 1960.

___. *Zarubezhnye slaviane i Rossiia; dokumenty arkhiva M. F. Raevskogo 40–80 gody XIX veka.* Moscow, 1975.

___. ed. *Slavianskii arkhiv; sbornik statei i materialov.* Moscow, 1962.

___. *Slavianskoe istochnikovedenie; sbornik statei i materialov.* Moscow, 1965.

Nol'de, B. E. *Iurii Samarin i ego vremia.* Paris, 1926.

Offord, Derek. *Portraits of Early Russian Liberals: A Study of the Thought of T. N. Granovsky, V. P. Botkin, P. V. Annenkov, A. V. Druzhinin, and K. D. Kavelin.* Cambridge, Eng., 1985.

Orton, L. D. *The Prague Slav Congress of 1848.* New York, 1978.

Ovsiannikov, M. F., et al., eds. *Russkie esteticheskie traktaty pervoi treti XIX veka.* 2 vols. Moscow, 1974.

Owen, T. C. *Capitalism and Politics in Russia: A Social History of the Moscow Merchants, 1855–1905.* Cambridge, Eng., 1981.

Pascal, Pierre. *Civilisation paysanne en Russie. Six esquisses.* Lausanne, 1969.

Pashkov, A., ed. *Istoriia russkoi ekonomicheskoi mysli.* Moscow, 1958.

Petrovich, M. B. *The Emergence of Russian Panslavism, 1856–1870.* New York, 1956.

Pintner, W. M. *Russian Economic Policy under Nicholas I.* Ithaca, N.Y., 1967.

Pipes, Richard. *Russia under the Old Regime.* London, 1975.

___. *Struve: Liberal on the Left, 1870–1905.* Cambridge, Mass., 1970.

___. *Struve: Liberal on the Right, 1905–1944.* Cambridge, Mass., 1980.

Pirozhkova, T. F. *Revoliutsionery-demodraty o slavianofil'stve i slavianofil'skoi zhurnalistike.* Moscow, 1984.

Pirumova, N. M. *Zemskoe liberal'noe dvizhenie. Sotsial'nye korni i evoliutsiia do nachala XX veka.* Moscow, 1977.

Plekhanov, G. V. *Sochineniia.* Edited by D. Riazanov, 24 vols. Moscow-Leningrad, 1920–1927. *Istoriia russkoi obschestvennoi mysli v XIX veke (materialy),* vol. 23, *kniga pervaia. Zapadniki i Slavianofily.*

Polozhenie 19 fevralia 1861 goda o krest'ianakh, vyshedshikh iz krepostnoi zavisimosti. . . . Moscow, 1916.

Ponomarev, S. I., ed. *Pis'ma M. P. Pogodina k M. A. Maksimovichu.* St. Petersburg, 1882.

Popov, A. N. *Materialy dlia istorii vozmushcheniia Sten'ki Razina.* Moscow, 1857.

___. *Shletser. Razsuzhdenie o russkoi istoriografii,* n.p., n.d.

Porokh, V. I. *Nekotorye voprosy otechestvennoi i vseobshchei istorii.* Saratov, 1971.

Porter, C. H. *Mikhail Petrovich Pogodin and the Development of Russian Nationalism, 1800–1856.* Ph.D. dissertation, 1974.

Poznansky, V. V. *Ocherk formirovaniia russkoi natsional'noi kul'tury. Pervaia polovina XIX veka.* Moscow, 1975.

Rabinowitch, Janet. *The Slavophiles and the Peasant Commune, 1840–1861.* Ph.D. dissertation, Georgetown Univ., 1965.

Rachinsky, S. A., ed. *Tatevskii sbornik.* St. Petersburg, 1899.

Raisky, Leonid. *Sotsial'nye vozzreniia petrashevtsev. Ocherk iz istorii utopicheskogo sotsializma v Rossii.* Leningrad, 1927.

Read, Christopher. *Religion, Revolution, and the Russian Intelligentsiia 1900–1912: The Vekhi Debate and Its Intellectual Background.* New York, 1980.

Reuel', A. L. *Russkaia ekonomicheskaia mysl' 60–70 kh godov XIX veka i marksizm.* Moscow, 1956.

Riasanovsky, Nicholas V. *The Image of Peter the Great in Russian History and Thought.* Oxford, 1985.

___. *Recent Soviet Scholarship on the Slavophiles.* Berkeley, Calif., 1985.

Rieber, A. J. *Merchants and Entrepreneurs in Imperial Russia.* Chapel Hill, N.C., 1982.

___. ed, *The Politics of Autocracy: Letters of Alexander II to Prince A. I. Bariatinskii, 1857–1868.* Paris and the Hague, 1966.

Ruckman, Jo Ann. *The Moscow Business Elite: A Social and Cultural Portrait of Two Generations, 1840–1905.* De Kalb, Ill., 1984.

Perepiska Iu. F. Samarina s baronessoiu E. F. Raden. 2nd. ed. Moscow, 1894.

Samarin, Iurii, and Dmitriev, Fedor. *Revoliutsionnyi konservatizm. Kiniga R. Fadeeva "Russkoe obshchestvo v nastoiashchem i budushchem" i pred-*

lozheniia Peterburgskikh dvorian ob organizatsii vsesoslovnoi volosti. Berlin, 1875.

Schierren, C. C. G. *Livlandische Antwort an Herrn Juri Samarin.* Leipzig, 1869.

Schreider, Alexander. *Ocherki filosofii narodnichestva.* Berlin, 1923.

Semenov, V. P., et al., eds. *Rossiia. Polnoe geograficheskoe opisanie nashego otechestva.* 19 vols. St. Petersburg, 1899–1913.

Senelick, Laurence. *Serf Actor: The Life and Art of Mikhail Shchepkin.* Westport, Conn., 1984.

Shchipanov, I. Ia., et al. *Iz istorii russkoi filosofii. Sbornik statei.* Leningrad, 1952.

Shkurinov, P. C. *Positivizm v Rossii XIX veka.* Moscow, 1980.

Shragin, Boris, ed. *Landmarks: A Collection of Essays on the Russian Intelligentsia 1909...* Translated by Marian Schwartz. New York, 1977.

Shtein, V. M. *Ocherki razvitiia russkoi obshchestvenno-ekonomicheskoi mysli XIX–XX vekov.* Leningrad, 1948.

Sofronenko, K. A., ed. *Krest'ianskaia reforma v Rossii 1861 goda. Sbornik zakonodatel'nykh aktov.* Moscow, 1954.

Solov'ev, A. V. *Holy Russia: The History of a Religious-Social Idea.* The Hague, 1959.

Solov'ev, E. A. *Aksakovykh, ikh zhizn.* St. Petersburg, 1895.

Solov'ev, V. A. *Sobranie sochinenii.* 10 vols., Edited by S. M. Solov'ev and E. L. Radlov. 2nd ed., St. Petersburg, 1873–1900.

Stein, Lorenz Jacob von. *Der Sozialismus und Kommunismus des heutigen Frankreichs. Ein Beitrag zur Zeitgeschichte.* Leipzig, 1842.

Strakhovskii, Iv. *Krest'ianskiia prava i uchrezhdeniia.* St. Petersburg, 1903.

Struve, Gleb. *Russkii evropeets. Materialy dlia biografii i kharakteristiki kniazia P. B. Kozlovskogo.* San Francisco, 1950.

Struve, P. B. *Dukh i slovo. Stat'i o russkoi i zapadno-evropeiskoi literature.* Paris, 1981.

Stupperich, Robert. *Die Anfänge der Bauernbefreiung in Russland.* Berlin, 1939.

___. *Jurij Samarin und die Anfänge der Bauernbefreiung in Russland.* Wiesbaden, 1969.

Thaden, E. C. *Conservative Nationalism in Nineteenth-Century Russia.* Seattle, 1964.

___, ed. *Russificaton in the Baltic Provinces and Finland, 1855–1914.* Princeton, N. J. 1981.

Thaden, E. C., and Thaden, M. F. *Russia's Western Borderlands, 1710–1870.* Princeton, N. J., 1984.

Timberlake, C. E., ed. *Essays on Russian Liberalism.* Columbia, Mo., 1972.

Todd, W. M., III. *Literature and Society in Imperial Russia, 1800–1914.* Stanford, Calif., 1978.

Tsagolov, N. A. *Ocherki russkoi ekonomicheskoi mysli perioda padeniia krepostnogo prava.* Moscow, 1965.

Tsamutali, A. N. *Bor'ba techenii v russkoi istoriografii vo vtoroi polovine XIX veka.* Leningrad, 1977.

Tschizewskij, D., and Osborne, J. C., trans.; Rice, M. P., ed. *Russian Intellectual History.* Ann Arbor, Mich., 1978.

Tsimbaev, N. I. *I. S. Aksakov v obshchestvennoi zhizni poreformennoi Rossii.* Moscow, 1978.

___. *Slavianofil'stvo. Iz istorii russkoi obshestvenno-politicheskoi mysli XIX veka.* Moscow, 1986.

Ursin, M. *Ocherki iz psikhologii slavianskago plemeni. Slavianofily.* St. Petersburg, 1887.

Utechin, S. V. *Russian Political Thought: A Concise History.* New York, 1963.

Valuev, D. A. *Izsledovanie o mestnichestve.* Moscow, 1845.

___. ed. *Sbornik istoricheskikh i statisticheskikh svedenii o Rossii i narodakh ei edinovernykh i edinoplemennykh.* Vol. 1, Moscow, 1845.

Vasil'ev, A., ed. *M. Iu. Lermontov v vospominaniiakh sovremennikov.* Penza, 1960.

Vasl'ev, Ath. *Khomiakov i slavianskoe delo.* St. Petersburg, 1877.

Vengerov, S. A., ed. *Glavnye deiateli osvobozhdeniia krest'ian.* St. Petersburg, 1903.

Venturi, Franco. *Studies in Free Russia.* Translated by F. S. Walsby and M. O. Dell. Chicago, 1982.

Vernadsky, George. *Russian Historiography: A History.* Edited by Sergei Pushkarev, translated by Nicholas Lupinin. Belmont, Mass., 1978.

Vucinich, Alexander. *Science in Russian Culture, 1861–1917.* Stanford, Calif., 1970.

Vucinich, W. S., ed. *The Peasant in Nineteenth-Century Russia.* Stanford, Calif., 1962.

Vucinich, W. S., and Emmons, Terence, eds. *The Zemstvo in Russia: An Experiment in Local Self-Government.* Cambridge, Eng., 1982.

Whittaker, Cynthia H. *The Origins of Modern Russian Education: An Intellectual Biography of Count Sergei Uvarov, 1786–1855.* De Kalb, Ill., 1984.

Whittaker, R. T. *Apollon Aleksandrovich Grigor'ev and the Evolution of "Organic Criticism".* Ph.D. dissertation, Indiana University. 1970.

Woehrlin, Richard. *Chernyshevskii: The Man and the Journalist.* Cambridge, Mass., 1971.

Wortman, Richard. *The Crisis of Russian Populism.* Cambridge, Eng., 1967.

Young, Alexey. *A Man Is His Faith: Ivan Kireevsky and Orthodox Christianity.* London, 1920.

Zaionchkovsky, P. A. *Otmena krepostnogo prava v Rossii.* Moscow, 1960.

___. *Provedenie v zhizn' krestianskoi reformy 1861 g.* Moscow, 1958.

___, ed. *Miliutin, Dmitrii Alekseevich, graf, 1861–1912 Dnevnik.* 4 vols. Moscow, 1947–1950.

___, ed. *Moskovskii universitet v vospominaniiakh sovremennikov.* Moscow, 1956.

Zarubezhnye slaviane i Rossiia. Dokumenty arkhiva M. F. Raevskogo, 40–80-e gody XIX v. Moscow, 1975.

Zeldin, Jesse, ed., trans. *Poems and Political Letters of F. I. Tiutchev.* Knoxville, Tenn., 1973.

Zeldin, Mary-Barbara, trans. *Peter Yakovlevich Chaadayev: Philosophical Letters and Apology of a Madman.* Knoxville, Tenn., 1969.

Zenkovsky, V. V. *O mnimoi materializme russkoi nauki i filosofii.* Munich, 1956.

Zor'kin, V. D. *Iz istorii burzhuazno-liberal'noi politicheskoi mysli Rossii vtoroi poloviny XIX – nachala XX v. (B. N. Chicherin).* Moscow, 1975.

Articles

Aksakov, I. S. "Fedor Ivanovich Tiutchev (1803–1873)." *Russkii arkhiv,* 1874, no. 10, pp. 6–407. [Complete issue.]

___. "Fedor Vasil'evich Chizhov. Iz rechi I. S. Aksakova 18 Dekabria 1877g." *Russkii arkhiv,* 1878, no. 1, pp. 129–137.

___. "Pis'mo k izdateliu po povodu predydushchei stat'i." *Russkii arkhiv,* 1873, no. 12, pp. 2508–2529. [About A. N. Pypin on Slavophilism.]

Aksakova, V. S. "O dispute Iu. F. Samarina. Iz pis'ma Very Sergeevny Aksakovoi v Astrakhan k bratu Ivanu Sergeevichu ot 3-go Iunia. 1844g." *Russkii arkhiv,* 1910, no. 2, pp. 301–303.

Aksakovykh. "Iz semeinoi perepiski starikov Aksakovykh." *Russkii arkhiv,* 1894, no. 9, pp. 99–136. [Thirty letters, 1818–1835.]

Ammon, E. A., ed. "Moskovskii universitet v vospominaniiakh A. N. Afanas'eva. 1843–1849gg." *Russkaia starina,* August, 1886, pp. 357–394.

Annensky, N. F. "N. G. Chernyshevsky i krest'ianskaia reforma." *Velikaia reforma,* vol. 4, pp. 220–279. Moscow, 1911.

Arsen'ev, K. K. "Valerian Maikov. Iz istorii kritiki sorokovykh godov." *Vestnik evropy,* 1886, no. 4, pp. 780–823. [On Maikov's anti-Slavophilism and Belinsky's reply to Maikov's "fantastic cosmopolitanism."]

B. [signed P.B.]. "F. V. Chizhov. K stoletiiu ego pamiati." *Russkii arkhiv,* 1911, book I, pp. 310–312.

Bartenev, Iu. P., ed. "Pis'mo Pal'mera k A. S. Khomiakovu. 1845." *Russkii arkhiv,* 1894, no. 11, pp. 433–444.

Bartenev, P. B. "Sochineniia Iu. F. Samarina. Tom dvenadtsatyi Pis'ma 1840–1853." *Russkii arkhiv,* 1912, no. 2. [Two columns on inside front cover.]

Bartenev, P. I. "A. I. Koshelev." *Russkii arkhiv,* 1884, no. 1, pp. 246–249.

___. *"Sochineniia Iu. F. Samarina. Tom dvenadtsatyi. Pisma 1840–1853."* M. 1911. [Book review.] *Russkii arkhiv,* 1912, no. 2 (inside front cover). [How Samarin felt a stranger in St. Petersburg; could not hear the voice of the peasant; objected to K. S. Aksakov's "Russian" dress.]

___, ed. "Dlia biografii grafa Sergiia Semenovicha Uvarova." *Russkii arkhiv,* 1871, no. 1–12, pp. 2078–2112.

___, ed. "Iz bumag N. P. Giliarova-Platonova." *Russkii arkhiv,* 1889, book III, pp. 263–269, 421–432; 1890, book I, pp. 316–324.

___, ed. "Iz pisem k N. F. Pavlovu ego priatelei." *Russkii arkhiv,* 1892, no. 2, pp. 214–219.

___, ed. "Pervyi priezd Vil'iama Pal'mera v Rossiiu, 1840–1841. (Iz ego zapisok)." *Russkii arkhiv,* 1894, no. 9, pp. 78–98.

___, ed. "Pis'mo I. S. Aksakova k K. P. Pobedonostsevu (o bumagakh A. N. Popova)." *Russkii arkhiv,* 1905, no. 8, pp. 591–592.

Beneš, Václav L. "Bakunin and Palacký's Concept of Austroslavism." *Indiana Slavic Studies,* Bloomington, Ind., 1958, vol. 2, pp. 79–111.

Berlin, Isaiah. "Russian Thought and the Slavophile Controversy." *Slavonic and East European Review,* 1981, no. 4, pp. 572–585.

Bestuzhev-Riumin, K. N. "Aleksander Nikolaevich Popov." *Russkaia starina,* May, 1882, pp. 463–464.

___. "Teoriia kul'turno-istoricheskikh tipov." In N. Ia. Danilevsky, *Rossiia i Evropa,* pp. 559–610. Reprint, New York, 1966.

Bludova. "Vospominaniia grafini Antoniny Dmitrievny Bludovoi (pisany v 1867 godu)." *Russkii arkhiv,* 1889, book I, pp. 39–106. [Favorable characterizations of the early Slavophils.]

Bochkarev, V. N. "Iurii Fedorovich Samarin." *Velikaia reforma.* Moscow, 1911, vol. 5, pp. 92–107.

Brooks, J. *"Vekhi* and the Vekhi Dispute." *Survey,* 1971, no. 1, pp. 41–58.

Buslaev, F. I. "Moi vospominaniia." *Vestnik Evropy,* December, 1890, pp. 513–548. [On Samarin's family in the 1840s.]

___. "M. P. Pogodin kak professor." In *Sochineniia Ivana Pososhkova,* ed. Mikhail Pogodin, pp. 3–19, Moscow, 1842. [On Pogodin's high opinion of Samarin as a student.]

Butkovsky, A. N. "Obshchinnoe vladenie i sobstvennost'." *Russkii vestnik,* 1858, book I, no. 7, pp. 5–59. [On Samarin's health; Haxthausen and Sain Simon's utopia in Russia.]

Chaadaev, P. Ia. "Neizdannyia rukopisi." *Vestnik Evopry.* 1871, no.11, pp. 324–344. [Chaadaev's reaction to Samarin's defense of his dissertation, 1844.]

Cherkassky, V. A. "Nekotorye obshchie cherty budushchego sel'skogo upravleniia." *Sel'skoe blagoustroistvo,* 1858, no. 2, pp. 250–260.

___. "O droblenii pozemel'noi sobstvennosti pis'mo kniaza V. A. Cherkaskago k kniaziu S. N. Urosovu." *Russkii arkhiv,* 1884, no. 4, pp. 270–279. [On dim future of commune.]

Chicherin, B. N. "O norodnosti v nauke." *Russkii vestnik,* 1856, May, book I, pp. 62–71; September, book I, pp. 8–27.

Chizov, F. V. "F. V. Chizhov k khudozhniku A. A. Ivanovu." ed. P. I. Bartenev, 1884, no. 2, pp. 391–422.

___. "Vospominaniia F. V. Chizhova." Intr. V. I. Lamansky. *Istoricheskii vestnik,* February, 1883, pp. 241–262.

___. "Zapiski o Gogole v dnevnikakh F. V. Chizhova." *Literaturnoe nasledstvo,* Moscow, 1952, no. 58, pp. 776–785.

Christoff, P. K. "A. S. Khomiakov on the Agricultural and Industrial Problem in Russia." In A. D. Ferguson and Alfred Levin, eds., *Essays in Russian History: A Collection Dedicated to George Vernadsky,* pp. 129–159, Hamden, Conn., 1964.

Davydov, V. D. "Samarin-opolchenets. (Iz vospominanii ego druzhinnago nachal'nika po opolcheniiu 1855g.)" *Russkii arkhiv,* 1877, no. 5, pp. 42–49.

De-Vollan, G. A. "Ocherki proshlago." *Golos munivshago,* 1914, no. 2, pp. 170–190; no. 4, pp. 122–153. [On Russia's support of war of 1877–1878; Slav committees.]

Dowler, Wayne. "Echoes of Pochvennichestvo in Solzhenitsyn's *August 1914.*" *Slavic Review,* March 1975, pp. 109–122.

Dudzinskaia, E. A. "Die Auslandsreisen A. I. Koselevs in den dreiziger und vierziger Jahren des 19. Jahrhunderts." In Wolfgang Kessler, ed., *Reisen und Reisenbeschreibungen im 18. und 19. Jahrhundert als Quellen der Kulturbeziehungsforschung,* pp. 101–116, Berlin, 1980.

___. "Die Bauernfrage in der Russischen Publizistik am Vorabend der Reform von 1861 in Russland" in Dan Berindei et al. *Der Bauer Mittel- und Osteuropas im Sozio-Okonomischen Wandel des 18. und 19. Jahrhunderts* . . . Koln Wien, 1973, pp. 327–350.

___. "Burzhuaznye tendentsii v teorii i praktike slavianofilov." *Voprosy istorii,* 1972, no. 1, pp. 49–64.

___. "Evropa glazami russkogo puteshestvennika." *Problemy istorii russkogo obshchestvennogo dvizheniia i istoricheskoi nauki,* pp. 68–76, Moscow, 1981. [On A. I. Koshelev.]

___. "Ideino-teoreticheskie pozitsii slavianofilov nakanune krest'ianskoi reformy." *Istoriia SSSR,* vol. 5, pp. 139–160. Moscow, 1972.

___. "Obshchestvennaia i khoziaistvennaia deiatel'nost' Slavianofila Iu F. Samarina v 40–50-kh godakh XIX v." *Istoricheskie zapiski,* 1984, no. 110, pp. 312–333.

___. "Der 'preussische Weg' in den Schriften des Slawophilen Ju. F. Samarin." In Wolfgang Kessler et al., trans., ed., *Kulturbeziehungen in*

Mittel-und Osteuropa im 18. und 19. Jahrhundert, pp. 245–250, Berlin, 1982.

___. Russkie slavianofily i zarubezhnoe slavianstvo." In V. A. Diakov et al., eds., *Metodologicheskie problemy istorii slavistiki,* pp. 261–281, Moscow, 1978.

___. "Slavianofily i istoricheskoe pravo krest'ian na zemliu." In V. P. Zagorovsky, ed., *Sotsial'no-politicheskoe i pravovoe polozhenie krest'ianstva v dorevoliutsionnoi Rossii,* pp. 24–31, Voronezh, 1983.

___. "Slavianofily na stranitsakh gertsenovskikh izdanii." In M. V. Nechkina et al., eds., *Revoliutsionnaia situatsiia v seredine XIX veka: deiateli i istoriki,* pp. 75–85, Moscow, 1986.

___. "U istokov formirovaniia antikrepostnicheskikh vozzrenii A. I. Kosheleva." In I. P. Popov, ed., *Obshchestvennoe dvizhenie v tsentral'nykh guberniiakh Rossii v vtoroi polovine XIX–nachale XX vv,* pp. 3–21, Riazan, 1984.

Efimova, M. T. "Iu. Samarin i ego otnoshenii k Lermontovu." *Pushkinskii sbornik,* pp. 40–47. Pskov, 1968.

___. "Iu. Samarin o Gogole." In E. A. Maimin, ed., *Pushkin i ego sovremenniki,* pp. 135–147. Pskov, 1970.

___. "Tema 'Pushkin i slavianofily' v Pushkinovedenie." *Pushkinskii sbornik,* pp. 15–22. Pskov, 1968.

Egorov, B. F. "Samarin, Iurii Fedorovich." In D. S. Likhachev et al., eds., *Russkie pisateli,* pp. 582–584. Moscow, 1971.

Engels, Friedrich. "Industrialism and Slums." In H. H. Rowen, ed., *From Absolutism to Revolution 1648–1848,* pp. 306–310. 2nd ed., New York, 1968.

"Epizod iz istorii Slavianofil'stva 1852–1853." *Russkaia starina,* October, 1875, pp. 367–379. [A review of the Slavophil "Moskovskii Sbornik" of 1852.]

Every, E. "Khomiakov and the Encyclical of the Eastern Patriarchs in 1848." *The Christian East,* London, 1984, no. 3, pp. 102–104.

Evreinov, B. A. "Iu. F. Samarin v Prage v 1867–68gg. (Po materialam prazhskoi politsii)." *Sbornik russkago instituta v Prage,* 1929, vol. I, pp. 333–350.

Florovsky, G. V. "The Historical Premonitions of Tyutchev. (For the 50th anniversary of His death, 15 July 1873)." *Slavonic Review,* December, 1924, pp. 337–349.

___. "Reason and Faith in the Philosophy of Solov'ev." In E. J. Simmons, ed., *Continuity and Change in Russian and Soviet Thought,* pp. 283–297. Cambridge, Mass., 1955.

Foerster, Freidrich W. "Pangermanism." In Feliks Gross, ed., *European Ideologies,* pp. 742–762. New York, 1948.

Frantsev, V. A. "Iz istorii slavianskoi literaturnoi vzaimnosti. Kollar i russkie uchenye v Zagrebe (1840–1841)." *Sbornik russkago instituta v Prage,* 1929, vol. I, pp. 91–118.

Gaidenkov, N. M. "Pavlova (Ianish) Karolina Karlovna." In D. S. Likhachev et al, eds., *Russkie pisateli,* pp. 502–505. Moscow, 1971.

Gerasimova, Iu. I. "Nachalo krizisa 'verkhov.' Pristup pravitel'stva k reformam (1853–1855gg.)." In M. V. Nechkina, ed., *Revoliutsionnaia situatsiia v Rossii v seredine XIX veka,* pp. 113–132. Moscow, 1978.

_____. "Otnoshenie pravitel'stva k uchastiiu pechati v obsuzhdenii krest'ianskogo voprosa v period revoliutsionnoi situatsii kontsa 50-kh – nachala 60-kh godov XIX v." *Revoliutsionnaia situatsiia v Rossii v 1859–1861 gg.,* pp. 81–105. Moscow, 1974.

_____. "Slavianofil'skii zhurnal "Sel'skoe blagoustroistvo' i ego krest'ianskaia programma (1858–1859 gg.)." In M. V. Nechkina, ed., *'Epokha Chernyshevskogo.' Revolutsionnaia situatsiia v Rossii v 1859–1861 gg.,* pp. 181–193. Moscow, 1978.

Gershtein, E. G. "Lermontov i 'kruzhok shestnadtsati'." In N. L. Brodsky et al, eds., *Zhizn' i tvorchestvo M. Iu. Lermontova. Issledovaniia i materialy,* vol. I, pp. 77–124. Moscow, 1941.

Gil'ferding, A. F. "Iz perepiski A. F. Gil'ferdinga s I. S. Aksakovym (K tridtsatiletiiu so dnia smerti I. S. Aksakova)." *Golos minuvshago,* 1916, no. 2, pp. 201–214. [First letter reveals disagreements between the two men.]

Giliarov-Platonov, N. P. "Iz bumag N. P. Giliarov-Platonova." *Russkii arkhiv,* 1889, book III, pp. 263–269. [On Khomiakov and Samarin; on the "neo-Slavophils."]

_____. "Iz bumag N. P. Giliarova-Platonova. Pis'ma k odnomu iz ego chitatelei." *Russkii arkhiv,* 1890, book I, pp. 316–324. [About Russian translation of Khomiakov's theological works.]

Glinsky, B. B. "A. S. Khomiakov pred sudom potomstva (K 100-letiiu so dnia ego rozhdeniia)." *Istoricheskii vestnik,* June, 1904, pp. 912–924.

Gogol', N. V. "Nikolai Vasil'evich Gogol' v ego neizdannykh pis'makh." Ed. V. I. Shenrok and A. A. Gatsuk, *Russkaia starina,* 1889, no. 1, pp. 141–158. [On Slavophil efforts to get Gogol' to contribute to Slavophil *zbornik,* 1846.]

Golitsyn, N. V., ed. "P. Ia. Chaadaev i E. A. Sverbeeva (Iz neizdannykh bumag Chaadaeva)." *Vestnik Evropy,* 1918, no. 1–4, pp. 233–254.

Golubev, A. N. "Poniatie lichnosti v etike Vladimira Solov'eva." *Voprosy filosofii,* 1978, no. 3, pp. 125–136.

Gol'berg, M. Ia. "K istorii polemiki vokrug slavianofil'skogo poslaniia 'K Serbam.'" In V. I. Freidzon, ed., *Voprosy pervonachal'nogo nakopleniia kapitala i natsional'nye dvizheniia v slavianskikh stranakh,* pp. 197–209. Moscow, 1972.

Gradovsky, A. D. "Liberalizm i zapadnichestvo." *Sobrannie sochinenii,* vol. 6, pp. 394–400. St. Petersburg, 1901.

___. "Pamiati Iuriia Fedorovicha Samarina." *Sobranie sochinenii,* vol. 9, pp. cxlv–cliii. St. Petersburg, 1904.

___. "Pervye slavianofily." *Sobranie sochinenii,* vol. 6, pp. 160–224. St. Petersburg, 1901. *[Four public lectures.]*

___. "Po povodu odnogo predisloviia, N. Strakhov. Bor'ba s Zapadom v nashei literature. Spb. 1882g." *Sobranie sochinenii,* vol. 6, pp. 424–440. St. Petersburg, 1901.

___. "Slavianofil'skaia teoriia gosudarstva (Pis'mo v redaktsiiu)." *Sobranie sochinenii,* vol. 6, pp. 412–423. St. Petersburg, 1901. [To *Golos.*]

___. "Staroe i novoe slavianofil'stvo." *Sobranie sochinenii,* vol. 6, pp. 265–272. St. Petersburg, 1901.

Granjard, Henri. "Du Romantisme politique: Slavophiles et Populistes." *Revue des etudes slaves,* 1957, vol. 34, pp. 73–80.

Grigorovich, D. V. "Literaturnyia vospominaniia." *Russkaia mysl',* 1893, no. 1, pp. 1–41; no. 2, pp. 49–82. [On Ostrovsky circle.]

Ia. [signed, V. Ia.]. "19 fevrialia 1861g." *Russkaia Starina,* 1911, no. 1–3, pp. 419–456. [On Samarin's and Cherkassky's appointment to editorial commissions; Samarin's part in the emancipation proclamation.]

Iakovlev, N., ed. "Faddei Bulgarin." *Epigrama i satira. Iz istorii literaturnoi borby XIXgo veka 1800–1840,* vol. 1, pp. 361–396. Moscow-Leningrad, 1931.

Iakushkin, V. E. "N. A. Miliutin i redaktsionnyia komissii." *Russkie starina,* October, 1897, pp. 139–158. [On Samarin-Miliutin relationship.]

Iakushin, N. I. "Sollogub, Vladimir Aleksandrovich." In D. S. Likhachev et al, eds., *Russkie pisateli,* pp. 600–601. Moscow, 1971.

Ianov, A. L. "Slavianofily i Konstantin Leont'ev (Russkaia konservativnaia mysl' XIXv. i ee interpretatory)." *Voprosy filosofii,* 1969, no. 8, pp. 97–106.

Iazykov, N. M. "Iz pisem N. M. Iazykova k bratu ego Aleksandru Mikhailovichu." Ed. Shenrok, V. I., *Russkaia starina,* March, 1903, pp. 529–539. [Young Samarin characterized.]

Ignatovich, I. I. "Krest'ianskiia volneniia." *Velikaia reforma. Russkoe obshchestvo i krest'ianskii vopros v proshlom i nastoiashchem,* Vol. 3, pp. 41–65. Moscow, 1911.

Ikonnikov, V. S. "Russkie universitety v sviazi s khodom obshchestvennago obrazovaniia." *Vestnik Evropy,* 1876, no. 9, pp. 161-2-6; no. 10, pp. 492–550; no. 11, pp. 73–132. [On Samarin's dissertation, 1844.]

Iudin, P. L. "Sem' let neurozhainykh (Iz istorii samarskikh golodovok)." *Russkaia starina,* October, 1909, pp. 140–152. [On Samarin's part in fighting hunger, turn of 1860s.]

Ivanov, I. "Kniaz, Vladimir Aleksandrovich Cherkasky," *Russkaia starina,* 1890, no. 11, p. 382. [Obituary notice.]

Ivantsov-Platonov, A. "Predislovie, " to Samarin's *Sochineniia.* vol. 5, pp. vii–xxxiv. [A biographical, religious, ideological essay.]

K. [signed A.P.K.]. "Ocherk istorii raskreposhcheniia pomeshchich'ikh krest'ian." *Russkii arkhiv,* 1911, book I, pp. 313–318. [On Slavophil views on emancipation.]

___. "Sviatoe delo raskreposhcheniia pomeshchich'ikh krest'ian." *Russkii arkhiv,* 1911, book I, pp. 97–504. [Samarin prominently mentioned.]

Karpovich, Michael. "Two Types of Russian Liberalism: Maklakov and Miliukov." In E. J. Simmons, ed., *Continuity and Change in Russian and Soviet Thought,* pp. 129–143. Cambridge, Mass., 1955.

Katkov, M. N. "Pis'ma M. N. Katkova k A. N. Popovu 1843–1847." *Russkii arkhiv,* 1888, book II, pp. 480–499. [Information about the early Slavophils.]

Kavelin, K. D. "Iurii Fedorovich Samarin. Nekrolog." *Vestnik Evropy,* 1876, no. 4, pp. 906–910.

___. "Pozemel'naia obshchina v drevnei i novoi Rossii." *Vestnik Evropy,* 1876, no.5, pp. 200–233.

___. "Psikhologicheskaia kritika. Zamechaniia Iu. F. Samarina na knigu 'Zadachi psikhologii.'" *Vestnik Evropy,* 1875, May, pp. 361–191; June, pp. 777–791; July, pp. 333–355.

Kerimov, V. I., Poliakov, L. V. V. A. Koshelev. Esteticheskie i literaturnye vozzreniia russkikh slavianofilov (1840–1850-e gody) Leningrad, 1984." *Voprosy filosofii,* 1986, no. 6, pp. 166–169. [Book review.]

Khomiakov, A. S. "Ob otmene krepostnago prava v Rossii, Pis'mo Alekseia Stepanovicha Khomiakova k (grafu) Ia. I. Rostovtsevu (1858)." *Russkii arkhiv,* 1878, no. 3, pp. 277–296.

___. "Otzyv A. S. Khomiakova o K. D. Kaveline." Ed. M. A. Venevitinov. *Russkii arkhiv,* 1885, book II, pp. 335–336. [On Khomiakov's attitude toward the younger Slavophils Samarin, A. N. Popov, and D. A. Valuev.]

___. "Pis'ma." Ed. I. S. Aksakov. *Russkii arkhiv,* 1879, no. 11, pp. 301–304.

___. "Pis'ma A. S. Khomiakova k Iu. F. Samarinu." Ed. I. S. Aksakov. *Russkii arkhiv,* 1879, no. 11, pp. 301–353.

___. "Pol'skii vopros. Pis'mo A. S. Khomiakova k A. O. Smirnovoi." *Russkaia mysl',* 1881, book III, pp. 305–308. Part II, pp. 309–326.

Kirpichnikov, A. I. "Mezhdu Slavianofilami i Zapadnikami. N. A. Mel'gunov. Istoriko-literaturnyi ocherk po neizdannym dokumentam." *Russkaia starina,* 1898, no. 11, pp. 297–330; no. 12, pp. 551–585.

Klier, J. D. "The Jewish Question in the Reform Era Russian Press, 1855–1865." *Russian Review,* July, 1980, pp. 301–319.

Kline, George L. "Darwinism and the Russian Orthodox Church." In E. J. Simmons, ed., *Continuity and Change in Russian and Soviet Thought,* pp. 307–328. Cambridge, Mass., 1955.

___. "Les Interpretations russes de Spinoza (1796–1862) et leurs sources allemandes." In *Spinoza entre lumiere et romantisme,* pp. 361–377. Les Cahiers de Fontenay, 1985.

___. "Russian Religious Thought." In *Nineteenth Century Religious Thought in the West,* vol. 2, pp. 179–229. Ninian Smart et al., eds., Cambridge, Eng., 1985.

Kohn, Hans. "Dostoevsky and Danilevsky: Nationalist Messianism." In E. J. Simmons, ed., *Continuity and Change in Russia and Soviet Thought,* pp. 500–515. Cambridge, Mass., 1955.

Kolchin, Peter. "In Defense of Servitude: American Proslavery and Russian Proserfdom Arguments, 1760–1860." *American Historical Review,* October, 1980, pp. 809–827.

Kornilov, A. A. "Iurii Fedorovich Samarin." *Ocherki po istorii obshchestvennago dvizheniia i krest'ianskago dela v Rossii,* pp. 453–473. St. Petersburg, 1905.

Korsakov, D. A. "Pogodin, Mikhail Petrovich." *Russkii biograficheskii slovar',* St. Petersburg, 1905, vol. Plavil'shchikov-Primo, pp. 154–166.

___. ed., "K 50-tiletiiu osvobozhdeniia krest'ian. Korlovskoe imenie Velikoi Kniagini Eleny Pavlovny. (Posviashchaetsia pamiati K. D. Kavelina)." *Russkaia starina,* 1912, February, pp. 303–307, March, pp. 633–651. [Korsakov states that up to 1912, 2170 of Samrarin's letters were collected.]

Korsakov, V. "Raden, baronessa Edita Fedorovna." *Russkii biograficheskii slovar',* St. Petersburg, 1910, vol. 15, pp. 369–371.

Koshelev, A. I. "Pis'ma A. I. Kosheleva k A. N. Popovu." Ed. P. I. Bartenev, *Russkii arkhiv,* 1886, no. 3, pp. 352–362.

___. "Poezdka russkago zemledel'tsa v Angliiu i na vsemirnuiu vystavku." *Moskovskii sbornik,* Moscow, 1852, pp. 145–243.

___. "Soobrazheniia kasatel'no ustroistva zheleznykh dorog v Rossii. (*Sovrem.* 1856 goda. No. 2-ii)." *Russkaia beseda,* 1856, Vol 1, kritika, pp. 148–157.

___. "Eshche soobrazheniia kasatel'no ustroistva zheleznykh dorog v Rossi. (*Sovremennik.* Sentiabr 1856. Otvet *Russkoi besede,* no. 1.)" *Russkaia beseda,* 1856, vol. 3, kritika, pp. 88–112.

Koshelev, V. A. "Novye raboty o russkom slavianofil'stve." *Russkaia literatura,* 1979, no. 1, pp. 199–211.

Kostomarov, N. I. "O Kazakakh. (Po povodu stat'i P. A. Kulisha, napechatannoi v 3-i i 6-i tetriadakh '*Russkago arkhiva*' izd. 1877 goda)." *Russkaia starina,* 1878, vol. 21, pp. 385–402. [Contains Kostomarov's high opinion of Samarin.]

Kozlovsky, L. S. "Mechty o Tsar'grade (Dostoevsky i K. Leont'ev)." *Golos Minuvshago*, 1915, no. 2, pp. 88–116; no. 11, pp. 44–74.

Koz'menko, I. V., ed. "Dnevnik F. K. Chizhova 'Puteshestvie po slavianskim zemliam' kak istochnik." *Slavianskii arkhiv. Sbornik statei i materialov*, pp. 127–260. Moscow, 1958.

Kuchumova, L. I. "Sel'skaia pozemel'naia obshchina evropeiskoi Rossii v 60–70-e gody XIX v." *Istoricheskie zapiski*, Moscow, 1981, no. 106, pp. 323–347.

Kuibyshev, K. S. "Krupnaia moskovskaia burzhuaziia v period revoliutsionnoi situatsii 1859–1861gg." *Revoliutsionnaia situatsiia v Rossii 1859–1861gg*, pp. 314–341. Moscow, 1965.

Kulesha, Stepan. "Aleksandr Viktorovich Rahcinsky." *Russkaia starina*, October, 1880, pp. 433–436. [Contains high praise of Samarin.]

Kuleshov, V. I. "Slavianofily i romantizm." In Iu. F. Mann et al., eds., *K istorii russkogo romantizma*, pp. 305–344. Moscow, 1973.

Lampert, E. "*Vekhi* and the Vekhovtsy: A Critical Re-examination." *New Zealand Slavonic Journal*, 1978, no. 2, pp. 41–58.

Laverychev, V. Ia. "Russkie kapitalisty i periodicheskaia pechat' vtoroi poloviny XIX v." *Istoriia SSSR*, 1972, no. 1, pp. 26–47.

Leskov, N. C. "Russkie deiateli v ostzeiskom krae (Svoi i chuzhiia nabliudeniia, opyty, zametki)." *Istoricheskii vestnik*, 1883, no. 11, pp. 238–263. [In this and other installments Samarin is often mentioned.]

Lilly, Ian, K. "N. M. Iazykov as a Slavophile Poet." *Slavic Review*, 1972, no. 4, pp. 797–804.

Lincoln, W. B. "The Circle of the Grand Duchess Yelena Pavlovna, 1847–1861." *Slavonic and East European Review*. July, 1970, pp. 373–387.

Linnichenko, I. A. "Patriarkh russkago slavianovedeniia. (Vladimir Ivanovich Lamansky)." *Golos minuvshago*, 1915, no. 2, pp. 244–253.

"Liubopytnyia pokazaniia o nekotorykh predstaviteliakh moskovskago obrazovannago obshchestva v nachale proshlago tsarstvovaniia." *Russkii arkhiv*, 1885, book II, pp. 447–452. [On the government's suspicions and mistrust of Slavophils.]

Lockhart, Robert Bruce, Sir. "The Russians and Ourselves: The Scots in Russia." *Penguin Russian Review*, 1948, no. 4, pp. 65–78.

Lossky, N. O. "The Philosophy of Vladimir Solovyev." *Slavonic Review*, December, 1923, pp. 346–358. [Solov'ev continued Slavophil work "on a wider scale."]

MacMaster, R. E. "Danilevsky and Spengler: A New Interpretation." *Journal of Modern History*, 1954, no. 2, pp. 154–161.

___. "The Question of H. Ruckert's Influence on Danilevskij." *American Slavic and East European Journal*, 1955, vol. 14, pp. 59–66.

Maikov, P. M. "Cherkassky, kniaz' Vladimir Aleksandrovich." *Russkii biograficheskii slovar'*, St. Petersburg, 1905, vol. 22, pp. 198–208.

____. "Popov, Aleksandr Nikolaevich." *Russkii biograficheskii slovar'*, St. Petersburg, 1905, vol. Plavil'shchikov-Primo, pp. 514–517.

Malia, M. E. "Herzen and the Peasant Commune." In E. J. Simmons, ed., *Continuity and Change in Russian and Soviet Thought*, pp. 197–217. Cambridge, Mass., 1955.

Mamonov, E. "Slavianofily. Istoriko-kriticheskii ocherk. (Po povodu stat'i g-na Pypina)." *Russkii arkhiv*, 1873, no. 12, pp. 2488–2508.

Matossian, Mary. "The Peasant Way of Life." In W. S. Vucinich, ed., *The Peasant in Nineteenth-Century Russia*, pp. 1–40. Stanford, Calif., 1968.

Mikhailovsky, N. K. "Pis'ma o pravde i nepravde." *Sochineniia*, vol. 4, pp. 381–464. St. Petersburg, 1897.

Miliutin, A. N. "Nikolai Alekseevich Miliutin v ego zabotakh o krest'ianskom i sudebnom dele v tsarstve Pol'skom. K Ia. A. Solov'evu." Ed. M. A. Stil', *Russkaia starina*, 1884, vol. 422 pp. 585–594. [Miliutin critical of Koshelev; his, Samarin's, and Cherkassky's dissatisfaction with emancipation reform.]

Miliutina, M. A. "Iz zapisok Marii Aggeevny Miliutinoi." *Russkaia starina*, 1899, no. 1, pp. 39–65; no. 2, pp. 264–288; no. 3, pp. 575–601; no. 4, pp. 105–127.

Modzalevsky, B. L. "Panov, Vasilii Alekseevich." *Russkii biograficheskii slovar'*, St. Petersburg, 1905, vol. 12, pp. 261–262.

Modzalevsky, Vadim. "Chizhov, Fedor Vasil'evich." *Russkii biograficheskii slovar'*, St. Petersburg, 1905, vol. 22, pp. 376–381.

Muller, Eberhard. "Zwischen Liberalismus und utopischem Sozialismus Slavophile sozialtheoretische Perspektiven zur Reform vor 1861." *Jarbucher fur Geschichte Osteuropas*, 1965, Heft 4, pp. 511–530.

Nikitin, S. A. "Slavianskie s"ezdy shestidesiatikh godov XIX veka." In N. M. Druzhinin, ed., *Slavianskii sbornik: Slavianskii vopros i russkoe obshchestvo v 1867–1878 godakh*, Moscow, 1948.

Nosov, S. N. "Dva istochnika po istorii rannego slavianofil'stva." (Zapiska A. S. Khomiakova 'O starom i novom' i otvet I. V. Kireevskogo)." *Vspomogatel'nye istoricheskie distsipliny*, Leningrad, 1978, X, pp. 252–268.

____. "K voprosu o formirovanii obshchinnoi teorii rannego slavianofil'stva (po sledam perepiski mezhdu A. S. Khomiakovym i A. I. Koshelevym)." *Vestnik leningradskogo universiteta*. Istoriia-iazyk-literatura. 1980, no. 20, pp. 16–20.

____. "Novye tendentsii i starye problemy (Obzor noveishei sovetskoi literatury o slavianofil'stve)." *Russkaia literatura*, 1984, no. 2, pp. 202–210.

____. "Pervye istoricheskie sochineniia Konstantina Aksakova." *Istoricheskie zapiski*, Moscow, 1981, no. 106, pp. 271–290.

___. "Pis'ma Apollona Grigor'eva kak istochnik po istorii slavianofil'stva." *Vspomogatel'nye istoricheskie distsipliny,* Leningrad, 1981, no. 12, pp. 110–140.

___. "Vazhnyi dokument ob otnoshenii slavianofilov k revoliutsii 1848 g." *Vspomogatel'nye istoricheskie distsipliny.* Leningrad, 1979, XI, pp. 163–171.

Novgorodtsev, Paul. "On Slavonic Reciprocity." *Slavonic Review,* March, 1923, pp. 447–503.

"O polednikh dniakh zhiznin i konchine kniazia V. A. Cherkasskago." *Russkii arkhiv,* 1878, book II,, pp. 227–239.

"Ob Ukraino-Slavianskom Obshchestve. (Graf S. S. Uvarov i graf S. S. Stroganov). 1847-god." *Russkii arkhiv,* 1893, no. 7, pp. 347–355.

Obelensky, D. A. "Moi vospominaniia o Velikoi Kniagine Elene Pavlovne." *Russkaia starina,* 1909, March, pp. 503–528; April, pp. 37–62; May, pp. 260–277. [On Samarin and the Slavophils.]

___. "Nabroski iz vospominanii kniazia D. a. Obolenskago." Ed. P. I. Bartenev, *Russkii arkhiv,* 1894, no. 12, pp. 581–589. [On Samarin and Slavophil defense of commune.]

Ostrovsky, A. A., ed. "Materialy po istorii russkoi literatury i kul'tury. Iz perepiski deiatelei epokhi osvobozhdeniia krest'ian." *Russkaia Mysl',* March, 1911, pp. 113–115. [Samarin on early peasant reaction to emancipation.]

Palmer, William. "Pis'mo Pal'mera k A. S. Khomiakovu." *Russkii arkhiv,* 1894, no. 11, pp. 433–456. [Written in 1845 in English.]

Panov, V. A. "Biografiia D. A. Volueva." *Russkii arkhiv,* 1899, no. 9, pp. 130–139.

Pavlov, N. M., ed. "Iz perepiski A. O. Smirnovoi s Aksakovymi." *Russkii arkhiv,* 1896, no. 1, pp. 142–160. [On conflict between K. Aksakov and Samarin over latter's government service.]

___. "Gogol' i slavianofily (Po povodu prilagaemykh pisem K. S. Aksakova)." *Russkii arkhiv,* 1890, book I, pp. 139–152.

Pavlov, V. N. "Recent Soviet Reinterpretations of Slavophilism: Debates on the Russian National Heritage." (Unpublished manuscript. 17p.)

___. "Spory o slavianofil'stve i russkom patriotizme v sovetskoi nauchnoi literature 1969–1970 gg." *Grani,* 1972, no. 82, pp. 183–211.

Pavlova, Karolina. "Moi vospominaniia." *Russkii arkhiv,* 1875, no. 10, pp. 222–240.

___. "Karolina Pavlova." *Karolina Pavlova. Polnoe sobranie stikhotvorenii,* ed. Pavel P. Gromov, Moscow-Leningrad, 1964, pp. 5–72.

Perovsky, V. A. "Pis'mo V. A. Perovskago k Iu. F. Samarinu." *Russkii arkhiv,* 1878, no. 3, pp. 379–380. [References to Samarin's imprisonment in 1849.]

Petrovich, M. B. "Russian Pan-Slavists and the Polish Uprising of 1863." *Harvard Slavic Studies*, vol. I, Cambridge, Mass., 1953, pp. 219–247.

Picheta, V. I., ed. "Pis'ma M. G. Cherniaeva i P. S. Kulikovskago k I. S. Aksakovu o Servii v 1880–1882 g." *Golos munuvshago*, 1915, no. 9, pp. 232–249. [Picheta stresses Slavophil negative attitude toward Catholic Poland, and Serbian desire for political and cultural independence.]

Pipes, Richard. "Russian Conservatism in the Second Half of the Nineteenth Century." *Slavic Review*, March, 1971, pp. 121–128.

Plakans, Andrejs. "Peasants, Intellectuals, and Nationalism in the Russian Baltic Provinces, 1820–1890." *Journal of Modern History*, 1974, no. 3, pp. 445–475.

Pogodin, M. P. "Petr Pervyi i natsional'noe organicheskoe razvitie." *Russkii vestnik*, 1862.

___. "Pis'ma M. P. Pogodina k V. A. Zhukovskomu 1829–1846." Ed. P. I. Bartenev. *Russkii arkhiv*, 1899, no. 10, pp. 300–310.

Pokrovsky, M. N. "Krest'ianskaia reforma." In A. I. Granat, ed., *Istoriia Rossii v XIX veke*, vol. 3, pp. 68–178. N.p. n.d.

___. "Vostochnyi vopros. Ot parizhskago mira do berlinskago kongresa. (1856–1878)." In A. I. Granat, ed., *Istoriia Rossii v XIX veke*, vol. 6, pp. 1–68. St. Petersburg, n.d., [Leont'ev considered a Slavophil.]

Popov, A. "General Moro na sluzhbe v russkikh voiskakh. (Biograficheskiia svedeniia o A. N. Popove)." *Russkaia starina*, January, 1910, pp. 191–197. [Information on A. N. Popov-Khomiakov relationship.]

Popov, I. P. "Liberal'no-burzhuaznyi lager' (1853–1858 gg.)" In M. V. Nechkina, ed., *Revoliutsionnaia situatsiia v Rossii v seredine XIX veka*, pp. 83–99. Moscow, 1978.

Popov, N. A. "Osip Maksimovich Bodiansky v 1831–1849 godakh." *Russkaia starina*, November, 1879, pp. 461–480.

Porokh, I. V., Porokh, Vl. I. "Gertsen i I. Aksakov na rubezhe 50–60-kh godov XIXv." In M. V. Nechkina et al., eds. *Revoliutsionnaia situatsiia v Rossii v seredine XIX veka: deiateli i istoriki*, pp. 85–102. Moscow, 1986.

Pospelovsky, D. "A Comparative Enquiry into Neo-Slavophilism and Its Antecedents." *Soviet Studies*, July, 1979, pp. 319–342.

Prokhorova, Aleksandra. "K zhizneopisaniiu F. V. Chizhova. Ego roditeli i sestry." *Russkii arkhiv*, 1907, no. 4, pp. 623–634.

Protopopov, M. A. "Zapiski i dnevnik (1826–1877 gg.) A. V. Nikitenka." *Russkaia mysl'*, 1893, no. 6, pp. 214–234; no. 7, pp. 186–203.

Pypin, A. N. "Kharakteristiki literaturnykh mnenii ot dvadtsatykh do piatidesiatykh godov. Istoricheskie ocherki." *Vestnik Evropy*, 1871, book IX, pp. 301–351, book XII, pp. 455–514; 1872, book XI, pp. 47–97; book XII, pp. 618–678. [The last two installments are devoted to Slavophilism.]

Raeff, Marc. "Georges Samarin et la commune paysanne apres 1861." *Revue des etudes slaves*, 1952, vol. 29, pp. 71–81.

Raevskaia, E. I. "Iz vospominanii E. I. Raevskoi." *Russkii arkhiv,* 1896, no. 2, pp. 220–240. [Cherkassky challenged to a duel.]

Riasanovsky, N. V. "Aleksander I. Koshelev." Introduction to Koshelev's *Zapiski 1803–1883,* (Berlin, 1884), reprinted Newtonville, Mass., 1976, pp. i–vi.

———. "Theory and Practice of Tsarism's Ideology." In H. H. Rowen, ed., *From Absolutism to Revolution, 1648–1848,* 2nd ed., pp. 259–264. New York, 1968.

Rieber, A. J. "The Formation of La Grande Societe des Chemins de Fer Russes." *Jahrbucher fur die Geschichte Osteuropas,* 1973, Band 21, Heft 3, pp. 375–391.

Rogger, Hans. "Reflections on Russian Conservatism: 1861–1905." *Jahrbucher fur die Geschichte Osteuropas,* 1966, Heft 2, pp. 195–212.

Rosset, A. O. "Iz pisem A. O. Rosseta k A. O. Smirnovoi. Pis'ma v Kalugu." *Russkii arkhiv,* March, 1896, pp. 361–392. [Information on Samarin, Chizhov and other Slavophils second half of 1840s to 1864, Khomiakov's death and Samarin.]

Rozental', V. M. "Ideinye tsentry liberal'nogo dvizheniia v Rossii nakanune revoliutsionnoi situatsii i Peterburgskii kruzhok "K. D. Kavelina v 1855–1857gg." *Revoliutsionnaia situatsiia v Rossii v 1859–1861gg.,* pp. 383–398. Moscow, 1963.

Rudd, C. A. "Censorship and the Peasant Question: The Contingencies of Reform under Alexander II (1855–1859)." *California Slavic Studies,* Berkeley, Calif., 1970, vol. 5, pp. 137–167.

Rusov, N. N. "Anarkhicheskie elementy v Slavianofil'stve (Istoricheskaia spravka)." In A. A. Borovoi, ed., *Mikhailu Bakuninu, 1876–1926: ocherk istorii anarkhisticheskogo dvizheniia v Rossii,* pp. 37–43. Moscow, 1926.

Samarin, Dmitrii. "Bogoroditsa v russkom narodnom pravoslavii." *Russkaia mysl',* March–June, 1918, pp. 1–38. [On the early Slavophils' neglect of pagan elements in the Orthodoxy of the Russian peasantry.]

———. "Iurii Fedorovich Samarin." *Russkii biograficheskii slovar,* St. Petersburg, 1904, vol. 18, pp. 133–146.

Samarin, Iu. F. "Dva pis'ma Iu. F. Samarina k S. P. Shevyrevu." *Russkii arkhiv,* 1907, no. 11, pp. 430–432.

———. "Iz dnevnika vedennago Iu. F. Samarinym v Kieve v 1850 godu." *Russkii arkhiv,* 1877, no. 6, pp. 229–232.

———. "Iz pis'em Iu. F. Samarina i kniazia V. A. Cherkasskago k K. K. Grotu." *Russkii arkhiv,* 1907, no. 1, pp. 157–162.

———. "Iz vospominanii ob universitete, 1834–1838g." *Rus',* 1880, no. 1, pp. 18–19.

———. "Perepiska Iu. F. Samarina s A. I. Gertsenom v 1864g." Ed. I. S. Aksakov, *Rus',* 1883, no. 1, pp. 30–42; no. 2, pp. 23–30.

___. "Pis'ma Iu. F. Samarina k A. N. Tatarinovu 1861." Ed. A. A. Ostrovsky, *Russkaia mysl'*, March, 1911, pp. 113–115. [Samarin's thoughts on emancipation.]

___. "Pis'ma Iu. F. Samarina i kniazia V. A. Cherkaskago k K. K. Grotu o vzimanii podatei v Rossii." *Russkii arkhiv*, 1907, no. 1, pp. 157–162.

___. "Pis'ma Iu. F. Samarina k kniaziu I. A. Meshcherskomu." *Russkii arkhiv*, 1877, no. 5, pp. 103–107.

___. "Pis'ma Iuriia Fedorovicha Samarina (1840–1845)." Ed. P. I. Bartenev, *Russkii arkhiv*, 1880, book II, pp. 241–332.

___. "Pis'ma (1840–1845)." Ed. D. F. Samarin, *Russkii arkhiv*, 1880, book II, pp. 241–330.

___. "Pis'mo Iu. F. Samarina k K. O. Smirnovu." *Russkii arkhiv*, 1908, no. 2, p. 297. [Letter contains feelings about his "unfulfilled duty," his introduction to Khomiakov's theological works, his feelings toward government and church.]

Samokhvalov, A. N., ed. "Molodaia redaktsiia Moskvitianina i Slavianofily." *Epigrama i satira. Iz istorii literaturnoi bor'by XIXgo veka 1840–1880*, pp. 87–89. Moscow-Leningrad, 1932.

Scherrer, Jutta. "Neoslavophilie et germanophobie: Vladimir Francevic Ern (1881–1917)." *Revue des etudes slaves*, 1979, no. 3, pp. 297–309.

Seddon, J. H. "The Petrashevtsy: A Reappraisal." *Slavic Review*, no. 3, 1984, pp. 434–452.

Seton-Watson, R. W. "Panslavism." *Contemporary Review*, October, 1916, pp. 419–429.

Shapiro, L. B. "The *Vekhi* Group and the Mystique of Revolution." *Slavonic and East European Review*, December, 1955, pp. 56–76.

Shenrok, V. I., ed. "Druz'ia i znakomye Nikolaia Vasil'evicha Gogolia v ikh k nemu pis'makh. F. V. Chizhov-N. V. Gogoliu." *Russkaia starina*, 1889, no. 7, pp. 163–176; no. 8, pp. 363–380.

Shevyrev, S. P. "Khristiianskaia filosofiia. Besedy Baadera." *Moskvitianin*, 1841, no. 3, pp. 378–437.

____. "Vzgliad russkago na sovremennoe obrazovanie Evropy." *Moskvitianin*, 1841, part 1, pp. 219–296.

Sinitsyn, A. A. "Iz vospominanii starago vracha A. A. Sinitsyna." Ed. N. D. Romanov, *Russkaia starina*, June, 1913, pp. 495–549. [In this installment the author states that in the 1850s some thought of Samarin and the Slavophils as radicals, "Marata".]

Sirotinin, Andrei. "Professor L. E. Vladimirov. Aleksei Stepanovich Khomiakov i ego etiko-sotsial'noe uchenie, Moskva, 1904." (Review.) *Istoricheskii vestnik*, November, 1904, pp. 769–772.

___. "V. Z. Zavitnevich. Aleksei Stepanovich Khomiakov. Tom I, kn. 1 i 2. Spb. 1902." (Review.) *Istoricheskii vestnik*, October, 1902, pp. 304–307.

Smirnova, A. C. "Iz perepiski A. O. Smirnovoi s Aksakovymi." Ed. P. I. Bartenev. *Russkii arkhiv,* 1896, no. 1, pp. 142–160. [On disagreements between Samarin and K. S. Aksakov.]

___. "Iz pisem A. O. Rosseta k a. O. Smirnovoi." *Russkii arkhiv,* 1896, no. 3, pp. 361–392. [On impact on Samarin of Khomiakov's death; Sverbeev's attitude toward Slavophils.]

___. "Iz zapisok A. O. Smirnovoi." Ed. P. I. Bartenev, *Russkii arkhiv,* 1895, no. 9, pp. 71–90. [On Samarin's imprisonment.]

___. "Nikolai Vasil'evich Gogol'. Pis'ma k nemu A. O. Smirnovoi, rozhd. Rosset. 1844–1851gg." Ed. V. I. Shenrok, *Russkaia starina,* 1890, no. 7, pp. 195–212. [In this and other installments there is much information about the Slavophils, including Samarin's problems with his father.]

Shmurlo, E. "From Krizanic to the Slavophils." *Slavonic Review,* 1927–1928, pp. 321–335.

Solov'ev, A. V. "Sviataia Rus' (Ocherk razvitiia religiozno-obshestvennoi idei." *Sbornik Russkago Arkheologicheskago Obshchestva v Korolevstve S. Kh. S.* Belgrade, 1927, pp. 77–112.

Stroev, V. "Koshelev, Aleksandr Ivanovich." *Russkii biograficheskii slovar',* St. Petersburg, 1903, vol. 9, pp. 385–390.

Struve, P. B. "Iurii Samarin. Opyt kharakteristiki i otsenki." *Vozrozhdenie,* Paris, 1926, June 13, no. 376, pp. 2–3.

___. "Konservatizm intelligentskoi mysli. Iz razmyshlenii o russkoi revoliutsii." *Russkaia mysl',* July, 1907, pp. 172–178. [On Samarin's "revolutionary conservatism," and Slavophilism and populism.]

___. "Konstantin Leont'ev." *Vozrozhdenie,* Paris, 1926, May, 30, no. 362, pp. 2–3.

___. "Russia." *Slavonic Review,* June, 1922, pp. 24–39.

___. "S. M. Solov'ev. Po povodu otdel'nago izdaniia ego zapisok." *Russkaia mysl',* October, 1915, pp. 20–22.

___. "Velikaia Rossiia i Sviataia Rus'." *Russkaia mysl',* 1914, no. 12, pp. 176–180. [On Dostoevsky's pro-Orthodox rather than pro-Slav stand.]

___. "Vladimir Solov'ev." [Obituary]. *Mir Bozhii,* September, 1900, part 2, pp. 13–15.

Stupperich, Robert. "Jurij Fedorovic Samarin. Seine geistesge-schichtliche Position und politische Bedeutung." *Jahrbucher fur die Geschichte Osteuropas,* 1974, Heft 2, pp. 288–289. [Review of Gerda Hucke's book on Samarin.]

Sverbeev, D. N. "iz zapisok D. N. Sverbeeva. D. A. Valuev." Ed. P. I. Bartenev, *Russkii arkhiv,* 1899, no. 9, pp. 140–149.

Tartak, E. L. "The Liberal Tradition in Russia: A. Herzen and V. Soloviev." In Feliks Gross, ed., *European Ideologies,* pp. 310–323. New York, 1948.

Thaden, E. C. "Iurii Fedorovich Samarin and Baltic History." in *Journal of Baltic Studies,* 1986, vol. XVII, no. 4, pp. 321–327.

___. "Samarin's 'Okrainy Rossii' and Official Policy in the Baltic Provinces." *Russian Review*, 1974, no. 4, pp. 405–415.

Tiutchev, F. I. "Papstvo i rimskii vopros s russkoi tochki zreniia." *Russkii arkhiv*, 1886, no. 5, pp. 33–51. [This article, published in French in Paris, is said to have inspired Khomiakov's essays on religion.]

Torgashev, P. I. "Zapiski Narodovol'tsa 1878–1883g.g." *Golos minuvshago*, 1914, no. 2, pp. 142–169.

Troitsky, M. M. "K. D. Kavelin (Stranitsa iz istorii filosofii v Rossii)." *Russkaia mysl'*, 1885, November, pp. 160–194. [On Samarin-Kavelin relationship.]

Trubetskaiia, O. N. "Kn. Vladimir Aleksandrovich Cherkassky." *Velikaia reforma*, Moscow, 1911, vol. 5, pp. 108–118.

Trubetskoi, S. N. "Pamiati K. N. Leont'eva." *Russkoe obozrenie*, 1892, no. 11, pp. 406–409.

___. "Razocharovanyi slavianofil." *Vestnik Evropy*, 1892, no. 10, pp. 772–810.

Tseitlin, S. Ia. "Zemskaia reforma." In A. I. Granat, *Istoriia Rossii v XIX veke*, vol. 3, pp. 179–213. St. Petersburg, n.d.

Tsimbaev, N. I. Review of E. Muller, *Russischer Intellekt in europaischer Krise. Voprosy istorii*, 1971, no. 4, pp. 192–194.

___. Review of "Literaturnye vzgliady i tvorchestvo slavianofilov. 1830–1850 gody." (Moscow, 1978). *Istoriia SSSR*, 1979, no. 4, pp. 222–225.

Turgenev, A. I. "Aleksander Ivanovich Turgenev v ego pis'makh. 1827–1845 gg." Ed. N. P. Barsukov, *Russkaia starina*, 1881, June, pp. 187–206; October, pp. 337–350; 1882, April, pp. 177–194; May, pp. 443–462. [Contains Samarin's evaluation of Baader, whom he did not consider particularly favorable to Orthodoxy.]

V... "Biografiia D. A. Volueva." *Russkii arkhiv*, 1899, no. 9, pp. 130–139.

V. "Biografiia D. A. Volueva." In S. A. Rachinsky, ed., *Tatevskii sbornik*, pp. 84–100. 1899.

Vinogradov, Paul. "A Prophetic Career." *British Review*, October, 1915, no. 1, pp. 3–14. [About Iu. F. Samarin.]

"V pribaltiiskom krae. Iz zapisok russkago chinovnika. 1856–1866." *Russkaia starina*, 1882, July, pp. 59–90. [Quotes Samarin.]

W. "Kniaz' V. A. Cherkasskii ob osvobozhdenii krest'ian." *Russkaia mysl'*, September, 1886, pp. 49–55.

Walicki, Andrzej. "The Paris Lectures of Mickiewicz and Russian Slavophilism." *Slavonic and East European Review*, January, 1986, pp. 155–175.

Weidemaier, W. C. "Herzen and the Existential World View: A New Approach to an Old Debate." *Slavic Review*, 1981, no. 4, pp. 557–569.

Whittaker, Robert. "'My Literary and Moral Wanderings': Apollon Grigor'ev and the Changing Cultural Topography of Moscow." *Slavic Review,* Fall 1983, pp. 390–407.

Zaionchkovsky, P. A. "Popytka sozyva zemskogo sobora i padenie ministerstva N. P. Ignat'eva." *Istoriia SSSR,* 1960, no. 5, pp. 126–139.

Zenkovsky, Serge A. "The Emancipation of the Serfs in Retrospect." *Russian Review,* October, 1961, pp. 280–293.

Zohrab, Irene. "'The Slavophiles' by M. P. Pogodin. An Introduction and Translation." *New Zealand Slavonic Journal,* 1982, pp. 29–87.

Zorn, Jonathan. "New Soviet Work on the Old-Russian Peasantry. Review Article." *Russian Review,* July, 1980, pp.339–347.

Zotov, V. P. "Liberal'nyi tsenzor i professor-pessimist. (Biograficheskii ocherk.) Nikitenko v tsarstvovanie Aleksandra I." *Istoricheskii vestnik,* 1893, no. 10, pp. 194–210; no. 11, pp. 511–558; no. 12, pp. 800–832. [Also one installment each on the reigns of Alexander I and II. Also information on Chizhov's arrest, his views of all-Slav union under the Russian tsar; the government's negative response and its distrust of the Slavophils; the tsar and Samarin after the latter's arrest.]

Index

Since the names of the early or Moscow Slavophiles: A.S. Khomiakov, I.V. Kireevsky, K.S. Aksakov and Iu. F. Samarin appear on most pages of this text they do not appear in this Index.

About the Book and Author

This work is the fourth volume of Peter Christoff's study of nineteenth-century Russian Slavophilism, which grew out of vigorous and prolonged debates between the Slavophils and proponents of Slavophilism's principal ideological rival, Westernism, in the mid-nineteenth century. As the names indicate, the Westerners looked to the West for the solution to Russia's political, social, and economic problems. The Slavophils, well-to-do members of the Russian gentry who knew the West well, chose to look inward. Both Slavophils and Westerners favored emancipation of the Russian serfs, which was finally achieved in 1861. In this crucial reform, the Slavophils—Iu. F. Samarin in particular—played a leading role.

Since the beginning of *glasnost'* and *perestroika*, Slavophilism has been experiencing a revival in the Soviet Union expressed in a number of ways, including the announced republication of the works of A. S. Khomiakov and I. V. Kireevsky. The original Slavophil circle included these two senior Slavophils as well as K. S. Aksakov and Samarin (1819–1876).

Samarin was the youngest and most active of the Moscow Slavophils. Endowed with an exceptional mind and character, he was fluent in several languages and attracted attention while still a young student at Moscow University. He played a leading role in the emancipation of the serfs and in other reforms, sometimes risking his own safety. He left more than eleven volumes of collected works and correspondence—the largest written legacy among the early Slavophils and an invaluable source for the study of Moscow Slavophilism as well as Samarin's life and activities.

Peter K. Christoff was, until his retirement in 1977, professor of Russian history at San Francisco State University. He was visiting professor at Cornell University, Mills College, Stanford University, and the University of Leiden; a Fulbright recipient; and a research fellow with the Kennan Institute and the U.S.–Soviet Union Cultural Exchange Program (IREX).